BARRON'S

AP*

CHINESE LANGUAGE AND CULTURE

2ND EDITION

Yan Shen, M.A.
Department of Asian Languages & Cultures
UCLA, Los Angeles

Contributing author:
Joanne Shang, B.S.
Chinese Language Teacher
Durham Academy
Durham, North Carolina

AP* is a registered trademark of the College Board, which was not involved in the production of, and does not endorse, this product.

ABOUT THE AUTHORS

Yan Shen has been a lecturer in Asian Languages and Cultures at UCLA, Los Angeles since 2005. She has a Masters in Sinology and Anthropology from University Trier, Trier, Germany and a Bachelor in Chinese Language and Literature from Capital Normal University, Beijing, China. She was born in China and has lived in Beijing for more than two decades. She taught Chinese as a second language at the International Chinese Language and Culture Center, Tsinghua University, China, during 1993 and 2004. She has been a certified Oral Proficiency Tester for the American Council on the Teaching of Foreign Languages since 2012. She has written numerous articles for journals and speaks regularly at national and global conferences. She has served as a reviewer for the Critical Language Scholarship Program (Chinese) for several years.

Joanne Shang teaches Mandarin Chinese at Durham Academy in North Carolina, and is professionally focused in Instructional Technology for 21st Century Learning. She speaks regularly at national and global conferences. She is a master teacher in Startalk Teachers Academies, and has served as the Chinese Language Director at Middlebury-Monterey Language Academy. Joanne previously taught in Raleigh Charter High School.

Both authors have been readers for the AP Chinese Language and Culture Exam.

ACKNOWLEDGMENTS

Thanks to my husband, Wei Li, for his support while I worked on the book. Thanks also to my daughter, Yunyi Li, for her help in translating much of the Chinese into English. Many thanks also to Joanne Shang for checking the manuscript and offering valuable suggestions for improvement. Special thanks are due to my editor at Barron's, Pat Hunter.

© Copyright 2014, 2009 by Barron's Educational Series, Inc.

All rights reserved.
No part of this product may be reproduced or distributed in any form or by any means without the written permission of the copyright owner.

All inquiries should be addressed to:
Barron's Educational Series, Inc.
250 Wireless Boulevard
Hauppauge, New York 11788
www.barronseduc.com

ISBN: 978-1-4380-7388-0

ISSN 2330-3263

PRINTED IN THE UNITED STATES OF AMERICA

9 8 7 6 5 4 3

10%
POST-CONSUMER WASTE
Paper contains a minimum of 10% post-consumer waste (PCW). Paper used in this book was derived from certified, sustainable forestlands.

Contents

Barron's *Essential 5*   v

1 Introduction   1

General Information   1
The AP Chinese Course   1
The AP Chinese Exam   2
Navigating the Computer   5
Suggested Resources   11
Using This Book   15

2 Listening Comprehension   17

General Information   17
Rejoinders   19
Listening Selections   22
Listening Strategies   23
Listening Comprehension Practice   55
Answers and Answer Explanations   70

3 Reading Comprehension   162

General Information   162
Reading Strategies   162
Reading Selections   178
Reading Comprehension Practice   181
Answers and Answer Explanations   210

4 Writing Skills   227

General Information   227
Evaluation Criteria   228
Scoring Guidelines   229
Types of Essays   240
Writing Strategies   261
Writing Skills Practice   270

5 Speaking Skills   331

General Information   331
Evaluation Criteria   332
Conversation Samples and Scores   336
Cultural Presentation Samples and
   Scores   350
Speaking Tips   355
Vocabulary Tips   356
Speaking Preparation   356
Presentation   359
Speaking Skills Practice   364
Speaking Skills   390

6 Grammar Review   399

Complements   399
Sentences with Special Predicates   405
The Passive Voice   407
The "把"—Sentences   408
Existential Sentences   410
Sentences with Verbal
   Constructions in a Series   411
Pivotal Sentences   412
Comparison   413
Expressing Emphasis   416
Complex Sentences   417
Common Sentence Patterns in
   Spoken Chinese   426

7 Cultural Notes   441

Physical Geography of China   441
Survey of Modern History   448
Festivals and Customs   450
Chinese Family Virtues   455
Chinese Mythology   458
Idiom Story   462
Four Grand Works in Chinese
   Literature   471

Chinese Character 476

Calligraphy 478

Chinese Arts and Crafts 480

Four Great Inventions of
Ancient China 482

Traditional Chinese Medicine 485

Traditional Chinese Architecture 487

Classical Gardens 490

Traditional Performing Arts 492

Education 495

Chinese Martial Arts 501

Traditional Entertainment 503

Cultural Heritage 507

Traditional Clothing 509

Traditional Food 512

Chinese Astrology 516

Chinese Taboos 518

Important Idioms 525

Useful Proverbs 531

8 Model Exam 1 541

Answers and Answer Explanations 558

9 Model Exam 2 577

Answers and Answer Explanations 594

As you work toward achieving that **5** on your AP Chinese Language and Culture exam, here are five essentials that you **MUST** know above everything else:

Barron's Essential

1

Familiarize yourself with the exam structure and the three modes of communication around which the course is structured.

● Understanding the various tasks in the exam is critical for success.
● Remember that communication can be interpersonal, interpretive, or presentational.
● All of the tasks in the exam are built upon these modes.
● Your success depends on a balanced mastery of language.

2

Listen and read critically.

● You will need to comprehend a variety of authentic Chinese texts, e-mails, letters, articles, conversations, interviews, announcements, and other items such as ads, charts, and instructions.
● Be sure you understand the purpose, the essential facts, and the tone of each of these items, as well as the puns and euphemisms used.

3

Complete the tasks in Free-Response Questions.

● The instructions to the Free-Response Questions are written in English.
● Read them carefully as they specify what *tasks* are expected of you.
● It is most important to complete the *right* task *correctly*.
● Overlooking a task or subtask will marginalize the score regardless of the rich language used.

4

Type correctly.

● The Writing sections include an *E-mail Response* and a *Story Narration*.
● Each must be completed in 15 minutes by typing Chinese characters.
● Practice typing on IME methods for proficiency and accuracy in choosing the characters after keying in the Hanyu Pinyin or Zhuyin Fuhao.

5

Use all elements of this guide.
● Read and pay attention to the suggested strategies and the explanations in the Answer Keys to strengthen or supplement your knowledge.
● Complete the exercises in all sections and the two Model Exams. Be sure you're familiar with the exam directions.

Introduction

CHAPTER 1

GENERAL INFORMATION

The AP Chinese program offers high school students an opportunity to earn credit for Chinese courses at the college level. Like other College Board programs, it is available to anyone worldwide who wishes to participate. The AP Chinese Language and Culture exam was first held in May 2007 and is used to assess a student's proficiency in Chinese equivalent to completing a fourth-semester Chinese course in college.

The AP Chinese exam consists of two essential aspects: Chinese language and Chinese culture. Because language and culture are so closely intertwined, culture is acquired in the process of learning a language, and language is learned when studying culture. As such, students should try to absorb as much Chinese culture as possible while learning the language, because it is impossible to separate the two.

THE AP CHINESE COURSE

The curriculum and assessment frameworks for the AP Chinese Language and Culture course undergo continuous improvement. In order to prepare for the AP Chinese exam, students are strongly encouraged, although not required, to enroll in an AP Chinese course in high school. Like other AP courses, the AP Chinese course should match the level of a fourth-semester university/college course in Mandarin/*Putonghua* Chinese. This level requires students to complete approximately 250 hours of classroom instruction.

In the AP Chinese course, students should intensively practice Chinese in three modes: interpersonal, interpretive, and presentational. In addition, they should develop Chinese language skills in the five goal areas: communication, cultures, connections, comparisons, and communities.

The first goal involves *communication* in Chinese. Students are expected:

1. to engage in conversations, provide and obtain information, express feelings and emotions, exchange opinions, and make presentations
2. to understand, write, and discuss a variety of topics

The second goal involves the acquisition of *cultural* knowledge. This includes:

1. understanding social patterns
2. the active practice of conventions
3. appropriate use of Chinese in cultural settings

In particular, students should understand significant components of Chinese culture, such as traditions, history, literature, art, and so on.

The third goal is to establish a *connection* between Chinese and other disciplines and to further acquire information and recognize distinctive viewpoints that are only available through Chinese language and culture.

The fourth goal concerns the student's ability to *compare* and contrast the Chinese language and culture with his or her native or other language and culture.

The fifth goal emphasizes that students should apply the Chinese language in *communities* both within and beyond the school setting.

THE AP CHINESE EXAM

The AP Chinese Language and Culture course and exam incorporate Chinese cultural information with listening, speaking, reading, and writing. Like other AP foreign language exams, the AP Chinese exam measures fluency. Students should be able to recognize and understand both spoken and written Chinese at a sophisticated level. In addition, they should demonstrate their ability to speak and write Chinese fluently and accurately in a culturally appropriate manner.

Format of the Exam

Here is a summary of the important information on the AP Chinese exam. Table I and Table II represent the format of the exam. The exam assesses the communication ability of AP Chinese students in two sections: multiple-choice and free-response questions. Each section of the AP Chinese exam contributes a specific portion to the final AP grade. Detailed rubrics for the Writing and Speaking free-response sections will be given in the related chapters. Table I and Table II list the time distribution and weight of each part on the final grade.

TABLE I

Section I: Multiple Choice

Section/ Weight of Final Score	Question Type	# of Problems	Knowledge/ Skills Assessed	Time
Part A: <u>Listening</u> 25%	<u>Rejoinders:</u> Listen to the beginning of a conversation, then determine an appropriate continuation of the conversation.	10–15	Interpersonal communication— Understanding 2$^+$-character phrases and sociocultural formulae; expressing opinion, attitude, intent	10 mins: 5 seconds response time per problem
	<u>Listening Selections:</u> Answer questions after listening to a variety of stimuli, e.g., conversation, instructions, voice message, report, announcement.	15–20	Interpretive communication— Comprehension, inference, application of basic cultural knowledge	10 mins: 12 seconds response time per problem
Part B: Reading 25%	<u>Reading Comprehension:</u> Answer questions after reading a variety of stimuli, e.g., note, public sign, poster, e-mail, letter, story, advertisement, article, brochure.	35–40	Interpretive communication— Comprehension, inference, application of basic cultural knowledge	60 mins

TABLE II

Section II: Free Response—Writing

Section/ Weight of Final Score	Question Type	# of Tasks	Knowledge/Skills Assessed	Time
Part A: Writing 25%	<u>Story Narration:</u> Write a story according to a series of picture prompts.	1	Presentational communication— Writing	15 mins
	<u>E-mail response:</u> Write an e-mail response after reading an e-mail message.	1	Interpersonal communication— Reading, writing	15 mins

看图说话

回信

TABLE III

Section II: Free Response—Speaking				
Section/ Weight of Final Score	**Question Type**	**# of Tasks**	**Knowledge/ Skills Assessed**	**Time**
Part B: Speaking 25%	Conversation: Engage in a 6-part conversation by responding in a culturally appropriate manner.	6	Interpersonal communication— Speaking	4 mins: 20 seconds response time per problem
	Cultural Presentation: Make an oral presentation describing and explaining the significance of a Chinese cultural practice or product.	1	Presentational communication— Speaking	7 mins: 4 minutes to prepare, 2 minutes to record the presentation

To do well on the exam, it is important to understand the structure of the AP Chinese Language and Culture exam.

SECTION I

Section I, as illustrated in Table I, is the multiple-choice section and covers listening and reading comprehension.

THE LISTENING SECTION consists of two types of multiple-choice questions developed to evaluate interpersonal and interpretive communication skills.

1. **Rejoinders**—AP students must
   - first listen to and fully understand the expressions in the beginning part of a conversation, then
   - listen to a list of choices and select a culturally acceptable discourse to continue or complete the conversation.

2. **Listening Selections**—AP students must
   - first listen to a selected discourse, which may be an instruction, voice message, report, announcement, or conversation, then
   - read the question and choices and make the correct choice within 12 seconds. (*Students will be told whether a selection will be played once or twice.*)

THE READING SECTION assesses interpretive communication skills through multiple-choice questions related to a variety of reading materials, such as a story, sign, poster, note, letter, e-mail, brochure, article, or advertisement.

SECTION II

Section II is the free-response section and covers writing and speaking.

THE WRITING SECTION assesses writing skills in both the presentational and interpersonal modes. It requires test-takers to complete two tasks by writing in Chinese for different purposes and to specific people.

Task 1: Narrate a complete story based on a four-picture sequence.

Task 2: Write an e-mail response.

THE SPEAKING SECTION assesses speaking skills in the interpersonal and presentational modes. It requires students to complete two tasks using their speaking skills.

Task 1: Participate in a simulated conversation with a Chinese speaker on a given topic.

Task 2: Make an oral presentation on one or more Chinese cultural practices, products, or customs.

Complete and appropriate cultural expressions are the important scoring standard for both writing and speaking tasks.

Standard time allowance for each section is listed in Table I and Table II. It also appears on the instructions for each section during the exam. If the scheduled time for the section is extended during the actual exam, the clock on the computer screen will be updated to show the adjusted time for all related sections.

The AP Chinese Language and Culture exam is a computer-based test. AP students are advised to practice using a computer with a multimedia system, and to familiarize themselves with Chinese input techniques. Test-takers will be seated in front of a desktop computer to work on the exam questions, which are burned on a CD.

Prior to starting the exam, you will be instructed to enter your student information into the computer. This information includes, but is not limited to, your heritage or background, date of birth, Social Security number, parents' education, first language, home address, and phone number or international phone number. These answers will not be graded.

NAVIGATING THE COMPUTER

Display Option:

During the course of the exam, you will read directly from a computer screen, listen through a headset, type on a keyboard, and speak into a microphone. The questions on the AP Chinese exam are formulated in both traditional and simplified characters. Chinese texts for the multiple-choice questions in Section I, Listening and Reading Comprehension, can be displayed in either traditional or simplified characters. You can click on an on-screen button, "Switch to Traditional" or "Switch to Simplified," to display the character version with which you are more familiar.

Input Option:

After inputting the student information described above, but before the exam begins, you will be presented with the Typing Options setup screen on the computers, which allows you to configure your typing options for the writing part of Section II, Free Response. Two input techniques are available:

1. Microsoft Pinyin IME (MSPY), which uses Hanyu Pinyin to type in either simplified or traditional characters, or
2. Microsoft New Phonetic IME, which uses Zhuyin Fuhao (Bopomofo) to type in traditional characters.

If you intend to use the Pinyin input, you can decide between traditional and simplified character by using the toggle button labeled 繁 (traditional) or 简 (simplified) on the IME toolbar on the Typing Options setup screen.

A white text box on the screen allows you to test your chosen setting. Be sure to try it out by inputting a few words and verify that, indeed, it is accepting the input in the chosen character version correctly. Be sure to notify the exam proctor immediately if you can't find the white text box, or the toggle button does not function as described.

Note that you ***must decide*** the input technique and character version you intend to use in the writing section ***on this screen***. *This configuration **cannot be changed** once you **exit** the screen and the exam starts.* It is highly recommended to also test the microphone and headset volumes before the test starts.

Clock / Timer

Throughout the exam, a digital clock is displayed at the top of the screen to show the remaining time to respond for each part.

In addition, a timer, in the form of a progress bar, is displayed to indicate the remaining time for each problem in the Listening section.

When a question in the Listening section has timed out, the screen automatically moves on to the next question. Note that you cannot go back to any previous question in the Listening section. However, in the Reading section, you may skip questions and go back to them later as long as there is sufficient time remaining on the clock.

Listening Controls

There are two parts in the Listening section: Rejoinders and Listening Selections. There are two buttons on the top right of the screen:

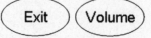

1. (Volume) Use this button to control the volume of the listening audio.

2. (Exit) Click this button to return to the previous screen.

In the *Rejoinders* part of the Listening section, you will listen to several short verbal exchanges and the four answer choices, and then choose the one that best continues/completes the conversation. A progress bar and the four selection bubbles are displayed on the screen. You have 5 seconds to answer each question.

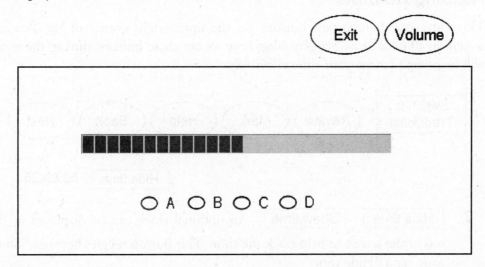

When the time expires, the exam automatically moves to the next task. You cannot return to the previous task once it is completed.

In the *Listening Selections* part of the Listening section, you will listen to several selections of audio recordings. For each selection, you will be told if the selection will be played once or twice. After listening to the selection for the number of times assigned, you will see the question in English on the screen. You then have 12 seconds to answer each question.

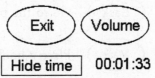

What is the purpose of the announcement?

○ To start boarding a flight

○ To announce a late arrival of a flight

○ To announce a delayed departure of a flight

○ To greet the passengers on board a flight

| Hide time | / | Show time |—An optional clock can be displayed at the top of the screen to indicate how much time is left to make a selection. This button toggles between "Show time" and "Hide time." The clock will not count down while the audio is played, but only when you are expected to answer the problem.

When the time expires, the exam automatically moves to the next task. You cannot return to the previous task once it is completed.

Reading Controls

There are several important buttons on the upper right corner of the Reading screen, as illustrated below. Knowing how to use these buttons during the exam will help you manage your time effectively.

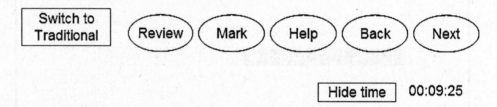

1. | Hide time | / | Show time |—An optional clock can be displayed at the top of the screen to help track the time. This button toggles between "Show time" and "Hide time."

2. | Switch to Traditional | / | Switch to Simplified |—The Chinese text can be displayed in either traditional or simplified characters. This button toggles between "Switch to Traditional" and "Switch to Simplified."

3. (Next)—Go to the next problem.

4. (Back)—Go to the previous problem.

5. (Mark)—Place a bookmark on the currently displayed problem to make it easy to return to later for revisions. A checkmark will also appear next to the problem on the Summary Review screen. The problem remains marked until it is unmarked. This button toggles between placing and removing the bookmark.

6. (Help)—Display help information on different topics. You are advised to use the Help button wisely because searching through the Help topics can be time-consuming.

7. (Review)—Go to the Summary Review screen, where all the problems within the Reading section are displayed along with their status (answered or not answered).

	Return	Go to Question

Hide time	00:09:25

Number	Problem Description	Marked	Status
1	*Problem 1 ....?*	✓	**Answered**
2	*Problem 2 ....?*	✓	**Not Answered**
3	*Problem 3 ....?*		**Answered**
4	Problem 4 ....?		Not Seen

From here, you may go directly to any of the active problems by highlighting the problem and clicking [Go to Question]. Otherwise, you may click [Return] to go back to the previous screen.

Break

There is a 10-minute break between Section I, Listening and Reading Comprehension (multiple-choice problems) and Section II, Writing and Speaking (free-response problems). The free-response section resumes after the break.

Writing Controls

Remember that whenever Chinese text is displayed, you may choose between displaying it in traditional or simplified characters simply by clicking the toggle button: [Switch to Traditional] or [Switch to Simplified].

There are two tasks in the Writing section: *Story Narration* and *E-mail Response*. You will type in a white text box displayed on the screen. Several function buttons will be displayed along the top of the screen.

Hide time	00:01:33

[Cut] [Paste] [Undo] [Redo]   [Hide Char Count] [#] [Pinyin ▼]

1. [Cut]—Highlight the text you typed, then click this button to remove the highlighted text.

2. [Paste]—Position the cursor at the place where you want the previously "cut" text to be, then click this button to insert it.

3. [Undo]—Click this button to undo, or reverse, the last action. Every click reverses one more previous action.

4. Redo—Click this button to reverse the last "Undo" action. Every click reverses one more "Undo" command.

5. Hide Char Count—Click this button to toggle between showing and hiding the character count at the # button.

6. Pinyin ▼ / Bopomofo —Click on this pull-down menu to select the desired input method, Pinyin or Bopomofo.

The following keyboard keys behave exactly the same as in the Microsoft Word program.

Use the **Tab** key to indent at the beginning of a line.
Use the **Backspace** key to remove the character to the left of the cursor.
Use the **Delete** key to remove the character to the right of the cursor.

The time displayed next to the Hide time button indicates how much time is left to complete the task at hand.

When the time expires, the exam automatically moves to the next task. You cannot return to the previous task once it is completed.

Speaking Controls

Before starting the Speaking section, check the headset and microphone again to make sure that they are functioning properly.

There are two tasks in the Speaking section: *Conversation* and *Cultural Presentation*. Each task specifies the amount of response time allowed. In the simulated conversation, you have 20 seconds to respond to each question. There are six questions in the simulated conversation. The seventh question is the cultural presentation.

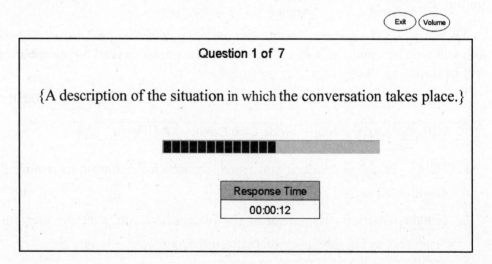

1. Question 1 of 7—This line shows that you are on the first of the seven speaking tasks.

2. ▬▬▬▬▬▬▬▬▬▬——The progress bar serves as a visual indicator of how much time is left to complete the task at hand.

3. Response Time 00:00:12—This timer, along with the progress bar above, counts down the remaining time left to complete the task.

When the time expires, the exam automatically moves to the next question. You cannot return to the previous question once it is completed.

For the Cultural Presentation task, you will first read and hear about the topic that you are asked to present. You have 4 minutes to prepare for the presentation, and 2 minutes to record it.

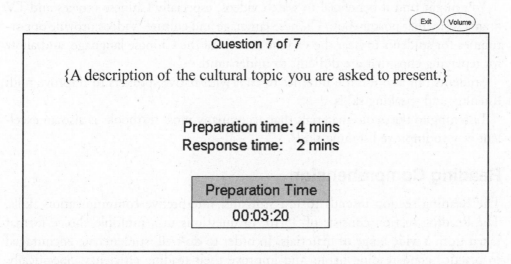

When the preparation time expires, the exam automatically moves to the next step: response time. The countdown timer will be reset to 2 minutes.

When the response time expires, the exam officially ends. You cannot return to the previous task or question, and should **NOT** touch the computer after completing the exam because it will be processing all exam responses.

Since changes to the exam can take place at any time, you should stay abreast of any updates by visiting the College Board's website at www.collegeboard.com/student/testing/ap/about.html.

SUGGESTED RESOURCES
Listening Comprehension

The Listening section of the AP exam intends to test students' interpersonal and interpretive communication skills. To do well on this section, students should practice listening comprehension in different ways and listen to as much Chinese as possible from different sources. Chinese radio and Chinese TV programs are good listening resources. For example:

1. China Radio International (CRI) is an overseas broadcast from China. It provides comprehensive information on both Chinese and international topics. website: *www.chinabroadcast.cn*
2. CCTV is the 24-hour news channel of China Central Television, the largest national TV network in China. It is dedicated to reporting news, with a special focus on China. website: *www.cctv.com.cn*
3. Radio Taiwan International—*www.rti.com.tw/default.htm*
4. Taipei Broadcasting Station—*www.radio.taipei.gov.tw*
5. Radio Singapore International—*www.rsi.sg/chinese/regionalpressreview_c/view/20080107185000/1/b5/.html*

You might find it beneficial to watch videos, especially Chinese movies and TV drama series that portray both Chinese language and culture. Videos provide opportunities for students to hear the various accents of the Chinese language, and allow for replaying clips that are difficult to understand.

Students can also use the Internet to chat with native speakers to improve both listening and speaking skills.

Listening to the audio materials that accompany most textbooks is also an excellent way to improve listening skills.

Reading Comprehension

The Reading section intends to test students' interpretive communication skills. The Reading section consists of 35 to 40 questions in a multiple-choice format taken from a wide range of materials. In order to do well, students are encouraged to practice good reading habits and improve their reading efficiency. Specifically, students should master the following comprehension skills:

1. grasp the main ideas of a reading passage;
2. understand the content and literal meaning of a reading passage;
3. find key points by skimming;
4. infer main themes;
5. determine the style of a reading passage and the attitude of the author.

The more students read, the better prepared they will be. In order to do well on this section, students should have a thorough knowledge of Chinese vocabulary and grammatical structures, and the ability to understand Chinese in a variety of contexts. It's a good idea for students to practice on a variety of reading materials from daily life, such as articles, letters, e-mails, instructions, advertisements, notes, posters, public signs, newspaper reports, and announcements, as well as stories. A variety of resources are available to help students improve their reading comprehension skills. Reading Chinese newspapers and magazines is an excellent way to enrich students' vocabulary. Chinese websites allow students to access a vast range of reading materials.

1. *United Daily News* (Traditional Char. 繁體), 聯合報 (联合报)
www.udn.com

2. *World Journal* (Traditional Char. 繁體), 世界日報 (世界日报)
   www.worldjournal.com
3. *People's Daily* (Simplified Char. 简体), 人民日報 (人民日报)
   http://web.peopledaily.com.cn

Visiting libraries regularly enables students to improve their skills using Chinese books and periodicals. In order to better understand Chinese culture, students should expand their reading to literary texts, such as novels, essays, and short stories in their original form. They should also familiarize themselves with the different registers of language, different styles of writing, and new vocabulary words and grammatical structures.

Writing

The Writing section intends to test students' presentational and interpersonal communication skills. Students should be able to understand the task they are being asked to complete, write essays fluently, express main points clearly, provide solid support for their arguments, and organize essays in a logical manner. Students should practice choosing appropriate vocabulary and idioms, using correct grammar, and employing culturally appropriate expressions.

Writing an essay is a relatively subjective task. Students should write in complete sentences with culturally appropriate expressions, taking into account the purpose of the essay and the characters described. Students should read the essay directions carefully, develop a theme, and stay on topic throughout the entire essay. Remember that changing the essay plan midway is not a wise idea due to the limited time.

It is a good idea for students to make a list of the main points before starting to write, so that readers will be able to easily identify the introduction, development, and conclusion. Students should use specific examples or details to support their ideas and arguments.

Speaking

The Speaking section intends to test students' interpersonal and presentational communication skills. Specifically, students should be sure to understand the task at hand, pronounce words correctly, respond to questions with a clear viewpoint, express ideas fluently and clearly, and adopt culturally appropriate expressions. Although most students know that, in order to speak Chinese fluently, one needs to practice speaking as much as possible, very few actually do. Students should take the opportunity to speak with teachers and peers in their Chinese classes.

In addition to actively practicing speaking in courses offered at school, students should also make an effort to improve their skills on their own. The best way to improve speaking skills is by interacting with native speakers and, ideally, by visiting China or Taiwan. This allows students to broaden their horizons with new views and to expand their knowledge of Chinese culture.

Vocabulary

Vocabulary is an extremely important aspect of the Chinese language. It is crucial for students to equip themselves with a wide-ranging vocabulary. Usually, new words are the key factors that prevent students from fast reading and precise listening comprehension. Guessing the meanings of unknown words based on context clues is a good way to speed up reading and to improve listening comprehension. Using a variety of vocabulary and sentence patterns correctly demonstrates the ability to master Chinese.

In order to express their thoughts clearly and effectively, students must have a rich and appropriate vocabulary and be able to master a wide range of grammatical structures. This book provides explanations to help students understand the vocabulary in each section. The vocabulary in the Reading Comprehension chapter is relatively abundant, so students should try to guess the meanings of unknown words and phrases according to context clues. The exercises in both the Writing and Speaking chapters require students to apply a variety of vocabulary words and phrases, as well as idioms.

Grammar Review

The grammar pointers collected in this book are at the level of a fourth-semester college course. Although grammar is not explicitly tested in an independent section of the AP Chinese exam, it is a factor in each section of the exam. The basic grammar topics in Chapter 6 empower students to identify and correct their persistent errors. The materials in the grammar chapter are compiled from a wide range of sources.

Cultural Notes

Chinese cultural knowledge is addressed in the last chapter of this book. On the AP exam, cultural aspects are tested along with the four basic skills. The more students know about Chinese culture, including geography, history, population, ethnicity, climate, social relationships, economics, and politics, the more vocabulary they are likely to master. When students have a strong base of cultural knowledge, they will be more confident on the exam.

Language comprehension and production use a variety of skills simultaneously and involve interactions between speaking, writing, reading, and listening. Improving one skill can actually enhance the other skills. Having good study habits and using effective testing techniques during the AP Chinese exam can help students improve their final grade.

Here are some helpful suggestions for establishing confidence in taking the exam:

1. **Develop good study habits by**
   - reviewing materials regularly from previous sessions and using time wisely while studying;
   - practicing speaking and listening skills whenever possible, and seeking help for standard pronunciation and intonation from native speakers;

- applying strategies suggested in this book to practice reading comprehension, and selecting reading materials from a variety of sources;
- practicing writing according to Chinese writing formats; and
- identifying and improving weak skills.

2. **Be familiar with exam procedure in advance.**

Be clear about the order and length of the sections, and the specific problem types in each section. Taking a practice test before the actual exam will allow you to get accustomed to the environment of the actual exam.

3. **Maintain a relaxed, natural mood during the exam.**

You may feel nervous before and during the exam, but anxiety and tension can put you at a disadvantage. By maintaining a relaxed mind and body, you may actually be more able to concentrate on the exam. Establishing self-confidence and developing excellent focus are essential for taking the exam. Don't let the outcome of a previous section disrupt the rest of the exam.

USING THIS BOOK

This book is intended for students who are preparing for the AP Chinese language and culture exam, and for teachers who are coaching students in preparation for the exam. This book will help students organize their thoughts, express them effectively, and use vocabulary accurately.

Each chapter in this book not only discusses a single skill area but also contains information that will be useful in other areas. For each of the four skills—listening, speaking, reading, and writing—this book provides practical strategies for approaching the exam, sample exercises, answer keys, and explanations.

The model exams and answers offer another valuable opportunity to prepare for the actual exam. This book also contains additional grammar reviews to enhance students' grasp of Chinese grammar. It provides a variety of cultural materials to help students understand Chinese culture and society. It also provides sample topics for preparing for the writing and speaking portions of the AP Chinese exam. The selected materials cover a variety of topics, including school, family, clothing, food, sports, entertainment, jobs, housing, transportation, education, festivities, customs, travel, art, literature, history, society, science, climate, environment, and animals.

The objective of the AP Chinese Language and Culture exam is for the student to express himself or herself as clearly, accurately, and fluently as possible in Chinese. This book contains review materials that students will find useful as a study aid and as a tool to succeed on the AP exam.

The AP Chinese Language and Culture exam allows students to read and write in either simplified or traditional characters. Therefore, this book also provides students first with traditional characters, followed by the simplified version.

The AP Chinese Language and Culture course and exam are designed to prepare students to study Chinese in college at an intermediate to advanced level. Each college or university has its own credit-awarding policy to define the number of credits, if any, that may be awarded to students with a given AP exam score. Information regarding college credits is available from the College Board. New information and any changes to the AP Chinese Language and Culture exam will also be announced on the official College Board website.

Listening Comprehension

CHAPTER 2

GENERAL INFORMATION

The Listening section of the AP Chinese exam assesses students' ability to understand spoken Chinese and their mastery of interpersonal and interpretive communication skills. AP Chinese students are expected to have attained enough listening skills to understand dialogues and narrations with good overall comprehension.

This chapter discusses several listening strategies. The listening materials in this chapter are collected from a variety of sources to help students prepare for the AP exam. The more students listen to a language, the better their listening skills will be. Active listening experiences should be structured into daily activities. Students learn to value listening when it is given a prominent role in the Chinese language classroom and meaningfully integrated with their speaking, writing, and reading.

Sentences used in oral communications typically have the following features:

1. They are usually short, and may not be as formal as those in the written language.
2. They may contain some unnecessary and redundant information. Therefore, it is important for students to determine essential words and phrases while listening so that they can understand the main ideas.

In reality, it is nearly impossible for students to understand every single word spoken when listening to a foreign language. The best way to practice listening comprehension is to focus on the general meaning of the entire conversation by ignoring unknown words while listening. Missing some words during oral communication doesn't always affect students' understanding of the general meaning, and these words or their synonyms may be repeated several times throughout the recording.

IMPORTANT NOTE

Whenever Chinese characters are used in this chapter, the traditional version is presented first, followed by the simplified version in parentheses. If there are no parentheses, the characters in both versions are identical.

Listening to and understanding oral language is a complex process in which listeners interact with a speaker to construct meaning within the context of their experiences and knowledge. To prepare students for the Listening section of the

AP Chinese exam, this chapter offers important strategies that can improve listening skills. The listening selections offer students an opportunity to practice with different types of listening materials at different levels, and the explanations provide students with the correct answers.

This chapter is organized into the following sections:

1. Rejoinders and Listening Selections
2. Listening Strategies
3. Answer Sheets and Printed Problems
   Section I – Conversation (no printed problems)
   Section II – Short Narration
   Section III – Dialogue
   Section IV – Long Narration
4. Answer Keys
   Section I – Conversation
   Section II – Short Narration
   Section III – Dialogue
   Section IV – Long Narration
5. Answers and Answer Explanations
   Section I – Conversation
   Section II – Short Narration
   Section III – Dialogue
   Section IV – Long Narration
6. Vocabulary Lists
   Section III – Dialogue
   Section IV – Long Narration
7. Scripts
   Section I – Conversation
   Section II – Short Narration
   Section III – Dialogue
   Section IV – Long Narration

Remember that the AP Chinese Language and Culture exam is a computer-based test. The Listening Comprehension section consists of Rejoinders and Listening Selections.

1. Rejoinders – For each problem, you will hear a part of a conversation, followed by four answer choices: (A), (B), (C), and (D). You will then choose one of the choices to complete the conversation most appropriately. Note that the choices will not be displayed on screen.
2. Listening Selections – After listening to each selection, you will see the question and choices in English, one question at a time. You will then choose the most appropriate answer based on the selection you just heard.

MULTIPLE-CHOICE SECTION: LISTENING

Type: Rejoinders
Number of problems: 10–15
Weight: 10%
Duration: 10 minutes

Directions: You will hear the beginning of several short, incomplete conversations. Each conversation will be followed by a list of 4 possible responses. Choose the response that completes the conversation in the most logical and culturally appropriate manner.

Important notes:
1. You will not see the 4 choices. You will hear them immediately after you hear the incomplete conversation.
2. You will hear the conversation and the choices only once.
3. You will see on the screen 4 bubbles labeled A, B, C, D. Click on the one that best completes the conversation.
4. You have 5 seconds to answer each problem.
5. You cannot move back and forth among problems.

Knowledge & Skills:
1. Interpersonal communication.
2. Using set phrases and social formulae.
3. Communicating opinion, attitude, or intent.

Strategies:
1. Stay focused throughout this section.
2. Pay attention to the speaker's mood: happy, sad, excited, etc.
3. Make culturally appropriate responses: response to compliments, addressing one's superior, etc.
4. Do NOT take notes. You won't have enough time.

Fig. 2-1 Rejoinders Task Breakdown

REJOINDERS

The first part of the Listening section on the AP Chinese exam requires students to reply with rejoinders. A **rejoinder** is a quick reply to a question or remark. For each problem, you will hear a part of a conversation, followed by four answer choices. You will then choose the answer that completes the conversation in a culturally and logically appropriate way.

In order to select an appropriate rejoinder to a statement or request, you may have to use several different strategies. For example, you may locate key words, make inferences about the topic of the conversation, refer to their previous experiences, or use a combination of these strategies. Focusing on stressed words and intonation will help you find the key words of the conversation. In longer conversations, you will have to process details and possibly ignore unimportant information. However, this will not be necessary for Rejoinders, as they are relatively short.

Rejoinder questions will typically be in one of these formats:

1. Some questions will directly use question words.

[Traditional-character version]

(Track 1)

(Woman)　　請問圖書館在哪兒？

(Man)　　　(A) 圖書館裏有很多中文書。

　　　　　　(B) 圖書館就在那邊。

　　　　　　(C) 圖書館十點開門。

　　　　　　(D) 圖書館裏有很多學生。

[Simplified-character version]

(Woman)　　请问图书馆在哪儿？

(Man)　　　(A) 图书馆里有很多中文书。

　　　　　　(B) 图书馆就在那边。

　　　　　　(C) 图书馆十点开门。

　　　　　　(D) 图书馆里有很多学生。

HINT: Listen for the question word. For example, after hearing "哪兒" ("哪儿"), you will only have to listen for the choice that responds with a place or direction, which is (B).

2. Some questions will be immediately answered and then followed by another question, which you will have to answer to complete the dialogue.

[Traditional-character version]

(Woman)　　你是從哪個城市來的？

(Man)　　　我是從華盛頓來的。你呢？

(Woman)　　(A) 什麼？你連華盛頓都沒去過？

　　　　　　(B) 我去過美國的很多城市。

　　　　　　(C) 我可不想去那兒。

　　　　　　(D) 我也是從那兒來的。

[Simplified-character version]

(Woman)　　你是从哪个城市来的？

(Man)　　　我是从华盛顿来的。你呢？

(Woman)　　(A) 什么？你连华盛顿都没去过？

　　　　　　(B) 我去过美国的很多城市。

　　　　　　(C) 我可不想去那儿。

　　　　　　(D) 我也是从那儿来的。

HINT: Listen for the question word. Choose the answer that relates to the question word—in this case, (D).

3. **Some questions will have you analyze a statement, then respond with an appropriate ending.**

[Traditional-character version]
(Man)　　　我哥哥一上網就什麼都忘了。
(Woman)　　(A) 他忘了看什麼？
　　　　　　(B) 他為什麼忘了上網？
　　　　　　(C) 他在網上太專心了。
　　　　　　(D) 他能記住什麼？

[Simplified-character version]
(Man)　　　我哥哥一上网就什么都忘了。
(Woman)　　(A) 他忘了看什么？
　　　　　　(B) 他为什么忘了上网？
　　　　　　(C) 他在网上太专心了。
　　　　　　(D) 他能记住什么？

HINT: Watch out for statements disguised as rhetorical questions. Although "什麼" ("什么") is a question word, it is used as a non-specific descriptive in this context. Students should be careful not to take it too literally. The appropriate response here is to follow up with empathy instead of further scrutiny, or (C).

4. **Some questions will require you to respond to a statement with a euphemism.**

[Traditional-character version]
(Woman)　　老趙最近好嗎？我好久沒有看見他了。
(Man)　　　什麼，你還不知道？他已經不在了。
(Woman)　　(A) 我也不知道他在不在。
　　　　　　(B) 怎麼會呢？他的身體一直那麼好。
　　　　　　(C) 他剛才還在這裏。
　　　　　　(D) 他去哪兒了？

[Simplified-character version]
(Woman)　　老赵最近好吗？我好久没有看见他了。
(Man)　　　什么，你还不知道？他已经不在了。
(Woman)　　(A) 我也不知道他在不在。
　　　　　　(B) 怎么会呢？他的身体一直那么好。
　　　　　　(C) 他刚才还在这里。
　　　　　　(D) 他去哪儿了？

HINT: Be sensitive to unpleasant topics such as death, divorce, and the like. "已經不在了" ("已经不在了") is a subtle way of saying someone has died, equivalent to "passed away" in English. Again, students should be careful not to take this phrase literally. The appropriate response here is to say something to ease the unpleasantness, which is (B).

Let's summarize what we learned about Rejoinder questions into some quick tips to improve listening skills.

1. Make connections between prior knowledge and the information at hand.
2. Identify key words and follow the sequence of ideas spoken.
3. Recognize the speaker's main ideas and identify the supporting details and examples.
4. Evaluate the speaker's motive (recognize the speaker's purpose) and determine the speaker's attitude.
5. Listen for the transitions between different thoughts or pieces of information. When speakers finish one thought and start a new one, their voices tend to fall to a lower pitch, and they may pause between thoughts.

LISTENING SELECTIONS

The Listening Selection questions in this book are grouped into four sections.

Section I – Conversation

You will listen to a series of short conversations or parts of conversations followed by questions about what they have heard. Each question will be played once. The questions are not printed on the answer sheet, but they are heard at the end of each conversation. You will have several seconds to respond after you hear each question.

Section II – Short Narration

You will listen to a series of short narratives. The questions for each narrative are given after each selection. Each selection will be played once. You will be given several seconds to respond after you hear each question. All questions are shown in English.

Section III – Dialogue

This section consists of several long dialogues that will be played twice. The questions for each dialogue are printed after each selection on the answer sheet. You will be given a few more seconds than in Section I to respond after you hear each question. All questions are shown in English.

Section IV – Long Narration

This section consists of several long narrations that will be played twice. The questions for each narration are printed after each selection on the answer sheet. You will be given a few more seconds than in Section II to respond. All questions are shown in English.

MULTIPLE-CHOICE SECTION: LISTENING

Type: Listening Selections–
Number of problems: 15–20
Weight: 15%
Duration: 10 minutes

Directions: You will listen to several selections in Chinese. For each selection, you will be told if it will play once or twice. After listening to the selection, you will then see the question and answer choices in English. Choose the answer that best matches the selection.

Important notes:
1. You have 12 seconds to answer each question.
2. You cannot move back and forth among questions.

Knowledge & Skills:
1. Interpretive communication.
2. Comprehension; inference.
3. Application of basic cultural knowledge.

Strategies:
1. Stay focused throughout this section.
2. Pay attention to the speaker's mood: happy, sad, excited, etc.
3. Make culturally appropriate responses: response to compliments, addressing one's superior, etc.
4. You may take notes, but they will not be graded.

Fig. 2-2 Listening Selections Task Breakdown

LISTENING STRATEGIES

Listening strategies are techniques that contribute directly to the comprehension and recall of listening input. Students can use listening strategies to maximize their comprehension of auditory input and identify relevant and non-relevant information. **Specific strategies** include:

1. Determining a speaker's attitude or feelings
2. Focusing on stressed words and intonation
3. Making inferences
4. Taking notes
5. Scanning questions and making predictions
6. Identifying key words and main ideas from the context
7. Processing details
8. Ignoring unimportant information
9. Following scripts

Note that the suggested strategies provided in this chapter are good for pre-exam practices. Although some may not be suitable for the actual exam (scanning, for example), they can nevertheless help you master the language.

Determining a speaker's attitudes or feelings

Questions regarding a person's opinion, attitude, feelings, outlook, or reaction to something are common on the Listening section of the test. Sometimes, the speakers will directly announce their attitudes or feelings. In most cases, however, speakers in a recording only imply them by their tone of voice, intonation, and word choice. Usually, if a speaker emphasizes a certain word or phrase, that word or phrase is important. Students should also listen for the thesis in the recording to grasp the purpose of the speech. The thesis will often be found in either the first or last sentence of the speech.

Common questions that require students to determine the speaker's attitude or opinion are below:

What is the woman's/man's attitude toward/opinion about . . . ?
What does the woman/man mean/imply (by saying . . .)?
What did the woman/man think of . . . ?
What does the woman's answer suggest?
What can be concluded from this conversation?

Track 2

[Traditional-character version]
(Woman)　　你好像有很多工作要做。我看你每天都做到很晚才下班。
(Man)　　　工作多有意思呀，我從來不在乎加班。

[Simplified-character version]
(Woman)　　你好像有很多工作要做。我看你每天都做到很晚才下班。
(Man)　　　工作多有意思呀，我从来不在乎加班。

1. How does the man feel about his job?

    (A) He hates working overtime.
    (B) He doesn't care much for it.
    (C) He enjoys it very much.
    (D) He doesn't mind it even though it is tedious.

(**C**) is correct because the man says his job is very interesting.

People are often very subtle when speaking. When one person disagrees with another person, he usually will not say so directly. He may first agree with the other person politely and euphemistically, but then counteract his statement using an adversative (a word that expresses opposition). Students should pay attention to adversatives to gauge the actual opinion of the speaker while listening to such a conversation. Note that adversatives may be introduced by certain adverbs and conjunctions, including "到底" ("到底") (in the end), "最終" ("最终") (finally), "但是" (but, however), "可是" (but, however), "不過" ("不过") (but, nevertheless), "然而" (yet), "儘管如此" ("尽管如此") (in spite of that), "另一方面" (on the other hand), and "除非" ("除非") (unless). Listen to the following dialogues:

[Traditional-character version]
(Woman)   爸爸，物理太難了，我不想學了。我想去讀商學院。
(Man)   你自己的事情自己決定吧。不過，你最好再想想。要知道，並不
是每一個讀商學院的人都能學好的。

[Simplified-character version]
(Woman)   爸爸，物理太难了，我不想学了。我想去读商学院。
(Man)   你自己的事情自己决定吧。不过，你最好再想想。要知道，并不
是每一个读商学院的人都能学好的。

2. What do we learn from the conversation?

    (A) The man insists that his daughter should pursue her physics degree.
    (B) The man thinks his daughter will be unsuccessful if she gets a business
         degree.
    (C) The man advises his daughter to think carefully before making her
         decision.
    (D) The man doesn't have money for his daughter's studies.

The word "不過" ("不过") in the man's statement expresses that his daughter should
consider her decision carefully, so the answer is (**C**).

[Traditional-character version]
(Woman)   你聽到那個消息了嗎？你覺得怎麼樣？
(Man)   現在，我終于可以睡一個好覺了。

[Simplified-character version]
(Woman)   你听到那个消息了吗？你觉得怎么样？
(Man)   现在，我终于可以睡一个好觉了。

3. How does the man feel when he hears the news?

    (A) Relaxed
    (B) Worried
    (C) Angry
    (D) Happy

"終於可以睡一個好覺了" ("终于可以睡一个好觉了") means "relaxed," so (**A**) is
the correct answer.

Adjectives that describe emotions in Chinese are limited, so students should
practice and become familiar with the following words:

興奮	(兴奋)	excited
高興	(高兴)	happy
生氣	(生气)	angry
擔心	(担心)	worried
失望	(失望)	disappointed
心煩	(心烦)	irritated
沮喪	(沮丧)	depressed

渴望	(渴望)	desirous
放鬆	(放松)	relaxed
緊張	(紧张)	nervous

Students should recognize the differences between actual and subjunctive conditional sentences while listening. Usually, it is not easy to understand subjunctive conditional sentences that express speakers' opinions and attitudes. Practice with the subjunctive conditional sentence in this dialogue:

[Traditional-character version]
(Woman)　　昨天的籃球比賽你們贏了嗎？
(Man)　　　要是我們再多得一分就好了。

[Simplified-character version]
(Woman)　　昨天的篮球比赛你们赢了吗？
(Man)　　　要是我们再多得一分就好了。

4. What does the man mean?

    (A) They lost by one point.
    (B) Their team was the best by far.
    (C) They won a very close game.
    (D) Their team didn't get one point.

The word "要是," with which conditional sentences often start, introduces a subjunctive sentence, meaning that the man's comment is actually the opposite of what happened, so the answer is (**A**).

Students should practice and become familiar with the following conjunctions, and pay attention to their grammatical and semantic meanings:

如果 . . .		if
要不是		if it were not for
要不然		otherwise
除非 . . .　(除非 . . .)		unless
不但 . . . 而且 . . .		not only . . . but also
不僅不 . . . 反而 . . . (不仅不 . . . 反而 . . .)		on the contrary
不是 . . . 就是		if not A, it's B; either A or B
要麼 . . . 要麼 . . . (要么 . . . 要么 . . .)		either . . . or
寧可 . . . , 也 . . . (宁可 . . . 也 . . .)		would rather; better
與其 . . . 不如 . . . (与其 . . . 不如 . . .)		it's better . . . than . . .
雖然　(虽然)		though; although
只是 . . .		it's just that
儘管 . . . 可是 . . . (尽管 . . . 可是 . . .)		even though
只要 . . . 就 . . .		so long as
只有 . . . 才 . . .		only if . . .
無論 . . . 都 . . .　　(无论 . . . 都 . . .)		no matter . . .
就是 . . . 也 . . .		even if . . . still . . .
即使 . . . 也 . . .		even . . . still . . .
因爲 . . . 所以 . . .　　(因为 . . . 所以 . . .)		because . . . , therefore . . .

所以 . . . 是因爲 . . . (所以 . . . 是因为)	the reason is that
既然 . . . 就	since; in the case
以便 . . .	so that
以免　　(以免)	in order to avoid; so as not to

The above conjunctions will be reviewed in Chapter 6 under "Complex Sentences." Students can find examples for each phrase in that chapter.

Distinguishing between interrogative and rhetorical questions is another key listening skill. Understanding rhetorical questions is especially difficult because the message can only be found between the lines. See the rhetorical question in the following dialogue.

[Traditional-character version]
(Woman)　　你爸爸說，你走路去上學不方便，他想給你買一輛自行車。
(Man)　　汽車不更方便嗎？

[Simplified-character version]
(Woman)　　你爸爸说，你走路去上学不方便，他想给你买一辆自行车。
(Man)　　汽车不更方便吗？

5. What does the man mean?

(A) He agrees with the woman.
(B) He should ask his father about it.
(C) Buying a bicycle is a good idea.
(D) He wants to get a car.

The father believes that it is inconvenient to go to school on foot, so he wants to buy a bicycle for his son. However, his son asks his father a rhetorical question that implies that he prefers a car, so the correct answer is (**D**).

STRATEGY

2　Focusing on stressed words and intonation

It is important for students to pay attention to the tone of the speaker's voice and to focus on the stressed words. Students should listen for stressed words, particularly in the Rejoinders section. Useful information and meanings are usually expressed by stressed syllables and intonation. For most listening tests, professional recordings will be provided, so a monotone voice will never express shock, and unimportant words will never be stressed.

Focusing on the stressed words will help students find key words and identify main ideas. Underline the stressed words while listening to the following selection.

[Traditional-character version]

中國人的名字往往都有一定的含義。有的名字包含著出生時的地點、時間或自然現象，如"京、滬、晨、冬、雪"　等；有的名字包含著父母對孩子的願望，如表示健康、漂亮、幸福、快樂的"健、美、興、樂"等等。男人的名字和女人的名字也不完全相同。男人的名字多用表示強壯、勇敢的字,如"虎、龍、偉、強"等;女人的名字多用表示溫柔、美麗、文靜的字,如花、玉、靜等。

[Simplified-character version]

中国人的名字往往都有一定的含义。有的名字包含着出生时的地点、时间或自然现象,如"京、沪、晨、冬、雪"等;有的名字包含着父母对孩子的愿望,如表示健康、漂亮、幸福、快乐的"健、美、兴、乐"等等。男人的名字和女人的名字也不完全相同。男人的名字多用表示强壮、勇敢的字,如"虎、龙、伟、强"等;女人的名字多用表示温柔、美丽、文静的字,如花、玉、静等。

Students should try to focus on the bold words in the above selection while listening, as each of them stresses an important detail. For example, "有…含義" ("有…含义") means "has a specific meaning." The leading sentence, "each Chinese name usually has a specific meaning," expresses the main idea of the selection. The stressed words used in the selection, such as, "地點" ("地点"), "時間" ("时间"), "現象" ("现象"), and "父母…願望" ("父母…愿望"), support the main idea. Another stressed word, "不," indicates that male names differ from female names, and vice versa. Moreover, the words "強壯" ("强壮"), and "勇敢" further specify some meanings of male names, while the words "溫柔" ("温柔"), "美麗" ("美丽"), and "文靜" ("文静") specify some meanings of female names. Focusing on different intonations will also help students understand listening passages more clearly.

STRATEGY

3　Making inferences

Making inferences is another important listening strategy. Inferring is the process of identifying the main idea of a listening passage based on evidence in the passage. It involves combining what is heard with relevant prior knowledge. Oftentimes, a speaker will imply something and leave it up for interpretation. Making inferences when listening is usually easier than when reading.

Understanding vocabulary that relates to the topic and the main ideas is an essential ingredient of making inferences. For example, words such as *medicine*, *patient*, *doctor*, and *recover* will relate to hospitals; words such as *check*, *interest*, *rate*, *account*, and *bank* will relate to money; and *returning* and *checking out* books will relate to a library. These key words, combined with common knowledge, can help students make inferences.

Here are some common inference questions that may appear in the Listening section:

What can be inferred from the passage?

What is the speaker most concerned about?

How does the writer feel about . . . ?

What does the author want to tell us?

Practice making inferences with the following conversation.

1. [Traditional-character version]

(Woman)　張林，你要的那本字典我帶來了，放在你的桌子上了。

(Man)　　是凱琳啊，謝謝你，我馬上去拿。你現在要回家嗎？

(Woman)　不，我先去圖書館借幾本書，然後再回家。

(Man)　　聽說你昨天去爬山了，怎麼樣？

(Woman)　不錯啊，天氣很好，就是山上的人太多了。你也要去？

(Man)　　要是人那麼多，我就再想想吧。對了，我有一道數學題想問問你，你什麼時候有時間？

(Woman)　今天晚上我家裏有點兒事，明天吧，你看明天怎麼樣？

(Man)　　沒問題，就明天吧。那明天見。

[Simplified-character version]

(Woman)　张林，你要的那本字典我带来了，放在你的桌子上了。

(Man)　　是凯琳啊，谢谢你，我马上去拿。你现在要回家吗？

(Woman)　不，我先去图书馆借几本书，然后再回家。

(Man)　　听说你昨天去爬山了，怎么样？

(Woman)　不错啊，天气很好，就是山上的人太多了。你也要去？

(Man)　　要是人那么多，我就再想想吧。对了，我有一道数学题想问问你，你什么时候有时间？

(Woman)　今天晚上我家里有点儿事，明天吧，你看明天怎么样？

(Man)　　没问题，就明天吧。那明天见。

Based on this piece of conversation, students can infer the answers to the following questions: 1) Who is talking? Two students. 2) Where are they talking? The woman is at the man's place returning a dictionary, but he is not there. 3) What are they talking about? Lending dictionaries, checking out books, climbing a mountain, and doing mathematics homework.

Making inferences helps students analyze information that is not directly expressed, but implied. Students not only have to listen for the literal meanings of individual words but also understand their implied meanings. Using this strategy, students can make guesses or assumptions about speakers' purposes and attitudes.

Here is another example:

[Traditional-character version]

(Man)　　快點走不好嗎，要不然就遲到了。

(Woman)　我的鞋跟太高了，你先走吧。

[Simplified-character version]

(Man)　　快点走不好吗，要不然就迟到了。

(Woman)　我的鞋跟太高了，你先走吧。

2. What does the woman mean by her statement?

(A) She can't walk any faster.

(B) Her heel broke.

(C) She has other errands to run.

(D) She likes to walk slowly.

This conversation states two facts: First, the man asks the woman to walk faster because they are going to be late; and second, the woman asks the man to go first because her heels are too high to walk on. From this information, students can infer that the woman cannot walk any faster, so (**A**) is the correct answer.

Listening to passages about daily activities, social life, culture, history, and fables requires students to know some background information, and to focus on important events, characters, and relationships, to infer the speaker's opinion. For example:

[Traditional-character version]

八十年代的時候，中國人過年、過節，或者拜訪親朋好友時，　總是送一些像蛋糕、糖果、水果之類的小禮物。後來，人們的生活水平提高了，送的禮物也就越來越好，像送咖啡、維生素等的已經不是少數了。隨著生活條件和文化素質的不斷提高，人們又開始注重精神生活水平，于是送書開始流行起來。現在，商店裏的東西應有盡有，買禮物卻成了人們頭疼的一件事。今後隨著計算機的普及，送學習軟件可能是最好不過的禮物了。

[Simplified-character version]

八十年代的时候，中国人过年、过节，或者拜访亲朋好友时，总是送一些像蛋糕、糖果、水果之类的小礼物。后来，人们的生活水平提高了，送的礼物也就越来越好，像送咖啡、维生素等的已经不是少数了。随着生活条件和文化素质的不断提高，人们又开始注重精神生活水平，于是送书开始流行起来。现在，商店里的东西应有尽有，买礼物却成了人们头疼的一件事。今后随着计算机的普及，送学习软件可能是最好不过的礼物了。

3. What did people give as presents in the '80s?

   (A) Candies and fruit
   (B) Coffee
   (C) Computers
   (D) Books

4. What will people probably give as presents in the future?

   (A) Fruit and candies
   (B) Books
   (C) Computer software
   (D) Vitamins

5. Why do people worry about buying presents?

   (A) There are too many people to buy presents for.
   (B) There are too many varieties of presents.
   (C) There aren't enough things to choose from.
   (D) Presents are too expensive.

Students should recognize some key words while listening to this passage. If they grasped the key words, which are a variety of presents, then they may well answer the first two questions easily: (**A**) for question 3 and (**C**) for question 4. If students notice the essential sentence "商店裏的東西應有盡有，買禮物却成了人們頭疼的一件事" ("商店里的东西应有尽有，买礼物却成了人们头疼的一件事"), they can make an inference to choose the correct answer for question 5. (**B**) is correct because the literal meaning of this sentence is that people don't know what to buy, but its contextual meaning is that there are too many varieties of presents to choose from.

Sometimes, students need to make inferences based on a series of actions, as in this example:

[Traditional-character version]
(Man)   我把名字寫在這兒了，這裏填的是出生日期和出生地，這裏填的是我的家庭地址。你看，還要填什麼？
(Woman)   我來看一下，嗯，沒有什麼了。請在這裏簽上你的名字。

[Simplified-character version]
(Man)   我把名字写在这儿了，这里填的是出生日期和出生地，这里填的是我的家庭地址。你看，还要填什么？
(Woman)   我来看一下，嗯，没有什么了。请在这里签上你的名字。

6. What is the man doing?

    (A) Asking for information
    (B) Filling out a form
    (C) Talking to a friend
    (D) Having a birthday party

If students are able to infer something from this series of actions—writing "名字," "出生日期," "出生地," filling out "家庭地址," and signing—"簽上…名字" ("签上…名字") they will be able to choose the correct answer, (**B**).

Making inferences is very useful in answering questions regarding "cause and effect." For example:

[Traditional-character version]
(Man)   爲什麼小張不在我們公司做了？
(Woman)   他被解聘了。

[Simplified-character version]
(Man)   为什么小张不在我们公司做了？
(Woman)   他被解聘了。

7. Why does Xiao Zhang not work?

    (A) He is tired of working.
    (B) He was dismissed from his job.
    (C) He's changing jobs.
    (D) The company is too big.

If students understand that this dialogue indicates the consequence of an event "被解聘," ("被解聘,") they will realize that the correct answer is (**B**). The passive voice in the woman's statement also indicates this answer.

[Traditional-character version]
(Man)   如果公司給你提薪，你還會換工作嗎？
(Woman)   我已經決定了，我想找個能發揮我能力的工作。

[Simplified-character version]
(Man)   如果公司给你提薪，你还会换工作吗？
(Woman)   我已经决定了，我想找个能发挥我能力的工作。

8. Why has the woman decided to leave the company?

   (A) She is too tired to work.
   (B) She is not sufficiently paid for her work.
   (C) The job isn't challenging enough.
   (D) She cannot keep her mind on her work.

In order to answer this question, students have to make an inference from the sentence "我想找個能發揮我能力的工作" ("我想找个能发挥我能力的工作"). This sentence implies "She doesn't think the job is challenging enough," so (**C**) is the answer.

Sometimes, long passages may appear in the Listening section of the exam. These passages are often simpler than shorter recordings because they may not be related to literature or academics, or include technical jargon. Instead, their topics, such as school life, family issues, entertainment, or animals, are usually general. Also, a longer passage may contain more useful information for making inferences. If students have a good general knowledge and vocabulary, they will feel confident when listening to long passages.

STRATEGY

4   Taking notes

Taking notes is important while listening. Students are allowed to take notes during the second part of the Listening section, but their notes will not be graded. Taking notes requires students to: 1) listen and analyze at the same time; and 2) identify the topic quickly and write down the main idea and supporting details. The speed of note-taking must match the speech rate.

Taking notes while listening differs from taking dictation. Using key words, simple, meaningful symbols, and figures is an important principle of note-taking. Names, places, numbers, and occupations, are essential information to include in notes. Efficient note-taking helps students better understand listening materials and remember content when answering the questions. The following example illustrates some techniques for taking notes.

[Traditional-character version]
(Man)   你知道物理老師的辦公時間是什麼時候嗎？我有一些問題想問問他。
(Woman)   請稍等，我幫你看一下。他的時間是星期一、三、四從下午1點到下午4點，星期二和星期五從下午6點到晚上8點。

[Simplified-character version]

(Man)　　　你知道物理老师的办公时间是什么时候吗？我有一些问题想问问他。

(Woman)　　请稍等，我帮你看一下。他的时间是星期一、三、四从下午1点到下午4点，星期二和星期五从下午6点到晚上8点。

1. When does the teacher have office hours?

   (A) From one to four in the afternoon on Friday
   (B) From six to eight in the afternoon on Monday
   (C) At ten in the morning on Wednesday
   (D) At seven in the evening on Tuesday

Students' notes might look like this: 1、3、4: 1PM → 4PM; 2、5: 6PM → 8PM. From these notes, they'll be able to choose the correct answer, (**D**).

Note-taking methods vary greatly between individuals. Different symbols, signs, and abbreviations, in Pinyin or English, can be adopted for taking notes. The important thing is for students to develop a note-taking technique that works for them.

STRATEGY

Scanning questions and making predictions

This strategy is intended as an exercise for practicing listening comprehension skills prior to the exam. During the Listening section of the AP Chinese exam, the questions and answer choices are not visible to students until after they listen to the audio; therefore, this strategy is not applicable during the exam.

When practicing for the exam, students can be given several seconds to hear or to read the questions before each recorded passage begins. Students should use this time to become familiar with the questions, scanning them instead of reading them word for word.

When scanning, students should underline key words and decide what they need to listen for. Students should pay attention to question words such as *where* and *who* that require specific details about places and people. Scanning the multiple-choice answers beforehand can help students predict the topics of the test questions and quickly refresh related vocabulary.

The following examples show how to apply the scanning technique on both short and long multiple-choice answers. For short multiple-choice answers, quickly looking over them may be sufficient to obtain the relevant information. However, for long multiple-choice answers, vertically scanning the list of choices may help students identify the differences between the choices. For example:

1. (A) Swimming
   (B) Cycling
   (C) Running
   (D) Hunting

2. (A) A single room
   (B) A double room
   (C) A room on the second floor
   (D) A room on the third floor

3. (A) The man had gone home.
   (B) The man had a fight with his colleague.
   (C) The man had finished loading the truck.
   (D) The man had just started loading the truck.

4. (A) His daughter must leave for school at 9:30.
   (B) His daughter must go to work at 9:30.
   (C) His wife must have breakfast at 9:30.
   (D) His wife must get to her office at 9:30.

The multiple-choice answers in question 1 are short. By looking over them, it is easy to identify all four as sports or games. Although the answers in question 2 are slightly longer, by looking at them quickly students can tell that the choices are all about apartments. The answer choices in question 3 are long. By comparing the answers vertically, students will see that all four answers contain "the man had" and the differences between the answers are:

(A) gone home
(B) a fight with his colleague
(C) finished loading the truck
(D) just started loading the truck

The choices in question 4 are also long. By looking over the answers, students will find the following commonalities:

1. the ending of all four answers is the same, "9:30;"
2. both (A) and (B) are about his daughter;
3. both (C) and (D) are about his wife.

By comparing the middle parts of the answers vertically, students can further identify the differences between the answers:

(A) daughter must leave for school
(B) daughter must go to work
(C) wife must have breakfast
(D) wife must get to her office

Listening materials contain a lot of information and prompt a variety of questions. While listening, some students hear individual words and sentences rather then the complete thoughts they express. Although they may understand each word or a single sentence, they sometimes fail to understand the conversation as a whole. In addition, students often forget an earlier part of a selection when listening to a later part. When they answer the questions, they may have difficulty recalling what they heard in each section.

Sometimes students risk losing a portion of a selection by thinking about the questions instead of about what they are hearing. On longer selections, it is probably better to focus on remembering what they hear. When listening, it is important to lock down some key words and important sentences. Understanding and remembering the key points is half the battle in choosing the correct answers.

Students should use the scanning strategy to make predictions about the selection before or while listening. Before listening, students should analyze the wording of the questions and answer choices and refer to their own knowledge and experience about the topic. Scanning some questions greatly helps students grasp the ideas of listening materials, such as speeches or conversations. While listening, students should pay attention to the leading sentence of the introductory paragraph, which usually states the topic of the essay and often outlines the rest of the work. Sometimes, the leading sentence of the conclusion paragraph also summarizes the key points of an essay. Grasping the topic is an important part of understanding the essay as a whole. Besides the topic, students should try to predict the author's purpose. An accurate prediction shows that the student has correctly aligned his or her thoughts with those of the speaker. An incorrect prediction implies that the student must learn to listen more carefully.

Scan questions 5–8 and their answer choices, based on a dialogue between a man and a woman, to practice predicting the ideas in a selection.

5. Why didn't the phone call go through the last two times?

   (A) The phone broke.
   (B) The line was busy.
   (C) The number was wrong.
   (D) No one picked up the phone.

6. Why does the man call the woman?

   (A) To watch a movie
   (B) To come over for dinner
   (C) To go shopping
   (D) To join a club

7. Why doesn't the woman accept the invitation?

   (A) She has a test the next day.
   (B) She already has a plan.
   (C) There aren't any good movies out.
   (D) She's sick.

8. Who is the man?

   (A) A student
   (B) A doctor
   (C) An actor
   (D) A patient

Students should be able to predict the topic by scanning these questions as a whole. By identifying the key words "phone call," "join a club," "watch a movie," "eat dinner," and "tests," students will easily recognize that the topic of the dialogue is "inviting someone to do something."

In the same way, scan questions 9–11 and their multiple-choice options to practice making predictions about an essay.

9. What is a good eating habit?

　(A) Eating an appropriate amount of food at a good time
　(B) Eating a lot
　(C) Eating very cold and very hot foods
　(D) Eating good foods sparingly

10. How should breakfast, lunch, and dinner be eaten?

　(A) Eat a lot at dinner.
　(B) Eat a lot at breakfast and dinner, and less during lunch.
　(C) Never eat breakfast.
　(D) Eat less at dinner.

11. What kind of problems will eating snacks bring?

　(A) Decreased appetite
　(B) Increased appetite
　(C) Disease
　(D) Obesity

Students should be able to predict the topic of the essay by scanning these questions as a whole. Identifying the key words "eating habits," "three meals," and "snacks" should enable students to predict the topic: "eating habits and health." Being able to predict the topic will help students comprehend the audio material and then predict its main idea while listening.

Practice making predictions by scanning the questions and the answer choices before listening to the following two selections.

[Traditional-character version]
　　缺水是世界各大城市的主要問題。到了2025年，世界上將有三分之二以上的人口生活在城市。目前世界上16%的城市人口缺少飲用水，尤其在非洲，缺水的城市更多。專家們說，讓城市人有水喝是人們生活的基本條件，也是城市發展的主要方面。爲了解決缺水問題，我們要重視水資源的管理，特別是解決好飲用水的保存和輸送等問題。

[Simplified-character version]
　　缺水是世界各大城市的主要问题。到了2025年，世界上将有三分之二以上的人口生活在城市。目前世界上16%的城市人口缺少饮用水，尤其在非洲，缺水的城市更多。专家们说，让城市人有水喝是人们生活的基本条件，也是城市发展的主要方面。为了解决缺水问题，我们要重视水资源的管理，特别是解决好饮用水的保存和输送等问题。

12. What is the main topic of the selection?

   (A) Social pressures
   (B) Citizens' needs
   (C) Shortage of drinking water
   (D) Population growth

The leading sentence, "缺水是世界各大城市的主要問題" ("缺水是世界各大城市的主要问题"), and the last sentence "爲了解決缺水問題" ("为了解决缺水问题"), of the passage indicate that the topic is related to the shortage of drinking water, so (**C**) is the correct answer.

[Traditional-character version]

　　電子游戲對人們生活的各個方面都有影響。一方面，當人們在學習和工作中感到壓力大的時候，適當地玩玩電子游戲，可以使精神得到放鬆；但另一方面，那些有殺人、搶劫內容的電子遊戲對人們，特別是對青少年會產生不好的影響，再加上一些青少年整天玩遊戲，使其學習成績不斷下降，讓他們對學習越來越沒有興趣。

[Simplified-character version]

　　电子游戏对人们生活的各个方面都有影响。一方面，当人们在学习和工作中感到压力大的时候，适当地玩玩电子游戏，可以使精神得到放松；但另一方面，那些有杀人、抢劫内容的电子游戏对人们，特别是对青少年会产生不好的影响，再加上一些青少年整天玩游戏，使其学习成绩不断下降，让他们对学习越来越没有兴趣。

13. What is the theme of the passage?

   (A) Video games cause grades to go down.
   (B) Video games have many positive aspects.
   (C) Video games influence people.
   (D) Video games are dangerous.

By scanning the question and answer choices, students will see that (A) and (D) have negative connotations, (C) has a neutral connotation, and (B) has a positive connotation. The scanning process should help students predict that (C) might be the correct answer since it covers both positive, (B), and negative, (A) and (D), aspects associated with playing video games. The first sentence, "電子遊戲對人們生活的各個方面都有影響"("电子游戏对人们生活的各个方面都有影响"), which has a neutral connotation, supports (C).

　　As you have seen, this listening strategy utilizes reading skills to help students find the general topic from the questions and answer choices. If students can identify the general topic beforehand, they will be under less pressure while listening to recordings. This strategy can really benefit students, helping them focus on the main ideas and specific information in the listening passages.

STRATEGY

6 Identifying key words and main ideas from the context

As discussed in the previous section, scanning questions and answer choices helps students understand the general topic of a speech or conversation. Knowing the topic may help students identify the main idea of the passage while listening. The main idea is the key point or thought expressed.

A key word is a word or a concept with special significance. In listening tests, key words usually express the key points in the speech or conversation. Some key words directly name places, people, or things. Some key words repeatedly appear in the speech or conversation. Students should underline or write down the key words while listening.

But remember: The answer choices will often use a substitution or an explanation, rather than the key word itself. Answering these questions requires students to master a wide range of vocabulary and listening skills. Listen to the following conversation and answer the question.

[Traditional-character version]
(Woman)	我找了你半天，你去哪兒了？
(Man)	我哪兒都沒去，我剛來。
(Woman)	你怎麼現在才來？
(Man)	我今天早上睡過頭了，只好坐下個航班的飛機了。

[Simplified-character version]
(Woman)	我找了你半天，你去哪儿了？
(Man)	我哪儿都没去，我刚来。
(Woman)	你怎么现在才来？
(Man)	我今天早上睡过头了，只好坐下个航班的飞机了。

1. Why was the man late?

(A) He got up later than usual.
(B) The flight was late.
(C) He forgot the appointment.
(D) His clock was slow.

"睡過頭了" ("睡过头了") is the key word, which indicates that the man got up later than usual, so the answer is (**A**).

Finding key words is an important strategy for understanding listening materials, especially in the Rejoinders section. For example, if students hear words and phrases from a conversation such as "菜單" ("菜单"), "點菜" ("点菜"), and "飲料" ("饮料"), they can infer that the place is a restaurant and the topic is related to food. Using this strategy, it should be easy for students to answer the questions.

Listening to the leading sentence of the introductory paragraph in an argumentative essay is helpful for identifying the main idea. Typical main idea questions include:

What is the main idea of this passage?
What is the passage mainly about?
What is the speaker talking about?
Which of these titles fits the passage best?

Use the listening selection below to practice focusing on key words and identifying the main idea.

[Traditional-character version]

　　體育已經進入現代人的生活之中，成爲人們日常生活中的一個重要部分。在中國，經常參加體育運動的人數是總人口的18%，而且這個比例還在不斷增長。在經濟比較發達的國家中，比如美國，經常參加體育運動的人更多。體育用它特有的內容和形式吸引了越來越多的人，豐富了人們的生活內容，增強了人們的體質。

[Simplified-character version]

　　体育已经进入现代人的生活之中，成为人们日常生活中的一个重要部分。在中国，经常参加体育运动的人数是总人口的18%，而且这个比例还在不断增长。在经济比较发达的国家中，比如美国，经常参加体育运动的人更多。体育用它特有的内容和形式吸引了越来越多的人，丰富了人们的生活内容，增强了人们的体质。

2. What is the main idea of this report?

   (A) More and more Chinese people are taking part in sports.
   (B) There are many reasons why people join sports.
   (C) Sports are a big part of life.
   (D) There are many different sports.

3. Which of the following titles fits the report best?

   (A) Sports and Economy
   (B) Sports and Life
   (C) Different Sports
   (D) People Who Play Sports

After listening to this report, students will find that the word "sport" appears frequently. Using "sport" as a key word, students should infer that the report topic is sports. After listening to the first sentence, "體育已經進入現代人的生活之中，成爲人們日常生活中的一個重要部分"（"体育已经进入现代人的生活之中，成为人们日常生活中的一个重要部分"）, and the last sentence, "體育用它特有的內容和形式吸引了越來越多的人，豐富了人們的生活內容，增強了人們的體質"（"体育用它特有的内容和形式吸引了越来越多的人，丰富了人们的生活内容，增强了人们的体质"）, students should be able to identify the main idea—"sports are a part of life"—so **(C)** is the correct answer for question 2. Once they have found the main idea, students should be able to determine the title of the report, choosing **(B)** as the answer for question 3.

　　Identifying main ideas based on key words can be a complex process, because key words do not always appear repeatedly in the audio materials. If this is the case, students can identify the main idea using other techniques—for example, inferring the main idea based on a contextual clue or determining the main idea by eliminating non-relevant information. The next selection will help students learn how to identify the main idea in a complicated news report.

[Traditional-character version]

　　在中國，由於不良的生活方式而引起的疾病死亡率很高。就拿北京來說吧，專家曾經對北京市兩萬多人進行調查，發現超過三分之一的疾病是由不好的飲食習慣、吸煙、喝酒以及不運動等不健康的生活方式所引起的。

[Simplified-character version]

　　在中国，由于不良的生活方式而引起的疾病死亡率很高。就拿北京来说吧，专家曾经对北京市两万多人进行调查，发现超过三分之一的疾病是由不好的饮食习惯、吸烟、喝酒以及不运动等不健康的生活方式所引起的。

4. What is the main idea of the report?

  (A) Many people in Beijing are getting sick.
  (B) Bad living habits cause disease.
  (C) Drinking and smoking are unhealthy.
  (D) Beijing conducted a survey of 20,000 people.

In this case, the questions do not include key words that suggest the main idea of the report. However, understanding the phrase "在中國" (在中国) in the leading sentence should help students find a context clue—"China"—even though "China" does not appear in the answer choices. Students can infer that the main idea of the report is related to "China" instead of "Beijing," as Beijing is just a part of China and taken as example. Consequently, students can exclude (A) and (D) related to "Beijing." Students can also eliminate (C), because it is too specific to be the main idea. Thus, only **(B)** represents the main idea of the report.

　　Students are strongly advised to practice finding key words and identifying main ideas. These skills are essential to comprehending listening materials accurately.

STRATEGY

7 Processing details

Processing the details of listening materials, such as time, places, characters, and numbers, is one of the most important strategies for the AP Chinese Listening test, especially for answering Rejoinders and "sample stimulus" questions. The art of processing details requires students to focus on detailed information once they have found the main idea and to constantly compare what they hear with what they know about the topic. They must listen closely for information that answers the questions what?, where?, who?, and when?, and for information about how something is done or why something is happening.

　　Students should remember that, when answering detailed questions, they can often find the answers directly stated in the passage. Also, the order of the subjects in the questions usually reflects the order of the passage. Therefore, take note of the setting, characters, plot, and so on as you go. Students should also identify relationships and occupations. Keeping track of details can be difficult. However, learning to write down as much detail as possible when taking notes will help tremendously. If students can sort and file this information as they hear it, they will remember it better.

Questions regarding **time and numbers** often appear in listening tests. Students tend to score very low in this area. This is because many students are not familiar with numbers in Chinese. Numbers such as dates, ages, and phone numbers are usually given directly, but sometimes students have to know the connection between numbers or do simple math problems in their heads. Recordings also may include comparison words such as "多," "少," "晚," "早," "快," "慢," "以前," "之後" ("之后"), and other number-related adjectives, prepositions, and adverbs. In general, visualizing the numerals instead of the words helps understanding. Students should practice numbers regularly so that they don't waste time translating words as they listen. The following passage will help students develop the skills needed to process details.

Track 8

[Traditional-character version]

　　大衛，我是珍妮。我給你打了幾次電話都沒有找到你。你今天中午看新聞了嗎？就是關於早上那場車禍的。電視上說，那是我們社區一所學校的校車，車上一名司機和兩個學生當時就死了，剩下的四位老師和六十三個學生也都受傷了。這場車禍真是太嚴重了，我很難過。我想下午到醫院去看看那些受傷的老師和學生們。你想跟我一起去嗎？請給我回個電話。

[Simplified-character version]

　　大卫，我是珍妮。我给你打了几次电话都没有找到你。你今天中午看新闻了吗？就是关于早上那场车祸的。电视上说，那是我们社区一所学校的校车，车上一名司机和两个学生当时就死了，剩下的四位老师和六十三个学生也都受伤了。这场车祸真是太严重了，我很难过。我想下午到医院去看看那些受伤的老师和学生们。你想跟我一起去吗？请给我回个电话。

1. How many people suffered in the car crash?

　　(A) 70　　　(B) 63　　　(C) 4　　　(D) 3

The important key word is "suffer." "Suffer" includes people who died and also people who were injured. The correct answer is **(A)** because $1 + 2 + 4 + 63 = 70$. In this case, solving a simple mathematic problem is necessary.

Listen to the following announcement and answer the question.

[Traditional-character version]

　　各位乘客請注意，我們每天早上7點發車，每兩個小時一趟，但是周末比平常晚半個小時發車。

[Simplified-character version]

　　各位乘客请注意，我们每天早上7点发车，每两个小时一趟，但是周末比平常晚半个小时发车。

2. When did the second bus leave on Saturday morning?

    (A) 7:30   (B) 8:00   (C) 9:00   (D) 9:30

Students must listen carefully for the two hard parts of the problem: "每兩個小時一趟" ("每两个小时一趟") and "周末比平常晚半個小時" ("周末比平常晚半个小时"). Students must also notice "the second bus" and "Saturday" in the question. Using this information, students can select the correct answer, **(D)**. To do so, a deduction in two steps needs to take place: 1) "每天早上7點發車" ("每天早上7点发车") and "每兩個小時一趟" ("每两个小时一趟") indicate that the second bus is at 9:00 AM; 2) "周末比平常晚半個小時" ("周末比平常晚半个小时") indicates that the bus is a half hour late on the "Saturday" in question, so the correct answer is 9:30 AM.

[Traditional-character version]
(Woman)   我想預訂兩張八月三號的民航984號班機的票。
(Man)   三號的已經訂完了，我們還有幾張四號的。

[Simplified-character version]
(Woman)   我想预订两张八月三号的民航984号班机的票。
(Man)   三号的已经订完了，我们还有几张四号的。

3. When does the woman want to leave?

    (A) August 4th
    (B) August 8th
    (C) August 3rd
    (D) August 13th

Students should try to listen for useful information and ignore words that are not necessarily relevant to the question. For example, the words "Flight 984" and "4th of August" are irrelevant here. Being familiar with the format of dates in Chinese will certainly help students answer this and similar questions.

    Remembering important adverbs, adjectives, and time-measure words, such as "快…了," "差不多" ("差不多"), "…點過…分" ("…点过…分"), "…點半" ("…点半"), and "幾個…" ("几个…"), is very helpful in correctly understanding listening materials.

[Traditional-character version]
(Woman)   小張，你下課後直接回宿舍嗎？
(Man)   我今天的課上到1點，下課以後我還得去圖書館看幾個小時的書，因為明天有個考試。

[Simplified-character version]
(Woman)   小张，你下课后直接回宿舍吗？
(Man)   我今天的课上到1点，下课以后我还得去图书馆看几个小时的书，因为明天有个考试。

4. Which of the following is more plausible?

(A) Xiao Zhang will go back to the dorm around 5:00.
(B) Xiao Zhang will go back to the dorm around 3:00.
(C) Xiao Zhang will go back to the dorm around 2:00.
(D) Xiao Zhang will go back to the dorm around 1:00.

If students clearly hear the information "課上到1點" ("课上到1点") and "去圖書館看幾個小時的書" ("去图书馆看几个小时的书"), they can use the word "幾" ("几"), which means "more than three," to find the correct answer, **(A)**.

The following skills are essential for correctly understanding prices expressed in Chinese:

1. being familiar with the format of prices in Chinese;

2. understanding prices for one item or a set of items;

3. knowing important words, such as "百分之…," "打…折," "原價" ("原价"), "降半價" ("降半价"), and "打X折";

4. using simple arithmetic.

[Traditional-character version]
(Woman)   我要買兩張票，我這兒有十美元。
(Man)   這是你的票，請拿好，這是找你的錢，一塊四。

[Simplified-character version]
(Woman)   我要买两张票，我这儿有十美元。
(Man)   这是你的票，请拿好，这是找你的钱，一块四。

5. How much does one ticket cost?

(A) $1.40
(B) $4.30
(C) $8.60
(D) $6.40

The key to this problem is to listen for "十美元," "兩張票" ("两张票"), "找," and "一塊四" ("一块四"). Students can use simple addition and subtraction to obtain the correct answer, **(B)**.

Questions regarding **location and direction** appear frequently in listening tests, so it's important for students to listen carefully for directional words. To help answer these questions, students should practice and remember words regarding location and direction. For example, if students hear "登記" ("登记"), "房間" ("房间"), "含早餐", and "退房" ("退房"), the conversation is related to a hotel; if students hear "大小," "肥瘦," "顏色" ("颜色"), and "打折," the conversation is related to a clothing store. Common questions for location include:

Where does the conversation most probably take place?
Where does this conversation most likely occur?
Where are the two speakers?

Such questions often appear in dialogues about daily life, including conversations about clothing, food, shelter, occupation, and studying. The related locations are often public places (banks, malls, airports, hospitals, clothing stores, and campuses) and homes. People employ different types of language at different places. Being familiar with the following words associated with specific places will be beneficial to students.

Campus

[Traditional-character version]

宿舍，圖書館、實驗室、教室、教學樓、運動場、教授，同學、指導教師、學期、考試、課程、學分、輔導、畢業、功課、報告、獎學金

[Simplified-character version]

宿舍，图书馆、实验室、教室、教学楼、运动场、教授，同学、指导教师、学期、考试、课程、学分、辅导、毕业、功课、报告、奖学金

Restaurant

[Traditional-character version]

飯館、服務員、位子、桌子、菜單、預定、點菜、上菜、主食、酒、果汁、素菜、葷菜、中餐、西餐、甜點、小費、好吃、餓、渴、味精、飲料

[Simplified-character version]

饭馆、服务员、位子、桌子、菜单、预定、点菜、上菜、主食、酒、果汁、素菜、荤菜、中餐、西餐、甜点、小费、好吃、饿、渴、味精、饮料

Airport

[Traditional-character version]

機場、登機口、座位、航空公司、班機、航班號、安全檢查、托運、飛行、起飛、晚點、行李、直飛、轉機

[Simplified-character version]

机场、登机口、座位、航空公司、班机、航班号、安全检查、托运、飞行、起飞、晚点、行李、直飞、转机

Train station

[Traditional-character version]

快車、慢車、直達、晚點、車廂、乘客、列車員、檢票、站臺、時刻表、高鐵

[Simplified-character version]

快车、慢车、直达、晚点、车厢、乘客、列车员、检票、站台、时刻表、高铁

Hospital

[Traditional-character version]

醫生、大夫、護士、病人、手術室、急症、身體、生病、感冒、發燒、咳嗽、頭疼、牙疼、檢查、探訪時間、處方、打針、吃藥、健康保險

[Simplified-character version]

　　医生、大夫、护士、病人、手术室、急症、身体、生病、感冒、发烧、咳嗽、头疼、牙疼、检查、探访时间、处方、打针、吃药、健康保险

Post office

[Traditional-character version]

　　郵局、營業員、平信、快信、郵票、信封、信、包裹、明信片、郵資、掛號、海運、陸運、聯邦快遞

[Simplified-character version]

　　邮局、营业员、平信、快信、邮票、信封、信、包裹、明信片、邮资、挂号、海运、陆运、联邦快递

Hotel

[Traditional-character version]

　　星級飯店、三星級、四星級、五星級、豪華套間、客房服務、前臺、服務員、訂房間、登記、單人房、雙人房、入住、結帳、單人床、雙人床、大床、沙發、電視、臺燈

[Simplified-character version]

　　星级饭店、三星级、四星级、五星级、豪华套间、客房服务、前台、服务员、订房间、登记、单人房、双人房、入住、结帐、单人床、双人床、大床、沙发、电视、台灯

Library

[Traditional-character version]

　　圖書館員、閱覽室、音像室、開架圖書、參考書、工具書、開門、關門、借書證、借書、還書、續借、過期、罰款

[Simplified-character version]

　　图书馆员、阅览室、音像室、开架图书、参考书、工具书、开门、关门、借书证、借书、还书、续借、过期、罚款

Shopping

[Traditional-character version]

　　購物中心、小賣部、商店、百貨商店、市場、早市、夜市、大排檔、售貨員、顧客、物美價廉、討價還價、打折、大減價、大拍賣、貴、便宜、大、小、長、短、肥、瘦、合適、號、換、退、付錢、找錢、現金、支票、信用卡

[Simplified-character version]

　　购物中心、小卖部、商店、百货商店、市场、早市、夜市、大排档、售货员、顾客、物美价廉、讨价还价、打折、大减价、大拍卖、贵、便宜、大、小、长、短、肥、瘦、合适、号、换、退、付钱、找钱、现金、支票、信用卡

The following conversations contain clues to help students determine the location of events.

[Traditional-character version]
(Man)   你剛才去哪兒了？指導老師找了你半天了。
(Woman)   我一直在這兒上課呢。

[Simplified-character version]
(Man)   你刚才去哪儿了? 指导老师找了你半天了。
(Woman)   我一直在这儿上课呢。

6. Where does the conversation most probably take place?

   (A) In a restaurant
   (B) At a bank
   (C) At a bookstore
   (D) At a school

The key point "在這兒上課" ("在这儿上课)" indicates that the correct answer is **(D)**.

[Traditional-character version]
(Man)   我看了今天報紙上的廣告，你們有房間要出租，是嗎？
(Woman)   是啊，就在二樓。要是你有興趣，我帶你上去看看。

[Simplified-character version]
(Man)   我看了今天报纸上的广告，你们有房间要出租，是吗？
(Woman)   是啊，就在二楼。要是你有兴趣，我带你上去看看。

7. Where does this conversation most likely occur?

   (A) At a bank
   (B) In a restaurant
   (C) In a post office
   (D) At an apartment building

"有房間要出租" ("有房间要出租") and "我帶你上去看看" ("我带你上去看看") indicate that the answer is **(D)**.

   There are only a few Chinese direction words to remember. It is a good idea to sketch out a map while listening to selections that include directions. Listening to the following selections will help students obtain information about direction.

[Traditional-character version]
   去圖書館很容易。你從這兒一直往南走，看到一個小書店往東拐，再一直走，看到郵局，就往南拐，走不了多遠，就可以看到一家銀行，銀行的後面就是圖書館。

[Simplified-character version]

去图书馆很容易。你从这儿一直往南走，看到一个小书店往东拐，再一直走，看到邮局，就往南拐，走不了多远，就可以看到一家银行，银行的后面就是图书馆。

8. Where is the bookstore?

    (A) East of the post office
    (B) West of the post office
    (C) South of the bank
    (D) Behind the bank

Students should sketch a map with directions and the building names while listening to the selection. This will help them determine that the correct answer is **(B)**.

[Traditional-character version]

我是一個新生，住在學校宿舍樓的3312房間。房門的兩邊是書架和沙發，書架在左邊，沙發在右邊。門的對面是一個大窗戶，窗戶底下有一張桌子，桌子前面擺著一把椅子，桌子上有一盞臺燈、一個電腦，還有一本字典，字典裏夾著一支筆。我的床在房間的西邊，床下是我的鞋。床的東邊有一個櫃子，櫃子裏掛著我的衣服。櫃子左邊擺著一個茶几，茶几上有一臺電視機，可是我沒有時間看電視。

[Simplified-character version]

我是一个新生，住在学校宿舍楼的3312房间。房门的两边是书架和沙发，书架在左边，沙发在右边。门的对面是一个大窗户，窗户底下有一张桌子，桌子前面摆着一把椅子，桌子上有一盏台灯、一个电脑，还有一本字典，字典里夹着一支笔。我的床在房间的西边，床下是我的鞋。床的东边有一个柜子，柜子里挂着我的衣服。柜子左边摆着一个茶几，茶几上有一台电视机，可是我没有时间看电视。

9. What's on either side of the door?

    (A) A bookshelf and a window
    (B) A table and a chair
    (C) A sofa and a bookshelf
    (D) A shelf and a bed

10. What's on top of the table?

    (A) A dictionary and other books
    (B) A television set and a lamp
    (C) A pen and a television
    (D) A lamp and a computer

Students should draw a map while listening to the positions of the furniture and other items. This will help them find the correct answers, **(C)** for question 9 and **(D)** for question 10.

Listening tests may contain some questions regarding **identity** and **relationship**. Using context clues can help students predict the identity of a speaker or the relationship between speakers. For example, a conversation about daily life could be between a husband and wife, disease is probably a conversation topic between a doctor and patient, and a school-related conversation usually occurs between students and/or teachers. Some common questions regarding identity and relationship include:

Who (what) is the man/woman?
What is the man's/woman's profession/occupation?
What is the probable relationship between the two speakers?

[Traditional-character version]
(Man)   二位小姐，晚上好。請到那邊坐。
(Woman)   謝謝。可以看看菜單嗎？

[Simplified-character version]
(Man)   二位小姐，晚上好。请到那边坐。
(Woman)   谢谢。可以看看菜单吗？

11. What is the relationship between the man and the woman?

    (A) Husband and wife
    (B) Waiter and customer
    (C) Salesman and customer
    (D) Host and guest

The key words "二位小姐," "晚上好," and "菜單" ("菜单") indicate that the relationship between the speakers is **(B)**, waiter and customer.

[Traditional-character version]
(Woman)   王主任，我想問一下，這個月底我可不可以休兩天假？
(Man)   你填休假單了嗎?

[Simplified-character version]
(Woman)   王主任，我想问一下，这个月底我可不可以休两天假？
(Man)   你填休假单了吗?

12. What is the probable relationship between the two speakers?

    (A) Doctor and patient
    (B) Manager and office worker
    (C) Travel agent and customer
    (D) Teacher and student

Key pieces of information such as "我想問一下" ("我想问一下") and "主任" establish a relationship between a boss and an employee, so **(B)** is the answer.

Comprehending **events** during listening tests is a difficult task, as some listening materials are very short and may consist of only one sentence, even though they describe a series of events or a complicated relationship between several people. Students should:

1. pay attention to the sequence of events;
2. remember the names of characters and their relationships; and
3. be familiar with special sentence structures.

Questions regarding events may appear in the following formats:

What are the speakers discussing?
What is the man/woman asking about?
What can you learn from the conversation?

Pay attention to the events in the following sentence, whose verbal construction is a series.

[Traditional-character version]
  她起床後喝了點兒水，拿起一個麵包，背上書包就往車站跑去。

[Simplified-character version]
  她起床后喝了点儿水，拿起一个面包，背上书包就往车站跑去。

13. What does she do last?

  (A) Put on her backpack
  (B) Drink water
  (C) Run to the bus stop
  (D) Get a piece of bread

The correct answer is **(C)** based on the sequence of events.

The next sentence tests if students can determine the correct answer based on a complicated statement.

[Traditional-character version]
  老張叫小馬告訴王力下午跟李新去買書。

[Simplified-character version]
  老张叫小马告诉王力下午跟李新去买书。

14. Who will go buy books this afternoon?

  (A) Li Xin and Xiao Ma
  (B) Wang Li and Li Xin
  (C) Xiao Ma and Lao Zhang
  (D) Lao Zhang and Wang Li

To determine that the correct answer is **(B)**, students need to remember the people's names and to understand the grammatical meaning of the sentence.

STRATEGY

8   Ignoring unimportant information

It is unlikely that students will understand 100 percent of the vocabulary in a listening text. When listening, students often come upon a word or phrase that they don't understand. When this happens, students should skip over the unknown words or phrases. It is necessary for students to determine the importance of the words or phrases they skip. Ignoring unimportant words does not affect a general understanding of listening materials. For instance:

1. Students should be aware of redundancy because they can use it to give themselves time to think and identify the important parts of the selection.

2. The author expresses just one opinion using several examples, described by long and complicated sentences. Understanding one example is enough to understand the opinion.

[Traditional-character version]

　　俗話說，生命在於運動。然而，生活中有人對這句話的理解太片面，以爲只要多運動就一定對身體健康有好處。爲此，有些人特別喜歡做跑步、打球這樣的運動，實際上這些運動方式很不適合中老年人做，很容易引起疾病，甚至帶來死亡。專家認爲，對多數中老年人來說，適當的體育運動是散步、慢跑、騎車、做操和游泳，除了這些以外，每天看看書，思考思考問題，都對身體和心理健康有幫助。所以說，人們要根據自己的情況，選擇適合自己的運動方式。

[Simplified-character version]

　　俗话说，生命在于运动。然而，生活中有人对这句话的理解太片面，以为只要多运动就一定对身体健康有好处。为此，有些人特别喜欢做跑步、打球这样的运动，实际上这些运动方式很不适合中老年人做，很容易引起疾病，甚至带来死亡。专家认为，对多数中老年人来说，适当的体育运动是散步、慢跑、骑车、做操和游泳，除了这些以外，每天看看书，思考思考问题，都对身体和心理健康有帮助。所以说，人们要根据自己的情况，选择适合自己的运动方式。

Before listening, scanning the questions and the answer choices should help students predict the topic of the report, which is "sports and health." Understanding the sentence "生活中有人對這句話的理解太片面" ("生活中有人对这句话的理解太片面") is the key to understanding the author's opinion.

STRATEGY

9   Following scripts

Scripts will accompany the listening materials in this book. Students can use the scripts to practice listening comprehension skills. For example, if students have difficulty understanding recordings, they can refer to the scripts to check the vocabulary they do not understand. However, students should not try to translate entire listening selections because it is more important to focus on the main ideas.

To answer questions correctly, students may have to use several of the listening strategies presented in this section. For example, students may need to find key words, and/or make inferences about the topic of the conversation, and/or use their previous experiences to reply. Focusing on stressed words and intonation will help students find the key words of the conversation. In longer conversations, students will have to process details and possibly ignore unimportant information. However, in the following section, this will not be necessary as the listening materials are relatively short.

Listening Comprehension Practice
ANSWER SHEET

Section I Conversation

1 Ⓐ Ⓑ Ⓒ Ⓓ
2 Ⓐ Ⓑ Ⓒ Ⓓ
3 Ⓐ Ⓑ Ⓒ Ⓓ
4 Ⓐ Ⓑ Ⓒ Ⓓ
5 Ⓐ Ⓑ Ⓒ Ⓓ
6 Ⓐ Ⓑ Ⓒ Ⓓ
7 Ⓐ Ⓑ Ⓒ Ⓓ
8 Ⓐ Ⓑ Ⓒ Ⓓ
9 Ⓐ Ⓑ Ⓒ Ⓓ
10 Ⓐ Ⓑ Ⓒ Ⓓ
11 Ⓐ Ⓑ Ⓒ Ⓓ
12 Ⓐ Ⓑ Ⓒ Ⓓ
13 Ⓐ Ⓑ Ⓒ Ⓓ
14 Ⓐ Ⓑ Ⓒ Ⓓ
15 Ⓐ Ⓑ Ⓒ Ⓓ
16 Ⓐ Ⓑ Ⓒ Ⓓ
17 Ⓐ Ⓑ Ⓒ Ⓓ
18 Ⓐ Ⓑ Ⓒ Ⓓ
19 Ⓐ Ⓑ Ⓒ Ⓓ
20 Ⓐ Ⓑ Ⓒ Ⓓ
21 Ⓐ Ⓑ Ⓒ Ⓓ
22 Ⓐ Ⓑ Ⓒ Ⓓ
23 Ⓐ Ⓑ Ⓒ Ⓓ
24 Ⓐ Ⓑ Ⓒ Ⓓ
25 Ⓐ Ⓑ Ⓒ Ⓓ

26 Ⓐ Ⓑ Ⓒ Ⓓ
27 Ⓐ Ⓑ Ⓒ Ⓓ
28 Ⓐ Ⓑ Ⓒ Ⓓ
29 Ⓐ Ⓑ Ⓒ Ⓓ
30 Ⓐ Ⓑ Ⓒ Ⓓ
31 Ⓐ Ⓑ Ⓒ Ⓓ
32 Ⓐ Ⓑ Ⓒ Ⓓ
33 Ⓐ Ⓑ Ⓒ Ⓓ
34 Ⓐ Ⓑ Ⓒ Ⓓ
35 Ⓐ Ⓑ Ⓒ Ⓓ
36 Ⓐ Ⓑ Ⓒ Ⓓ
37 Ⓐ Ⓑ Ⓒ Ⓓ
38 Ⓐ Ⓑ Ⓒ Ⓓ
39 Ⓐ Ⓑ Ⓒ Ⓓ
40 Ⓐ Ⓑ Ⓒ Ⓓ
41 Ⓐ Ⓑ Ⓒ Ⓓ
42 Ⓐ Ⓑ Ⓒ Ⓓ
43 Ⓐ Ⓑ Ⓒ Ⓓ
44 Ⓐ Ⓑ Ⓒ Ⓓ
45 Ⓐ Ⓑ Ⓒ Ⓓ
46 Ⓐ Ⓑ Ⓒ Ⓓ
47 Ⓐ Ⓑ Ⓒ Ⓓ
48 Ⓐ Ⓑ Ⓒ Ⓓ
49 Ⓐ Ⓑ Ⓒ Ⓓ
50 Ⓐ Ⓑ Ⓒ Ⓓ

51 Ⓐ Ⓑ Ⓒ Ⓓ
52 Ⓐ Ⓑ Ⓒ Ⓓ
53 Ⓐ Ⓑ Ⓒ Ⓓ
54 Ⓐ Ⓑ Ⓒ Ⓓ
55 Ⓐ Ⓑ Ⓒ Ⓓ
56 Ⓐ Ⓑ Ⓒ Ⓓ
57 Ⓐ Ⓑ Ⓒ Ⓓ
58 Ⓐ Ⓑ Ⓒ Ⓓ
59 Ⓐ Ⓑ Ⓒ Ⓓ
60 Ⓐ Ⓑ Ⓒ Ⓓ
61 Ⓐ Ⓑ Ⓒ Ⓓ
62 Ⓐ Ⓑ Ⓒ Ⓓ
63 Ⓐ Ⓑ Ⓒ Ⓓ
64 Ⓐ Ⓑ Ⓒ Ⓓ
65 Ⓐ Ⓑ Ⓒ Ⓓ
66 Ⓐ Ⓑ Ⓒ Ⓓ
67 Ⓐ Ⓑ Ⓒ Ⓓ
68 Ⓐ Ⓑ Ⓒ Ⓓ
69 Ⓐ Ⓑ Ⓒ Ⓓ
70 Ⓐ Ⓑ Ⓒ Ⓓ
71 Ⓐ Ⓑ Ⓒ Ⓓ
72 Ⓐ Ⓑ Ⓒ Ⓓ
73 Ⓐ Ⓑ Ⓒ Ⓓ
74 Ⓐ Ⓑ Ⓒ Ⓓ
75 Ⓐ Ⓑ Ⓒ Ⓓ

76 Ⓐ Ⓑ Ⓒ Ⓓ
77 Ⓐ Ⓑ Ⓒ Ⓓ
78 Ⓐ Ⓑ Ⓒ Ⓓ
79 Ⓐ Ⓑ Ⓒ Ⓓ
80 Ⓐ Ⓑ Ⓒ Ⓓ
81 Ⓐ Ⓑ Ⓒ Ⓓ
82 Ⓐ Ⓑ Ⓒ Ⓓ
83 Ⓐ Ⓑ Ⓒ Ⓓ
84 Ⓐ Ⓑ Ⓒ Ⓓ
85 Ⓐ Ⓑ Ⓒ Ⓓ
86 Ⓐ Ⓑ Ⓒ Ⓓ
87 Ⓐ Ⓑ Ⓒ Ⓓ
88 Ⓐ Ⓑ Ⓒ Ⓓ
89 Ⓐ Ⓑ Ⓒ Ⓓ
90 Ⓐ Ⓑ Ⓒ Ⓓ
91 Ⓐ Ⓑ Ⓒ Ⓓ
92 Ⓐ Ⓑ Ⓒ Ⓓ
93 Ⓐ Ⓑ Ⓒ Ⓓ
94 Ⓐ Ⓑ Ⓒ Ⓓ
95 Ⓐ Ⓑ Ⓒ Ⓓ
96 Ⓐ Ⓑ Ⓒ Ⓓ
97 Ⓐ Ⓑ Ⓒ Ⓓ
98 Ⓐ Ⓑ Ⓒ Ⓓ
99 Ⓐ Ⓑ Ⓒ Ⓓ
100 Ⓐ Ⓑ Ⓒ Ⓓ

Section II Short Narration

101 Ⓐ Ⓑ Ⓒ Ⓓ
102 Ⓐ Ⓑ Ⓒ Ⓓ
103 Ⓐ Ⓑ Ⓒ Ⓓ
104 Ⓐ Ⓑ Ⓒ Ⓓ
105 Ⓐ Ⓑ Ⓒ Ⓓ

106 Ⓐ Ⓑ Ⓒ Ⓓ
107 Ⓐ Ⓑ Ⓒ Ⓓ
108 Ⓐ Ⓑ Ⓒ Ⓓ
109 Ⓐ Ⓑ Ⓒ Ⓓ
110 Ⓐ Ⓑ Ⓒ Ⓓ

111 Ⓐ Ⓑ Ⓒ Ⓓ
112 Ⓐ Ⓑ Ⓒ Ⓓ
113 Ⓐ Ⓑ Ⓒ Ⓓ
114 Ⓐ Ⓑ Ⓒ Ⓓ
115 Ⓐ Ⓑ Ⓒ Ⓓ

116 Ⓐ Ⓑ Ⓒ Ⓓ
117 Ⓐ Ⓑ Ⓒ Ⓓ
118 Ⓐ Ⓑ Ⓒ Ⓓ
119 Ⓐ Ⓑ Ⓒ Ⓓ
120 Ⓐ Ⓑ Ⓒ Ⓓ

Listening Comprehension Practice
ANSWER SHEET

Section III Dialogues

121 Ⓐ Ⓑ Ⓒ Ⓓ	134 Ⓐ Ⓑ Ⓒ Ⓓ	147 Ⓐ Ⓑ Ⓒ Ⓓ	160 Ⓐ Ⓑ Ⓒ Ⓓ
122 Ⓐ Ⓑ Ⓒ Ⓓ	135 Ⓐ Ⓑ Ⓒ Ⓓ	148 Ⓐ Ⓑ Ⓒ Ⓓ	161 Ⓐ Ⓑ Ⓒ Ⓓ
123 Ⓐ Ⓑ Ⓒ Ⓓ	136 Ⓐ Ⓑ Ⓒ Ⓓ	149 Ⓐ Ⓑ Ⓒ Ⓓ	162 Ⓐ Ⓑ Ⓒ Ⓓ
124 Ⓐ Ⓑ Ⓒ Ⓓ	137 Ⓐ Ⓑ Ⓒ Ⓓ	150 Ⓐ Ⓑ Ⓒ Ⓓ	163 Ⓐ Ⓑ Ⓒ Ⓓ
125 Ⓐ Ⓑ Ⓒ Ⓓ	138 Ⓐ Ⓑ Ⓒ Ⓓ	151 Ⓐ Ⓑ Ⓒ Ⓓ	164 Ⓐ Ⓑ Ⓒ Ⓓ
126 Ⓐ Ⓑ Ⓒ Ⓓ	139 Ⓐ Ⓑ Ⓒ Ⓓ	152 Ⓐ Ⓑ Ⓒ Ⓓ	165 Ⓐ Ⓑ Ⓒ Ⓓ
127 Ⓐ Ⓑ Ⓒ Ⓓ	140 Ⓐ Ⓑ Ⓒ Ⓓ	153 Ⓐ Ⓑ Ⓒ Ⓓ	166 Ⓐ Ⓑ Ⓒ Ⓓ
128 Ⓐ Ⓑ Ⓒ Ⓓ	141 Ⓐ Ⓑ Ⓒ Ⓓ	154 Ⓐ Ⓑ Ⓒ Ⓓ	167 Ⓐ Ⓑ Ⓒ Ⓓ
129 Ⓐ Ⓑ Ⓒ Ⓓ	142 Ⓐ Ⓑ Ⓒ Ⓓ	155 Ⓐ Ⓑ Ⓒ Ⓓ	168 Ⓐ Ⓑ Ⓒ Ⓓ
130 Ⓐ Ⓑ Ⓒ Ⓓ	143 Ⓐ Ⓑ Ⓒ Ⓓ	156 Ⓐ Ⓑ Ⓒ Ⓓ	169 Ⓐ Ⓑ Ⓒ Ⓓ
131 Ⓐ Ⓑ Ⓒ Ⓓ	144 Ⓐ Ⓑ Ⓒ Ⓓ	157 Ⓐ Ⓑ Ⓒ Ⓓ	170 Ⓐ Ⓑ Ⓒ Ⓓ
132 Ⓐ Ⓑ Ⓒ Ⓓ	145 Ⓐ Ⓑ Ⓒ Ⓓ	158 Ⓐ Ⓑ Ⓒ Ⓓ	171 Ⓐ Ⓑ Ⓒ Ⓓ
133 Ⓐ Ⓑ Ⓒ Ⓓ	146 Ⓐ Ⓑ Ⓒ Ⓓ	159 Ⓐ Ⓑ Ⓒ Ⓓ	172 Ⓐ Ⓑ Ⓒ Ⓓ

Section IV Long Narration

173 Ⓐ Ⓑ Ⓒ Ⓓ	185 Ⓐ Ⓑ Ⓒ Ⓓ	197 Ⓐ Ⓑ Ⓒ Ⓓ	209 Ⓐ Ⓑ Ⓒ Ⓓ
174 Ⓐ Ⓑ Ⓒ Ⓓ	186 Ⓐ Ⓑ Ⓒ Ⓓ	198 Ⓐ Ⓑ Ⓒ Ⓓ	210 Ⓐ Ⓑ Ⓒ Ⓓ
175 Ⓐ Ⓑ Ⓒ Ⓓ	187 Ⓐ Ⓑ Ⓒ Ⓓ	199 Ⓐ Ⓑ Ⓒ Ⓓ	211 Ⓐ Ⓑ Ⓒ Ⓓ
176 Ⓐ Ⓑ Ⓒ Ⓓ	188 Ⓐ Ⓑ Ⓒ Ⓓ	200 Ⓐ Ⓑ Ⓒ Ⓓ	212 Ⓐ Ⓑ Ⓒ Ⓓ
177 Ⓐ Ⓑ Ⓒ Ⓓ	189 Ⓐ Ⓑ Ⓒ Ⓓ	201 Ⓐ Ⓑ Ⓒ Ⓓ	213 Ⓐ Ⓑ Ⓒ Ⓓ
178 Ⓐ Ⓑ Ⓒ Ⓓ	190 Ⓐ Ⓑ Ⓒ Ⓓ	202 Ⓐ Ⓑ Ⓒ Ⓓ	214 Ⓐ Ⓑ Ⓒ Ⓓ
179 Ⓐ Ⓑ Ⓒ Ⓓ	191 Ⓐ Ⓑ Ⓒ Ⓓ	203 Ⓐ Ⓑ Ⓒ Ⓓ	215 Ⓐ Ⓑ Ⓒ Ⓓ
180 Ⓐ Ⓑ Ⓒ Ⓓ	192 Ⓐ Ⓑ Ⓒ Ⓓ	204 Ⓐ Ⓑ Ⓒ Ⓓ	216 Ⓐ Ⓑ Ⓒ Ⓓ
181 Ⓐ Ⓑ Ⓒ Ⓓ	193 Ⓐ Ⓑ Ⓒ Ⓓ	205 Ⓐ Ⓑ Ⓒ Ⓓ	217 Ⓐ Ⓑ Ⓒ Ⓓ
182 Ⓐ Ⓑ Ⓒ Ⓓ	194 Ⓐ Ⓑ Ⓒ Ⓓ	206 Ⓐ Ⓑ Ⓒ Ⓓ	218 Ⓐ Ⓑ Ⓒ Ⓓ
183 Ⓐ Ⓑ Ⓒ Ⓓ	195 Ⓐ Ⓑ Ⓒ Ⓓ	207 Ⓐ Ⓑ Ⓒ Ⓓ	219 Ⓐ Ⓑ Ⓒ Ⓓ
184 Ⓐ Ⓑ Ⓒ Ⓓ	196 Ⓐ Ⓑ Ⓒ Ⓓ	208 Ⓐ Ⓑ Ⓒ Ⓓ	220 Ⓐ Ⓑ Ⓒ Ⓓ

Listening Comprehension Practice

SECTION I – CONVERSATIONS

Track 10 — You will hear several short conversations. Each conversation will be played once along with four choices of response (A), (B), (C), and (D). You will have 5 seconds to choose a response that completes the conversation in a logical and culturally appropriate way. Please remember to mark your answers on the answer sheet.

Conversations 1 through 10

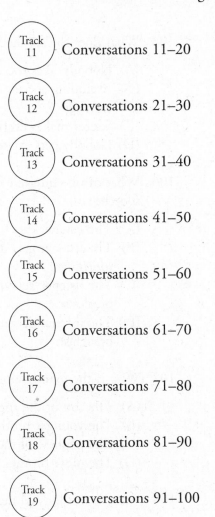

Track 11 — Conversations 11–20

Track 12 — Conversations 21–30

Track 13 — Conversations 31–40

Track 14 — Conversations 41–50

Track 15 — Conversations 51–60

Track 16 — Conversations 61–70

Track 17 — Conversations 71–80

Track 18 — Conversations 81–90

Track 19 — Conversations 91–100

SECTION II – SHORT NARRATIONS

 You will listen to several short narrations. Each narration will be played once. You may take notes. After each narration, you will have 5 seconds to read the question and choose the most appropriate response (A), (B), (C) or (D) in English, from the answer sheet. Please be reminded that during the AP Chinese Exam, the question will be displayed only *after* you hear the narration; therefore, in this practice, previewing the printed questions prior to listening to the narration is not recommended.

Narrations for Questions 101 to 110.

101. Which statement is correct?

    (A) The difference between the highest and lowest temperatures is 4°C.
    (B) This city freezes every day in the winter.
    (C) The difference between the highest and lowest temperatures is 35°C.
    (D) Today's average temperature is 18°C.

102. What happened?

    (A) Xiao Li is sick.
    (B) Xiao Li is in the hospital.
    (C) Xiao Li's mom is in the hospital.
    (D) Xiao Li's younger sister is in the hospital.

103. What is the speaker's attitude?

    (A) Angry
    (B) Doubtful
    (C) Apathetic
    (D) Surprised

104. What is the flaw of the clothing?

    (A) Bad quality
    (B) High price
    (C) Ugly color
    (D) Out of style

105. What does the speaker mean?

    (A) Nobody likes soccer.
    (B) Excluding soccer, all other sports are exciting.
    (C) Soccer makes everyone excited.
    (D) Nobody gets excited over soccer.

106. What can be inferred from the woman's speech?

    (A) The listener eats breakfast every day.
    (B) The listener gets up early every morning.
    (C) The listener gets up too late to eat breakfast.
    (D) The listener gets up early and eats breakfast.

107. Who is the man behind the older brother?

    (A) The son of the speaker
    (B) The younger brother of the speaker
    (C) The nephew of the speaker
    (D) The older brother of the speaker

108. What is not located next to the dorm?

    (A) Clothes shop
    (B) Post office
    (C) Grocery store
    (D) Bookstore

109. Which sequence is right?

    (A) Eating snacks, shopping, going to the post office
    (B) Shopping, going to the post office, eating snacks
    (C) Eating snacks, going to the post office, shopping
    (D) Going to the post office, shopping, eating snacks

110. What is the main reason for the good health of the speaker?

    (A) Frequently walking
    (B) Doing Taiji
    (C) Keeping an exercise routine
    (D) No smoking, but a little drinking

111. Where does the speaker work?

    (A) A hospital
    (B) An English school
    (C) A post office
    (D) A high school

112. Where did they travel?

    (A) Shanghai, Guangzhou
    (B) Nanjing, Shanghai
    (C) Xi'an, Nanjing
    (D) Guangzhou, Xi'an

113. How are they going to Los Angeles?

    (A) They want to go from Washington, D.C., to New York by train and then fly to Los Angeles by airplane.
    (B) They are planning to fly from Washington, D.C., to New York and then fly to Los Angeles.
    (C) They plan to take the train from Washington, D.C., to Los Angeles.
    (D) They plan to fly directly from Washington, D.C., to Los Angeles.

114. What is the speaker's mother's occupation?

    (A) Teacher
    (B) Doctor
    (C) Reporter
    (D) Student

115. What does he plan to do after he finishes school?

    (A) He wants to go abroad.
    (B) He wants to get a job.
    (C) He wants to make money.
    (D) He wants to study computer science.

116. What is this room?

    (A) Office
    (B) Library
    (C) Classroom
    (D) Dorm

117. Who ends up fixing the computer?

    (A) Father
    (B) Mother
    (C) Elder brother
    (D) Friend

118. How many *yuan* did the woman pay for the shoes?

    (A) 150
    (B) 50
    (C) more than 200
    (D) 280

119. Which phone number is most likely Li Laoshi's home number?

    (A) 82301968
    (B) 62386786
    (C) 86974253
    (D) 83657106

120. How long does it take to get to school by car?

    (A) 10 minutes
    (B) 40 minutes
    (C) 25 minutes
    (D) 90 minutes

SECTION III—DIALOGUES

Directions: You will listen to several dialogues for questions 121 through 172. Each dialogue should be played twice. You may take notes. After replaying each dialogue, students will be given 12 seconds on the actual exam to read the question and choose the most appropriate response—(A), (B), (C) or (D) in English from the answer sheet. Please be reminded that during the AP Chinese Exam, the question will be displayed only *after* you hear the narration; therefore, in this practice, previewing the printed questions prior to listening to the narration is not recommended.

121. Where does the interview take place?

    (A) Near a pool
    (B) At a university
    (C) In a cinema
    (D) In a shopping center

122. Which statement is incorrect?

    (A) The woman dances very well.
    (B) The woman works in a bookstore.
    (C) The interview takes place in a ballroom.
    (D) They are talking at her workplace.

123. Which statement about the woman is correct?

    (A) She worked in a computer company.
    (B) She comes from Tianjing.
    (C) She studied in Beijing.
    (D) She is working in Beijing.

124. Where is the woman from?

    (A) Beijing
    (B) Nanjing
    (C) Tianjin
    (D) Shanghai

125. Which Chinese arts is the man studying?

    (A) *wushu* and folk song
    (B) calligraphy and folk song
    (C) Beijing opera and calligraphy
    (D) calligraphy and *wushu*

126. Which art is the woman not interested in?

    (A) *wushu*
    (B) calligraphy
    (C) Beijing opera
    (D) folk song

127. What is the woman's hobby?

    (A) Listening to music
    (B) Watching TV
    (C) Dancing
    (D) Traveling

128. What does the woman do in the evening?

    (A) She teaches her students.
    (B) She goes shopping.
    (C) She cooks dinner for her family.
    (D) She tutors her son in English.

129. What does the man do every day?

    (A) Swim
    (B) Play ping pong
    (C) Play tennis
    (D) Play soccer

130. What is the man's occupation?

    (A) He is an athlete.
    (B) He is a coach.
    (C) He is a journalist.
    (D) He doesn't say.

Track 22
Track 23
Track 24
Track 25
Track 26
Track 27

131. What is not a requirement when the man buys clothes?

    Track 28

    (A) Fabric
    (B) Brand
    (C) Appearance
    (D) Comfort

132. How much did the woman spend for her sweater?

    (A) $5
    (B) $10
    (C) $39
    (D) $89

133. What is the conversation about?

    Track 29

    (A) A maid talking to a guest
    (B) Picking up someone at the airport
    (C) Taking someone to the train station
    (D) A host saying good-bye to a guest

134. Where could the conversation take place?

    (A) A house
    (B) A hotel
    (C) An airport
    (D) A train station

135. Who is the speaker calling for?

    Track 30

    (A) Xiao Li
    (B) A doctor
    (C) Professor Zhang
    (D) Mrs. Zhang

136. Why does the man make the phone call?

    (A) He wants to talk to Mrs. Zhang about seeing a doctor.
    (B) He wants to tell Mrs. Zhang that he is busy.
    (C) He suggests that Mrs. Zhang should go to see a doctor.
    (D) There is something he wants to talk to professor Zhang about.

137. What does the man ask the woman?

    Track 31

    (A) How long dinner should take
    (B) How to invite someone to a party
    (C) Her preferred place to eat dinner
    (D) Her favorite food

138. What is the woman's response to the man's question?

    (A) In China, people eat very slowly, and usually take about two hours to eat.
    (B) It's not very polite if the guest hasn't finished eating and the host is done.
    (C) If the guest has finished eating, the host can eat as slowly as he wants to.
    (D) To spend time with the guests, the host should eat very quickly.

139. Who goes to the park daily?

    Track 32

    (A) The man
    (B) The woman
    (C) The man's father
    (D) The woman's father

140. Did their fathers retire?

    (A) Both fathers are retired.
    (B) Both fathers are not retired.
    (C) The woman's father is retired, but the man's father is not.
    (D) The woman's father is retired, but it doesn't say whether the man's father is retired or not.

141. Which activity does the woman's father not do?

    (A) Walk
    (B) Practice Taiji
    (C) Exercise
    (D) Go fishing

142. Which reason for the man's father serving as a president of the fishing club is incorrect?

    (A) He fishes very well.
    (B) He has a lot of time.
    (C) He is the oldest member in the club.
    (D) He wants to be.

143. Where is the woman living right now?

    (Track 33)

    (A) Her parents' home
    (B) A new apartment
    (C) A friend's apartment
    (D) A dorm

144. What is an advantage for girls to living in a dorm?

    (A) Inexpensive
    (B) Safe
    (C) Freedom
    (D) Roommate

145. Why does the woman want to move out?

    (A) Living in a dorm is not free.
    (B) Living in a dorm is not safe.
    (C) She does not like her roommate.
    (D) Her dorm is too expensive.

146. Which statement is not correct?

    (A) The roommate watches TV late into the evening.
    (B) The roommate likes to chat on the phone.
    (C) The roommate can't study and sleep.
    (D) The roommate sometimes shouts on the phone.

147. Where is the man now?

    (Track 34)

    (A) Chicago
    (B) Taiwan
    (C) East Coast
    (D) West Coast

148. Which preparation for traveling abroad is not mentioned?

    (A) Applying for a passport
    (B) Applying for a visa
    (C) Packing
    (D) Buying plane tickets

149. Where does the man want to buy plane tickets?

    (A) A travel agency
    (B) At the airport
    (C) On the Internet
    (D) Undecided

150. Who has been to Taiwan?

    (A) The woman's sister
    (B) The man's girlfriend
    (C) The woman
    (D) The man

151. Where does this conversation most likely occur?

    (Track 35)

    (A) A restaurant
    (B) A bakery
    (C) A food store
    (D) A house

152. What is the relationship between the two speakers?

    (A) Master and apprentice
    (B) Waiter and customer
    (C) Manager and staff
    (D) Salesperson and customer

153. Which of the following items does the woman order?

    (A) Wine
    (B) Juice
    (C) Rice
    (D) Soup

154. Which dish does the woman not order?

    (A) Shrimp
    (B) Pork rib
    (C) Fish
    (D) Tofu

155. What does the woman want to drink?

    (A) Tea
    (B) Coffee
    (C) Both tea and coffee
    (D) Neither tea nor coffee

156. What kind of tea does the woman prefer?

    (A) Jasmine tea
    (B) Black tea
    (C) Green tea
    (D) It doesn't matter

157. Which statement is correct?

    (A) China has the most types of tea in the world.
    (B) China has the most tea drinkers in the world.
    (C) China has the most tea shops in the world.
    (D) China was the first country to discover the tea plant.

158. Which city has the most tea shops? *

    (A) Beijing
    (B) Shanghai
    (C) Guangzhou
    (D) Not mentioned

159. Which city does the man come from?

    (A) Beijing
    (B) Shanghai
    (C) Guangzhou
    (D) Not mentioned

160. How long have they not seen each other?

    (A) Two years
    (B) Less than two years
    (C) More than two years
    (D) Four years

161. Where does the man live now?

    (A) He lives with his parents.
    (B) He lives with his wife's parents.
    (C) He lives with the old people.
    (D) He lives in his own house.

162. Which statement is correct?

    (A) The woman has her own house.
    (B) The woman wants to live with the elderly.
    (C) The woman bought a house last year.
    (D) The man thinks that people can benefit from their parents' help.

163. What caused the woman's family to be unhappy?

    (A) Conflicting schedules
    (B) Financial problems
    (C) Children's education
    (D) Housework

164. Where does the conversation take place?

    (A) On the way
    (B) The woman's home
    (C) The man's home
    (D) Their workplace

165. What happened to the man?

    (A) He went on a business trip.
    (B) He caught a cold.
    (C) He saw snow for the first time.
    (D) He changed his workplace.

166. Which season does the man dislike?

    (A) Spring
    (B) Summer
    (C) Fall
    (D) Winter

167. Where is the man from?

    (A) Beijing
    (B) Shanghai
    (C) Guangzhou
    (D) Not mentioned

168. Where is the woman from?

    (A) Beijing
    (B) Shanghai
    (C) Guangzhou
    (D) Not mentioned

169. Where was the man yesterday afternoon?

    (A) At a train station
    (B) In a park
    (C) In a factory
    (D) At home

170. What did the man do in the factory?

    (A) Pick up trash
    (B) Protest
    (C) Work
    (D) Take a break

171. Which type of pollution was not mentioned?

    (A) The factory polluted the water.
    (B) The factory polluted the air.
    (C) Because of the air pollution, all the birds died.
    (D) Because of the water pollution, all the fish died.

172. Why doesn't the factory find a solution to the pollution problem?

    (A) They don't have enough money.
    (B) They don't want to.
    (C) The government doesn't want to help them.
    (D) They don't have the time.

SECTION IV—LONG NARRATION

Directions: You will listen to several long narrations of passages for questions 173 to 220. Each passage should be played twice. You may take notes. After replaying each passage, students will be given 12 seconds on the actual exam to read the question and choose the most appropriate response (A), (B), (C) or (D) in English from the answer sheet. Please be reminded that during the AP Chinese Exam, the question will be displayed only *after* you hear the narration; therefore, in this practice, previewing the printed questions prior to listening to the narration is not recommended.

173. Why does Xiao Min plan on quitting his job?

 (A) His boss is not nice to him.
 (B) He cannot keep working and studying at the same time.
 (C) Customers don't tip enough.
 (D) The restaurant doesn't have many customers.

174. Which statement is correct?

 (A) Xiao Min moved from Taiwan in the '50s.
 (B) Xiao Min and his boss moved from Taiwan 50 years ago.
 (C) Xiao Min and his boss moved from Taiwan together in the '50s.
 (D) Xiao Min's boss moved from Taiwan in the '50s.

175. What is tonight's temperature?

 (A) The low is 23°C.
 (B) The high is 14°C.
 (C) The high is 27°C.
 (D) The low is 24°C.

176. Which statement describes tomorrow's weather during the day?

 (A) Cloudy and chance of rain
 (B) South wind with 1–2 levels
 (C) North wind with 3–4 levels
 (D) North wind turning to south with 2–3 levels

177. Which statement is correct?

 (A) Qi Baishi learned to draw at a very young age.
 (B) Qi Baishi learned to draw as an adult.
 (C) Qi Baishi observed animals under trees, because he liked them.
 (D) Qi Baishi raised animals, because he liked them.

178. Which animal is not mentioned in the passage?

 (A) Insects
 (B) Horses
 (C) Birds
 (D) Fish

179. What doesn't interest Peter?

 (A) Living in China
 (B) Traveling in China
 (C) Eating Chinese food
 (D) Learning Chinese

180. How is Peter at the end of the passage?

 (A) Mad
 (B) Happy
 (C) Embarrassed
 (D) Apologetic

181. What is the passage mainly about?

(Track 44)

(A) How to use chopsticks
(B) Table manners
(C) The difference between chopsticks and spoons
(D) Rude eating habits

182. Which is a rude eating habit according to the passage?

(A) Using hands to get food from a dish
(B) Using one's own chopsticks to receive food offered by others
(C) Taking food from a dish across someone's chopsticks
(D) Avoiding touching one's chopsticks with someone else's

183. What is the passage mainly about?

(Track 45)

(A) Flu and precautions
(B) Flu virus
(C) Flu symptoms
(D) Flu and climate

184. Which idea is not mentioned in the passage?

(A) People should select clothes according to weather changes.
(B) People should exercise to strengthen their bodies.
(C) People should close windows before sleeping.
(D) People should avoid contact with flu patients.

185. What does the author suggest to flu patients?

(A) Stay home
(B) Get plenty of sleep
(C) Listen to the weather forecast
(D) Wear more clothes

186. Who likes *wulong* tea?

(Track 46)

(A) People from Beijing
(B) People from Shanghai
(C) People from Guangdong
(D) People from Tibet

187. What kinds of tea sets are good for making tea?

(A) Porcelain
(B) Ceramic
(C) Both porcelain and ceramic
(D) Not mentioned

188. What is the advantage of making tea with a ceramic tea set?

(A) Appealing
(B) Cheap
(C) Convenient
(D) Keeps the heat in

189. When do people drink the spring tea?

(A) When a baby completes his first month of life
(B) Before the spring season
(C) During a wedding ceremony
(D) During the Spring Festival

190. Who likes to watch Beijing operas?

(Track 47)

(A) The grandfather
(B) The father
(C) The mother
(D) The older sister

191. Which TV programs does the father like the most?

(A) Sports programs
(B) Soccer games
(C) Television plays
(D) American movies

192. What are the narrator's favorite TV programs?

    (A) Soccer games
    (B) American movies
    (C) Cartoons
    (D) Foreign programs

193. What is his older sister's occupation?

    (A) Retiree
    (B) Doctor
    (C) Nurse
    (D) Teacher

194. What is the passage mainly about?

    (A) Differences in parenting techniques between Chinese and American families
    (B) Differences in expectations regarding college between Chinese and American families
    (C) Attitudes toward education in American families in China
    (D) Attitudes toward education in Chinese families in the United States

195. What do some Chinese parents not want their children to study?

    (A) Law
    (B) Medicine
    (C) Science
    (D) Humanities

196. Which statement is correct?

    (A) All Chinese parents want their children to go to good colleges.
    (B) Many Chinese parents want their children to go to good colleges.
    (C) After graduating from a good college, one can earn more money.
    (D) Parents want their children to go to good colleges for their own pride.

197. What is the author's attitude toward Chinese parents' expectations of their children's education?

    (A) He offers a suggestion.
    (B) He is in total agreement with the parents.
    (C) He believes the parents' expectations are very harmful to their children's education.
    (D) He is indifferent toward what the parents do.

198. What is the purpose of this message?

    (A) To ask Xiao Li if she has a class
    (B) To invite Xiao Li for coffee
    (C) To invite Xiao Li for a movie
    (D) To ask Xiao Li where she is

199. Who will be going to the movie?

    (A) Only Zhang Hua and her cousin
    (B) At least Zhang Hua and her cousin
    (C) Zhang Hua and Xiao Li
    (D) None of the above

200. What time does the movie start?

    (A) 3:00 P.M.
    (B) 3:30 P.M.
    (C) 4:00 P.M.
    (D) 4:30 P.M.

201. Where will they meet?

    (A) At the speaker's home
    (B) At their school
    (C) At a movie theater
    (D) At a coffee shop

202. What is a "複姓" ("复姓")?

    (A) A single-character surname
    (B) A two-character surname
    (C) A duplicate-character surname
    (D) A two-or-more-character surname

203. How many surnames are commonly used or seen currently?

    (A) 60
    (B) 200
    (C) 500
    (D) Nobody knows.

204. Which common family name is not mentioned in the passage?

    (A) Zhūgě
    (B) Ōuyáng
    (C) Dōngfāng
    (D) Sītú

205. What is the topic of this passage?

    (A) Chinese first names
    (B) Chinese surnames
    (C) The meaning of Chinese names
    (D) The history of Chinese names

206. What is the passage mainly about?

    Track 51

    (A) Visiting patients in the hospital
    (B) A patient's situation
    (C) Presents for a patient
    (D) Visitation time

207. Which idea is mentioned in the passage?

    (A) People like to give patients candies now.
    (B) People should talk about something pleasant around patients.
    (C) Visiting hours are usually in the evenings.
    (D) Visitors are welcome any time of the day on the weekends.

208. What does "跟病人說話要注意" ("跟病人说话要注意") mean?

    (A) People should not talk about disease.
    (B) People should talk about disease a lot.
    (C) People should avoid provoking the patient.
    (D) People should talk about a lot of different topics.

209. Which is the correct visitation time?

    (A) Visitation time on weekdays is usually three to four hours.
    (B) Normally, patients can be visited in the morning.
    (C) Wednesdays and Thursdays are open for visitation.
    (D) Visitation time on weekends is longer.

210. What is the topic of this passage?

    Track 52

    (A) Invitation time
    (B) Formality of visiting
    (C) Manners as a guest
    (D) Manners as a host

211. How do Chinese people invite guests to their homes in their everyday lives?

    (A) Phone call
    (B) Oral invitation or phone call
    (C) Formal invitation and then a phone call
    (D) Formal invitation

212. When should one arrive at a host's home?

    (A) It's best to arrive at the appointed time.
    (B) One should arrive at the appointed time or earlier.
    (C) One has to arrive exactly on time.
    (D) One should come either a little earlier or later.

213. Why do hosts say things like "沒做什麼好吃的" ("没做什么好吃的") when eating with guests?

    (A) They don't want to provide sumptuous meals for guests.
    (B) They are polite.
    (C) They want their guests to be relaxed.
    (D) They don't provide good meals for guests.

214. What is the passage mainly about?

   (A) Comparisons between Chinese and American college exams
   (B) Comparisons between Chinese and American college exam systems
   (C) Comparisons between majors
   (D) Comparisons between test opportunities

215. Which statement is correct?

   (A) In China, college exams cover many subjects.
   (B) In China, SAT scores are very important.
   (C) In China, students can take the college exams many times a year.
   (D) In China, colleges look at grades from the three years of high school.

216. What can be inferred from the passage?

   (A) In China, colleges don't require interviews.
   (B) In China, only certain majors require interviews.
   (C) China should do interviews like America does.
   (D) In China, there are problems with doing interviews.

217. What medium is this passage about?

   (A) Television program
   (B) Radio program
   (C) Newspaper article
   (D) Magazine article

218. How many generations live together in a traditional Chinese family?

   (A) One generation
   (B) Two generations
   (C) More than two generations
   (D) Not mentioned

219. Where do small or medium-sized families exist?

   (A) City
   (B) Countryside
   (C) City and countryside
   (D) City or countryside

220. Which statement is correct?

   (A) Young people don't expect to live independently after marriage.
   (B) Young people expect to live independently after marriage, but their parents disagree.
   (C) Some young people and their parents expect to live separately.
   (D) Young people want to live with their parents, but their parents don't.

Listening Comprehension Practice
ANSWER KEY

Section I—Conversation

1. D	26. B	51. C	76. D
2. B	27. D	52. B	77. C
3. C	28. B	53. D	78. B
4. C	29. B	54. A	79. A
5. B	30. B	55. C	80. B
6. A	31. C	56. B	81. A
7. B	32. D	57. C	82. A
8. D	33. A	58. B	83. C
9. D	34. D	59. A	84. C
10. A	35. B	60. C	85. B
11. C	36. B	61. D	86. A
12. B	37. A	62. B	87. C
13. C	38. B	63. A	88. D
14. D	39. C	64. B	89. A
15. C	40. D	65. B	90. B
16. C	41. A	66. C	91. B
17. B	42. B	67. D	92. C
18. D	43. B	68. D	93. D
19. B	44. B	69. D	94. C
20. A	45. B	70. C	95. D
21. A	46. B	71. A	96. B
22. B	47. B	72. D	97. C
23. D	48. A	73. A	98. C
24. C	49. B	74. B	99. C
25. B	50. D	75. C	100. B

Section II—Short Narration

101. C	106. C	111. A	116. D
102. C	107. C	112. B	117. D
103. D	108. D	113. A	118. B
104. C	109. D	114. B	119. B
105. C	110. C	115. D	120. A

Listening Comprehension Practice
ANSWER KEY

Section III—Dialogues

121. B	134. A	147. C	160. C
122. D	135. C	148. C	161. D
123. D	136. D	149. D	162. D
124. B	137. A	150. D	163. A
125. D	138. B	151. A	164. D
126. D	139. D	152. B	165. B
127. A	140. A	153. C	166. D
128. D	141. D	154. C	167. C
129. A	142. A	155. A	168. B
130. C	143. D	156. C	169. C
131. B	144. B	157. D	170. B
132. C	145. C	158. C	171. C
133. D	146. C	159. B	172. A

Section IV—Long Narration

173. B	185. B	197. A	209. D
174. D	186. C	198. C	210. B
175. D	187. C	199. B	211. B
176. A	188. D	200. D	212. A
177. B	189. D	201. D	213. B
178. B	190. A	202. D	214. B
179. D	191. B	203. B	215. A
180. C	192. C	204. C	216. C
181. B	193. D	205. B	217. B
182. C	194. D	206. A	218. C
183. A	195. D	207. B	219. C
184. B	196. B	208. C	220. C

ANSWERS AND ANSWER EXPLANATIONS

In this section, the correct answer to each question is given, along with supporting information from the passages. Detailed explanations are provided after the "Why not" label in cases that are not obvious to illustrate why the other choices are incorrect.

Section I—Conversation

1. **(D)** The man answers that he is from San Francisco, and turns the same question around for the woman by asking "你呢？" The woman's response should address the question appropriately. Why not:

   (A) She misunderstands the man's response and completely misses the question.
   (B) She misunderstands the question, thinking he has asked if she would like to go somewhere.
   (C) She misunderstands the question, thinking that it is an invitation to visit San Francisco.

2. **(B)** It responds to the question "Where is the bookstore?" Why not:

   (A) tells what's inside the bookstore.
   (C) indicates when the bookstore opens.
   (D) comments that the books are expensive.

3. **(C)** The man is taken a bit by surprise because he does not even hear anything, let alone identify whose voice it is. Why not:

   (A) The woman can certainly hear someone calling her; she just cannot make out who is calling. This response asks about "what" she hears instead of "who" is producing the sound she hears.
   (B) Similar to (A), this response asks about where the sound she hears is coming from instead of who is producing the sound. The woman, in fact, already knows that the sound is coming from outside of the dormitory.
   (D) This response is redundant because it restates what the woman is wondering about.

4. **(C)** "什麼都忘了" ("什么都忘了") is a statement, not a question, meaning *lose track of everything*. Although "什麼" ("什么") is a question word, it is used as a non-specific descriptive in this context. The appropriate response here is to follow up with empathy and bring closure instead of further scrutiny. Why not:

(A) The "什麼" ("什么") is taken too literally by the woman, who misunderstands that the man forgets to watch something.

(B) She mistakenly mixes up the three keywords "電視" ("电视"), "什麼" ("什么"), and "忘了" that she hears, and goes off on a tangent with her own word "爲什麼" ("为什么").

(D) There is a sarcastic tone to this response: "What CAN you remember?" Although this may conceivably be a response in some situations, it is generally not appropriate.

5. **(B)** This is a polite way of saying "no" by offering an alternative suggestion, "Why don't I go to your house to meet you instead?" Why not:

(A) This is irrelevant to her asking if she can go to his house. "你知道我家在哪兒嗎?" ("你知道我家在哪儿吗") would have been a logical response as a follow-up to her question.

(C) "I went to your house yesterday" does not answer her question.

(D) "Where shall we meet?" is ignoring her suggestion of meeting him at his house.

6. **(A)** He indirectly accepts her suggestion of making Chinese friends to improve his Chinese language studies by commenting that he has a lot of Chinese friends. Why not:

(B) His response is off topic of her recommendation, asking what she thinks of his Chinese friends.

(C) He explains that he met his Chinese friends in Chinatown, which doesn't respond to her recommendation.

(D) He is stating an opinion that is irrelevant to her recommendation.

7. **(B)** She responds to his statement that he must find a place to buy a Chinese dictionary by giving him specific directions to a nearby bookstore. Why not:

(A) She asks if *that* bookstore is big, but he did not say anything about a bookstore.

(C) She comments that the bookstore is not far, even though he has not said anything about a bookstore.

(D) She asks him how to get to a bookstore when he seems to have a little trouble finding one himself.

8. **(D)** A straightforward, direct response to "How come you got up so late?" Why not:

(A) His response, "I like to go to bed early and get up early," contradicts what she says.
(B) He sounds defensive by saying, "I went to bed as early as eight last night," but it still does not address her question.
(C) "I like to sleep eight hours every night" might have answered her question if he had indeed just gone to bed eight hours ago, but it is not clear if that is what he intends to say.

9. **(D)** He directly responds to her compliment, that he speaks Chinese so well she wonders if he has studied it for a long time.
Why not:

(A), (B) Both only state who can speak Chinese.
(C) He explains why he studies Chinese, but does not answer her question about how long.

10. **(A)** He confirms what she heard about the winter in New York. Why not:

(B) He talks about how he likes to go skiing in winter, but she is seeking feedback about what she heard.
(C) He comments on how beautiful winter is in New York instead of giving feedback on what she heard.
(D) He tells her that winter is long in New York instead of addressing the low temperature she is talking about.

11. **(C)** He explains that his girlfriend went to visit her best friend after the trip when she asks, "How come yourself . . . ?" Why not:

(A) His response, "The trip with my girlfriend was great," does not address the woman's concern. It would have been a great response had she asked him how the trip went.
(B) He only restates what she observed—that he came back alone—without answering her questions.
(D) That his girlfriend bought a lot of clothes on the trip doesn't answer her question regarding his girlfriend's whereabouts.

12. **(B)** She apologizes for not being able to take him to the airport because she has to stay home and wait for a friend. Why not:

(A) Her proclamation that she is a much better driver than him does not answer his request for her to take him to the airport.
(C) Her opinion about her car does not answer his request for her to take him to the airport.
(D) Asking why he is heading to the airport does not answer his request for her to take him to the airport. Besides, he already said he is going on a business trip.

13. **(C)** His response, "Yes, she does, but she's not very good at it," directly answers her question about whether his mother makes Chinese food. Why not:

    (A), (D) These responses talk about who likes to *eat* Chinese food without addressing whether his mother knows how to *make* Chinese food.

    (B) He shares his opinion that Chinese food is more delicious than Japanese food without addressing her inquiry.

14. **(D)** He directly responds to her question about whether he went to the soccer game yesterday by telling her that his son was sick, so he had to take him to the hospital. Why not:

    (A), (B) He talks about how well he plays soccer and that he likes soccer very much without addressing her question.

    (C) His comment on some soccer players does not answer her question.

15. **(C)** This problem tests students' ability to differentiate "教" and "叫." His response, "That teacher teaches physics," not only answers her question but also makes clear that the teacher with glasses is called Zhang LaoShi. Why not:

    (A) He clearly misunderstands her question and responds with the teacher's name.

    (B) Instead of saying *what* that teacher teaches, he describes *what grade* the teacher with glasses teaches.

    (D) He tells us that all the students call him Zhang LaoShi without telling us what subject he teaches.

16. **(C)** When asked about who bought her the computer, she directly answers that her brother bought it for her as a birthday gift. Why not:

    (A) She tells us that she really needs a computer, but does not answer the man's question.

    (B) She tells us that her brother and sister both like the computer; however, she does not say who bought the computer.

    (D) Her sister really wanted to give her a computer, but she does not say if she actually gave it to her.

17. **(B)** This problem tests students' ability to identify the woman's rhetorical statement, "Who else would I be looking for?" As long as they understand that this is not really meant to be a question, the obvious response can only be, "What do you need me for?" Why not:

    (A) He asks who she is looking for after she just implied that she was looking for him.

    (C) The question "Who is looking for you?" is irrelevant.

    (D) He contradicts himself by asking when she looked for him when he starts the dialogue, "Were you looking for me just now?"

18. **(D)** She says, "Don't worry, we can definitely solve this problem," to which he responds, "Not necessarily." He seems to have no faith that the problem can be solved. It makes a lot of sense for her to respond, "Why is it that you have no faith?" Why not:

   (A) "Can't you see the problem?" is not correct because "不見得" ("不见得") means *not necessarily* and "看不見" ("看不见") means *cannot see*. They are not the same.
   (B) "What do you think of this problem?" is irrelevant and out of the blue.
   (C) "I agree with you" conflicts with her first statement.

19. **(B)** His "What's there to watch?" is another rhetorical statement, meaning that he does not believe there is anything worth watching. As expected, her response counters his opinion: "I think all of the programs are pretty good." Why not:

   (A) "Which channel do you think has something worth watching?" seems inappropriate when he just said that there is nothing worth watching.
   (C) "Do you have any good programs?" makes no sense.
   (D) "Do you like to watch television?" is unacceptable, especially when he already implied that he does not like to watch television.

20. **(A)** "不在了" is a euphemism for *deceased*. The response, therefore, is "How could it be! He has been very healthy all along." Why not:

   (B) "I don't know either if he's here or not" assumes the more literal definition of the homonym "在," *at*.
   (C) "Where did he go?" also assumes the more literal definition of "在."
   (D) "He was just here" makes no sense. It also erroneously takes the more literal definition "在."

21. **(A)** "Not that many" is a logical and accurate response to the question, "You must have a lot of people taking Chinese at your school this semester?" Why not:

   (B) "Chinese is too hard" doesn't answer her question directly. At best, it may be indirect feedback, implying a low enrollment.
   (C) This response goes beyond her question about the enrollment of this school, and stretches it out to cover the entire United States.
   (D) "They study Chinese at school" answers where the students study, but not how many.

22. **(B)** He elaborates on why Wang LaoShi is one of the best teachers. Why not:

   (A) Teaching for a long time does not always translate to a better teacher.
   (C) The subject she teaches is irrelevant to how she became one of the best.
   (D) The number of classes she teaches is irrelevant to how she became one of the best.

23. **(D)** He is definitely coming. Why not:

(A) He describes how they met.
(B) He explains that he has never been to his house without saying if he will come this time.
(C) He reiterates that he is his best friend but falls short of saying if he is coming or not.

24. **(C)** She makes it clear that she'd rather take the bus than drive to the museum. Why not:

(A) "We are going to the museum" does not address how to get there.
(B) "I've already been to the museum" does not address how to get there this time.
(D) "The museum is very famous" is irrelevant.

25. **(B)** He offers what he knows about the weather when she says she forgot to check the weather forecast. Why not:

(A) "I listen to the weather report every day" doesn't answer the question.
(C) "The weather is usually pretty good" tells how the weather is generally, but not how it is going to be tomorrow specifically.
(D) "Some people don't think the weather report is accurate" only shows that some people don't believe in the weather report, and it does not help her in this case.

26. **(B)** She says, "You all like to come to big cities, but I don't see what's so great about big cities." He says, "I think it's because there are more opportunities in big cities." Why not:

(A) He reiterates her viewpoint, and doesn't answer the question.
(C) "We all like big cities" confirms what she says without giving any supporting reasons.
(D) "How do we get to a big city?" is irrelevant.

27. **(D)** "I'm not sure" sounds like a believable response from someone who spends all day watching television and going on the Internet when it's almost time for finals. Why not:

(A) He claims that the break is coming soon, but doesn't answer when finals will be.
(B) "I get nervous when people talk about finals" is a diversion to dodge the question.
(C) "I won't be late to finals" is quite irrelevant.

28. **(B)** He disagrees with her assessment by saying "我覺得那家餐館還不錯" ("我觉得那家餐馆还不错"). Why not:

(A) The structure of "That restaurant is really good" seems to suggest that this is a conclusion he draws from her experience, but the conclusion contradicts her experience.

(C) "Is the restaurant far from here?" doesn't respond to the woman's statement. It would have worked better if he had continued by saying, "我親自去嘗一嘗" ("我亲自去尝一尝").

(D) He asks, "How is that restaurant," when the woman clearly expressed her dislike of it.

29. **(B)** He says, "Finding a good job is harder than anything." She says, "Well, that depends on what your major is." He rebuts, "It doesn't matter what my major is, companies aren't short of staff." Why not:

(A) He agrees with her by saying, "It's easier to find jobs with a good major," but that is not aligned with his initial concerns.

(C) "I have a major" is irrelevant.

(D) "I don't like my major" is also irrelevant.

30. **(B)** The phrase "一個比一個貴" ("一个比一个贵") literally means that each item is more expensive than the last, but what it actually means in context is "everything is expensive." Why not:

(A), (C), (D) All use the literal meaning of "一個比一個貴" ("一个比一个贵").

31. **(C)** She complains, "If you don't come right now, we're not going to wait anymore." It is only appropriate that he apologize for being late. Why not:

(A) He talks about next time "下次" ("下次") but doesn't say anything about the current situation.

(B) "Why do you not want to wait for me?" is illogical because she apparently already has been waiting and is getting upset that he is not there yet.

(D) "If you're not going to wait for me, I'm leaving" is illogical. How is he going to leave if he has not arrived yet?

32. **(D)** She can't find the bookstore, and he gives her the obvious landmark close to it. Why not:

(A) He reiterates what she already told him.

(B) He does not seem to have heard her when she said she could not find the bookstore no matter where she looked. "好找嗎? ("好找吗?") means *easy to find*?

(C) "Did you find the bookstore?" doesn't make sense when the woman clearly said that she can't find it.

33. **(A)** He says, "When my girlfriend heard the news, she couldn't believe her own ears." She wonders, "Why didn't she believe the news?" Why not:

    (B) "Did she believe the news?" isn't correct because he already said that she didn't.

    (C), (D) She takes "can't believe her own ears" literally thinking that there is something wrong with her ears.

34. **(D)** "When are you going?" is a natural response after she announces, "I'm going to China to study Chinese and visit historic sites."
    Why not:

    (A), (B), (C) All three are wrong because the woman has already stated the answers to all of the man's questions.

35. **(B)** The man wants to know why Ana is always late to class. Why not:

    (A) He asks how late Ana is when she already said "three, four minutes."

    (C) He wonders if Ana is really that good after she said that Ana is always late.

    (D) He wonders when Ana was ever later, even though she already said that she is always late to class.

36. **(B)** After he shares his plan, she responds with a very reasonable scenario: "What if your parents don't agree with your plan, what do you do?"
    Why not:

    (A) He says his parents don't want him to get a job first.

    (C) He says he has not graduated yet.

    (D) He says he hasn't started working yet.

37. **(A)** Based on what she says, he concludes, "I see that your parents are very satisfied with your brother." Why not:

    (B) The subject and objects are switched.

    (C), (D) These responses are the opposite of what she said.

38. **(B)** She asks about the bathroom because he did not say anything about it.
    Why not:

    (A), (B), (D) These were already mentioned in his first statement.

39. **(C)** She is avoiding going to the hospital by claiming her illness is a minor one. He appropriately follows up with, "Regardless of if it's major or minor, you should always go to the hospital."
Why not:

   (A) He is making a judgment by saying "this disease" before she even sees a doctor.
   (B) He is questioning her self-diagnosis, and urges her to go to the hospital.
   (D) He agrees that she has a minor illness, but still urges her to go to the hospital. While similar to the correct answer, this response is less convincing grammatically. It would have been more appropriate if he had said, "就算是小病，也得去醫院看看" ("就算是小病，也得去医院看看").

40. **(D)** He apologizes for being late. Why not:

   (A) Her question is rhetorical; she is not actually expecting a response to "都幾點了" ("都几点了").
   (B), (C) Both responses are impolite.

41. **(A)** He says, "I want to, but I have class, so I can't," when she asks him if he is going to the basketball game. Why not:

   (B) The basketball game hasn't happened yet.
   (C) He asks who is going when she just wants to know if he is going. It doesn't answer her question.
   (D) "Do you like watching basketball games?" doesn't answer her question either.

42. **(B)** He agrees with her assessment by using "又乾燥又悶熱" ("又干燥又闷热"). Why not:

   (A), (C), (D) All are wrong because they contradict her first statement.

43. **(B)** She relays, "Miss Zhang asked Mr. Wang to give Huang Laoshi a letter." He wonders when Ms. Zhang wrote this letter.

44. **(B)** She says that Xiao Zhang came forty minutes after 7:30. This means that he came at 8:10. Why not:

   (A) It is redundant; she did say that Xiao Zhang came, although 40 minutes late.
   (C) She already states that she came first.
   (D) This is not a valid question because she was not late.

45. **(B)** He apologizes for calling so late. Why not:

(A) "How do I call" restates part of her question using "怎麼打電話" ("怎么打电话").

(C) One cannot make a call as one is receiving a call. "I will call you as soon as I receive your message" would have been a better response— "我一接到你的留言就給你打了" (我一接到你的留言就给你打了").

(D) He says, "Who is calling you?" as he is calling her.

46. **(B)** He articulates why he is so tired when he says, "I had three periods of classes, then I worked four hours in the media center." Why not:

(A) He complains that the prices are too high at the shopping center, which is irrelevant.

(C) He says again, "I don't want to go shopping when I'm tired," which is redundant and offers no new information.

(D) He asks her if she can go shopping by herself, which, again, is redundant.

47. **(B)** She says that she has three classes, and he replies, "I have four classes, and one of them is a Chinese class. What about you?" Why not:

(A) It is completely irrelevant.

(C), (D) The woman doesn't answer the man's question.

48. **(A)** She says, "I see that you're a regular customer here," and he says, "我來了多少趟了" ("我来了多少趟了"), which means "I've been here many times." Why not:

(B) Her first comment actually implies that they both know where the restaurant is.

(C) His statement "我來了多少趟了" ("我来了多少趟了") is not a question and it does not expect a response.

(D) She repeats what he said.

49. **(B)** After he compliments her, "Your French is very good," she tries to be modest by saying, "Good? I've only been studying for one year." He continues to compliment her, saying, "That's really good for only studying for one year." Why not:

(A) He seems surprised to discover that she speaks French.

(C) He contradicts himself by saying, "So it's okay if you're not very good."

(D) Her "好什麼" ("好什么") is a rhetorical question, but he goes on to point out what is good and what is not that good.

50. **(D)** They are talking about soccer. Why not: (A), (B), (C)—"踢" only refers to soccer, so these are wrong because they refer to the wrong sports.

51. **(C)** He explains that his older sister drove him. Why not:

    (A), (B) He talks about his driving skills, but doesn't answer how he got here.

    (D) He talks about the crowded bus, but doesn't answer the question.

52. **(B)** The key word "雙" ("双") is a measure word, and the other key word, "戴," is a verb. Both indicate that the item they are talking about is a pair of gloves. Why not:

    (A), (C), (D) These responses don't fit the man's description.

53. **(D)** She indicates that she likes running, too, but she has been too busy to run. It is most logical that he asks her what she's been busy with. Why not:

    (A) She already said that she's too busy to run.

    (B), (C) She wasn't talking about movies or Chinese food.

54. **(A)** He is not happy that she is always late. When she explains that she lives far away, he then complains, "Then why can't you leave earlier?"
    Why not:

    (B) She says that her house is far away.

    (C) It is irrelevant and out of the blue.

    (D) He is talking about his own house.

55. **(C)** She is looking for birthday gift ideas for her roommate. He suggests food or clothing. Why not: (A), (B), (D)—These choices contradict his suggestions.

56. **(B)** He says it was five years ago when he last visited Shanghai.
    Why not:

    (A), (C), (D) These responses don't answer the woman's question.

57. **(C)** "還可以吧" ("还可以吧") means *it's OK.* "一般" also means *OK, ordinary.* He agrees with her that the movie is mediocre, and nothing stood out.
    Why not:

    (A), (B), (D) All of these contradict the woman's statement.

58. **(B)** "說不好" ("说不好") = "說不定" ("说不定") = "不一定," which means that "小張" ("小张") is not sure. Why not:

    (A) Xiao Wang is fine; he can come.

    (C) There is no problem between the man and Xiao Wang.

    (D) "小張" ("小张") is not sure if he can make it.

59. **(A)** This is a very typical scene in the marketplace. She likes the size and color, but not the price. So the vendor offers to lower the price. Why not:

(B) He offers other colors, but she does not have a problem with the color.
(C), (D) The man offers to give her a different size when it already fits.

60. **(C)** She turns down his suggestion to eat at a new restaurant by gently saying, "Maybe some other time." Later, she says that she has too much homework. Why not:

(A) He points out that the restaurant is next to the movie theatre.
(B), (D) Neither answer addresses why she does not want to go this evening.

61. **(D)** She likes swimming, basketball, and volleyball, but her favorite is tennis. His favorite is volleyball. Why not:

(A), (B), (C) Both must be in agreement when the character "也" is involved.

62. **(B)** She explains that the shoes were too small so she just got rid of them decisively. "說 (说) verb 就 verb" indicates a sense of determination on the action verb. Why not:

(A), (C), (D) All are irrelevant because they don't answer the man's question.

63. **(A)** He is impressed by her ability to drive everywhere, so he concludes that she must be a very good driver. Why not:

(B) The statements must be in agreement to include "也" in the same sentence.
(C), (D) They are incorrect because they contradict her own statement.

64. **(B)** She decides to buy five pounds of apples. Why not:

(A) She asks about the quality of the bananas and does not answer the question.
(C), (D) She talks about the price of the fruit and doesn't answer the question.

65. **(B)** They are sharing their views about clothes shopping. She goes after name brands regardless of style, price, or quality. He looks for quality. Why not:

(A), (C) He is making statements about name brands and styles.
(D) It is an error to use "也" in non-agreements.

66. **(C)** According to the context, students can infer that the relationship between the two speakers is a mother and her son. The mother asks her son, "How did you do on your test?" The son says, "If I tell you, you must promise that you won't get mad." This implies that he has received a bad mark. The mother then says, "When you're not watching television, you're out playing soccer. How can you get a good grade that way!" Why not:

   (A), (D) On the contrary, he did not do well.
   (B) She already knows what he got.

67. **(D)** From "這裏" ("这里") and "來上班" ("来上班"), students can infer that the man and the woman are at the hospital, and that Doctor Li is not at work. Why not:

   (A) Dr. Li is not at the hospital because that is where the woman and the man are.
   (B) Dr. Li has already graduated from college.
   (C) She has nothing to do with a company.

68. **(D)** She asks if everyone in his family wears glasses. He says that he and his younger brother wear glasses, but his sister doesn't. The woman then concludes, "I see that your sister's vision is pretty good." Why not:

   (A) His sister doesn't wear glasses.
   (B) He and his brother wear glasses.
   (C) His brother doesn't have good vision.

69. **(D)** She is here to study Chinese, then she will go back and be a translator. He works in China.

70. **(C)** He is to meet Xiao Wang at 5:00 to go shopping. He came at 4:50 and waited until 5:30, but ended up going shopping alone. Xiao Wang never came. Why not:

   (A), (B), (D) These are wrong because Xiao Wang never showed up.

71. **(A)** She explains that she does not have a table, so she put her TV on the floor. He shows his understanding by saying, "Not having a table is very inconvenient." Why not:

   (B) The woman already said, "There is not so much stuff in my room."
   (C) The woman already explained why she put her TV on the floor.
   (D) The woman explained this in her statement.

72. **(D)** He likes to play soccer and tennis. She wonders if he plays every day. He says, "As if I have the time!" Why not:

   (A) He doesn't answer the question.
   (B) She asks about the frequency of his play, not for him to choose between soccer and tennis.
   (C) They are talking about how well he plays scoccer, not how often, as she asked.

73. **(A)** He sees her sister going to an English school behind the post office. She elaborates that her sister is planning to travel abroad, so she is studying English to improve her language skills. Why not:

(B) They are not discussing where the man was.
(C), (D) These responses are irrelevant.

74. **(B)** She says, "No wonder your health is so good," when the man talks about the things he does to keep himself healthy. Why not:

(A) It is out of the blue.
(C), (D) They contradict the man's statement.

75. **(C)** She wonders when Xiao Zhang's mom retired when he says Xiao Zhang's mother used to be a salesperson before she retired. Now she lives at Xiao Zhang's house and helps take care of the kids. Why not:

(A), (B) He makes it quite clear that Xiao Zhang's mother had already retired.
(D) He says Xiao Zhang's mother used to work in a store.

76. **(D)** She asks, "What's wrong? You don't look too good." "臉色這麼不好看" ("脸色这么不好看") means that Lao Zhang either looks mad or sick. In this case, he is mad. He says why he is mad. Why not:

(A), (C) "不好看" doesn't mean that he is not good looking, which is the literal meaning.
(B) It takes the word "色" too literally, to mean *color*.

77. **(C)** He agrees when she says, "After all these years, I don't even recognize Xiao Wang anymore." Why not:

(A), (B), (D) These are wrong because "認不出來" ("认不出来") means that Xiao Wang looks different, not that the man doesn't know him.

78. **(B)** He says he doesn't like to read even when he's not watching basketball games in response to her statement, "If only you could watch fewer games, you'd have the time to read." Why not:

(A) He hasn't missed any games yet.
(C) It contradicts her hypothesis.
(D) When she says "兩場" ("两场"), she means it figuratively, that he watches too many games, not that he should miss exactly two of them.

79. **(A)** She says, "No matter what you say, I won't agree." He asks her why she won't agree. Why not:

(B), (D) She already said that she won't agree, no matter what he says.
(C) It makes no sense.

80. **(B)** He compliments a shirt she is wearing. She explains that it is a gift made by a friend for her birthday. He wonders what her friend does for a living. Why not:

    (A) She already said it was for her birthday.
    (C) She already said that her friend made it and didn't buy it.
    (D) She just said that her friend made the shirt.

81. **(A)** He says, "If I can't get an A, who else could get an A?" The man's question is rhetorical, so she says, "You may not necessarily get an A."

82. **(A)** She says, "Just listen to Xiao Zhang talk. I can tell he is from Shanghai." He responds with "我也覺得是" ("我也觉得是"), which means that he is thinking the same thing. Then she asks, "When did he move out of Shanghai?" Why not:

    (B), (C), (D) These are wrong because they already agreed that Shanghai is Xiao Zhang's hometown.

83. **(C)** He asks if she'd like to go out to lunch. She answers, "What do you think?" This is a rhetorical question that implies agreement, so he asks, "What do you want to eat?" Why not:

    (A), (B), (D) These are wrong because she already agreed with the suggestion.

84. **(C)** She says, "They all said that you are going to work as a volunteer in China; is that true?" He says, "I have this plan," so she asks him when he plans to leave. Why not:

    (A), (B), (D) These are wrong because the woman already answered the questions.

85. **(B)** He asks, "How many people are there in your family?" She says, "Four. My husband and I, and we have a daughter and a son. My husband is a college teacher. I teach elementary school. My daughter is a nurse." He then asks, "Where does your son work?"

86. **(A)** From the conversation, students can infer that the relationship between the two speakers should be mother and son. The son assures his mom, "Mom, don't worry. No problem." This means that he is ready for the test. Then the mom says, "Are you sure?" Why not:

    (B) The son says, "No problem."
    (C), (D) The mom does not need to prepare for a test.

87. **(C)** From the dialogue, we know that her daughter is not only good at singing and dancing, she is also a good student. Why not:

    (A) It repeats the previous statements.
    (B), (C) These responses contradict the previous statement.

88. **(D)** She asks, "Are we going to watch a Chinese movie or an American movie?" He replies, "隨便吧" ("随便吧") ("It doesn't matter"), meaning that he doesn't have a strong opinion either way. So the woman decides, "Let's go to watch an American movie." Why not:

    (A), (B), (C) These are wrong because he doesn't care what kind of movie they watch.

89. **(A)** She says, "不錯" ("不错") ("Not bad") when he asks her how her interview went. Then he says, "Terrific." Why not:

    (B), (C), (D) All contradict the woman's statement.

90. **(B)** She says, "I didn't go to class. I wasn't feeling well yesterday, so I went to the hospital and then went to my parents' house." Why not:

    (A), (C), (D) All contradict the woman's statement.

91. **(B)** "那還用說" ("那还用说") has a positive connotation—*that goes without saying*. It implies that the man did well on the exam. Then she comments, "You are always so confident." Why not:

    (A), (C), (D) All use the literal meaning of the phrase.

92. **(C)** The man's statement is a rhetorical question, so what he actually means is that it wasn't supposed to rain. The woman then says, "How can you trust the weather forecast?" Then the man asks, "Why don't you trust the weather forecast?" Why not:

    (A), (D) These responses misinterpret the rhetorical question.
    (B) This is incorrect because the man actually heard the weather forecast.

93. **(D)** She is looking for a grocery store nearby. He says, "See the white building? There is a grocery store right behind it." Then she chats about what she is getting from the store: "I want to buy milk and bread there." Why not:

    (A) She already asked the question.
    (B), (C) He said that the grocery store is behind the white building.

94. **(C)** He asks for her opinion regarding majoring in literature or statistics. She recommends, "I think nothing is better than medicine," so he says, "Studying medicine is too expensive." Why not:

    (A), (B), (D) These are wrong because she already stated that studying medicine is the best choice.

95. **(D)** He says, "你看著辦吧" ("你看着办吧"), which shows that he is leaving it to the woman to decide. So she says, "Then let's get one."

96. **(B)** "你看我哪有時間呀" ("你看我哪有时间呀") is a rhetorical question and shows that he doesn't have time to watch a movie, so she asks, "Why are you so busy?"

97. **(C)** She asks him if he will travel with them during the summer vacation. He explains that he will only if his roommate is going, too. She responds, "Your roommate is definitely going." Why not:

    (A), (B), (D) These are incorrect because he indicates that he will go only if his roommate goes.

98. **(C)** She asks, "Can you please tell me why the bus is just coming now?" which implies that the bus is late. The man, who is probably the bus driver, informs her that he waited for a long time because there was a car accident in the intersection of the street. Why not:

    (B) She already commented that the bus is late.
    (A), (D) She already learned about the accident from the driver.

99. **(C)** She asks, "How did you do on your exam?" He says, "Li Yun only got a 65, let alone me," which implie Li Yun did poorly, but he did worse. Why not:

    (A), (B) He implied that Li Yun did poorly, but he did worse.
    (D) It has nothing to do with the topic.

100. **(B)** He asks, "Where is the restaurant?" The woman says, "There are lots of restaurants around here, which one are you talking about?" He then says, "I am asking about the Sichuan restaurant." Why not:

    (A) "經常" ("经常") is *frequently, often*—for example, he comments that she goes out to eat in restaurants very often.
    (C) He points out that no one knows where restaurants are (i.e., non-specific restaurants).
    (D) He comments that no one knows who owns the restaurant.

Section II—Short Narration

101. **(C)** The difference can be obtained by subtracting 4°C (*lowest*) from 39°C (*highest*). Why not:

    (A) The lowest temperature is 4°C.
    (B) There is no mention of "freezing."
    (D) The average temperature is for a year, instead of just today.

102. **(C)** The voice message says, "Xiao Zhang, this is your roommate Xiao Li. I could not go to class this afternoon because my mother was sick, and I am going to visit her at the hospital with my little sister. Please let the teacher know that I'll be taking this afternoon off."

103. **(D)** The narrator says, "I couldn't even imagine in my dreams that he could get such a good job." This shows that she is surprised.

104. **(C)** "糟糕" is *horrific, appalling, ghastly*. The narrator says, "The shirt my sister bought was of good quality, not expensive, and in style. The only problem was that the color was too appalling." This shows that the color of the shirt wasn't good.

105. **(C)** "再也沒有" ("再也没有") means *there cannot possibly be*. "讓…激動" ("让…激动") means *be excited*. The man says, "Soccer gets people excited like no other sport."

106. **(C)** The sentence starting with "要是" usually is a subjunctive conditional. The question "怎麼會沒有時間呢" ("怎么会没有时间呢?") is a rhetorical one, meaning *how could there be no time?*

107. **(C)** Her younger brother's son (nephew) is behind her older brother.

108. **(D)** "就是沒有書店" ("就是没有书店") indicates that there is no bookstore.

109. **(D)** It is based on the sequence of events.

110. **(C)** The statements (A) and (B) are not wrong, but they are just examples of (C). (D) is wrong, as the speaker does not drink, either.

111. **(A)** The phrase "我們醫院" ("我们医院")—*our hospital, the hospital that we work in*—indicates that the speaker works in a hospital. As another example, "我們學校" ("我们学校") means *our school, the school that we go to*.

112. **(B)** Originally, the speaker planned to travel to Nanjing, Shanghai, Guangzhou, and Xi'an, but he went back to Beijing from Shanghai because they could not get the train tickets to Guangzhou while they were in Shanghai.

113. **(A)** She is suggesting an alternative to a challenge they are facing: "Our problem is that there isn't a direct flight from Washington, D.C., to Los Angeles, but going by train is too slow, so we have to take the train from Washington, D.C., to New York and fly to Los Angeles from there."

114. **(B)** This passage states that the title "老師" ("老师") can sometimes be applied to people who aren't actually *teachers*. The narrator says that her mother is sometimes called "李老師" ("李老师") instead of "李醫生" ("李医生"), indicating that she actually is a doctor.

115. **(D)** The narrator says, "After I graduate, I plan to study computer science for two years to gain some knowledge. As for getting a job, making money, or going abroad, etc., they are not so important to me."

116. **(D)** In addition to a desk and a bookcase, there are also a bed and a TV. There wouldn't be a bed in an (A) office, (B) library, or (C) classroom.

117. **(D)** The father is too busy, the brother has to go see his girlfriend, and the mother doesn't know how to fix the computer. A friend ends up fixing the computer.

118. **(B)** The sentence "我只花了50元就買來了" ("我只花了50元就买来了") indicates that she only paid 50 *yuan* for the shoes.

119. **(B)** "最後兩位數是86" ("最后两位数是86")—the last two digits are 86.

120. **(A)** "開車比較快，也就十分鐘" ("开车比较快，也就十分钟")—*driving a car to school takes only about 10 minutes.*

Section III—Dialogues

121. **(B)** "您是這個大學的學生嗎" ("您是这个大学的学生吗") means "Are you a student at this university?" This implies that they are at a school.

122. **(D)** The woman works at a bookstore. "一家書店" ("一家书店"), and the dialogue happens at a place that she "不常來" ("不常来"). Both clues tell us that they are not at the bookstore now.

123. **(D)** The woman introduces herself as follows: She works at a bank, she is from Nanjing, she studied in Shanghai. After she graduated, she came to Beijing to work.

124. **(B)** The woman's statement "我是南京人" ("我是南京人") means that she is from Nanjing.

125. **(D)** He says so directly.

126. **(D)** The woman says that she likes calligraphy and Beijing opera, but not folk songs.

127. **(A)** She says "我喜歡聽音樂" ("我喜欢听音乐"), but doesn't have a lot of time to do so.

128. **(D)** She says "晚上還得輔導兒子英語" ("晚上还得辅导儿子英语"), which means *tutors her son in English in the evening.*

129. **(A)** She asks him if he comes to swim in the pool often, and he says, "每天都來" ("每天都来").

130. **(C)** She asks him about his job, and he says, "跟你一樣，是記者" ("跟你一样，是记者").

131. **(B)** He doesn't care about the brand as long as the clothing item looks good and is comfortable.

132. **(C)** She said that the price of her sweater was originally $89, but "打折後才39元" ("打折后才39元"). She bought it on sale for $39.

133. **(D)** Based on "有時間也到我們家坐坐吧" ("有时间也到我们家坐坐吧"), students can infer that the relationship between the speakers is a host and a guest. The conversation is about the man leaving the woman's house after a visit.

134. **(A)** The phrases "以後常來玩" ("以后常来玩") and "不遠送了" ("不远送了") show that the speakers are in a house.

135. **(C)** Ms. Zhang asks Xiao Li if he is looking for Lao Zhang (Professor Zhang), and Xiao Li answers, "對，我找張教授有點兒事" ("对，我找张教授有点儿事").

136. **(D)** "我找張教授有點兒事" ("我找张教授有点儿事") is what he told Mrs. Zhang directly.

137. **(A)** The man asks the teacher how long dinner should take in the first sentence: "中國人吃飯的時間總是那麼長嗎?" ("中国人吃饭的时间总是那么长吗?").

138. **(B)** The woman explains that a host tends to pace himself or herself and would avoid finishing the meal before the guest.

139. **(D)** The woman says that her father goes to the park every day to stay healthy.

140. **(A)** The woman's father is retired, so he goes to the park every day. The man's father is also retired and is the president of a fishing club.

141. **(D)** The man's father is the one who fishes, not the woman's father.

142. **(A)** "好什麼" ("好什么") is a rhetorical question indicating quite the opposite of what it sounds like—"不好" is *not good*—that his father is not good at fishing.

143. **(D)** She is currently living in a dorm but wants to move out.

144. **(B)** The answer is directly stated by the man , "比較安全" ("比较安全"), and agreed to by the woman, "我同意你的說法" ("我同意你的说法"). Why not:

    (A) Dorms are expensive, "住在公寓也比住在宿舍便宜得多" ("住在公寓也比住在宿舍便宜得多")
    (C) The woman thinks that living in a dorm is "不自由," *lacks freedom.*
    (D) Having a roommate is a fact, not an advantage or a disadvantage.

145. **(C)** The woman says so directly.

146. **(C)** The woman is the one who can't sleep or study, not her roommate. (A), (C), and (D) are what her roommate does a lot, causing the woman to want to move out.

147. **(C)** When she asks him if he has any plans for the break, he says that he wants to stay on the East Coast and rest, which shows that *East Coast* is where he is.

148. **(C)** Although packing is an important step in preparing for a trip, it is not mentioned in the dialogue.

149. **(D)** He says that plane tickets from the travel agencies are not necessarily cheaper, and he got his tickets from the Internet last time. In conclusion, he says, "我還得再看看" ("我还得再看看"), meaning that he has not made up his mind yet.

150. **(D)** The man says that the last time he went to Taiwan, he bought his ticket from the Internet, which shows that he has been there before.

151. **(A)** The key words "糖醋排骨" ("糖醋排骨") and "我們飯館" ("我们饭馆") show that the conversation takes place in a restaurant.

152. **(B)** From "我們飯館" ("我们饭馆") and "請你給我們推薦推薦吧" ("请你给我们推荐推荐吧"), students can infer that he is the waiter and she is the customer.

153. **(C)** After ordering the main courses, she asks for "再要兩碗米飯" ("再要两碗米饭").

154. **(C)** The man says that "有兩個菜特別有名：一個是麻婆豆腐，另一個是糖醋排骨" ("有两个菜特别有名：一个是麻婆豆腐，另一个是糖醋排骨"). Then the woman says, "那就點這兩個吧" ("那就点这两个吧"), (D) and (B). After that, the man recommends "我們這兒的紅燒魚和油燜大蝦做得都不錯" ("我们这儿的红烧鱼和油焖大虾做得都不错"). The woman says, "點個油燜大蝦吧" ("点个油焖大虾吧") (A), which means that she doesn't order "紅燒魚" ("红烧鱼").

155. **(A)** The woman says that since she is in China, of course she wants to drink tea.

156. **(C)** She says, "我最愛喝綠茶" ("我最爱喝绿茶").

157. **(D)** The man says, "中國還是世界上第一個發現茶的國家呢" ("中国还是世界上第一个发现茶的国家呢").

158. **(C)** The man says that there are many teashops in Beijing, Shanghai, and Guangzhou—"尤其是廣州" ("尤其是广州"), *especially Guangzhou*.

159. **(B)** "我請你跟我回上海" ("我请你跟我回上海"). The man invites the woman to go back to Shanghai with him for tea. This implies that he is from Shanghai.

160. **(C)** When the woman says that they haven't seen each other for two years, the man says that it has actually been more than two years, "兩年多了" ("两年多了").

161. **(D)** The man says that he bought a house last year, and moved out of his in-laws' house.

162. **(D)** The man comments that "跟老人一起生活好，很方便" ("跟老人一起生活好，很方便").

163. **(A)** The woman says that she and her husband like to go to bed late and wake up late, while her in-laws like to go to bed and wake up early; "大家常常爲這些小事不高興" ("大家常常为这些小事不高兴").

164. **(D)** The man says, "一直沒來上班" ("一直没来上班"), *haven't come to work*.

165. **(B)** He explained, "我感冒了，一直沒來上班" ("我感冒了，一直没来上班") to the woman's question, "出差啦?" ("出差啦？") Why not:

(A) His phrase "我感冒了，一直沒來上班" ("我感冒了，一直没来上班") shows that the man didn't go on a business trip.
(C) He comments, "我沒見過雪" ("我没见过雪") when she describes the winter weather in Beijing.
(D) Her phrase "你剛來" ("你刚来") indicates that the man just changed his living place. Although it might indirectly imply that he also changed his workplace recently, it is not her most immediate concern.

166. **(D)** This is directly expressed by "最不喜歡這裏的冬天了" ("最不喜欢这里的冬天了").

167. **(C)** The sentence "我們廣州從來不下雪" ("我们广州从来不下雪") indicates that the man is from Guangzhou.

168. **(B)** She says, "我從上海來北京工作" ("我从上海来北京工作").

169. **(C)** It was directly stated in the conversation: "下午去工廠了" ("下午去工厂了").

170. **(B)** It was directly stated in the conversation: "到工廠抗議去了" ("到工厂抗议去了").

171. **(C)** The man says, "那家工廠排出的廢水和廢氣...造成了嚴重的污染,...廢水把河裏的魚都毒死了" ("那家工厂排出的废水和废气...造成了严重的污染,...废水把河里的鱼都毒死了"). Choices (A), (B), and (D) are all covered in the above statements. Although birds may die from the air pollution, it is not directly mentioned or indirectly inferable from the dialogue.

172. **(A)** The man explains that they do want to solve the problem, but "解決這個問題需要花很多錢" ("解决这个问题需要花很多钱"). Why not:

(B) This contradicts what he says in the dialogue.
(C) "如果政府不幫助他們，他們也沒有辦法" ("如果政府不帮助他们，他们也没有办法") is meant to be a hypothetical statement; the man is *not* saying that *the government does not want to help.*
(D) The time factor is not mentioned in the dialogue.

Section IV—Long Narration

173. **(B)** Xiao Min says, "一邊打工，一邊學習，我受不了了" ("一边打工，一边学习，我受不了了"). Why not:

(A) On the contrary, "餐館的老闆...對小民非常好" ("餐馆的老板...对小民非常好").
(C) On the contrary, "來吃飯的客人給小民的小費也比給別人的多" ("来吃饭的客人给小民的小费也比给别人的多").
(D) On the contrary, "小民打工的那家餐館，生意一直都很好" ("小民打工的那家餐馆，生意一直都很好").

174. **(D)** As directly stated in the passage, "餐館的老闆是一位五十年代移民來美國的臺灣人" ("餐馆的老板是一位五十年代移民来美国的台湾人").

175. **(D)** The weather report indicates, "最低氣溫攝氏24度" ("最低气温摄氏24度").

176. **(A)** The weather report states, "多雲轉陰，有小雨" ("多云转阴，有小雨"). Why not:

(B) "風向偏南，風力一、二級" ("风向偏南，风力一、二级") is the forecast for tonight.
(C) The wind direction is inconsistent with the passage—"南風，風力三、四級" ("南风，风力三、四级").
(D) "風向北轉南，風力二、三級" ("风向北转南，风力二、三级") is the forecast for "明天夜間" ("明天夜间").

177. **(B)** The sentence "齊白石從小就喜歡畫畫兒，可是到了27歲他才正式開始學習繪畫" ("齐白石从小就喜欢画画儿，可是到了27岁他才正式开始学习绘画") indicates that he liked to draw when he was very young, but he formally started to learn drawing at age 27. Why not:

(C) The purpose for observing the animals under the tree is "爲了畫好動物" ("为了画好动物"), not because he liked them.
(D) The purpose for raising the animals at home is "爲了更好地觀察動物" ("为了更好地观察动物"), not because he liked them, either.

178. **(B)** The animals Qi liked to draw were "鳥、魚、蟲什麽的" ("鸟、鱼、虫什么的").

179. **(D)** It is stated in the first sentence that he "對學中文沒有什麽興趣" ("对学中文没有什么兴趣"). But he likes "在中國生活、吃中國菜和在中國旅行" ("在中国生活、吃中国菜和在中国旅行").

180. **(C)** At the end of the passage, Peter "臉紅了" ("脸红了"). This phrase means that he is embarrassed.

181. **(B)** The main idea of this passage is in the first sentence: "中國人請客吃飯有很多講究" ("中国人请客吃饭有很多讲究"). Why not:

(A), (C) These are not mentioned in the passage.
(D) This is only mentioned in the passage for comparison.

182. **(C)** Note the "千萬" ("千万") in "千萬不要跨過別人的筷子去夾食物" ("千万不要跨过别人的筷子去夹食物"). It signifies that crossing over someone else's chopsticks is a serious offense. Why not:

(A) Although a rude eating habit, it is not mentioned in this passage.
(B) When someone offers it is advised that one shall not "用筷子或勺子去接" ("用筷子和勺子去接").
(D) This is, in fact, a good eating habit.

183. **(A)** The main idea is expressed in the first sentence, "感冒是生活中常見的病，預防感冒是不容忽視的" ("感冒是生活中常见的病，预防感冒是不容忽视的").

184. **(B)** Although it is logical, it is not mentioned in the passage.

185. **(B)** The last sentence in the passage indicates that the author advises to get sufficient sleep. Why not:
    (A) This is not mentioned in the passage. One may interpret "把窗戶關好" ("把窗户关好") or "充足的睡眠" to be *staying home*; however, (B) is more specific, and therefore a better choice.
    (C) The narrator suggests "聽天氣預報" ("听天气预报") as a precaution, not what a flu patient should do.
    (D) The author also suggests "注意衣服保暖問題" ("注意衣服保暖问题") as a precaution (to dress appropriately after listening to the forecast), not what a flu patient should do.

186. **(C)** It is stated in the passage that "廣東人偏愛烏龍茶" ("广东人偏爱乌龙茶"). Why not:
    (A) "北京人愛喝茉莉花茶" ("北京人爱喝茉莉花茶"), *people from Beijing like jasmine tea.*
    (B) "上海人喜歡綠茶" ("上海人喜欢绿茶"), *people from Shanghai like green tea.*
    (D) "藏族人離不開酥油茶" ("藏族人离不开酥油茶"), *people from the Zang ethnic group cannot part with the suyou tea (they like suyou tea).*

187. **(C)** From "中國人大多喜歡用陶器茶具和瓷器茶具沏茶" ("中国人大多喜欢用陶器茶具和瓷器茶具沏茶"), we learn that both porcelain and ceramic are favorable choices for making tea.

188. **(D)** "這兩種茶具可以保持水的溫度" ("这两种茶具可以保持水的温度"), *both of these tea sets keep the heat in very well.*

189. **(D)** "慶祝春節的時候" ("庆祝春节的时候") is when people drink the spring tea "春茶". Why not:
    (A) "滿月茶" ("满月茶") is for "孩子滿月的時候" ("孩子满月的时候").
    (B) There is no mention in the passage of any specific tea designated for before the spring season.
    (C) "喜茶" is for "結婚的時候" ("结婚的时候").

190. **(A)** The narrator says "我爺爺…喜歡看京劇…常常一邊看一邊跟著唱" ("我爷爷…喜欢看京剧…常常一边看一边跟着唱"), *his grandfather likes to watch the opera and sing along with it.*

191. **(B)** The narrator says, "爸爸喜歡看體育節目，特別是足球比賽" ("爸爸喜欢看体育节目，特别是足球比赛"), *his father likes to watch sports programs, particularly soccer games.*

192. **(C)** As stated in the last sentence, "我只對動畫片感興趣" ("我只对动画片感兴趣"), *I'm only interested in the animations* (cartoons).

193. **(D)** The narrator says, "我姐姐是一個中學的英語老師" ("我姐姐是一个中学的英语老师"), my sister is an English teacher at a secondary school.

194. **(D)** The main idea of the passage can be found in the first sentence, "與美國家長相比，在美國的中國家庭對孩子的期望比較高" ("与美国家长相比，在美国的中国家庭对孩子的期望比较高"). This indicates that Chinese families in the United States have higher expectations for their children's education than American families, particularly when it comes to choosing a college or major. Why not:

(A) The passage presents Chinese parents' expectations for their children's college education in the United States, but there is no mention of parenting techniques.

(B) Although there is a brief mention of American families at the end of the passage, the passage mainly focuses on Chinese families in the United States. There is no compare-and-contrast between the two.

(C) There is no mention of American families in China.

195. **(D)** As stated in the passage, "不希望他們學文科" ("不希望他们学文科").

196. **(B)** As stated in the passage, "很多中國家長不僅要求自己的孩子上大學，而且希望他們考上名牌大學" ("很多中国家长不仅要求自己的孩子上大学，而且希望他们考上名牌大学"). Why not:

(A) The narrator never says "all parents."

(C) The narrator explains that "上名牌大學對以後找工作有好處" ("上名牌大学对以后找工作有好处"), but "好處" ("好处") does not necessarily translate to *earn more money*.

(D) From the phrase "另外" ("另外"), this is understood as an added benefit, but it does not serve as the main reason for attending a famous college.

197. **(A)** The last passage, "中國家長也許應該學習美國家長，把選擇的權利還給孩子，給孩子更多的自由" ("中国家长也许应该学习美国家长，把选择的权利还给孩子，给孩子更多的自由"), is a suggestion that children should be given more freedom to make their own choices.

198. **(C)** The narrator and some of her friends and classmates are going to a movie, and she is asking Xiao Li if she wants to come along.

199. **(B)** This is stated by the speaker: "我表姊和我都去" ("我表姐和我都去"). Why not:

(A) The use of "都" indicates that, in addition to "咱們同學準備一起去看場電影" ("咱们同学准备一起去看场电影"), the speaker, Zhang Hua, and her cousin are also going, so they are not the only two.

(C) This is a phone message from Zhang Hua to Xiao Li asking if Xiao Li would like to join them to see the movie.

200. **(D)** As stated by Zhang Hua, "電影是下午四點半的" ("电影是下午四点半的"), *4:30 P.M. is when the movie will start*. Why not:

(A) 3:00 PM is not explicitly mentioned, although it is before 3:30 PM that Xiao Li should call with a response.
(B) "請在三點半以前給我打個電話" ("请在三点半以前给我打个电话") indicates that before 3:30 PM is when Xiao Li should call with a response.
(C) 4:00 PM is when they will be meeting at the coffee shop.

201. **(D)** The speaker says, "在電影院旁邊的那家咖啡館見面" ("在电影院旁边的那家咖啡馆见面"), *they are going to meet at a coffee shop next to the movie theater.*

202. **(D)** As stated in the passage, "兩個或兩個字以上的姓叫複姓" ("两个或两个字以上的姓叫复姓").

203. **(B)** As described in the passage, "現在常見的姓有兩百個" ("现在常见的姓有两百个").

204. **(C)** Although "東方" ("东方"), *Dōngfāng* is a common family name, it is not mentioned in the passage.

205. **(B)** The passage is a general discussion of surnames. It does not talk about the *meaning* or the *history* of the names.

206. **(A)** This passage is a general discussion about visiting patients in the hospital, including a brief mention of gifts for patients and the visitation time.

207. **(B)** As stated in the passage, "跟病人說話要注意，多談愉快的話題" ("跟病人说话要注意，多谈愉快的话题"). Why not:

(A) It is mentioned in the passage that "以前. . .探訪病人時..帶一些吃的東西，現在..喜歡給病人送鮮花" ("以前. . .探访病人时. . .带一些吃的东西，现在. . .喜欢给病人送鲜花").
(C) In general, "上午. . .不能探訪，所以探訪病人都在下午" ("上午. . .不能探访，所以探访病人都在下午").
(D) As indicated, "周末的時候，探訪病人的時間可以長一些" ("周末的时候，探访病人的时间可以长一些"), *the visiting hours may be longer on the weekends,* but this does not mean that people can visit *any time* they wish.

208. **(C)** As stated in the passage, "跟病人說話要注意" ("跟病人说话要注意"), *be mindful while talking to the patient* by "多談愉快的話題，不說刺激病人的話" ("多谈愉快的话题，不说刺激病人的话"), *talking about something pleasant around the patient, and nothing offensive or upsetting.*

209. **(D)** As stated in the passage, "周末的時候，探訪病人的時候可以長一些" ("周末的时候, 探访病人的时候可以长一些"). Why not:

(A), (C) The "三" and "四" are mentioned in this statement: "每星期有三、四個下午可以探訪" ("每星期有三、四个下午可以探访"), *one may visit the patient three or four afternoons per week.*

(B) Mornings are typically reserved for treatment.

210. **(B)** The passage is a general discussion of the host's role, the visitor's role, and the interaction between the two. The last sentence, "如果是關係比較近的人，那麼，主人和客人之間就不必太客氣了" ("如果是关系比较近的人，那么，主人和客人之间就不必太客气了"), suggests that the *formality* of the host-guest interaction can be omitted when the parties are close friends.

211. **(B)** As stated in the passage, "大多用打電話或者口頭邀請的方式" ("大多用打电话或者口头邀请的方式"). Why not:

(A) The phone call option is included in the correct answer, (B).

(C), (D) A *formal* invitation is only issued for an *important* or *formal* event "如果是比較重要的活動，就會發請貼邀請客人" ("如果是比较重要的活动，就会发请贴邀请客人").

212. **(A)** As stated in the passage, "到中國人家裏做客，最好在約定的時間裏到達" ("到中国人家里做客，最好在约定的时间里到达"), and also "提前或者遲到都是不禮貌的" ("提前或者迟到都是不礼貌的").

213. **(B)** As stated in the passage, "這些都是中國人的禮貌" ("这些都是中国人的礼貌").

214. **(B)** The main topic is stated in the first sentence, "中國大學招生...美國大學招生..." ("中国大学招生...美国大学招生...").

215. **(A)** As stated in the beginning, "主要看4-9門學科的高考成績" ("主要看4-9门学科的高考成绩").

216. **(C)** When talking about *interviews*, the speaker highly recommended "值得推薦" ("值得推荐"), *that Chinese high schools follow suit.*

217. **(B)** This is indicated from the greeting of the passasge, "各位聽眾" ("各位听众").

218. **(C)** This was expressed by the statement "幾代人一起生活是很常見的事情" ("几代人一起生活是很常见的事情"), as "幾代人" ("几代人") typically means more than two generations.

219. **(C)** The statement "無論是城市還是農村，幾代人共同生活的大家庭逐漸變成了中小家庭" ("无论是城市还是农村，几代人共同生活的大家庭逐渐变成了中小家庭") means "No matter in the city or rural areas, big families, being composed of several generations, are gradually replaced with medium- and small-sized families."

220. **(C)** The statement indicates the mutual desire to live separately: "多數年輕人希望結婚以後能和老人分開生活，這也是一部分老年人的願望" ("多数年轻人希望结婚以后能和老人分开生活，这也是一部分老年人的愿望").

VOCABULARY LIST

Section III—Dialogues

Question 121

貴姓	(贵姓)	guì xìng	May I ask your name?
逛商店	(逛商店)	guàng shāngdiàn	go shopping

Question 122

舞廳	(舞厅)	wǔtīng	ballroom
售貨員	(售货员)	shòuhuòyuán	salesperson

Questions 123 to 124

南京	（南京）	Nánjīng	name of a city
天津	（天津）	Tiānjīn	name of a city

Questions 125 to 126

武術	(武术)	wǔshù	martial arts such as shadowboxing, swordplay, etc.
書法	(书法)	shūfǎ	calligraphy
京劇	(京剧)	Jīngjù	Beijing opera
民歌	(民歌)	míngē	folk song

Questions 127 to 128

愛好	(爱好)	àihào	hobby
輔導	(辅导)	fǔdǎo	tutor

Questions 129 to 130

運動員	(运动员)	yùndòngyuán	athlete
教練	(教练)	jiàoliàn	coach
記者	(记者)	jìzhě	journalist

Questions 131 to 132

名牌	(名牌)	míngpái	name brand
質量	(质量)	zhìliàng	quality
標準	(标准)	biāozhǔn	standard

Questions 133 to 134

耽誤	(耽误)	dānwu	delay
聊		liáo	chat

Questions 135 to 136

感冒		gǎnmào	cold; flu
厲害	(厉害)	lìhai	serious

Questions 137 to 138

邀請	(邀请)	yāoqǐng	invite; invitation
陪		péi	to go with someone
禮貌	(礼貌)	lǐmào	polite
怪不得		guài bu de	no wonder

Questions 139 to 142

釣魚	(钓鱼)	diàoyú	go fishing
魚竿兒	(鱼竿儿)	yúgānr	fishing rod
協會	(协会)	xiéhuì	club; association
會長	(会长)	huìzhǎng	president
技術	(技术)	jìshù	technique; skill

Questions 143 to 146

公寓		gōngyù	apartment
大喊大叫		dàhǎn dàjiào	yell and scream
吵		chǎo	disturb; make a noise

Questions 147 to 150

結束	(结束)	jiéshù	end
安排	(安排)	ānpái	arrange
旅行社	(旅行社)	lǚxíngshè	travel agency
網	(网)	wǎng	Internet
芝加哥	(芝加哥)	Zhījiāgē	Chicago
臺灣	(台湾)	Táiwān	Taiwan

Questions 151 to 154

推薦	(推荐)	tuījiàn	recommend
麻婆豆腐		mápó dòufu	name of a dish
糖醋排骨	(糖醋排骨)	tángcù páigǔ	name of a dish
海味		hǎiwèi	seafood
紅燒魚	(红烧鱼)	hóngshāoyú	name of a dish
油燜大蝦	(油焖大虾)	yóumèn dàxiā	name of a dish
酒		jiǔ	wine
果汁		guǒzhī	juice

Questions 155 to 159

茶館	(茶馆)	cháguǎn	teahouse
尤其		yóuqí	especially

Questions 160 to 163

結婚	(结婚)	jiéhūn	get married
搬出來	(搬出来)	bān chūlai	move out

Questions 164 to 168

出差	(出差)	chūchāi	business trip
颶風	(刮风)	guāfēng	blow (of the wind)

Questions 169 to 172

環保	(环保)	huánbǎo	environmental protection
俱樂部	(俱乐部)	jùlèbù	club
活動	(活动)	huódòng	activity
撿	(捡)	jiǎn	pick up
垃圾		lājī	trash
抗議	(抗议)	kàngyì	protest
排出	(排出)	páichū	discharge
廢水	(废水)	fèishuǐ	waste water
廢氣	(废气)	fèiqì	waste gas
毒	(毒)	dú	toxin, poison
解決	(解决)	jiějué	solve
政府		zhèngfǔ	government

Section IV—Long Narration

Questions 173 to 174

老闆	(老板)	lǎobǎn	boss
小費	(小费)	xiǎofèi	tips
辭職	(辞职)	cízhí	quit
實驗室	(实验室)	shíyànshì	laboratory

Questions 175 to 176

播送	(播送)	bōsòng	broadcast
偏	(偏)	piān	tilt
攝氏度	(摄氏度)	shèshìdù	centigrade
轉	(转)	zhuǎn	turn

Questions 177 to 178

畫家	(画家)	huàjiā	painter; artist
繪畫	(绘画)	huìhuà	drawing; painting
蟲	(虫)	chóng	insect
觀察	(观察)	guānchá	observe
養	(养)	yǎng	raise
逼真	(逼真)	bīzhēn	realistic; clearly
齊白石	(齐白石)	Qí Báishí	name of a person

Questions 179 to 180

隨便	(随便)	suíbiǎn	accord with wishes
彼得		Bǐdé	Peter

Questions 181 to 182

講究	(讲究)	jiǎngjiu	pay attention to; strive for
筷子		kuàizi	chopsticks
盛		chéng	get (food)
碟子		tiézi	plate
夾	(夹)	jiā	use chopsticks to pick up food
碰撞		pèngzhuàng	touch
跨越		kuàyuè	across

Questions 183 to 185

預防	(预防)	yùfáng	prevent; prevention
保暖		bǎonuǎn	dress warmly
避免	(避免)	bìmiǎn	avoid
接觸	(接触)	jiēchù	contact
指導	(指导)	zhǐdǎo	guide; advise
充足		chōngzú	enough
保證	(保证)	bǎozhèng	guarantee; ensure

Questions 186 to 189

根據	(根据)	gēnjù	according to
口味		kǒuwèi	individual taste
偏愛	(偏爱)	piān'ài	prefer
酥油茶		sūyóuchá	a kind of tea
茶具		chájù	tea set
陶器		táoqì	porcelain; chinaware
瓷器		cíqì	pottery; earthenware
沏		qī	infuse; pour hot water over
滿月	(满月)	mǎnyuè	a baby's completion of its first month of life
祝賀	(祝贺)	zhùhè	congratulation; congratulate
藏族		Zàngzú	a nationality of China

Questions 190 to 193

退休	(退休)	tuìxiū	retire; retirement
電視劇	(电视剧)	diànshìjù	television play
動畫片	(动画片)	dònghuàpiàn	cartoon

Questions 194 to 197

期望		qīwàng	expect
重視	(重视)	zhòngshì	take something seriously
嚴	(严)	yán	strict; rigid
優秀	(优秀)	yōuxiù	outstanding; excellent
面子		miànzi	self-respect; face
學習	(学习)	xuéxí	learn; study
權利	(权利)	quánlì	right

Questions 198 to 201

直接	(直接)	zhíjiē	directly
小麗	(小丽)	Xiǎo Lì	name of a person
張華	(张华)	Zhāng Huá	name of a person

Questions 202 to 205

準確	(准确)	zhǔnquè	exact
統計	(统计)	tǒngjì	count; statistics
文獻	(文献)	wénxiàn	document; literature
《百家姓》		Bǎijiāxìng	name of a book

Questions 206 to 209

探訪	(探访)	tànfǎng	visit
刺激		cìjī	provoke
規定	(规定)	guīdìng	regulate
治療	(治疗)	zhìliáo	treat

Questions 210 to 213

口頭	(口头)	kǒutóu	oral
請貼	(请帖)	qǐngtiě	invitation
約定	(约定)	yuēdìng	appoint
豐盛	(丰盛)	fēngshèng	sumptuous
禮貌	(礼貌)	lǐmào	polite
謙虛	(谦虚)	qiānxū	modest
告辭	(告辞)	gàocí	take leave; say goodbye
歉意		qiànyì	apology; regret
打擾	(打扰)	dǎrǎo	disturb

Questions 214 to 216

招生		zhāoshēng	open enrollment
學科	(学科)	xuékē	subject
高考		gāokǎo	college exam
命運	(命运)	mìngyùn	fate
期間	(期间)	qījiān	period
面試	(面试)	miànshì	interview
值得	(值得)	zhídé	be worth
推薦	(推荐)	tuījiàn	recommend
社區	(社区)	shèqū	community
記錄	(记录)	jìlù	record
遺憾	(遗憾)	yíhàn	regretful

Questions 217 to 220

聽眾	(听众)	tīngzhòng	audience; listeners
熱門話題	(热门话题)	rèmén huàtí	hot topic
觀念	(观念)	guānniàn	idea; concept
影響	(影响)	yǐngxiǎng	influence; affect
常見	(常见)	chángjiàn	common
結構	(结构)	jiégòu	structure
逐漸	(逐渐)	zhújiàn	gradually
代替		dàitì	replace
屋檐		wūyán	roof
寥寥無幾	(寥寥无几)	liáoliáo-wújǐ	very few; scanty
分開	(分开)	fēnkāi	separate
重視	(重视)	zhòngshì	emphasize
尊敬	(尊敬)	zūnjìng	respect
照顧	(照顾)	zhàogù	take care of; look after
力所能及		lìsuǒ-néngjí	in one's power
家務	(家务)	jiāwù	household duties
禮品	(礼品)	lǐpǐn	present; gift

Scripts*

The passages in this section are clearly labeled as either traditional or simplified.

> Track 10
>
> Narrator: Chapter 2 Listening Comprehension Practice, Section 1 Conversations
> You will hear several short conversations. Each conversation will be played once along with four choices of response (A), (B), (C), and (D). You will have 5 seconds to choose a response that completes the conversation in a logical and culturally appropriate way. Please remember to mark your answers on the answer sheet.

1.

[Traditional-character version]

(Woman)	你是從哪個城市來的？
(Man)	我是從舊金山來的。你呢？
(Woman)	(A) 什麼？你沒去過舊金山？
	(B) 我哪兒都不想去。
	(C) 我可不想去那兒。
	(D) 我也是從那兒來的。

[Simplified-character version]

(Woman)	你是从哪个城市来的？
(Man)	我是从旧金山来的。你呢？
(Woman)	(A) 什么？你没去过旧金山？
	(B) 我哪儿都不想去。
	(C) 我可不想去那儿。
	(D) 我也是从那儿来的。

2.

[Traditional-character version]

(Woman)	請問書店在哪兒？
(Man)	(A) 書店裏有很多中文書。
	(B) 書店就在那邊。
	(C) 書店十點開門。
	(D) 書店裏的書都很貴。

[Simplified-character version]

(Woman)	请问书店在哪儿？
(Man)	(A) 书店里有很多中文书。
	(B) 书店就在那边。
	(C) 书店十点开门。
	(D) 书店里的书都很贵。

---

* *Tracks 1–9 are part of the review material and are printed within the appropriate sections.*

3.

[Traditional-character version]

(Woman) 宿舍外面有人叫我的名字，但是我聽不出來是誰。

(Man) (A) 你聽不見嗎？

(B) 叫你的人在哪兒？

(C) 我怎麼沒聽見有人叫你。

(D) 誰在叫你？

[Simplified-character version]

(Woman) 宿舍外面有人叫我的名字，但是我听不出来是谁。

(Man) (A) 你听不见吗？

(B) 叫你的人在哪儿？

(C) 我怎么没听见有人叫你。

(D) 谁在叫你？

4.

[Traditional-character version]

(Man) 我一看起電視來就什麼都忘了。

(Woman) (A) 你忘了看什麼？

(B) 你為什麼忘了看電視？

(C) 你看電視太專心了。

(D) 你能記住什麼？

[Simplified-character version]

(Man) 我一看起电视来就什么都忘了。

(Woman) (A) 你忘了看什么？

(B) 你为什么忘了看电视？

(C) 你看电视太专心了。

(D) 你能记住什么？

5.

[Traditional-character version]

(Woman) 我下午可以去你家找你嗎？

(Man) (A) 我不知道你家住哪兒。

(B) 我去你家找你吧。

(C) 我昨天去你家了。

(D) 我們在哪兒見面？

[Simplified-character version]

(Woman) 我下午可以去你家找你吗？

(Man) (A) 我不知道你家住哪儿。

(B) 我去你家找你吧。

(C) 我昨天去你家了。

(D) 我们在哪儿见面？

6.

[Traditional-character version]

(Woman)　　多跟中國人交朋友對你學中文有好處。

(Man)　　　(A) 我有很多中國朋友。

　　　　　　(B) 你覺得我的中國朋友怎麼樣？

　　　　　　(C) 我是在中國城認識我的中國朋友的。

　　　　　　(D) 中國人都很友好。

[Simplified-character version]

(Woman)　　多跟中国人交朋友对你学中文有好处。

(Man)　　　(A) 我有很多中国朋友。

　　　　　　(B) 你觉得我的中国朋友怎么样？

　　　　　　(C) 我是在中国城认识我的中国朋友的。

　　　　　　(D) 中国人都很友好。

7.

[Traditional-character version]

(Man)　　　我得找個地方買本中文字典，明天上課就要用了。

(Woman)　　(A) 那家書店大不大？

　　　　　　(B) 從這兒一直走，到了第一個路口，向右轉，就有一家書店。

　　　　　　(C) 書店離這兒不遠。

　　　　　　(D) 對不起，怎麼去書店？

[Simplified-character version]

(Man)　　　我得找个地方买本中文字典，明天上课就要用了。

(Woman)　　(A) 那家书店大不大？

　　　　　　(B) 从这儿一直走，到了第一个路口，向右转，就有一家书店。

　　　　　　(C) 书店离这儿不远。

　　　　　　(D) 对不起，怎么去书店？

8.

[Traditional-character version]

(Woman)　　你怎麼這麼晚才起床？

(Man)　　　(A) 我喜歡早睡、早起。

　　　　　　(B) 我昨天晚上8點就睡了。

　　　　　　(C) 我每天睡8小時。

　　　　　　(D) 我昨天睡得太晚了。

[Simplified-character version]

(Woman)　　你怎么这么晚才起床？

(Man)　　　(A) 我喜欢早睡、早起。

　　　　　　(B) 我昨天晚上8点就睡了。

　　　　　　(C) 我每天睡8小时。

　　　　　　(D) 我昨天睡得太晚了。

9.

[Traditional-character version]

(Woman)　　你的中文說得那麼好，你學中文學了很長時間吧？

(Man)　　　(A) 我會說中文。

　　　　　　(B) 我爸爸媽媽都會說中文。

　　　　　　(C) 學中文對我以後找工作有好處。

　　　　　　(D) 我4歲就開始學中文了。

[Simplified-character version]

(Woman)　　你的中文说得那么好，你学中文学了很长时间吧？

(Man)　　　(A) 我会说中文。

　　　　　　(B) 我爸爸妈妈都会说中文。

　　　　　　(C) 学中文对我以后找工作有好处。

　　　　　　(D) 我4岁就开始学中文了。

10.

[Traditional-character version]

(Woman)　　我聽說紐約的冬天溫度很低。

(Man)　　　(A) 紐約的冬天冷極了。

　　　　　　(B) 我在紐約的時候,冬天特別喜歡去滑雪。

　　　　　　(C) 紐約的冬天很漂亮。

　　　　　　(D) 紐約的冬天很長。

[Simplified-character version]

(Woman)　　我听说纽约的冬天温度很低。

(Man)　　　(A) 纽约的冬天冷极了。

　　　　　　(B) 我在纽约的时候,冬天特别喜欢去滑雪。

　　　　　　(C) 纽约的冬天很漂亮。

　　　　　　(D) 纽约的冬天很长。

11.

Track 11

[Traditional-character version]

(Woman)　　你怎麼一個人回來了？你的女朋友呢？

(Man)　　　(A) 我跟我女朋友的這次旅行很愉快。

　　　　　　(B) 我自己回來的。

　　　　　　(C) 我女朋友旅行以後去看她的好朋友了。

　　　　　　(D) 我女朋友旅行的時候買了很多衣服。

[Simplified-character version]

(Woman)　　你怎么一个人回来了？你的女朋友呢？

(Man)　　　(A) 我跟我女朋友的这次旅行很愉快。

　　　　　　(B) 我自己回来的。

　　　　　　(C) 我女朋友旅行以后去看她的好朋友了。

　　　　　　(D) 我女朋友旅行的时候买了很多衣服。

12.

[Traditional-character version]

(Man) 我要出差，今天晚上你能不能開車送我去機場？

(Woman) (A) 我開車比你好多了。

(B) 對不起，我得在家等朋友。

(C) 我有一輛很好的車。

(D) 你爲什麼要去機場？

[Simplified-character version]

(Man) 我要出差，今天晚上你能不能开车送我去机场？

(Woman) (A) 我开车比你好多了。

(B) 对不起，我得在家等朋友。

(C) 我有一辆很好的车。

(D) 你为什么要去机场？

13.

[Traditional-character version]

(Woman) 你媽媽會做中國飯嗎？

(Man) (A) 我喜歡吃中國飯。

(B) 中國飯比日本飯好吃。

(C) 她會做，可是做得不太好。

(D) 我家裏的人都喜歡吃中國飯。

[Simplified-character version]

(Woman) 你妈妈会做中国饭吗？

(Man) (A) 我喜欢吃中国饭。

(B) 中国饭比日本饭好吃。

(C) 她会做，可是做得不太好。

(D) 我家里的人都喜欢吃中国饭。

14.

[Traditional-character version]

(Woman) 昨天的足球比賽真是精彩，就是門票太貴了。你去了嗎?

(Man) (A) 我踢足球踢得不太好。

(B) 我特別喜歡足球。

(C) 有些運動員踢得很不好。

(D) 沒有。兒子病了，我得帶他去醫院。

[Simplified-character version]

(Woman) 昨天的足球比赛真是精彩，就是门票太贵了。你去了吗?

(Man) (A) 我踢足球踢得不太好。

(B) 我特别喜欢足球。

(C) 有些运动员踢得很不好。

(D) 没有。儿子病了，我得带他去医院。

15.
[Traditional-character version]
(Woman)　　　那位戴眼鏡的老師教什麼？
(Man)　　　　(A) 那位老師叫張學民。
　　　　　　(B) 那位老師教二年級。
　　　　　　(C) 那位老師教物理。
　　　　　　(D) 我們都叫他 "張老師"。

[Simplified-character version]
(Woman)　　　那位戴眼镜的老师教什么？
(Man)　　　　(A) 那位老师叫张学民。
　　　　　　(B) 那位老师教二年级。
　　　　　　(C) 那位老师教物理。
　　　　　　(D) 我们都叫他"张老师"。

16.
[Traditional-character version]
(Man)　　　　這臺電腦是你哥哥給你買的還是你姐姐給你買的？
(Woman)　　　(A) 我真需要一臺電腦。
　　　　　　(B) 我哥哥姐姐都喜歡這臺電腦。
　　　　　　(C) 我哥哥買了這臺電腦給我當生日禮物。
　　　　　　(D) 我姐姐說她真的想送給我一臺電腦。

[Simplified-character version]
(Man)　　　　这台电脑是你哥哥给你买的还是你姐姐给你买的？
(Woman)　　　(A) 我真需要一台电脑。
　　　　　　(B) 我哥哥姐姐都喜欢这台电脑。
　　　　　　(C) 我哥哥买了这台电脑给我当生日礼物。
　　　　　　(D) 我姐姐说她真的想送给我一台电脑。

17.
[Traditional-character version]
(Man)　　　　你剛才是找我嗎？
(Woman)　　　不找你找誰。
(Man)　　　　(A) 你想找誰？
　　　　　　(B) 你找我有什麼事嗎？
　　　　　　(C) 誰找你？
　　　　　　(D) 你什麼時候找我的？

[Simplified-character version]
(Man)　　　　你刚才是找我吗？
(Woman)　　　不找你找谁。
(Man)　　　　(A) 你想找谁？
　　　　　　(B) 你找我有什么事吗？
　　　　　　(C) 谁找你？
　　　　　　(D) 你什么时候找我的？

18.

[Traditional-character version]

(Woman)	別擔心，這個問題我們一定能解決。
(Man)	那可不見得。
(Woman)	(A) 你看不見這個問題？
	(B) 你怎麼看這個問題？
	(C) 我同意你的看法。
	(D) 你爲什麼沒有信心？

[Simplified-character version]

(Woman)	别担心，这个问题我们一定能解决。
(Man)	那可不见得。
(Woman)	(A) 你看不见这个问题？
	(B) 你怎么看这个问题？
	(C) 我同意你的看法。
	(D) 你为什么没有信心？

19.

[Traditional-character version]

(Woman)	咱們看一會兒電視吧。
(Man)	有什麼好看的。
(Woman)	(A) 你覺得哪個頻道的節目好看？
	(B) 哪個頻道的節目都不錯呀。
	(C) 你有什麼好節目嗎？
	(D) 你也喜歡看電視嗎？

[Simplified-character version]

(Woman)	咱们看一会儿电视吧。
(Man)	有什么好看的。
(Woman)	(A) 你觉得哪个频道的节目好看？
	(B) 哪个频道的节目都不错呀。
	(C) 你有什么好节目吗？
	(D) 你也喜欢看电视吗？

20.

[Traditional-character version]

(Woman)	老王最近身體怎麼樣？
(Man)	你不知道嗎？他已經不在了。
(Woman)	(A) 怎麼會呢？他的身體一直都很好。
	(B) 我也不知道他在不在。
	(C) 他去哪兒了？
	(D) 他剛才還在這裏。

[Simplified-character version]

(Woman) 老王最近身体怎么样？

(Man) 你不知道吗？他已经不在了。

(Woman) (A) 怎么会呢？他的身体一直都很好。

(B) 我也不知道他在不在。

(C) 他去哪儿了？

(D) 他刚才还在这里。

21.

(Track 12)

[Traditional-character version]

(Woman) 你們學校這學期選中文課的學生一定很多吧？

(Man) (A) 不太多。

(B) 中文太難學了。

(C) 在美國，學中文的人越來越多。

(D) 他們在學校學中文。

[Simplified-character version]

(Woman) 你们学校这学期选中文课的学生一定很多吧？

(Man) (A) 不太多。

(B) 中文太难学了。

(C) 在美国，学中文的人越来越多。

(D) 他们在学校学中文。

22.

[Traditional-character version]

(Woman) 大家都說王老師是我們學校最好的老師之一。

(Man) (A) 她在這兒工作十年了。

(B) 她對學生很負責。

(C) 她上個學期給我們上英語課。

(D) 她每天都有五個小時的課。

[Simplified-character version]

(Woman) 大家都说王老师是我们学校最好的老师之一。

(Man) (A) 她在这儿工作十年了。

(B) 她对学生很负责。

(C) 她上个学期给我们上英语课。

(D) 她每天都有五个小时的课。

23.

[Traditional-character version]

(Woman) 你過生日的時候你朋友會來嗎？

(Man) (A) 我們是在火車上認識的。

(B) 他從來沒有來過我家。

(C) 他是我最好的朋友。

(D) 他一定來。

[Simplified-character version]

(Woman)　你过生日的时候你朋友会来吗？

(Man)　(A) 我们是在火车上认识的。

　　　(B) 他从来没有来过我家。

　　　(C) 他是我最好的朋友。

　　　(D) 他一定来。

24.

[Traditional-character version]

(Man)　我們開車去那家博物館嗎？

(Woman)　(A) 我們要去那家博物館。

　　　(B) 我以前去過那家博物館。

　　　(C) 我寧願坐公共汽車去。

　　　(D) 那家博物館很有名。

[Simplified-character version]

(Man)　我们开车去那家博物馆吗？

(Woman)　(A) 我们要去那家博物馆。

　　　(B) 我以前去过那家博物馆。

　　　(C) 我宁愿坐公共汽车去。

　　　(D) 那家博物馆很有名。

25.

[Traditional-character version]

(Woman)　我明天要出門，不知道天氣怎麼樣，忘了看天氣預報了。

(Man)　(A) 我每天都聽天氣預報。

　　　(B) 明天的天氣很好。

　　　(C) 這兒的天氣一般都不錯。

　　　(D) 有些人不相信天氣預報。

[Simplified-character version]

(Woman)　我明天要出门，不知道天气怎么样，忘了看天气预报了。

(Man)　(A) 我每天都听天气预报。

　　　(B) 明天的天气很好。

　　　(C) 这儿的天气一般都不错。

　　　(D) 有些人不相信天气预报。

26.

[Traditional-character version]

(Woman)　你們都喜歡來大城市，可是我看不出來大城市有什麼好的。

(Man)　(A) 我不知道大城市好什麼。

　　　(B) 我覺得在大城市的機會比較多。

　　　(C) 我們都喜歡來大城市。

　　　(D) 怎麼才能來大城市？

[Simplified-character version]

(Woman)   你们都喜欢来大城市，可是我看不出来大城市有什么好的。

(Man)   (A) 我不知道大城市好什么。

(B) 我觉得在大城市的机会比较多。

(C) 我们都喜欢来大城市。

(D) 怎么才能来大城市？

27.

[Traditional-character version]

(Woman)   你整天都在看電視、上網，要考試了吧，怎麼也不見你學習？哪
一天考？

(Man)   (A) 我們快放假了。

(B) 一說考試我就緊張。

(C) 我考試不會遲到。

(D) 我不太清楚。

[Simplified-character version]

(Woman)   你整天都在看电视、上网，要考试了吧，怎么也不见你学习？哪
一天考？

(Man)   (A) 我们快放假了。

(B) 一说考试我就紧张。

(C) 我考试不会迟到。

(D) 我不太清楚。

28.

[Traditional-character version]

(Woman)   我真不想再到那家飯館吃飯了。

(Man)   (A) 那家飯館的菜好吃極了。

(B) 我覺得那家飯館還不錯。

(C) 那家飯館遠不遠？

(D) 那家飯館怎麼樣？

[Simplified-character version]

(Woman)   我真不想再到那家饭馆吃饭了。

(Man)   (A) 那家饭馆的菜好吃极了。

(B) 我觉得那家饭馆还不错。

(C) 那家饭馆远不远？

(D) 那家饭馆怎么样？

29.

[Traditional-character version]

(Man)   要想找到一份好工作比什麼都難。

(Woman)   那就要看你學什麼專業了。

(Man)   (A) 好專業對找工作有好處。

(B) 學什麼都沒有用，現在哪個公司都不缺人。

(C) 我有專業。

(D) 我不喜歡我的專業。

[Simplified-character version]
(Man)   要想找到一份好工作比什么都难。
(Woman)   那就要看你学什么专业了。
(Man)   (A) 好专业对找工作有好处。
           (B) 学什么都没有用，现在哪个公司都不缺人。
           (C) 我有专业。
           (D) 我不喜欢我的专业。

30.
[Traditional-character version]
(Woman)   這家購物中心的東西一個比一個貴。
(Man)   (A) 你說得對，那個東西沒有這個東西貴。
           (B) 他們的東西是很貴。
           (C) 我也覺得這個東西比那個東西貴。
           (D) 你覺得這個貴，那個不太貴嗎？

[Simplified-character version]
(Woman)   这家购物中心的东西一个比一个贵。
(Man)   (A) 你说得对，那个东西没有这个东西贵。
           (B) 他们的东西是很贵。
           (C) 我也觉得这个东西比那个东西贵。
           (D) 你觉得这个贵，那个不太贵吗？

31.

Track 13

[Traditional-character version]
(Woman)   你要是再不來，我們就不等你了。
(Man)   (A) 我下次不來了，你們不用等我了。
           (B) 你們爲什麼不想等我？
           (C) 家裏有點事兒，讓你們久等了。
           (D) 你們不等我，我就走了。

[Simplified-character version]
(Woman)   你要是再不来，我们就不等你了。
(Man)   (A) 我下次不来了，你们不用等我了。
           (B) 你们为什么不想等我？
           (C) 家里有点事儿，让你们久等了。
           (D) 你们不等我，我就走了。

32.
[Traditional-character version]
(Woman)   我找了好半天，也不知道你說的那家書店到底在哪兒。
(Man)   (A) 你不知道那家書店嗎？
           (B) 那家書店好找嗎？
           (C) 你找到那家書店了嗎？
           (D) 就在電影院旁邊。

[Simplified-character version]
(Woman)　　我找了好半天，也不知道你说的那家书店到底在哪儿。
(Man)　　　(A) 你不知道那家书店吗？
　　　　　　(B) 那家书店好找吗？
　　　　　　(C) 你找到那家书店了吗？
　　　　　　(D) 就在电影院旁边。

33.
[Traditional-character version]
(Man)　　　我女朋友聽到這個消息的時候，簡直不相信自己的耳朵了。
(Woman)　(A) 她爲什麼不相信這個消息呢？
　　　　　　(B) 她相信這個消息嗎？
　　　　　　(C) 她聽不見嗎？
　　　　　　(D) 因爲她的耳朵不好，所以她聽不清楚。

[Simplified-character version]
(Man)　　　我女朋友听到这个消息的时候，简直不相信自己的耳朵了。
(Woman)　(A) 她为什么不相信这个消息呢？
　　　　　　(B) 她相信这个消息吗？
　　　　　　(C) 她听不见吗？
　　　　　　(D) 因为她的耳朵不好，所以她听不清楚。

34.
[Traditional-character version]
(Woman)　我到中國去，一是爲了學中文，二是可以游覽一下中國的名勝古
　　　　　　迹。
(Man)　　　(A) 你去中國學什麼？
　　　　　　(B) 你去中國做什麼？
　　　　　　(C) 你去中國除了旅游以外還打算做什麼？
　　　　　　(D) 你打算什麼時候去？

[Simplified-character version]
(Woman)　我到中国去，一是为了学中文，二是可以游览一下中国的名胜古
　　　　　　迹。
(Man)　　　(A) 你去中国学什么？
　　　　　　(B) 你去中国做什么？
　　　　　　(C) 你去中国除了旅游以外还打算做什么？
　　　　　　(D) 你打算什么时候去？

35.
[Traditional-character version]
(Woman)　安娜什麼都好，就是每次上課總是遲到個三、四分鐘。
(Man)　　　(A) 安娜遲到多長時間？
　　　　　　(B) 安娜爲什麼總是遲到？
　　　　　　(C) 安娜真的沒有缺點嗎？
　　　　　　(D) 安娜什麼時候遲到？

[Simplified-character version]

(Woman)　安娜什么都好，就是每次上课总是迟到个三、四分钟。

(Man)　(A) 安娜迟到多长时间？

　　　　(B) 安娜为什么总是迟到？

　　　　(C) 安娜真的没有缺点吗？

　　　　(D) 安娜什么时候迟到？

36.

[Traditional-character version]

(Man)　我父母希望我大學畢業以後上研究所，可是我打算先找一個工作，賺點錢，有了一點兒工作經驗，然後再去念研究所。

(Woman)　(A) 你父母希望你找什麼樣的工作？

　　　　(B) 要是你父母不同意，你怎麼辦？

　　　　(C) 你是什麼時候大學畢業的？

　　　　(D) 你有哪些工作經驗？

[Simplified-character version]

(Man)　我父母希望我大学毕业以后上研究所，可是我打算先找一个工作，赚点钱，有了一点儿工作经验，然后再去念研究所。

(Woman)　(A) 你父母希望你找什么样的工作？

　　　　(B) 要是你父母不同意，你怎么办？

　　　　(C) 你是什么时候大学毕业的？

　　　　(D) 你有哪些工作经验？

37.

[Traditional-character version]

(Woman)　我弟弟從來沒讓父母失望過。

(Man)　(A) 看來你父母對你弟弟很滿意。

　　　　(B) 你弟弟爲什麼對父母這麼失望？

　　　　(C) 你父母對你弟弟不滿意嗎？

　　　　(D) 你父母對你弟弟哪方面不滿意？

[Simplified-character version]

(Woman)　我弟弟从来没让父母失望过。

(Man)　(A) 看来你父母对你弟弟很满意。

　　　　(B) 你弟弟为什么对父母这么失望？

　　　　(C) 你父母对你弟弟不满意吗？

　　　　(D) 你父母对你弟弟哪方面不满意？

38.

[Traditional-character version]

(Man)　我找的那套公寓，臥室挺大，還帶家具，就是廚房和客廳得跟別人一起用。

(Woman)　(A) 臥室怎麼樣？

　　　　(B) 廁所大不大？

　　　　(C) 沒有客廳嗎？

　　　　(D) 廚房也要跟別人一起用嗎？

[Simplified-character version]
(Man) 我找的那套公寓，卧室挺大，还带家具，就是厨房和客厅得跟别
人一起用。
(Woman) (A) 卧室怎么样？
(B) 厕所大不大？
(C) 没有客厅吗？
(D) 厨房也要跟别人一起用吗？

39.
[Traditional-character version]
(Woman) 這點小病也用去醫院嗎？
(Man) (A) 這種病應該去醫院。
(B) 你得了小病嗎？去醫院看看吧。
(C) 不管大病小病都應該去醫院看看。
(D) 這是小病，得去醫院看看。

[Simplified-character version]
(Woman) 这点小病也用去医院吗？
(Man) (A) 这种病应该去医院。
(B) 你得了小病吗？去医院看看吧。
(C) 不管大病小病都应该去医院看看。
(D) 这是小病，得去医院看看。

40.
[Traditional-character version]
(Woman) 都幾點了？你怎麼才來？大家都在等你一個人。
(Man) (A) 快十點了。
(B) 你來得比我早嗎？
(C) 你是什麼時候來的？
(D) 對不起，家裏有一點兒事情。

[Simplified-character version]
(Woman) 都几点了？你怎么才来？大家都在等你一个人。
(Man) (A) 快十点了。
(B) 你来得比我早吗？
(C) 你是什么时候来的？
(D) 对不起，家里有一点儿事情。

41.
Track 14
[Traditional-character version]
(Woman) 聽說周末的籃球比賽特別好，很多有名的球星都會來。我是肯定
要去看的，你呢？
(Man) (A) 我想去，可是我有課，去不了。
(B) 那場比賽誰贏了？
(C) 誰去看比賽？
(D) 你喜歡看籃球比賽嗎？

[Simplified-character version]

(Woman)　听说周末的篮球比赛特别好，很多有名的球星都会来。我是肯定
要去看的，你呢？

(Man)　(A) 我想去，可是我有课，去不了。

　　(B) 那场比赛谁赢了？

　　(C) 谁去看比赛？

　　(D) 你喜欢看篮球比赛吗？

42.

[Traditional-character version]

(Woman)　洛杉磯的夏天不但乾燥而且悶熱。

(Man)　(A) 是的，洛杉磯的夏天雖然不太熱，但很乾燥。

　　(B) 我也覺得洛杉磯的夏天又乾燥又悶熱。

　　(C) 是的，洛杉磯的夏天不乾燥也不悶熱。

　　(D) 你說得對。洛杉磯的夏天不太乾燥，但很悶熱。

[Simplified-character version]

(Woman)　洛杉矶的夏天不但干燥而且闷热。

(Man)　(A) 是的，洛杉矶的夏天虽然不太热，但很干燥。

　　(B) 我也觉得洛杉矶的夏天又干燥又闷热。

　　(C) 是的，洛杉矶的夏天不干燥也不闷热。

　　(D) 你说得对。洛杉矶的夏天不太干燥，但很闷热。

43.

[Traditional-character version]

(Woman)　張小姐托王先生給黃老師帶一封信。

(Man)　(A) 王先生寫信做什麼？

　　(B) 張小姐什麼時候寫的信？

　　(C) 黃老師什麼時候寫的信？

　　(D) 張小姐跟王先生一起寫的信嗎？

[Simplified-character version]

(Woman)　张小姐托王先生给黄老师带一封信。

(Man)　(A) 王先生写信做什么？

　　(B) 张小姐什么时候写的信？

　　(C) 黄老师什么时候写的信？

　　(D) 张小姐跟王先生一起写的信吗？

44.

[Traditional-character version]

(Woman)　我是七點半到的，等了四十分鐘小張才來。

(Man)　(A) 小張來了嗎？

　　(B) 小張爲什麼八點十分才來？

　　(C) 你和小張誰先來的？

　　(D) 你爲什麼遲到四十分鐘？

[Simplified-character version]

(Woman)   我是七点半到的，等了四十分钟小张才来。
(Man)   (A) 小张来了吗？
         (B) 小张为什么八点十分才来？
         (C) 你和小张谁先来的？
         (D) 你为什么迟到四十分钟？

45.

[Traditional-character version]

(Woman)   你怎麼現在才給我打電話？
(Man)   (A) 我怎麼打電話？
         (B) 對不起，我剛才在開車，打電話不方便。
         (C) 我一接到你的電話就給你打了。
         (D) 誰給你打電話了？

[Simplified-character version]

(Woman)   你怎么现在才给我打电话？
(Man)   (A) 我怎么打电话？
         (B) 对不起，我刚才在开车，打电话不方便。
         (C) 我一接到你的电话就给你打了。
         (D) 谁给你打电话了？

46.

[Traditional-character version]

(Man)   我今天太累了，不能陪你去購物中心買東西了。
(Woman)   你今天做什麼了，爲什麼這麼累？
(Man)   (A) 購物中心的東西太貴了。
         (B) 我上了三節課，又在圖書館工作了四個小時。
         (C) 我累的時候不想買東西。
         (D) 你能自己去買東西嗎？

[Simplified-character version]

(Man)   我今天太累了，不能陪你去购物中心买东西了。
(Woman)   你今天做什么了，为什么这么累？
(Man)   (A) 购物中心的东西太贵了。
         (B) 我上了三节课，又在图书馆工作了四个小时。
         (C) 我累的时候不想买东西。
         (D) 你能自己去买东西吗？

47.

[Traditional-character version]

(Woman)   我的朋友們這學期都很累，因爲他們選的課都太多了。你選得多
         嗎？
(Man)   我選了四門，其中一門是中文課。你呢？
(Woman)   (A) 我沒選電腦課。
         (B) 我只選了三門。
         (C) 中文課難不難？
         (D) 我也想選課。

[Simplified-character version]

(Woman)   我的朋友们这学期都很累，因为他们选的课都太多了。你选得多吗？

(Man)   我选了四门，其中一门是中文课。你呢？

(Woman)   (A) 我没选电脑课。

    (B) 我只选了三门。

    (C) 中文课难不难？

    (D) 我也想选课。

48.

[Traditional-character version]

(Woman)   你對中國城的這家飯館很熟悉啊！

(Man)   我來了多少趟了。

(Woman)   (A) 看來你是這裏的常客了。

    (B) 這家飯館在哪兒？

    (C) 你忘了你來了幾趟了？

    (D) 你經常來嗎？

[Simplified-character version]

(Woman)   你对中国城的这家饭馆很熟悉啊！

(Man)   我来了多少趟了。

(Woman)   (A) 看来你是这里的常客了。

    (B) 这家饭馆在哪儿？

    (C) 你忘了你来了几趟了？

    (D) 你经常来吗？

49.

[Traditional-character version]

(Man)   你的法文說得真好。

(Woman)   好什麼！我學法文只學了一年。

(Man)   (A) 原來你會說法文。

    (B) 學了一年就說得這麼好啊！

    (C) 剛學了一年，說不好沒關係。

    (D) 聽和說不錯，讀和寫不太好。

[Simplified-character version]

(Man)   你的法文说得真好。

(Woman)   好什么！我学法文只学了一年。

(Man)   (A) 原来你会说法文。

    (B) 学了一年就说得这么好啊！

    (C) 刚学了一年，说不好没关系。

    (D) 听和说不错，读和写不太好。

50.

[Traditional-character version]

(Man)　　　你看那位4號運動員踢得多好！

(Woman)　　只要他參加比賽，我們女孩子都愛看。

(Man)　　　(A) 他是那個籃球隊裏最好的運動員。

　　　　　　(B) 他們游泳隊的運動員，個個都不錯。

　　　　　　(C) 我也喜歡網球運動。

　　　　　　(D) 只要他參加，他們足球隊一定能贏。

[Simplified-character version]

(Man)　　　你看那位4号运动员踢得多好！

(Woman)　　只要他参加比赛，我们女孩子都爱看。

(Man)　　　(A) 他是那个篮球队里最好的运动员。

　　　　　　(B) 他们游泳队的运动员，个个都不错。

　　　　　　(C) 我也喜欢网球运动。

　　　　　　(D) 只要他参加，他们足球队一定能赢。

51.

Track 15

[Traditional-character version]

(Man)　　　你是開車來的嗎？

(Woman)　　我的車被弟弟開走了，我是坐公共汽車來的。你呢？

(Man)　　　(A) 我也不會開車。

　　　　　　(B) 我開車開得不太好。

　　　　　　(C) 我姐姐開車送我來的。

　　　　　　(D) 公共汽車上的人太多了。

[Simplified-character version]

(Man)　　　你是开车来的吗？

(Woman)　　我的车被弟弟开走了，我是坐公共汽车来的。你呢？

(Man)　　　(A) 我也不会开车。

　　　　　　(B) 我开车开得不太好。

　　　　　　(C) 我姐姐开车送我来的。

　　　　　　(D) 公共汽车上的人太多了。

52.

[Traditional-character version]

(Man)　　　你要是想買樣子好的，我看這雙就很適合你，你戴著一定好看。

(Woman)　　我買東西雖然在乎樣子，可是我也得看看質量怎麼樣。

(Man)　　　(A) 我們這兒的牛仔褲沒有質量不好的。

　　　　　　(B) 這種手套，如果質量有問題，能有那麼多人買嗎？

　　　　　　(C) 我們賣的衣服，質量都很好。

　　　　　　(D) 這你放心，我們賣的鞋質量都不錯。

[Simplified-character version]

(Man)   你要是想买样子好的，我看这双就很适合你，你戴着一定好看。

(Woman)   我买东西虽然在乎样子，可是我也得看看质量怎么样。

(Man)   (A) 我们这儿的牛仔裤没有质量不好的。

           (B) 这种手套，如果质量有问题，能有那么多人买吗？

           (C) 我们卖的衣服，质量都很好。

           (D) 这你放心，我们卖的鞋质量都不错。

53.

[Traditional-character version]

(Man)   周末的時候，我常常一個人待在家裏，做做中國飯、跑跑步，有時也跟朋友去看看電影什麽的。

(Woman)   我也喜歡跑步，不過太忙，好長時間沒跑了。

(Man)   (A) 你天天跑步嗎？

           (B) 你喜歡看什麽電影？

           (C) 你也喜歡做中國飯呀？

           (D) 你忙什麽呢？

[Simplified-character version]

(Man)   周末的时候，我常常一个人待在家里，做做中国饭、跑跑步，有时也跟朋友去看看电影什么的。

(Woman)   我也喜欢跑步，不过太忙，好长时间没跑了。

(Man)   (A) 你天天跑步吗？

           (B) 你喜欢看什么电影？

           (C) 你也喜欢做中国饭呀？

           (D) 你忙什么呢？

54.

[Traditional-character version]

(Man)   你怎麽又來晚了？

(Woman)   我家離這兒太遠了。

(Man)   (A) 你不能早一點兒出來嗎？

           (B) 你家離這兒遠不遠？

           (C) 你的家大不大？

           (D) 我家離這兒不太遠。

[Simplified-character version]

(Man)   你怎么又来晚了？

(Woman)   我家离这儿太远了。

(Man)   (A) 你不能早一点儿出来吗？

           (B) 你家离这儿远不远？

           (C) 你的家大不大？

           (D) 我家离这儿不太远。

55.
[Traditional-character version]
(Woman)   我同屋要過生日了，你說我送她什麼禮物？
(Man)   我覺得吃的、穿的都可以。
(Woman)   (A) 好，我就給她買本書吧。
      (B) 那我送她一台小電視。
      (C) 那我就送她一盒巧克力吧。
      (D) 行，我請她看一場電影。

[Simplified-character version]
(Woman)   我同屋要过生日了，你说我送她什么礼物？
(Man)   我觉得吃的、穿的都可以。
(Woman)   (A) 好，我就给她买本书吧。
      (B) 那我送她一台小电视。
      (C) 那我就送她一盒巧克力吧。
      (D) 行，我请她看一场电影。

56.
[Traditional-character version]
(Woman)   你這次來上海，覺得上海怎麼樣？
(Man)   我幾乎都認不出來上海了，跟上次看到的完全不同。
(Woman)   你上次是什麼時候來的？
(Man)   (A) 上海發展太快。
      (B) 大概五年以前。
      (C) 我在上海幾乎沒有認識的人了。
      (D) 我兩次來上海沒有什麼不同的感受。

[Simplified-character version]
(Woman)   你这次来上海，觉得上海怎么样？
(Man)   我几乎都认不出来上海了，跟上次看到的完全不同。
(Woman)   你上次是什么时候来的？
(Man)   (A) 上海发展太快。
      (B) 大概五年以前。
      (C) 我在上海几乎没有认识的人了。
      (D) 我两次来上海没有什么不同的感受。

57.
[Traditional-character version]
(Man)   你認為那部電影怎麼樣？
(Woman)   還可以吧。你覺得呢？
(Man)   (A) 我也覺得特別好。
      (B) 我和你看法一樣，好極了。
      (C) 跟你的看法差不多，一般吧。
      (D) 我也覺得不怎麼樣。

[Simplified-character version]

(Man) 你认为那部电影怎么样？

(Woman) 还可以吧。你觉得呢？

(Man) (A) 我也觉得特别好。

(B) 我和你看法一样，好极了。

(C) 跟你的看法差不多，一般吧。

(D) 我也觉得不怎么样。

58.

[Traditional-character version]

(Woman) 明天的會你們都能參加嗎？

(Man) 小王跟我沒問題，至於小張，我說不好。

(Woman) (A) 小王怎麼了？

(B) 小張怎麼了？

(C) 你跟小王有什麼問題？

(D) 太好了，大家都能來。

[Simplified-character version]

(Woman) 明天的会你们都能参加吗？

(Man) 小王跟我没问题，至于小张，我说不好。

(Woman) (A) 小王怎么了？

(B) 小张怎么了？

(C) 你跟小王有什么问题？

(D) 太好了，大家都能来。

59.

[Traditional-character version]

(Man) 你試的那件衣服怎麼樣？

(Woman) 大小、肥瘦都挺合適的，顏色也不錯，就是價錢不理想。

(Man) (A) 真想買的話，我可以便宜一點兒。

(B) 我這兒有別的顏色的。

(C) 你再試試這件小號的。

(D) 這件太肥了，買那件瘦的吧。

[Simplified-character version]

(Man) 你试的那件衣服怎么样？

(Woman) 大小、肥瘦都挺合适的，颜色也不错，就是价钱不理想。

(Man) (A) 真想买的话，可以便宜一点儿。

(B) 我这儿有别的颜色的。

(C) 你再试试这件小号的。

(D) 这件太肥了，买那件瘦的吧。

60.

[Traditional-character version]

(Man) 聽說電影院旁邊新開了一家餐館，晚上去吃一頓吧？
(Woman) 以後吧。
(Man) 怎麼了？
(Woman) (A) 那家餐館在哪兒？
(B) 那家餐館的飯好吃。
(C) 今天的功課太多了。
(D) 聽說那兒的東西很便宜。

[Simplified-character version]

(Man) 听说电影院旁边新开了一家餐馆，晚上去吃一顿吧？
(Woman) 以后吧。
(Man) 怎么了？
(Woman) (A) 那家餐馆在哪儿？
(B) 那家餐馆的饭好吃。
(C) 今天的功课太多了。
(D) 听说那儿的东西很便宜。

61.

Track 16

[Traditional-character version]

(Man) 你最喜歡什麼體育運動？
(Woman) 游泳、排球、籃球什麼的，我都喜歡，不過最拿手的還是網球。
你呢？
(Man) (A) 我最喜歡的也是籃球。
(B) 我也不喜歡游泳。
(C) 跟你一樣，我也不太喜歡籃球。
(D) 我最喜歡的是排球。

[Simplified-character version]

(Man) 你最喜欢什么体育运动？
(Woman) 游泳、排球、篮球什么的，我都喜欢，不过最拿手的还是网球。
你呢？
(Man) (A) 我最喜欢的也是篮球。
(B) 我也不喜欢游泳。
(C) 跟你一样，我也不太喜欢篮球。
(D) 我最喜欢的是排球。

62.

[Traditional-character version]

(Man) 你昨天穿的那雙鞋挺好看的，怎麼說不要就不要了？
(Woman) (A) 你覺得那雙鞋不好看嗎？
(B) 那雙鞋有點小。
(C) 那雙鞋在哪兒買的？
(D) 那雙鞋貴不貴？

[Simplified-character version]

(Man)   你昨天穿的那双鞋挺好看的, 怎么说不要就不要了?

(Woman)   (A) 你觉得那双鞋不好看吗?

                  (B) 那双鞋有点小。

                  (C) 那双鞋在哪儿买的?

                  (D) 那双鞋贵不贵?

63.

[Traditional-character version]

(Man)   你能在紐約開車呀?我聽說在紐約開車可不容易了。

(Woman)   在哪兒我都能開。

(Man)   (A) 這麼說,你開車的技術不錯。

                  (B) 在紐約我也不能開。

                  (C) 在紐約你不能,在這兒呢?

                  (D) 你能在哪兒開?

[Simplified-character version]

(Man)   你能在纽约开车呀?我听说在纽约开车可不容易了。

(Woman)   在哪儿我都能开。

(Man)   (A) 这么说,你开车的技术不错。

                  (B) 在纽约我也不能开。

                  (C) 在纽约你不能,在这儿呢?

                  (D) 你能在哪儿开?

64.

[Traditional-character version]

(Woman)   你這水果怎麼賣?

(Man)   蘋果一元一磅,香蕉一元三磅。你買點兒什麼?

(Woman)   (A) 香蕉看起來怎麼樣?

                  (B) 要五磅蘋果。

                  (C) 要是蘋果太貴,我就不買了。

                  (D) 香蕉比蘋果便宜。

[Simplified-character version]

(Woman)   你这水果怎么卖?

(Man)   苹果一元一磅,香蕉一元三磅。你买点儿什么?

(Woman)   (A) 香蕉看起来怎么样?

                  (B) 要五磅苹果。

                  (C) 要是苹果太贵,我就不买了。

                  (D) 香蕉比苹果便宜。

65.

[Traditional-character version]

(Woman)　　我買衣服，樣子、價錢、質量什麼的都不在乎，我主要看是不是
　　　　　　名牌。我買的衣服，非名牌不可。你呢？

(Man)　　　(A) 名牌的衣服都很貴。
　　　　　　(B) 我主要是看質量，質量不好的我不買。
　　　　　　(C) 樣子好的衣服都不便宜。
　　　　　　(D) 我也都無所謂。

[Simplified-character version]

(Woman)　　我买衣服，样子、价钱、质量什么的都不在乎，我主要看是不是
　　　　　　名牌。我买的衣服，非名牌不可。你呢？

(Man)　　　(A) 名牌的衣服都很贵。
　　　　　　(B) 我主要是看质量，质量不好的我不买。
　　　　　　(C) 样子好的衣服都不便宜。
　　　　　　(D) 我也都无所谓。

66.

[Traditional-character version]

(Woman)　　你這次考試考得怎麼樣？

(Man)　　　媽媽，我要是告訴你，你可千萬別生氣。

(Woman)　　(A) 你一直都考得不錯。
　　　　　　(B) 你什麼時候能知道成績？
　　　　　　(C) 你每天不是看電視就是踢足球，能考好嗎！
　　　　　　(D) 你考得那麼好，我很高興。

[Simplified-character version]

(Woman)　　你这次考试考得怎么样？

(Man)　　　妈妈，我要是告诉你，你可千万别生气。

(Woman)　　(A) 你一直都考得不错。
　　　　　　(B) 你什么时候能知道成绩？
　　　　　　(C) 你每天不是看电视就是踢足球，能考好吗！
　　　　　　(D) 你考得那么好，我很高兴。

67.

[Traditional-character version]

(Man)　　　請問，你是李醫生嗎？

(Woman)　　不是，我是這裏的護士，李醫生還沒來上班。你找她有事嗎？

(Man)　　　我們公司的一位同事是李醫生的大學同學。我來這裏出差，那位
　　　　　　同事讓我給李醫生帶點東西。

(Woman)　　(A) 她現在應該在醫院，這是她的電話號碼。
　　　　　　(B) 她在大學，你給她打電話吧。
　　　　　　(C) 她現在不在公司。
　　　　　　(D) 你往她家打電話吧，我這兒有她家裏的電話號碼。

[Simplified-character version]
(Man)　　　请问，你是李医生吗？
(Woman)　　不是，我是这里的护士，李医生还没来上班。你找她有事吗？
(Man)　　　我们公司的一位同事是李医生的大学同学。我来这里出差，那位
　　　　　　同事让我给李医生带点东西。
(Woman)　　(A) 她现在应该在医院，这是她的电话号码。
　　　　　　(B) 她在大学，你给她打电话吧。
　　　　　　(C) 她现在不在公司。
　　　　　　(D) 你往她家打电话吧，我这儿有她家里的电话号码。

68.
[Traditional-character version]
(Woman)　　你家裏的人都戴眼鏡嗎？
(Man)　　　我和弟弟戴眼鏡，妹妹不戴。
(Woman)　　(A) 你們都戴眼鏡呀。
　　　　　　(B) 你們都不戴眼鏡。
　　　　　　(C) 你弟弟的眼睛怎麼那麼好？
　　　　　　(D) 看來你妹妹的眼睛不錯。

[Simplified-character version]
(Woman)　　你家里的人都戴眼镜吗？
(Man)　　　我和弟弟戴眼镜，妹妹不戴。
(Woman)　　(A) 你们都戴眼镜呀。
　　　　　　(B) 你们都不戴眼镜。
　　　　　　(C) 你弟弟的眼睛怎么那么好？
　　　　　　(D) 看来你妹妹的眼睛不错。

69.
[Traditional-character version]
(Man)　　　你來中國是學習還是旅遊？
(Woman)　　我是來學中文的，回國以後當翻譯。你呢？
(Man)　　　(A) 你在哪個大學？
　　　　　　(B) 當中文翻譯很難。
　　　　　　(C) 我也是來旅遊的。
　　　　　　(D) 我來中國工作。

[Simplified-character version]
(Man)　　　你来中国是学习还是旅游？
(Woman)　　我是来学中文的，回国以后当翻译。你呢？
(Man)　　　(A) 你在哪个大学？
　　　　　　(B) 当中文翻译很难。
　　　　　　(C) 我也是来旅游的。
　　　　　　(D) 我来中国工作。

70.

[Traditional-character version]

(Man)　　　我跟小王說好下午5:00一起去買東西。我4:50就回宿舍等他了，一直等到5:30，最後還是我一個人去的。

(Woman)　　(A) 小王幾點到的？

　　　　　　(B) 小王什麼時候到的？

　　　　　　(C) 小王爲什麼沒來？

　　　　　　(D) 小王等了你很長時間嗎？

[Simplified-character version]

(Man)　　　我跟小王说好下午5:00一起去买东西。我4:50就回宿舍等他了，一直等到5:30，最后还是我一个人去的。

(Woman)　　(A) 小王几点到的？

　　　　　　(B) 小王什么时候到的？

　　　　　　(C) 小王为什么没来？

　　　　　　(D) 小王等了你很长时间吗？

71.

Track 17

[Traditional-character version]

(Woman)　　我的房間裏東西不多，只有一張床和兩個書架，可是書架上的書卻不少。我還有一臺小電視，因爲沒有桌子，只好放在地上了。

(Man)　　　(A) 房間裏沒有桌子是很不方便。

　　　　　　(B) 你房間裏的東西多嗎？

　　　　　　(C) 你爲什麼把電視放在地上？

　　　　　　(D) 你的書架上有書嗎？

[Simplified-character version]

(Woman)　　我的房间里东西不多，只有一张床和两个书架，可是书架上的书却不少。我还有一台小电视，因为没有桌子，只好放在地上了。

(Man)　　　(A) 房间里没有桌子是很不方便。

　　　　　　(B) 你房间里的东西多吗？

　　　　　　(C) 你为什么把电视放在地上？

　　　　　　(D) 你的书架上有书吗？

72.

[Traditional-character version]

(Man)　　　我喜歡踢足球，也愛打網球。

(Woman)　　你每天都踢足球或打網球嗎？

(Man)　　　(A) 踢踢足球，打打網球，對身體健康有好處。

　　　　　　(B) 我更喜歡踢足球。

　　　　　　(C) 我有時候踢得不太好。

　　　　　　(D) 我哪有那麼多時間。

[Simplified-character version]

(Man)　　　　我喜欢踢足球，也爱打网球。

(Woman)　　　你每天都踢足球或打网球吗？

(Man)　　　　(A) 踢踢足球，打打网球，对身体健康有好处。

　　　　　　　(B) 我更喜欢踢足球。

　　　　　　　(C) 我有时候踢得不太好。

　　　　　　　(D) 我哪有那么多时间。

73.

[Traditional-character version]

(Man)　　　　我們醫院的旁邊是一家郵局，郵局的後邊是一所英語學校。每個星期六下午，我都看見你妹妹去那所學校。

(Woman)　　　(A) 她想出國，所以去那兒學英語。

　　　　　　　(B) 我昨天看見你去郵局了。

　　　　　　　(C) 你妹妹去嗎？

　　　　　　　(D) 醫院在郵局的旁邊對病人不太好。

[Simplified-character version]

(Man)　　　　我们医院的旁边是一家邮局，邮局的后边是一所英语学校。每个星期六下午，我都看见你妹妹去那所学校。

(Woman)　　　(A) 她想出国，所以去那儿学英语。

　　　　　　　(B) 我昨天看见你去邮局了。

　　　　　　　(C) 你妹妹去吗？

　　　　　　　(D) 医院在邮局的旁边对病人不太好。

74.

[Traditional-character version]

(Man)　　　　我每天都會做運動，比如散散步、打打太極拳什麼的。另外，我從不吸煙，也不喝酒。

(Woman)　　　(A) 難怪你喜歡散步。

　　　　　　　(B) 怪不得你身體這麼好。

　　　　　　　(C) 你每天都吸煙嗎？

　　　　　　　(D) 你喜歡喝什麼酒？

[Simplified-character version]

(Man)　　　　我每天都会做运动，比如散散步、打打太极拳什么的。另外，我从不吸烟，也不喝酒。

(Woman)　　　(A) 难怪你喜欢散步。

　　　　　　　(B) 怪不得你身体这么好。

　　　　　　　(C) 你每天都吸烟吗？

　　　　　　　(D) 你喜欢喝什么酒？

75.
[Traditional-character version]
(Man)　　　小張的媽媽退休以前是一家商店的售貨員，現在住在小張家，幫
　　　　　　助小張照顧孩子。
(Woman)　　(A) 小張的媽媽爲什麼不工作了？
　　　　　　(B) 小張的媽媽還做售貨員嗎？
　　　　　　(C) 小張的媽媽什麼時候退休的？
　　　　　　(D) 小張的媽媽在哪兒當售貨員？

[Simplified-character version]
(Man)　　　小张的妈妈退休以前是一家商店的售货员，现在住在小张家，帮
　　　　　　助小张照顾孩子。
(Woman)　　(A) 小张的妈妈为什么不工作了？
　　　　　　(B) 小张的妈妈还做售货员吗？
　　　　　　(C) 小张的妈妈什么时候退休的？
　　　　　　(D) 小张的妈妈在哪儿当售货员？

76.
[Traditional-character version]
(Woman)　　老張，你怎麼了？臉色這麼不好看。
(Man)　　　(A) 我的臉長得不漂亮嗎？
　　　　　　(B) 我的臉本來就是這種顏色。
　　　　　　(C) 我的臉本來就長得不好看。
　　　　　　(D) 怎麼了？讓兒子氣的。

[Simplified-character version]
(Woman)　　老张，你怎么了？脸色这么不好看。
(Man)　　　(A) 我的脸长得不漂亮吗？
　　　　　　(B) 我的脸本来就是这种颜色。
　　　　　　(C) 我的脸本来就长得不好看。
　　　　　　(D) 怎么了？让儿子气的。

77.
[Traditional-character version]
(Woman)　　幾年沒見，我簡直認不出來小王了。
(Man)　　　(A) 你認識小王嗎？
　　　　　　(B) 你不認識小王嗎？
　　　　　　(C) 我也覺得小王的變化很大。
　　　　　　(D) 我也不認識小王。

[Simplified-character version]
(Woman)　　几年没见，我简直认不出来小王了。
(Man)　　　(A) 你认识小王吗？
　　　　　　(B) 你不认识小王吗？
　　　　　　(C) 我也觉得小王的变化很大。
　　　　　　(D) 我也不认识小王。

78.

[Traditional-character version]

(Woman) 你只要少看兩場籃球比賽就有時間看書了。

(Man) (A) 我少看了兩場籃球比賽。

(B) 就是不看籃球比賽，我也不喜歡看書。

(C) 我沒有時間看籃球比賽。

(D) 我看一場籃球比賽就可以有時間看書了。

[Simplified-character version]

(Woman) 你只要少看两场篮球比赛就有时间看书了。

(Man) (A) 我少看了两场篮球比赛。

(B) 就是不看篮球比赛，我也不喜欢看书。

(C) 我没有时间看篮球比赛。

(D) 我看一场篮球比赛就可以有时间看书了。

79.

[Traditional-character version]

(Woman) 你說什麼我也不能答應你。

(Man) (A) 你到底爲什麼不同意？

(B) 我說什麼你才能答應我？

(C) 我不說話，你能答應我嗎？

(D) 我怎麼說你才同意？

[Simplified-character version]

(Woman) 你说什么我也不能答应你。

(Man) (A) 你到底为什么不同意？

(B) 我说什么你才能答应我？

(C) 我不说话，你能答应我吗？

(D) 我怎么说你才同意？

80.

[Traditional-character version]

(Man) 你身上穿的這件衣服真漂亮，在哪兒買的？

(Woman) 不是買的，是一個朋友做的，送給我當生日禮物。

(Man) (A) 你朋友爲什麼送你這件衣服？

(B) 你的朋友是做什麼工作的？

(C) 你的朋友在哪兒買的這件衣服？

(D) 你的朋友會做衣服嗎？

[Simplified-character version]

(Man) 你身上穿的这件衣服真漂亮，在哪儿买的？

(Woman) 不是买的，是一个朋友做的，送给我当生日礼物。

(Man) (A) 你朋友为什么送你这件衣服？

(B) 你的朋友是做什么工作的？

(C) 你的朋友在哪儿买的这件衣服？

(D) 你的朋友会做衣服吗？

81.

[Traditional-character version]

(Woman)　　你這學期能得A嗎？

(Man)　　　我不得A，誰得A呀。

(Woman)　　(A) 我看你不一定得A。

　　　　　　(B) 我不知道誰能得A。

　　　　　　(C) 你肯定得A。

　　　　　　(D) 你不得A，那麼誰可以得A？

[Simplified-character version]

(Woman)　　你这学期能得A吗？

(Man)　　　我不得A，谁得A呀。

(Woman)　　(A) 我看你不一定得A。

　　　　　　(B) 我不知道谁能得A。

　　　　　　(C) 你肯定得A。

　　　　　　(D) 你不得A，那么谁可以得A？

82.

[Traditional-character version]

(Woman)　　一聽小張說話就知道他是上海人。

(Man)　　　我也覺得是。

(Woman)　　(A) 他是什麼時候離開上海的？

　　　　　　(B) 你說他是上海人嗎？

　　　　　　(C) 你是怎麼知道他不是上海人的？

　　　　　　(D) 你覺得他是哪里人？

[Simplified-character version]

(Woman)　　一听小张说话就知道他是上海人。

(Man)　　　我也觉得是。

(Woman)　　(A) 他是什么时候离开上海的？

　　　　　　(B) 你说他是上海人吗？

　　　　　　(C) 你是怎么知道他不是上海人的？

　　　　　　(D) 你觉得他是哪里人？

83.

[Traditional-character version]

(Man)　　　一起去吃個飯吧。今天我請客，去不去？

(Woman)　　你說呢？

(Man)　　　(A) 我們一起去嗎？

　　　　　　(B) 你餓不餓？

　　　　　　(C) 你想吃什麼？

　　　　　　(D) 你想去嗎？

[Simplified-character version]

(Man)	一起去吃个饭吧。今天我请客，去不去？
(Woman)	你说呢？
(Man)	(A) 我们一起去吗？
	(B) 你饿不饿？
	(C) 你想吃什么？
	(D) 你想去吗？

84.

[Traditional-character version]

(Woman)	他們都說你要去中國做義工，是真的嗎？
(Man)	有這計劃。
(Woman)	(A) 你打算去哪個國家？
	(B) 你真的想去中國嗎？
	(C) 你打算什麼時候去？
	(D) 你去中國做什麼？

[Simplified-character version]

(Woman)	他们都说你要去中国做义工，是真的吗？
(Man)	有这计划。
(Woman)	(A) 你打算去哪个国家？
	(B) 你真的想去中国吗？
	(C) 你打算什么时候去？
	(D) 你去中国做什么？

85.

[Traditional-character version]

(Man)	你家有幾口人？
(Woman)	四口。丈夫和我，還有一個兒子、一個女兒。我丈夫是大學老師，我在小學工作，女兒在一家醫院做護士。
(Man)	(A) 女兒在哪兒工作？
	(B) 兒子在什麼地方工作？
	(C) 你也是大學老師嗎？
	(D) 你丈夫在學校工作嗎？

[Simplified-character version]

(Man)	你家有几口人？
(Woman)	四口。丈夫和我，还有一个儿子、一个女儿。我丈夫是大学老师，我在小学工作，女儿在一家医院做护士。
(Man)	(A) 女儿在哪儿工作？
	(B) 儿子在什么地方工作？
	(C) 你也是大学老师吗？
	(D) 你丈夫在学校工作吗？

86.

[Traditional-character version]

(Woman)	你考試準備得怎麼樣了？
(Man)	媽媽，放心吧，沒問題。
(Woman)	(A) 你真的準備好了嗎？
	(B) 你怎麼還沒準備好？
	(C) 我已經準備好了。
	(D) 我考試沒問題。

[Simplified-character version]

(Woman)	你考试准备得怎么样了？
(Man)	妈妈，放心吧，没问题。
(Woman)	(A) 你真的准备好了吗？
	(B) 你怎么还没准备好？
	(C) 我已经准备好了。
	(D) 我考试没问题。

87.

[Traditional-character version]

(Man)	聽說你女兒既會唱歌又會跳舞，樣樣都不錯。
(Woman)	學習也很好啊。
(Man)	(A) 除了學習以外，你女兒唱歌也好。
	(B) 你女兒不會跳舞嗎？
	(C) 你女兒真是多才多藝。
	(D) 你女兒學習好，但是唱歌不太好。

[Simplified-character version]

(Man)	听说你女儿既会唱歌又会跳舞，样样都不错。
(Woman)	学习也很好啊。
(Man)	(A) 除了学习以外，你女儿唱歌也好。
	(B) 你女儿不会跳舞吗？
	(C) 你女儿真是多才多艺。
	(D) 你女儿学习好，但是唱歌不太好。

88.

[Traditional-character version]

(Woman)	我們去看中國電影還是看美國電影？
(Man)	隨便吧。
(Woman)	(A) 你爲什麼不喜歡美國電影？
	(B) 你不想看中國電影嗎？
	(C) 那你想看哪國電影？
	(D) 那我們就看美國電影吧。

[Simplified-character version]

(Woman)	我们去看中国电影还是看美国电影？
(Man)	随便吧。
(Woman)	(A) 你为什么不喜欢美国电影？
	(B) 你不想看中国电影吗？
	(C) 那你想看哪国电影？
	(D) 那我们就看美国电影吧。

89.

[Traditional-character version]

(Man)　　　　你今天上午的面試怎麼樣？

(Woman)　　　不錯。

(Man)　　　　(A) 那太好了。

　　　　　　　(B) 沒關係，還有機會。

　　　　　　　(C) 你什麼問題回答錯了？

　　　　　　　(D) 你哪個問題回答得不清楚？

[Simplified-character version]

(Man)　　　　你今天上午的面试怎么样？

(Woman)　　　不错。

(Man)　　　　(A) 那太好了。

　　　　　　　(B) 没关系，还有机会。

　　　　　　　(C) 你什么问题回答错了？

　　　　　　　(D) 你哪个问题回答得不清楚？

90.

[Traditional-character version]

(Man)　　　　我昨天下午給你宿舍打了幾次電話都沒找到你，你去上課了？

(Woman)　　　沒去。我昨天身體不舒服，下午去了醫院，完了以後直接回父母家了。

(Man)　　　　(A) 原來你去上課了。

　　　　　　　(B) 原來你回父母家啦。

　　　　　　　(C) 原來你陪父母去醫院了。

　　　　　　　(D) 原來你在宿舍呀。

[Simplified-character version]

(Man)　　　　我昨天下午给你宿舍打了几次电话都没找到你，你去上课了？

(Woman)　　　没去。我昨天身体不舒服，下午去了医院，完了以后直接回父母家了。

(Man)　　　　(A) 原来你去上课了。

　　　　　　　(B) 原来你回父母家啦。

　　　　　　　(C) 原来你陪父母去医院了。

　　　　　　　(D) 原来你在宿舍呀。

Track
19

91.

[Traditional-character version]

(Woman)　　　你這次考試考得怎麼樣？

(Man)　　　　那還用說。

(Woman)　　　(A) 爲什麼不能說說考試的事情呢？

　　　　　　　(B) 你總是這麼自信。

　　　　　　　(C) 我得跟你說說考試的事情。

　　　　　　　(D) 我很快跟你說說這件事情。

[Simplified-character version]

(Woman)　你这次考试考得怎么样？

(Man)　那还用说。

(Woman)　(A) 为什么不能说说考试的事情呢？

　　　　(B) 你总是这么自信。

　　　　(C) 我得跟你说说考试的事情。

　　　　(D) 我很快跟你说说这件事情。

92.

[Traditional-character version]

(Man)　天氣預報不是說今天沒有雨嗎？

(Woman)　你能相信天氣預報嗎？

(Man)　(A) 我可以借給你一把雨傘。

　　　　(B) 我沒有聽天氣預報。

　　　　(C) 你爲什麼不相信天氣預報呢？

　　　　(D) 帶把雨傘吧，要下雨了。

[Simplified-character version]

(Man)　天气预报不是说今天没有雨吗？

(Woman)　你能相信天气预报吗？

(Man)　(A) 我可以借给你一把雨伞。

　　　　(B) 我没有听天气预报。

　　　　(C) 你为什么不相信天气预报呢？

　　　　(D) 带把雨伞吧，要下雨了。

93.

[Traditional-character version]

(Woman)　請問，這兒附近有沒有食品店？

(Man)　你看到那座白色的樓了嗎？後邊的就是。

(Woman)　(A) 我想找一家食品店。

　　　　(B) 白樓的後邊是什麼？

　　　　(C) 食品店在白樓裏面嗎？

　　　　(D) 我想買點牛奶和麵包。

[Simplified-character version]

(Woman)　请问，这儿附近有没有食品店？

(Man)　你看到那座白色的楼了吗？后边的就是。

(Woman)　(A) 我想找一家食品店。

　　　　(B) 白楼的后边是什么？

　　　　(C) 食品店在白楼里面吗？

　　　　(D) 我想买点牛奶和面包。

94.

[Traditional-character version]

(Man)　　　你看我是學文學好還是學統計學好？

(Woman)　　我覺得都不如上醫學院。

(Man)　　　(A) 我也覺得學統計學不錯。

　　　　　　(B) 你覺得學文學好啊。

　　　　　　(C) 學醫太貴了。

　　　　　　(D) 你覺得學醫不好啊？

[Simplified-character version]

(Man)　　　你看我是学文学好还是学统计学好？

(Woman)　　我觉得都不如上医学院。

(Man)　　　(A) 我也觉得学统计学不错。

　　　　　　(B) 你觉得学文学好啊。

　　　　　　(C) 学医太贵了。

　　　　　　(D) 你觉得学医不好啊？

95.

[Traditional-character version]

(Woman)　　你穿這件襯衫一定很帥，買一件吧？

(Man)　　　你看著辦吧。

(Woman)　　(A) 你想怎麼辦？

　　　　　　(B) 你還想再看看呀？

　　　　　　(C) 你想買一件嗎？

　　　　　　(D) 那就買一件。

[Simplified-character version]

(Woman)　　你穿这件衬衫一定很帅，买一件吧？

(Man)　　　你看着办吧。

(Woman)　　(A) 你想怎么办？

　　　　　　(B) 你还想再看看呀？

　　　　　　(C) 你想买一件吗？

　　　　　　(D) 那就买一件。

96.

[Traditional-character version]

(Woman)　　咱們晚上去看場電影吧？

(Man)　　　你看我哪有時間呀。

(Woman)　　(A) 有時間的話我們去看電影。

　　　　　　(B) 你怎麼這麼忙？

　　　　　　(C) 我想跟你去看電影。

　　　　　　(D) 我也沒有時間去看電影。

[Simplified-character version]
(Woman)   咱们晚上去看场电影吧?
(Man)   你看我哪有时间呀。
(Woman)   (A) 有时间的话我们去看电影。
           (B) 你怎么这么忙?
           (C) 我想跟你去看电影。
           (D) 我也没有时间去看电影。

97.
[Traditional-character version]
(Woman)   這個暑假你能不能跟我們去旅遊?
(Man)   除非我同屋去我才去,要不然我就不去。
(Woman)   (A) 你同屋不去,你去嗎?
           (B) 你不想跟同屋一起去呀?
           (C) 你同屋肯定去。
           (D) 你同屋去,你就不去。

[Simplified-character version]
(Woman)   这个暑假你能不能跟我们去旅游?
(Man)   除非我同屋去我才去,要不然我就不去。
(Woman)   (A) 你同屋不去,你去吗?
           (B) 你不想跟同屋一起去呀?
           (C) 你同屋肯定去。
           (D) 你同屋去,你就不去。

98.
[Traditional-character version]
(Woman)   請問這輛車怎麼才來?
(Man)   剛才在那個路口發生了一場車禍,等了半天。
(Woman)   (A) 你們等了很長時間嗎?
           (B) 車晚了嗎?
           (C) 車禍嚴重嗎?
           (D) 哪兒有車禍?

[Simplified-character version]
(Woman)   请问这辆车怎么才来?
(Man)   刚才在那个路口发生了一场车祸,等了半天。
(Woman)   (A) 你们等了很长时间吗?
           (B) 车晚了吗?
           (C) 车祸严重吗?
           (D) 哪儿有车祸?

99.

[Traditional-character version]

(Woman) 你這次考試考得怎麼樣？

(Man) 李雲才考了65分，我就不用說了。

(Woman) (A) 李雲考試總是那麼好。

(B) 你比李雲考得好。

(C) 這麼說，你考得更糟糕啦？

(D) 李雲不知道你考多少。

[Simplified-character version]

(Woman) 你这次考试考得怎么样？

(Man) 李云才考了65分，我就不用说了。

(Woman) (A) 李云考试总是那么好。

(B) 你比李云考得好。

(C) 这么说，你考得更糟糕啦？

(D) 李云不知道你考多少。

100.

[Traditional-character version]

(Man) 請問，飯館在哪兒？

(Woman) 飯館到處都是，你問的是哪家飯館？

(Man) (A) 你經常去飯館吃飯。

(B) 那家四川飯館。

(C) 沒有人知道飯館在哪兒。

(D) 沒有人知道是誰的飯館。

[Simplified-character version]

(Man) 请问，饭馆在哪儿？

(Woman) 饭馆到处都是，你问的是哪家饭馆？

(Man) (A) 你经常去饭馆吃饭。

(B) 那家四川饭馆。

(C) 没有人知道饭馆在哪儿。

(D) 没有人知道是谁的饭馆。

Section II—Short Narration

The passages in this section are clearly labeled as either traditional or simplified.

Track 20

You will listen to several short narrations. Each narration will be played once. You may take notes. After each narration, you will have 5 seconds to read the question and choose the most appropriate response (A), (B), (C), or (D) in English, from the answer sheet. Please be reminded that during the AP Chinese Exam, the question will be displayed only *after* you hear the narration; therefore, in this practice, previewing the printed questions prior to listening to the narrations is not recommended.

101.
[Traditional-character version]
(Man) 我住的那個城市，常年平均氣溫18℃，最高氣溫39℃，最低氣溫4℃。很多人對那裏的氣候不適應，我已經習慣了。

[Simplified-character version]
(Man) 我住的那个城市，常年平均气温18℃，最高气温39℃，最低气温4℃。很多人对那里的气候不适应，我已经习惯了。

102.
[Traditional-character version]
(Woman) 小張，我是你的同屋小李。我媽媽昨天晚上住院了，我今天要跟妹妹去醫院看媽媽，所以下午上不了課了。麻煩你到老師那兒幫我請個假。

[Simplified-character version]
(Woman) 小张，我是你的同屋小李。我妈妈昨天晚上住院了，我今天要跟妹妹去医院看妈妈，所以下午上不了课了。麻烦你到老师那儿帮我请个假。

103.
[Traditional-character version]
(Woman) 張小天平時學習不努力，考試成績一直都不好。今年大學畢業生又特別多，工作很難找。我做夢也沒想到張小天找到了一個那麼好的工作。

[Simplified-character version]
(Woman) 张小天平时学习不努力，考试成绩一直都不好。今年大学毕业生又特别多，工作很难找。我做梦也没想到张小天找到了一个那么好的工作。

104.

[Traditional-character version]

(Woman) 我妹妹買的那件衣服，質量不錯，也不太貴，樣子特別好，就是顏色太糟糕了。

[Simplified-character version]

(Woman) 我妹妹买的那件衣服，质量不错，也不太贵，样子特别好，就是颜色太糟糕了。

105.

[Traditional-character version]

(Man) 每當有足球比賽的時候，運動場上總是坐滿了人。我真是覺得，世界上再也沒有比足球更讓我們激動的體育運動了。

[Simplified-character version]

(Man) 每当有足球比赛的时候，运动场上总是坐满了人。我真是觉得，世界上再也没有比足球更让我们激动的体育运动了。

106.

[Traditional-character version]

(Woman) 你總是說你忙得沒有時間吃早飯。其實，你要是每天早一點兒起床，怎麼會沒有時間呢？

[Simplified-character version]

(Woman) 你总是说你忙得没有时间吃早饭。其实，你要是每天早一点儿起床，怎么会没有时间呢？

107.

[Traditional-character version]

(Woman) 我有一個哥哥、兩個姊姊，還有一個弟弟。你看，前邊那個坐著的人是我哥哥，站在他後邊的長得挺帥的男孩子是我弟弟的兒子。

[Simplified-character version]

(Woman) 我有一个哥哥、两个姐姐，还有一个弟弟。你看，前边那个坐着的人是我哥哥，站在他后边的长得挺帅的男孩子是我弟弟的儿子。

108.

[Traditional-character version]

(Woman) 我今年住在學校的宿舍裏。我們宿舍的旁邊有郵局、服裝店、食品店、咖啡館什麼的，就是沒有書店，我覺得不太方便。

[Simplified-character version]

(Woman) 我今年住在学校的宿舍里。我们宿舍的旁边有邮局、服装店、食品店、咖啡馆什么的，就是没有书店，我觉得不太方便。

109.

[Traditional-character version]

(Woman)　昨天我沒有課。上午，我一直待在家裏做功課，下午先去了一趟郵局，寄了兩封信，又到商店買了點兒文具，最後在一家飯館吃了點兒小吃。

[Simplified-character version]

(Woman)　昨天我没有课。上午，我一直待在家里做功课，下午先去了一趟邮局，寄了两封信，又到商店买了点儿文具，最后在一家饭馆吃了点儿小吃。

110.

[Traditional-character version]

(Man)　我天天做運動，像散步、打太極拳什麼的。我從來不抽煙，也不喝酒。我這個人很注意身體，也沒有什麼壞的生活習慣，所以誰都看不出來我已經八十歲了，他們都說我最多六十歲。聽了這些話以後，我別提有多高興了。

[Simplified-character version]

(Man)　我天天做运动，像散步、打太极拳什么的。我从来不抽烟，也不喝酒。我这个人很注意身体，也没有什么坏的生活习惯，所以谁都看不出来我已经八十岁了，他们都说我最多六十岁。听了这些话以后，我别提有多高兴了。

111.

Track 21

[Traditional-character version]

(Man)　我們醫院的旁邊是一家郵局，郵局的後邊是一所中學，中學校園裏有一個英語班，每個星期六我都去那兒上英文課。

[Simplified-character version]

(Man)　我们医院的旁边是一家邮局，邮局的后边是一所中学，中学校园里有一个英语班，每个星期六我都去那儿上英文课。

112.

[Traditional-character version]

(Man)　我們本來打算先去南京、上海旅行，再去廣州，最後再到西安玩幾天。可是在上海，我們沒有買到去廣州的火車票，只好回北京了。

[Simplified-character version]

(Man)　我们本来打算先去南京、上海旅行，再去广州，最后再到西安玩几天。可是在上海，我们没有买到去广州的火车票，只好回北京了。

113.

[Traditional-character version]

(Woman) 我們的問題是沒有從華盛頓直飛洛杉磯的航班，坐火車吧，又太慢，所以只好先從華盛頓坐火車到紐約，再從紐約坐飛機到洛杉磯。

[Simplified-character version]

(Woman) 我们的问题是没有从华盛顿直飞洛杉矶的航班，坐火车吧，又太慢，所以只好先从华盛顿坐火车到纽约，再从纽约坐飞机到洛杉矶。

114.

[Traditional-character version]

(Woman) 在中國，"老師" 是一個常用的稱呼。比如，大家叫我媽媽 "李老師"，而不叫她 "李醫生"，還有很多人叫我爸爸 "張老師"，其實，他根本不是老師，而是一個記者。

[Simplified-character version]

(Woman) 在中国，"老师" 是一个常用的称呼。比如，大家叫我妈妈 "李老师"，而不叫她 "李医生"，还有很多人叫我爸爸 "张老师"，其实，他根本不是老师，而是一个记者。

115.

[Traditional-character version]

(Man) 我打算畢業後再學兩年電腦課程，爲的是多學一些知識。至於能不能找到一個好工作，可不可以掙很多錢，要不要出國什麼的，對我來說都不重要。

[Simplified-character version]

(Man) 我打算毕业后再学两年电脑课程，为的是多学一些知识。至于能不能找到一个好工作，可不可以挣很多钱，要不要出国什么的，对我来说都不重要。

116.

[Traditional-character version]

(Man) 這個房間裏有一張床和一張桌子，桌子上放著幾本書和一個筆記本電腦。靠窗戶的地方擺著一個很大的書架，書架旁邊有個小桌子，桌子上面放著一臺小電視。

[Simplified-character version]

(Man) 这个房间里有一张床和一张桌子，桌子上放着几本书和一个笔记本电脑。靠窗户的地方摆着一个很大的书架，书架旁边有个小桌子，桌子上面放着一台小电视。

117.

[Traditional-character version]

(Woman)　　　王小美的電腦壞了。小美請爸爸幫忙，爸爸沒有時間；請哥哥幫忙，哥哥說得去見女朋友；請媽媽幫忙，媽媽說她不會。最後，還是朋友幫小美把電腦修好了。

[Simplified-character version]

(Woman)　　　王小美的电脑坏了。小美请爸爸帮忙，爸爸没有时间；请哥哥帮忙，哥哥说得去见女朋友；请妈妈帮忙，妈妈说她不会。最后，还是朋友帮小美把电脑修好了。

118.

[Traditional-character version]

(Woman)　　　這雙鞋原來的價錢是280元，我只花了50元就買來了，少花200多呢。我不說你們也能猜出來爲什麼：新年了，東西都打折了。

[Simplified-character version]

(Woman)　　　这双鞋原来的价钱是280元，我只花了50元就买来了，少花200多呢。我不说你们也能猜出来为什么：新年了，东西都打折了。

119.

[Traditional-character version]

(Man)　　　　李老師剛把他家的電話號碼告訴我，我就忘了，只記得最後兩位數是86。

[Simplified-character version]

(Man)　　　　李老师刚把他家的电话号码告诉我，我就忘了，只记得最后两位数是86。

120.

[Traditional-character version]

(Man)　　　　到我們學校，騎自行車要四十分鐘；坐公共汽車二十五分鐘；自己開車比較快，也就十分鐘；要是走路的話，那就不好說了，至少得一個半小時。

[Simplified-character version]

(Man)　　　　到我们学校，骑自行车要四十分钟；坐公共汽车二十五分钟；自己开车比较快，也就十分钟；要是走路的话，那就不好说了，至少得一个半小时。

Section III—Dialogues

In this section, the traditional version will appear first, followed by the simplified version, without labels.

You will listen to several dialogues for questions 121 through 172. Each dialogue should be played twice. You may take notes. After replaying each dialogue, students will be given 12 seconds to read the question and choose the most appropriate response (A), (B), (C), or (D) in English, from the answer sheet. Please be reminded that during the AP Chinese Exam, the question will be displayed only *after* you hear the dialogue; therefore, in this practice, previewing the printed questions prior to listening to the dialogues is not recommended.

121.

(Man)	您貴姓？
	您贵姓？
(Woman)	我姓丁。
	我姓丁。
(Man)	丁小姐，您是這個大學的學生嗎？
	丁小姐，您是这个大学的学生吗？
(Woman)	是的。
	是的。
(Man)	您的愛好是什麼？
	您的爱好是什么？
(Woman)	很多呀，比如看電影、逛商店、旅遊什麼的。不過，我最喜歡游泳。
	很多呀，比如看电影、逛商店、旅游什么的。不过，我最喜欢游泳。

122.

(Man)	小姐的舞跳得真好。
	小姐的舞跳得真好。
(Woman)	謝謝！
	谢谢！
(Man)	我可以請你跳個舞嗎？
	我可以请你跳个舞吗？
(Woman)	當然可以。
	当然可以。
(Man)	小姐常來這兒跳嗎？
	小姐常来这儿跳吗？
(Woman)	不常來，這家舞廳比較貴。
	不常来，这家舞厅比较贵。
(Man)	請問小姐做什麼工作？
	请问小姐做什么工作？
(Woman)	我是一家書店的售貨員。
	我是一家书店的售货员。

Track 22

Track 23

Track 24

123–124
(Man) 請自我介紹一下，好嗎？
請自我介紹一下，好吗？

(Woman) 好的。我叫王美麗，在銀行工作。
好的。我叫王美丽，在银行工作。

(Man) 聽起來，你好像不是北京人吧？
听起来，你好像不是北京人吧？

(Woman) 不是，我是南京人。我是在上海讀的大學，畢業後來到北京工作的。
不是，我是南京人。我是在上海读的大学，毕业后来到北京工作的。

(Man) 旁邊這位是…
(Man) 旁边这位是…

(Woman) 她是我的朋友，叫張華，在一家電腦公司工作。她也不是北京人，她是天津人。
她是我的朋友，叫张华，在一家电脑公司工作。她也不是北京人，她是天津人。

Track 25

125–126
(Woman) 聽說你正在跟中國人學武術？
听说你正在跟中国人学武术？

(Man) 對。我很喜歡中國的武術，也喜歡看武術方面的電影。
对。我很喜欢中国的武术，也喜欢看武术方面的电影。

(Woman) 除了武術以外還喜歡什麼？
除了武术以外还喜欢什么？

(Man) 還喜歡中國的書法、京劇和中國民歌。
还喜欢中国的书法、京剧和中国民歌。

(Woman) 會書法嗎？
会书法吗？

(Man) 也在學呢。我每星期跟一位書法家學習三個小時。
也在学呢。我每星期跟一位书法家学习三个小时。

(Woman) 我也喜歡書法和京劇，不過，我對民歌不感興趣。
我也喜欢书法和京剧，不过，我对民歌不感兴趣。

Track 26

127–128
(Man) 可以問你一個問題嗎？
可以问你一个问题吗？

(Woman) 你請問。
你请问。

(Man) 你知道什麼是愛好嗎？
你知道什么是爱好吗？

(Woman) 愛好就是人們在業餘時間有興趣做的事情吧，比如說聽音樂、看電視、跳舞、旅遊什麼的。
爱好就是人们在业余时间有兴趣做的事情吧，比如说听音乐、看电视、跳舞、旅游什么的。

(Man) 說得真好。那麼請問，您的業餘愛好是什麼？
说得真好。那么请问，您的业余爱好是什么？

(Woman) 我喜歡聽音樂，可是我很忙，沒有多少時間聽。我是小學老師，
白天得上課，下班後還要買菜、做飯，晚上還得輔導兒子英語。
我喜欢听音乐，可是我很忙，没有多少时间听。我是小学老师，
白天得上课，下班后还要买菜、做饭，晚上还得辅导儿子英语。

129–130

(Woman) 你是張先生吧？
你是张先生吧？

Track 27

(Man) 對，我姓張。
对，我姓张。

(Woman) 聽說你經常來這個游泳館游泳。
听说你经常来这个游泳馆游泳。

(Man) 我每天都來。
我每天都来。

(Woman) 除了游泳以外，你還喜歡什麼體育運動？
除了游泳以外，你还喜欢什么体育运动？

(Man) 打乒乓球、打網球，還喜歡踢足球。
打乒乓球、打网球，还喜欢踢足球。

(Woman) 你是運動員吧？
你是运动员吧？

(Man) 不是。
不是。

(Woman) 教練？
教练？

(Man) 也不是。跟你一樣，是記者。
也不是。跟你一样，是记者。

131–132

(Man) 我看你總是穿名牌衣服，看來你很有錢。
我看你总是穿名牌衣服，看来你很有钱。

Track 28

(Woman) 不是因爲我有錢，而是因爲名牌衣服質量都不錯，所以我只買名
牌的。
不是因为我有钱，而是因为名牌衣服质量都不错，所以我只买名
牌的。

(Man) 我買衣服的標準跟你不一樣。我沒有名牌衣服，我買的衣服都是
純棉的。只要穿著舒服、好看就行了。名牌太貴了。
我买衣服的标准跟你不一样。我没有名牌衣服，我买的衣服都是
纯棉的。只要穿着舒服、好看就行了。名牌太贵了。

(Woman) 名牌衣服打折以後也很便宜。你看我這件毛衣，原來賣89元，打
折後才39元。我腳上的鞋打了5折，才10元。
名牌衣服打折以后也很便宜。你看我这件毛衣，原来卖89元，打
折后才39元。我脚上的鞋打了5折，才10元。

<table>
<tr><td rowspan="16">Track 29</td><td>133–134</td></tr>
</table>

133–134

Track 29

(Man) 　我們得走了。
　　　　我们得走了。

(Woman) 急什麼，還早呢。
　　　　急什么，还早呢。

(Man) 　不早了，耽誤你們這麼長時間。
　　　　不早了，耽误你们这么长时间。

(Woman) 你們能來家裏坐坐，我們也很高興。
　　　　你们能来家里坐坐，我们也很高兴。

(Man) 　能一起聊聊天兒確實是件愉快的事情，不過真得走了，我們也還
　　　　有事。
　　　　能一起聊聊天儿确实是件愉快的事情，不过真得走了，我们也还
　　　　有事。

(Woman) 非要走，我們也不留了，以後常來玩。
　　　　非要走，我们也不留了，以后常来玩。

(Man) 　一定再來。有時間也到我們家坐坐吧。
　　　　一定再来。有时间也到我们家坐坐吧。

(Woman) 一定去。請慢走，不遠送了。
　　　　一定去。请慢走，不远送了。

135–136

Track 30

(Man) 　喂，張太太，你好，我是小李。
　　　　喂，张太太，你好，我是小李。

(Woman) 噢，小李，你好啊。這麼長時間也不來家裏坐坐。
　　　　噢，小李，你好啊。这么长时间也不来家里坐坐。

(Man) 　最近比較忙，也沒能抽出時間去看你們，真是不好意思。怎麼
　　　　樣，身體挺好的吧？
　　　　最近比较忙，也没能抽出时间去看你们，真是不好意思。怎么
　　　　样，身体挺好的吧？

(Woman) 身體還可以，就是這兩天有點兒感冒。
　　　　身体还可以，就是这两天有点儿感冒。

(Man) 　厲害嗎？要不要看看醫生？
　　　　厉害吗？要不要看看医生？

(Woman) 不太厲害，吃點藥就行了。謝謝你這麼關心我。你是找老張吧？
　　　　不太厉害，吃点药就行了。谢谢你这么关心我。你是找老张吧？

(Man) 　對，我找張教授有點兒事。
　　　　对，我找张教授有点儿事。

(Woman) 你等一下，我這就去叫他接電話。老張，你的電話。
　　　　你等一下，我这就去叫他接电话。老张，你的电话。

137–138

(Man) 　老師，中國人吃飯的時間總是那麼長嗎？
　　　　老师，中国人吃饭的时间总是那么长吗？

Track 31

(Woman) 爲什麼問起這個問題了？
　　　　为什么问起这个问题了？

(Man)　昨天，我的一個中國朋友邀請我去他家吃晚飯，一頓飯吃了兩個
多小時。

昨天，我的一个中国朋友邀请我去他家吃晚饭，一顿饭吃了两个
多小时。

(Woman)　中國人平常吃飯也不會吃那麼久，但是請客的時候，爲了陪客人
就吃得比較慢。如果客人還沒吃完，主人先吃完了，那就不禮貌
了。

中国人平常吃饭也不会吃那么久，但是请客的时候，为了陪客人
就吃得比较慢。如果客人还没吃完，主人先吃完了，那就不礼貌
了。

(Man)　要是客人先吃完了，主人還在慢慢吃，這樣禮貌嗎？

要是客人先吃完了，主人还在慢慢吃，这样礼貌吗？

(Woman)　那也不太好。要是客人先吃完了，主人就應該快點兒吃了。

那也不太好。要是客人先吃完了，主人就应该快点儿吃了。

(Man)　怪不得呢，昨天在他家，我剛一吃完，他們一家四口也都很快地
吃完了。

怪不得呢，昨天在他家，我刚一吃完，他们一家四口也都很快地
吃完了。

Track 32

139–142

(Man)　昨天早上我在公園看見你爸了。

昨天早上我在公园看见你爸了。

(Woman)　他退休後每天早上都去鍛煉身體。在那兒散散步、打打太極拳什
麼的。你爸也去公園鍛煉嗎？

他退休后每天早上都去锻炼身体。在那儿散散步、打打太极拳什
么的。你爸也去公园锻炼吗？

(Man)　我爸除了釣魚以外什麼都不喜歡。最近，他買了個美國魚竿兒，
特別貴。他們還成立了釣魚協會，我爸做會長。

我爸除了钓鱼以外什么都不喜欢。最近，他买了个美国鱼竿儿，
特别贵。他们还成立了钓鱼协会，我爸做会长。

(Woman)　那他釣魚的技術一定很好。

那他钓鱼的技术一定很好。

(Man)　好什麼。

好什么。

(Woman)　不好怎麼能當會長？

不好怎么能当会长？

(Man)　他年紀最大，退了休，又有時間，人家就請他做了會長。

他年纪最大，退了休，又有时间，人家就请他做了会长。

Track 33

143–146

(Man)　你跟父母一起住嗎？

你跟父母一起住吗？

(Woman)　不，我住在學校的宿舍，可是打算搬出去。

不，我住在学校的宿舍，可是打算搬出去。

(Man)　住在宿舍很方便，你爲什麼要搬出去？搬到哪兒？

住在宿舍很方便，你为什么要搬出去？搬到哪儿？

(Woman)　或者搬到朋友的公寓去，或者找個新的公寓。住在宿舍方便是方
便，可是不自由。再說，住在公寓也比住在宿舍便宜得多。

或者搬到朋友的公寓去，或者找個新的公寓。住在宿舍方便是方
便，可是不自由。再說，住在公寓也比住在宿舍便宜得多。

(Man)　宿舍貴是貴，可是對女孩子來說比較安全。
　　　　宿舍贵是贵，可是对女孩子来说比较安全。

(Woman)　我同意你的說法。其實我想搬出去，主要是因爲我現在的同屋。
　　　　　我同意你的说法。其实我想搬出去，主要是因为我现在的同屋。

(Man)　她怎麼了？
　　　　她怎么了？

(Woman)　她每天晚上不是看電視看到很晚，就是打電話跟朋友聊天，有時
　　　　　還在電話裏大喊大叫，吵得我看不了書，睡不好覺。
　　　　　她每天晚上不是看电视看到很晚，就是打电话跟朋友聊天，有时
　　　　　还在电话里大喊大叫，吵得我看不了书，睡不好觉。

Track 34 147–150

(Man)　這個學期就要結束了，你假期有什麼安排嗎？
　　　　这个学期就要结束了，你假期有什么安排吗？

(Woman)　或者去西岸看姑媽，或者去芝加哥看姊姊。你呢？
　　　　　或者去西岸看姑妈，或者去芝加哥看姐姐。你呢？

(Man)　我本來哪兒都不想去，就待在東岸好好休息，可是我女朋友沒有
　　　　去過臺灣，非讓我跟她去旅行不可。
　　　　我本来哪儿都不想去，就待在东岸好好休息，可是我女朋友没有
　　　　去过台湾，非让我跟她去旅行不可。

(Woman)　出國旅行很麻煩吧，聽說要辦很多手續。
　　　　　出国旅行很麻烦吧，听说要办很多手续。

(Man)　沒有那麼麻煩。先到郵局辦護照，再到領事館辦簽證。
　　　　没有那么麻烦。先到邮局办护照，再到领事馆办签证。

(Woman)　還有機票呢？哪家旅行社的機票便宜？
　　　　　还有机票呢？哪家旅行社的机票便宜？

(Man)　旅行社的機票不見得便宜。上次去臺灣的機票我是在網上買的，
　　　　比哪家旅行社的都便宜。所以，我還得再看看。
　　　　旅行社的机票不见得便宜。上次去台湾的机票我是在网上买的，
　　　　比哪家旅行社的都便宜。所以，我还得再看看。

Track 35 151–154

(Man)　兩位小姐吃點兒什麼？
　　　　两位小姐吃点儿什么？

(Woman)　請你給我們推薦推薦吧。
　　　　　请你给我们推荐推荐吧。

(Man)　我們飯館的菜都不錯，有兩個菜特別有名：一個是麻婆豆腐，另
　　　　一個是糖醋排骨。
　　　　我们饭馆的菜都不错，有两个菜特别有名：一个是麻婆豆腐，另
　　　　一个是糖醋排骨。

(Woman)　那就點這兩個吧。
　　　　　那就点这两个吧。

(Man)　看看要不要再點點兒別的？
　　　　看看要不要再点点儿别的？

(Woman)	有海味嗎？
	有海味吗？
(Man)	我們這兒的紅燒魚和油燜大蝦做得都不錯。
	我们这儿的红烧鱼和油焖大虾做得都不错。
(Woman)	點個油燜大蝦吧，再要兩碗米飯。
	点个油焖大虾吧，再要两碗米饭。
(Man)	喝點兒什麼？酒還是果汁？
	喝点儿什么？酒还是果汁？
(Woman)	就喝水吧。
	就喝水吧。

Track 36 155–159

(Man)	安娜，你喝咖啡還是喝茶？
	安娜，你喝咖啡还是喝茶？
(Woman)	當然喝茶了。你想啊，到了中國，怎麼能不喝中國茶呢。
	当然喝茶了。你想啊，到了中国，怎么能不喝中国茶呢。
(Man)	對呀。你想喝什麼茶？紅茶、綠茶、茉莉花茶什麼的，我這兒都有。
	对呀。你想喝什么茶？红茶、绿茶、茉莉花茶什么的，我这儿都有。
(Woman)	我最愛喝綠茶。我聽說中國茶有很多種，是嗎？
	我最爱喝绿茶。我听说中国茶有很多种，是吗？
(Man)	是的。你知道嗎，中國還是世界上第一個發現茶的國家呢。
	是的。你知道吗，中国还是世界上第一个发现茶的国家呢。
(Woman)	我當然知道了。對了，中國人都在家裏喝茶嗎？
	我当然知道了。对了，中国人都在家里喝茶吗？
(Man)	也不是，有人就喜歡到茶館去喝茶。北京、上海、廣州等城市都有很多茶館，尤其是廣州。以後有時間的話，我請你跟我回上海，請你去喝喝我們上海茶館裏的茶。
	也不是，有人就喜欢到茶馆去喝茶。北京、上海、广州等城市都有很多茶馆，尤其是广州。以后有时间的话，我请你跟我回上海，请你去喝喝我们上海茶馆里的茶。

Track 37 160–163

(Woman)	小李，我們有兩年沒見了吧？
	小李，我们有两年没见了吧？
(Man)	兩年多了。你好嗎？孩子多大了？
	两年多了。你好吗？孩子多大了？
(Woman)	孩子一歲多了。你的呢？
	孩子一岁多了。你的呢？
(Man)	我兒子四歲了。
	我儿子四岁了。
(Woman)	你現在住哪兒？
	你现在住哪儿？

(Man)	剛結婚時，我們住在我妻子的父母家，去年買了房子就搬出來了。你們呢？
	刚结婚时，我们住在我妻子的父母家，去年买了房子就搬出来了。你们呢？
(Woman)	我們一直住在我丈夫的父母家呢。
	我们一直住在我丈夫的父母家呢。
(Man)	跟老人一起生活好，很方便。
	跟老人一起生活好，很方便。
(Woman)	方便什麼。我們喜歡晚睡、晚起，可是兩位老人喜歡早睡、早起。大家常常爲這些小事不高興。
	方便什么。我们喜欢晚睡、晚起，可是两位老人喜欢早睡、早起。大家常常为这些小事不高兴。

Track 38

164–168

(Woman)	好久沒有看到你，出差啦？
	好久没有看到你，出差啦？
(Man)	我感冒了，一直沒來上班。
	我感冒了，一直没来上班。
(Woman)	北京的冬天白天暖和，可是早上、晚上還是挺冷的。你剛來，要注意這兒的天氣變化。
	北京的冬天白天暖和，可是早上、晚上还是挺冷的。你刚来，要注意这儿的天气变化。
(Man)	我是從南方來的，最不喜歡這裏的冬天了。
	我是从南方来的，最不喜欢这里的冬天了。
(Woman)	北京的冬天常常颳風，還經常下雪，不太方便。
	北京的冬天常常刮风，还经常下雪，不太方便。
(Man)	我沒見過雪，我們廣州從來不下雪。
	我没见过雪，我们广州从来不下雪。
(Woman)	我從上海來北京工作，第一次看到雪的時候就很高興。
	我从上海来北京工作，第一次看到雪的时候就很高兴。

Track 39

169–172

(Woman)	我昨天給你打了幾次電話，你都不在。你去哪兒了？
	我昨天给你打了几次电话，你都不在。你去哪儿了？
(Man)	我們環保俱樂部有活動。上午我們去了公園和火車站撿垃圾，下午去工廠了。
	我们环保俱乐部有活动。上午我们去了公园和火车站捡垃圾，下午去工厂了。
(Woman)	到工廠做什麼？打工嗎？
	到工厂做什么？打工吗？
(Man)	到工廠抗議去了。那家工廠排出的廢水和廢氣給我們這個城市造成了嚴重的污染，他們排放的廢水把河裏的魚都毒死了。
	到工厂抗议去了。那家工厂排出的废水和废气给我们这个城市造成了严重的污染，他们排放的废水把河里的鱼都毒死了。

(Woman)	這個問題很嚴重，他們不想解決嗎？
	这个问题很严重，他们不想解决吗？
(Man)	想是想，可是沒有能力解決，因爲解決這個問題需要花很多錢。
	他們說如果政府不幫助他們，他們也沒有辦法。
	想是想，可是没有能力解决，因为解决这个问题需要花很多钱。
	他们说如果政府不帮助他们，他们也没有办法。

Section IV—Long Narration

The passages in this section are clearly labeled as either traditional or simplified.

You will listen to several long narrations of passages for questions 173 to 220. Each passage should be played twice. You may take notes. After replaying each passage, students will be given 12 seconds to read the question and choose the most appropriate response (A), (B), (C), or (D) in English, from the answer sheet. Please be reminded that during the AP Chinese Exam, the question will be displayed only *after* you hear the narration; therefore, in this practice, previewing the printed questions prior to listening to the narrations is not recommended.

173–174

[Traditional-character version]

(Man)　　小民打工的那家餐館，生意一直都很好。餐館的老闆是一位五十年代移民來美國的臺灣人，對小民非常好。來吃飯的客人給小民的小費也比給別人的多，可是小民突然不做了。老闆想來想去，也想不明白小民爲什麼要辭職。小民說：“我這學期選了一門化學課，功課特別多，還得經常去實驗室做試驗。一邊打工，一邊學習，我受不了了。”

[Simplified-character version]

(Man)　　小民打工的那家餐馆，生意一直都很好。餐馆的老板是一位五十年代移民来美国的台湾人，对小民非常好。来吃饭的客人给小民的小费也比给别人的多，可是小民突然不做了。老板想来想去，也想不明白小民为什么要辞职。小民说：“我这学期选了一门化学课，功课特别多，还得经常去实验室做试验。一边打工，一边学习，我受不了了。”

175–176

[Traditional-character version]

(Woman)　　現在播送北京地區天氣預報：今天夜間，風向偏南，風力一、二級，最低氣溫攝氏24度。明天白天，多雲轉陰，有小雨，南風，風力三、四級，最高氣溫攝氏27度。明天夜間，風向北轉南，風力二、三級，最低氣溫攝氏23度。

[Simplified-character version]

(Woman) 现在播送北京地区天气预报：今天夜间，风向偏南，风力一、二级，最低气温摄氏24度。明天白天，多云转阴，有小雨，南风，风力三、四级，最高气温摄氏27度。明天夜间，风向北转南，风力二、三级，最低气温摄氏23度。

177–178

[Traditional-character version]

(Man) 齊白石是中國的一位著名畫家。齊白石從小就喜歡畫畫兒，可是到了27歲他才正式開始學習繪畫。齊白石最喜歡畫動物，如鳥、魚、蟲什麼的。爲了畫好動物，齊白石經常站在樹下觀察動物，一站就是幾個小時。爲了更好地觀察動物，齊白石也經常在家裏養一些動物，因此，他筆下的動物都非常逼真。

[Simplified-character version]

(Man) 齐白石是中国的一位著名画家。齐白石从小就喜欢画画儿，可是到了27岁他才正式开始学习绘画。齐白石最喜欢画动物，如鸟、鱼、虫什么的。为了画好动物，齐白石经常站在树下观察动物，一站就是几个小时。为了更好地观察动物，齐白石也经常在家里养一些动物，因此，他笔下的动物都非常逼真。

179–180

[Traditional-character version]

(Man) 美國學生彼得對學中文沒有什麼興趣，可是他很喜歡在中國生活，尤其是對吃中國菜和在中國旅行特別感興趣。有一天，彼得到學校附近的一家飯館吃飯。他坐下來以後，服務員小姐拿來菜單請他點菜，可是他不認識菜單上的中文字。彼得想：反正中國菜都很好吃，吃什麼都一樣。于是，他隨便指了指菜單上的一行字，用英文對服務員說："我就點這個吧。"小姐用英文回答他說："對不起，先生，這個不能吃！" 彼得不高興地說："怎麼不能吃，我已經吃過兩次了。"小姐笑著說："你吃過兩次了？不可能吧，這是我們飯店的名字呀！"彼得的臉紅了。

[Simplified-character version]

(Man) 美国学生彼得对学中文没有什么兴趣，可是他很喜欢在中国生活，尤其是对吃中国菜和在中国旅行特别感兴趣。有一天，彼得到学校附近的一家饭馆吃饭。他坐下来以后，服务员小姐拿来菜单请他点菜，可是他不认识菜单上的中文字。彼得想：反正中国菜都很好吃，吃什么都一样。于是，他随便指了指菜单上的一行字，用英文对服务员说："我就点这个吧。"小姐用英文回答他说："对不起，先生，这个不能吃！"彼得不高兴地说："怎么不能吃，我已经吃过两次了。"小姐笑着说："你吃过两次了？不可能吧，这是我们饭店的名字呀！"彼得的脸红了。

Track 44

181–182

[Traditional-character version]

(Woman) 中國人請客吃飯有很多講究。比如說：吃飯的時候，如果有人用筷子或勺子盛食物給你的時候，你不能也用筷子或勺子去接，而是要用碗或碟子；最好不要用自己的筷子去夾食物，而是應該用公用的勺子或筷子去取；另外，當兩個人同時夾桌子上的食物時，要盡量避免雙方的筷子互相碰撞，千萬不要跨過別人的筷子去夾食物。

[Simplified-character version]

(Woman) 中国人请客吃饭有很多讲究。比如说：吃饭的时候，如果有人用筷子或勺子盛食物给你的时候，你不能也用筷子或勺子去接，而是要用碗或碟子；最好不要用自己的筷子去夹食物，而是应该用公用的勺子或筷子去取；另外，当两个人同时夹桌子上的食物时，要尽量避免双方的筷子互相碰撞，千万不要跨过别人的筷子去夹食物。

Track 45

183–185

[Traditional-character version]

(Woman) 感冒是生活中常見的病，預防感冒是不容忽視的。預防感冒的最好方法是每天聽天氣預報，根據天氣的變化注意衣服的保暖問題。另外，白天要多開窗戶，以便室內空氣流通，但是晚上睡覺以前應該把窗戶關好，以免受涼。還有，生活中要儘量避免跟感冒病人的接觸。如果發現自己已經感冒了，最好去看醫生，並在醫生的指導下吃藥。要多喝水，並保證充足的睡眠時間。

[Simplified-character version]

(Woman) 感冒是生活中常见的病，预防感冒是不容忽视的。预防感冒的最好方法是每天听天气预报，根据天气的变化注意衣服的保暖问题。另外，白天要多开窗户，以便室内空气流通，但是晚上睡觉以前应该把窗户关好，以免受凉。还有，生活中要尽量避免跟感冒病人的接触。如果发现自己已经感冒了，最好去看医生，并在医生的指导下吃药。要多喝水，并保证充足的睡眠时间。

Track 46

186–189

[Traditional-character version]

(Woman) 中國人根據自己的口味選擇茶葉。一般來說，北京人愛喝茉莉花茶，上海人喜歡綠茶，廣東人偏愛烏龍茶，藏族人離不開酥油茶。中國茶的種類很多，茶具的種類也不少。中國人大多喜歡用陶器茶具和瓷器茶具沏茶，因爲這兩種茶具可以保持水的溫度。在中國，喝茶已經成爲一種習俗。慶祝春節的時候，人們會喝春茶；孩子滿月的時候，大家要去喝滿月茶；結婚的時候，親朋好友都要去喝喝表示祝賀新婚的喜茶。

[Simplified-character version]

(Woman)　中国人根据自己的口味选择茶叶。一般来说，北京人爱喝茉莉花茶，上海人喜欢绿茶，广东人偏爱乌龙茶，藏族人离不开酥油茶。中国茶的种类很多，茶具的种类也不少。中国人大多喜欢用陶器茶具和瓷器茶具沏茶，因为这两种茶具可以保持水的温度。在中国，喝茶已经成为一种习俗。庆祝春节的时候，人们会喝春茶；孩子满月的时候，大家要去喝满月茶；结婚的时候，亲朋好友都要去喝喝表示祝贺新婚的喜茶。

Track 47

190–193

[Traditional-character version]

(Man)　我家裏的人都喜歡看電視。我爺爺是一個退休工人，他喜歡看京劇。爺爺看京劇的時候，常常一邊看一邊跟著唱。在一家大醫院做醫生的爸爸喜歡看體育節目，特別是足球比賽。只要電視上有足球節目，爸爸非看不可。媽媽跟爸爸在同一家醫院工作，但她不是醫生，而是一個護士。媽媽跟爸爸不一樣，她一點兒也不喜歡看體育節目，她愛看電視劇。看電視劇的時候，媽媽常常是跟著電視裏的人物，一會兒哭一會兒笑，讓我們都哭笑不得。我姊姊是一個中學的英語老師，她愛看英語節目，最喜歡看美國電影。我跟他們的興趣完全不一樣，我只對動畫片感興趣。

[Simplified-character version]

(Man)　我家里的人都喜欢看电视。我爷爷是一个退休工人，他喜欢看京剧。爷爷看京剧的时候，常常一边看一边跟着唱。在一家大医院做医生的爸爸喜欢看体育节目，特别是足球比赛。只要电视上有足球节目，爸爸非看不可。妈妈跟爸爸在同一家医院工作，但她不是医生，而是一个护士。妈妈跟爸爸不一样，她一点儿也不喜欢看体育节目，她爱看电视剧。看电视剧的时候，妈妈常常是跟着电视里的人物，一会儿哭一会儿笑，让我们都哭笑不得。我姐姐是一个中学的英语老师，她爱看英语节目，最喜欢看美国电影。我跟他们的兴趣完全不一样，我只对动画片感兴趣。

Track 48

194–197

[Traditional-character version]

(Woman)　與美國家長相比，在美國的中國家庭對孩子的期望比較高，因此，家長對孩子的學習特別重視，在學習上管得比美國家長嚴得多。多數中國家長希望孩子學習成績優秀，有些家庭甚至要求孩子各門考試非得A不可。很多中國家長不僅要求自己的孩子上大學，而且希望他們考上名牌大學，這主要是因爲上名牌大學對以後找工作有好處。另外，子女考上名牌大學，家長也有面子。在選擇大學專業上，中國家長多半希望孩子學理科或者讀醫學院、法律學院什麽的，而不希望他們學文科。在家庭教育方面，中國家長也許應該學習美國家長，把選擇的權利還給孩子，給孩子更多的自由。

[Simplified-character version]

(Woman) 与美国家长相比，在美国的中国家庭对孩子的期望比较高，因此，家长对孩子的学习特别重视，在学习上管得比美国家长严得多。多数中国家长希望孩子学习成积优秀，有些家庭甚至要求孩子各门考试非得A不可。很多中国家长不仅要求自己的孩子上大学，而且希望他们考上名牌大学，这主要是因为上名牌大学对以后找工作有好处。另外，子女考上名牌大学，家长也有面子。在选择大学专业上，中国家长多半希望孩子学理科或者读医学院、法律学院什么的，而不希望他们学文科。在家庭教育方面，中国家长也许应该学习美国家长，把选择的权利还给孩子，给孩子更多的自由。

Track 49

198–201

[Traditional-character version]

(Woman) 喂，小麗，我是張華。我給你打了兩次電話，你都不在家。你去哪兒了？去上課了嗎？咱們同學準備一起去看場電影。我表姊和我都去。電影是下午四點半的，我們準備四點鐘的時候在電影院旁邊的那家咖啡館見面。你想不想跟我們一起去看電影？如果想去，請在三點半以前給我打個電話或者四點鐘的時候直接去那家咖啡館找我們吧。好，再見。

[Simplified-character version]

(Woman) 喂，小丽，我是张华。我给你打了两次电话，你都不在家。你去哪儿了？去上课了吗？咱们同学准备一起去看场电影。我表姐和我都去。电影是下午四点半的，我们准备四点钟的时候在电影院旁边的那家咖啡馆见面。你想不想跟我们一起去看电影？如果想去，请在三点半以前给我打个电话或者四点钟的时候直接去那家咖啡馆找我们吧。好，再见。

Track 50

202–205

[Traditional-character version]

(Man) 中國人的姓有一個字的，也有兩個或兩個以上的。一個字的姓叫單姓，兩個或兩個字以上的姓叫複姓。中國到底有多少姓，至今沒有準確的數字。據說，在很早以前，有一個讀書人寫了一本書，叫《百家姓》，書裏提到的中國姓有五百多個，其中六十個是複姓。有人統計，在中國的歷史文獻中，出現過的中國姓有五千多個。現在常見的姓有兩百個。張、王、李、趙、劉是其中最常見的單姓，而諸葛、歐陽、司徒等是中國最常見的複姓。

[Simplified-character version]

(Man) 中国人的姓有一个字的，也有两个或两个以上的。一个字的姓叫单姓，两个或两个字以上的姓叫复姓。中国到底有多少姓，至今没有准确的数字。据说，在很早以前，有一个读书人写了一本书，叫《百家姓》，书里提到的中国姓有五百多个，其中六十个是复姓。有人统计，在中国的历史文献中，出现过的中国姓有五千多个。现在常见的姓有两百个。张、王、李、赵、刘是其中最常见的单姓，而诸葛、欧阳、司徒等是中国最常见的复姓。

Track 51

206–209

[Traditional-character version]

(Woman) 病人住院的時候，親人或朋友會到醫院探訪，這是一種禮貌。以前，中國人到醫院探訪病人時，常常會給病人帶一些吃的東西，現在越來越多的人喜歡給病人送鮮花。到醫院探訪病人的時候，時間不要太長，否則會影響醫生工作和病人休息。跟病人說話要注意，多談愉快的話題，不說刺激病人的話。在中國，每家醫院都規定了探訪病人的時間。一般情況下，上午是治療的時間，不能探訪，所以探訪病人都在下午。每星期有三、四個下午可以探訪，時間大多是在下午三點鐘以後。周末的時候，探訪病人的時間可以長一些。

[Simplified-character version]

(Woman) 病人住院的时候，亲人或朋友会到医院探访，这是一种礼貌。以前，中国人到医院探访病人时，常常会给病人带一些吃的东西，现在越来越多的人喜欢给病人送鲜花。到医院探访病人的时候，时间不要太长，否则会影响医生工作和病人休息。跟病人说话要注意，多谈愉快的话题，不说刺激病人的话。在中国，每家医院都规定了探访病人的时间。一般情况下，上午是治疗的时间，不能探访，所以探访病人都在下午。每星期有三、四个下午可以探访，时间大多是在下午三点钟以后。周末的时候，探访病人的时间可以长一些。

Track 52

210–213

[Traditional-character version]

(Woman) 在日常生活中，中國人邀請別人到家裏做客大多用打電話或者口頭邀請的方式。如果是比較重要的活動，就會發請貼邀請客人。到中國人家裏做客，最好在約定的時間裏到達，提前或者遲到都是不禮貌的。中國人請客總是用豐盛的飯菜招待客人，可是主人往往還會對客人說"沒做什麼好吃的，請隨便吃"之類的話，這些都是中國人的禮貌。在中國人家裏吃飯，每當一道菜端上飯桌以後，主人總是會熱情地請客人先吃。每當這時，客人就會說些感謝的話或者請主人先吃。客人告辭的時候，主人會禮貌地說"還早哪，再坐一會兒吧"，"怎麼剛來就要走呀"什麼的。如果客人發現主人還有事情做，就應該主動告辭。告辭時，要再一次向主人表示感謝和歉意，比如說"感謝你們"、"打擾您了"等等。當然，如果是關係比較近的人，那麼，主人和客人之間就不必太客氣了。

[Simplified-character version]

(Woman)　　在日常生活中，中国人邀请别人到家里做客大多用打电话或者口头邀请的方式。如果是比较重要的活动，就会发请贴邀请客人。到中国人家里做客，最好在约定的时间里到达，提前或者迟到都是不礼貌的。中国人请客总是用丰盛的饭菜招待客人，可是主人往往还会对客人说"没做什么好吃的，请随便吃"之类的话，这些都是中国人的礼貌。在中国人家里吃饭，每当一道菜端上饭桌以后，主人总是会热情地请客人先吃。每当这时，客人就会说些感谢的话或者请主人先吃。客人告辞的时候，主人会礼貌地说"还早哪，再坐一会儿吧"，"怎么刚来就要走呀"什么的。如果客人发现主人还有事情做，就应该主动告辞。告辞时，要再一次向主人表示感谢和歉意，比如说"感谢你们"、"打扰您了"等等。当然，如果是关系比较近的人，那么，主人和客人之间就不必太客气了。

Track 53

214–216

[Traditional-character version]

(Woman)　　中國大學招生，主要看4–9門學科的高考成績；美國大學招生，要看SATI的考試成績，一些學校和專業還要看SATII的考試成績。因爲中國大學招生，完全看學生的高考成績，那麼大學考試考得好壞就決定一個學生一生的命運。美國的學生在高中期間可以多次參加SAT考試，一次考不好還有第二次。美國大學除了看學生的SAT成績以外，也要看高中期間的考試成績，也就是說，在美國，能不能上個好大學，除了大學考試以外，平時的學習成績也很重要。我認爲這很有道理，對學生來說也很公平。中國大學招生，除了少數專業外，大部分專業不進行面試，而美國高校特別注重對學生的面試，這一點值得推薦。美國大學招生時會考慮學生的社區活動記錄，令人遺憾的是中國高校却不重視學生在這些方面的表現。

[Simplified-character version]

(Woman)　　中国大学招生，主要看4–9门学科的高考成绩；美国大学招生，要看SATI的考试成绩，一些学校和专业还要看SATII的考试成绩。因为中国大学招生，完全看学生的高考成绩，那么大学考试考得好坏就决定一个学生一生的命运。美国的学生在高中期间可以多次参加SAT考试，一次考不好还有第二次。美国大学除了看学生的SAT成绩以外，也要看高中期间的考试成绩，也就是说，在美国，能不能上个好大学，除了大学考试以外，平时的学习成绩也很重要。我认为这很有道理，对学生来说也很公平。中国大学招生，除了少数专业外，大部分专业不进行面试，而美国高校特别注重对学生的面试，这一点值得推荐。美国大学招生时会考虑学生的社区活动记录，令人遗憾的是中国高校却不重视学生在这些方面的表现。

Track
54

217–220
[Traditional-character version]

(Woman) 　各位聽眾，家庭問題是一個熱門話題。受傳統家庭觀念的影響，中國人幾代人一起生活是很常見的事情。隨著社會生活水平的提高，家庭結構也改變了。在今天，無論是城市還是農村，幾代人共同生活的大家庭逐漸變成了中小家庭。特別是城市中，幾代人生活在一個屋簷下的現象已經很少了。多數年輕人希望結婚以後和老人分開生活，這也是一部分老年人的願望。這不能說中國人不再重視家庭了，實際上，分開生活的年輕人還是尊敬、照顧老人的，老人也經常到子女家裏幫助照顧孩子，幫子女做一些家務。大家平時做自己的事情，到了節假日，子女們會帶著禮品去看望老人，與老人一起過節度假。

[Simplified-character version]

(Woman) 　各位听众，家庭问题是一个热门话题。受传统家庭观念的影响，中国人几代人一起生活是很常见的事情。随着社会生活水平的提高，家庭结构也改变了。在今天，无论是城市还是农村，几代人共同生活的大家庭逐渐变成了中小家庭。特别是城市中，几代人生活在一个屋檐下的现象已经很少了。多数年轻人希望结婚以后和老人分开生活，这也是一部分老年人的愿望。这不能说中国人不再重视家庭了，实际上，分开生活的年轻人还是尊敬、照顾老人的，老人也经常到子女家里帮助照顾孩子，帮子女做一些家务。大家平时做自己的事情，到了节假日，子女们会带着礼品去看望老人，与老人一起过节度假。

Reading Comprehension CHAPTER 3

GENERAL INFORMATION

The Reading Comprehension section of the test assesses the student's interpretive communication skills. The student will read a variety of written texts—such as advertisements, articles, e-mails, letters, notes, posters, signs, and stories—before answering multiple-choice questions about the texts.

This chapter is organized into the following sections:

- Reading Strategies
- Reading Selections and Sample Questions
- Answer Keys
- Answers and Answer Explanations

All passages in this chapter are presented in both traditional and simplified characters. Phrases referenced in the Answer Explanation section are first written in the traditional-character version and immediately followed by the simplified counterpart in parentheses. If there is no parenthesized phrase, the presented characters are common in both the traditional and simplified versions.

READING STRATEGIES

This section presents nine reading strategies that students can use to hone their reading comprehension skills prior to taking the test. Students may find that some strategies are more applicable than others in different contexts, or that certain strategies are more helpful given their individual reading styles.

The nine reading strategies are:

1. Prediction
2. Skimming
3. Scanning
4. Understanding main ideas
5. Ignoring unimportant words
6. Guessing and analyzing
7. Detailed reading
8. Inferring ideas
9. Determining the writer's attitude

Prediction

During the pre-reading phase, students are encouraged to identify what they already know about the topic and use that knowledge to predict what they may learn from the reading. They may even begin to formulate questions that they may be asked to answer after reading the text.

1. What information might students predict before reading the following passage?

[Traditional-character version]

　　近日，一份上海校園學生零用錢調查報告顯示：有86.7%的學生平時有零用錢，而且隨著年齡的增長，他們的零用錢越來越多。

[Simplified-character version]

　　近日，一份上海校园学生零用钱调查报告显示：有86.7%的学生平时有零用钱，而且随着年龄的增长，他们的零用钱越来越多。

This passage is a survey report about the amount of allowance students receive. It is highly likely that students already know something about the discussed topic, "零用錢" ("零用钱"), from personal experience, and also because it may be widely talked about among peers. Before students finish reading the entire text, they may be able to predict the main ideas of the investigation and formulate some possible questions. Then, they can compare their predictions with the results of the investigation while reading the passage.

2.

[Traditional-character version]

　　美國的教育重視讓孩子自由發展，注意發揮孩子的想象力。中國的教育不太考慮學生的特點，對每位學生的要求都一樣。在中國，升學的壓力很大，使許多學生變成了只會死讀書的考試機器。美國老師認爲，學生，特別是小學生，應該在輕鬆、愉快的環境中學習，而不應該讓他們感到有太大壓力，可是很多中國家長對此不以爲然。他們認爲小學的基礎一定得打好。如果基礎打不好，將來就沒有能力跟別人競爭。

[Simplified-character version]

　　美国的教育重视让孩子自由发展，注意发挥孩子的想象力。中国的教育不太考虑学生的特点，对每位学生的要求都一样。在中国，升学的压力很大，使许多学生变成了只会死读书的考试机器。美国老师认为，学生，特别是小学生，应该在轻松、愉快的环境中学习，而不应该让他们感到有太大压力，可是很多中国家长对此不以为然。他们认为小学的基础一定得打好。如果基础打不好，将来就没有能力跟别人竞争。

This passage is about the major differences of opinion between Chinese and Americans on the topic of education. Students may have years of experience in the American educational system and/or some experience in the Chinese educational system. As they are reading the passage, they may mentally summarize what they already know about American schools and Chinese families. They can compare their predictions with the passage as they read, which may help them grasp the main differences between the two educational systems.

If this article were preceded by the title "中美教育的差異" ("中美教育的差异"), the prediction strategy would enable students to glean important information from the title and to more effectively focus on the main ideas before, or as they finish, reading.

STRATEGY

2 Skimming

Skimming is a fast-reading skill that does not require reading word by word, but it does require a high degree of concentration. Skimming may involve reading only the title, subheading, illustrations, and the first and last paragraphs of a passage, or the first, second, and last sentence of each paragraph. Instead of a detailed reading, students are encouraged to try the skimming technique to identify the overall idea of the text.

Consider the title of the next text, "Bicycle Kingdom," "自行車王國" ("自行车王国"). Students should start skimming, and then decide if the title is appropriate.

[Traditional-character version]

自行車王國

人們說，中國是一個"自行車王國"，這是因爲中國的自行車特別多。

在城市，每當上下班的時候，大街小巷的自行車就像潮水一樣湧來。在農村，人們常常可以看到丈夫騎著自行車，妻子抱著孩子，坐在後面的架子上，一家人高高興興地去買東西。中國的大學校園多半都很大，從宿舍到教室，從圖書館到餐廳，距離都很遠。如果騎自行車，就方便多了。

人們的生活離不開自行車，自行車是中國人常用的交通工具。

[Simplified-character version]

自行车王国

人们说，中国是一个"自行车王国"，这是因为中国的自行车特别多。

在城市，每当上下班的时候，大街小巷的自行车就像潮水一样涌来。在农村，人们常常可以看到丈夫骑着自行车，妻子抱着孩子，坐在后面的架子上，一家人高高兴兴地去买东西。中国的大学校园多半都很大，从宿舍到教室，从图书馆到餐厅，距离都很远。如果骑自行车，就方便多了。

人们的生活离不开自行车，自行车是中国人常用的交通工具。

While skimming, students should underline the key words, "特別多," "像潮水," "離不開" ("离不开"), and "常用," paying attention to the first two sentences of the introductory paragraph, as well as the concluding paragraph. This should give students an overall idea of China as the "Bicycle Kingdom."

In the next passage, consider the phrases "中國的傳統節日" ("中国的传统节日") in the first line, followed by "春節、元宵節、端午節和中秋節" ("春节、元宵节、端午节和中秋节"). The introductory paragraph directly addresses the main topic of the passage.

[Traditional-character version]

中國的傳統節日有春節、元宵節、端午節和中秋節等。

春節是農曆的新年，是一年中最重要的節日。過春節的時候，家家戶戶放鞭炮，親朋好友互相拜年。結了婚的子女帶著自己的孩子回家看望父母，父母也會給晚輩們壓歲錢。全家老小，坐在一起，熱熱鬧鬧地吃餃子。

農曆正月十五是元宵節，也叫燈節。元宵節那一天，人們在門前掛上燈籠，圍在一起吃元宵。農曆五月五日是端午節。中國人有端午節吃粽子、賽龍舟的習俗。農曆八月十五日是中秋節，這是中國人家庭團圓的日子。中秋節的晚上，月亮又圓又亮。全家人圍坐在一起，一邊賞月，一邊吃著象徵團圓的月餅。

[Simplified-character version]

中国的传统节日有春节、元宵节、端午节和中秋节等。

春节是农历的新年，是一年中最重要的节日。过春节的时候，家家户户放鞭炮，亲朋好友互相拜年。结了婚的子女带着自己的孩子回家看望父母，父母也会给晚辈们压岁钱。全家老小，坐在一起，热热闹闹地吃饺子。

农历正月十五是元宵节，也叫灯节。元宵节那一天，人们在门前挂上灯笼，围在一起吃元宵。农历五月五日是端午节。中国人有端午节吃粽子、赛龙舟的习俗。农历八月十五日是中秋节，这是中国人家庭团圆的日子。中秋节的晚上，月亮又圆又亮。全家人围坐在一起，一边赏月，一边吃着象征团圆的月饼。

Students should then pay attention to the first line of each of the following paragraphs. They may also want to take notes on the activities of each festival, such as "放鞭炮" (set up firecrackers), "拜年" (pay a New Year call), "賽龍舟" ("赛龙舟") (the dragon boat competition), "賞月" ("赏月") (admire the full moon), "吃餃子" ("吃饺子") (eat dumplings), "吃元宵" (eat sweet dumplings), "吃粽子" (eat glutinous rice dumplings), and "吃月餅" ("吃月饼") (eat moon cake). By skimming, students will understand the overall idea of the passage.

STRATEGY

 Scanning

Scanning is a helpful technique when students are looking for the answer to a particular question. Unlike skimming, scanning involves moving quickly through the passage seeking specific words and phrases. Scanning is also useful for determining whether a particular piece of information will answer one of the questions. While scanning, it may be a good idea to look for organizers such as numbers, letters, steps, or the words *first*, *second*, or *next*.

Scanning off a computer screen has become increasingly important. Although this may be an unfamiliar skill for some students, with regular practice, they should become comfortable with it.

The following example is a program guide for a TV station in Taiwan. Students should scan the program guide and find the necessary information to answer the following four comprehension questions.

[Traditional-character version]

時間	播出節目
00:00	中視夜線新聞
01:00	冰冰好料理
02:00	我猜，我猜，我猜猜猜
03:30	國光異校
04:00	世界非常奇妙
05:00	歌仔戲:江南四才子
06:00	院線搶先看： 曼哈頓奇緣
06:30	中視早安新聞
08:00	淨覺法語
08:30	快樂生活王
09:00	全民大講堂
10:00	超級星光大道
12:00	中視午間新聞
12:30	MIT台灣誌
13:30	蝴蝶飛
15:00	院線搶先看:瘋狂理髮師
15:30	院線搶先看:把愛找回來
16:00	我猜，我猜，我猜猜猜
17:30	神奇寶貝鑽石&珍珠
18:00	大陸尋奇
19:00	中視新聞全球報導
20:00	周日八點黨
22:15	蝴蝶飛
23:45	卡通動畫: 死亡筆記本

[Simplified-character version]

时间	播出节目
00:00	中视夜线新闻
01:00	冰冰好料理
02:00	我猜,我猜,我猜猜猜
03:30	国光异校
04:00	世界非常奇妙
05:00	歌仔戏:江南四才子
06:00	院线抢先看: 曼哈顿奇缘
06:30	中视早安新闻
08:00	净觉法语
08:30	快乐生活王
09:00	全民大讲堂
10:00	超级星光大道
12:00	中视午间新闻
12:30	MIT台湾志
13:30	蝴蝶飞
15:00	院线抢先看:疯狂理发师
15:30	院线抢先看:把爱找回来
16:00	我猜,我猜,我猜猜猜
17:30	神奇宝贝钻石&珍珠
18:00	大陆寻奇
19:00	中视新闻全球报导
20:00	周日八点党
22:15	蝴蝶飞
23:45	卡通动画: 死亡笔记本

1. If students are interested in watching an animation program, what time should they watch?

2. If students are interested in watching a program about Taiwan, when should they watch?

3. If students are interested in watching a program about traveling in mainland China, when should they watch?

4. If students are interested in news programs, how many times each day does the station provide news broadcasting?

ANSWERS:

1. 11:45 PM   2. 12:30 PM   3. 6:00 PM   4. four times

The following is the table of contents of a phone book for a Chinese community. Refer to the table of contents to find the necessary pages.

[Traditional-character version]

生活廣場		分類總目錄	
社安局	2	法律	103
車管局	3	理財	140
郵政局	5	服務	202
圖書館	6	商店	270
博物館	8	交通	412
航空公司	11	住房	484
國際機廠	12	製造	536
領館簽證	13	醫藥	548
美國宗教	14	娛樂	672
主要節日	22	食飲	698
美國教育	28	文教	761
社會保障	32	貿易	813
投資科技	37	招商	822
買車駕照	38	緊急電話　911	
駕照試題	42	特別危急情況使用	
影院藝團	46	任何電話免費直撥	
購物指南	49	火警	
國際貨運	53	警察	
旅遊覽勝	55	救護車	

[Simplified-character version]

生活广场		分类总目录	
社安局	2	法律	103
车管局	3	理财	140
邮政局	5	服务	202
图书馆	6	商店	270
博物馆	8	交通	412
航空公司	11	住房	484
国际机厂	12	制造	536
领馆签证	13	医药	548
美国宗教	14	娱乐	672
主要节日	22	食饮	698
美国教育	28	文教	761
社会保障	32	贸易	813
投资科技	37	招商	822
买车驾照	38	紧急电话　911	
驾照试题	42	特别危急情况使用	
影院艺团	46	任何电话免费直拨	
购物指南	.49	火警	
国际货运	53	警察	
旅游览胜	55	救护车	

Find the page numbers for the following categories:

1. Theaters _____

2. Libraries _____

3. Museums _____

4. Medicines _____

5. Airline flight schedules _____

6. Restaurants _____

ANSWERS:

1. Page 46   2. Page 6   3. Page 8
4. Page 548   5. Page 11   6. Page 698

4 Understanding main ideas

The main idea of a passage can usually be found in the title or the topic sentence. The main idea may also be found elsewhere in the passage—for example, in the body or the conclusion. Read the following two passages carefully and try the questions.

[Traditional-character version]

旅美的中國大熊貓美香一直受到中美兩國人民的關注。當地時間7月9日，熊貓媽媽美香在位于華盛頓的美國國家動物園順利生下一隻小寶寶。動物園的專家和工作人員都非常高興。目前，熊貓媽媽美香正在精心地照顧這個可愛的熊貓寶寶。

[Simplified-character version]

旅美的中国大熊猫美香一直受到中美两国人民的关注。当地时间7月9日，熊猫妈妈美香在位于华盛顿的美国国家动物园顺利生下一只小宝宝。动物园的专家和工作人员都非常高兴。目前，熊猫妈妈美香正在精心地照顾这个可爱的熊猫宝宝。

1. Which of the following is the most appropriate title for this news story?

   (A) Chinese Pandas Living in the United States
   (B) People of the World Love Pandas Very Much
   (C) The Panda Is One of the Scarcest Animals
   (D) Panda Gives Birth at the National Zoo

The first sentence of this passage states that both Chinese and Americans have been paying a considerable amount of attention to a panda that is currently living in the United States. Throughout the passage, though, the focus is on "熊貓媽媽…華盛頓…國家動物園…生下…小寶寶"("熊猫妈妈…华盛顿…国家动物园…生下…小宝宝"), which illustrates the main idea. Therefore, the answer is **(D)**.

[Traditional-character version]

電影和電視對人們生活的影響很大。人們看了電影和電視上的廣告以後，很容易就去購買廣告中的商品。看了新聞或教育性的節目，人們可以學到很多新知識，知道許多新事物。看了娛樂節目，可能會讓人覺得世界上的人大都很有錢，而且長得都很漂亮，這就容易使一些人對自己的生活感到不滿意。兒童看了電影和電視以後，可能會去模仿片中的人物，還可能因此而學壞。

[Simplified-character version]

电影和电视对人们生活的影响很大。人们看了电影和电视上的广告以后，很容易就去购买广告中的商品。看了新闻或教育性的节目，人们可以学到很多新知识，知道许多新事物。看了娱乐节目，可能会让人觉得世界上的人大都很有钱，而且长得都很漂亮，这就容易使一些人对自己的生活感到不满意。儿童看了电影和电视以后，可能会去模仿片中的人物，还可能因此而学坏。

2. Which of the following titles most appropriately describes the main idea of this passage?

(A) How Do Movies and Television Educate People?
(B) Watching Movies or Television Induces People to Buy Certain Products
(C) The Influence of Television and Movies
(D) Children Try to Imitate Acts They See on TV or in Movies

In this passage, the leading sentence, "電影和電視對人們生活的影響很大" ("电影和电视对人们生活的影响很大"), expresses the main idea directly. The answer is **(C)**.

STRATEGY

5   Ignoring unimportant words

The reality is that, when reading a text, students may often come upon words or phrases that are unfamiliar to them. Before resorting to a dictionary, though, students should first try to determine whether the word or phrase is a critical piece of information or not. In order to show an emotion or to emphasize an opinion, writers may use synonyms to express the same or similar meaning as another word in the passage. Thus, understanding one of the synonyms allows students to guess the meaning of another word within the context. For example:

[Traditional-character version]
　　對昨天發生的事情，她一直感到惶恐和不安。

[Simplified-character version]
　　对昨天发生的事情，她一直感到惶恐和不安。

In this sentence, after the verb "感到," there are two adjectives with similar meanings. Knowing one of the two adjectives provides a reasonable clue for the other, and for understanding the entire sentence.

Sometimes writers may use several examples to express one opinion. These examples can make sentences long and complicated. Therefore, understanding just one example may be sufficient to pinpoint the writer's opinion.

[Traditional-character version]
　　最近幾年，市場上的化妝品越來越多，比如說，防曬霜、去斑霜、美白面膜什麼的，應有盡有。

[Simplified-character version]
　　最近几年，市场上的化妆品越来越多，比如说，防晒霜、去斑霜、美白面膜什么的，应有尽有。

In this sentence, the key word "比如說" ("比如说") introduces all types of cosmetics, "化妝品" ("化妆品"). As long as students know one of the items after "比如說" ("比如说"), it is likely that they will understand the sentence without necessarily recognizing all the items on the list.

STRATEGY

Guessing and analyzing

Guessing the meaning of unknown words from context is a very important strategy while reading. Analyzing the meaning of sentences is also critical.

Based on the context, students can guess the meaning of some unknown words in reading passages. When an unfamiliar word or phrase is encountered, students should not stop. On the contrary, continuing to read through the entire passage often helps to decipher the meaning of those unfamiliar words and phrases. Once students feel comfortable with the new words, they can look them up in the dictionary to check their guesses. This strategy helps students better understand the guessed words and increase their vocabulary.

Guessing from context is particularly helpful when students come across idioms and proverbs. For example:

[Traditional-character version]

麥克的中國朋友小張，工作特別忙，根本沒有時間管兒子。爲了孩子的教育問題，小張的妻子小夏常常跟他吵架。要不是小夏覺得單親家庭對孩子的影響不好的話，她早就跟小張離婚了。麥克一直以爲只有美國的家庭才有那麼多的問題，其實，哪個國家都一樣，真是家家有本難念的經。

[Simplified-character version]

麦克的中国朋友小张，工作特别忙，根本没有时间管儿子。为了孩子的教育问题，小张的妻子小夏常常跟他吵架。要不是小夏觉得单亲家庭对孩子的影响不好的话，她早就跟小张离婚了。麦克一直以为只有美国的家庭才有那么多的问题，其实，哪个国家都一样，真是家家有本难念的经。

Looking up the proverb "家家有本難念的經" ("家家有本难念的经") in the dictionary may result in the definition "Every family has skeletons in the closet." However, contextual clues provide detailed information regarding "家庭" and "孩子," which yield a more direct definition of this unfamiliar proverb: "Every family has its own problem."

Sometimes, by considering the grammatical structure of a sentence and normal word order rules in Chinese, students may be able to guess the meaning of the sentence. This guessing skill is extremely important for reading comprehension because it also requires students to abstract and summarize ideas and facts presented in the text. Read and analyze the following sentence:

[Traditional-character version]

中國運動員在本屆奧林匹克運動會上拿到了那麼多金牌和銀牌，作爲一個中國人，我感到多麼驕傲、多麼自豪啊！

[Simplified-character version]

中国运动员在本届奥林匹克运动会上拿到了那么多金牌和银牌，作为一个中国人，我感到多么骄傲、多么自豪啊！

In this sentence, students might not know words such as "奧林匹克," "金牌," "銀牌" ("银牌"), "驕傲" ("骄傲"), and "自豪," but they might be familiar with the nouns, like "運動員" ("运动员") and "運動會" ("运动会"), and the verbs, like "拿" and "感到." With the help of the word-order rule—subject + place word + adverbials + verb-complement + (attributive) object—students might guess that the sentence is related to a "sport meeting," and possibly even understand the sentence meaning: "The Chinese athletes won medals at a sport meeting and strived for honor, and I was very proud."

Using the Chinese word-order rules to make inferences is an invaluable skill, especially when it comes to guessing the meanings of place names, technical terms, and other words that even native speakers might not be familiar with.

Analyzing Chinese characters based on the relationships and connections between the radicals and components is also a valuable skill that can provide clues to decode unknown words. Read the following passage.

[Traditional-character version]

　　臺灣高山族人，性格豪放，熱情好客。他們喜歡在節日或者喜慶日子的時候請客和舉行歌舞表演。高山族節日中最有代表性的食物是用糯米做的各種各樣的糕點和糍粑。

[Simplified-character version]

　　台湾高山族人，性格豪放，热情好客。他们喜欢在节日或者喜庆日子的时候请客和举行歌舞表演。高山族节日中最有代表性的食物是用糯米做的各种各样的糕点和糍粑。

What does the word "豪放" mean? If students have learned the word "性格" and the grammatical structure of *topic + comment*, they can guess that "豪放" is a description of a certain personality, which is enough to understand the first sentence. Even though students may not recall words such as "糕" and "糍粑," if they remember that the radical "米" means *food*, they may guess that the unknown words are names for types of food. That may be enough information to understand the last sentence.

STRATEGY

7 Detailed reading

Before doing a detailed reading, students should quickly read through the passage using the reading strategies discussed above. Doing this will help them grasp the main idea of the text. When students read the text for the second or third time, the focus shifts to the secondary ideas and the details that support the main idea. Detailed reading is a slower and more careful reading process.

　　The AP exam sometimes requires students to find details concerning when, where, what, who, or how in a piece of writing. In searching for these data, students must be careful to look for the exact information specified in the question. Read the following passage carefully and answer the question.

[Traditional-character version]

今天的孩子無法理解他們父母創業的艱辛，而只知道去分享父母創造的成果。這些孩子，衣來伸手，飯來張口，而造成這一個後果的竟是辛辛苦苦了一輩子的父母。父母經歷過了生活的艱辛，就不想再讓自己的孩子去吃苦了，於是把孩子像小皇帝一樣高高地捧在手中，孩子要什麼，他們就給什麼。孩子變得越來越自私，一切以自己爲中心。這種情況引起了社會學家的高度重視。

[Simplified-character version]

今天的孩子无法理解他们父母创业的艰辛，而只知道去分享父母创造的成果。这些孩子，衣来伸手，饭来张口，而造成这一个后果的竟是辛辛苦苦了一辈子的父母。父母经历过了生活的艰辛，就不想再让自己的孩子去吃苦了，于是把孩子像小皇帝一样高高地捧在手中，孩子要什么，他们就给什么。孩子变得越来越自私，一切以自己为中心。这种情况引起了社会学家的高度重视。

1. Who should take responsibility for the children's attitude problems?

   (A) The kids should take responsibility for the problems.
   (B) The emperor should take responsibility for the problems.
   (C) The parents should take responsibility for the problems.
   (D) Society should take responsibility for the problems.

After reading the text, students will be able to answer the question if they have comprehended the writer's point of view. The writer tries to inform people of a common phenomenon within some Chinese families. He observes that children today do not work as hard as their parents but expect to enjoy the luxurious lives provided for them. He points out that the cause of this phenomenon is that the parents tend to spoil their children, so the answer is **(C)**.

STRATEGY

Inferring ideas

Inferring means drawing conclusions from the evidence or premises offered in a piece of writing. Often, the writer implies something and leaves it up to you to infer the rest. This involves combining and sorting out what is read. Read the following passage and answer the question.

[Traditional-character version]

尊敬的賓客：

歡迎您來南京友誼飯店。南京友誼飯店是一家歷史悠久的四星級飯店，建於1956年。本飯店地處市中心，環境優美，交通方便。無論外出旅遊，開商務會議，還是探親訪友，我們都熱情地歡迎你們的到來。

南京友誼飯店總經理

王必成

[Simplified-character version]
尊敬的宾客：

欢迎您来南京友谊饭店。南京友谊饭店是一家历史悠久的四星级饭店，建于1956年。本饭店地处市中心，环境优美，交通方便。无论您外出旅游，开商务会议，还是探亲访友，我们都热情地欢迎你们的到来。

南京友谊饭店总经理

王必成

1. What is the purpose of the manager's letter?

   (A) He asks the guests for their advice.
   (B) He is welcoming the guests.
   (C) He asks the guests to stay longer.
   (D) He asks the guests to pay attention to the good service.

Answer: **(B)**

While reading a text, students should remember to pay close attention to cultural perspectives, especially those of foreign cultures. Note that written texts may sometimes produce different interpretations by people with different cultures. Students who are highly aware of the differences between American and Chinese culture will find it easier to infer answers from a cross-cultural point of view.

STRATEGY

9 Determining the writer's attitude

Identifying the writer's point of view, or his purpose and attitude, can help students comprehend the underlying objective of the text.

Writers are not necessarily neutral when they write, particularly if they are trying to persuade readers to agree with their opinions. It is important for students to recognize what a writer's attitude is in relation to the ideas or information being presented. Students should practice this by reading the following passages and answering the questions below.

[Traditional-character version]

　　從前，有一隻青蛙住在一口井裏。有一天，一隻大鼈從海裏走來，路過井邊的時候，它看見了井底的青蛙。青蛙很熱情地對大鼈說：“大鼈兄弟，你看，我住在這兒多快樂呀！世界上再也找不到比這兒更好的地方了。你看吧，我高興了，就到井邊玩玩，玩累了呢就回來睡一會兒。在井裏，我是主人，我想做什麼就做什麼，多好啊！”

　　大鼈聽了青蛙的話，就走到井裏，仔細看了看，並不覺得井裏有什麼好玩的，于是大鼈說：“青蛙小弟，你見過大海嗎？鬧水災的時候，海水不會增加多少。鬧旱災的時候，海水也減少不了多少。難道你不覺得住在大海才是真正的自由和快樂嗎？”

　　青蛙聽了大鼈的話很不好意思。它終於明白了一個道理：原來世界很大，而自己知道的事情卻很少。

[Simplified-character version]

　　从前，有一只青蛙住在一口井里。有一天，一只大鳖从海里走来，路过井边的时候，它看见了井底的青蛙。青蛙很热情地对大鳖说："大鳖兄弟，你看，我住在这儿多快乐呀！世界上再也找不到比这儿更好的地方了。你看吧，我高兴了，就到井边玩玩，玩累了呢就回来睡一会儿。在井里，我是主人，我想做什么就做什么，多好啊！"

　　大鳖听了青蛙的话，就走到井里，仔细看了看，并不觉得井里有什么好玩的，于是大鳖说："青蛙小弟，你见过大海吗？闹水灾的时候，海水不会增加多少。闹旱灾的时候，海水也减少不了多少。难道你不觉得住在大海才是真正的自由和快乐吗？"

　　青蛙听了大鳖的话很不好意思。它终于明白了一个道理：原来世界很大，而自己知道的事情却很少。

1. What is the purpose of this story?

(A) The story tells how the frog bragged about his well to the turtle.
(B) The story teaches that people ought to have a broad and far-reaching vision of life.
(C) The story tells how the frog lives in the well and thinks of the world based only on what he can see.
(D) The story tells where the frog and the turtle came from.

This Chinese fable criticizes people with a very narrow outlook. Traditionally, a Chinese fable or an idiom imparts an important philosophical lesson by way of a story that is easy to understand. After reading the story, students should use their understanding of the writer's point of view to identify the underlying idea, **(B)**.

[Traditional-character version]

　　只要你走進大學的電腦房，無論是什麼時候，早上也好，晚上也罷，總有一批大學生泡在網上。雖然有一部分學生是在尋找學習資料，但大部分人卻是在網上自得其樂。我問他們長期下去是不是會影響學習，那些學生告訴我，其實他們也知道整天上網，確實耽誤了不少時間，但是他們已經習慣了上網。如果有一天沒上網，他們就會覺得全身上下不舒服。大學生是這樣，那麼中學生爲什麼也喜歡泡在網上呢？我看主要是好玩兒。面對網上各種各樣的內容，好奇心總是讓他們很想知道下面是什麼，到了下面，又想知道再下面的是什麼。從網上的內容看，大多是一些新聞、廣告什麼的，對學習真正有幫助的資料其實很少。

　　事實證明，學生長時間呆在網上難免影響學習，對他們的身體健康也沒有好處。不少大學生在這方面都不能自我控制，何況是中學生呢。所以，我要勸勸青年學生，最好以學習爲主要任務，不要過分沉於"網海"。

[Simplified-character version]

　　只要你走进大学的电脑房，无论是什么时候，早上也好，晚上也罢，总有一批大学生泡在网上。虽然有一部分学生是在寻找学习资料，但大部分人却是在网上自得其乐。我问他们长期下去是不是会影响学习，那些学生告诉我，其实他们也知道整天上网，确实耽误了不少时间，但是他们已经习惯了上网。如果有一天没上网，他们就会觉得全身上下不舒服。大学生是这样，那么中学生为什么也喜欢泡在网上呢？我看主要是好玩儿。面对网上各种各样的内容，好奇心总是让他们很想知道下面是什么，到了下面，又想知道再下面的是什么。从网上的内容看，大多是一些新闻、广告什么的，对学习真正有帮助的资料其实很少。

　　事实证明，学生长时间呆在网上难免影响学习，对他们的身体健康也没有好处。不少大学生在这方面都不能自我控制，何况是中学生呢。所以，我要劝劝青年学生，最好以学习为主要任务,不要过分沉于"网海"。

2. What is the purpose of this passage?

(A) To find out why students spend so much time on the Internet
(B) To find out how students can make the best use of the Internet
(C) To advise students not to waste time on the Internet
(D) To discuss the function of the Internet with students

3. How does the author feel about materials on the Internet for students?

(A) They are useless.
(B) They are not helpful.
(C) They are helpful.
(D) They are very helpful.

ANSWERS:
2. **(C)**　　　3. **(B)**

After skimming and scanning the text, students should try to guess the opinion of the writer, which can help them understand the topic of the text. The main idea can be found in the first sentence: regardless of the time of day, "有一批大學生泡在網上" ("有一批大学生泡在网上"). The writer expresses his opinion by using certain phrases and by modifying key words. In this case, the modifiers are adjectives and adverbs, such as "好玩兒" ("好玩儿"), "主要", "真正," and "其實" ("其实"). These words tell us if the writer is for or against certain behaviors. The writer may also use some words to indicate the appropriateness or the frequency of something, such as "大多," "很少," "總是" ("总是"), "整天," and "過分" ("过分"). Assessing the purposes of these words is helpful for understanding the writer's attitude. The purpose of the passage can be inferred from the final paragraph: Because surfing the Net directly "影響學習" ("影响学习") and "對身體健康也沒有好處" (对身体健康也没有好处"), students should therefore refrain from "沉於'網海'"("沉于'网海'").

　　As we complete this section, students should review these helpful tips:

1. Do look at the questions first before reading the corresponding passage. You may be able to find the answers as you read.

2. Do read the text from beginning to end without interruptions. This helps you capture the main idea of the text as a whole.

3. Do not waste too much time on deciphering new words or a single sentence.

READING SELECTIONS

To familiarize students with the typical format of the AP exam, this section offers a selection of reading materials followed by sample problems that allow students to practice what they have learned. The selected materials are either excerpts or adaptations from a variety of sources, from newspaper articles to contemporary literature. The materials cover a variety of topics and learning tasks, and may include advertisements, posters, letters, e-mails, signs, and so on. Students who regularly read a broad range of materials are at an advantage on the AP exam. All exercises in the Reading Selections section are presented in the form of multiple-choice questions.

AP students are strongly advised to familiarize themselves with the graphical user interface elements described in Chapter 1. The (**Help**) button is available during the Reading section if the student needs to review the function of these interface elements.

MULTIPLE-CHOICE SECTION: READING

Type: Reading Selections
Number of problems: 35–40
Weight: 25%
Duration: 60 minutes

Directions: You will read several selections in Chinese. For each selection, there will be one or more multiple-choice questions in English. Choose an answer that best matches the selection.

Important Notes:
1. You **may** move back and forth among problems.
2. There is no time limit to answer each problem. You have a total of 60 minutes to answer all the problems in the Reading section.

Knowledge & Skills:
1. Interpretive communication.
2. Comprehension; inference.
3. Application of basic cultural knowledge.

Strategies:
1. Remain focused throughout this section.
2. Be familiar with the functions of the buttons, and use them to your advantage.
3. Move quickly on the problems that you are confident with; "Mark" the ones you wish to return to later.
4. Note-taking is unnecessary since you can go back to the reading and the problems.

Fig. 3-1 Reading Selections Task Breakdown

Answer keys and explanations are included at the end of the chapter.

Now, use the reading strategies discussed in this chapter to complete the following sample problems.

Reading Comprehension Practice
ANSWER SHEET

1 Ⓐ Ⓑ Ⓒ Ⓓ
2 Ⓐ Ⓑ Ⓒ Ⓓ
3 Ⓐ Ⓑ Ⓒ Ⓓ
4 Ⓐ Ⓑ Ⓒ Ⓓ
5 Ⓐ Ⓑ Ⓒ Ⓓ
6 Ⓐ Ⓑ Ⓒ Ⓓ
7 Ⓐ Ⓑ Ⓒ Ⓓ
8 Ⓐ Ⓑ Ⓒ Ⓓ
9 Ⓐ Ⓑ Ⓒ Ⓓ
10 Ⓐ Ⓑ Ⓒ Ⓓ
11 Ⓐ Ⓑ Ⓒ Ⓓ
12 Ⓐ Ⓑ Ⓒ Ⓓ
13 Ⓐ Ⓑ Ⓒ Ⓓ
14 Ⓐ Ⓑ Ⓒ Ⓓ
15 Ⓐ Ⓑ Ⓒ Ⓓ
16 Ⓐ Ⓑ Ⓒ Ⓓ
17 Ⓐ Ⓑ Ⓒ Ⓓ
18 Ⓐ Ⓑ Ⓒ Ⓓ
19 Ⓐ Ⓑ Ⓒ Ⓓ
20 Ⓐ Ⓑ Ⓒ Ⓓ
21 Ⓐ Ⓑ Ⓒ Ⓓ
22 Ⓐ Ⓑ Ⓒ Ⓓ
23 Ⓐ Ⓑ Ⓒ Ⓓ
24 Ⓐ Ⓑ Ⓒ Ⓓ
25 Ⓐ Ⓑ Ⓒ Ⓓ

26 Ⓐ Ⓑ Ⓒ Ⓓ
27 Ⓐ Ⓑ Ⓒ Ⓓ
28 Ⓐ Ⓑ Ⓒ Ⓓ
29 Ⓐ Ⓑ Ⓒ Ⓓ
30 Ⓐ Ⓑ Ⓒ Ⓓ
31 Ⓐ Ⓑ Ⓒ Ⓓ
32 Ⓐ Ⓑ Ⓒ Ⓓ
33 Ⓐ Ⓑ Ⓒ Ⓓ
34 Ⓐ Ⓑ Ⓒ Ⓓ
35 Ⓐ Ⓑ Ⓒ Ⓓ
36 Ⓐ Ⓑ Ⓒ Ⓓ
37 Ⓐ Ⓑ Ⓒ Ⓓ
38 Ⓐ Ⓑ Ⓒ Ⓓ
39 Ⓐ Ⓑ Ⓒ Ⓓ
40 Ⓐ Ⓑ Ⓒ Ⓓ
41 Ⓐ Ⓑ Ⓒ Ⓓ
42 Ⓐ Ⓑ Ⓒ Ⓓ
43 Ⓐ Ⓑ Ⓒ Ⓓ
44 Ⓐ Ⓑ Ⓒ Ⓓ
45 Ⓐ Ⓑ Ⓒ Ⓓ
46 Ⓐ Ⓑ Ⓒ Ⓓ
47 Ⓐ Ⓑ Ⓒ Ⓓ
48 Ⓐ Ⓑ Ⓒ Ⓓ
49 Ⓐ Ⓑ Ⓒ Ⓓ
50 Ⓐ Ⓑ Ⓒ Ⓓ

51 Ⓐ Ⓑ Ⓒ Ⓓ
52 Ⓐ Ⓑ Ⓒ Ⓓ
53 Ⓐ Ⓑ Ⓒ Ⓓ
54 Ⓐ Ⓑ Ⓒ Ⓓ
55 Ⓐ Ⓑ Ⓒ Ⓓ
56 Ⓐ Ⓑ Ⓒ Ⓓ
57 Ⓐ Ⓑ Ⓒ Ⓓ
58 Ⓐ Ⓑ Ⓒ Ⓓ
59 Ⓐ Ⓑ Ⓒ Ⓓ
60 Ⓐ Ⓑ Ⓒ Ⓓ
61 Ⓐ Ⓑ Ⓒ Ⓓ
62 Ⓐ Ⓑ Ⓒ Ⓓ
63 Ⓐ Ⓑ Ⓒ Ⓓ
64 Ⓐ Ⓑ Ⓒ Ⓓ
65 Ⓐ Ⓑ Ⓒ Ⓓ
66 Ⓐ Ⓑ Ⓒ Ⓓ
67 Ⓐ Ⓑ Ⓒ Ⓓ
68 Ⓐ Ⓑ Ⓒ Ⓓ
69 Ⓐ Ⓑ Ⓒ Ⓓ
70 Ⓐ Ⓑ Ⓒ Ⓓ
71 Ⓐ Ⓑ Ⓒ Ⓓ
72 Ⓐ Ⓑ Ⓒ Ⓓ
73 Ⓐ Ⓑ Ⓒ Ⓓ
74 Ⓐ Ⓑ Ⓒ Ⓓ
75 Ⓐ Ⓑ Ⓒ Ⓓ

76 Ⓐ Ⓑ Ⓒ Ⓓ
77 Ⓐ Ⓑ Ⓒ Ⓓ
78 Ⓐ Ⓑ Ⓒ Ⓓ
79 Ⓐ Ⓑ Ⓒ Ⓓ
80 Ⓐ Ⓑ Ⓒ Ⓓ
81 Ⓐ Ⓑ Ⓒ Ⓓ
82 Ⓐ Ⓑ Ⓒ Ⓓ
83 Ⓐ Ⓑ Ⓒ Ⓓ
84 Ⓐ Ⓑ Ⓒ Ⓓ
85 Ⓐ Ⓑ Ⓒ Ⓓ
86 Ⓐ Ⓑ Ⓒ Ⓓ
87 Ⓐ Ⓑ Ⓒ Ⓓ
88 Ⓐ Ⓑ Ⓒ Ⓓ
89 Ⓐ Ⓑ Ⓒ Ⓓ
90 Ⓐ Ⓑ Ⓒ Ⓓ
91 Ⓐ Ⓑ Ⓒ Ⓓ
92 Ⓐ Ⓑ Ⓒ Ⓓ
93 Ⓐ Ⓑ Ⓒ Ⓓ
94 Ⓐ Ⓑ Ⓒ Ⓓ
95 Ⓐ Ⓑ Ⓒ Ⓓ
96 Ⓐ Ⓑ Ⓒ Ⓓ
97 Ⓐ Ⓑ Ⓒ Ⓓ
98 Ⓐ Ⓑ Ⓒ Ⓓ
99 Ⓐ Ⓑ Ⓒ Ⓓ
100 Ⓐ Ⓑ Ⓒ Ⓓ

Reading Comprehension Practice

Directions: Read the following passages in Chinese. Each of them is followed by a number of questions in English. For each question, choose the most appropriate answer, and record on the answer sheet.

Public sign for question 1.

[Traditional-character version]

請不要在室內大聲說話。

[Simplified-character version]

请不要在室内大声说话。

1. Where would you most likely see the sign?

(A) In a park
(B) In a library
(C) On a bus
(D) In a cafeteria

Poster for questions 2 and 3.

[Traditional-character version]
狗年到，新年好。新年新事少不了：
一家健康身體好，孩子勤奮學習好，
夫妻恩愛從不吵，一年到頭樣樣好！

[Simplified-character version]
狗年到，新年好。新年新事少不了：
一家健康身体好，孩子勤奋学习好，
夫妻恩爱从不吵，一年到头样样好！

2. What is the poster about?

(A) Family togetherness
(B) Good health
(C) New Year greetings
(D) Children's education

3. What does "一年到頭" ("一年到头") mean?

(A) End of the year
(B) Whole year
(C) Beginning of the year
(D) Every year

Note for questions 4 and 5.

[Traditional-character version]

雲雲：

　　媽媽接到醫院裏打來的電話，說我的一個病人病得很厲害，非馬上動手術不可。我得趕快去醫院。你放學回家後快一點做功課。另外，給爸爸學校的辦公室打個電話，讓他早點回來，帶你去飯館吃晚飯。

媽媽

[Simplified-character version]

云云：

　　妈妈接到医院里打来的电话，说我的一个病人病得很厉害，非马上动手术不可。我得赶快去医院。你放学回家后快一点做功课。另外，给爸爸学校的办公室打个电话，让他早点回来，带你去饭馆吃晚饭。

妈妈

4. What could be the father's occupation?

    (A) The father could be a doctor.
    (B) The father could be a patient.
    (C) The father could be a student.
    (D) The father could be a teacher.

5. Where could the mother be right now?

    (A) The mother could be in the hospital.
    (B) The mother could be at her home.
    (C) The mother could be in a school.
    (D) The mother could be in a restaurant.

Advertisement for question 6.

[Traditional-character version]

　　請有家教經驗的大學生輔導高中女孩數學及英文。能教中文更佳。如有興趣，請打電話：555-586-1234。

[Simplified-character version]

　　请有家教经验的大学生辅导高中女孩数学及英文。能教中文更佳。如有兴趣，请打电话：555-586-1234。

6. What should the tutor teach?

    (A) The tutor should teach Chinese and English.
    (B) The tutor should teach mathematics, Chinese, and English.
    (C) The tutor should teach Chinese, English, and mathematics.
    (D) The tutor should teach English and mathematics, and preferably Chinese as well.

Sign for questions 7 and 8.

[Traditional-character version]

請對號入座

[Simplified-character version]

请对号入座

7. Where would the sign most likely appear?

(A) On a bus
(B) In a library
(C) In a theatre
(D) At a high school football game

8. What is the purpose of the sign?

(A) To inform people that they cannot sit wherever they want
(B) To inform people that there are no more available seats
(C) To inform people where not to sit
(D) To inform people of the business hours

Passage for questions 9 through 11.

[Traditional-character version]
張大慶先生/女士：

歡迎你應聘本店 服務員 職位。你的專業知識和工作經驗都給我們留下了深刻的印象。爲了加強進一步的瞭解，現在邀請你於 3 月 15 日 9 時 30 分前來本店參加：

1. 面談 (x)　　　　2. 專業考試 ( )

如果上邊的時間不合適，請你事先與本店人事部陳先生/女士聯繫，電話：6555.6555。謝謝合作！

人事部
2013年3月10日

[Simplified-character version]
张大庆先生/女士：

欢迎你应聘本店 服务员 职位。你的专业知识和工作经验都给我们留下了深刻的印象。为了加强进一步的了解，现在邀请你于 3 月 15 日 9 时 30 分前来本店参加：

1. 面谈 (x)　　　　2. 专业考试 ( )

如果上边的时间不合适，请你事先与本店人事部陈先生/女士联系，电话：6555.6555。谢谢合作！

人事部
2013年3月10日

9. What kind of a document is this?

(A) This is a notification for a test.
(B) This is an ad for a store.
(C) This is a notification for a scheduled interview.
(D) This is a notification to tell someone that he is hired.

10. The store is most impressed by the applicant's _____.

(A) test scores
(B) professional knowledge
(C) degrees
(D) interview results

11. Which statement is correct?

(A) The interview is scheduled for March 15, 10:00 PM.
(B) The applicant is seeking a position in the Human Resources department.
(C) The applicant has past work experience.
(D) The applicant must contact Ms. Chen before March 15.

Note for questions 12 through 13.

[Traditional-character version]

今天早上，我媽媽得了急病，被鄰居送到了醫院。由於我爸爸出差不在家，我得到醫院照顧媽媽。今天我不能上中文課了，很抱歉。

您的學生：王小平
2013年4月22日

[Simplified-character version]

今天早上，我妈妈得了急病，被邻居送到了医院。由于我爸爸出差不在家，我得到医院照顾妈妈。今天我不能上中文课了，很抱歉。

您的学生：王小平
2013年4月22日

12. Why did Wang Xiaoping write this note?

(A) To explain why she is good friends with her neighbor
(B) To explain why she can't attend class today
(C) To notify that she is ill and in the hospital
(D) To notify that her father is out of town

13. What is Wang Xiaoping's occupation?

(A) Wang Xiaoping is a doctor.
(B) Wang Xiaoping is a nurse.
(C) Wang Xiaoping is a teacher.
(D) Wang Xiaoping is a student.

Passage for questions 14 and 15.

[Traditional-character version]

　　本博物館全年對外開放，星期一閉館，寒暑假、法定節假日將有調整，敬請關注網站公告。如有變動，以本館官方發佈的最新資訊爲准。

　　開放時間：星期二至星期天　9:00—17:00（16:00停止入館）。

　　參觀內容：爬行動物廳、恐龍公園、鳥類廳等。

[Simplified-character version]

　　本博物館全年对外开放，星期一闭馆，寒暑假、法定节假日将有调整，敬请关注网站公告。如有变动，以本馆官方发布的最新信息为准。

　　开放时间：星期二至星期天　9:00—17:00（16:00停止入馆）。

　　参观内容：爬行动物厅、恐龙公园、鸟类厅等。

14. What is the brochure about?

(A) A planetarium
(B) An art museum
(C) A natural history museum
(D) An air and space museum

15. Which statement is correct?

(A) The museum is open seven days a week.
(B) Last entry is at 5:00 PM before closing.
(C) Open hours will change during holidays.
(D) The museum website updates every day.

Passage for questions 16 through 18.

[Traditional-character version]

一、用本校學生證進入本室。

二、室內書刊只能在本室內閱讀。除了筆及筆記本外，其他物品不能帶入室內。

三、愛護室內資料。

四、保持室內安靜與清潔。

五、關門前15分鐘停止借閱。

[Simplified-character version]

一、用本校学生证进入本室。

二、室内书刊只能在本室内阅读。除了笔及笔记本外，其他物品不能带入室内。

三、爱护室内资料。

四、保持室内安静与清洁。

五、关门前15分钟停止借阅。

16. These are the policies likely to be seen at a _____.

(A) restaurant
(B) bookstore
(C) reading room
(D) classroom

17. What item do you need to enter the room?

    (A) Notebook
    (B) Pen
    (C) Student I.D.
    (D) Newspaper/magazine

18. Which of the following is correct?

    (A) Students from other schools can enter the reading room.
    (B) Students are allowed to take notes.
    (C) The reading material in the room can be taken out of the room.
    (D) Noise is allowed as long as it is within the room.

E-mail for questions 19 and 20.

[Traditional-character version]
發件人：馬克
郵件主題：找語伴
發件日期：2012年12月10日

　　本人正在選修中文課程，想找一位母語是中文的朋友作爲語言交換伴侶，互相提高中文和英語水平。男女都可以，彼此不收費。有興趣的朋友請打電話：555-0118， 或發電子信：make@email.com

[Simplified-character version]
发件人：马克
邮件主题：找语伴
发件日期：2012年12月10日

　　本人正在选修中文课程，想找一位母语是中文的朋友作为语言交换伴侣，互相提高中文和英语水平。男女都可以，彼此不收费。有兴趣的朋友请打电话：555-0118， 或发电子信：make@email.com

19. What is this e-mail mainly about?

    (A) Finding a Chinese tutor
    (B) Finding a language partner
    (C) Finding a boyfriend
    (D) Finding a girlfriend

20. Which statement below is correct about the sender?

    (A) He is studying Chinese and English.
    (B) He is looking for someone who speaks Chinese.
    (C) He will pay.
    (D) He does not care if the respondent is a man or a woman.

Passage for questions 21 through 24.

[Traditional-character version]
主要材料：糖，味精，鹽，麵粉
使用方法：1. 把300克豬肉切成絲。
　　　　　2. 鍋裏放油，加熱到370 ºF 左右，把肉絲炒熟。
　　　　　3. 把本品放到鍋裏，繼續炒一分鐘。

保存：24個月
注意：本品適合放在乾燥、陰涼的地方

[Simplified-character version]
主要材料：糖，味精，盐，面粉
使用方法：1. 把300克猪肉切成丝。
　　　　　2. 锅里放油，加热到370 ºF 左右，把肉丝炒熟。
　　　　　3. 把本品放到锅里，继续炒一分钟。

保存：24个月
注意：本品适合放在干燥、阴凉的地方

21. Where would this passage most likely appear?

  (A) In front of a food store
  (B) In a butcher shop
  (C) On the packaging of a food item
  (D) In a newspaper

22. What is the purpose of the passage?

  (A) To advertise a new food
  (B) To remind people of the expiration date
  (C) To tell how to make a dish
  (D) To tell people how to use a certain product

23. Which item is not mentioned in the passage?

  (A) Salt
  (B) Vinegar
  (C) Flour
  (D) MSG

24. Which statement is correct?

  (A) The packaged product lasts two years.
  (B) The packaged product should be stored in direct sunlight.
  (C) Water cannot be added to make this dish.
  (D) The temperature when cooking with this packaged product should be over 370 degrees.

Degree certificate for questions 25 and 26.

[Traditional-character version]

學生王小平，江蘇南京市人，性別女，　生於一九七四年五月十八日。一九九二年九月至一九九六年六月在本校外語系法國語言文學專業學習，完成四年制本科教學計劃規定的學習任務，成績合格，准予畢業。經審核符合《中華人民共和國學位條例》規定，授予法國文學學士學位。

雲州語言文化大學校長　張偉
一九九六年七月八日

[Simplified-character version]

学生王小平，江苏南京市人，性别女，生于一九七四年五月十八日。一九九二年九月至一九九六年六月在本校外语系法国语言文学专业学习，完成四年制本科教学计划规定的学习任务，成绩合格，准予毕业。经审核符合《中华人民共和国学位条例》规定，授予法国文学学士学位。

云州语言文化大学校长　张伟
一九九六年七月八日

25. When did the degree recipient start going to college?

    (A) May 1974
    (B) June 1996
    (C) September 1992
    (D) July 1996

26. What is the degree recipient's major?

    (A) Foreign language
    (B) French language and literature
    (C) Chinese language and literature
    (D) Language and culture

Article for questions 27 through 29.

[Traditional-character version]

冰箱是現代人家庭中不可缺少的生活用品，差不多每家都有冰箱。有的人爲了方便，有的人爲了好看，也有的人因爲家裏房間太少、太小，就把冰箱放到了臥室。冰箱放在房間裏會產生三種污染：一是聲音污染；二是電子污染；三是化學污染。專家提醒人們：爲了家人的身體健康，最好不要把冰箱放在臥室裏。

[Simplified-character version]

冰箱是现代人家庭中不可缺少的生活用品，差不多每家都有冰箱。有的人为了方便，有的人为了好看，也有的人因为家里房间太少、太小，就把冰箱放到了卧室。冰箱放在房间里会产生三种污染：一是声音污染；二是电子污染；三是化学污染。专家提醒人们：为了家人的身体健康，最好不要把冰箱放在卧室里。

27. What issue is presented in the text?

    (A) Problems refrigerators can cause
    (B) How refrigerators affect people's daily lives
    (C) The convenience refrigerators have brought to people
    (D) How refrigerators affect people's health

28. What kinds of pollution could be caused by placing the refrigerator in the bedroom?

    (A) Electric and air
    (B) Chemical and air
    (C) Chemical and noise
    (D) Noise and water

29. Why do experts recommend that people take refrigerators out of their bedrooms?

    (A) Bedrooms are too small.
    (B) It is for convenience.
    (C) It makes bedrooms look bad.
    (D) It is for health reasons.

Letter for questions 30 through 32.

[Traditional-character version]

爺爺：

　　你好！我來美國快十年了，一直沒有機會回國看望您老人家。一個月後，我要到上海出差，想順便到蘇州看看您和老家的親朋好友。中國最近十幾年的變化太大了，我想趁這次出差的機會帶妻子和兩個孩子回去一趟，看看中國的變化，游覽一些名勝古蹟。我還沒有買機票，等買好了機票，我再寫信告訴您回去的具體時間。您需要我在這邊買什麼，一定不要客氣，請寫信告訴我。

　　祝您
健康長壽！

孫子：小文
2013年4月10日

[Simplified-character version]

爷爷：

　　你好！我来美国快十年了，一直没有机会回国看望您老人家。一个月后，我要到上海出差，想顺便到苏州看看您和老家的亲朋好友。中国最近十几年的变化太大了，我想趁这次出差的机会带妻子和两个孩子回去一趟，看看中国的变化，游览一些名胜古迹。我还没有买机票，等买好了机票，我再写信告诉您回去的具体时间。您需要我在这边买什么，一定不要客气，请写信告诉我。

　　祝您
健康长寿！

孙子：小文
2013年4月10日

30. How long has Xiao Wen been in the United States?

    (A) Somewhere between 10 and 20 years
    (B) Several decades
    (C) Less than 10 years
    (D) 2 months

31. What is Xiao Wen's main reason for going back to China?

    (A) Visit grandfather
    (B) Business travel
    (C) Visit friends
    (D) Tour

32. Where does Xiao Wen live currently?

    (A) United States
    (B) China
    (C) Suzhou
    (D) Shanghai

Advertisement for questions 33 through 35.

[Traditional-character version]

　　有公寓房一套，位於東城區，交通方便，環境安全、安靜。兩室一廳，一個浴室。不帶家具，有地毯、洗衣機。月租$1800，不包水電。房客不得吸煙與養寵物，夫妻無小孩或女生優先考慮。有興趣者請打電話：555-627-3794。

[Simplified-character version]

　　有公寓房一套，位于东城区，交通方便，环境安全、安静。两室一厅，一个浴室。不带家具，有地毯、洗衣机。月租$1800，不包水电。房客不得吸烟与养宠物，夫妻无小孩或女生优先考虑。有兴趣者请打电话：555-627-3794。

33. How many bedrooms are there in this apartment?

    (A) One
    (B) Two
    (C) Three
    (D) Four

34. What kind of people definitely cannot rent the apartment?

    (A) Couples with kids
    (B) Female students
    (C) Smokers
    (D) Couples without kids

35. Which of the following descriptions of the apartment's amenities is correct?

   (A) Comes with furniture, but no water or electricity
   (B) No furniture or carpet
   (C) Comes with a washing machine
   (D) Safe, but transportation is inconvenient

Sign for questions 36 through 37.

[Traditional-character version]
   貴重物品，隨身攜帶。

[Simplified-character version]
   贵重物品，随身携带。

36. Where would the sign most likely appear?

   (A) In a furniture store
   (B) In a housewares store
   (C) At a railway station
   (D) In a jewelry shop

37. What is the purpose of the sign?

   (A) To advertise a valuable item
   (B) To remind people to be mindful of their valuables
   (C) To advertise a new piece of furniture
   (D) To encourage people to buy jewelry

News article for questions 38 through 42.

[Traditional-character version]
   上海青山大學龍舟隊參加了“第17屆中國雲海清湖國際龍舟比賽”。這次比賽在江蘇省雲海市清湖舉行。參加這次比賽的16個隊的226名運動員分別來自國內外、港澳台不同地區，其中包括獲得上一屆龍舟比賽冠軍的香港明珠龍舟隊，歷史悠久的台北同仁大學龍舟隊和我們上海青山大學龍舟隊等。今年的龍舟賽除了原來有的500米、1000米和5000米比賽以外，還增加了800米的比賽。另外，比賽期間還增加了一項表現南方風景民俗的水上交藝表演。本次比賽，各龍舟隊，技術水平高，競爭激烈。最後，青山大學龍舟隊和明珠隊分別獲得第一、二名。

[Simplified-character version]
   上海青山大学龙舟队参加了“第17届中国云海清湖国际龙舟比赛”。这次比赛在江苏省云海市清湖举行。参加这次比赛的16个队的226名运动员分别来自国内外、港澳台不同地区，其中包括获得上一届龙舟比赛冠军的香港明珠龙舟队，历史悠久的台北同仁大学龙舟队和我们上海青山大学龙舟队等。今年的龙舟赛除了原来有的500米、1000米和5000米比赛以外，还增加了800米的比赛。另外，比赛期间还增加了一项表现南方风景民俗的水上文艺表演。本次比赛，各龙舟队，技术水平高，竞争激烈。最后，青山大学龙舟队和明珠队分别获得第一、二名。

38. Where did this competition take place?

    (A) Yunhai
    (B) Hong Kong
    (C) Taiwan
    (D) Shanghai

39. Which event did not take place at the previous competition?

    (A) 500 meters
    (B) 800 meters
    (C) 1,000 meters
    (D) 5,000 meters

40. What kind of entertainment will be provided?

    (A) Popular Hong Kong musical
    (B) Traditional South Chinese concert
    (C) Taiwan folk performance
    (D) Shanghai ballet

41. Where was the 16th champion team from?

    (A) Shanghai
    (B) Hong Kong
    (C) Taiwan
    (D) Not mentioned

42. Which statement is correct?

    (A) There are 226 teams competing.
    (B) The Shanghai Qingshan dragon boating team has a long history.
    (C) Most competitors have very high skill.
    (D) The Hong Kong Mingzhu team won this competition.

Passage for questions 43 and 44.

[Traditional-character version]

　　一個健康的人每天至少要喝七到八杯水，運動量大或者天氣熱的時候還應該喝得更多。早晨是補充身體水分的關鍵時刻，所以要養成早晨喝水的好習慣。早晨喝水，非空腹喝不可，而且要慢慢地喝。喝水喝得太快，對身體健康沒有好處。

[Simplified-character version]

　　一个健康的人每天至少要喝七到八杯水，运动量大或者天气热的时候还应该喝得更多。早晨是补充身体水分的关键时刻，所以要养成早晨喝水的好习惯。早晨喝水，非空腹喝不可，而且要慢慢地喝。喝水喝得太快，对身体健康没有好处。

43. What is the main topic of the text?

   (A) How much water one should drink
   (B) How to drink water correctly
   (C) The best time to drink water
   (D) How water affects health

44. What does "早晨喝水，非空腹喝不可" mean?

   (A) Do not drink water when your stomach is empty.
   (B) If people drink water in the morning, it must be on an empty stomach.
   (C) People should drink water on an empty stomach.
   (D) People drink water on a very empty stomach.

Passage for questions 45 through 47.

[Traditional-character version]
親愛的筆友，

你好！我的名字是Mary，中文名字叫瑪麗。我是你們在美國的姐妹學校的學生，現住在美國的第二大城市洛杉磯。中文老師告訴我你住在中國最大的城市之一南京。我喜歡吃中國飯、寫中國字、聽中國音樂，也特別喜歡看中國電影。

我的中文老師告訴我們，最近幾十年中國的發展很快。她希望我們去看看。我打算今年暑假去中國旅行，順便去看看生活在北京的外公和外婆。我希望能早一點看看北京的故宮，遊遊上海的豫園，逛逛南京的夫子廟和西安的兵馬俑，也希望能早日見到你。

請你儘快回信。

祝

學習進步！

瑪麗
四月十五日

[Simplified-character version]
亲爱的笔友，

你好！我的名字是Mary，中文名字叫玛丽。我是你们在美国的姐妹学校的学生，现住在美国的第二大城市洛杉矶。中文老师告诉我你住在中国最大的城市之一南京。我喜欢吃中国饭、写中国字、听中国音乐，也特别喜欢看中国电影。

我的中文老师告诉我们，最近几十年中国的发展很快。她希望我们去看看。我打算今年暑假去中国旅行，顺便去看看生活在北京的外公和外婆。我希望能早一点看看北京的故宫，游游上海的豫园，逛逛南京的夫子庙和西安的兵马俑，也希望能早日见到你。

请你尽快回信。

祝

学习进步！

玛丽
四月十五日

45. What do the writer and the recipient of the letter have in common?

    (A) Both of them have sisters.
    (B) They both live in big cities.
    (C) They are the same age.
    (D) They will both graduate high school soon.

46. What will be the writer's Chinese travel activity?

    (A) Listening to Chinese music
    (B) Eating Chinese food
    (C) Visiting the Forbidden City
    (D) Writing Chinese characters

47. What Chinese historical spot is the writer most looking forward to visiting?

    (A) The Yuyuan Garden in Xi'an
    (B) The Terracotta Army in Beijing
    (C) The Forbidden City in Shanghai
    (D) The Confucius Temple in Nanjing

Story for questions 48 through 51.

[Traditional-character version]

　　小張是北京網球隊的運動員。幾天前，小張到上海去參加比賽，比賽後他給父母寫了一封信。信中說："我打敗了一個上海的運動員，得了第一名。"父母看完信後非常高興，他媽媽還自豪地對他爸爸說："老張，兒子比你強。你當籃球運動員的時候得過第一名嗎？"老張不好意思地說："別說第一了，能取得前三名的成績就不錯了。"

　　小張今天要回家了。父母一早就忙著做好吃的東西，爲的是歡迎兒子。沒有想到，兒子一到家就難過地對父母說："不好意思，我打敗了。"而老張很奇怪，馬上叫妻子把信拿來，又仔細地看了一遍，對兒子說："你的信上說你得了第一名啊！"小張接過信一看，臉紅了。他說："對不起。我把標點符號的位置寫錯了。我是想說：我打敗了，一個上海的運動員得了第一名。"

[Simplified-character version]

　　小张是北京网球队的运动员。几天前，小张到上海去参加比赛，比赛后他给父母写了一封信。信中说："我打败了一个上海的运动员，得了第一名。"父母看完信后非常高兴，他妈妈还自豪地对他爸爸说："老张，儿子比你强。你当篮球运动员的时候得过第一名吗？"老张不好意思地说："别说第一了，能取得前三名的成绩就不错了。"

　　小张今天要回家了。父母一早就忙着做好吃的东西，为的是欢迎儿子。没有想到，儿子一到家就难过地对父母说："不好意思，我打败了。"老张很奇怪，马上叫妻子把信拿来，又仔细地看了一遍，对儿子说："你的信上说你得了第一名啊！"小张接过信一看，脸红了。他说："对不起。我把标点符号的位置写错了。我是想说：我打败了，一个上海的运动员得了第一名。"

48. Xiao Zhang is an athlete on which team?

   (A) Beijing basketball team
   (B) Shanghai basketball team
   (C) Beijing tennis team
   (D) Shanghai tennis team

49. Why is the mom proud?

   (A) Her husband placed first.
   (B) Her son always places first.
   (C) Her husband and son both have placed first.
   (D) Her son outperformed her husband.

50. Which of the following statements regarding Lao Zhang is correct?

   (A) He has placed first.
   (B) He has placed in the top three.
   (C) He has never gotten in the top three.
   (D) He has placed third.

51. Why did the parents think their son placed first?

   (A) Xiao Zhang lied in a letter he wrote.
   (B) Lao Zhang read the letter wrong.
   (C) Xiao Zhang put a comma in the wrong place in the letter.
   (D) Xiao Zhang was winning at first, but lost at the end.

Passage for questions 52 through 55.

[Traditional-character version]

到過中國的外國人常說：不到長城非好漢，不吃北京烤鴨真遺憾。

北京烤鴨是明朝的宮廷食品，到今天已經有三百多年的歷史了。明朝的時候，宮廷的廚師把生長在南京湖中的鴨子放到火上，做成烤鴨。烤熟以後的鴨子，又香又脆，雖然很肥，但是一點兒也不膩。後來，明朝的首都從南京搬到北京，烤鴨的技術也從南京帶到了北京。廚師用北京填鴨做的烤鴨，皮兒很薄，肉非常嫩，更加好吃。北京烤鴨很快變成北方風味中的一道名菜。

[Simplified-character version]

到过中国的外国人常说：不到长城非好汉，不吃北京烤鸭真遗憾。

北京烤鸭是明朝的宫廷食品，到今天已经有三百多年的历史了。明朝的时候，宫廷的厨师把生长在南京湖中的鸭子放到火上，做成烤鸭。烤熟以后的鸭子，又香又脆，虽然很肥，但是一点儿也不腻。后来，明朝的首都从南京搬到北京，烤鸭的技术也从南京带到了北京。厨师用北京填鸭做的烤鸭，皮儿很薄，肉非常嫩，更加好吃。北京烤鸭很快变成北方风味中的一道名菜。

52. What can be inferred from the first sentence?

   (A) China has the Great Wall and Beijing duck.
   (B) The Great Wall and Beijing duck are very famous.
   (C) It's regretful that I didn't eat Beijing duck.
   (D) Good men must go to the Great Wall.

53. Regarding the capital of China, which statement is correct?

    (A) The capital of the Ming Dynasty is Nanjing, and the next dynasty's capital is Beijing.
    (B) The Ming Dynasty had two capitals, first in Nanjing and then in Beijing.
    (C) The Ming Dynasty had two capitals, Nanjing and Beijing.
    (D) The Ming Dynasty had two capitals, first in Beijing and then in Nanjing.

54. Which description of Beijing duck is false?

    (A) Nice-smelling and crisp
    (B) Thin skin and tender meat
    (C) Thin skin and lean meat
    (D) A lot of fat but not greasy

55. What is the main topic of this passage?

    (A) The smell of Beijing duck
    (B) People who eat Beijing duck
    (C) The history behind Beijing duck and its characteristics
    (D) Famous places that serve Beijing duck

Story for questions 56 through 60.

[Traditional-character version]

　　“狗不理”包子是天津的傳統小吃，在全國也非常有名。

　　很早以前，一個叫高小貴的小男孩兒，因爲性格太強，父母就叫他“狗不理”。小貴十四歲的時候離開了家鄉，到天津的一家包子店打工。那家包子店在天津很有名，已經有幾十年的歷史了。過了不久，包子店的老闆看小貴人雖然不大，但是聰明好學，就決定教他做包子，于是小貴就跟著師傅學起了做包子。小貴做事非常認真，學得很快，沒過多長時間就都學會了。十六、七歲的時候，高小貴用掙來的錢開了一家自己的包子店。小貴做的包子，比師傅的更受歡迎。因爲高小貴的外號叫“狗不理”，大家就把他做的包子叫“狗不理”包子。現在，天津的“狗不理”包子已經有一百多年的歷史了。

　　“狗不理”包子店越開越大，生意也越做越好。天津有一句俗語說：到天津，不嘗一嘗“狗不理”包子，就等於沒有來過天津。

[Simplified-character version]

　　“狗不理”包子是天津的传统小吃，在全国也非常有名。

　　很早以前，一个叫高小贵的小男孩儿，因为性格太强，父母就叫他“狗不理”。小贵十四岁的时候离开了家乡，到天津的一家包子店打工。那家包子店在天津很有名，已经有几十年的历史了。过了不久，包子店的老板看小贵人虽然不大，但是聪明好学，就决定教他做包子，于是小贵就跟着师傅学起了做包子。小贵做事非常认真，学得很快，没过多长时间就都学会了。十六、七岁的时候，高小贵用挣来的钱开了一家自己的包子店。小贵做的包子，比师傅的更受欢迎。因为高小贵的外号叫“狗不理”，大家就把他做的包子叫“狗不理”包子。现在，天津的“狗不理”包子已经有一百多年的历史了。

　　"狗不理"包子店越开越大，生意也越做越好。天津有一句俗语说：到天津，不尝一尝"狗不理"包子，就等于没有来过天津。

56. What is this article mainly about?

    (A) The history behind a food
    (B) A proverb regarding a food
    (C) The biography of a person
    (D) The development of a food

57. How old is this particular type of baozi?

    (A) 14 years
    (B) About 16 years
    (C) 90 years
    (D) Over 100 years

58. Who named the food "goubuli?"

    (A) The boss
    (B) The boy himself
    (C) Everyone
    (D) Parents

59. Which statement is correct?

    (A) His boss's restaurant was not famous.
    (B) The boss was very patient.
    (C) The boy opened a restaurant with his former boss.
    (D) The boy learned how to make baozi very quickly.

60. What does the saying at the end of the story mean?

    (A) One cannot eat baozi in Tianjin.
    (B) There are no baozi in Tianjin.
    (C) When in Tianjin, one must eat baozi.
    (D) Everyone in Tianjin enjoys baozi.

Passage for questions 61 through 64.

[Traditional-character version]

　　故宮地處北京市中心，又叫紫禁城，是目前世界上最大的宮殿建築。

　　故宮從東到西750米，由南到北960米。故宮的面積72萬平方米，是由9000多個房間組成的。宮殿的周圍是近10米高、3公里長的城牆，牆外是寬52米、深6米的河。城牆的四面都有門，其中南邊的叫午門，是故宮的正門；北邊的門是神武門；東邊的門叫東華門；還有西邊的西華門。故宮城牆的四個角上各有一座小樓，叫角樓。

　　故宮主要分爲兩大部分：南邊的區域是皇帝工作的地方，叫外朝；北邊的區域是皇帝及家人生活的地方，叫內廷。

[Simplified-character version]

故宫地处北京市中心，又叫紫禁城，是目前世界上最大的宫殿建筑。

故宫从东到西750米，由南到北960米。故宫的面积72万平方米，是由9000多个房间组成的。宫殿的周围是近10米高、3公里长的城墙，墙外是宽52米、深6米的河。城墙的四面都有门，其中南边的叫午门，是故宫的正门；北边的门是神武门；东边的门叫东华门；还有西边的西华门。故宫城墙的四个角上各有一座小楼，叫角楼。

故宫主要分为两大部分：南边的区域是皇帝工作的地方，叫外朝；北边的区域是皇帝及家人生活的地方，叫内廷。

61. How many meters is the Imperial Palace from the north to the south?

    (A) 9,000
    (B) 960
    (C) 750
    (D) 720,000

62. The main gate of the Imperial Palace faces _____.

    (A) east
    (B) south
    (C) west
    (D) north

63. How long is the wall that surrounds the Imperial Palace?

    (A) 52 meters
    (B) 3 kilometers
    (C) 10 meters
    (D) 6 meters

64. What function does the southern complex of the Imperial Palace serve?

    (A) The Emperor and family members' workplace
    (B) The Emperor and family members' living area
    (C) The Emperor's family members' living area
    (D) The Emperor's workplace

Advertisement for questions 65 through 68.

[Traditional-character version]

順美客運公司每日提供往返洛杉磯與舊金山之間的客車。請預先訂票，可上車後買票。未訂票者坐後排。

票價：單程 $60/$45 (小孩)；往返 $110/$80 (小孩)。當天生日者、兩歲以下(含兩歲) 幼兒免費。

服務：提供午餐；400萬保險；客車後部有廁所

電話： (555)555-3062； (555)555-0190 (中文)

主頁：www.shunmeikeyun.com

[Simplified-character version]

順美客运公司每日提供往返洛杉矶与旧金山之间的客车。请预先订票，可上车后买票。未订票者坐后排。

票价：单程 $60/$45 (小孩)；往返 $110/$80 (小孩)。当天生日者、两岁以下(含两岁) 幼儿免费。

服务：提供午餐；400万保险；客车后部有厕所

电话：(555)555-3062; (555) 555-0190 (中文)

主页：www.shunmeikeyun.com

65. What kind of business does this advertise?

   (A) Restaurant
   (B) Long-distance bus
   (C) Insurance company
   (D) Public restroom

66. Which statement is correct?

   (A) People must buy tickets before boarding the bus.
   (B) Lunch is free for people with birthdays on that day.
   (C) Passengers without reservations sit at the front of the bus.
   (D) A bathroom is available on the bus.

67. Who may ride the bus for free?

   (A) 2-year-olds
   (B) Kids about 2 years old
   (C) Kids older than 2 years old
   (D) 2-year-olds and under

68. How much does a round-trip ticket cost for an adult?

   (A) $45
   (B) $60
   (C) $80
   (D) $110

Passage for questions 69 and 70.

[Traditional-character version]

李成龍，男，24歲，未婚，本屆大學畢業。電腦、英文寫作及口語水平高。希望在電腦公司工作，月薪不低於3000元。

[Simplified-character version]

李成龙，男，24岁，未婚，本届大学毕业。电脑、英文写作及口语水平高。希望在电脑公司工作，月薪不低于3000元。

69. What kind of advertisement is this?

    (A) A help-wanted ad
    (B) A dating ad
    (C) A job-seeker ad
    (D) A public notice

70. Which statement is not correct?

    (A) The man is graduating this year.
    (B) He has good computer skills.
    (C) He is proficient at writing both in English and Chinese.
    (D) He is looking for a job that pays more than 3,000 yuan a month.

News article for questions 71 through 73.

[Traditional-character version]

　　根據本市氣象台的報告，　最近幾天本市平均氣溫在10˚C以上，比常年氣溫高4˚C左右，最高溫度已達12˚C。這表明，本市已經提前十天進入春天。據氣象專家介紹，平均氣溫超過10˚C就是進入春天的開始。專家建議，這樣好的天氣適合人們到室外活動。由於這個時候的空氣很乾燥，專家特別提醒人們注意多喝水。

[Simplified-character version]

　　根据本市气象台的报告，最近几天本市平均气温在10°C以上，比常年气温高4°C左右，最高温度已达12°C。这表明，本市已经提前十天进入春天。据气象专家介绍，平均气温超过10°C就是进入春天的开始。专家建议，这样好的天气适合人们到室外活动。由于这个时候的空气很干燥，专家特别提醒人们注意多喝水。

71. What was the highest temperature for the last few days in the city?

    (A) 4°C
    (B) 10°C
    (C) Above 10°C
    (D) 12°C

72. What is the average temperature to indicate the arrival of spring?

    (A) 10°C
    (B) Above 10°C
    (C) 12°C
    (D) About 10°C

73. Why do experts suggest that people should exercise outdoors?

    (A) Because the weather is dry and humid
    (B) Because the temperature is appropriate
    (C) Because people can get dehydrated
    (D) Because people can drink more water

Passage for questions 74 through 76.

[Traditional-character version]

　　隨著手機的普及和功能的增多，手機已成爲人們生活中不可缺少的一部分。近日，《校園之聲》網站在10所中學的校園裡針對高中學生使用手機情況的問題做了一項調查。結果如下：在受訪學生中，擁有手機的學生數量超過沒有手機的人數。四分之三的人稱自己會隨時隨地攜帶手機。超過二分之一的人即使在睡覺的時候也不會關機，以免錯過電話和短信。至於購買手機的原因，45%左右的人說是爲了跟家人聯絡，26%的人稱便於查找學習資料，近10%的人稱用於檢查郵箱、流覽網頁，只有8%的受訪者提到交結新朋友，這其中以女生居多。

[Simplified-character version]

　　随着手机的普及和功能的增多，手机已成为人们生活中不可缺少的一部分。近日，《校园之声》网站在10所中学的校园里针对高中学生使用手机情况的问题做了一项调查。结果如下：在受访学生中，拥有手机的学生数量超过没有手机的人数。四分之三的人称自己会随时随地携带手机。超过二分之一的人即使在睡觉的时候也不会关机，以免错过电话和短信。至于购买手机的原因，45%左右的人说是为了跟家人联络，26%的人称便于查找学习资料，近10%的人称用于检查邮箱、浏览网页，只有8%的受访者提到交结新朋友，这其中以女生居多。

74. What is the purpose of the survey?

   (A) To explain why high school students purchase mobile phones
   (B) To analyze how high school students use mobile phones
   (C) To calculate how many high school students have mobile phones
   (D) To find out why high school has become the main market for mobile phones

75. Which statement is correct?

   (A) 75 percent of respondents said they take their phone with them everywhere.
   (B) 8 percent of female respondents mentioned that they make new friends through mobile phones.
   (C) The survey was made by a radio station.
   (D) More than 10 percent of respondents said they use their mobile phones to check their e-mails and browse websites.

76. Why do some respondents go to bed with their phones nearby?

   (A) They use their phones as alarms.
   (B) They said they couldn't live without their phone.
   (C) They are afraid they'll lose contact with their family members.
   (D) They are afraid they'll miss phone calls and text messages.

Passage for questions 77 through 79.

[Traditional-character version]

　　各班同學請注意，由於近日連續下雪，我校原定本週五下午2:00舉行的足球比賽將推遲，本周五下午各班照常上課。如果天氣條件允許，足球比賽將在下個星期二下午相同的時間內舉行。

[Simplified-character version]

　　各班同学请注意，由于近日连续下雪，我校原定本周五下午2:00举行的足球比赛将推迟，本周五下午各班照常上课。如果天气条件允许，足球比赛将在下个星期二下午相同的时间内举行。

77. What kind of passage is this?

(A) Advertisement
(B) Announcement
(C) Sports news
(D) Poster

78. Why was the soccer game rescheduled?

(A) Some soccer players were not available.
(B) There were conflicts with classes.
(C) Weather conditions were unfavorable.
(D) Students had to go to their classes.

79. Which statement is correct?

(A) The soccer game was postponed until further notice.
(B) The time of the game will be posted on Tuesday.
(C) It has been snowing for several days.
(D) The classes and the game are all cancelled this Friday.

Advertisement for questions 80 through 83.

[Traditional-character version]

　　爲了讓美國學生有機會利用暑期去中國學習中文及感受中國文化，我華美文化中心今年將繼續舉辦"中國之行"夏令營活動。年齡在16歲到20歲之間身體健康的學生都可參加。今年的夏令營一共6個星期，6月4日至7月8日。夏令營設在北京體育大學。在北京期間，除了開設中文課以外，我中心還將組織觀看文藝表演、體育比賽、品嘗風味小吃和欣賞中國電影等活動，並將組織學生到上海、南京、杭州等地進行一個星期的旅遊活動。

[Simplified-character version]

　　为了让美国学生有机会利用暑期去中国学习中文及感受中国文化，我华美文化中心今年将继续举办"中国之行"夏令营活动。年龄在16岁到20岁之间身体健康的学生都可参加。今年的夏令营一共6个星期，6月4日至7月8日。夏令营设在北京体育大学。在北京期间，除了开设中文课以外，我中心还将组织观看文艺表演、体育比赛、品尝风味小吃和欣赏中国电影等活动，并将组织学生到上海、南京、杭州等地进行一个星期的旅游活动。

80. Where is the Huamei Cultural Center located?

    (A) Beijing
    (B) Nanjing
    (C) America
    (D) Shanghai

81. How old do you have to be to be in the program?

    (A) Younger than 16 or older than 20
    (B) 16 or 20 years old
    (C) Between 16 and 20
    (D) Everyone is eligible

82. Where is the camp located this year?

    (A) Beijing
    (B) Shanghai
    (C) Nanjing
    (D) Hangzhou

83. Which activity is not included at the camp?

    (A) Watching performances
    (B) Participating in competitions
    (C) Visiting places
    (D) Sampling local delicacies

Advertisement for questions 84 through 87.

[Traditional-character version]

　　明日之星運動學校將舉辦第十屆青少年籃球夏令營。報名時間：5月15日到5月31日，6月15日開始上課。訓練班分初、中、高三級，學員按年齡分班訓練，由專業教練員授課，並邀請著名籃球運動員指導。學員一律住校，兩位經驗豐富的老師將對學員的日常生活進行管理。

[Simplified-character version]

　　明日之星运动学校将举办第十届青少年篮球夏令营。报名时间：5月15日到5月31日，6月15日开始上课。训练班分初、中、高三级，学员按年龄分班训练，由专业教练员授课，并邀请著名篮球运动员指导。学员一律住校，两位经验丰富的老师将对学员的日常生活进行管理。

84. Who sponsors this camp?

    (A) A sport school
    (B) A basketball team
    (C) A group of professional coaches
    (D) Several famous basketball players

85. When does the camp start?

    (A) May 15
    (B) May 31
    (C) June 15
    (D) July 18

86. Which levels are offered at the camp?

    (A) Elementary
    (B) Intermediate
    (C) Advanced
    (D) All levels are offered

87. Who were invited to be the guest coaches?

    (A) Professional coaches
    (B) Famous athletes
    (C) Two experienced counselors
    (D) Basketball fans

Passage for questions 88 through 91.

[Traditional-character version]

改革開放使中國社會發生了很大的變化，也給家庭結構帶來了影響，社會上出現了"丁克家庭"。"丁克家庭"就是可以生孩子的夫妻自願不要孩子的家庭。這些家庭不願意要孩子，主要有下面幾個原因：一是沒有孩子，夫妻兩人都可以專心做自己的事業，而不用在業餘的時間裏還得爲子女操心；二是沒有孩子對夫妻雙方的發展都有好處。過去在中國，婦女們一切都依靠男人，結婚後整天忙於家務事，在個人的發展上很難有什麼選擇。現在時代不同了，婦女們再也不必依靠什麼人了。她們可以和男人一樣，在事業上有一定的發展；三是沒有孩子，夫妻兩人可以自由地生活，可以追求新的生活方式，享受兩人世界的輕鬆感覺。而一旦離婚，他們也不會有太多的後顧之憂。

[Simplified-character version]

改革开放使中国社会发生了很大的变化，也给家庭结构带来了影响，社会上出现了"丁克家庭"。"丁克家庭"就是可以生孩子的夫妻自愿不要孩子的家庭。这些家庭不愿意要孩子，主要有下面几个原因：一是没有孩子，夫妻两人都可以专心做自己的事业，而不用在业余的时间里还得为子女操心；二是没有孩子对夫妻双方的发展都有好处。过去在中国，妇女们一切都依靠男人，结婚后整天忙于家务事，在个人的发展上很难有什么选择。现在时代不同了，妇女们再也不必依靠什么人了。她们可以和男人一样，在事业上有一定的发展；三是没有孩子，夫妻两人可以自由地生活，可以追求新的生活方式，享受两人世界的轻松感觉。而一旦离婚，他们也不会有太多的后顾之忧。

88. What kind of family is this passage mainly about?

    (A) A couple with one child
    (B) A couple who can have children but don't want to
    (C) Two people in one family
    (D) A couple who wants children but can't have them

89. Which of the following is not a reason for the couple to be "丁克家庭"?

    (A) The couple doesn't want to care for a child.
    (B) The wife wants a good career.
    (C) They want a new lifestyle.
    (D) All of the above.

90. What does "婦女們再也不必依靠什麼人了"("妇女们再也不必依靠什么人了")
    mean?

    (A) Women worry about who they should depend on.
    (B) Women became independent.
    (C) Women should not depend on their husbands.
    (D) Women have no one to depend on.

91. From the context, what does "後顧之憂" ("后顾之忧") mean?

    (A) Couples without children can separate more easily.
    (B) What happens to the children when parents divorce?
    (C) Two people want to enjoy life.
    (D) Modern women don't want to get married.

E-mail for questions 92 through 94.

[Traditional-character version]
發件人：林森
收件人：傑克
主題：NBA小巨人—— 姚明
發件日期：2012年12月10日

傑克：

　　你好！你信中問起姚明，正好我是他的球迷，讓我給你介紹一下吧。

　　姚明1980年在上海出生。他爸爸身高2.08米，原來在上海男子籃球隊打球。媽媽1.88米，曾當過中國國家籃球隊的隊長。姚明身高2.26米，所以外號叫"小巨人"。姚明有一個漂亮的妻子，也是籃球運動員，高1.90米。姚明4歲生日的時候有了自己的第一個籃球；6歲在上海看美國籃球隊比賽時知道了NBA；9歲在上海少年體校開始籃球訓練。1997年，他加入上海籃球隊；2002年，上海隊贏得了CBA冠軍，他獲得了那次比賽的最佳球員的榮譽；同一年，到美國加入休士頓火箭隊，成爲NBA的第三位中國球員。

　　看了我的信，你是不是對姚明更感興趣了？

祝好！
林森

[Simplified-character version]
发件人：林森
收件人：杰克
主题：NBA小巨人—— 姚明
发件日期: 2012年12月10日

杰克：

　　你好！你信中问起姚明，正好我是他的球迷，让我给你介绍一下吧。

　　姚明1980年在上海出生。他爸爸身高2.08米，原来在上海男子篮球队打球。妈妈1.88米，曾当过中国国家篮球队的队长。姚明身高2.26米，所以外号叫"小巨人"。姚明有一个漂亮的妻子，也是篮球运动员，高1.90米。姚明4岁生日的时候有了自己的第一个篮球；6岁在上海看美国篮球队比赛时知道了NBA；9岁在上海少年体校开始篮球训练。1997年，他加入上海篮球队；2002年，上海队赢得了CBA冠军，他获得了那次比赛的最佳球员的荣誉；同一年，到美国加入休士顿火箭队，成为NBA的第三位中国球员。

　　看了我的信，你是不是对姚明更感兴趣了？

祝好！
林森

92. Who was once the captain of the Chinese national basketball team?

(A) Yao Ming
(B) Yao Ming's father
(C) Yao Ming's mother
(D) Yao Ming's wife

93. When did Yao Ming learn about the NBA?

(A) When he was 4 years old
(B) When he was 6 years old
(C) When he entered the Shanghai Junior Sports School
(D) When he came to the United States

94. When did Yao Ming join the NBA?

(A) 1980
(B) 1981
(C) 1997
(D) 2002

Passage for questions 95 and 96.

[Traditional-character version]
　　中國城是指海外華人生活的地區，也叫"唐人街"。美國最著名的中國城在紐約和舊金山。舊金山的中國城已有一百五十年的歷史了。那裏的華人幾乎佔了美國華人總數的1/4。在舊金山的中國城裏，中國飯館不計其數，各種風味，應有盡有。紐約的中國城，附近有地鐵車站，交通方便。目前美國各地的唐人街，已經不完全是中國人的市場了，越來越多的韓國人、越南人、泰國人等也開始在那些地方發展了。

[Simplified-character version]

　　中国城是指海外华人生活的地区，也叫"唐人街"。美国最著名的中国城在纽约和旧金山。旧金山的中国城已有一百五十年的历史了。那里的华人几乎占了美国华人总数的1/4。在旧金山的中国城里，中国饭馆不计其数，各种风味，应有尽有。纽约的中国城，附近有地铁车站，交通方便。目前美国各地的唐人街，已经不完全是中国人的市场了，越来越多的韩国人、越南人、泰国人等也开始在那些地方发展了。

95. What is the topic of the passage?

　　(A) Chinatowns of the world
　　(B) Chinatowns in New York
　　(C) Development of Chinatowns
　　(D) Chinatowns in the United States

96. Which statement is true?

　　(A) All Chinese people live in Chinatowns.
　　(B) There are many different restaurants in Chinatown in San Francisco.
　　(C) There are only two Chinatowns in the United States.
　　(D) Everyone who does business in Chinatown is Chinese.

Passage for questions 97 and 98.

[Traditional-character version]

　　代溝就是不同年齡的人因爲思想觀念的不同而産生的文化距離。在家庭中，由於父母和子女兩代人的成長過程不同，社會環境不一樣，受教育的方式和內容都有差異，再加上經濟條件的改善和生活質量的提高，使得兩代人在對問題的看法和做事的方法上都不完全一樣，形成了父母與子女之間的代溝。

　　根據調查，86%的學生在穿衣服問題上跟父母的看法不一樣。有70%以上的學生在課外書的選擇上跟父母不同。多半的學生在使用零用錢方面受到父母的干涉。有57%的學生在愛好方面與父母的要求不一樣。在父母偷偷看自己的信件、日記、關注孩子與異性同學交往的問題上，有將近20%的學生對父母的做法表示不滿意。

[Simplified-character version]

　　代沟就是不同年龄的人因为思想观念的不同而产生的文化距离。在家庭中，由于父母和子女两代人的成长过程不同，社会环境不一样，受教育的方式和内容都有差异，再加上经济条件的改善和生活质量的提高，使得两代人在对问题的看法和做事的方法上都不完全一样，形成了父母与子女之间的代沟。

　　根据调查，86%的学生在穿衣服问题上跟父母的看法不一样。有70%以上的学生在课外书的选择上跟父母不同。多半的学生在使用零用钱方面受到父母的干涉。有57%的学生在爱好方面与父母的要求不一样。在父母偷偷看自己的信件、日记、关注孩子与异性同学交往的问题上，有将近20%的学生对父母的做法表示不满意。

97. According to the passage, what is a "代溝" (代沟)?

   (A) Different thoughts
   (B) Different age groups
   (C) Cultural differences
   (D) Different genders

98. According to research, what percentage of kids have different hobbies from their parents' expectations?

   (A) 20%
   (B) 57%
   (C) 70%
   (D) 86%

Passage for questions 99 and 100.

[Traditional-character version]

　　人口老齡化是中國的一個社會問題。引起人口老齡化的原因是出生率和死亡率的下降，其中出生率是最主要的因素。隨著出生率的下降，少年兒童人口越來越少，成年人和老年人越來越多，整個社會的人口逐漸走向老齡化。老年人口比率的提高嚴重地影響了社會經濟的發展。目前，人口老齡化在全世界也是一個不可避免的問題。不同的國家，人口老齡化的過程、時間、速度和發展的趨勢都不完全相同。

[Simplified-character version]

　　人口老龄化是中国的一个社会问题。引起人口老龄化的原因是出生率和死亡率的下降，其中出生率是最主要的因素。随着出生率的下降，少年儿童人口越来越少，成年人和老年人越来越多，整个社会的人口逐渐走向老龄化。老年人口比率的提高严重地影响了社会经济的发展。目前，人口老龄化在全世界也是一个不可避免的问题。不同的国家，人口老龄化的过程、时间、速度和发展的趋势都不完全相同。

99. What is the main reason for the aging population?

   (A) Birth rates rising
   (B) Birth rates decreasing
   (C) Death rates rising
   (D) Death rates decreasing and birth rates rising

100. What does the phrase "不可避免" mean?

   (A) evitable
   (B) inevitable
   (C) should be avoided
   (D) should not be avoided

Reading Comprehension Practice
ANSWER KEY

1. B	26. B	51. C	76. D
2. C	27. D	52. B	77. B
3. B	28. C	53. B	78. C
4. D	29. D	54. C	79. C
5. A	30. C	55. C	80. C
6. D	31. B	56. A	81. C
7. C	32. A	57. D	82. A
8. A	33. B	58. C	83. B
9. C	34. C	59. D	84. A
10. B	35. C	60. C	85. C
11. C	36. C	61. B	86. D
12. B	37. B	62. B	87. A
13. D	38. A	63. B	88. B
14. C	39. B	64. D	89. D
15. C	40. B	65. B	90. B
16. C	41. B	66. D	91. B
17. C	42. C	67. D	92. C
18. B	43. D	68. D	93. B
19. B	44. B	69. C	94. D
20. D	45. B	70. C	95. D
21. C	46. C	71. D	96. B
22. D	47. D	72. B	97. C
23. B	48. C	73. B	98. B
24. A	49. D	74. B	99. B
25. C	50. C	75. A	100. B

ANSWERS AND ANSWER EXPLANATIONS

This section provides the correct answer to each question, along with supporting information from the selected materials. Detailed explanations will also be provided, in cases that are not obvious, to illustrate why the other choices are incorrect after the "Why not" label. Students who self-check their understanding of the problems and answers are more likely to learn from their mistakes.

1. **(B)** This public sign means "Do not talk loudly in the room." People who are in a library should be quiet, so it is reasonable to expect this sign to appear in a library. Why not:

   (A), (D) People are usually allowed to talk loudly in a park or in a cafeteria.
   (C) "室內" is not applicable to a bus.

2. **(C)** The poster is a New Year's greeting and includes all the wishes stated in (A), (B), and (D).

3. **(B)** "一年到頭" ("一年到头") is a time-duration phrase that means "sustains the entire year." Why not:

   (D) "Every year" is a frequency phrase, not a duration phrase.
   (A), (C) *End of year* and *beginning of the year* are both specific points in time, not duration.

4. **(D)** The note mentions to call the father at his office in the school. Why not:

   (A) This is most likely the mother's occupation.
   (C) A student doesn't have a "辦公室" ("办公室") in the school.
   (B) The patient is whom the mother will be operating on.

5. **(A)** "Right now" is when the note is being read. So it is safe to assume that the mother left the house after she wrote the note and is now at the hospital. Why not:

   (B) This is where the mother was when she left the note.
   (C) This is where the father is.
   (D) This is where the father will take the child for dinner.

6. **(D)** This is an advertisement looking for a tutor to teach mathematics and English, "數學及英文" ("数学及英文"). However, someone who can teach Chinese, "能教中文更佳," is preferred. Why not:

   (A) This response fails to include mathematics.
   (B), (C) Both require the tutor to teach all three subjects, whereas the advertisement indicates that it's even better if the tutor can teach only Chinese.

7. (**C**) There are usually no assigned seats on a bus (A), in a library (B), or in a stadium (D).

8. (**A**) The sign says "Please be seated according to your assigned seats." People who are in a theatre should be seated in that fashion.

9. (**C**) It says "請你...來本店參加...面談"("请你...来本店参加...面谈"). The interview, "面談"("面谈"), is the activity checked.

10. (**B**) It is stated in the first line that the store is very impressed by his "專業知識"("专业知识"). Why not:

    (A) The applicant has not taken the test yet.
    (D) The interview has not taken place yet.
    (C) The applicant's degree is not mentioned in the passage.

11. (**C**) As stated in the first line of the invitation letter, the store is happy with his work experience. Why not:

    (A) The interview is scheduled for 9:30 PM, not 10:00 PM.
    (B) The applicant is applying for a position as a waiter, "服務員"("服务员"), not in the HR department.
    (D) The applicant may contact Ms. Chen only if he has a problem with the proposed interview schedule.

12. (**B**) This note explains why Wang Xiaoping cannot attend class. Why not:

    (A) The neighbor took Wang's mother to the hospital, but it is not clear if the neighbor is a "good friend."
    (C) Wang's mother is ill, not Wang herself.
    (D) The fact that Wang's father is out of town makes Wang the only person who can take care of her mother.

13. (**D**) Wang's signature at the end of the note indicates that Wang is a student, which invalidates the other options.

14. (**C**) The brochure states that people can visit the reptile hall, the dinosaur park, and bird hall, all of which are related to natural history. Why not:

    (A) The brochure does not state anything regarding astronomy.
    (B) The brochure does not mention the museum's artwork.
    (D) The brochure does not state anything regarding space travel or technology.

15. **(C)** The announcement states that during winter breaks, summer vacation, and national holidays, hours will change. Why not:

    (A) The museum will close on Monday.
    (B) Although the closing time is 5:00 PM, people are not permitted to enter the museum after 4:00 PM.
    (D) The website updates only if there are changes in hours of operation.

16. **(C)** The answer is *reading room* since the word "閱" ("阅"), in rules 2 and 5, means "reading."

    Why not:
    (A) Through "閉館前15分鐘停止借閱" ("闭馆前15分钟停止借阅"), "restaurant" is out of the question, because this rule is only related to reading.
    (B) The next clue is "借," instead of "買" ("买"), so "bookstore" can be eliminated.
    (D) Through rule 2 (二) "除了筆和筆記本外，其他物品不能帶入室內" ("除了笔和笔记本外，其它物品不能带入室内"), it is understood that all school supplies, not only notebooks and pens, can be brought into a classroom.

17. **(C)** Policy #1, "用本校學生證進入本室" ("用本校学生证进入本室"), mandates that the student I.D. of the school is required for admission. Why not:

    (A), (B) "Notebook" and "pen" are the two things you can bring into the reading room, but they are not required.
    (D) There are magazines and newspapers in the room, but they are not required to enter the room.

18. **(B)** Policy #2, "除了筆及筆記本以外，其他物品不能帶入室內" ("除了笔及笔记本以外，其他物品不能带入室内"), implies that taking notes is allowed in the reading room. Why not:

    (A) Policy #1, "用本校學生證進入本室" ("用本校学生证进入本室"), mandates that the student I.D. of the school is required. Students from other schools cannot be admitted.
    (C) Policy #2, "室內書刊只能在本室內閱讀" ("室内书刊只能在本室内阅读"), mandates that the reading material in the room stays in the room.
    (D) Policy #4, "保持室內安靜" ("保持室内安静"), states that noise is not allowed.

19. **(B)** As directly stated in both the subject line, "找語伴" ("找语伴"), and in the e-mail itself, "想找一位母語是中文的朋友作爲語言交換伴侶" ("想找一位母语是中文的朋友作为语言交换伴侣"). Why not:

    (A) A tutor only teaches one way.
    (C), (D) These responses are irrelevant.

20. **(D)** As stated, "男女都可以." Why not:

    (A) "本人正在選修中文課程" ("本人正在选修中文课程") means he is currently studying Chinese.

    (B) The sender is looking for a native speaker, "母語是中文的朋友" ("母语是中文的朋友"), not just anyone who can speak Chinese.

    (C) He says, "彼此不收費" ("彼此不收费"), indicating that he will not pay.

21. **(C)** "主要材料," "使用方法" indicate that this is some kind of instruction, like a recipe, that lists the ingredients in a product and its usage. "本品" and "保存" indicate that this product can be added to cooking for another minute, and that it can be stored.

22. **(D)** The passage talks about how to use this product, "本品," including the ingredients, how to make a dish with it (C), when it expires (B), and how to store it.

23. **(B)** The other three items can be found in the ingredients section.

24. **(A)** 24 months = 2 years. Why not:

    (B) It goes on to say that this packaged product is best kept in a dry, cool place, "本品適合放在乾燥、陰涼的地方" ("本品适合放在干燥、阴凉的地方").

    (C) Water is not mentioned in the recipe, so it is irrelevant.

    (D) "加熱到370 °F左右" ("加热到370 °F左右") suggests that the temperature should be kept around 370° F, not to exceed it.

25. **(C)** As a reader is scanning the certificate, he should look for the very important word "至," which connects two dates in a period of time. The first date is when the recipient started college, and the second date is when the recipient finished. Also, in China, most schools start a new school year in September. Look for a date in the answers that is around that time. Why not:

    (A) This is the birth date of the recipient.
    (B) This is when she finished college.
    (D) This is when the certificate was issued.

26. **(B)** Between "系" and "專業" ("专业"), the degree recipient's major can be found. "法國語言文學" (法国语言文学) means French language and literature. Why not:

    (A) Usually, *foreign language* is used for the name of a department, and it is too general to be a major.
    (C) This is not mentioned in the certificate.
    (D) This is the name of the school.

27. **(D)** This passage is about a refrigerator in a bedroom. The main idea is how it affects people's health. (D) includes the other three choices. Why not:

    (A) This is not entirely correct because only the second half of the passage discusses the problems.
    (B) This is not entirely correct either because it covers only the first half of the passage.
    (C) This only points out the specific benefits, like convenience, that refrigerators bring to our lives.

28. **(C)** The answer is stated in the last few lines of the passage. Why not:

    (A), (B) Air pollution is not mentioned in the passage.
    (D) Water is not mentioned in the passage.

29. **(D)** As stated in the last sentence of the passage, "爲了家人的身體健康" ("为了家人的身体健康"), so (D) is the only correct answer. Why not:

    (A) "房間太少、太小" ("房间太少、太小") says that there are not enough rooms, and that the house is small in general.
    (B) This is one of the reasons why people have refrigerators in their bedrooms in the first place.
    (C) This is not mentioned in the passage and is irrelevant.

30. **(C)** As indicated in the opening line, "快十年了," almost 10 years!—that is, not quite 10 years yet.

31. **(B)** According to his letter, he is going to Shanghai for a business trip. Why not:

    (A), (C) "順便" ("顺便") means he wants to do these things, but they are not the primary reasons.
    (D) From "趁這次出差的機會帶妻子和兩個孩子回去一趟" ("趁这次出差的机会带妻子和两个孩子回去一趟"), we know that he is bringing his wife and kids as well, but only as an added bonus.

32. **(A)** Since he is going to China in a month, it is safe to conclude that he is not in China at this time, so that rules out (B), (C), and (D). The only choice that makes sense is the United States.

33. **(B)** This is an advertisement for an apartment for rent. The phrase "兩室一廳" ("两室一厅") indicates that there are two bedrooms. "室" refers to bedrooms. Why not:

    (A) 1 is the number of bathrooms or living rooms.
    (C) 3 is the answer only if one takes "兩室一廳" ("两室一厅") into account.
    (D) 4 is the total number of rooms.

34. **(C)** The ad clearly states "房客不得吸煙" ("房客不得吸烟"). Why not:

    (A) *couples with kids* may rent because the passage does not directly address them.
    (B), (D) "夫婦無小孩" ("夫妇无小孩"), "或女生," are preferred, "優先考慮" ("优先考虑").

35. **(C)** As stated, "不帶家具，有地毯、洗衣機" ("不带家具，有地毯、洗衣机"). The washing machine is included. Why not:

    (A) The ad makes it clear that "不帶家具" ("不带家具").
    (B) "有地毯," carpet is included.
    (D) "交通方便，環境安全" ("交通方便，环境安全") means that transportation is very convenient, and the neighborhood is safe.

36. **(C)** This public sign means "Please keep valuable items on your person." People who are on a public transport should be careful with their own goods. Why not: Goods in a furniture store (A) and a houseware store (B) may be heavy, but not necessarily expensive. Even most jewelry is valuable; people are not allowed to take items prior to purchase.

37. **(B)** It is reasonable to expect this sign to appear at a public transport. Why not:

    (A), (C), (D) The text does not give any indication of encouraging people to buy something.

38. **(A)** The first line of the article clearly states "第17屆中國雲海清湖國際龍舟比賽" ("第17届中国云海清湖国际龙舟比赛"). Why not:

    (B), (C), (D) These are the hometowns of some of the contestants, not where the competition took place.

39. **(B)** As stated in the article, "還增加了800米的比賽" ("还增加了800米的比赛").

40. **(B)** As directly stated in the article, "還增加了一項表現南方風景民俗的水上文藝表演" ("还增加了一项表现南方风景民俗的水上文艺表演").

41. **(B)** As stated in the article, "其中包括獲得上一屆龍舟比賽冠軍的香港明珠龍舟隊" ("其中包括获得上一届龙舟比赛冠军的香港明珠龙舟队"). The team is from "香港," Hong Kong.

42. **(C)** The answer is found in the text "各龍舟隊，技術水平高" ("各龙舟队，技术水平高"). Why not:

   (A) There are 16 teams made up of 226 athletes.
   (B) The team that has a long history is from Taiwan.
   (D) The Hong Kong team was the champion last year, but it placed second this time.

43. **(D)** The first sentence of the text, "一個健康的人每天至少要喝七到八杯水" ("一个健康的人每天至少要喝七到八杯水"), provides a clue using two key words, "水"and "健康." After reading the article, one would confirm that these key words indeed represent the main idea. All of the other three choices address some aspects about how drinking water affects health.

44. **(B)** Here, the phrase "非...不可" means "have to" and "must." Why not:

   (A) This contradicts the phrase in question.
   (C) This only partially addresses the phrase by leaving out "only in the morning."
   (D) This basically restates the same argument as in (C).

45. **(B)** The writer states that she lives in the second biggest city in America, and that the recipient lives in Nanjing, one of the biggest cities in China. Why not:

   (A) The term sister school means that the two schools in different nations have established a collaborative international partnership.
   (C) and (D) are not correct because there is no related information in the letter.

46. **(C)** The writer states that she wishes to visit the Forbidden City in Beijing. Why not:

   (A), (B), and (D) are the writer's hobbies and interests, not her travel plans.

47. **(D)** The letter implies that the Confucius Temple is in Nanjing. Why not:

   (A) and (B) are incorrect because the Yuyuan Garden is in Shanghai, and the Terracotta Army is in Xi'an. The Forbidden City is in Beijing, so (C) is also wrong.

48. **(C)** The answer can be found in the first sentence, "小張是北京網球隊的運動員" ("小张是北京网球队的运动员"). Why not:

   (A), (B) Xiao Zhang plays tennis, and has never been on a basketball team. But his father was on a basketball team.
   (D) Shanghai is the place where Xiao Zhang's team competed, not the city that his team represents.

49. **(D)** The phrase "兒子比你強" ("儿子比你强") explains why the mom is particularly proud of the son's achievement. Also, according to traditional Chinese cultures, it is something to be proud of when students surpass their teachers, apprentices surpass their masters, and a son surpasses his father. A Chinese proverb describes this situation as "青出於藍而勝於藍" ("青出于蓝而胜于蓝"). Why not:

(A) Her husband is not an athlete anymore, and also the sentence "你當籃球運動員的時候得過第一名嗎" ("你当篮球运动员的时候得过第一名吗") is a rhetorical question. It is clear that he has never placed first.

(B) The text doesn't mention whether Xiao Zhang places first often, so it cannot be verified.

(C) Her husband and son were athletes at different periods. At the present time, only her son is an athlete.

50. **(C)** Lao Zhang's comment "別說第一了，能取得前三名的成績就不錯了"("别说第一了，能取得前三名的成绩就不错了") implies that he has never gotten in the top three. The pattern "別說…了，能…就不錯了" ("别说…了，能…就不错了") is a hypothetical sentence, about something that would never happen. Why not:

(A), (B), (D) The key word "不好意思" expresses that Lao Zhang is not pleased with his performance as an athlete. He has never gotten in the top three.

51. **(C)** Xiao Zhang explains that he meant to write "我打敗了，一個上海的運動員得了第一名" ("我打败了，一个上海的运动员得了第一名"), which means "I lost. An athlete from the Shanghai team placed first." But he put the comma in the wrong place, and the sentence became "我打敗了一個上海的運動員，得了第一名" ("我打败了一个上海的运动员，得了第一名"), meaning "I beat an athlete from Shanghai, and got first place." Why not:

(A), (B) These cannot be correct based on the explanation above.

(D) In the letter, no details are given regarding the process of the competition, so what is suggested in (D) is irrelevant.

52. **(B)** The first part of the sentence comes from a poem by Mao Zedong, the former Chairman of China, and the last part is what travel enthusiasts say after visiting the country. The Great Wall and Beijing duck are what many consider to be the two most important aspects of China. Why not:

(A) This states a fact without emphasizing its significance.

(C) The second part of the sentence is figurative and can apply to anyone, but (C) makes it too personal.

(D) The first part of the sentence is a simile, but (D) interprets it literally.

53. **(B)** In the passage, the sentence "後來，明朝的首都從南京搬到北京" ("后来，明朝的首都从南京搬到北京"), indicates that the capital of the Ming Dynasty started out at Nanjing, but later was moved to Beijing. Why not:

(A) This explains that the different dynasties have different capitals—that is, the capital of the Ming Dynasty was Nanjing, and the capital of the next dynasty, Qing, was Beijing. In reality, the Qing Dynasty inherited the second capital, Beijing, from the Ming Dynasty.

(C) This response is wrong in claiming that the Ming Dynasty had two different capitals at the same time.

(D) This response has the time sequence reversed.

54. **(C)** The text describes Beijing duck as "又香" (smells good), "又脆" (crisp), (A); "皮兒很薄" ("皮儿很薄") (thin skin), "肉非常嫩" (tender meat), (B); and "雖然很肥，但是一點兒也不膩" ("虽然很肥，但是一点儿也不腻"), (though a lot of fat, not greasy), (D).

55. **(C)** The time phrases "明朝" ("明朝"), "到今天," "三百多年," and "後來" ("后来"), and the key word "歷史" ("历史"), all illustrate that the main topic of the passage is the history of Beijing duck. Why not:

(A), (D) These are merely subtopics of the passage.

(B) This is not mentioned in the text.

56. **(A)** This answer Encompasses the other three choices, making it the most complete and appropriate.

57. **(D)** As stated in the essay, "天津的 '狗不理' 包子已經有一百多年的歷史了" ("天津的'狗不理'包子已经有一百多年的历史了").

58. **(C)** As stated in the essay, "大家就把他做的包子叫狗不理包子." "大家" means *everybody*.

59. **(D)** The boy is described as "做事非常認真，學得很快" ("做事非常认真，学得很快"). Why not:

(A) His boss's restaurant was already quite popular at the time.

(B) This is not confirmed in the story, although the boss had actually said that the boy was very patient.

(C) The boy opened his own restaurant with the money he saved.

60. **(C)** His statement "到天津，不嘗一嘗 '狗不理' 包子，就等於沒有來過天津" ("到天津，不尝一尝'狗不理'包子，就等于没有来过天津") indicates the significance of baozi in Tianjin. Without trying it, a trip to Tianjin seems wasted.

61. **(B)** As stated, "由南到北960米." "米" is a meter. Why not:

    (A) This is the number of rooms.
    (C) This is the length from east to west.
    (D) The area is 720,000 square meters.

62. **(B)** As stated, "南邊的叫午門，是故宮的正門" ("南边的叫午门，是故宫的正门").

63. **(B)** As stated, "宮殿的周圍是近10米高、3公里長的城牆" ("宫殿的周围是近10米高、3公里长的城墙"). Why not:

    (A) This is the width of the moat.
    (C) This is the height of the wall.
    (D) This is the depth of the moat.
    Notes: 米 = meter (m), 公里 = kilometer (km)

64. **(D)** The function of the southern complex of the palace can be understood from the description "南邊的區域是皇帝工作的地方" ("南边的区域是皇帝工作的地方"). You may think of this as the "South Wing," similar to the West Wing of the White House in the United States, which is the workplace of the president. Why not:

    (A) It is not the family members' workplace. Their living area is located in the north wing.
    (B), (C) As stated, "北邊的區域是皇帝及家人生活的地方" ("北边的区域是皇帝及家人生活的地方").

65. **(B)** The term "客運" ("客运") indicates that the ad is about transportation. "客" is "乘客" (passengers). Why not:

    (A) Although lunch is provided, the ad is not about a restaurant.
    (C) $4,000,000 insurance coverage is included in the bus fare, but it is not about an insurance company, either.
    (D) Although a restroom facility is available in the back of the bus, this is not an ad for a public restroom.

66. **(D)** "客車後部有廁所" ("客车后部有厕所"). Why not:

    (A) Reservations are recommended, but tickets are also available after you board the bus.
    (B) Lunch is provided regardless of birthdays. Passengers whose birthdays are on the same day of the ride can ride free. Children who are two years old or younger also ride free.
    (C) As stated, "未訂票者坐後排" ("未订票者坐后排"). Passengers without reservations must sit in the back.

67. **(D)** The ad says that kids two years old or under can ride for free: "當天生日者、兩歲以下(含兩歲) 幼兒免費" ("当天生日者、两岁以下(含两岁) 幼儿免费"). Why not:

    (A) This misses those under two.
    (B) Two and a quarter years old is *about* two years old, but children of this age are ineligible for free rides.
    (C) This contradicts the policy.

68. **(D)** "往返," also known as "來回" ("来回"), means *round-trip*, and "單程" ("单程") is *one-way*. As stated, "往返" $110/80 (小孩). $80 is immediately followed by "小孩" within parentheses, which indicates that $80 is the round-trip bus fare for a child. The reader should infer that the first amount is the adult's round-trip fare. Why not:

    (A) $45 is the child's one-way bus fare.
    (B) $60 is the adult's one-way bus fare.
    (C) $80 is the child's round-trip bus fare.

69. **(C)** As stated, Li hopes to find a job in a computer company, "希望在電腦公司工作" ("希望在电脑公司工作"). Why not:

    (A) *Help wanted* is an advertisement issued by someone who wants to hire people.
    (B) The words "男，24歲，未婚" ("男，24岁，未婚") in the text may make it seem like a *personal* or *dating* advertisement. In fact, in most Asian countries, it is not uncommon to include gender, age, and marital status on a resume or job application.
    (D) The advertisement text starts with the name "李成龍" ("李成龙"). This may seem like a public *wanted* notice that the authorities are looking for this person. However, a public notice should include the notice issuer, which is not found in this ad. Moreover, the "希望在電腦公司工作" ("希望在电脑公司工作") clarifies that the individual by this name is trying to find a job in a computer company.

70. **(C)** The text indicates that the individual is "英文寫作及口語水平高" ("英文写作及口语水平高"), "proficient at speaking and writing English," but his Chinese skills are not mentioned in the passage. Why not:

    (A) As stated, "本屆大學畢業" ("本届大学毕业"). "本屆" is the current year, and "大學畢業" ("大学毕业") means graduating from college.
    (B) As stated, "電腦…水平高" ("电脑…水平高"), meaning computer proficiency is high.
    (D) As stated, "月薪不低於3000元" ("月薪不低于3000元") literally means "monthly salary no lower than RMB3000 yuan."

71. **(D)** As stated, the recent temperature averages above 10°C, i.e., 10°C 以上. "最高溫度已達12°C" ("最高温度已达12°C") says the highest it has reached is 12°C. Why not:

   (A) As stated, 4°C is how much this year's average is higher than the previous year's, "比常年氣溫高4°C左右" ("比常年气温高4°C左右").
   (B) As stated, "最近幾天本市平均氣溫在10°C以上" ("最近几天本市平均气温在10°C以上"), meaning the average these days is above 10°C.
   (C) As stated, this is the same as in (B).

72. **(B)** When "平均氣溫超過10°C就是進入春天的開始" ("平均气温超过10°C就是进入春天的开始"), the average temperature reaches above 10°C, it indicates that spring is here. Please refer to the explanation in #71 above for "Why not."

73. **(B)** As stated, "這樣好的天氣適合人們到室外活動" ("这样好的天气适合人们到室外活动"). Why not:

   (A) As stated, "由於這個時候的空氣很乾燥，專家特別提醒人們注意多喝水" ("由于这个时候的空气很干燥，专家特别提醒人们注意多喝水")—that is, experts advised that the weather is dry, so everybody should be mindful and drink more water.
   (C), (D) As stated in (A) above, (C) presents a potential risk, and (D) is a precaution to prevent that risk. Neither is the reason why people should engage in outdoor activities.

74. **(B)** The second sentence clearly states "針對高中學生使用手機情況的問題做了一項調查"("针对高中学生使用手机情况的问题做了一项调查".) Why not:

   (A) and (C) are only parts of the questionnaire.
   (D) The survey is not mentioned, so it is irrelevant.

75. **(A)** The news states "四分之三的人稱自己會隨時隨地携帶手機"("四分之三的人称自己会随时随地携带手机"). Three-quarters is 75 percent. Why not:

   (B) is incorrect because 8% of respondents (who want to make friends through mobile phones) refers to the total number of respondents, not just female students.
   (C) is wrong because this survey was made by a website, as it states in the passage "《校園之聲》網站......做了一項調查》(《校园之声》网站......做了一项调查)."
   (D) is incorrect because "近10%" means "nearly 10% of respondents."

76. **(D)** The clause "以免錯過電話和短信"("以免错过电话和短信") shows that they go to bed with their phones nearby, so as not to miss something.

Why not: Both (A) and (B) are irrelevant because the following two issues may be true but are not mentioned in the text: First, many people use a mobile phone as an alarm clock, and second, some people can't live without their phones. (C) is incorrect because it is the reason why many students buy mobile phones.

77. **(B)** The key points "各班同學" ("各班同学"), "我校," and "各班照常上課" ("各班照常上课") show that it is a school announcement.

78. **(C)** Due to "連續下雪" ("连续下雪") means consistently snowing and "如果天氣條件允許" ("如果天气条件允许"), *weather permits*, is also related to weather. Why not:

(A), (B) The announcement offers no supporting information for these choices.

(D) This is the outcome of postponing the game: Students remain in class as normally scheduled.

79. **(C)** As stated directly in the announcement, to "連續下雪" ("连续下雪").

80. **(C)** In the beginning of the text, one finds out that some group is going to organize a camp to travel to China. This camp is especially for American students who want to learn Chinese language and Chinese culture during the summer vacation. "爲了讓美國學生有機會利用暑期去中國學習中文及感受中國文化，我華美文化中心今年將繼續舉辦'中國之行'夏令營活動" ("为了让美国学生有机会利用暑期去中国学习中文及感受中国文化，我华美文化中心今年将继续举办'中国之行'夏令营活动"). From the description, the organization is located somewhere other than China, based on the directional word "去" instead of "來" ("来"). Why not:

(A) Beijing is the location of the camp, "夏令營設在北京體育大學" ("夏令营设在北京体育大学").

(B), (D) Nanjing and Shanghai are the Chinese cities that they will visit during the trip: "並將組織學生到上海、南京、杭州等地進行一個星期的旅遊活動" ("并将组织学生到上海、南京、杭州等地进行一个星期的旅游活动").

81. **(C)** As stated, the age requirement for this program is "年齡在10歲到22歲" ("年龄在10岁到22岁"), i.e., the qualified student must be between the ages of 10 and 22. Why not:

(A) Younger than 16 or older than 20 is out of the requirement range.

(B) Either exactly 16 or 20 is also out of the requirement range.

(D) As stated, there is an age requirement; therefore, it is not open to everyone.

82. **(A)** See #80 above. The location of the camp is "北京體育大學" ("北京体育大学") (Beijing Physical Education University). Why not:

    (B), (C), (D) These are merely some cities that the campers will visit during the trip.

83. **(B)** After detailed reading, we learn that the only activity the campers are not participating in is the competition. Why not:

    (A) As stated, "我中心還將組織觀看文藝表演…等活動" ("我中心还将组织观看文艺表演…等活动"), i.e., they will watch some cultural performances.
    (C) As stated, "並將組織學生到上海、南京、杭州等地進行一個星期的旅遊活動" ("并将组织学生到上海、南京、杭州等地进行一个星期的旅游活动"), i.e., they will visit places.
    (D) As stated, "還將組織…品嘗風味小吃等活動" ("还将组织…品尝风味小吃等活动"), i.e., they will sample local delicacies.

84. **(A)** As stated, "明日之星運動學校將舉辦…" ("明日之星运动学校将举办…"), the camp is sponsored by the sport school.

85. **(C)** As stated, "報名時間：5月15日到5月31日，6月15日開始上課" ("报名时间：5月15日到5月31日，6月15日开始上课"). Why not:

    (A) May 15 is the beginning of the application period.
    (B) May 31 is the last date of the application period.
    (D) July 18 is irrelevant.

86. **(D)** As stated, "訓練班分初、中、高三級" ("训练班分初、中、高三级"), i.e., all levels are offered.

87. **(A)** "專業教練員授課" ("专业教练员授课") means that professional coaches normally teach classes. Why not:

    (B) *Famous athletes* are special guest instructors: "並邀請著名籃球運動員指導" ("并邀请著名篮球运动员指导").
    (C) *Two experienced counselors* are responsible for the campers' daily routines, but they do not coach: "兩位經驗豐富的老師將對學員的日常生活進行管理" ("两位经验丰富的老师将对学员的日常生活进行管理").
    (D) *Basketball fans* is not mentioned in the text and therefore is irrelevant.

88. **(B)** As stated, "丁克家庭" is a transliteration of the imported English term *DINK*, i.e., *double-income-no-kids*, a working couple who are able to be parents but decide not to. Why not:

    (A) One child per family is the current policy in China for families that want to raise a child.
    (C) *Two people in one family* is overly general and does not indicate that they are *a couple*.
    (D) This actually contradicts the definition of *DINK*.

89. **(D)** All three reasons were stated in the passage. Why not:

    (A) As stated, "夫妻…不用在業餘的時間裏還得爲子女操心" ("夫妻…不用在业余的时间里还得为子女操心").
    (B) As stated, "她們可以和男人一樣，在事業上有一定的發展" ("她们可以和男人一样，在事业上有一定的发展").
    (C) As stated, "夫妻兩人可以自由地…追求新的生活方式" ("夫妻两人可以自由地…追求新的生活方式").

90. **(B)** "婦女們再也不必依靠什麽人了"("妇女们再也不必依靠什么人了") can be translated as "women do not need to depend on anybody anymore." Why not:

    (A) This is a misinterpretation of the line. "不必" is *no need to*, and "什麽人" ("什么人") is *whoever*.
    (C) The passage does not take a position on what women *should* or *should not* do.
    (D) The key word is "不必," *no need to*, as explained in (A) above, not that they have *no one to*.

91. **(B)** The idiom "後顧之憂" ("后顾之忧") literally means "troubles back at home," and the specific meaning of "troubles" depends on the context. The context here is illustrated by the third reason why a couple might not want children: because they want to enjoy a modern and carefree lifestyle. At the end of the passage, the sentence "而一旦離婚，他們也不會有太多的後顧之憂" ("而一旦离婚，他们也不会有太多的后顾之忧") means "just in case that they divorce, they do not have a lot of troubles." One of those troubles in this context is what may happen to the child if the couple gets a divorce. Why not:

    (A) This may be an important and believable reason, but it is overly general and does not pinpoint the "憂" ("忧"), the actual *worry*.
    (C) *Two people* is too general to be considered *a couple*, and it fails to identify the worry associated with divorce.
    (D) This is not mentioned in the passage, and therefore is irrelevant.

92. **(C)** As stated, "媽媽…曾當過中國國家籃球隊的隊長" ("妈妈…曾当过中国国家篮球队的队长").

93. **(B)** As stated, "6歲在上海看美國籃球隊比賽時知道了NBA" ("6岁在上海看美国篮球队比赛时知道了NBA").

94. **(D)** As stated, "2002年，上海贏得了…同一年…成爲NBA的第三位中國球員" ("2002年，上海队赢得了…同一年…成为NBA的第三位中国球员"). "同一年" refers to the same year, 2002.

95. **(D)** "美國最著名的中國城在紐約和舊金山" ("美国最著名的中国城在纽约和旧金山"), and later towards the end, "目前美國各地的唐人街，…" ("目前美国各地的唐人街，…") show that the passage is mainly about Chinatowns in the United States. Why not:

(A) The passage doesn't specify any Chinatowns outside of the United States.

(B) The passage includes the Chinatown in San Francisco, in addition to the one in New York.

(C) The development of Chinatowns is just one aspect of the passage, which also includes the demographics of the residents in Chinatowns. Again, this option fails to identify that the Chinatowns described in the passage are within the United States only.

96. **(B)** As stated, "在舊金山的中國城裏，中國飯館不計其數。" ("在旧金山的中国城里，中国饭馆不计其数。"). "不計其數" ("不计其数") means *too many to be all accounted for*. Why not:

(A) As stated, "舊金山的中國城…裏的華人幾乎佔了美國華人總數的¼" ("旧金山的中国城…里的华人几乎占了美国华人总数的¼"), i.e., the Chinese population in the San Francisco Chinatown is only ¼ of all the Chinese in the United States. Common sense also tells us that the majority of Chinese people live in China.

(C) As stated, "美國最著名的中國城在紐約和舊金山" ("美国最著名的中国城在纽约和旧金山"). The Chinatowns in New York and San Francisco are the two most famous Chinatowns in the United States, but there are also many other Chinatowns.

(D) "目前美國各地的唐人街，已經不完全是中國人的市場了" ("目前美国各地的唐人街，已经不完全是中国人的市场了") indicates that other Asians are also doing business in Chinatowns these days.

97. **(C)** As stated, "代溝就是不同年齡的人因爲思想觀念的不同而產生的文化距離" ("代沟就是不同年龄的人因为思想观念的不同而产生的文化距离"). In this passage, "代溝" ("代沟") (generation gap) is described as *cultural differences* between a younger generation and their elders and is attributed to the difference in their thoughts. Why not:

(A) *Different thoughts*, "思想觀念的不同" ("思想观念的不同"), is only a part of the definition of *generation gap*.

(B) *Differences of age*, "不同年齡" ("不同年龄"), is also just a part of the *generation gap* definition, as the gap exists between parents and their children.

(D) *Different genders* is not associated with the *generation gap* definition.

98. **(B)** As stated, "有57%的學生在愛好方面與父母的要求不一樣" ("有57%的學生在爱好方面与父母的要求不一样"), i.e., 57% of kids disagree with their parents on the choice of their hobbies. Why not:

(A) As stated, "在父母偷偷看自己的信件、日記，關注孩子與异性同學交往的問題上，有將近20%的學生對父母的做法表示不滿意" ("在父母偷偷看自己的信件、日记，关注孩子与异性同学交往的问题上，有将近20%的学生对父母的做法表示不满意"), i.e., close to 20% of kids disagree with their parents' views of privacy.

(C) As stated, "有70%以上的學生在課外書的選擇上跟父母不同" ("有70%以上的学生在课外书的选择上跟父母不同"), i.e., over 70% of kids disagree with the choice of books outside of school.

(D) As stated, "86%的學生在穿衣服問題上跟父母的看法不一樣" ("86%的学生在穿衣服问题上跟父母的看法不一样"), i.e., 86% of kids disagree with their parents on the choice of clothing.

99. **(B)** As stated, "引起人口老齡化的原因是出生率和死亡率的下降，其中出生率是最主要的因素" ("引起人口老龄化的原因是出生率和死亡率的下降，其中出生率是最主要的因素"). The sentence explains that the primary reason for the increase of the aging population is, indeed, the drop in birth rates.

100. **(B)** The idiom "不可避免" means something is inevitable and definitely will happen.

Writing Skills

CHAPTER 4

GENERAL INFORMATION

The Writing section of the AP Chinese exam evaluates a student's presentational writing ability and mastery of interpretive communication skills. Students are expected to have attained sufficient reading skills to understand the prompts and to:

1. communicate information and ideas in a story narration and a response to an e-mail inquiry;
2. express their feelings and emotions, and exchange personal opinions;
3. demonstrate an understanding of Chinese culture;
4. apply appropriate grammatical structures to express ideas; and
5. exhibit a considerably wide variety of vocabulary that allows them to write fluently and accurately.

There are two tasks in the Writing section of the AP Chinese exam:

1. **Story Narration** is presentational writing. Students will have 15 minutes to write a story according to a four-picture set of prompts. Students should narrate the story as completely as possible, in a culturally appropriate fashion.

2. **E-mail Response** is interpersonal writing with an interpretive element. Students will be presented with an e-mail inquiry from a friend. They will then have 15 minutes to read the e-mail and write a response, addressing the inquiry as completely and appropriately as possible.

The Writing section will take about 30 minutes in total.

To help students prepare for the Writing test, this chapter includes important test information, evaluation criteria, writing strategies, common writing mistakes, and practice prompts. The various topics suggested in this chapter are carefully chosen to help students practice drawing from their own experiences, and to express not only their creativity, but also their views and opinions. Students are encouraged to fully address the prompts with fluency and accuracy, and to elaborate with rich vocabulary, idioms, and grammatical structures.

All writing samples in this chapter are presented in both traditional and simplified Chinese characters. Each sample will be clearly labeled as traditional or simplified. Answer explanations and examples are written first in traditional characters and immediately followed by the simplified counterpart in parentheses. When there is no parenthesized phrase, the presented characters are common in both traditional and simplified versions.

EVALUATION CRITERIA

The Writing free-response section will be evaluated according to the College Board's scoring guidelines. As students prepare for this section, they should familiarize themselves with the scoring guidelines, which are described in this chapter.

The evaluation criteria for the AP Chinese exam include three main factors: task completion, delivery, and language use. It is important for students to understand the task at hand and to complete their responses fully and correctly. Incomplete or incorrect answers will lower their task completion score, even if they manage to deliver a perfect piece of writing featuring advanced language.

While evaluating students' writing, the exam readers check for specific items in each of the three main categories.

Task Completion

1. **Completeness:** Is the prompt fully addressed and the response on topic?

2. **Elaboration:** Is the main idea clearly communicated with enough supporting details?

3. **Organization:** Is the writing properly organized, coherent, and logically connected by appropriate transitional elements?

Delivery

Some of the writing styles students may use on the exam include formal, consultative, casual, and intimate. The choice of style depends on the context of the communication. While using casual slang is probably fine when writing an e-mail to a friend, it may be deemed inadequate for a story narration. Here, the reader examines if the style of language is appropriate to the context, and if it is consistently demonstrated throughout the writing sample.

Language Use

This category is where students can showcase their advanced knowledge of grammar, sentence structure, vocabulary, and idioms. Adequate language use enhances the overall effectiveness of a piece of writing, and thus will be rewarded with high marks.

Overall suggestions:

1. Choose words carefully. For example, use synonyms to avoid unnecessary repetition, and try a variety of grammatical structures.
2. Include a thesis and an appropriate and meaningful conclusion.
3. Use characters, punctuation, and grammar to show language mastery.
4. Master Chinese typing. The AP Writing test requires students to type an essay on a computer instead of handwriting the essay. Students must be careful to select the correct characters according to the Pinyin or Bopomofo formats, particularly with homonyms.
5. Include advanced language, such as Chinese idioms, proverbs, and metaphors, for an added bonus. A list of suggested idioms and proverbs for specific topics is provided later in this book.

SCORING GUIDELINES

Based on the student's performance in task completion, delivery, and language use, scores will be awarded in 7 levels, level 0 to level 6. A description of each level follows, along with examples illustrating the corresponding level for Story Narration and for E-mail Response.

Similar to the conversation samples described in the last chapter, a response that earns the highest mark does not necessarily mean it is perfect or error-free. On the contrary, some samples are deliberately chosen to illustrate that they may still deserve a high mark, as a whole, regardless of some minimal errors, infrequent hesitation, or occasional repetition.

Some characters or phrases in the samples below are intentionally left uncorrected to illustrate the authenticity in the responses.

The **Story Narration** example is based on these pictures:

1.

2.
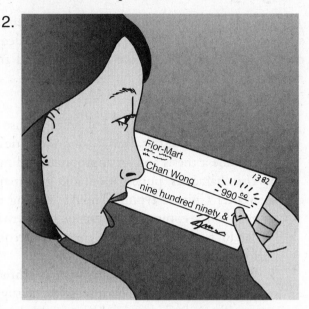

3.

4.

The **E-mail Response** example is based on this incoming e-mail:

[Traditional-character version]
發件人：趙剛
郵件主題：請朋友看電影

　　這個星期天下午的功夫電影，我買好了兩張票。既然你去不了，我打算請我的同屋去，可是我的兩個同屋都跟我關係不錯。我只能請一個去。你認為我請其中的一個同屋去的時候應該考慮哪些因素？另外，對於那位沒有被邀請的同屋，我應該怎麼做才能讓他不生氣？你有什麼具體的建議？

[Simplified-character version]
发件人：赵刚
邮件主题：请朋友看电影

　　这个星期天下午的功夫电影，我买好了两张票。既然你去不了，我打算请我的同屋去，可是我的两个同屋都跟我关系不错。我只能请一个去。你认为我请其中的一个同屋去的时候应该考虑哪些因素？另外，对于那位没有被邀请的同屋，我应该怎么做才能让他不生气？你有什么具体的建议？

LEVEL 6—EXCELLENT

Demonstrates excellence in both presentational and interpersonal writing.

Task Completion
- Written responses address all aspects of the tasks thoroughly.
  - ○ Narration—complete with elaboration and detail, and consistent with the prompt; includes a distinct introduction, middle, and conclusion.
  - ○ E-mail Response—complete with detail.
- Present ideas completely and logically, providing facts or examples if necessary.
- Well-organized and coherent; use appropriate transitional words and cohesive devices to connect paragraphs smoothly.

Delivery
- Narration and E-mail Response—Consistent use of words and phrases appropriate to the situation.

Language Use
- Narration and E-mail Response—Rich and appropriate use of vocabulary and idioms; wide variety of grammatical structures; minimal errors.

Level 6 Story Narration Example:

[Traditional-character version]
　　陳先生和言小姐一起在花落市場的服務台工作。言小姐是一位做使用心的人，每一件事都要弄得好好的才行。陳先生是一位懶洋洋的人，什麼事都不按時昨完。有一天，言小姐不小心拿到了陳先生的支票了。言小姐看到的時候，緊壓得說不出話來了。她就請了宏是宏公司的律師來幫她去告他們公司的董事長。公司的董事長不理不睬地說言小姐為什麼應該和陳先生拿一樣的新水呢？律師說，"因為言小姐和陳先生一樣用心，應該同工同酬！"法官後來就決定言小姐不僅得到了她應該得的薪水，公司還要加倍付她以前少給的薪水。

[Simplified-character version]
　　陈先生和言小姐一起在花落市场的服务台工作。言小姐是一位做使用心的人，每一件事都要弄得好好的才行。陈先生是一位懒洋洋的人，什么事都不按时昨完。有一天，言小姐不小心拿到了陈先生的支票了。言小姐看到的时候，紧压得说不出话来了。她就请了宏是宏公司的律师来帮她去告他们公司的董事长。公司的董事长不理不睬地说言小姐为什么应该和陈先生拿一样的新水呢？律师说，"因为言小姐和陈先生一样用心，应该同工同酬！"法官后来就决定言小姐不仅得到了她应该得的薪水，公司还要加倍付她以前少给的薪水。

COMMENT: The narration tells a complete story that includes a thorough and detailed beginning, middle, and end. The content is well organized and well connected with the use of conjunctions. It uses a variety of rich and appropriate vocabulary, idioms, and grammatical structures, e.g., "懶洋洋"（"懒洋洋"）, "按時"（"按时"）, "不理不睬", "同工同酬." Minimal errors—such as "做事", "做完", "緊壓得"（"紧压得"）—are acceptable as long as they do not obscure the meaning.

Level 6 E-mail Response Example:

[Traditional-character version]

趙剛：

　　你好！收到你的信後我很不好意思。真沒有想到，我的失約給你帶來了這麼大的麻煩，我很過意不去。

　　怎麼在兩個同屋中選擇一個跟你去看電影呢？我覺得最好找一個兩全其美的辦法。首先，你想想看，他們兩人中間哪一個喜歡看功夫片，並問問他們誰星期天下午有空兒。如果一個喜歡另一個不喜歡，或者只有一個那天有時間，問題就容易解決了。可是，如果兩個人都喜歡看這類片子，而且他們都有時間，那問題就會麻煩一些。那麼，你應該看看他們兩個中誰跟你的關係更近一些。我認為你應該邀請那位跟你關係不太近的同屋去。我想那位跟你關係更好的同屋是能理解你的這一做法的。俗話說，物以類聚，人以群分。你這個人這麼大方，我相信你的同屋們也不會是太小氣的人。放心吧，他們不會因為這點兒小氣而生你的氣的。當然，不管你最終邀請了誰，你都應該對那位沒有被邀請的同屋做些補償，比如請他吃頓中國飯，下次請他聽音樂會或者送他一份小禮物什麼的。

　　以上是我的一點兒看法，希望能對你有幫助。

[Simplified-character version]

赵刚：

　　你好！收到你的信后我很不好意思。真没有想到，我的失约给你带来了这么大的麻烦，我很过意不去。

　　怎么在两个同屋中选择一个跟你去看电影呢？我觉得最好找一个两全其美的办法。首先，你想想看，他们两人中间哪一个喜欢看功夫片，并问问他们谁星期天下午有空儿。如果一个喜欢另一个不喜欢，或者只有一个那天有时间，问题就容易解决了。可是，如果两个人都喜欢看这类片子，而且他们都有时间，那问题就会麻烦一些。那么，你应该看看他们两个中谁跟你的关系更近一些。我认为你应该邀请那位跟你关系不太近的同屋去。我想那位跟你关系更好的同屋是能理解你的这一做法的。俗话说，物以类聚，人以群分。你这个人这么大方，我相信你的同屋们也不会是太小气的人。放心吧，他们不会因为这点儿小气而生你的气的。当然，不管你最终邀请了谁，你都应该对那位没有被邀请的同屋做些补偿，比如请他吃顿中国饭，下次请他听音乐会或者送他一份小礼物什么的。

　　以上是我的一点儿看法，希望能对你有帮助。

COMMENT: The response addresses all aspects of the inbound e-mail inquiry in detail. It is a well-organized and well-connected discourse, and demonstrates appropriate transitional elements. It also exhibits a wide range of grammatical structures and rich vocabulary such as "兩全其美"（"两全其美"）, "物以類聚"（"物以类聚"）, and "人以群分"（"人以群分"）.

LEVEL 5—VERY GOOD

Suggests excellence in both presentational and interpersonal writing.

Task Completion
- Written responses address all aspects of the given tasks.
  - Narration—complete and consistent with the prompt; includes an introduction, middle, and conclusion.
  - E-mail Response—addresses all aspects of the prompt.
- Generally good development of ideas; provide facts or examples if necessary.
- Well-organized and coherent; use transitional words and cohesive devices to connect different paragraphs.

Delivery
- Narration and E-mail Response—Generally consistent style of language that is appropriate to situation. A few inconsistencies may occur.

Language Use
- Narration and E-mail Response—Appropriate use of vocabulary, idioms, and grammatical structures; however, a few infrequent errors may occur.

Level 5 Story Narration Example:

[Traditional-character version]

　　小燕在花店已經做了十幾年了．她每天很早就起床上班，做了一整天才回到家做家事煮飯．她每天都這樣心心苦苦地做下去，還只有免免強強地参住家庭．她每個月都在等發薪水的那一天．有一天小燕不小心拿到了大陳的支票，她不小心瞇到支票上的薪水遠遠超過她自己的薪水！小燕想也想不通爲什麽大陳比她的高．那天晚上，小燕打電話給她表哥，因爲表哥是厥資團的律師，小燕就求表哥幫她去告花店的老闆．下一天，表哥跟小燕去跟老闆說．老闆不聽，所以小燕就上法官告花店．過了幾個月小燕已經找到別的工作，法律也打贏了這場官司，小燕得到了補償．

[Simplified-character version]

　　小燕在花店已经做了十几年了．她每天很早就起床上班，做了一整天才回到家做家事煮饭．她每天都这样心心苦苦地做下去，还只有免免强强地参住家庭．她每个月都在等发薪水的那一天．有一天小燕不小心拿到了大陈的支票，她不小心瞇到支票上的薪水远远超过她自己的薪水！小燕想也想不通为什么大陈比她的高．那天晚上，小燕打电话给她表哥，因为表哥是厥资团的律师，小燕就求表哥帮她去告花店的老板．下一天，表哥跟小燕去跟老板说．老板不听，所以小燕就上法官告花店．过了几个月小燕已经找到别的工作,法律也打赢了这场官司，小燕得到了补偿．

COMMENT: The narration includes a beginning, middle, and end, complete with details and elaboration. The content is well organized using transitional elements and cohesive devices, e.g., "有一天", "因爲" ("因为"), "所以", "過了幾個月" ("过了几个月"). The vocabulary and idioms are appropriate in general, but the narration does contain sporadic errors such as "心心苦苦" instead of "辛辛苦苦", "免免強強"("免免强强") instead of "勉勉強強" ("勉勉强强"). "参"("参") instead of "撐",."下一天" instead of "第二天", and an unusual—yet arguably proper—noun "厥資團" ("厥资团").

Level 5 E-mail Response Example:

[Traditional-character version]

　　你請同屋去看電影是一個好主意。不過，兩個人中只能請一個是有點兒讓你左右爲難了。你可以先了解了解，看看兩個同屋中那個喜歡看功夫電影，那個喜歡就請那個去。要是他們兩個都喜歡，那你就自己決定吧。我另外那個你可以請他看別個電影，還是請他吃一次飯。這樣他就不會生氣了。怎麼樣，我的建議不錯吧！

[Simplified-character version]

　　你请同屋去看电影是一个好主意。不过，两个人中只能请一个是有点儿让你左右为难了。你可以先了解了解，看看两个同屋中那个喜欢看功夫电影，那个喜欢就请那个去。要是他们两个都喜欢，那你就自己决定吧。我另外那个你可以请他看别个电影，还是请他吃一次饭。这样他就不会生气了。怎么样，我的建议不错吧！

COMMENT: The response addresses all aspects of the inquiry. The content is well organized and connected with transitional elements. It contains a wide range of grammatical structures and appropriate vocabulary, although there are sporadic errors, e.g., "別個電影" ("别个电影") instead of "別的電影" ("别的电影") and "還是請他" ("还是请他") instead of "或者請他" ("或者请他").

LEVEL 4—GOOD

Demonstrates competence in both presentational and interpersonal writing.

Task Completion
- Writing responses fulfill the task given.
  - Narration—although complete, lacks detail or elaboration; contains minor inconsistencies in story development.
  - E-mail response—includes all aspects of the prompt, but lacks details and elaboration.
- Generally organized and coherent; some use of transitional elements; paragraphs may include loosely connected sentences.

Delivery
- Narration and E-mail Response—although generally consistent in language use, several inconsistencies occur.

Language Use
- Narration and E-mail Response—mostly appropriate vocabulary, idioms, and grammatical structures; some errors, but they generally do not obscure meaning.

Level 4 Story Narration Example:

[Traditional-character version]

　　小楊以經在花店做了好幾年．每天早上六點半起床上ban．做得很累．整天都在幫客人chu li3 事情 到了很晚 才回到家．她zhuan 來的錢，mian3 qiang2夠用．有一天小楊不小心看到張王的薪水比自己的多．她就找律師告公司，最後她贏了，拿回來的錢多到以後都不需要上ban 了．

[Simplified-character version]

小杨以经在花店做了好几年. 每天早上六点半起床上ban. 做得很累. 整天都在帮客人chu li3 事情 到了很晚 才回到家. 她zhuan 来的钱, mian3 qiang2够用. 有一天小杨不小心看到张王的薪水比自己的多. 她就找律师告公司, 最后她赢了, 拿回来的钱多到以后都不需要上ban 了.

COMMENT: The narration tells a complete story with a beginning, middle, and end, but it lacks detail from pictures #1 and #3. It includes some transitional elements and loosely connected sentences, e.g., "到了很晚", "有一天", "最後" ("最后"). Vocabulary and grammatical structures are mostly appropriate.

Level 4 E-mail Response Example:

[Traditional-character version]

我不好意思。你請同污去吧。他們是你的朋友嗎？很好，請那一個去都OK。喜歡看功夫電影的去吧。不喜歡的去吃飯，兩張票給兩個同污，這是我的意見。

[Simplified-character version]

我不好意思。你请同污去吧。他们是你的朋友吗？很好，请那一个去都OK。喜欢看功夫电影的去吧。不喜欢的去吃饭，两张票给两个同污。这是我的意见。

COMMENT: The response completes the task but lacks detail. The content is generally organized, and the discourse is loosely connected. The language use is adequate but there are some errors that do not obscure meaning, such as "同污" instead of "同屋".

LEVEL 3—ADEQUATE

Suggests competence in both presentational and interpersonal writing.

Task Completion
- Written responses fit the given tasks.
  - Narration—basic story, may be inconsistent in story development.
  - E-mail Response—missing some aspects of the prompt.
- May lack organization and coherence; infrequent use of transitional elements; may include disconnected sentences.

Delivery
- Narration and E-mail Response—inconsistent use of language, and may include many errors.

Language Use
- Narration and E-mail Response—limited use of appropriate vocabulary and idioms, mostly simple grammatical structures; errors sometimes obscure meaning, some errors may be interference from another language.

Level 3 Story Narration Example:

[Traditional-character version]

    Yan小姐和Chan先生工作一樣，在花商店。他們在的地方回答問題，customer有什麼問題。Yan小姐工作用工特別，和Chan先生工作not hard as 她。她不高興看Chan先生check。她根husband 找她的Law, 和她最後win, 花商店的boss 給Yan小姐多錢。

[Simplified-character version]

    Yan小姐和Chan先生工作一样，在花商店。他们在的地方回答问题，customer有什么问题。Yan小姐工作用工特别，和Chan先生工作not hard as 她。她不高兴看Chan先生check。她根husband 找她的Law, 和她最后win, 花商店的boss 给Yan小姐多钱。

COMMENT: The narration tells a basic story, but " "她根" husband "找她的" Law" is not entirely consistent with picture #3. The content is somewhat organized but lacks transitional elements. The vocabulary is insufficient and is intermittently interrupted by another language.

Level 3 E-mail Response Example:

[Traditional-character version]

    我想你不請的兩個同屋，而請我的一個朋友去看電影。我的朋友很好的人和星期天有空兒，但是他喜不喜看功夫電影。我覺得，你還是請兩個同屋裡一個區吧。

[Simplified-character version]

    我想你不请的两个同屋，而请我的一个朋友去看电影。我的朋友很好的人和星期天有空儿，但是他喜不喜看功夫电影。我觉得，你还是请两个同屋里一个区吧。

COMMENT: The response addresses the inquiry directly, but it does not address all aspects of the prompt. The content lacks organization, and limited appropriate vocabulary makes it hard to follow, e.g., "但是他喜不喜看功夫電影" ("但是他喜不喜看功夫电影").

> ## LEVEL 2–WEAK
>
> Suggests lack of competence in both presentational and interpersonal writing.
>
> ### Task Completion
> * Written responses may not fit the task given.
>   * Narration—description or a listing instead of narration; may be inconsistent with prompt.
>   * E-mail Response—addresses only some aspects of the prompt.
> * Lack organization and coherence; scattered information, minimal or no use of transitional elements; fragmented sentences.
>
> ### Delivery
> * Narration and E-mail Response—frequent use of language inappropriate to the situation.
>
> ### Language Use
> * Narration and E-mail Response—minimal appropriate vocabulary; plenty of errors that obscure meaning, repeated interference from another language; limited grammatical structures.

Level 2 Story Narration Example:

[Traditional-character version]

    Chan 先生和 Yan 太太一起在Flor 市場的服物台打功．他們一樣的用功 他們的老闆不喜歡女人，chan 先生的新水很多了。他們都去lawyer. Yan太太高興，因爲她多新水。

[Simplified-character version]

    Chan 先生和 Yan 太太一起在Flor 市场的服物台打功. 他们一样的用功 他们的老板不喜欢女人，chan 先生的新水很多了。他们都去lawyer. Yan太太高兴，因为她多新水。

COMMENT: The narration can be characterized as a description of the pictures, but shows little narrative skill. "他們都去lawyer" ("他们都去lawyer") is not consistent with picture #3. The content contains scattered information and lacks organization. It suffers from fragmented sentences and minimal use of transitional elements. Vocabulary and grammatical structures are minimal. There are also interruptions from another language.

Level 2 E-mail Response Example:

[Traditional-character version]

    你情我看電影 我不能去 和你可以 去看電影 馬？同屋喜歡電影 如果 不喜歡 功夫 他生氣 也 許 兩個同屋 跟你的 好馬？我真高興建議你。

[Simplified-character version]

    你情我看电影 我不能去 和你可以 去看电影 马？同屋喜欢电影 如果 不喜欢 功夫 他生气 也 许 两个同屋 跟你的 好马？我真高兴建议你。

COMMENT: The response addresses the inquiry only marginally. The content lacks organization, and it contains scattered information with minimal transitional elements and fragmented sentences. It also includes minimal appropriate vocabulary and limited grammatical structures, with frequent errors such as "情我" instead of "請我" ("请我"), and "好馬" ("好马") instead of "好嗎" ("好吗").

LEVEL 1–VERY WEAK

Demonstrates lack of competence in both presentational and interpersonal writing.

Task Completion
- Written responses are incomplete and difficult to follow.
  - Narration—weak or no narration, inconsistent with the prompt.
  - E-mail Response—very minimally addresses the prompt.
- No organization or coherence; disjointed sentences or isolated words.

Delivery
- Narration and E-mail Response—constant misuse of language; writing style inappropriate to the situation.

Language Use
- Narration and E-mail Response—inappropriate vocabulary; severe interference from another language; poor grammatical structures; frequent errors significantly obscure meaning.

Level 1 Story Narration Example:

[Traditional-character version]

  嚴買東西，Chan是在Flor-Mart也．他們 生氣都．一個check 是990， 嚴不想到那樣，不高興．她去Law with中國朋友．出Court，她是高興．

[Simplified-character version]

  严买东西，Chan是在Flor-Mart也. 他们looks like 生气都. 一个check 的钱是990， 严不想到那样, 不高兴. 她去Law with中国朋友. 出Court，她是高兴.

COMMENT: The narration is incomplete and inconsistent with the picture prompts. The content lacks organization and is made up of disconnected sentences and isolated phrases. Insufficient vocabulary and inadequate grammatical structures make it very difficult to follow the story.

Level 1 E-mail Response Example:

[Traditional-character version]
    星期天 你買票。你請我吃飯，謝謝你，和我 不喜歡 吃中國飯，另外人 去 看 電影。

[Simplified-character version]
    星期天 你买票。你请我吃饭，谢谢你，和我 不喜欢 吃中国饭，另外人 去 看 电影。

COMMENT: The response only minimally addresses the inquiry using very disconnected phrases like "另外人", "謝謝你"("谢谢你"). The content exhibits insufficient vocabulary and grammatical structures, resulting in a largely incomprehensible text.

LEVEL 0—UNACCEPTABLE

Contains nothing that earns credit.

Task Completion
- Written responses completely misunderstand the task given; respond in a different language or dialect other than Mandarin Chinese; no response.

Level 0 Story Narration Example:

[Traditional-character version]
    換年將幫和

[Simplified-character version]
    换年将帮和

COMMENT: The narration is irrelevant to the pictures.

Level 0 E-mail Response Example:

[Traditional-character version]
    你有什麼具體的建議？

[Simplified-character version]
    你有什么具体的建议？

COMMENT: The response is merely a restatement of the question.

> **Free-Response Section: Writing**
>
> **Type:** Free Response-Writing
> **Number of problems:** 2
> **Weight:** 25%
> **Duration:** 30 minutes
>
> ***Directions:*** You will be asked to complete the following two writing tasks.
> 1. Story Narration: Write a narrative story based on a series of 4 pictures given as the main topic. (15 minutes)
> 2. E-mail response: Read an e-mail inquiry from a friend and write a response accordingly. (15 minutes)
>
> ***Important Notes:***
> 1. You cannot move back and forth between the two tasks.
> 2. After the 15 minutes is up from the first task, you will be moved automatically to the second task.
>
> ***Knowledge & Skills:***
> 1. Presentational, interpersonal, interpretive communication.
> 2. Application of basic cultural knowledge.
> 3. Keyboard inputting.
>
> ***Strategies:***
> 1. Be focused, and stay on topic.
> 2. The text displayed in the incoming e-mail can be switched between simplified and traditional characters.
> 3. Select your preferred input method from the pull-down list.
> 4. Use the displayed clock to gauge the remaining time.
> 5. Story Narration – include a beginning, a middle, and an end; narrate key elements from each picture.
> 6. E-mail Response – answer the question in detail.

Fig. 4-1 Writing Task Breakdown

TYPES OF ESSAYS

Based on the College Board's AP Chinese Course Description 2009–2011, students should develop skills to write in a variety of styles, including narrative, descriptive, expository, and persuasive. Each type of writing invokes different aspects of the language that students will want to master. This section presents the necessary writing skills for each type of essay.

Narrative Essay

A narrative essay is an essay that tells a story. There are three important factors when it comes to writing narrative essays: setting, characters, and plot. A story should also have a conclusion and a theme. Each of these factors should be clear and well organized. Mostly, the plot of a story is organized chronologically, leading to a conclusion at the end. The advantage of writing a story this way is that the structure is very clear, and this method is the easiest to work with. In the Writing section of the AP Chinese exam, this method would be most appropriate for narrating a story based on a series of pictures, as in the Story Narration question.

When writing a narrative essay, students should keep in mind the following points.

1. **Captivating**: Capture the reader's attention by doing more than just telling the story. Keep the reader's interest by adding details and/or personal observations that invite the reader into the writer's world. This way, the story is more personal and interesting.

2. **Detailed**: Be sure to include all the essential parts of a story, including a plot, characters, setting, and resolution. Adding internal and external conflicts can make the story more attractive. The details must be carefully thought out to support, explain, and improve the story.

3. **Third-person voice**: A narrative essay is typically written either in the first person, using "我," or in the third person, using "他," "她," or "它." Although the first person point of view seems more personal, it presents a limited knowledge of events. The third person point of view is omniscient, but it may appear less personal, and readers may not relate to it as much. Since the Writing section requires students to narrate a story from beginning to end according to a series of pictures, using the third person point of view would, in fact, be most appropriate.

Practice makes perfect, which is why we encourage students to practice writing narrative stories with a series of pictures.

First, students should outline the story according to the pictures.

Second, they will begin writing an essay with a paragraph that introduces the story and communicates the significance of the subject.

Next, they will use the outline to describe each part of the essay, and add specific details to these parts to breathe life into the story.

Generally, a narrative essay describes a series of events or a process in some sort of order—for example, chronological order. Students write their narratives by following the events as they unfurl.

Before we begin, let's look at each of these steps in detail. Narrating a story by looking at a series of pictures tests one's observation, imagination, reasoning, self-expression, and presentational communication skills. The first thing to do is determine the topic by looking at the pictures and identifying the main point of each picture. Be aware of the sequence of the pictures and pay close attention to the important parts. It is extremely important for students to notice what happens in each picture, the differences between the pictures, and how they relate to one another. This helps students organize the sequence of events they want to present in the essay.

It is also essential to know which details to focus on, such as characters, objects, and settings that relate to the main topic. Some details provide helpful information for completing the story. For example, a character's clothing may indicate what time or season it is; a character's pose or gesture may indicate what he is doing or how he feels. Naming the characters in the story makes it easier to refer to them in the narration. Students should use vocabulary they are familiar with and a lot of conjunctions to ensure a connected flow between sentences and paragraphs, such as "然後" ("然后"), "接著" ("接着"), "可是," "然而," "除此…之外," and "因此." Students should also use adjectives to describe the action and confine their story to the plot shown in the pictures; irrelevant embellishments may distract students from the main ideas and prevent them from completing the task within the allotted time.

While using the following picture prompt to practice writing, students will also improve their vocabularies. In addition, students can practice their speaking skills by telling the story aloud according to the pictures. Oral storytelling can help students exercise their imaginations and give them ideas of how to narrate the story.

The following four pictures present a story about a Chinese idiom, "掩耳盜鈴" ("掩耳盗铃"). Students should first write the story according to the pictures, and then compare their own narration to the sample. The time for writing the story is limited to 15 minutes.

[Traditional-character version]

　　從前有個小偷叫李四。有一天，李四看到一家人的院子裏掛著一口大鐘。那口大鐘是用銅製造的，大鐘的樣子和鐘上的畫兒都很漂亮。李四心想：要是把這口大鐘偷走，然後把它賣掉，一定能賺很多錢。可是鐘又大又重，李四怎麼搬也搬不動。他想啊想，最後終於想出一個好辦法，那就是把鐘打碎，然後再一塊一塊地搬回家。

　　李四找來一把大錘子，用力朝鐘砸去，"咣"的一聲響，把他嚇了一大跳。他想，聲音這麼大，不就是告訴人們他正在這裏偷鐘了嗎？李四越想越害怕，突然，他想出一個主意：要是把耳朵堵起來，不就聽不到鐘的聲音了嗎。李四找東西來把兩隻耳朵堵起來，果然，他什麼聲音都聽不到了。於是李四放心地砸起鐘來。

　　鐘聲傳到了很遠的地方，人們聽到鐘聲後，跑來把李四抓住了。

[Simplified-character version]

　　从前有个小偷叫李四。有一天，李四看到一家人的院子里挂着一口大钟。那口大钟是用铜制造的，大钟的样子和钟上的画儿都很漂亮。李四心想：要是把这口大钟偷走，然后把它卖掉，一定能挣很多钱。可是钟又大又重，李四怎么搬也搬不动。他想啊想，最后终于想出一个好办法，那就是把钟打碎，然后再一块一块地搬回家。

　　李四找来一把大锤子，用力朝钟砸去，"咣"的一声响，把他吓了一大跳。他想，声音这么大，不就是告诉人们他正在这里偷钟了吗？李四越想越害怕，突然，他想出一个主意：要是把耳朵堵起来，不就听不到钟的声音了吗。李四找东西来把两只耳朵堵起来，果然，他什么声音都听不到了。于是李四放心地砸起钟来。

　　钟声传到了很远的地方，人们听到钟声后，跑来把李四抓住了。

The Story Narration task tests students' writing ability in the presentational communication mode. Whether a student receives a good score depends on if he or she is able to write a well-organized story with a clear progression of ideas—namely, a beginning, middle, and end with as much detail as possible. It also depends on whether the student can showcase his or her mastery of proper transitional elements and a cohesive strategy. The above sample essay demonstrates that the author understood the pictures completely and used good techniques to write the story. For convenience, the author named the character "李四." The author paid attention to the differences between pictures, then adopted the proper adverbs and conjunctions, such as "要是," "然後"("然后"), "突然," "果然," "於是" ("于是"), and "以後" ("以后"), to produce a coherent discourse.

In Chinese, some common words are used to describe sequence. The following conjunctions and adverbs are widely used in narration. Students should practice using these words in their own writing.

Conjunctions indicating coordination, transition, succession, progression, or causality

和	hé	and
跟	gēn	and
同	tóng	and
與　（与）	yǔ	and
及	jí	and; as well as

以及		yǐjí	and; as well as
並且	(并且)	bìngqiě	and; besides
但是		dànshì	but; yet
可是		kěshì	but
不過	(不过)	búguò	but; however
這樣	(这样)	zhèyàng	so; in this way
那麼	(那么)	nàme	then; in that case
接著	(接着)	jiēzhe	then; followed by
而且		érqiě	and also; moreover
因此		yīncǐ	therefore; so
然後	(然后)	ránhòu	then; after that; afterwards
於是	(于是)	yúshì	hence; consequently; as a result

Adverbs indicating time and frequency

不斷	(不断)	búduàn	continuously; constantly
常		cháng	often; frequently
常常		chángcháng	often; frequently; usually
曾		céng	once; formerly
曾經	(曾经)	céngjīng	once; formerly
重新		chóngxīn	again; once more
趕緊	(赶紧)	gǎnjǐn	in a hurry
趕快	(赶快)	gǎnkuài	in a hurry
剛	(刚)	gāng	just
剛才	(刚才)	gāngcái	just now
剛剛	(刚刚)	gānggāng	just
後來	(后来)	hòulái	afterwards
漸漸	(渐渐)	jiànjiàn	gradually; little by little
將	(将)	jiāng	be going to; only just; will
將要	(将要)	jiāngyào	will; close to (a certain period of time)
經常	(经常)	jīngcháng	often; frequent
就		jiù	emphasizes that something occurs early
就要		jiùyào	will; shall; close to (a certain of time)
快		kuài	almost
立即		lìjí	immediately; as soon as
立刻		lìkè	immediately; as soon as; at once
屢次	(屡次)	lǚcì	repeatedly; time and again
馬上	(马上)	mǎshàng	immediately; at once
其間	(其间)	qíjiān	meanwhile
然後	(然后)	ránhòu	then; after that
始終	(始终)	shǐzhōng	all along
突然		tūrán	suddenly
已		yǐ	already
已經	(已经)	yǐjīng	already
以後	(以后)	yǐhòu	after; afterwards; later
以前		yǐqián	before; formerly
又		yòu	again
再		zài	again; once more

再三		zàisān	over and over
正在		zhèngzài	indicates an action in progress
終於	（终于）	zhōngyú	finally; at last
總是	（总是）	zǒngshì	always
總算	（总算）	zǒngsuàn	at last; finally
最後	（最后）	zuìhòu	final; in the end

NARRATIVE ESSAY WRITING TIPS

1. The story should contain all three essential factors: plot, characters, and setting.
2. The story should be written in complete paragraphs, with a logically structured content.
3. The story should demonstrate the student's ability to choose the appropriate vocabulary and to adopt a wide range of grammatical structures.
4. The progression of the story should be narrated with a suitable selection of transitional elements.
5. The story should contain few, if any, typographic errors. Students should avoid mistakes like typing the correct pronunciation but choosing the wrong character, or typing an incorrect pronunciation to start with and consequentially choosing the wrong character.

Descriptive Essay

A descriptive essay is an essay that describes a person, place, or thing. It can be either *objective* or *subjective*. In an objective descriptive essay, students describe physical objects by providing facts, not opinions. In a subjective descriptive essay, students write about what they perceive in all five senses, including details such as height, weight, color, and smell, and their feelings toward the object. The purpose of a descriptive essay is to capture the reader's imagination so that he or she can visualize the things being described. It is important for students to carefully select specific, concrete details to support their dominant impression.

Descriptive essay writing techniques may be useful in Story Narration or E-mail Response questions. For example, the pictures in a Story Narration may present an opportunity to depict people, animals, or scenery.

When writing a descriptive essay, students should keep in mind the following points.

1. A descriptive essay focuses on a person, a place, a memory, an event, or an experience. Students should start with the obvious, then develop and describe.
2. Students should provide plenty of specific descriptions to give readers a complete and vivid perception and impression.
3. Students should choose appropriate words that convey their emotions or perspectives, and use words that appeal to the reader's senses.
4. Students should create a clear pattern of organization and use a wide range of grammatical structures.

Describing an Animal:

Students might need to describe an animal when narrating a story or introducing an animal in one of the four pictures. Describing an animal is a good topic for a descriptive essay. The following is a sample essay describing a cat.

[Traditional-character version]

　　我最喜愛的小動物是貓，因爲它們漂亮,溫和，也很獨立。

　　我家有一隻可愛的小貓，我給它起了一個有意思的名字叫"白胖胖"，因爲它胖胖的身上長了一層又長又軟的白毛。白胖胖有一雙又大又亮的藍眼睛和一個紅紅的小鼻子，讓人喜愛。白胖胖是一隻特別愛乾淨的貓。它每天都要用爪子給自己洗好幾次臉，每次大小便也總會在同一個地方。白胖胖的作息時間跟我完全不一樣。它白天的大部分時間都在我的沙發上或者床下睡覺，因此，我常常罵它是"懶貓"。到了半夜，我睡覺睡得很香的時候，它又常常把我吵醒。

　　我喜歡白胖胖，把它看成我生活中的一個好朋友。

[Simplified-character version]

　　我最喜爱的小动物是猫，因为它们漂亮，温和，也很独立。

　　我家有一只可爱的小猫，我给它起了一个有意思的名字叫"白胖胖"，因为它胖胖的身上长了一层又长又软的白毛。白胖胖有一双又大又亮的蓝眼睛和一个红红的小鼻子，让人喜爱。白胖胖是一只特别爱干净的猫。它每天都要用爪子给自己洗好几次脸，每次大小便也总会在同一个地方。白胖胖的作息时间跟我完全不一样。它白天的大部分时间都在我的沙发上或者床下睡觉，因此，我常常骂它是"懒猫"。到了半夜，我睡觉睡得很香的时候，它又常常把我吵醒。

　　我喜欢白胖胖，把它看成我生活中的一个好朋友。

In the first sentence, the writer begins with a confession that cats are his favorite animal, because they are "漂亮，溫和，也很獨立" ("漂亮，温和，也很独立"). Then, the writer describes his lovely cat with specific details, such as its appearance, daily routine, and habits. The conclusion paragraph summarizes the writer's sentiment about the cat: "把它看成我生活中的一個好朋友" ("把它看成我生活中的一个好朋友").

Describing a Place:

When asked to describe a place, such as a room or a park, try to use sentences that indicate the existence of certain objects at the given place. The following is a sample essay that describes a room.

[Traditional-character version]

　　這是我的房間，它是我在大學居住和學習的地方。

　　我的房間在大樓的第二層。房間的前面有一個大窗戶，窗戶的下面是我的書桌，書桌的前邊有一把椅子，書桌上面放著一個筆記本電腦，電腦的旁邊有一個漂亮的小臺燈。書桌的右邊放著一個很大的書架，書架上邊有很多英文書，也有幾本中文書。書桌的左邊是一個小沙發，沙發上放滿了衣服。床放在房間的右邊，床對面的牆上有一幅大照片，照片裏面是一個漂亮的女孩子，那是我的朋友給我照的。照片的下面有一個小櫃子，櫃子上放著一臺小小的電視機。我學習累了，就看一會兒電視。

　　我的房間不很大，也不太整齊，但是我很喜歡它。我總是把它打掃得很乾淨。

[Simplified-character version]

这是我的房间，它是我在大学居住和学习的地方。

我的房间在大楼的第二层。房间的前面有一个大窗户，窗户的下面是我的书桌，书桌的前边有一把椅子，书桌上面放着一个笔记本电脑，电脑的旁边有一个漂亮的小台灯。书桌的右边放着一个很大的书架，书架上边有很多英文书，也有几本中文书。书桌的左边是一个小沙发，沙发上放满了衣服。床放在房间的右边，床对面的墙上有一幅大照片，照片里面是一个漂亮的女孩子，那是我的朋友给我照的。照片的下面有一个小柜子，柜子上放着一台小小的电视机。我学习累了，就看一会儿电视。

我的房间不很大，也不太整齐，但是我很喜欢它。我总是把它打扫得很干净。

This essay includes the three types of sentences: sentences with "有," "是," and "Verb-著"("Verb-着"). For example: "窗戶的下面是我的書桌，書桌的前邊有一把椅子，書桌上面放著一個筆記本電腦" ("窗户的下面是我的书桌，书桌的前边有一把椅子，书桌上面放着一个笔记本电脑").

Writing a descriptive essay requires students to master a variety of descriptive vocabulary and appropriate expressions. A wide-ranging vocabulary helps students create vivid images and enhance readers' interest in the essay. Adjectives, prepositions, directional words, directional complements, descriptive complements, and sentences are very important and practical for writing this type of essay.

Describing a Country or City:

It is likely that students will be asked to describe a country or a city in an E-mail Response. Students might also need to describe a place in the Cultural Presentation part of the Speaking section. When describing countries and cities, students should communicate the significance of the place, its physical location, size, geography, climate, culture, population, and so on. The following is a sample essay.

[Traditional-character version]

新加坡位於東南亞的中心，是由幾十個小島組成的，面積大約600多平方公里，人口300多萬。新加坡是一個多民族的國家，一半以上的人口是華人。新加坡的政府官方語言是英語，但是每個民族都有自己的語言，例如華語，也就是中文。新加坡是一個有名的花園城市國家，又乾淨又漂亮。新加坡也是一個有名的旅遊中心，每年從世界各地去那裏旅遊的人很多。新加坡有很多有名的購物中心。在那裏，差不多世界上所有的名牌都可以買到。新加坡還是一個美食中心，遊客可以吃到各種各樣風味的小吃。

[Simplified-character version]

新加坡位于东南亚的中心，是由几十个小岛组成的，面积大约600多平方公里，人口300多万。新加坡是一个多民族的国家，一半以上的人口是华人。新加坡的政府官方语言是英语，但是每个民族都有自己的语言，例如华语，也就是中文。新加坡是一个有名的花园城市国家，又干净又漂亮。新加坡也是一个有名的旅游中心，每年从世界各地去那里旅游的人很多。新加坡有很多有名的购物中心。在那里，差不多世界上所有的名牌都可以买到。新加坡还是一个美食中心，游客可以吃到各种各样风味的小吃。

For practice, students can describe their own cities, towns, or somewhere they want to live. They should make an effort to tell their readers where the city is located and why it is special. Students may also want to explain the history behind the place or predict what the city might be like in the future.

The following words and phrases related to directions can be useful when describing a place:

東	(东)	dōng	east
南		nán	south
西		xī	west
北		běi	north
東北	(东北)	dōngběi	northeast
東南	(东南)	dōngnán	southeast
西北		xīběi	northwest
西南		xīnán	southwest
前		qián	front
後	(后)	hòu	back; behind
左		zuǒ	left
右		yòu	right
中間	(中间)	zhōngjiān	center; middle
裏面	(里面)	lǐmian	inside
外面		wàimian	outside
對面	(对面)	duìmiàn	opposite
上面		shàngmian	above; over; top
下面		xiàmian	below; under
頂上	(顶上)	dǐngshang	top
底下		dǐxia	bottom
角上	(角上)	jiǎoshang	corner
旁邊	(旁边)	pángbiān	side
四周		sìzhōu	around
遠處	(远处)	yuǎnchù	beyond
近處	(近处)	jìnchù	nearby
向上		xiàngshàng	up
向下		xiàngxià	down
朝上		cháoshàng	up
朝下		cháoxià	down
在…之上		zài…zhīshàng	over
在…之下		zài…zhīxià	beneath
在附近		zài fùjìn	round about
周圍	(周围)	zhōuwéi	round about
挨著	(挨着)	āizhe	next to
緊挨著	(紧挨着)	jǐnāizhe	close to
沿著	(沿着)	yánzhe	along
順著	(顺着)	shùnzhe	along

Describing a Person:

Describing people requires students to record not only their physical characteristics, but also their movements, postures, emotions, personalities, and idiosyncrasies. Everyone's family background, profession, class, and experience is different, and they may all affect people's appearances. Sometimes, describing a person's physical appearance may reveal a lot about a person's personality. Describing people also requires students to depict what people are wearing or carrying.

The following is a passage that describes a person.

[Traditional-character version]

王麗麗是一個17歲的女孩子，個子不高也不矮，看起來有一點兒胖。麗麗的眼睛又大又亮，嘴唇兒紅紅的。她的身上穿著一件藍色的T恤衫，下面配的是一條牛仔褲，腳上穿著一雙白色的運動鞋。她的肩上背著一個漂亮的小包，手裏拿著幾本書。麗麗不僅人長得漂亮，還是一個對別人特別好的女孩子。

[Simplified-character version]

王丽丽是一个17岁的女孩子，个子不高也不矮，看起来有一点儿胖。丽丽的眼睛又大又亮，嘴唇儿红红的。她的身上穿着一件蓝色的T恤衫，下面配的是一条牛仔裤，脚上穿着一双白色的运动鞋。她的肩上背着一个漂亮的小包，手里拿着几本书。丽丽不仅人长得漂亮，还是一个对别人特别好的女孩子。

The following words and phrases can be used to describe the physical characteristics of a person:

年齡	（年龄）	niánlíng	age
多歲	（多岁）	. . . duōsuì	more than . . . years old
…上下		. . . shàngxià	about . . . years old
…左右		. . . zuǒyòu	about . . . years old
身高		shēngāo	height
矮個子	（矮个子）	ǎigèzi	short man; to be short
高個兒	（高个儿）	gāogèr	big man; to be big
身材		shēncái	figure
苗條	（苗条）	miáotiao	slender
胖		pàng	fat
亭亭玉立		tíngtíng yùlì	to stand tall and graceful
小巧玲瓏	（小巧玲珑）	xiǎoqiǎo línglóng	small and nimble
高大魁梧		gāodà kuíwú	tall and strong
人高馬大	（人高马大）	réngāo mǎdà	tall and strong
身強力壯	（身强力壮）	shēnqiáng lìzhuàng	healthy and strong
矯健	（矫健）	jiǎojiàn	strong and vigorous
瘦小枯乾	（瘦小枯干）	shòuxiǎo kūgān	thin, small, and emaciated
皮膚	（皮肤）	pífū	skin
白淨	（白净）	bájìng	fair and clear
光滑	（光滑）	guānghuá	smooth
光潔	（光洁）	guāngjié	clear
粗糙		cūcāo	rough skin
皺紋	（皱纹）	zhòuwén	wrinkle
臉色	（脸色）	liǎnsè	complexion

紅潤	（红润）	hóngrùn	rosy
蒼白	（苍白）	cāngbái	pale
灰暗		huī'àn	ashen and gray
眼睛		yǎnjing	eyes
明亮		míngliàng	bright
清澈		qīngchè	clear
水汪汪		shuǐwāngwāng	bright and sparkling
亮晶晶		liàngjīngjīng	bright
髮型	（发型）	fàxíng	hairstyle
長髮	（长发）	chángfà	long hair
短髮	（短发）	duǎnfà	short hair
捲髮	（卷发）	juǎnfà	curly
直髮	（直发）	zhífà	straight
劉海兒	（刘海儿）	liúhǎir	bangs
穿著	（穿着）	chuānzhuó	clothing
樸素	（朴素）	pǔsù	simple; plain
整潔	（整洁）	zhěngjié	clear
破破爛爛	（破破烂烂）	pòpò lànlàn	worn-out clothes
髒乎乎	（脏乎乎）	zānghūhū	dirty
時髦	（时髦）	shímáo	stylish; in vogue
土氣	（土气）	tǔqì	rustic; uncouth
精神		jīngshén	psychosis
活潑	（活泼）	huópō	natural and lively
開朗	（开朗）	kāilǎng	open; cheerful
樂觀	（乐观）	lèguān	hopeful; optimistic
文靜	（文静）	wénjìng	gentle and quiet
呆板		dāibǎn	stiff; rigid
沉默寡言		chénmò guǎyán	of few words; reticent
無精打采	（无精打采）	wújīng dǎcǎi	listless; out of sorts
精神抖擻	（精神抖擞）	jīngshén dǒusǒu	spirits

The AP Chinese exam will not require students to write an entire essay describing a person. However, the ability to do so might be necessary when describing a character in a Story Narration. When practicing, students should try to describe people they know, such as family members, friends, classmates, teachers, and famous people. To write a good description, students must observe people's physical characteristics, especially how one person differs from another. Students should focus their descriptions on the senses, and provide vivid and specific details that *show*, rather than *tell*, readers what they are describing.

Describing Scenery:

When writing a Story Narration, students may need to describe scenery according to the pictures. The most important thing is to be extremely observant. Students need to leave a lingering impression with their descriptions. Write what you "see" rather than what you "know," and organize the essay by what is seen first through what is seen last. Correctly used adjectives and adverbs will make the essay's structure clear. Students may also present an opinion or feeling through their description. The following is a writing sample by a Chinese language learner, which contains a structure deficiency. Understanding the structural error in the essay will help students improve their writing skills.

[Traditional-character version]

　　雪後的校園特別漂亮。那條去校園的小路上好像蓋了一條白白的地毯，路兩邊整整齊齊的大樹，像士兵一樣認真地保護著校園。小風吹來，樹上的雪慢慢地飄下來，掉在同學們的頭上、臉上，涼涼的。

　　教室前的小松樹上都是白白的小雪球。小風吹來，樹枝一搖一搖的，好像向大家點頭問好。教室的房頂上，挂滿了亮亮的冰條兒，非常美麗。

　　學校的運動場上，男孩子們生龍活虎，女孩子們歡天喜地，個個快樂得像小鳥一樣。運動場中間，同學們堆起了一個大大的雪人：黑黑大大的眼睛，紅紅長長的鼻子。

　　雪讓校園更漂亮，讓同學們更快樂！

[Simplified-character version]

　　雪后的校园特别漂亮。那条去校园的小路上好像盖了一条白白的地毯，路两边整整齐齐的大树，像士兵一样认真地保护着校园。小风吹来，树上的雪慢慢地飘下来，掉在同学们的头上、脸上，凉凉的。

　　教室前的小松树上都是白白的小雪球。小风吹来，树枝一摇一摇的，好像向大家点头问好。教室的房顶上，挂满了亮亮的冰条儿，非常美丽。

　　学校的运动场上，男孩子们生龙活虎，女孩子们欢天喜地，个个快乐得像小鸟一样。运动场中间，同学们堆起了一个大大的雪人：黑黑大大的眼睛，红红长长的鼻子。

　　雪让校园更漂亮，让同学们更快乐！

This is a description about a schoolyard after snowfall. The author carefully uses metaphors to describe the beauty of this scene. The writer also uses idioms, such as "生龍活虎"("生龙活虎") and "歡天喜地" ("欢天喜地"), and exclamatory sentences correctly. The essay reveals that the author appreciates the beauty of the scenery and how snow brings joy to people. However, the essay structure does not present his observations in a clear order. The following rewrite reconstructs the order, giving the essay a proper structure.

[Traditional-character version]

　　雪後的校園漂亮而充滿歡笑。

　　遠遠望去，那條去校園的小路上好像蓋了一條白白的地毯，路兩邊整整齊齊的大樹，像士兵一樣認真地保護著校園。微風吹來，樹上的雪慢慢地飄下來，掉在同學們的頭上、臉上，涼涼的。

　　看，教室前的小松樹上都是白白的小雪球。微風吹來，樹枝一搖一搖的，好像向大家點頭問好。教室的房頂上，挂滿了亮亮的冰條兒，非常美麗。

　　瞧，運動場中間，同學們堆起了一個大大的雪人：黑黑大大的眼睛，紅紅長長的鼻子。

　　聽，學校的運動場上，男孩子們這邊生龍活虎，女孩子們那邊歡天喜地，個個快樂得像小鳥一樣。

　　雪讓校園更漂亮，讓同學們更快樂！

[Simplified-character version]

雪后的校园漂亮而充满欢笑。

远远望去，那条去校园的小路上好像盖了一条白白的地毯，路两边整整齐齐的大树，像士兵一样认真地保护着校园。微风吹来，树上的雪慢慢地飘下来，掉在同学们的头上、脸上，凉凉的。

看，教室前的小松树上都是白白的小雪球。微风吹来，树枝一摇一摇的，好像向大家点头问好。教室的房顶上，挂满了亮亮的冰条儿，非常美丽。

瞧，运动场中间，同学们堆起了一个大大的雪人：黑黑大大的眼睛，红红长长的鼻子。

听，学校的运动场上，男孩子们这边生龙活虎，女孩子们那边欢天喜地，个个快乐得像小鸟一样。

雪让校园更漂亮，让同学们更快乐！

The difference between the two sample essays lies in their structure. The new essay adds the verbs "遠遠望去" ("远远望去"), "看," and "聽" ("听"), which appeal to the senses. The writer invites readers into the scene, which makes people happy. When writing about the classroom, the author makes orderly observations, from the ceiling to the floor, and from far to near. When writing about the field, the author uses "這邊" ("这边") and "那邊" ("那边") to describe the scene in a more orderly fashion. The first sentence is changed to "雪後的校園漂亮而充滿歡笑" ("雪后的校园漂亮而充满欢笑"), which connects it to the last sentence, "雪讓校園更漂亮，讓同學們更快樂！" ("雪让校园更漂亮，让同学们更快乐！"), making the essay more vivid and meaningful.

Note that the AP Chinese exam does not require students to write a descriptive essay about scenery, but again, the ability to do so might be necessary in Story Narrations. Students should be mindful that, while the scenery may not be the main point of an essay, it may well be a crucial supporting detail. Therefore, although one may not need to describe every aspect of the scenery, picking out a couple of features that seem the most important can add depth to the essay.

The four seasons are often used in descriptive essays. The following are the idioms for each season. Students should understand these idioms, and learn how to use them in written and spoken language.

春天

春暖花開	（春暖花开）	chūnnuǎn huākāi	spring blossoms
百花盛開	（百花盛开）	bǎihuā shèngkāi	blaze of flowers
風和日麗	（风和日丽）	fēnghé rìlì	fine and warm
鳥語花香	（鸟语花香）	niǎoyǔ huāxiāng	birds sing and flowers release fragrance
雨後春筍	（雨后春笋）	yǔhòu chūnsǔn	mushroom like bamboo shoots after a spring rain

夏天

烈日炎炎		lièrì yányán	extremely hot
滿頭大汗	（满头大汗）	mǎntóu dàhàn	profusely hairy
寸草不生		cùncǎo bùshēng	lane is not long grass
烈日當空	（烈日当空）	lièrì dānkōng	scorching hot and dry
暴風驟雨	（暴风骤雨）	bàofēng zhòuyǔ	a prodigious storm

秋天

秋高氣爽	（秋高气爽）	qiūgāo qìshuǎng	high sky and bright autumn
景色宜人		jǐngsè yírén	offering enchanting views
秋風落葉	（秋风落叶）	qiūfēng luòyè	autumn leaves
五穀豐登	（五谷丰登）	wǔgǔ fēngdēng	have a bumper harvest
秋風蕭瑟	（秋风萧瑟）	qiūfēng xiāosè	autumn wind is sighing

冬天

冰天雪地		bīngtiān xuědì	world of ice and snow
白雪茫茫		báixuě mángmáng	snow everywhere
寒冬臘月	（寒冬腊月）	hándōng làyuè	severe winter
漫天飛雪	（漫天飞雪）	màntiān fēixuě	snow all over the sky
天寒地凍	（天寒地冻）	tiānhán dìdòng	the weather is cold and the ground is frozen

---

DESCRIPTIVE ESSAY WRITING TIPS

1. When planning, students should know what or whom they want to describe and the particular qualities they will focus on.
2. When drafting, students should consider the importance of the senses and include details that give readers a vivid impression.
3. When revising, students should add sufficient details and descriptions.
4. Finally, students should make sure that the essay focuses on one topic and that it is structured in the most effective way.

Expository Essay

An expository essay shares, explains, suggests, or explores information and ideas without any bias. The expository essay is formatted the same way as any other essay; it should be clear in its purpose and have a distinct main idea. The function of the expository essay is to present other people's views or to report an event or situation. The expository essay should:

1. Capture the significance of the topic. A certain topic might have several different facets, but not all of them have to be included in the essay.
2. Be aware of the audience. The same topic can be written differently depending on who's reading it. Students should remember the age, gender, class, level of education, occupation, and so forth of their intended readers. For example, the harmful effects of smoking are an important issue for many people. However, the effects are different for different people.
3. Make sure that the facts, especially numerical data regarding quantity, level, quality, and space, are accurate.
4. Introduce knowledge without being too literal.
5. Organize information well. Words such as "首先," "其次," "再者," and "最後" ("最后") are useful for presenting facts in a clear and orderly fashion.

The two different tasks in the Writing free-response portion of the AP Chinese exam—Story Narration and E-mail Response—both require strong expository writing skills.

There are a variety of ways to develop an expository essay. It is important to fully understand the topic, to focus on the most important characteristics of the topic, and to keep the audience in mind.

First analyze the essay topic. The task prompt presents a broad topic, and students can expand on this topic as much as they want to, within reason. This also allows students to write about a particular aspect of the topic that is familiar to them. In other words, the exam provides a broad topic that can be seen from a number of perspectives. Students simply need to define the aspect of the topic they are writing about and present it straightforwardly.

For example, the AP Chinese exam might require students to respond to an e-mail by introducing their school library, which contains elements of an expository essay. Classifying multiple subjects by certain criteria is a good technique to use in this kind of writing. The following sample is written without using the classification technique.

[Traditional-character version]

　　學校圖書館的書有中文的，英文的，科技的，文學的，現代的，古代的以及政治、經濟方面的。

[Simplified-character version]

　　学校图书馆的书有中文的，英文的，科技的，文学的，现代的，古代的以及政治、经济方面的。

The sample is revised and clarified below:

[Traditional-character version]

　　圖書館的書，按語言分，有中文的、英文的；按時代分，有現代的，古代的；按性質分，有科技的、文學的以及政治經濟方面的。

[Simplified-character version]

　　图书馆的书，按语言分，有中文的、英文的；按时代分，有现代的，古代的；按性质分，有科技的、文学的以及政治经济方面的。

Comparing the two versions of the sample, classifying the books into different categories makes the topic clear and logical. Note that the books here are classified more than once, but only one criterion is applied for each class.

Using graphs, statistics, and charts in an essay can also help students express their ideas more clearly. Sometimes, using quotes from famous writers, idioms, proverbs, and other materials makes the essay more concrete. Students should practice writing expository essays by combining several of these techniques. In some cases, it is hard to write an effective essay using a single technique. Which technique or how many techniques to apply should be determined by the writer's treatment of the topic.

Sometimes, the prompt may ask for *instructions*, which means the student needs to provide step-by-step instructions to teach readers to complete a task. The following sample essay gives step-by-step instructions for making a Christmas card.

[Traditional-character version]

聖誕節要到了，你可以自己給朋友做一張聖誕卡片。

你應該準備的東西有一張A4紙，一盒彩筆，一支鉛筆，一把剪刀和一把尺子。

首先，你把A4紙對著折起來，用尺子對著紙裏面畫幾條綫，那是爲了留出地方寫祝賀話用的。然後，你對著紙的中間畫一個“心”的符號，再沿著它的邊兒把它剪開。你拿出紅筆來，給“心”劃上紅色，再在紅心的周圍畫一個綠色的方框，方框的周圍再畫一個藍色的方框。在方框上寫上“聖誕節”三個字。接著，你在紙的左邊畫一頂聖誕帽子，再在紙的右邊畫一朵黃色的玫瑰花。這樣，聖誕卡的背景就做完了。現在，你可以寫祝賀的話了。你可以在畫好的線上寫上你想寫的話，比如“聖誕節快樂！”“祝你聖誕節愉快”什麼的。最後，在下面的一行線上，你把自己的名字和日期再寫上。

一張精美的聖誕卡片做完了。現在，你趕快去郵局給朋友寄去吧。

[Simplified-character version]

圣诞节要到了，你可以自己给朋友做一张圣诞卡片。

你应该准备的东西有一张A4纸，一盒彩笔，一支铅笔，一把剪刀和一把尺子。

首先，你把A4纸对着折起来，用尺子对着纸里面画几条线，那是为了留出地方写祝贺话用的。然后，你对着纸的中间画一个“心”的符号，再沿着它的边儿把它剪开。你拿出红笔来，给“心”划上红色，再在红心的周围画一个绿色的方框，方框的周围再画一个蓝色的方框。在方框上写上“圣诞节”三个字。接着，你在纸的左边画一顶圣诞帽子，再在纸的右边画一朵黄色的玫瑰花。这样，圣诞卡的背景就做完了。现在，你可以写祝贺的话了。你可以在画好的线上写上你想写的话，比如“圣诞节快乐！”“祝你圣诞节愉快”什么的。最后，在下面的一行线上，你把自己的名字和日期再写上。

一张精美的圣诞卡片做完了。现在，你赶快去邮局给朋友寄去吧。

The essay first lists the materials that are required to do this project. Then, the essay guides readers carefully through the instructions to ensure that the outcome is correct. The language is simple, the structure is clear.

Careful wording and usage make instructions in an essay more understandable and vivid. The following sample essay shows how to apply this technique to describe the procedures for carving and eating Peking duck. Pay close attention to the sentence structures, which are widely used in expository essays.

[Traditional-character version]

鴨子烤好以後，烤鴨店的師傅把一輛小車推到餐桌的旁邊，他要在顧客面前爲他們片烤鴨。師傅先讓顧客看看完整的鴨子，然後用一把特別的刀子，把鴨子連皮帶肉一片一片地片下來，再把片好的鴨肉整齊地擺在一個盤子裏，最後把盤子端到顧客的桌子上。盤中的鴨肉，每一片上都帶皮，肉薄得像紙一樣。師傅還會把剩下的鴨架子拿回廚房，把它做成一鍋味道鮮美的鴨湯。

吃烤鴨有很多講究。顧客拿起一張薄餅，把它鋪在一隻手上，再用筷子夾起鴨肉，蘸一點兒甜麵醬，把鴨肉放到薄餅上，然後夾上幾根葱絲和黃瓜條兒，最後用另一隻手把它們捲起來。如果顧客一隻手捲不好，也可以把餅放到盤子裏，用兩隻手來捲。

[Simplified-character version]

鸭子烤好以后，烤鸭店的师傅把一辆小车推到餐桌的旁边，他要在顾客面前为他们片烤鸭。师傅先让顾客看看完整的鸭子，然后用一把特别的刀子，把鸭子连皮带肉一片一片地片下来，再把片好的鸭肉整齐地摆在一个盘子里，最后把盘子端到顾客的桌子上。盘中的鸭肉，每一片上都带皮，肉薄得像纸一样。师傅还会把剩下的鸭架子拿回厨房，把它做成一锅味道鲜美的鸭汤。

吃烤鸭有很多讲究。顾客拿起一张薄饼，把它铺在一只手上，再用筷子夹起鸭肉，蘸一点儿甜面酱，把鸭肉放到薄饼上，然后夹上几根葱丝和黄瓜条儿，最后用另一只手把它们卷起来。如果顾客一只手卷不好，也可以把饼放到盘子里，用两只手来卷。

This essay is very specific and easy to understand. The verbs used in the essay were carefully chosen. For example, the author uses "片" (carve) instead of "切" (cut), which shows the quality of the cutting; the writer also uses "鋪"("铺"), "夾"("夹"), "蘸," "放," and "捲" ("卷") to explain eating ducks. Each of those verbs indicates a specific action. The nouns and measure words are very appropriate, such as "葱絲"("葱丝"), "黃瓜條兒" ("黄瓜条儿"), "一輛小車" ("一辆小车"), "一把刀子," "一鍋鴨湯" ("一锅鸭汤"), and "一張薄餅"("一张薄饼"). The writer uses idioms, such as "肉薄如紙"("肉薄如纸") (which is actually a simile) and "味道鮮美"("味道鲜美"), to make the descriptions vivid. Note that the author also uses the "把" sentence structure a couple of times: "把鴨子片下來" ("把鸭子片下来"), "把餅鋪在一隻手上" ("把饼铺在一只手上"), "把鴨肉放到薄餅上" ("把鸭肉放到薄饼上"), and "把它捲起來" ("把它卷起来"). Another sentence structure used in the essay is a resultative complement construction, as in "烤好," "片下來," "拿回," "熬成," "拿起," "夾起" ("夹起"), "夾上"("夹上"), and "捲起來"("卷起来"), which describes the actions accurately and vividly. "把" sentences and resultative complement constructions are commonly used in expository essays. Overall, this sample essay is quite advanced. It is well organized and coherent, with a clear progression of ideas. Its use of proper transitional elements and consistent devices is very good.

EXPOSITORY ESSAY WRITING TIPS

Attention to the following points:
1. The thesis statement should be defined narrowly enough to be supportable within the essay.
2. Each supporting paragraph should have a distinct controlling topic and all other sentences should be data directly and factually supporting the topic. Transitional elements and cohesive devices should help the reader follow along and support the essay's logic.
3. The concluding paragraph should restate the thesis and the main ideas.
4. The essay should finish with a statement that reinforces the key topics.
5. New material should never be introduced in the conclusion.

Persuasive Essay

A persuasive essay tries to prove a point by making a logical, ethical, and emotional appeal to readers. Persuasive essays present information about a controversial subject and also an argument debating the pros and cons of the subject. The author has to clearly take a stand and write as if he or she is trying to persuade an opposing audience to accept new beliefs.

Persuasive writing skills may come in handy on the E-mail Response task in the Writing free-response section of the exam. The task assesses students' interpretive communication skills (understanding what is being asked of them) and their presentational and interpersonal communication skills (delivering the response). When approaching this task, students should discuss the topic in general first, then choose one feature of that topic and describe the details, such as what they like or dislike about it. Students should justify their opinions with strong examples that befit the persuasive essay style.

The following is an e-mail about "chasing stars" and a sample response.

E-mail:

[Traditional-character version]

發件人：陳軍

郵件主題：中學生追星好不好

　　中學生追星已經成爲一種潮流，也是校園中的一個熱門話題。有些人覺得追星對青年學生的學習及生活都造成不好的影響，有些人認爲追星可以幫助學生樹立學習、生活目標，利於培養學生的興趣與愛好。你是一個追星族嗎？談談你追星的經歷或者對追星問題的看法。謝謝！

[Simplified-character version]

发件人：陈军

邮件主题：中学生追星好不好

　　中学生追星已经成为一种潮流，也是校园中的一个热门话题。有些人觉得追星对青年学生的学习及生活都造成不好的影响，有些人认为追星可以帮助学生树立学习、生活目标，利于培养学生的兴趣与爱好。你是一个追星族吗？谈谈你追星的经历或者对追星问题的看法。谢谢！

Response:

[Traditional-character version]

　　隨著社會的變化和科技的發展以及電影、電視的影響，年輕學生總是走在時代的前面。如果你認真觀察，你就會發現，走在最前面的往往都是我們中學生。但是我身邊的同學，因爲追星而影響了學習的人不在少數。

　　一些同學的衣服上、書包上、手機上都掛有一些明星的照片。宿舍的墙上，也常常能看到明星們照片：有電影明星，歌星，運動員什麼的。在教室裏，一些學生口中念的不是中文課文，也不是英語生詞，而是流行歌曲。這些影迷、歌迷們，爲了追星，花了很多錢和時間。還有一些學生學著明星的言語、動作和打扮，完全沒有了自己的個性。這些學生完全不考慮因爲追星而影響了學習怎麼辦。

　　我從來都沒有追過哪位明星，因爲我覺得中學生追星有很多危害。追星不但花了很多錢，也浪費了不少時間。中學生追星的錢大多是父母給的。俗話說：一寸光陰一寸金，寸金難買寸光陰。追星的中學生們把學習的時間都用在追星上，實在太可惜了。學生時代的主要任務是學知識，再說，爲了追星而失去了自己的個性，也就是生活失去了自己的目標。

　　也許會有一些學生覺得，學生學習負擔那麼重，在課餘時間追星可以讓自己放鬆。很多人喜歡成龍，成龍的吃苦精神會給學生帶來好的影響。但是在現實生活中，學生追星並不是被他們的精神所感動，而是被他們的外貌和歌聲所吸引。所以我覺得中學生追星沒有好處。

中學時代是攝取知識最好的時代。如果爲了追星而失去自己學習的機會，以後後悔也來不及了。到那時不但對不起自己，也對不起父母，更不用說將來到社會上與人競爭了。所以說，我勸那些盲目追星的同學們趕快停止追星吧！

[Simplified-character version]

随着社会的变化和科技的发展以及电影、电视的影响，年轻学生总是走在时代的前面。如果你认真观察，你就会发现，走在最前面的往往都是我们中学生。但是我身边的同学，因为追星而影响了学习的人不在少数。

一些同学的衣服上、书包上、手机上都挂有一些明星的照片。宿舍的墙上，也常常能看到明星们照片：有电影明星，歌星，运动员什么的。在教室里，一些学生口中念的不是中文课文，也不是英语生词，而是流行歌曲。这些影迷、歌迷们，为了追星，花了很多钱和时间。还有一些学生学着明星的言语、动作和打扮，完全没有了自己的个性。这些学生完全不考虑因为追星而影响了学习怎么办。

我从来都没有追过哪位明星，因为我觉得中学生追星有很多危害。追星不但花了很多钱，也浪费了不少时间。中学生追星的钱大多是父母给的。俗话说：一寸光阴一寸金，寸金难买寸光阴。追星的中学生们把学习的时间都用在追星上，实在太可惜了。学生时代的主要任务是学知识，再说，为了追星而失去了自己的个性，也就是生活失去了自己的目标。

也许会有一些学生觉得，学生学习负担那么重，在课余时间追星可以让自己放松。很多人喜欢成龙，成龙的吃苦精神会给学生带来好的影响。但是在现实生活中，学生追星并不是被他们的精神所感动，而是被他们的外貌和歌声所吸引。所以我觉得中学生追星没有好处。

中学时代是摄取知识最好的时代。如果为了追星而失去自己学习的机会，以后后悔也来不及了。到那时不但对不起自己，也对不起父母，更不用说将来到社会上与人竞争了。所以说，我劝那些盲目追星的同学们赶快停止追星吧！

As shown in the sample response, the essential factors of the persuasive essay include the thesis, the argument, opposing viewpoints, and the conclusion. The thesis, which is the key point the writer wants to present, must be clear, accurate, and concise. Usually, the thesis is extensively discussed in the middle of the essay and stated again in the conclusion, along with the supporting arguments. The argument should include evidence that appeals to logic, ethics, and emotions.

The argument of the above essay is that students are wasting valuable time chasing after stars, not to mention their parents' hard-earned money. The essay begins by restating the problem, then presenting an analysis, and finally proposing a solution. In this case, the author offers his analysis of the kind of damage "chasing the stars" could cause and makes an effort to persuade readers to accept his proposal to stop this behavior.

The AP Chinese exam does not require students to write a persuasive essay. However, having the ability to do so improves students' overall writing skills. Since the time allotted for each writing task is 15 minutes, it is unrealistic to expect students to write a thoroughly persuasive essay during the exam. However, the following outline can be used to structure a streamlined persuasive essay that adequately addresses the key points.

I. Introduction
   A. Capture readers' attention with a "hook"
II. Analysis
   A. Offer own opinions
   B. Present opposing arguments
III. Conclusion
   A. Present rebuttal evidence in favor of own viewpoints
   B. Add a personal call to action or solution

PERSUASIVE ESSAY WRITING TIPS

Because a persuasive essay requires logical, concise, and powerful language, the following three types of sentence structures will be particularly helpful when writing one:

1. The conditional sentence structure using "假如"(*if–then*). This structure usually describes a hypothetical case.
2. The sentence structure with "可是," "但是," or "然而." This structure may appear to agree with the opposing view in the first sentence, but turns the argument around completely using "可是," "但是," or "然而."
3. The rhetorical sentence structure with "難道" ("难道"). This structure usually emphasizes a key point.

Besides sentence structure, some words and phrases used for transitioning from one idea to the next are important in persuasive writing.

Adding Information

並且（并且）	bìngqiě	and
不但…而且	búdàn . . . érqiě	not only . . . but also
還（还）	hái	also; still
而且	érqiě	moreover; furthermore
此外	cǐwài	moreover; furthermore (more formal)
另外	lìngwài	in addition (more formal)

Giving Examples

例如	lìrú	for example; for instance
以…爲例（以…为例）	yǐ . . . wéilì	for example
特別是…	tèbiéshì	specifically; in particular
首先	shǒuxiān	first
其次	qícì	second; another
最後（最后）	zuìhòu	last; finally
第一	dìyī	the first
第二	dì'èr	the second

Showing a Contrast

但是	dànshì	but
可是	kěshì	but
不過（不过）	búguò	however; but

一方面	yì fāngmiàn	on the one hand
另一方面	lìng yì fāngmiàn	on the other hand
否則（否则）	fǒuzé	otherwise (more formal)
要不然	yàoburán	otherwise
相反	xiāngfǎn	in contrast
反之	fǎnzhī	otherwise; in contrast (more formal)
反而	fǎn'ér	instead; on the contrary; but

Showing a Concession

然而	rán'ér	however; nevertheless; yet (more formal)
但是	dànshì	yet
仍然	réngrán	nevertheless (more formal)
雖然（虽然）	suīrán	even; although
雖然如此（虽然如此）	suīrán rúcǐ	even so
儘管（尽管）	jǐnguǎn	although; despite
即使	jíshǐ	even though

Showing a Similarity

同樣（同样）	tóngyàng	likewise
與此同時（与此同时）	yǔcǐ tóngshí	similarly (more formal)

Showing a Result

那樣（那么）	nàme	so
因此	yīncǐ	so; therefore; consequently
所以	suǒyǐ	therefore
因而	yīn'ér	thus (more formal)
結果（结果）	jiéguǒ	as a consequence; as a result
從而（从而）	cóng'ér	consequently (more formal)

Showing a Supposition

是否	shìfǒu	whether . . . or
假如	jiǎrú	if . . . (then)
如果	rúguǒ	if
要是	yàoshì	if

Explaining or Emphasizing

實際上（实际上）	shíjìshang	in fact; actually
換句話說（换句话说）	huàn jùhuàshuō	in other words
換言之	huànyánzhī	in other words (more formal)
也就是	yějiùshì	namely
即	jí	namely (more formal)

Giving an Alternative

或	huò	or
或者…或者	huòzhě	either . . . or
既不…也不	jìbù . . . yěbù	neither . . . nor

WRITING STRATEGIES

On the AP Chinese Writing test, it is very important to understand the task at hand before starting to write. For the Story Narration task, students should ask themselves, what is the main topic of the picture prompt? For the E-mail Response task, what is the subject of the e-mail prompt that requires a response? Before writing, determine which elements from the various types of essays, as described in the previous sections, may work well for the task. Drafting an outline of the main points from the prompts also helps. Identify the introduction, development, and conclusion and introduce facts, details, and examples to develop the body of the essay. Appropriate transition words are needed to connect the sentences and paragraphs so that the essay is easy to read. Use the concluding paragraph to summarize the main ideas of the essay or restate them in different words.

Applying a variety of grammatical structures correctly increases the likelihood of receiving high marks. Double-check the Chinese characters, as incorrect homonyms may obscure the original intent.
Keep in mind that:

1. Adding too much unnecessary information may waste precious time that you will need to complete the task.
2. Practice writing on a variety of topics. Be creative and flexible when selecting essay types.
3. Regardless of the writing prompts, stay on topic and provide supporting details or specific examples whenever possible.
4. Avoid repetition by applying a rich variety of vocabulary, idioms, and grammatical structures. A collection of Chinese idioms and proverbs is included later in the book.

COMMON WRITING MISTAKES

The most common mistakes on written tests and ones that can lower scores are:
1. The writing style or language is incorrect.
2. The essay is off-topic.
3. The logic is unclear.
4. Grammatical errors obscure meanings.

Each common writing problem is explained with one or more examples.

Subject/Verb Disagreement (1–3)

[Traditional-character version]
1. 每天早上，同學們在學校的操場上奔馳。

[Simplified-character version]
　　每天早上，同学们在学校的操场上奔驰。

The noun "同學們" ("同学们") and the verb "奔馳" ("奔驰") in the sentence "同學們奔馳" ("同学们奔驰") disagree. The verb "奔馳" ("奔驰") means "horses run fast"; this word can also refer to a car, but not to a person. Students should use "跑步" or "奔跑" instead.

[Traditional-character version]
2. 狂風暴雨下了起來，但是我的同屋還是趕到學校去上課。

[Simplified-character version]
　　狂风暴雨下了起来，但是我的同屋还是赶到学校去上课。

The subject in the first part is not clear. The verb "下" should be paired with "暴雨," not "狂風" ("狂风"). To correct this sentence, students should get rid of "狂風" ("狂风"), which changes the sentence to "暴雨下了起來." Another way to fix this sentence is to add another verb, "刮," which changes the original sentence into "狂風刮起來，暴雨下起來" ("狂风刮起来，暴雨下起来").

[Traditional-character version]
3. 很多公司和工作的職位歧視女人。

[Simplified-character version]
　　很多公司和工作的职位歧视女人。

The subject in the sentence is not clear. The verb "歧視" ("歧视") should be paired with "公司," not "職位" ("职位"). To correct this sentence, address "公司," and "職位" ("职位") separately. This changes the sentence to "很多公司歧視女人，不給她們工作的職位" ("很多公司歧视女人，不给她们工作的职位").

Verb/Object Disagreement (4–5)

[Traditional-character version]
4. 在訪問期間，我們還參觀了他們中學生科技小組設計網頁的經驗。

[Simplified-character version]
　　在访问期间，我们还参观了他们中学生科技小组设计网页的经验。

"參觀 . . . 經驗" ("参观...经验") is the part that disagrees in this sentence because "參觀" ("参观") cannot apply to "經驗" ("经验"). Instead, the sentence should be "在訪問期間，我們參觀了他們中學生科技小組，並且分享了他們設計網頁的經驗" ("在访问期间，我们参观了他们中学生科技小组，并且学习分享了他们设计网页的经验").

[Traditional-character version]
5. 到了美麗的太平洋邊，我迫不及待地張開嘴巴盡情呼吸著海水、陽光和新鮮的空氣。

[Simplified-character version]
　　到了美丽的太平洋边，我迫不及待地张开嘴巴尽情呼吸着海水、阳光和新鲜的空气。

"海水" and "陽光" ("阳光") cannot be used with "呼吸." Each object should be given its own verb. The original sentence is corrected to read "到了美麗的太平洋

邊，我對著海水，迎著陽光，迫不及待地張開嘴巴盡情地呼吸著新鮮的空氣"
（"到了美丽的太平洋边，我对着海水，迎着阳光，迫不及待地张开嘴巴尽情地呼吸着新鲜的空气"）.

Misplaced Modifiers (6–10)

[Traditional-character version]

6. 我們每個人都有一雙聰明能幹的手，爲什麼還要靠父母呢？

[Simplified-character version]

我们每个人都有一双聪明能干的手，为什么还要靠父母呢？

The noun "手" can be modified by "能幹的" ("能干的"), not "聰明" ("聪明"). "聰明" ("聪明") should be deleted.

[Traditional-character version]

7. 中學時代打下的基礎知識，爲以後上大學創造了條件。

[Simplified-character version]

中学时代打下的基础知识，为以后上大学创造了条件。

The verb phrase "中學時代打下的" ("中学时代打下的") used as a modifier does not match the noun, i.e., "知識" ("知识") cannot be "打下." There are two ways to correct the sentence:

1) "打下" is changed to "掌握" or "學到" ("学到") as the modifier of "基礎知識" ("基础知识");
2) "知識" ("知识") is deleted. The correct sentence would be "中學時代打下的基礎，爲以後上大學創造了條件" ("中学时代打下的基础，为以后上大学创造了条件").

[Traditional-character version]

8. 他口口聲聲地欺騙了大家，卻還說是爲了大家好。

[Simplified-character version]

他口口声声地欺骗了大家，却还说是为了大家好。

The idiom "口口聲聲" ("口口声声") indicates *keeping on saying*, and the word "欺騙" ("欺骗") means *deceiving*, so "口口聲聲" ("口口声声") cannot modify "欺騙" ("欺骗"). "口口聲聲" ("口口声声") can be replaced by "三番兩次."

[Traditional-character version]

9. 你上次來美國，正趕上我考試，對你照顧得太不周全了，很不好意思。我一直盼望你能再來，這一次，我一定好好招待。

[Simplified-character version]

你上次来美国，正赶上我考试，对你照顾得太不周全了，很不好意思。我一直盼望你能再来，这一次，我一定好好招待。

"周全" should be replaced with "周到" ("周到"), as it cannot be used with "照顧" ("照顾").

[Traditional-character version]

10. 一到周末，我們宿舍的人就一起動手，把公寓打掃得乾乾淨淨、整整齊齊。

[Simplified-character version]

　　一到周末，我们宿舍的人就一起动手，把公寓打扫得干干净净、整整齐齐。

"打掃"("打扫") can be used with "乾乾淨淨" ("干干净净"), but not with "整整齊齊" ("整整齐齐"). "整整齊齊" ("整整齐齐") can be used with another verb, such as "收拾得."

Redundancy and Fragments (11–14)

[Traditional-character version]

11. 從大量的事實中告訴我們，要想今後找到一個好工作，必須在中學時代就打好基礎。

[Simplified-character version]

　　从大量的事实中告诉我们，要想今后找到一个好工作，必须在中学时代就打好基础。

This sentence is a fragment because it is missing a subject. Deleting "從" ("从") and "中" can fix this problem, as "大量的事實" ("大量的事实") becomes the subject.

[Traditional-character version]

12. 在美國的公司不給大家買保險。

[Simplified-character version]

　　在美国的公司不给大家买保险。

This sentence is a fragment because it uses prepositions instead of a subject. Deleting "在" fixes this problem.

[Traditional-character version]

13. 我朋友張大力在去指導教師辦公室的路上，突然一個穿得很漂亮的女生向他微笑。

[Simplified-character version]

　　我朋友张大力在去指导教师办公室的路上，突然一个穿得很漂亮的女生向他微笑。

This sentence is a fragment because the predicate isn't completed and the second half of the sentence has changed the subject from 张大力 to 漂亮的女生. Adding a verb after "突然," such as "發現" ("发现") or "看見" ("看见"), fixes this problem. The original sentence is changed to "我朋友張大力在去指導教師辦公室的路上，突然看見一個穿得很漂亮的女生向他微笑" ("我朋友张大力在去指导教师办公室的路上，突然看见一个穿得很漂亮的女生向他微笑").

[Traditional-character version]
14. 我們應該發揚我們父母那一代人勇於吃苦。

[Simplified-character version]
　　我们应该发扬我们父母那一代人勇于吃苦。

In Chinese, some verbs require a noun-phrase object. Missing this object turns a sentence into a fragment. The verb "發揚" ("发扬") misses its object. Adding the object "精神" corrects the sentence: "我們應該發揚我們父母那一代人勇於吃苦的精神" ("我们应该发扬我们父母那一代人勇于吃苦的精神").

Missing Modifiers (15–16)

[Traditional-character version]
15. 中國朋友告訴我，在中國要想考上大學，必須付出勞動。

[Simplified-character version]
　　中国朋友告诉我，在中国要想考上大学，必须付出劳动。

"勞動" ("劳动") needs a modifier to express that getting into college is extremely hard. The absence of "艱苦的" ("艰苦的") before "勞動" ("劳动") in the sentence makes it seem that getting into college is easy.

[Traditional-character version]
16. 去年聖誕節，父母給姐姐、弟弟和我都送了我們喜愛的禮物。我們三個人的禮物是一雙漂亮的皮鞋，一個遊戲機和一個新書包。

[Simplified-character version]
　　去年圣诞节，父母给姐姐、弟弟和我都送了我们喜爱的礼物。我们三个人的礼物是一双漂亮的皮鞋，一个游戏机和一个新书包。

The second sentence is missing the word "分別" (respectively). This mistake may cause confusion (it is unknown which gift is given to whom) or a misunderstanding (each person receives all three things). The correct sentence is "我們三個人的禮物分別是一雙漂亮的皮鞋，一個遊戲機和一個新書包" ("我们三个人的礼物分别是一双漂亮的皮鞋，一个游戏机和一个新书包").

Redundancy in Subject, Predicate, and Object (17–19)

[Traditional-character version]
17. 我們女孩子在穿衣服方面，一般來說，我們都很喜歡名牌服裝。

[Simplified-character version]
　　我们女孩子在穿衣服方面，一般来说，我们都很喜欢名牌服装。

This sentence is redundant because it has an extra "我們" ("我们"). Deleting "我們" ("我们") corrects the sentence: "我們女孩子，在穿衣服方面，一般來說，都很喜歡名牌服裝。" ("我们女孩子，在穿衣服方面，一般来说，都很喜欢名牌服装。").

[Traditional-character version]
18. 我對洛杉磯交通擁擠的狀況已經感到習以爲常了。

[Simplified-character version]
我对洛杉矶交通拥挤的状况已经感到习以为常了。

The idiom "習以爲常" ("习以为常") working as a verb means *being used to something*, so "感到" is redundant. Deleting "感到" changes the original sentence into "我對洛杉磯交通擁擠的狀況已經習以爲常了" ("我对洛杉矶交通拥挤的状况已经习以为常了"). An alternative correction is "我對洛杉磯交通擁擠的狀況已經感到習慣了" ("我对洛杉矶交通拥挤的状况已经感到习惯了"), in which "感到" is followed by the idiom "習慣" ("习惯").

[Traditional-character version]
19. 那天，我們幾個孩子從不同的地方趕回家，慶祝爸爸媽媽結婚25周年的到來。

[Simplified-character version]
那天，我们几个孩子从不同的地方赶回家，庆祝爸爸妈妈结婚25周年的到来。

The verb "慶祝" ("庆祝") already contains the object "結婚25周年" ("结婚25周年"), so the second object, "到來," ("到来") is redundant.

Redundant Modifiers (20–22)

[Traditional-character version]
20. 在回家的路上，發生了一件不大但是讓我難以忘記的小事。

[Simplified-character version]
在回家的路上，发生了一件不大但是让我难以忘记的小事。

"不大" and "小" have the same meaning. Deleting either one of the modifiers fixes the redundancy problem. For example, "在回家的路上，發生了一件不大但是讓我難以忘記的事。" ("在回家的路上，发生了一件不大但是让我难以忘记的事。")

[Traditional-character version]
21. 經過多次反復地實驗，我們終於成功了。

[Simplified-character version]
经过多次反复地实验，我们终于成功了。

"多次" and "反復" ("反复") have the same meaning. Deleting either one of the modifiers eliminates the redundancy. For example, "經過反復地實驗，我們終於成功了。"("经过反复地实验，我们终于成功了。")

[Traditional-character version]
22. 我爸爸做任何工作都非常認真得很。

[Simplified-character version]
  我爸爸做任何工作都非常认真得很。

Two modifiers "非常" "得很" for "認真" ("认真") cause a redundancy problem. Deleting one of the two corrects the sentence: "我爸爸做任何工作都非常認真" ("我爸爸做任何工作都非常认真"), or "我爸爸做任何工作都認真得很" ("我爸爸做任何工作都认真得很").

Incorrect Word Order (23)

[Traditional-character version]
23. 你可以買醫療保險從政府、學校、公司。

[Simplified-character version]
  你可以买医疗保险从政府、学校、公司。

The word order in this sentence is incorrect because, in Chinese, the modifier cannot be placed at the end of the sentence. The correct sentence is "你可以從政府、學校、公司買醫療保險" ("你可以从政府、学校、公司买医疗保险").

Conjunction Mistakes (24–26)

[Traditional-character version]
24. 美國的交通不很方便,得經常坐飛機。要不是就坐火車就是公共汽車。

[Simplified-character version]
  美国的交通不很方便,得经常坐飞机。要不是就坐火车就是公共汽车。

In the second sentence, the writer confuses "要不是" with "要不然," and "就是" with "或者." "要不是" has a hypothetical meaning, which does not fit the context. The correct sentence is "美國的交通不很方便,得經常坐飛機。要不然就坐火車或者公共汽車" ("美国的交通不很方便,得经常坐飞机。要不然就坐火车或者公共汽车。")

[Traditional-character version]
25. 姐姐哭了,不知道是因爲高興而是因爲難過。

[Simplified-character version]
  姐姐哭了,不知道是因为高兴而是因为难过。

The structure "不是A而是B" means that *it is not A, but B*. In this case, the writer misuses the conjunction "而是" for "還是" ("还是"). The correct sentence should be "姐姐哭了,不知道是因爲高興還是因爲難過" ("姐姐哭了,不知道是因为高兴还是因为难过").

[Traditional-character version]

26. 其實我一直認爲，只有天天運動，少吃一點兒肉，就不會太胖。

[Simplified-character version]

其实我一直认为，只有天天运动，少吃一点儿肉，就不会太胖。

Both "只有 ... 才" and "只要 ... 就" describe conditions, but "只有 ... 才" tends to be limiting and negative (*it won't happen unless*) while "只要...就" tends to be expansive and positive (*it will happen as long as*). Here, the context and logic call for "只要," not "只有."

Pronoun Mistakes (27)

[Traditional-character version]

27. 如果她們嫁人了，她的丈夫就不會幫她們。

[Simplified-character version]

如果她们嫁人了，她的丈夫就不会帮她们。

In this sentence, the writer confuses plural and singular words. Changing "她的丈夫" to "她們的丈夫" ("她们的丈夫") fixes the problem.

Misuse of Measure Words (28–29)

[Traditional-character version]

28. 她的兩個哥哥是從美國東岸的同一家有名的大學畢業的。

[Simplified-character version]

她的两个哥哥是从美国东岸的同一家有名的大学毕业的。

The measure word is misused. Instead of "家," it should be "所."

[Traditional-character version]

29. 那家服裝店裏的東西打折，小美一下子買了好幾件襯衫和牛仔褲。

[Simplified-character version]

那家服装店里的东西打折，小美一下子买了好几件衬衫和牛仔裤。

The author only provides a measure word for the first object, but leaves out the measure word for the second object. Adding "幾條" ("几条") for the second object fixes the problem.

Misuse of Idioms and Proverbs (30)

[Traditional-character version]

30. 春節期間，我們家家戶戶過著花天酒地的日子。

[Simplified-character version]

春节期间，我们家家户户过着花天酒地的日子。

The author misuses "花天酒地" to describe the spring festival because this idiom has a negative connotation. Changing it to "喜氣洋洋" ("喜气洋洋") fixes the problem.

Mistranslations (31–32)

[Traditional-character version]

31. 在美國，男人做錢比女人多。

[Simplified-character version]

　　在美国，男人做钱比女人多。

　　The writer translates "make money" into Chinese as "做錢" ("做钱"). However "做錢" ("做钱") in Chinese means making counterfeit money. The correct translation is "掙錢" ("挣钱") or "賺錢" ("赚钱").

[Traditional-character version]

32. 可是貴人有醫療保險。

[Simplified-character version]

　　可是贵人有医疗保险。

The writer translates "rich people" to "貴人" ("贵人"). However, "貴人" ("贵人") means a person with power or with influence over people. The correct translation is "富人" or "有錢人" ("有钱人").

Unprofessional Language (33)

[Traditional-character version]

33. 很多人覺得，帶孩子是女的的事，可是他們不想想，如果沒有女的，我們就完了。

[Simplified-character version]

　　很多人觉得带孩子是女的的事，可是他们不想想，如果没有女的，我们就完了。

Written formal language doesn't allow for words such as "帶孩子," "女的," and "完了." Substitute them with the more formal terms "照顧孩子" ("照顾孩子"), "女性," and "無法生存" ("无法生存").

Writing Skills Practice

The following section provides a variety of topics for essay-writing practice. For each topic, there is a picture stimulus for Story Narration and an e-mail inquiry for E-mail Response.

The Story Narration is designed to determine whether students can write a well-organized story with a comprehensible progression of thoughts (a beginning, middle, and end), together with as many details as possible. It also tests students' ability to use proper transitional elements and consistent devices, as well as their mastery of sentence structure and vocabulary.

The E-mail Response is designed to determine whether students are able to understand an e-mail and then respond to it, addressing all the questions raised in the incoming message.

Along the way, this section provides students with pictures, reminders, outlines, suggestions, and samples.

Topic One: School

Story Narration
The following pictures present a sequence of events. Write a complete story based on the pictures.

1.

2.

3.

4.

REMINDERS

Write a complete narration, including people's feelings, facial expressions, and gestures, according to these pictures. Using appropriate verbs, adverbs and adjectives, idioms, and grammatical structures will help make the narration accurate and lively.

OUTLINE

FIRST PARAGRAPH: Introduce characters, setting, and plot. The following words, phrases, and sentences may be helpful:

[Traditional-character version]

　　校園，更衣室，頭上留著短髮，身上穿著一條裙子，背著一個背包，兩腳併攏，看起來很害羞，不敢抬頭看別人，常常孤獨地站在一旁

[Simplified-character version]

　　校园，更衣室，头上留着短发，身上穿着一条裙子，背着一个背包，两脚并拢，看起来很害羞，不敢抬头看别人，常常孤独地站在一旁

SECOND PARAGRAPH: Describe how the story progresses, focusing on the characters' actions and expressions; be aware of transitional elements. The following phrases and idioms may be helpful:

[Traditional-character version]

　　有一天，突然看見，梳著辮子的女孩子，急急忙忙，跑走，掉在地上，毫無知覺，趕快走過去，撿起來，然後遞給......，物歸原主，非常感激，於是他們相識了

[Simplified-character version]

　　有一天，突然看见，梳着辫子的女孩子，急急忙忙，跑走，掉在地上，毫无知觉，赶快走过去，捡起来，然后递给......，物归原主，非常感激，于是他们相识了

THIRD PARAGRAPH: Conclude. The following phrases and idioms can be used:

[Traditional-character version]

　　漸漸地，越來越開朗，於是他們成為 ......，無話不談，形影不離

[Simplified-character version]

　　渐渐地，越来越开朗，于是他们成为 ......，无话不谈，形影不离

E-mail Response

Read this e-mail from a friend and then type a response.

[Traditional-character version]

發件人：高強
郵件主題：該選什麼？

　　下個學期的課程安排已經出來了。我想在下午的文化選修課與課外體育活動中選一項。從時間上看沒有什麼問題，一個是星期一、星期三課後上文化課，一個是星期二、星期四以後參加一項體育活動。但是我擔心要是兩項都參加，會影響到主科的學習。你覺得我應該選哪一項？為什麼？你去年是怎麼選擇的？非常感謝。

[Simplified-character version]
发件人：高强
邮件主题：该选什么？

　　下个学期的课程安排已经出来了。我想在下午的文化选修课与课外体育活动中选一项。从时间上看没有什么问题，一个是星期一、星期三课后上文化课，一个是星期二、星期四以后参加一项体育活动。但是我担心要是两项都参加，会影响到主科的学习。你觉得我应该选哪一项？为什么？你去年是怎么选择的？非常感谢。

SUGGESTIONS FOR WRITING AN E-MAIL RESPONSE

This e-mail is mainly about the balance between schoolwork and extracurricular activities. When responding, keep this outline in mind:

1. Briefly repeat the sender's main points. For example:

[Traditional-character version]
　　高强，你好！從來信中知道你正在爲如何處理文化課與課外活動的問題發愁，....

[Simplified-character version]
　　高强，你好！从来信中知道你正在为如何处理文化课与课外活动的问题发愁，....

2. Respond to any and all of the sender's questions in detail. Find the answers to these questions. For example:

[Traditional-character version]
　　你在信中提到高中文化課程，關於這個問題，有的人覺得......， 而有的人認爲......，我個人覺得......。我在選課的時候，......。是否參加課外活動，以我個人的經驗來看......，至於它與申請大學的關係問題，我覺得......。當然，如果能夠......， 那麼......。總之，......

[Simplified-character version]
　　你在信中提到高中文化课程，关于这个问题，有的人觉得......， 而有的人认为......，我个人觉得......。我在选课的时候， ......。是否参加课外活动，以我个人的经验来看......， 至于它与申请大学的关系问题，我觉得......。当然，如果能够......， 那么........。总之，......

3. Any closing statements should be sincere. For example:

[Traditional-character version]
　　希望我的經驗與看法能對你有所幫助。祝你選課順利。

[Simplified-character version]
　　希望我的经验与看法能对你有所帮助。祝你选课顺利。

Topic Two: Sports

Story Narration
The following pictures present a sequence of events. Write a complete story based on the pictures.

1.

2.

3.

4.

REMINDERS

Write a complete narration that includes the key elements of a story: characters, setting, and plot. Explain the relationships between the characters, and describe their physical appearances and feelings as well as their facial expressions. Be sure to address the sequence of events accordingly. Use proper complements—such as resultative complements, directional complements, and descriptive complements with 得—to make the narration livelier.

OUTLINE

FIRST PARAGRAPH: Introduce characters, setting, and plot. The following words, phrases, sentences, and idioms may be helpful:

[Traditional-character version]

　　身上穿著運動服，T恤衫，短褲，頭上戴著帽子，梳著兩根短辮子，腳上穿著運動鞋，身強體壯，人高馬大，身材矮小，站在起跑綫前不屑一顧，滿懷信心，

[Simplified-character version]

　　身上穿着运动服，T恤衫，短裤，头上戴着帽子，梳着两根短辫子，脚上穿着运动鞋，身强体壮，人高马大，身材矮小，站在起跑线前不屑一顾，满怀信心，

SECOND PARAGRAPH: Describe how the story progresses, focusing on the characters' actions and expressions; use proper transitional elements. The following phrases, sentences, and idioms may be helpful:

[Traditional-character version]

　　開始的時候.....一直領先，漸漸地就落後了。天氣炎熱，運動員們又累又渴，他們個個汗流浹背，有的人停下來擦汗，有的人......。到供水站的時候，......，只有......還繼續往前跑。

[Simplified-character version]

　　开始的时候.....一直领先，渐渐地就落后了。天气炎热，运动员们又累又渴，他们个个汗流浃背，有的人停下来擦汗，有的人......。到供水站的时候，......，只有......还继续往前跑。

THIRD PARAGRAPH: Conclude the story. The following words, phrases, idioms, and proverb can be used:

[Traditional-character version]

　　馬上就要到終點綫了，只見......。終於......　總算.......。取得了優異成績，拿到了冠軍，高興地揮舞雙臂，臉上露出喜悅之情。失望，難爲情，堅持不懈的精神，不放棄，達到目標，堅持就是勝利的道理

[Simplified-character version]

　　马上就要到终点线了，只见......。终于......　总算........。取得了优异成绩，拿到了冠军，高兴地挥舞双臂，脸上露出喜悦之情。失望，难为情，坚持不懈的精神，不放弃，达到目标，坚持就是胜利的道理

E-mail Response

Read this e-mail from a friend and then type a response.

[Traditional-character version]

發件人：王偉
郵件主題：體育活動

　　上學期末，學校籃球隊和網球隊招收新隊員，我都報名了，沒有想到他們都錄取我了。籃球和網球都是我喜歡的，我很想都參加，可是又擔心同時參加

兩項體育活動，哪一項都做不好。再說，父母也不願意我把太多的時間花在課外活動上。你覺得我應該參加哪個隊比較好？你參加過哪些課外活動？請談談你的經驗或者看法。非常感謝。

[Simplified-character version]

发件人：王伟

邮件主题：体育活动

　　上学期末，学校篮球队和网球队招收新队员，我都报名了，没有想到他们都录取我了。篮球和网球都是我喜欢的，我很想都参加，可是又担心同时参加两项体育活动，哪一项都做不好。再说，父母也不愿意我把太多的时间花在课外活动上。你觉得我应该参加哪个队比较好？你参加过哪些课外活动？请谈谈你的经验或者看法。非常感谢。

SUGGESTIONS FOR WRITING AN E-MAIL RESPONSE

This e-mail is mainly about a friend who needs help choosing between joining two sports teams. When responding, keep this outline in mind:

1. Briefly repeat the sender's main points and congratulate your friend for being accepted on both teams. For example:

[Traditional-character version]

王偉：

　　你好！知道你......，我真爲你高興，　在這裏向你表示祝賀。在信中，你談到了......和......的問題，你想知道我對這些問題是怎麼看的，我就談談我的看法吧。

[Simplified-character version]

王伟：

　　你好！知道你......，我真为你高兴，　在这里向你表示祝贺。在信中，你谈到了......和......的问题，你想知道我对这些问题是怎么看的，我就谈谈我的看法吧。

2. Respond to any and all of the sender's questions in detail. Find solutions for these questions. For example:

[Traditional-character version]

　　關于......的問題，我覺得你的擔心是有道理的，你父母的態度，我也非常能理解。據我所知，........，如果你兩個隊都參加，一是......，二是........，　　況且你父母......。比如我有一朋友，他......，結果，不但......，　而且.......。可見，......。　至于在兩個隊中選擇哪一個的問題，這就要看......了。另外，還要看.......。根據我的經驗，首先要看......，其次還要考慮......。總而言之，.......。

[Simplified-character version]

　　关于......的问题，我觉得你的担心是有道理的，你父母的态度，我也非常能理解。据我所知，........，如果你两个队都参加，一是......，二是........，　　况且你父母......。比如我有一朋友，他......，结果，不但......，　而且.......。可见，......。至于在两个队中选择哪一个的问题，这就要看......了。另外，还要看.......。根据我的经验，首先要看......，其次还要考虑......。总而言之，.......。

3. Any closing statements should be sincere. For example:

[Traditional-character version]

　　以上只是我個人的一些看法，希望能對你有幫助。你最後是怎麼決定，一定來信告訴我。不管你參加哪個隊，祝你有段愉快的時光！

[Simplified-character version]

　　以上只是我个人的一些看法，希望能对你有帮助。你最后是怎么决定，一定来信告诉我。不管你参加哪个队，祝你有段愉快的时光！

Topic Three: Lifestyle

Story Narration

The following pictures present a sequence of events. Write a complete story based on these pictures.

1.

2.

3.

4.

REMINDERS

Write a complete narration. Note the girl's facial expressions and actions.

OUTLINE

FIRST PARAGRAPH: Introduce characters and plot. In this particular story, the setting may not be that important. The following phrases and sentences may be helpful:

[Traditional-character version]

　　頭上梳著披肩髮，長得胖乎乎的，看起來有些粗壯，對自己的體型不滿意，稱體重，磅，臉上露出難過的表情

[Simplified-character version]

　　头上梳着披肩发，长得胖乎乎的，看起来有些粗壮，对自己的体型不满意，称体重，磅，脸上露出难过的表情

SECOND PARAGRAPH: Describe how the story progresses, focusing on the characters' actions and expressions; be aware of transitional elements. Students can embellish the story beyond what is shown in the pictures by including other details, like exercises the girl in the pictures did besides running. The following words, phrases, and sentences may be helpful:

[Traditional-character version]

　　爲了……，她制定了一個減肥計畫。每天進行體育鍛煉，堅持長跑。每當旭日東升的時候，她總是……。空氣十分清新，街上乾乾淨淨，十分安靜。她沿著筆直的小道……。心情愉快，面帶微笑。不但……，而且還……，並……。她改變了飲食習慣，注意生活的規律性，吃清淡而健康的食物，像……什麼的。隨著……，她漸漸地……，身材一天比一天苗條了，終於變成了一個……。

[Simplified-character version]

　　为了……，她制定了一个减肥计划。每天进行体育锻炼，坚持长跑。每当旭日东升的时候，她总是……。空气十分清新，街上干干净净，十分安静。她沿着笔直的小道……。心情愉快，面带微笑。不但……，而且还……，并……。她改变了饮食习惯，注意生活的规律性，吃清淡而健康的食物，像……什么的。随着……，她渐渐地……，身材一天比一天苗条了，终于变成了一个……。

THIRD PARAGRAPH: Conclude the story. The following words, phrases, idioms, and proverbs can be used:

[Traditional-character version]

　　出乎意料，驚喜，喜悅之情，表露出來，預料之中，如願以償，體重下降了，有志者事竟成

[Simplified-character version]

　　出乎意料，惊喜，喜悦之情，表露出来，预料之中，如愿以偿，体重下降了，有志者事竟成

E-mail Response
Read this e-mail from a friend and then type a response.

[Traditional-character version]
發件人：劉希
郵件主題：該怎麽樣安排作息？

　　我喜歡在自己精神狀態好的時候學習，而不管是白天還是晚上，甚至半夜。因爲我覺得只要學習效率高就可以了。可是有人認爲青少年應該有規律地生活和有計劃地學習，這樣才能保證充足的睡眠和均衡的營養，這才是健康的生活方式。你覺得我該怎麽樣安排作息？爲什麽？你是怎麽做的？謝謝。

[Simplified-character version]
发件人：刘希
邮件主题：该怎么样安排作息？

　　我喜欢在自己精神状态好的时候学习，而不管是白天还是晚上，甚至半夜。因为我觉得只要学习效率高就可以了。可是有人认为青少年应该有规律地生活和有计划地学习，这样才能保证充足的睡眠和均衡的营养，这才是健康的生活方式。你觉得我该怎么样安排作息？为什么？你是怎么做的？谢谢。

SUGGESTIONS FOR WRITING AN E-MAIL RESPONSE

This e-mail is mainly about what teenagers should do to stay happy and healthy. In the response, keep this outline in mind:

1. Briefly repeat the sender's main points. For example:

[Traditional-character version]
　　劉希，收到你的來信我很高興。你在信中談到了生活方式問題，我想談談自己對這個問題的看法。

[Simplified-character version]
　　刘希，收到你的来信我很高兴。你在信中谈到了生活方式问题，我想谈谈自己对这个问题的看法。

2. Respond to any and all questions from the sender in detail. Find solutions for these questions. For example:

[Traditional-character version]
　　什麽是健康的生活方式？針對這個問題，不同的人可能有不一樣的答案。你在信中提到，有人認爲有規律地生活和有計劃地學習很重要，我很同意這種觀點。因爲要想健康地生活，人們首先要......，其次還應該......，另外......也必不可少。至於你說到的充足的睡眠和均衡的營養什麽的，我的看法是　......。具體到對我們中學生來說，健康的生活方式應當是......。當然，生活中的很多事都是說起來容易做起來難，不過在這方面我做得還是不錯的。除了你信中提到的......和......，我平時比較注意......，對....也很注意。

[Simplified-character version]
　　什么是健康的生活方式？针对这个问题，不同的人可能有不一样的答案。你在信中提到，有人认为有规律地生活和有计划地学习很重要，我很同意这种观点。因为要想健康地生活，人们首先要......，其次还应该......，另外......也必不

可少。至于你说到的充足的睡眠和均衡的营养什么的，我的看法是 ......。具体到对我们中学生来说，健康的生活方式应当是......。当然，生活中的很多事都是说起来容易做起来难，不过在这方面我做得还是不错的。除了你信中提到的......和......，我平时比较注意......，对....也很注意。

3. Give personal advice. The following phrases can be used:

[Traditional-character version]
　　我建議你.......。

[Simplified-character version]
　　我建议你.......。

Topic Four: Entertainment

Story Narration
The following pictures present a sequence of events. Write a complete story based on these pictures.

1.

2.

3.

4.

REMINDERS

Write a complete narration according to the pictures. Be sure to include some of the characters' facial expressions, and what some of the changes are from one picture to the other.

OUTLINE

FIRST PARAGRAPH: Introduce characters, setting, and plot. The following phrases and sentences may be helpful:

[Traditional-character version]

　　電影開始之前，兩個年輕的男孩子坐在電影院裏。他們愉快地⋯⋯。坐在他們旁邊的是一對青年男女。那個女孩子身上穿著⋯⋯，那個男孩子臉上戴著⋯⋯，身上穿著⋯⋯，手裏拿著⋯⋯。

[Simplified-character version]

　　电影开始之前，两个年轻的男孩子坐在电影院里。他们愉快地⋯⋯。坐在他们旁边的是一对青年男女。那个女孩子身上穿着⋯⋯，那个男孩子脸上戴着⋯⋯，身上穿着⋯⋯，手里拿着⋯⋯。

SECOND PARAGRAPH: Describe how the story progresses, focusing on the characters' expressions. The following phrases and sentences may be helpful:

[Traditional-character version]

　　正當他們⋯⋯的時候，來了另外一對青年男女。這對男女，　每人手上都⋯⋯。坐在他們後面的⋯⋯很著急，因爲⋯⋯⋯⋯。不管怎麼⋯⋯，還是看不見。就在這時，戴眼鏡的那位男士站了起來，友好地對⋯⋯說⋯⋯⋯⋯。于是他們跟旁邊的那對男女交換了座位。

[Simplified-character version]

　　正当他们⋯⋯的时候，来了另外一对青年男女。这对男女, 每人手上都⋯⋯。坐在他们后面的⋯⋯很着急，因为⋯⋯⋯⋯。不管怎么⋯⋯，还是看不见。就在这时，戴眼镜的那位男士站了起来，友好地对⋯⋯说⋯⋯⋯⋯。于是他们跟旁边的那对男女交换了座位。

THIRD PARAGRAPH: Conclude the story. The following phrases and idioms can be used:

[Traditional-character version]

　　助人爲樂，感激不盡，皆大歡喜，度過了一個愉快的夜晚

[Simplified-character version]

　　助人为乐，感激不尽，皆大欢喜，度过了一个愉快的夜晚

E-mail Response

Read this e-mail from a friend and then type a response.

[Traditional-character version]
發件人：楊力雄
郵件主題：娛樂活動

　　學校的合唱隊和小提琴樂隊都在招收新隊員，我都報名了，而且也都被接收了。這兩個隊都在星期三下午活動，所以我只能參加一個。我最好的兩個朋友分別在這兩個隊裏。不管我選擇哪一個，兩個好朋友中總會有一個高興。你說我應該選擇？爲什麼？另外，請你幫我想幾個理由來說服那個可能不高興的朋友。希望早日收到回信。

[Simplified-character version]
发件人：杨力雄
邮件主题：娱乐活动

　　学校的合唱队和小提琴乐队都在招收新队员，我都报名了，而且也都被接收了。这两个队都在星期三下午活动，所以我只能参加一个。我最好的两个朋友分别在这两个队里。不管我选择哪一个，两个好朋友中总会有一个高兴。你说我应该选择？为什么？另外，请你帮我想几个理由来说服那个可能不高兴的朋友。希望早日收到回信。

SUGGESTIONS FOR WRITING AN E-MAIL RESPONSE

This e-mail is mainly about a friend who needs help choosing between joining the choir or the orchestra. When responding, keep this outline in mind:

1. Briefly repeat the sender's main points. For example:

[Traditional-character version]
　　力雄，你信中提到參加學校的藝文社團，我真是羨慕你，因爲你有那麼豐富的業餘文化生活。

[Simplified-character version]
　　力雄，你信中提到参加学校的艺文社团，我真是羨慕你，因为你有那么丰富的业余文化生活。

2. Respond to any and all questions from the sender in detail. Find solutions for these questions. For example:

[Traditional-character version]
　　兩個社團的活動時間有衝突，你只能選擇一個，而這個選擇對你來說很難，因爲……。關于這個問題，我覺得應該……，並且……。我也曾經有過這樣的經歷，讓我左右爲難。記得那是……。我是……做的，最後兩位朋友也都……。所以，我認爲你也應該……。當然，如果能夠……，那就更……。總而言之，……

[Simplified-character version]
　　两个社团的活动时间有冲突，你只能选择一个，而这个选择对你来说很难，因为……。关于这个问题，我觉得应该……，并且……。我也曾经有过这样的经历，让我左右为难。记得那是……。我是……做的，最后两位朋友也都……。所以，我认为你也应该……。当然，如果能够……，那就更……。总而言之，……

3. Any closing statements should be sincere. For example:

[Traditional-character version]

希望我的經驗與看法能對你有一些幫助。我相信，不管你最後參加了哪個社團，你的兩位朋友都會為你高興的。

[Simplified-character version]

希望我的经验与看法能对你有一些帮助。我相信，不管你最后参加了哪个社团，你的两位朋友都会为你高兴的。

Topic Five: Jobs

Story Narration

The following pictures present a sequence of events. Write a complete story based on these pictures.

REMINDERS

Write a complete narration. Be sure to take note of the girl's facial expressions.

OUTLINE

FIRST PARAGRAPH: Introduce characters, setting, and plot. The following words, phrases, and idiom may be helpful:

[Traditional-character version]
人事部門，面試，年輕女孩兒，等待，雙腿併攏，焦急等待，惶恐不安

[Simplified-character version]
人事部门，面试，年轻女孩儿，等待，双腿并拢，焦急等待，惶恐不安

SECOND PARAGRAPH: Describe how the story progresses, focusing on the characters' expressions (as there are no changes in setting, and no major actions are made). You can elaborate on the story by talking about why the girl is looking for a job, details of the job, and so on. The following words, phrases, and idiom may be helpful:

[Traditional-character version]
中年婦女，表情嚴肅，坐得端端正正，對答如流，摘下眼鏡，面帶微笑，放鬆，自然

[Simplified-character version]
中年妇女，表情严肃，坐得端端正正，对答如流，摘下眼镜，面带微笑，放松，自然

THIRD PARAGRAPH: Conclude the story. The following phrases and idiom can be used:

[Traditional-character version]
站起來，遞過來，雙手接過去，激動，如願以償

[Simplified-character version]
站起来，递过来，双手接过去，激动，如愿以偿

E-mail Response
Read this e-mail from a Chinese friend and then type a response.

[Traditional-character version]
發件人：孫小雨
郵件主題：理想的工作

　　真沒有想到，我一下子找到了兩份暑期工作。一個是在學校旁邊的一家麥當勞餐館工作，雖然錢不多，但是很容易做，就是賣賣快餐。另一個是在離學校較遠的一家書店當收款員。錢比較多，不過工作不太容易做。你覺得我應該選擇哪一份工作？爲什麼？另外，請你告訴我，你今年暑期打算做什麼。

[Simplified-character version]
发件人：孙小雨
邮件主题：理想的工作

　　真没有想到，我一下子找到了两份暑期工作。一个是在学校旁边的一家麦当劳餐馆工作，虽然钱不多，但是很容易做，就是卖卖快餐。另一个是在离学校较远的一家书店当收款员。钱比较多，不过工作不太容易做。你觉得我应该选择哪一份工作？为什么？另外，请你告诉我，你今年暑期打算做什么。

SUGGESTIONS FOR WRITING AN E-MAIL RESPONSE

This e-mail is from a friend who is having a hard time choosing between two jobs. When responding, keep this outline in mind:

1. Briefly repeat the sender's main points and congratulate your friend for being hired. For example:

[Traditional-character version]
　　小雨，你的運氣真不錯，一下子找到了兩份工作，我真羨慕你，在這裏祝賀你啦！

[Simplified-character version]
　　小雨，你的运气真不错，一下子找到了两份工作，我真羡慕你，在这里祝贺你啦！

2. Respond to any and all questions from the sender in detail. Find solutions for these questions. For example:

[Traditional-character version]
　　我覺得你在做出決定之前要看......，也要看......。如果你比較在乎......，你可以選擇麥當勞的那份工作。如果......對你很重要，那就去書店工作。這就要看......。

[Simplified-character version]
　　我觉得你在做出决定之前要看......，也要看......。如果你比较在乎......，你可以选择麦当劳的那份工作。如果......对你很重要，那就去书店工作。这就要看......。

3. Give direct advice on which job your friend should take. For example:

[Traditional-character version]
　　如果我是你，我就會選擇書店的那份工作，除了掙的錢比較多以外，也可以借此機會培養培養自己的責任心。

[Simplified-character version]
　　如果我是你，我就会选择书店的那份工作，除了挣的钱比较多以外，也可以借此机会培养培养自己的责任心。

Topic Six: Friendship

Story Narration

The following pictures present a sequence of events. Write a complete story based on these pictures.

1.

2.

3.

4.

REMINDERS

Write a complete narration, including each character's actions in each picture. Pay attention to the setting as well. Make sure to clarify the sequence of events.

OUTLINE

FIRST PARAGRAPH: Introduce characters, setting, and plot. The following words, phrases, and idioms may be helpful:

[Traditional-character version]

馬上就要放學了，一位媽媽把車停在學校門前。媽媽坐在駕駛座上，身上系著安全帶。她一會兒......，一會兒......。

[Simplified-character version]

马上就要放学了，一位妈妈把车停在学校门前。妈妈坐在驾驶座上，身上系着安全带。她一会儿......，一会儿........。

SECOND PARAGRAPH: Describe how the story progresses, focusing on the characters' actions and expressions; use proper transitional elements. The following words, phrases, sentences, and idioms may be helpful:

[Traditional-character version]

突然，她看見車窗外邊......摔倒了，女兒扔下書包，快步跑過去，......，先把......扶起來，再把......扶上車。事不宜遲，馬上把......送到醫院，在急診室裏，......，坐在輪椅上，......，總算松了一口氣

[Simplified-character version]

突然，她看见车窗外边......摔倒了，女儿扔下书包，快步跑过去，......，先把......扶起来，再把......扶上车。事不宜迟，马上把......送到医院，在急诊室里，......，坐在轮椅上，......，总算松了一口气

THIRD PARAGRAPH: Conclude the story. The following phrases and idiom can be used:

[Traditional-character version]

回到車裏以後，媽媽給......打電話，助人為樂的美德值得學習

[Simplified-character version]

回到车里以后，妈妈给......打电话，助人为乐的美德值得学习

E-mail Response
Read this e-mail from a classmate and then type a response.

[Traditional-character version]
發件人：許林
郵件主題：處理朋友關係

我的一個朋友希望我放假以後跟他／她去旅行，另一個朋友希望我跟他／她去做義工。他們兩個人還因為這件事情吵了架。我們三個人的這種關係讓我很為難，也不知道應該選擇跟誰去。我想聽聽你的看法。另外，我想知道你有沒有遇到過這樣的情況。

[Simplified-character version]
发件人：许林
邮件主题：处理朋友关系

我的一个朋友希望我放假以后跟他／她去旅行，另一个朋友希望我跟他／她去做义工。他们两个人还因为这件事情吵了架。我们三个人的这种关系让我很为难，也不知道应该选择跟谁去。我想听听你的看法。另外，我想知道你有没有遇到过这样的情况。

SUGGESTIONS FOR WRITING AN E-MAIL RESPONSE

This e-mail is mainly about a conflict between friends. When responding, keep this outline in mind:

1. Briefly repeat the sender's main points. For example:

[Traditional-character version]

　　許林：看了你的來信，我很同情你現在處境，也特別能理解你此時此刻的心情。如何處理你跟兩個朋友的關係，確實不太容易。

[Simplified-character version]

　　许林：看了你的来信，我很同情你现在处境，也特别能理解你此时此刻的心情。如何处理你跟两个朋友的关系，确实不太容易。

2. Respond to any and all questions from the sender in detail. Find answers to these questions. For example:

[Traditional-character version]

　　衆所周知，三角形在幾何圖形中是最穩固的，可是三人的友情卻是最不穩定的感情。因此，在處理上，你一定要小心。如何解決好這個問題呢？我認爲，首先要想想你跟他們是什麼關係，同時還要看看你的兩個朋友是什麼程度上的關係。因爲......，所以......。另外，他們爲什麼吵架？你信中說是"很小的事情"，瞭解他們吵架的具體原因跟過程也很重要。要是他們......你就最好不要......，否則會......。我就遇到過類似的事情，也曾把我弄得......。那是......，他們因爲......而彼此不再來往了，我夾在他們中間別提多難受了。剛開始的時候，......，　　後來，我......，慢慢地就......了。

[Simplified-character version]

　　众所周知，三角形在几何图形中是最稳固的，可是三人的友情却是最不稳定的感情。因此，在处理上，你一定要小心。如何解决好这个问题呢？我认为，首先要想想你跟他们是什么关系，同时还要看看你的两个朋友是什么程度上的关系。因为......，所以......。另外，他们为什么吵架？你信中说是"很小的事情"，了解他们吵架的具体原因跟过程也很重要。要是他们......你就最好不要......，否则会......。我就遇到过类似的事情，也曾把我弄得......。那是......，他们因为......而彼此不再来往了，我夹在他们中间别提多难受了。刚开始的时候，......，后来，我......，慢慢地就......了。

3. Give your friend advice about how to resolve the conflict. For example:

[Traditional-character version]

　　解決問題的關鍵在於對症下藥，我建議你......。如果他們是真正的朋友，我想最後一定會彼此諒解，重新和好的。

[Simplified-character version]

　　解决问题的关键在于对症下药，我建议你......。如果他们是真正的朋友，我想最后一定会彼此谅解，重新和好的。

Topic Seven: Clothing

Story Narration
The following pictures present a sequence of events. Write a complete story based on these pictures.

1.

2.

3.

4.

REMINDERS

Write a complete narration, including each character's facial expressions and gestures. Also be aware of the setting.

OUTLINE

FIRST PARAGRAPH: Introduce characters, setting, and plot. The following words and phrases may be helpful:

[Traditional-character version]

　　服裝店，顧客服務中心，櫃檯，售貨員，顧客，披肩髮，盤髮，牛仔褲，退，換，拉鎖，開綫，質量問題

[Simplified-character version]

　　服装店，顾客服务中心，柜台，售货员，顾客，披肩发，盘发，牛仔裤，退，换，拉锁，开线，质量问题

SECOND PARAGRAPH: Describe each character's actions and expressions; use proper transitional elements. The following phrases, sentences, and proverb may be helpful:

[Traditional-character version]

　　搖頭，擺手，拒人千里之外，拿出收據，指著墻上的退換條例，無話可說，仍然拒絕退換

[Simplified-character version]

　　摇头，摆手，拒人千里之外，拿出收据，指着墙上的退换条例，无话可说，仍然拒绝退换

THIRD PARAGRAPH: Conclude the story. The following words and phrases can be used:

[Traditional-character version]

　　經理，身穿西裝，面帶笑容，照章辦事，妥善解決

[Simplified-character version]

　　经理，身穿西装，面带笑容，照章办事，妥善解决

E-mail Response
Read this e-mail from a Chinese exchange student and then type a response.

[Traditional-character version]
發件人：程偉
郵件主題：該買哪一件衣服？

　　我在網上看到兩件衣服都很喜歡，也都有我穿的號碼和喜歡的顏色。一件是名牌的，樣子好看，質量很好，但是八十多塊錢一件，對我來說太貴了。另一件價錢便宜得多，不到三十塊。不過那件衣服的牌子我從來沒聽說過，從圖片上質量好像也不太好。一下子買兩件，我有點兒捨不得。我想聽聽你的看法。另外，我知道你很會買衣服，請你談談你買衣服的經驗。

[Simplified-character version]

发件人：程伟

邮件主题：该买哪一件衣服？

　　我在网上看到两件衣服都很喜欢，也都有我穿的号码和喜欢的颜色。一件是名牌的，样子好看，质量很好，但是八十多块钱一件，对我来说太贵了。另一件价钱便宜得多，不到三十块。不过那件衣服的牌子我从来没听说过，　从图片上质量好像也不太好。一下子买两件，我有点儿舍不得。我想听听你的看法。另外，我知道你很会买衣服，请你谈谈你买衣服的经验。

SUGGESTIONS FOR WRITING AN E-MAIL RESPONSE

This e-mail is mainly about choosing between two items of clothing. When responding, keep this outline in mind:

1. Briefly repeat the sender's main points. For example:

[Traditional-character version]

　　小偉：你信中提到在網上同時看中兩件衣服，你很難放棄其中的一件，又不能兩件都買了。從信中看出你正在爲這事煩惱。別發愁了，我來給你參謀參謀吧。

[Simplified-character version]

　　小伟：你信中提到在网上同时看中两件衣服，你很难放弃其中的一件，又不能两件都买了。从信中看出你正在为这事烦恼。别发愁了，我来给你参谋参谋吧。

2. Respond to any and all questions from the sender in detail. Find solutions for these questions. For example:

[Traditional-character version]

　　至於你買哪件，就要看你買衣服的標準是什麼了。因爲......，所以......。另外，我也想知道，你看上的那兩件衣服你打算在什麼場合穿？一般來說，人們上課或者上班的時候穿得比較正式，而在家裏的時候就穿得比較隨意、舒服。如果是爲了出門穿，我寧願多花點兒錢買那件名牌的。我之所以這樣做，是因爲一是......；二是......。如果只是在家裏穿，買那件便宜的就夠了，因爲你沒有必要......。當然，要是你家裏面類似第二件的很多，那你就應該買名牌的那件，畢竟......。

[Simplified-character version]

　　至于你买哪件，就要看你买衣服的标准是什么了。因为......，所以......。另外，我也想知道，你看上的那两件衣服你打算在什么场合穿？一般来说，人们上课或者上班的时候穿得比较正式，而在家里的时候就穿得比较随意、舒服。如果是为了出门穿，我宁愿多花点儿钱买那件名牌的。我之所以这样做，是因为一是......；二是......。如果只是在家里穿，买那件便宜的就够了，因为你没有必要......。当然，要是你家里面类似第二件的很多，那你就应该买名牌的那件，毕竟......。

3. Give advice as to which item of clothing you would personally choose. For example:

[Traditional-character version]

據我所知，你的衣服並不少，只是名牌的衣服沒有多少。如果我是你的話，我就把那件名牌的買回來，或者乾脆兩件都買了，最多這個月不再買化妝品罷了。

[Simplified-character version]

据我所知，你的衣服并不少，只是名牌的衣服没有多少。如果我是你的话，我就把那件名牌的买回来，或者干脆两件都买了，最多这个月不再买化妆品罢了。

Topic Eight: Food

Story Narration
The following pictures present a sequence of events. Write a complete story based on these pictures.

1.

2.

3.

4.

Ideas are like children, there are none as wonderful as your own.

REMINDERS

Write a complete narration. Include the characters, setting, and plot. Be sure to explain the relationships between the characters, and describe their physical appearances, feelings, and facial expressions.

OUTLINE

FIRST PARAGRAPH: Introduce characters, setting, and plot. The following words and phrases may be helpful:

[Traditional-character version]
　　中國餐館，賓客滿座，服務員忙忙碌碌，乾淨，明亮，竹子，菜單，點菜

[Simplified-character version]
　　中国餐馆，宾客满座，服务员忙忙碌碌，干净，明亮，竹子，菜单，点菜

SECOND PARAGRAPH: Describe how the story progresses, focusing on the characters' actions and expressions. Pay attention to the setting. Add descriptions of the décor of the restaurant, what people are eating, and so forth. The following phrases and proverb may be helpful:

[Traditional-character version]
　　豐盛的晚餐，教……用筷子，夾不住，有耐心，反復練習，功夫不負有心人，終于夾住了……，滿懷喜悅之情

[Simplified-character version]
　　丰盛的晚餐，教……用筷子，夹不住，有耐心，反复练习，功夫不负有心人，终於夹住了……，满怀喜悦之情

THIRD PARAGRAPH: Conclude the story. The following sentences can be used:

[Traditional-character version]
　　打開幸運餅，清晰地寫著："主意像孩子一樣，總是自己的最好。"

[Simplified-character version]
　　打开幸运饼，清晰地写着："主意像孩子一样，总是自己的最好。"

E-mail Response
Read this e-mail from a Chinese exchange student and then type a response.

[Traditional-character version]
發件人：張力軍
郵件主題：去哪一家餐館吃飯？

　　我們學校的國際交換學生小强和小紅就要回中國了，大家想在中國城請他們吃飯。我們找了兩家餐館，一家餐館是四川風味的，另一家是廣東風味的。但是不能確定他們會喜歡哪一家。你跟他們倆都是好朋友，一定比我們更瞭解他們。你覺得他們會更喜歡去哪一家？爲什麼？另外，聽說你是一位美食專家，請你談談點菜的經驗。

[Simplified-character version]

发件人：张力军

邮件主题：去哪一家餐馆吃饭？

我们学校的国际交换学生小强和小红就要回中国了，大家想在中国城请他们吃饭。我们找了两家餐馆，一家餐馆是四川风味的，另一家是广东风味的。但是不能确定他们会喜欢哪一家。你跟他们俩都是好朋友，一定比我们更了解他们。你觉得他们会更喜欢去哪一家？为什么？另外，听说你是一位美食专家，请你谈谈点菜的经验。

SUGGESTIONS FOR WRITING AN E-MAIL RESPONSE

This e-mail is mainly about inviting two friends to dinner, but the writer is having a hard time choosing a restaurant because he is not sure about the kind of food each may like. When responding, keep this outline in mind:

1. Briefly repeat the sender's main points.
2. Respond to any and all questions from the sender in detail. Find solutions for these questions.
3. Tell your friend what you would do if you were in this situation.

The following is a sample:

[Traditional character version]

力軍：

你好！謝謝你在信中稱我是“美食專家”。其實，我哪是什麼“專家”，不過是特別好吃罷了。

你準備請朋友吃飯，可是不知道去哪家餐館，也不知道怎麼點菜才能讓朋友滿意。根據我的經驗，你何不直接問問他們喜歡什麼樣的菜呢？或者請他們來選個餐館，說不定更省事。點菜的時候，兩個人的口味盡可能都照顧到。說到點菜，我覺得還要注意幾點：一是要請你的客人先點，如果客人謙讓，你也不必太客氣，畢竟是你作東；二是點有特殊口味的菜以前，應該問一下客人是否喜歡。不要點太辣或者太油膩的菜，因爲有些人不吃辣的，有些女孩子因爲怕胖，一點兒油膩的都不吃；三是點菜前要先想一下點幾個菜比較合適，不要同一類型的菜同時點上好幾道。

以上是我對請客、點菜的一點兒經驗和看法。希望對你有所幫助。

[Simplified-character version]

力军：

你好！谢谢你在信中称我是“美食专家”。其实，我哪是什么“专家”，不过是特别好吃罢了。

你准备请朋友吃饭，可是不知道去哪家餐馆，也不知道怎么点菜才能让朋友满意。根据我的经验，你何不直接问问他们喜欢什么样的菜呢？或者请他们来选个餐馆，说不定更省事。点菜的时候，两个人的口味尽可能都照顾到。说到点菜，我觉得还要注意几点：一是要请你的客人先点，如果客人谦让，你也不必太客气，毕竟是你作东；二是点有特殊口味的菜以前，应该问一下客人是否喜欢。不要点太辣或者太油腻的菜，因为有些人不吃辣的，有些女孩子因为怕胖，一点儿油腻的都不吃；三是点菜前要先想一下点几个菜比较合适，不要同一类型的菜同时点上好几道。

以上是我对请客、点菜的一点儿经验和看法。希望对你有所帮助。

Topic Nine: Housing

Story Narration
The following pictures present a sequence of events. Write a complete story based on these pictures.

1.

2.

3.

4.

REMINDERS

Write a complete narration including the characters, setting, and plot. Explain the relationships between the characters; also describe their physical appearances, feelings, and facial expressions. Make sure to clarify the sequence of events. Use proper complements.

OUTLINE

FIRST PARAGRAPH: Introduce characters, setting, and plot. The following words, phrases, and idioms may be helpful:

[Traditional-character version]

公寓，一對夫婦，旅行，出發，行李箱，手提包，機票，梳妝檯，鏡子，化妝盒，化妝品，化妝刷，精細，不耐煩，無可奈何，

[Simplified-character version]

公寓，一对夫妇，旅行，出发，行李箱，手提包，机票，梳妆台，镜子，化妆盒，化妆品，化妆刷，精细，不耐烦，无可奈何，

SECOND PARAGRAPH: Describe how the story progresses, focusing on the characters' actions and expressions; use proper transitional elements. Include each person's facial expressions and their inner thoughts. The following words and phrases may be helpful:

[Traditional-character version]

馬路上，出租汽車，招手，照鏡子，運營高峰期，繁忙，堵車，行駛緩慢，

[Simplified-character version]

马路上，出租汽车，招手，照镜子，运营高峰期，繁忙，堵车，行驶缓慢，

THIRD PARAGRAPH: Conclude the story. The following words, phrases, and sentences can be used:

[Traditional-character version]

飛機場，登機口，晚點，起飛，互相埋怨，互相指責，吵架

[Simplified-character version]

飞机场，登机口，晚点，起飞，互相埋怨，互相指责，吵架

E-mail Response
Read this e-mail from a Chinese friend and then type a response.

[Traditional-character version]
發件人：向靜
郵件主題：該住在哪里？

　　我秋季學期就要到美國去讀大學了，除了住宿問題還沒有解決以外，其他手續都辦好了。從美國大學那邊寄來的資料中知道，我可以申請學校的新生宿舍，也可以選擇住在美國人的家裏。你對美國大學的瞭解一定比我多，你覺得我應該住在新生宿舍還是住到美國人的家裏？爲什麼？你今年秋天也要上大學了，你是想住在學生宿舍還是自己找房子呢？

[Simplified-character version]

发件人：向静

邮件主题：该住在哪里？

　　我秋季学期就要到美国去读大学了，除了住宿问题还没有解决以外，其他手续都办好了。从美国大学那边寄来的资料中知道，我可以申请学校的新生宿舍，也可以选择住在美国人的家里。你对美国大学的了解一定比我多，你觉得我应该住在新生宿舍还是住到美国人的家里？为什么？你今年秋天也要上大学了，你是想住在学生宿舍还是自己找房子呢？

SUGGESTIONS FOR WRITING AN E-MAIL RESPONSE

This e-mail is from a friend who needs help choosing between two places to live. When responding, keep this outline in mind:

1. Briefly repeat the sender's main points.
2. Respond to any and all questions from the sender in detail. Find solutions for these questions.
3. Tell your friend what you would do if you were in her situation.

The following is a sample:

[Traditional-character version]

向靜：

　　你好！聽到你要來美國上大學的消息，我真高興。至於到美國以後住在哪兒比較好，這還真是個兩難選擇的問題。

　　住在學校和住在美國人家裏各有利弊。住在新生宿舍，既方便又安全，還可以認識很多朋友，對熟悉校園環境有幫助。不過，住在宿舍比較貴，也不太自由。住在美國人家裏，雖然房租會便宜一些，也很安全，但是生活不太方便，特別是每天坐公共汽車上學很麻煩。不過，住在美國人家裏，對瞭解美國人的文化有好處。你問我以後上學住在哪里，這要看我的大學在哪兒了。如果還在這個城市，我想先住在家裏，因爲我想給父母省點兒錢。要是離開這個城市，到別的地方去讀書，那我既不想住在新生宿舍，也不會住在別人家裏，我可能會找兩個同屋，合租一套公寓。當然，如果我是你，我會先住在新生宿舍，等熟悉了環境以後，再住到美國人家裏。

　　以上只是我個人的一點兒看法，希望能對你有所幫助。

[Simplified-character version]

向静：

　　你好！听到你要来美国上大学的消息，我真高兴。至于到美国以后住在哪儿比较好，这还真是个两难选择的问题。

　　住在学校和住在美国人家里各有利弊。住在新生宿舍，既方便又安全，还可以认识很多朋友，对熟悉校园环境有帮助。不过，住在宿舍比较贵，也不太自由。住在美国人家里，虽然房租会便宜一些，也很安全，但是生活不太方便，特别是每天坐公共汽车上学很麻烦。不过，住在美国人家里，对了解美国人的文化有好处。你问我以后上学住在哪里，这要看我的大学在哪儿了。如果还在这个城市，我想先住在家里，因为我想给父母省点儿钱。要是离开这个城市，到别的地方去读书，那我既不想住在新生宿舍，也不会住在别人家里，我可能会找两个同屋，合租一套公寓。当然，如果我是你，我会先住在新生宿舍，等熟悉了环境以后，再住到美国人家里。

　　以上只是我个人的一点儿看法，希望能对你有所帮助。

Topic Ten: Transportation

Story Narration

The following pictures present a sequence of events. Write a complete story based on these pictures.

1.

2.

3.
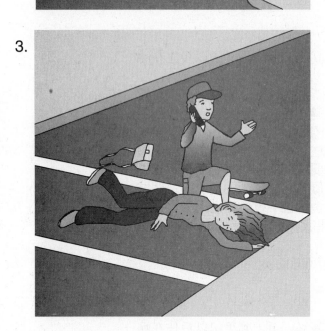

4.

REMINDERS

Write a complete narration, including the characters, the setting, and the plot. Explain the relationships between the characters; describe their physical appearances, and also their feelings and facial expressions. Make sure to clarify the sequence of events. Use proper complements.

OUTLINE

FIRST PARAGRAPH: Introduce characters, setting, and plot. The following words and phrases may be helpful:

[Traditional-character version]
　　從青年公園裏出來，十字路口，行人，人行橫道，披肩髮，身上挎著包

[Simplified-character version]
　　从青年公园里出来，十字路口，行人，人行横道，披肩发，身上挎着包

SECOND PARAGRAPH: Describe how the story progresses, focusing on the characters' actions and expressions; use proper transitional elements. The following phrases, sentences, and idiom may be helpful:

[Traditional-character version]
　　突然一輛黑色的小車疾駛而來，撞倒，昏迷過去，不停車，違章開車，逃跑，一場車禍發生了，驚慌失措，當機立斷，掏出手機，撥打911

[Simplified-character version]
　　突然一辆黑色的小车疾驶而来，撞倒，昏迷过去，不停车，违章开车，逃跑，一场车祸发生了，惊慌失措，当机立断，掏出手机，拨打911

THIRD PARAGRAPH: Conclude the story. The following words, phrases, sentences, and idiom can be used:

[Traditional-character version]
　　救護車，昏迷不醒，擡到擔架上，醫院急診室，及時搶救，助人爲樂

[Simplified-character version]
　　救护车，昏迷不醒，抬到担架上，医院急诊室，及时抢救，助人为乐

E-mail Response
Read this e-mail from a Chinese exchange student and then type a response.

[Traditional-character version]
發件人：趙亮
郵件主題：該不該買車？

　　我要作爲交換學生到你們的城市大學學習一年，但是他們提供的宿舍離大學不是很近。你一直生活在那個城市，一定很瞭解那兒的情況，請你告訴我到美國該不該買車？爲什麼？另外，請你談談在那個城市生活應該注意哪些交通方面的事情。謝謝你！

[Simplified-character version]
发件人：赵亮
邮件主题：该不该买车？

　　我要作为交换学生到你们的城市大学学习一年，但是他们提供的宿舍离大学不是很近。你一直生活在那个城市，一定很了解那儿的情况，请你告诉我到美国该不该买车？为什么？另外，请你谈谈在那个城市生活应该注意哪些交通方面的事情。谢谢你！

SUGGESTIONS FOR WRITING AN E-MAIL RESPONSE

This e-mail is mainly about whether or not to buy a car in the city, when the sender will only stay there for one year. When responding, keep this outline in mind:

1. Briefly recap the sender's main points.
2. Respond to any and all questions from the sender in detail. Find solutions for these questions.
3. Directly give advice on what you would do if you were in the sender's situation.

The following is a sample:

[Traditional-character version]
趙亮：

你好！知道你將作爲交換學生來我們城市，我很高興。歡迎你早日到來。你在來信中提到買車問題，那我來談談這個城市的交通狀況以及我對買車問題的看法。

我們城市是一個中等城市，公共交通比較發達。公共汽車和地鐵是城市裏最主要的交通工具，其中一條地鐵綫和三條公共汽車綫都經過大學，對學生來說非常方便。而且，不管是公共汽車還是地鐵，車票的價格都不貴，學生票更便宜。你作爲交換學生，只來這個城市一年，我覺得你沒有必要買車。現在美國的汽油很貴，停車費也貴，你不如坐公共汽車或地鐵去學校好了，既安全，又方便。

以上只是我個人的意見，供你參考。其實你不必急著做決定，等來了以後，先親眼看看這裏的情況，再來決定是不是需要買輛車。

[Simplified-character version]
赵亮：

你好！知道你将作为交换学生来我们城市，我很高兴。欢迎你早日到来。你在来信中提到买车问题，那我来谈谈这个城市的交通状况以及我对买车问题的看法。

我们城市是一个中等城市，公共交通比较发达。公共汽车和地铁是城市里最主要的交通工具，其中一条地铁线和三条公共汽车线都经过大学，对学生来说非常方便。而且，不管是公共汽车还是地铁，车票的价格都不贵，学生票更便宜。你作为交换学生，只来这个城市一年，我觉得你没有必要买车。现在美国的汽油很贵，停车费也贵，你不如坐公共汽车或地铁去学校好了，既安全，又方便。

以上只是我个人的意见，供你参考。其实你不必急着做决定，等来了以后，先亲眼看看这里的情况，再来决定是不是需要买辆车。

Topic Eleven: Family

Story Narration
The following pictures present a sequence of events. Write a complete story based on these pictures.

1.

2.

3.

4.

REMINDERS

Write a complete narration, to include the characters, the setting, and the plot. Explain the relationships between the characters; describe their physical appearances, as well as their feelings and facial expressions. Make sure to clarify the sequence of events. Use proper complements.

OUTLINE

FIRST PARAGRAPH: Introduce characters, setting, and plot. The following words, phrases, and idioms may be helpful:

[Traditional-character version]
氣球，出乎預料，跳出來，歡呼，給……驚喜，生日晚會

[Simplified-character version]
气球，出乎预料，跳出来，欢呼，给……惊喜，生日晚会

SECOND PARAGRAPH: Describe how the story progresses, focusing on the characters' actions and expressions; use proper transitional elements. Include each character's inner thoughts. The following words, phrases, sentences, and idioms may be helpful:

[Traditional-character version]
和藹可親的父親，禮品盒，昂貴的計算器機，無動于衷，並沒有被感動，年輕漂亮的母親，名牌包，欣喜之情掛在臉上

[Simplified-character version]
和蔼可亲的父亲，礼品盒，昂贵的计算器机，无动于衷，并没有被感动，年轻漂亮的母亲，名牌包，欣喜之情挂在脸上

THIRD PARAGRAPH: Conclude the story. The following words and phrases can be used:

[Traditional-character version]
激烈爭吵，衝突，家庭教育方式

[Simplified-character version]
激烈争吵，冲突，家庭教育方式

E-mail Response
Read this e-mail and then type a response.

[Traditional-character version]
發件人：安寧
郵件主題：我該怎麼辦？

　　我父母的感情一直不太好，最近他們的關係變得越來越差。前幾天，父母告訴我他們準備離婚了，問我對這件事情的看法。同意他們離婚吧，我就會失去一個完整的家。不同意吧，他們整天吵架，我也無法專心學習。你覺得我該同意他們離婚還是不同意？爲什麼？另外，請問你的朋友中有沒有父母離了婚的？

[Simplified-character version]
发件人：安宁
邮件主题：我该怎么办？

　　我父母的感情一直不太好，最近他们的关系变得越来越差。前几天，父母告诉我他们准备离婚了，问我对这件事情的看法。同意他们离婚吧，我就会失

去一个完整的家。不同意吧，他们整天吵架，我也无法专心学习。你觉得我该同意他们离婚还是不同意？为什么？另外，请问你的朋友中有没有父母离了婚的？

SUGGESTIONS FOR WRITING AN E-MAIL RESPONSE

This e-mail is mainly about a girl whose parents are going through a divorce. When responding, keep this outline in mind:

1. Briefly repeat the sender's main points, and empathize with your friend.
2. Respond to any and all questions from the sender in detail. Discuss the possible pros and cons of divorce.
3. Tell a personal story about you or a friend who has gone through a similar situation, and give advice on what you think your friend should do.
4. Comfort your friend and wish her luck.

The following is a sample:

[Traditional-character version]
安寧：

你好！得知你的父母要離婚了，我也爲你感到難過。我父母在我很小的時候就離婚了，所以我很理解你現在的心情。

父母離婚對子女來說確實是一件既痛苦又難辦的事情。沒有人希望這會發生在自己的家裏。可是，事情已經發展成這樣，你就應該學會面對現實了。你要相信父母一定是經過認真考慮才提出離婚的，我覺得你應該尊重他們的選擇，因爲孩子不是父母生活的全部，大人有重新選擇生活的權利。況且，他們整天爭吵，你也無法安心學習。雖然這段日子裏你會不太好受，但這只是暫時的。我相信，父母都是愛你的，他們一定會把你以後的生活安排好。

我現在跟著媽媽和繼父住，週末、節假日的時候就看望爸爸和他的妻子。你看我現在生活得也很開心啊。父母各自找到了幸福，不也是一件令人高興的事情嗎？請多多保重自己！

[Simplified-character version]
安宁：

你好！得知你的父母要离婚了，我也为你感到难过。我父母在我很小的时候就离婚了，所以我很理解你现在的心情。

父母离婚对子女来说确实是一件既痛苦又难办的事情。没有人希望这会发生在自己的家里。可是，事情已经发展成这样，你就应该学会面对现实了。你要相信父母一定是经过认真考虑才提出离婚的，我觉得你应该尊重他们的选择，因为孩子不是父母生活的全部，大人有重新选择生活的权利。况且，他们整天争吵，你也无法安心学习。虽然这段日子里你会不太好受，但这只是暂时的。我相信，父母都是爱你的，他们一定会把你以后的生活安排好。

我现在跟着妈妈和继父住，周末、节假日的时候就看望爸爸和他的妻子。你看我现在生活得也很开心啊。父母各自找到了幸福，不也是一件令人高兴的事情吗？请多多保重自己！

Topic Twelve: Education

Story Narration

The following pictures present a sequence of events. Write a complete story based on these pictures.

1.

2.

3.

4.

REMINDERS

Write a complete narration to include the characters, the setting, and the plot. Explain the relationships between the characters; describe their physical appearances, and also their feelings and facial expressions. Use proper complements.

OUTLINE

FIRST PARAGRAPH: Introduce characters, setting, and plot. The following words and phrases may be helpful:

[Traditional-character version]
短髮，白襯衫，花格短裙，鋼琴，督促……練琴，嚴厲，精神壓力

[Simplified-character version]
短发，白衬衫，花格短裙，钢琴，督促……练琴，严厉，精神压力

SECOND PARAGRAPH: Describe how the story progresses, focusing on characters' actions and expressions. Be sure to include the inner thoughts and ideas of each character. The following words, phrases, and idioms may be helpful:

[Traditional-character version]
放鬆，迫不及待，復習書，輕鬆，做不完的作業，跳舞，成才，多才多藝，成名成家，觀念，設計孩子的未來

[Simplified-character version]
放松，迫不及待，复习书，轻松，做不完的作业，跳舞，成才，多才多艺，成名成家，观念，设计孩子的未来

THIRD PARAGRAPH: Conclude the story. The following words, phrases, and idiom can be used:

[Traditional-character version]
管教嚴，限制，社會交往，輕鬆，快樂，順其自然，樂趣，身心成長，注重自由發展

[Simplified-character version]
管教严，限制，社会交往，轻松，快乐，顺其自然，乐趣，身心成长，注重自由发展

E-mail Response
Read this e-mail from a Chinese friend and then type a response.

[Traditional-character version]
發件人：周新
郵件主題：我該選什麼專業？

　　最近我在申請大學的事情上跟父母發生了一些不愉快。我喜歡文科，所以想申請幾所大學的歷史專業，可是父母覺得學文科沒有前途，畢業後難以找到工作。他們很希望我能學工科，覺得工科畢業生找到高薪工作的機會多一些。我知道父母說的話有一定道理，但是我不想選擇自己不喜歡的專業。你覺得我該怎麼辦？另外，你申請大學的事情怎麼樣了？你是怎麼選擇專業的？

[Simplified-character version]
发件人：周新
邮件主题：我该选什么专业？

　　最近我在申请大学的事情上跟父母发生了一些不愉快。我喜欢文科，所以想申请几所大学的历史专业，可是父母觉得学文科没有前途，毕业后难以找到工作。他们很希望我能学工科，觉得工科毕业生找到高薪工作的机会多一些。我知道父母说的话有一定道理，但是我不想选择自己不喜欢的专业。你觉得我该怎么办？另外，你申请大学的事情怎么样了？你是怎么选择专业的？

SUGGESTIONS FOR WRITING AN E-MAIL RESPONSE

This e-mail is about the sender's parents interfering with choosing majors. When responding, keep this outline in mind:

1. Briefly repeat the sender's main points. For example:

[Traditional-character version]
　　你在選擇專業問題上跟父母產生了矛盾，我知道你現在心裏一定很難過。這件事情的確不太好辦，處理不好難免影響你跟父母的關係和感情。

[Simplified-character version]
　　你在选择专业问题上跟父母产生了矛盾，我知道你现在心里一定很难过。这件事情的确不太好办，处理不好难免影响你跟父母的关系和感情。

2. Respond to any and all questions from the sender in detail. Relate a personal experience about such issues. For example:

[Traditional-character version]
　　我覺得要想處理好這件事情，需要……。勉強接受父母的安排，學了自己沒有興趣的專業，以後可能會自食其果。完全不聽從父母的意見，一味地……，肯定會傷害父母的感情。要想做到兩全其美，你最好……。我雖然沒有經歷過這樣的事情，但是我身邊的朋友們卻經歷過。就拿張三來說吧，他想讀……專業，可是他父母覺得學……將來不好找工作，非讓他學……不可，於是他聽從了父母的安排，結果……。相比之下，我的另一個朋友李四就處理得不錯。跟張三的父母一樣，李四的父母希望他……，而李四感興趣的卻是……。爲了說服父母，他先……，然後……。他還……。功夫不負有心人，他的父母終於……。你看，對同一事情的處理方法不同，它們的結果也大不一樣。

[Simplified-character version]
　　我觉得要想处理好这件事情，需要……。勉强接受父母的安排，学了自己没有兴趣的专业，以后可能会自食其果。完全不听从父母的意见，一味地……，肯定会伤害父母的感情。要想做到两全其美，你最好……。我虽然没有经历过这样的事情，但是我身边的朋友们却经历过。就拿张三来说吧，他想读……专业，可是他父母觉得学……将来不好找工作，非让他学……不可，于是他听从了父母的安排，结果……。相比之下，我的另一个朋友李四就处理得不错。跟张三的父母一样，李四的父母希望他……，而李四感兴趣的却是……。为了说服父母，他先……，然后……。他还……。功夫不负有心人，他的父母终于……。你看，对同一事情的处理方法不同，它们的结果也大不一样。

3. Give advice as to what you think your friend should do. For example:

[Traditional-character version]

　　在無關緊要的小事上，我們應該聽從大人的安排，但在選專業這樣的問題上，應該堅持自我，有自己的主見，不能總是走父母給的路。所以，我建議你……。

[Simplified-character version]

　　在无关紧要的小事上，我们应该听从大人的安排，但在选专业这样的问题上，应该坚持自我，有自己的主见，不能总是走父母给的路。所以，我建议你……。

Topic Thirteen: Festivities

Story Narration

The following pictures present a sequence of events. Write a complete story based on these pictures.

1.

2.

3.

4.

REMINDERS

Write a complete narration, including characters, setting, and plot. Explain the relationships between the characters; describe their physical appearances, and also their feelings and facial expressions. Make sure to clarify the sequence of events. Use proper complements.

OUTLINE

FIRST PARAGRAPH: Introduce characters, setting, and plot. The following words and phrases may be helpful:

[Traditional-character version]
　　年輕人，又高又帥，手裏捧著一個盒子，快步走進郵局

[Simplified-character version]
　　年轻人，又高又帅，手里捧着一个盒子，快步走进邮局

SECOND PARAGRAPH: Describe how the story progresses, focusing on the characters' actions and expressions; use proper transitional elements. Include the characters' personal thoughts. The following words, phrases, and idioms may be helpful:

[Traditional-character version]
　　進進出出，排隊的人很多，男女老幼，寄，包裹，郵票，掛號信，明信片，等了半天才輪到……．，櫃檯，工作人員，繁忙，母親節，給……寄禮物，表達心意

[Simplified-character version]
　　进进出出，排队的人很多，男女老幼，寄，包裹，邮票，挂号信，明信片，等了半天才轮到……．，柜台，工作人员，繁忙，母亲节，给……寄礼物，表达心意

THIRD PARAGRAPH: Conclude the story. The following words and idioms can be used:

[Traditional-character version]
　　驚訝地發現，原來，粗心大意

[Simplified-character version]
　　惊讶地发现，原来，粗心大意

E-mail Response
Read this e-mail from a Chinese exchange student and then type a response.

[Traditional-character version]
發件人：李向東
郵件主題：該接受誰的邀請？

　　因爲我圣誕節不回中國了，我的一個同學杰克邀請我跟他的家人一起吃圣誕晚餐，而另一個同學大卫邀请我聖誕節夜的時候跟他的家人去教堂。他們兩人不僅是我的同学，也都是我的好朋友。你觉得我应该接受谁的邀请？为什么？另外，你的家人一般是怎么过圣诞夜的？

[Simplified-character version]
发件人：李向东
邮件主题：该接受谁的邀请？

　　因为我圣诞节不回中国了，我的一个同学杰克邀请我跟他的家人一起吃圣诞晚餐，而另一个同学大卫邀请我圣诞节夜的时候跟他的家人去教堂。他们两人不仅是我的同学，也都是我的好朋友。你觉得我应该接受谁的邀请？为什么？另外，你的家人一般是怎么过圣诞夜的？

SUGGESTIONS FOR WRITING AN E-MAIL RESPONSE

This e-mail is mainly about having to choose between two invitations for Christmas Eve. When responding, keep this outline in mind:

1. Greet your friend and briefly repeat the sender's main points. For example:

[Traditional-character version]
　　聖誕節就要到了，先向你表示節日的問候。兩位朋友都是好心，你不想辜負人家的一片心意，覺得很難拒絕其中的一方，這種心情我很理解。

[Simplified-character version]
　　圣诞节就要到了，先向你表示节日的问候。两位朋友都是好心，你不想辜负人家的一片心意，觉得很难拒绝其中的一方，这种心情我很理解。

2. Respond to any and all questions from the sender in detail. Find solutions for these questions. You can also tell a story about a similar experience you or someone else had. For example:

[Traditional-character version]
　　爲了找到一個兩全其美的解決方式，首先，你應該考慮……。其次，你看看他們……。另外也要……。還有……因素也要考慮到。我哥哥在中國留學的時候，正好趕上了你們中國的春節。好幾個中國朋友都邀請他……。我哥哥就……，最後大家都過了一個愉快的新年。雖然過去兩、三年了，我哥哥至今仍記憶猶新。

[Simplified-character version]
　　为了找到一个两全其美的解决方式，首先，你应该考虑……。其次，你看看他们……。另外也要……。还有……因素也要考虑到。我哥哥在中国留学的时候，正好赶上了你们中国的春节。好几个中国朋友都邀请他……。我哥哥就……，最后大家都过了一个愉快的新年。虽然过去两、三年了，我哥哥至今仍记忆犹新。

3. Give direct advice as to what you think your friend should do. For example:

[Traditional-character version]

你可以把兩位朋友叫到一起，跟他們一起商量，找出一個解決辦法。我相信，他們都是善解人意的朋友，不管你做出什麼決定，他們都會理解你的。說不定到最後你發現，原來自己的顧慮是多餘的呢。

[Simplified-character version]

你可以把两位朋友叫到一起，跟他们一起商量，找出一个解决办法。我相信，他们都是善解人意的朋友，不管你做出什么决定，他们都会理解你的。说不定到最后你发现，原来自己的顾虑是多余的呢。

Topic Fourteen: Travel

Story Narration

The following pictures present a sequence of events. Write a complete story based on these pictures.

REMINDERS

Write a complete narration, including characters, setting, and plot. Pay special attention to the setting. Explain the relationships between the characters; describe their physical appearances, and also their feelings and facial expressions. Make sure to clarify the sequence of events. Use proper complements.

OUTLINE

FIRST PARAGRAPH: Introduce characters, setting, and plot. The following phrases and idioms may be helpful:

[Traditional-character version]

父子，遊覽長城，興高采烈，激動得跳了起來

[Simplified-character version]

父子，游览长城，兴高采烈，激动得跳了起来

SECOND PARAGRAPH: Describe how the story progresses, focusing on the characters' actions and expressions; use proper transitional elements. Include what each character might be saying and thinking. The following words, phrases, and idioms may be helpful:

[Traditional-character version]

萬里長城，雄偉，壯觀，古代人民創造的奇蹟，迫不及待，爬，累，不到長城非好漢，加油，打起精神，繼續往上爬

[Simplified-character version]

万里长城，雄伟，壮观，古代人民创造的奇迹，迫不及待，爬，累，不到长城非好汉，加油，打起精神，继续往上爬

THIRD PARAGRAPH: Conclude the story. The following phrase and proverb can be used:

[Traditional-character version]

堅持到底就是勝利，感到無比高興和自豪

[Simplified-character version]

坚持到底就是胜利，感到无比高兴和自豪

E-mail Response

Read this e-mail from a friend and then type a response.

[Traditional-character version]

發件人：小雪
郵件主題：旅遊

我將作爲交換學生到你們學校學習一年。除了學習以外，我還打算在寒假或者暑假的時候旅遊一次。我對美國旅遊方面的情況不太瞭解，請你告訴我怎麼旅遊最省錢？去哪些地方旅遊最合適？寒假去好還是暑假去比較好？爲什麼？另外，請你談談在美國旅遊要注意些什麼。

[Simplified-character version]
发件人：小雪
邮件主题：旅游

　　我将作为交换学生到你们学校学习一年。除了学习以外，我还打算在寒假或者暑假的时候旅游一次。我对美国旅游方面的情况不太了解，请你告诉我怎么旅游最省钱？去哪些地方旅游最合适？寒假去好还是暑假去比较好？为什么？另外，请你谈谈在美国旅游要注意些什么。

SUGGESTIONS FOR WRITING AN E-MAIL RESPONSE

This e-mail is mainly about a friend who wants to travel in America while being an exchange student. When responding, keep this outline in mind:

1. Greet your friend and repeat the sender's main points. For example:

[Traditional-character version]
　　聽到你要我們學校學習真高興。你想瞭解美國旅遊方面的情況，我大概給你介紹介紹吧。

[Simplified-character version]
　　听到你要我们学校学习真高兴。你想了解美国旅游方面的情况，我大概给你介绍介绍吧。

2. Respond to any and all questions from the sender in detail. Tell your friend about experiences you have had traveling in the States. For example:

[Traditional-character version]
　　在美國旅遊有各種各樣的方式，至于哪種旅遊方式最省錢，就要看……了。如果……，那你可以參加一個旅行社，由導遊安排你的行程。這樣做的好處是……，而且也……。當然不利的是……。如果……，你不妨自己坐飛機或者火車去。不僅可以……，而且還能……。可以說是一舉兩得。不過，……。還有就是自己開車旅行。既省錢，又自由。但是開車也有開車的……，……的時候就不方便了。至于什麼季節去什麼地方，對我來說，冬天的時候我會去……，暑假呢，我就去……。春天時最好去……看看，秋天的時候，……是非去不可的。我這個人，旅遊的時候不是太講究，不過，我會特別注意穿上合適的鞋，要不然走長路的時候會覺得累。還有，帶些常用藥也有必要。最好帶上一部手機，隨時向家人、好友報告行程，免得他們爲你擔心。

[Simplified-character version]
　　在美国旅游有各种各样的方式，至于哪种旅游方式最省钱，就要看……了。如果……，那你可以参加一个旅行社，由导游安排你的行程。这样做的好处是……，而且也……。当然不利的是……。如果……，你不妨自己坐飞机或者火车去。不仅可以……，而且还能……。可以说是一举两得。不过，……。还有就是自己开车旅行。既省钱，又自由。但是开车也有开车的……，……的时候就不方便了。至于什么季节去什么地方，对我来说，冬天的时候我会去……，暑假呢，我就去……。春天时最好去……看看，秋天的时候，……是非去不可的。我这个人，旅游的时候不是太讲究，不过，我会特别注意穿上合适的鞋，要不然走长路的时候会觉得累。还有，带些常用药也有必要。最好带上一部手机，随时向家人、好友报告行程，免得他们为你担心。

3. List places that you think she should visit. Add some general advice about traveling. For example:

[Traditional-character version]

根據你的情況，我大概給你做了一個旅行計劃，供你參考。你到美國以後，也可以先……再做決定。

[Simplified-character version]

根据你的情况，我大概给你做了一个旅行计划，供你参考。你到美国以后，也可以先……再做决定。

Topic Fifteen: Art

Story Narration

The following pictures present a sequence of events. Write a complete story based on these pictures.

1.

2.

3.

4.

REMINDERS

Write a complete narration, including characters, setting, and plot. Describe the physical appearances of characters, and their feelings and facial expressions. Make sure to clarify the sequence of events. Use proper complements.

OUTLINE

FIRST PARAGRAPH: Introduce characters, setting, and plot. The following words, phrases, and idioms may be helpful:

[Traditional-character version]

電視屏幕，武功，對……感興趣，功夫電影，少林武功，僧人，運動員，聚精會神

[Simplified-character version]

电视屏幕，武功，对……感兴趣，功夫电影，少林武功，僧人，运动员，聚精会神，

SECOND PARAGRAPH: Describe how the story progresses, focusing on the characters' actions and expressions; use proper transitional elements. The following words, phrases, and proverbs may be helpful:

[Traditional-character version]

武術雜誌，閱讀，廣爲流傳的健身方法，武術愛好者，武術學校，訓練班，教練，教學經驗豐富，打拳，練武，拳術，刀術，氣功，各種動作，勤學苦練，強身健體，只要功夫深，鐵杵磨成針，成功

[Simplified-character version]

武术杂志，阅读，广为流传的健身方法，武术爱好者，武术学校，训练班，教练，教学经验丰富，打拳，练武，拳术，刀术，气功，各种动作，勤学苦练，强身健体，只要功夫深，铁杵磨成针，成功

THIRD PARAGRAPH: Conclude the story. The following phrases and proverb can be used:

[Traditional-character version]

下決心，一分耕耘一分收穫，武術館，武術電影節，參加武術比賽，實現目標，功夫電影明星

[Simplified-character version]

下决心，一分耕耘一分收获，武术馆，武术电影节，参加武术比赛，实现目标，功夫电影明星

E-mail Response

Read this e-mail from a friend and then type a response.

[Traditional-character version]
發件人：唐雲
郵件主題：該選哪一門課程？

　　我很喜歡上藝術課，特別是油畫和藝術史。我本來打算下學期把這兩門課都選上，可是我的老師說，我只能選其中的一門，因爲有一門數學課下學期一定要選。油畫和藝術史都是我喜歡的課，你覺得我下學期是選油畫課還是應該上藝術史課？爲什麼？你下學期會選哪些課？

[Simplified-character version]
发件人：唐云
邮件主题：该选哪一门课程？

　　我很喜欢上艺术课，特别是油画和艺术史。我本来打算下学期把这两门课都选上，可是我的老师说，我只能选其中的一门，因为有一门数学课下学期一定要选。油画和艺术史都是我喜欢的课，你觉得我下学期是选油画课还是应该上艺术史课？为什么？你下学期会选哪些课？

SUGGESTIONS FOR WRITING AN E-MAIL RESPONSE

This e-mail is mainly about your friend who is having a hard time deciding which arts class to drop. When responding, keep this outline in mind:

1. Repeat the sender's main points.
2. Respond to any and all questions from the sender in detail. Tell a story about yourself or a friend who has gone through a similar situation.
3. Tell what you would do if you were in her situation.

The following is a sample:

[Traditional-character version]
唐雲：
　　我想人們對自己心愛的東西總是很難割捨的，所以你現在的心情我能理解。
　　其實，事情並沒有你想得那麼難辦。你根本不是什麼放棄，只不過是等待一年嘛。你今年先選一門油畫或者藝術史，明年再把另一門課選了。至於先選什麼，後選什麼，我倒覺得有點兒學問。據我所知，油畫課需要大量的課後練習，而藝術史需要記憶很多東西。所以，你在選課之前，這些因素都應該考慮進去。我去年的課就選得不太好，其中有兩門課，雖然都不太難，但是作業多，考試也不少，都是需要花很多時間去記憶的那種課。結果，一學期下來，我疲憊不堪，而成績也不太理想。
　　我希望你能接受我的教訓，盡可能考慮得全面一些。我要是你的話，我就先選油畫課，把藝術史留到明年再上。我聽說，咱們學校很多學生會利用暑假去社區大學上藝術史，也是一個不錯的選擇呀。

[Simplified-character version]
唐云：
　　我想人们对自己心爱的东西总是很难割舍的，所以你现在的心情我能理解。
　　其实，事情并没有你想得那么难办。你根本不是什么放弃，只不过是等待一年嘛。你今年先选一门油画或者艺术史，明年再把另一门课选了。至于先选什么，后选什么，我倒觉得有点儿学问。据我所知，油画课需要大量的课后练习，而艺术史需要记忆很多东西。所以，你在选课之前，这些因素都应该考虑进去。我去年的课就选得不太好，其中有两门课，虽然都不太难，但是作业多，考试也不少，都是需要花很多时间去记忆的那种课。结果，一学期下来，我疲惫不堪，而成绩也不太理想。

我希望你能接受我的教训，尽可能考虑得全面一些。我要是你的话，我就先选油画课，把艺术史留到明年再上。我听说，咱们学校很多学生会利用暑假去社区大学上艺术史，也是一个不错的选择呀。

Topic Sixteen: Literature & History

Story Narration
The following pictures present a sequence of events. Write a complete story based on these pictures.

1.

2.

3.

4.

REMINDERS

Write a complete narration, including characters, setting, and plot. Describe the physical appearances of the characters, and also their feelings and facial expressions. Make sure to clarify the sequence of events.

OUTLINE

FIRST PARAGRAPH: Introduce characters, setting, and plot. The following words, phrases, and idioms may be helpful:

[Traditional-character version]
　　書店，圖書，琳瑯滿目，分類，各種讀物，適合不同閱讀水平的讀者，學習參考書，小說

[Simplified-character version]
　　书店，图书，琳琅满目，分类，各种读物，适合不同阅读水平的读者，学习参考书，小说

SECOND PARAGRAPH: Describe how the story progresses, focusing on the characters' actions and expressions. Describe what each character is thinking. The following words, phrases, idioms, and proverb may be helpful:

[Traditional-character version]
　　古典文學作品，意外地發現，夢寐以求的小說，喜上眉梢，欣喜若狂，真是踏破鐵鞋無覓處，得來全不費功夫，收款台，交款，錢包裏空空的

[Simplified-character version]
　　古典文学作品，意外地发现，梦寐以求的小说，喜上眉梢，欣喜若狂，真是踏破铁鞋无觅处，得来全不费功夫，收款台，交款，钱包里空空的

THIRD PARAGRAPH: Conclude the story. The following words, phrases, and sentences can be used:

[Traditional-character version]
　　無可奈何，懷著戀戀不捨的心情，放回原處，沒精打采，愁眉苦臉

[Simplified-character version]
　　无可奈何，怀着恋恋不舍的心情，放回原处，没精打采，愁眉苦脸

E-mail Response
Read this e-mail from a friend and then type a response.

[Traditional-character version]
發件人：趙朋朋
郵件主題：服飾文化藝術

　　一年一度的校園文化節就要開始了，到時將有豐富多彩的文化藝術活動。我準備參加其中的傳統服裝藝術表演節目，想通過服飾藝術展現我們的家庭文化特色。媽媽建議我穿旗袍參加服裝表演，而姐姐認爲穿長褲更能體現我的風格。你在服裝方面一向很講究，你覺得我應該穿什麼衣服參加表演？另外，你參加過傳統文化方面的表演嗎？請談談你的經驗或者看法。

[Simplified-character version]
发件人：赵朋朋
邮件主题：服饰文化艺术

　　一年一度的校园文化节就要开始了，到时将有丰富多彩的文化艺术活动。我准备参加其中的传统服装艺术表演节目，想通过服饰艺术展现我们的家庭文化特色。妈妈建议我穿旗袍参加服装表演，而姐姐认为穿长裤更能体现我的风格。你在服装方面一向很讲究，你觉得我应该穿什么衣服参加表演？另外，你参加过传统文化方面的表演吗？请谈谈你的经验或者看法。

SUGGESTIONS FOR WRITING AN E-MAIL RESPONSE

This e-mail is mainly about choosing between two costumes for a cultural festival. When responding, keep this outline in mind:

1. Repeat the sender's main points.
2. Respond to any and all questions from the sender in detail.
3. Give your friend some advice on this topic.

The following is a sample:

[Traditional-character version]
朋朋：

　　真羨慕你呀，可以參加這麼有意義的文化藝術表演。你知道嗎，我一直都希望能有機會參加這類活動，可惜沒有。

　　我想學校舉辦傳統服裝藝術表演比賽，目的不過是增強學生對不同文化的興趣，給學生提供一個多種文化交流的環境。只要參賽的服裝能夠體現民族文化特色就够了。至於你的服裝，我覺得你可以把旗袍作爲參加比賽的服裝。我之所以這樣建議，一來是因爲你爸爸是中國人，旗袍是中國典型的傳統服裝之一，是中國傳統文化的一個重要組成部分；二來是你的身材很適合穿旗袍。你看你，身材高挑，不胖不瘦，骨肉匀稱。可以想象得出來，你穿上旗袍一定會給人美麗、優雅的美好印象。當然，選擇西式服裝出場也很不錯，對你熱情奔放的氣質很合適。

　　希望我的建議能對你有所幫助。別忘了在現場拍些照片，寄給我分享呀！

[Simplified-character version]
朋朋：

　　真羡慕你呀，可以参加这么有意义的文化艺术表演比赛。你知道吗，我一直都希望能有机会参加这类活动，可惜没有。

　　我想学校举办传统服装艺术表演比赛，目的不过是增强学生对不同文化的兴趣，给学生提供一个多种文化交流的环境。只要参赛的服装能够体现民族文化特色就够了。至于你的服装，我觉得你可以把旗袍作为参加比赛的服装。我之所以这样建议，一来是因为你爸爸是中国人，旗袍是中国典型的传统服装之一，是中国传统文化的一个重要组成部分；二来是你的身材很适合穿旗袍。你看你，身材高挑，不胖不瘦，骨肉匀称。可以想象得出来，你穿上旗袍一定会给人美丽、优雅的美好印象。当然，选择西式服装出场也很不错，对你热情奔放的气质很合适。

　　希望我的建议能对你有所帮助。别忘了在现场拍些照片，寄给我分享呀！

Topic Seventeen: Society

Story Narration

The following pictures present a sequence of events. Write a complete story based on these pictures. Although this set of pictures was used to explain the scoring guidelines earlier in the book, students are advised to compose their own story here.

1.

2.
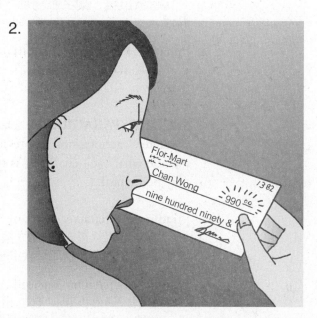

3.

4.

REMINDERS

Write a complete narration. Remember to include the characters, the setting, and the plot. Explain the relationships between the characters; describe their physical appearances, as well as their feelings and facial expressions. Make sure to clarify the sequence of events. Use proper complements.

OUTLINE

FIRST PARAGRAPH: Introduce characters, setting, and plot. The following phrases may be helpful:

[Traditional-character version]
　　超級市場，顧客服務部，聽取顧客意見，負責商品退換，反饋信息，工作繁忙

[Simplified-character version]
　　超级市场，顾客服务部，听取顾客意见，负责商品退换，反馈信息，工作繁忙

SECOND PARAGRAPH: Describe how the story progresses, focusing on the characters' actions and expressions; use proper transitional elements. Be sure to include what each character is thinking. The following words, phrases, and idioms may be helpful:

[Traditional-character version]
　　支票，偶然發現，職位相同，薪水却不一樣，出乎意料，不公平，歧視婦女，維護自己的權益，解決問題，律師事務所，起訴

[Simplified-character version]
　　支票，偶然发现，职位相同，薪水却不一样，出乎意料，不公平，歧视妇女，维护自己的权益，解决问题，律师事务所，起诉

THIRD PARAGRAPH: Conclude the story. The following words, phrases, and idioms can be used:

[Traditional-character version]
　　要求同工同酬，判決，大獲全勝，官司贏了，維護男女平等

[Simplified-character version]
　　要求同工同酬，判决，大获全胜，官司赢了，维护男女平等

E-mail Response
Read this e-mail from a friend from China and then type a response.

[Traditional-character version]
發件人：謝明
郵件主題：應該選擇什麼社會話題？

　　今天我們英文老師要我們下一個星期做一個有關社會話題的口頭報告，具體題目要自己選，可是我不知道寫什麼。請你幫我想一個社會問題作爲我口頭報告的題目，並告訴我爲什麼你覺得這個題目好。另外，請你談談做好一個口頭報告應該注意什麼。希望早日收到你的回信。謝謝！

[Simplified-character version]
发件人：谢明
邮件主题：应该选择什么社会话题？

　　今天我们英文老师要我们下一个星期做一个有关社会话题的口头报告，具体题目要自己选，可是我不知道写什么。请你帮我想一个社会问题作为我口头

报告的题目，并告诉我为什么你觉得这个题目好。另外，请你谈谈做好一个口头报告应该注意什么。希望早日收到你的回信。谢谢！

SUGGESTIONS FOR WRITING AN E-MAIL RESPONSE

This e-mail asks about an oral presentation on current social issues in the United States. When responding, keep this outline in mind:

1. Repeat the sender's main points. For example:

你來信中詢問有關口頭報告的題目，我想向你推薦同性戀這個社會話題，因爲它是目前世界上很多國家都在討論的一個熱門話題，尤其是美國。

你来信中询问有关口头报告的题目，我想向你推荐同性恋这个社会话题，因为它是目前世界上很多国家都在讨论的一个热门话题，尤其是美国。

2. Respond to any and all questions addressed by the sender in detail. Discuss both sides of the argument and then choose your own position on this topic. For example:

在美國同性戀能否結婚，各個地方不一樣。有些州已經合法化了，如新澤西州和加利福尼亞州等。之所以有這樣的不同，是因爲美國人對同性戀的看法各異。有些人覺得……，另外一些卻認爲……。我個人認爲，同性戀應該有結婚的權利。因爲第一，……，第二，……。另外，作爲公民，他們只不過是生理上跟別人不一樣，公民的平等權力他們爲什麼不能有呢？當然，同性戀結婚，也會給……帶來負面的影響，因爲……。所以法律上對同性戀結婚慎重一些也是應該的。

在美国同性恋能否结婚，各个地方不一样。有些州已经合法化了，如新泽西州和加利福尼亚州等。之所以有这样的不同，是因为美国人对同性恋的看法各异。有些人觉得……，另外一些却认为……。我个人认为，同性恋应该有结婚的权利。因为第一，……，第二，……。另外，作为公民，他们只不过是生理上跟别人不一样，公民的平等权力他们为什么不能有呢？当然，同性恋结婚，也会给……带来负面的影响，因为……。所以法律上对同性恋结婚慎重一些也是应该的。

3. Provide any additional thoughts you may have on this topic.

在此，我想向你推薦……，都是關於美國同性戀，是目前最流行的兩本書。聽說在中國也可以買到或者在圖書館借到。如果找不到，就告訴我，我給你寄去。至於做口頭報告要注意什麼，我覺得你報告的內容要豐富一些，多給一些實例。另外，你報告時的語速不能太快，也不應太慢，語速要適中。還有，你做報告那天最好穿得正式一點兒。

在此，我想向你推荐……，都是关于美国同性恋，是目前最流行的两本书。听说在中国也可以买到或者在图书馆借到。如果找不到，就告诉我，我给你寄去。至于做口头报告要注意什么，我觉得你报告的内容要丰富一些，多给一些实例。另外，你报告时的语速不能太快，也不应太慢，语速要适中。还有，你做报告那天最好穿得正式一点儿。

Topic Eighteen: Geography & Climate

Story Narration

The following pictures present a sequence of events. Write a complete story based on these pictures.

1.

2.

3.

4.

REMINDERS

Write a complete narration. Be sure to include the characters, the setting, and the plot. Explain the relationships between the characters; describe their physical appearances as well as their feelings and facial expressions. Make sure to clarify the sequence of events. Use proper complements.

OUTLINE

FIRST PARAGRAPH: Introduce characters, setting, and plot. The following words, phrases, and idioms may be helpful:

[Traditional-character version]

    路易斯安那，幽靜的海岸，海面上風平浪靜，漂亮的別墅，尖尖的屋頂在陽光下格外醒目，優美的環境，鄉村風情，讓人心曠神怡

[Simplified-character version]

    路易斯安那，幽静的海岸，海面上风平浪静，漂亮的别墅，尖尖的屋顶在阳光下格外醒目，优美的环境，乡村风情，让人心旷神怡

SECOND PARAGRAPH: Describe how the story progresses, focusing on the characters' actions and expressions; use proper transitional elements. Be sure to describe what each person is thinking. Give detailed descriptions of the weather and setting. The following words, phrases, and idioms can be used:

[Traditional-character version]

    大西洋，傾盆大雨，洪水，電閃雷鳴，澎湃洶湧，**襲擊**，建築物、房屋被摧毀，劫後餘生，恐懼，惴惴不安，憂心忡忡，撤離，逃難

[Simplified-character version]

    大西洋，倾盆大雨，洪水，电闪雷鸣，澎湃汹涌，袭击，建筑物、房屋被摧毁，劫后余生，恐惧，惴惴不安，忧心忡忡，撤离，逃难

THIRD PARAGRAPH: Conclude the story. The following words and phrases can be used:

[Traditional-character version]

    親戚，熱情招待，互相幫助

[Simplified-character version]

    亲戚，热情招待，互相帮助

E-mail Response

Read this e-mail from a friend from China and then type a response.

[Traditional-character version]

發件人：劉東

郵件主題：什麼時候去夏威夷比較好？

    夏威夷不僅是美國人的旅遊景點，也是世界著名的旅遊勝地之一。我打算利用在美國學習的這一年中去夏威夷玩一玩。但是對我來說，夏威夷之行只能安排在寒假或者暑假裏。你覺得我是該冬天去還是夏天去？為什麼？另外，請你談談到夏威夷旅遊應該注意什麼事情。謝謝你！

[Simplified-character version]

发件人：刘东

邮件主题：什么时候去夏威夷比较好？

夏威夷不仅是美国人的旅游景点，也是世界著名的旅游胜地之一。我打算利用在美国学习的这一年中去夏威夷玩一玩。但是对我来说，夏威夷之行只能安排在寒假或者暑假里。你觉得我是该冬天去还是夏天去？为什么？另外，请你谈谈到夏威夷旅游应该注意什么事情。谢谢你！

SUGGESTIONS FOR WRITING AN E-MAIL RESPONSE

This e-mail is mainly about a trip to Hawaii. When responding, keep this outline in mind:

1. Repeat the sender's main points.
2. Respond to any and all questions from the sender in detail. If you have been to Hawaii before, discuss your experience there.
3. Say what you would do if you were in your friend's position.

The following is a sample:

[Traditional-character version]

劉東：

這真是一個不錯的旅遊計劃，我相信夏威夷之行會讓你終生難忘的。夏威夷的氣候得天獨厚，十分宜人。全年的氣溫變化不大，冬夏氣溫在攝氏25度到30度左右。從十月到第二年的四月雨比較多。由於你提到你只能在寒暑假去，那我得告訴你，夏威夷旅遊的旺季正是那段時間，飯店住宿費比較貴，你可要提前把旅費準備好呀。

我以前去夏威夷是在春假期間去的，那個時間遊客比較少，相應的費用就低得多，還可以更真切地感受到當地民風。如果你也有春假，安排在春假更合適。

[Simplified-character version]

刘东：

这真是一个不错的旅游计划，我相信夏威夷之行会让你终生难忘的。夏威夷的气候得天独厚，十分宜人。全年的气温变化不大，冬夏气温在摄氏25度到30度左右。从十月到第二年的四月雨比较多。由于你提到你只能在寒暑假去，那我得告诉你，夏威夷旅游的旺季正是那段时间，饭店住宿费比较贵，你可要提前把旅费准备好呀。

我以前去夏威夷是在春假期间去的，那个时间游客比较少，相应的费用就低得多，还可以更真切地感受到当地民风。如果你也有春假，安排在春假更合适。

Topic Nineteen: Science & Technology

Story Narration

The following pictures present a sequence of events. Write a complete story based on these pictures.

1.

2.
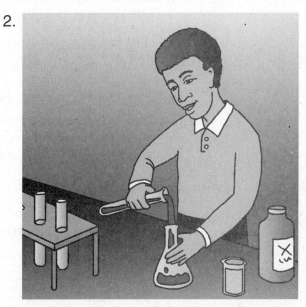

3.
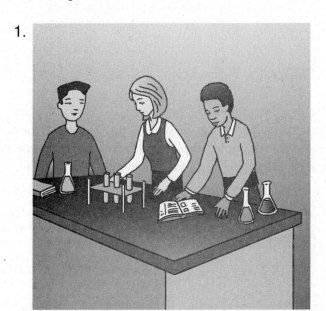

4.

REMINDERS

Write a complete narration. Be sure to include the characters, the setting, and the plot. Describe the physical appearances of characters as well as their feelings and facial expressions. Make sure to clarify the sequence of events. Using proper complements will make the narration livelier.

OUTLINE

FIRST PARAGRAPH: Introduce characters, setting, and plot. The following words, phrases, and idioms may be helpful:

[Traditional-character version]
　　化學課，實驗室，實驗台，實驗小組，試管，燒杯，做實驗，聚精會神

[Simplified-character version]
　　化学课，实验室，实验台，实验小组，试管，烧杯，做实验，聚精会神

SECOND PARAGRAPH: Describe how the story progresses, focusing on the characters' actions and expressions; use proper transitional elements. You can elaborate by giving extra information—for example, explaining why the explosion occurred or why they are not wearing safety goggles. The following words, phrases, and idioms may be helpful:

[Traditional-character version]
　　液體，把……倒入燒杯，不按要求做，安全鏡，危險，驚慌失措，嚇出一身冷汗，事故

[Simplified-character version]
　　液体，把……倒入烧杯，不按要求做，安全镜，危险，惊慌失措，吓出一身冷汗，事故

THIRD PARAGRAPH: Conclude the story. The following words, phrases, and sentences can be used:

[Traditional-character version]
　　發生爆炸，緊急處理，慶幸，嚴厲地批評，這個教訓終生難忘

[Simplified-character version]
　　发生爆炸，紧急处理，庆幸，严厉地批评，这个教训终生难忘

E-mail Response
Read this e-mail from a friend and then type a response.

[Traditional-character version]
發件人：郭燕
郵件主題：哪種學習方法更科學？

　　我學習一直很努力，每天都學到很晚才睡覺。但是我覺得學習效果沒有那麼好，成績提高得也沒有那麼快。我想可能是因爲我的學習方法不對吧。請你給我一些建議。另外，表面上你學習沒有我刻苦，可是你的成績卻一直都比我好，請你談談你的學習方法。謝謝！

[Simplified-character version]
发件人：郭燕
邮件主题：哪种学习方法更科学？

　　我学习一直很努力，每天都学到很晚才睡觉。但是我觉得学习效果没有那么好，成绩提高得也没有那么快。我想可能是因为我的学习方法不对吧。请你给我一些建议。另外，表面上你学习没有我刻苦，可是你的成绩却一直都比我好，请你谈谈你的学习方法。谢谢！

SUGGESTIONS FOR WRITING AN E-MAIL RESPONSE

This e-mail is mainly about different methods of learning. When responding, keep this outline in mind:

1. Repeat the sender's main points.
2. Respond to any and all questions from the sender in detail.
3. Choose which learning method you prefer.

The following is a sample:

[Traditional-character version]
郭燕：
　　你好！很高興能在信中與你討論學習方法的問題。
　　我覺得科學的學習方法就是根據自己的個性特點選擇學習時間和學習方式。比如，根據自己的智力特點和性格特徵制定一個相應的學習計劃，並要求自己一定按照計劃去做。這樣做，不僅提高了學習效率，還能充分發揮自己的特長。要想提高學習效率，就要注意科學地運用時間。無論是在學校的正常學習還是在家的自學，都不例外。對我來說，我的頭腦最清醒的時候是上午9點左右和下午3點前後，那是我學習效率最高的時候，我會抓緊學習。你說我沒有你刻苦，成績比你好一些，我想可能是因爲我掌握了一些用腦的藝術吧。我從不讓大腦過度疲勞，累了就休息，否則學習沒有效果。所以說，正確的學習方法可以得到事半功倍的作用。
　　什麼是科學的學習方法，這個問題因人而異。對我來說，適合自己的方法就是科學的。

[Simplified-character version]
郭燕：
　　你好！很高兴能在信中与你讨论学习方法的问题。
　　我觉得科学的学习方法就是根据自己的个性特点选择学习时间和学习方式。比如，根据自己的智力特点和性格特征制定一个相应的学习计划，并要求自己一定按照计划去做。这样做，不仅提高了学习效率，还能充分发挥自己的特长。要想提高学习效率，就要注意科学地运用时间。无论是在学校的正常学习还是在家的自学，都不例外。对我来说，我的头脑最清醒的时候是上午9点左右和下午3点前后，那是我学习效率最高的时候，我会抓紧学习。你说我没有你刻苦，成绩比你好一些，我想可能是因为我掌握了一些用脑的艺术吧。我从不让大脑过度疲劳，累了就休息，否则学习没有效果。所以说，正确的学习方法可以得到事半功倍的作用。
　　什么是科学的学习方法，这个问题因人而异。对我来说，适合自己的方法就是科学的。

Topic Twenty: Humans & Nature

Story Narration

The following pictures present a sequence of events. Write a complete story based on these pictures.

REMINDERS

Write a complete narration. Be sure to include the characters, the setting, and the plot. Explain the relationships between the characters; describe their physical appearances as well as their feelings and facial expressions. Make sure to clarify the sequence of events. Use proper complements.

OUTLINE

FIRST PARAGRAPH: Introduce characters, setting, and plot. The following words and phrases may be helpful:

[Traditional-character version]
工廠，煙囪，排放廢氣，污染天空，大自然，樹木，人類，飛走

[Simplified-character version]
工厂，烟囱，排放废气，污染天空，大自然，树木，人类，飞走

SECOND PARAGRAPH: Describe how the story progresses, focusing on the characters' actions and expressions; use proper transitional elements. Personify the birds and give them thoughts and personalities. The following words, phrases, and sentences may be helpful:

[Traditional-character version]
環境污染日趨嚴重，生存空間越來越小，悲哀，無奈，尋找新的家園

[Simplified-character version]
环境污染日趋严重，生存空间越来越小，悲哀，无奈，寻找新的家园

THIRD PARAGRAPH: Conclude the story. The following words, phrases, and sentences can be used:

[Traditional-character version]
遠離人類，藍色的天空，動物的樂園

[Simplified-character version]
远离人类，蓝色的天空，动物的乐园

E-mail Response
Read this e-mail from a friend and then type a response.

[Traditional-character version]
發件人：李冬
郵件主題：該不該用動物做實驗？

　　最近，我因爲科學家用動物做實驗的問題跟哥哥爭論了起來。哥哥認爲，爲了醫治人類的病痛，科學家應該先用動物做實驗，因爲人類的生命是最重要的。但是在我看來用動物做實驗是一種野蠻的行爲。你覺得我跟我哥哥的看法，誰的更有道理？爲什麼？另外，對科學家用動物做實驗這個問題，你有什麼建議？

[Simplified-character version]
发件人：李冬
邮件主题：该不该用动物做实验？

　　最近，我因为科学家用动物做实验的问题跟哥哥争论了起来。哥哥认为，为了医治人类的病痛，科学家应该先用动物做实验，因为人类的生命是最重要的。但是在我看来用动物做实验是一种野蛮的行为。你觉得我跟我哥哥的看

法，谁的更有道理？为什么？另外，对科学家用动物做实验这个问题，你有什么建议？

SUGGESTIONS FOR WRITING AN E-MAIL RESPONSE

This e-mail is mainly about using animals in the lab for testing. When responding, keep this outline in mind:

1. Repeat the sender's main points.
2. Respond to any and all questions from the sender in detail. Discuss the pros and cons of animal testing.
3. Make a suggestion.

The following is a sample:

[Traditional-character version]

李冬：

　　這個問題一直以來都是一個有爭議的話題，很難找到明確的答案。

　　我個人對動物實驗的問題，也一直都很矛盾。一方面，我覺得人類應該保護動物，而不應該拿他們去做實驗。我讀過一篇文章，上面說世界上每年會用成千上萬的動物來做實驗，引起動物保護組織的抗議。我同意人類對動物應該講人道，應該尊重它們的生命。另一方面，我也明白很多藥都是通過了多次的動物實驗，才保證了人們用藥的安全。如果不用動物，很多生命科學的研究就無法進行。

　　正是因為上面的那些考慮，你們兩個人的看法我都同意。我只能建議，科學家在用動物做實驗的時候，應該儘量減少所用動物的數量，並減少動物的精神緊張和痛苦。

[Simplified-character version]

李冬：

　　这个问题一直以来都是一个有争议的话题，很难找到明确的答案。

　　我个人对动物实验的问题，也一直都很矛盾。一方面，我觉得人类应该保护动物，而不应该拿他们去做实验。我读过一篇文章，上面说世界上每年会用成千上万的动物来做实验，引起动物保护组织的抗议。我同意人类对动物应该讲人道，应该尊重它们的生命。另一方面，我也明白很多药都是通过了多次的动物实验，才保证了人们用药的安全。如果不用动物，很多生命科学的研究就无法进行。

　　正是因为上面的那些考虑，你们两个人的看法我都同意。我只能建议，科学家在用动物做实验的时候，应该尽量减少实验中所用动物的数量，并减少动物的精神紧张和痛苦。

Speaking Skills

CHAPTER 5

GENERAL INFORMATION

The Speaking portion of the AP Chinese exam evaluates students' ability to participate in conversations and their mastery of interpersonal and interpretive communication skills. Students are expected to understand the scenario established by the spoken or written prompts, and to:

1. communicate information and ideas to an audience on a variety of topics;
2. express their feelings and emotions, and exchange personal opinions;
3. demonstrate an understanding of Chinese culture;
4. apply appropriate grammatical structures to express ideas; and
5. exhibit a considerably broad range of vocabulary that allows them to speak fluently and accurately.

Speaking skills are tested last on the AP Chinese exam. By the final section of the exam, emotional and psychological factors may be weighing on students. For example:

- If students feel that they performed poorly on the earlier sections, they may put more pressure on themselves to do better in this section, or they may give up altogether.
- After working on the earlier sections for about two hours, students may be fatigued when they get to this section. This may have a negative effect on their concentration and reaction time.

These situations are not uncommon, and students should prepare themselves mentally and physically for testing. Practice is the best way to build confidence. Students should also have realistic expectations of the exam.

There are two tasks in the Speaking portion of the AP Chinese exam:

Conversation is interpersonal speaking. Students will participate in a simulated conversation according to six prompts. Each student will have 20 seconds to record his or her response for each prompt. Students should respond as completely as possible, and in a culturally appropriate manner.

The Cultural Presentation is presentational speaking. Students will be asked to make a presentation to an audience about a Chinese cultural practice, tradition, or product. After reading and hearing the topic for this presentation, students will be given 4 minutes to prepare and another 2 minutes to deliver the presentation.

To help students improve their speaking skills and exam scores, this chapter includes important test information, evaluation criteria, and practice tests. The sample topics in this chapter are carefully chosen so that students can practice expressing their views and opinions on a variety of subjects. During the Conversation tasks, students should not only address the prompts but aim for fluency, accuracy, and cultural appropriateness. During the Speaking free-response, students should draw on their personal experiences and be creative. The more they elaborate with rich vocabulary and sentence structures, the higher the score they will achieve.

The selected topics are generally related to students' daily lives and to the cultural knowledge that students have probably learned. Students should find these topics interesting and relevant; after all, most people are more motivated to communicate in another language if the topics are of interest to them.

Chapter 7 provides additional cultural information to better prepare students to describe and explain the importance of each Chinese cultural practice or product.

All passages in this chapter are presented in both traditional and simplified characters. Phrases in the Answer Explanation and Vocabulary List sections are first written in traditional characters and immediately followed by the simplified counterpart in parentheses. If there is no parenthesized phrase, the presented characters are common in both traditional and simplified versions.

EVALUATION CRITERIA

The Speaking free-response part of the exam will be evaluated according to the College Board's scoring guidelines. As students prepare for this section, they should familiarize themselves with the scoring criteria described in this chapter.

The evaluation criteria include three main factors: task completion, delivery, and language use. It is important for students to understand the task at hand and to state their responses correctly. Incomplete or incorrect answers lower their task completion ratings, even if they manage to deliver a perfect presentational or interpersonal speaking performance using advanced language.

While evaluating students' performances, the exam scorers check for specific details within each of the main categories.

Task Completion

1. **Completeness:** Is the prompt fully addressed and the content on topic?

2. **Elaboration:** Is the main idea clearly communicated with enough supporting details?

3. **Organization:** Is the response properly organized, coherent, and logically connected by appropriate transitional elements?

4. **Cultural content:** Does the cultural element contain correct and sufficient detail?

Delivery

1. **Rhythm:** Does the speaker have a natural rhythm? Does the speaker stop frequently or repeat? Does the speaker express emotions appropriately?

2. **Pronunciation:** Does the speaker pronounce words correctly, with the right intonation?

3. **Style of language:** Does the speaker choose style appropriate to the context? Is this style consistently demonstrated throughout the response?

Language Use

This is where students can showcase their advanced knowledge of grammar, sentence structure, vocabulary, and idioms. Adequate use of language enhances the overall effectiveness of the response, and will be rewarded with high marks.

SCORING GUIDELINES

Based on the student's performance in task completion, delivery, and language use, scores will be awarded at 7 levels, level 0 to level 6. At the end of the following scoring descriptions, an example of each level is provided for both Conversation and Cultural Presentation.

Level 6—EXCELLENT

Demonstrates excellence in presentational and interpersonal speaking and cultural knowledge.

Task Completion
- Speaking responses address all aspects of the tasks thoroughly.
  - Conversation—includes elaboration and detail.
  - Cultural Presentation—includes ample, accurate, and detailed information.
- The responses present ideas completely and logically, by providing facts or examples if necessary.
- The responses are well organized and coherent; exhibit the student's ability to use appropriate transitional words and cohesive devices to connect different paragraphs smoothly.

Delivery
- The responses are delivered at a natural pace and intonation, with accurate pronunciation and tones, and exhibit consistent use of vocabulary appropriate to the situation; minimal errors, hesitation, or repetition are acceptable.

Language Use
- The responses demonstrate a rich and appropriate vocabulary and idioms, including a wide range of grammatical structures; minimal errors are acceptable.

Level 5—VERY GOOD

Suggests excellence in presentational and interpersonal speaking and cultural knowledge.

Task Completion

- Speaking responses address all aspects of the tasks given.
  - Conversation—includes some elaboration and detail.
  - Cultural Presentation—includes ample, accurate, and detailed information.
  - Event plan—reflects insightful awareness of cultural elements.
- The responses generally present a good development of ideas, providing facts or examples if necessary.
- The responses are well organized and coherent; they exhibit the student's ability to use transitional words and cohesive devices to connect different paragraphs.

Delivery

- The responses are delivered at a smooth pace and intonation, and exhibit consistent use of vocabulary appropriate to the situation, with infrequent errors in pronunciation and tones; occasional hesitation and repetition are acceptable.

Language Use

- The responses demonstrate appropriate vocabulary and idioms, including a variety of grammatical structures; infrequent errors are acceptable.

Level 4—GOOD

Demonstrates competence in presentational and interpersonal speaking and cultural knowledge.

Task Completion

- Speaking responses address all aspects of the tasks given; may lack detail or elaboration; may contain minor inconsistencies in development.
- The responses are generally organized and coherent; the student's use of transitional elements may be inconsistent; paragraphs are somewhat cohesive.

Delivery

- The responses are delivered at a generally consistent pace and intonation, with sporadic hesitation and repetition; may have several errors in pronunciation and tones; may include several lapses in otherwise consistent use of vocabulary appropriate to the situation.

Language Use

- The responses demonstrate mostly appropriate vocabulary and idioms, as well as mostly appropriate grammatical structures; may include some errors that do not generally obscure meaning.

Level 3—ADEQUATE

Suggests competence in presentational and interpersonal speaking and cultural knowledge.

Task Completion
- Speaking responses address most aspects of prompt; may contain inconsistencies in development.
- The responses may lack organization or coherence; the student infrequently uses transitional elements and cohesive devices; the sentences may be disconnected.

Delivery
- The responses are delivered at an inconsistent pace and intonation, with hesitation and repetition that interfere with comprehension; may have some errors in pronunciation and tones; may include inconsistent use of appropriate vocabulary, or many errors.

Language Use
- The responses demonstrate limited appropriate vocabulary and idioms, including intermittent interference from another language; simple grammatical structures; frequent errors sometimes obscure meaning.

Level 2—WEAK

Suggests lack of competence in presentational and interpersonal speaking and cultural knowledge.

Task Completion
- Speaking responses address only some aspects of the task; generally lack organization and coherence; the student exhibits minimal or no use of transitional elements in mosly incoherent, fragmented sentences.

Delivery
- The responses are delivered at a labored pace and intonation, with frequent hesitation and repetition; frequent errors in pronunciation and tones; and frequent use of vocabulary inappropriate to the situation.

Language Use
- The responses demonstrate minimal appropriate vocabulary; repeated interference from another language; limited grammatical structures; frequent errors that obscure meaning.

Level 1—VERY WEAK

Demonstrates lack of competence in presentational and interpersonal speaking and cultural knowledge.

Task Completion
- Speaking responses barely address the task; lack organization and coherence; consist of very disjointed sentences or isolated words.

Delivery

- The responses are delivered at a very labored pace and intonation, with constant hesitation and repetition; frequent errors in pronunciation and tones; constant use of vocabulary inappropriate to the situation.

Language Use

- The responses demonstrate insufficient, inappropriate vocabulary; constant interference from another language; little or no control of grammatical structures; frequent errors that significantly obscure meaning.

Level 0—UNACCEPTABLE

Contains nothing that earns credit.

Task Completion

- Speaking responses may:
  - repeat the task prompt,
  - be completely irrelevant to the topic,
  - be in a language or dialect other than Mandarin Chinese,
  - not be attempted at all.

CONVERSATION SAMPLES AND SCORES

The **Conversation** samples below are based on the following prompt.

You will have a conversation with Zhang Jian, the manager of a Chinese arts and crafts shop in Chinatown, about a part-time job. The questions will be spoken during the test. For illustration, both the questions and the responses are printed here for reference. Some words in the samples are intentionally left incorrect to illustrate mispronunciations and incorrect tone.

A response that earns the highest mark does not necessarily mean it is perfect or error-free. On the contrary, some samples are deliberately chosen to illustrate that they may still deserve a high mark, as a whole, regardless of some minimal errors, infrequent hesitation, or occasional repetition.

Comments are provided after most samples to further explain how the evaluation is conducted. Some samples may be self-explanatory, and therefore comments are not needed.

{Conversation Question 1}

[Traditional-character version]
你爲什麼想申請這個工作?

[Simplified-character version]
你为什么想申请这个工作?

Sample Response for Level 6—Excellent

[Traditional-character version]

　　我之所以要申請這份工作，一方面是因爲我對中國的傳統工藝有興趣，也有一定的研究。俗話說，學以致用，我希望能通過這工作，向顧客介紹中國工藝品，向美國人傳播中國的工藝文化。另外，我需要利用課餘時間掙一些錢，減輕我父母的經濟負擔。

[Simplified-character version]

　　我之所以要申请这份工作，一方面是因为我对中国的传统工艺有兴趣，也有一定的研究。俗话说，学以致用，我希望能通过这工作，向顾客介绍中国工艺品，向美国人传播中国的工艺文化。另外，我需要利用课余时间挣一些钱，减轻我父母的经济负担。

COMMENTS: This response addresses the question directly and completely. It provides thorough details in connected sentences. The pace is smooth with no noticeable errors or hesitation. It exhibits excellent language skills in choosing rich vocabulary, idioms, and transitional conjunctions and a variety of grammar structures, such as "之所以" ("之所以"), "俗話說" ("俗话说"), "學以致用" ("学以致用"), "另外", and "一方面", "經濟負擔" ("经济负担").

Sample Response for Level 5—Very Good

[Traditional-character version]

　　我想乘學習不是怎麼忙找一個工作，可以轉一些錢，正好一個朋友說，你們在找一個人。我一直都好喜歡藝術品，特別是中國的藝術的東西。所以我覺得你的工作一定合適我，這是一舉兩得的事。我希望張老闆，你能給我一個工作的機會。

[Simplified-character version]

　　我想乘学习不是怎么忙找一个工作，可以转一些钱，正好一个朋友说，你们在找一个人。我一直都好喜欢艺术品，特别是中国的艺术的东西。所以我觉得你的工作一定合适我，这是一举两得的事。我希望张老板，你能给我一个工作的机会。

COMMENTS: The response addresses the question directly and completely. It is delivered in connected sentences, with a steady pace and infrequent errors in pronunciation. It exhibits very good language skills: very good vocabulary, transitional conjunctions, and a variety of grammar structures, such as "乘", "正好", "特別是", "一舉兩得" ("一举两得"), and "所以". Although there are some minor awkward phrases—"中國的藝術的東西" ("中国的艺术的东西"), "找一個人" ("找一个人"), "轉一些錢" ("转一些钱")—they do not interfere with understanding the response.

Sample Response for Level 4—Good

[Traditional-character version]

　　我喜歡你的商店工作，嗯，賣的東西有意思，很有意思的東西。商店到我家房子不遠，我的意思，沒有那麼遠的路，我可以不要開車來你的店。還有，我要經驗這樣的事，是很好的事對我。

[Simplified-character version]

　　我喜欢你的商店工作，嗯，卖的东西有意思，很有意思的东西。商店到我家房子不远，我的意思，没有那么远的路，我可以不要开车来你的店。还有，我要经验这样的事，是很好的事对我。

COMMENTS: The response addresses all aspects of the question. It is delivered at a generally consistent pace with sporadic hesitation and repetition. It includes several errors in the use of vocabulary, such as "沒有那麼遠的路" ("没有那么远的路") "不要開車來" ("不要开车来"), "是很好的事對我" ("是很好的事对我").

Sample Response for Level 3—Adequate

[Traditional-character version]

　　你好，你的工作正有意思。你是一個boss，　爲這個店嗎？那是太好事情。(a long pause) 和你的一個店正是很大店。如果我可不可以在你商店做一個工作。請相信我會工作很好，比別的人。

[Simplified-character version]

　　你好，你的工作正有意思。你是一个boss，为这个店吗？那是太好事情。 (a long pause) 和你的一个店正是很大店。如果我可不可以在你商店做一个工作。请相信我会工作很好，比别的人。

COMMENTS: The response provides a basic answer to the question. It is delivered at an inconsistent pace with frequent hesitation and repetition. It includes several errors in the use of vocabulary and grammar, such as "你是一個boss，爲這個店" ("你是一个boss，爲这个店"), "和你的一個店正是很大店" ("和你的一个店正是很大店"), "如果我可不可以," "正有," "正是," "比別的人". The limited appropriate vocabulary, the misuse of "和," and other intermittent interference from another language sometimes obscure meaning.

Sample Response for Level 2—Weak

[Traditional-character version]

　　你要有很多錢，就是一個很大商店，錢很多。And，我是喜歡做一家interesting事。還說什么？我是一個學生，認識你，在一個商店，我是高興。

[Simplified-character version]

　　你要有很多钱，就是一个很大商店，钱很多。And，我是喜欢做一家interesting事。还说什么？我是一个学生，认识你，在一个商店，我是高兴。

COMMENTS: The response only addresses some aspects of the question, and it lacks organization and coherence. There are fragmented sentences, and it lacks transitional elements. It exhibits minimal appropriate vocabulary and repeated interference from another language. Frequent grammatical errors and frequent errors in pronunciation and tone obscure meaning.

Sample Response for Level 1—Very Weak

[Traditional-character version]

　　你是不是好？生請一件工作，like這個，一件工作。東西在這裏很多，你的上地東西一些多。

[Simplified-character version]

你是不是好？生请一件工作，like这个，一件工作。东西在这里很多，你的上地东西一些多。

COMMENTS: The response barely addresses the question. The pace of delivery is very labored, with lots of hesitation. The response is delivered in very disjointed sentences that are not comprehensible. It is characterized by insufficient vocabulary and inadequate control of grammatical structures.

Sample Response for Level 0—Unacceptable

I don't understand.

COMMENTS: The response is completely irrelevant. It is not in the targeted test language, Mandarin Chinese.

{Conversation Question 2}

[Traditional-character version]

你能談談你對中國工藝品有什麼瞭解嗎？

[Simplified-character version]

你能谈谈你对中国工艺品有什么了解吗？

Sample Response for Level 6—Excellent

[Traditional-character version]

中國的工藝品，種類很多，其中景泰藍舉世聞名。我看到了，你的商店裏賣了很多景泰藍。我以前看書知道了，景泰藍是用金和銀那樣金屬做出來。工人通過把那些金屬先燒藍了，再磨得好看一些，然後做成了工藝品，也有繪畫和雕刻技藝在裏面。中國人喜歡用這些種東西打扮家庭，真是漂亮極了。

[Simplified-character version]

中国的工艺品，种类很多，其中景泰蓝举世闻名。我看到了，你的商店里卖了很多景泰蓝。我以前看书知道了，景泰蓝是用金和银那样金属做出来。工人通过把那些金属先烧蓝了，再磨得好看一些，然后做成了工艺品，也有绘画和雕刻技艺在里面。中国人喜欢用这些种东西打扮家庭，真是漂亮极了。

COMMENTS: This response addresses the question directly, completely, and with lots of elaboration to demonstrate knowledge of this cultural product. The pace is smooth. It exhibits excellent language skills in choosing rich vocabulary, idioms, and transitional conjunctions and a variety of grammar structures, such as "其中", "舉世聞名" ("举世闻名"), "以前", "先．．了", "再", "然後" ("然后").

Sample Response for Level 5—Very Good

[Traditional-character version]

我很喜歡中國工藝品，因爲會使我的房間看起來有..文化，比如我房間牆上掛著一個..uh..風帳。放風帳是中國傳統的..玩的..事情，家喻戶曉。據說中國人們放風帳，uh.. 爲的是給生活帶來一個吉利。人把風帳fa..得, ..fang..放得高，等它飛上天很高了，就讓風帳飛走了，uh..能把不好的事情帶走了。

[Simplified-character version]

我很喜欢中国工艺品，因为会使我的房间看起来有..文化，比如我房间墙上挂着一个..uh..风帐。放风帐是中国传统的..玩的..事情，家喻户晓。据说中国人们放风帐，uh..为的是给生活带来一个吉利。人把风帐fa..得，..fang..放得高，等它飞上天很高了，就让风帐飞走了，uh..能把不好的事情带走了。

COMMENTS: The response addresses the prompt directly and appropriately. It tells the legend of flying the kites. The delivery is generally smooth with occasional hesitation. The language used is adequately rich, including proverbs and transitional words such as "因爲" ("因为"), "比如", "家喻戶曉" ("家喻户晓"), "據說" ("据说"), "爲的是" ("为的是"), and "就讓" ("就让"). The pronunciation is generally accurate, although "風箏" ("风筝") was mispronounced as "風帳" ("风帐").

Sample Response for Level 4—Good

[Traditional-character version]

很多中國人，也美國人，喜歡買那些工藝品。一個中國朋友，是心靈手巧的女孩子，她剪紙很好，給我很多。那朋友說，剪紙是中國流行。你可以用剪dǎo，和也可以用小刀dào。以前在中國農村裏，個個的女孩子得會這skill。中國人把剪紙放在牆和門，..和窗戶。

[Simplified-character version]

很多中国人，也美国人，喜欢买那些工艺品。一个中国朋友，是心灵手巧的女孩子，她剪纸很好，给我很多。那朋友说，剪纸是中国流行。你可以用剪dǎo，和也可以用小刀dào。以前在中国农村里，个个的女孩子得会这skill。中国人把剪纸放在墙和门，..和窗户。

COMMENTS: The response addresses the prompt with an appropriate cultural product. It contains several errors in grammar and pronunciation, but these do not obscure meaning, e.g., "也美國人" ("也美国人"), "她剪纸很好", "個個的女孩子" ("个个的女孩子"), and "*dǎo*" or "*dào*" instead of "刀" "*dāo*".

Sample Response for Level 3—Adequate

[Traditional-character version]

工藝品東西很多，...中國結、扇子什麼的，uh ...很好看的東西，我想...是好看。...還有什麼？...我也看很多東西，在電視看，我...很喜歡看。我不知道你的商店有沒有...這樣東西嗎？

[Simplified-character version]

工艺品东西很多，...中国结、扇子什么的，uh ...很好看的东西，我想...是好看。.....还有什么？...我也看很多东西，在电视看，我...很喜欢看。我不知道你的商店有没有...这样东西吗？

COMMENTS: The response provides a basic answer to the question, including a list of some cultural products, but without elaboration. The delivery is uneven; the vocabulary and grammatical structures seem limited.

Sample Response for Level 2—Weak

[Traditional-character version]

　　你問我工藝品什麼。我想，..你的商店很好，也東西..工藝品是很好，..很多東西。你是一個很好老闆，我想..你也是一個..很好人。

[Simplified-character version]

　　你问我工艺品什么。我想，.. 你的商店很好，也东西.. 工艺品是很好，..很多东西。你是一个很好老板，我想.. 你也是一个.. 很好人。

COMMENTS: The response attempts to address the question, by mentioning the products in the store, but it is incomplete. It contains minimal vocabulary and limited grammatical structures.

Sample Response for Level 1—Very Weak

[Traditional-character version]

　　你吻我，.. 我一點 ..一點.. 知道，..工藝..瓶..工藝..瓶..歷時，一點..長..在中國。我喜歡...好了。

[Simplified-character version]

　　你吻我，..我一点.. 一点.. 知道，.. 工艺.. 瓶.. 工艺.. 瓶.. 历时，一点.. 长.. 在中国。我喜欢...好了。

COMMENTS: The response minimally addresses the question with disjointed sentences. The delivery is labored, with constant hesitation and repetition. It uses insufficient vocabulary and grammatical structures that seriously affect the meaning.

Sample Response for Level 0—Unacceptable

Blank

COMMENTS: No response.

{Conversation Question 3}

[Traditional-character version]

　　如果顧客買工藝品作爲禮物送人，你會給他們什麼建議？

[Simplified-character version]

　　如果顾客买工艺品作为礼物送人，你会给他们什么建议？

Sample Response for Level 6—Excellent

[Traditional-character version]

　　我告訴顧客送禮物要因人而異。送給誰和送禮的原因，要清楚。文化背景和愛好也應該瞭解一下。還有，要委婉地問顧客打算花什麼錢買東西，方便幫忙他挑選。要是買結婚禮物送朋友，我會建議他買這兩個手工繡的枕頭。你看，這些紅花增加多新房子的喜慶，上面的"百年好合"四個字，是多好祝福。

[Simplified-character version]

我告诉顾客送礼物要因人而异。送给谁和送礼的原因，要清楚。文化背景和爱好也应该了解一下。还有，要委婉地问顾客打算花什么钱买东西，方便帮忙他挑选。要是买结婚礼物送朋友，我会建议他买这两个手工绣的枕头。你看，这些红花增加多新房子的喜庆，上面的"百年好合"四个字，是多好祝福。

COMMENTS: The response directly addresses the question with detailed and culturally appropriate elaboration. The pace is natural with connected sentences and correct pronunciation. It displays excellent use of vocabulary, such as "因人而異" ("因人而异"), "手工繡的" ("手工绣的"), "百年好合" ("百年好合"), and grammatical structures with minimal errors such as "委婉地", "增加多", "是多好祝福".

Sample Response for Level 5—Very Good

[Traditional-character version]

我不會給古客一個租意，以免他不滿意我。但是，我給他說說我們商店的工藝品，也說說這裏面的中國文化的指使。還告訴顧客，什麼東西他不要買。好像說，不能買一個鐘送給一個老人，給他過生日，因爲 "送終" 不好意思，老人要生氣。你也不得買一個金泰藍小刀，給你的中國女朋友，她想你要 "一刀兩斷"，她要哭死。

[Simplified-character version]

我不会给古客一个租意，以免他不满意我。但是，我给他说说我们商店的工艺品，也说说这里面的中国文化的指使。还告诉顾客，什么东西他不要买。好像说，不能买一个钟送给一个老人，给他过生日，因为"送终"不好意思，老人要生气。你也不得买一个金泰蓝小刀，给你的中国女朋友，她想你要"一刀两断"，她要哭死。

COMMENTS: The response provides a thorough and appropriate answer in connected sentences. The pace of delivery is smooth with few pronunciation errors. The vocabulary and grammatical structures are mostly appropriate with sporadic errors, such as "古客" instead of "顧客" ("顾客"), "租意" instead of "主意", and "金泰藍" ("金泰蓝") instead of "景泰藍" ("景泰蓝").

Sample Response for Level 4—Good

[Traditional-character version]

選的東西應該讓朋友能高興。我讓顧客看店裏的各個好看東西。我問問顧客，想花很多錢買東西給朋友。要是他很有錢，和他朋友喜歡音樂，我請他買這些好像古代的彈琴。要是他一點兒有錢，買一個茶壺和杯子，就可以。

[Simplified-character version]

选的东西应该让朋友能高兴。我让顾客看店里各个好看东西。我问问顾客，想花很多钱买东西给朋友。要是他很有钱，和他朋友喜欢音乐，我请他买这些好像古代的弹琴。要是他一点儿有钱，买一个茶壶和杯子，就可以。

Sample Response for Level 3—Adequate

[Traditional-character version]

　　這是重要的東西。買東西送誰人，很重要的東西。你想建議什麼，你的顧客買喜歡東西，也他們不想花多錢，買的東西很貴，他們生氣很。你應該給他們說說，要是他買東西。

[Simplified-character version]

　　这是重要的东西。买东西送谁人，很重要的东西。你想建议什么，你的顾客买喜欢东西，也他们不想花多钱，买的东西很贵，他们生气很。你应该给他们说说，要是他买东西。

COMMENTS: The response provides a basic answer but with disconnected sentences. It is delivered with very limited appropriate vocabulary and grammatical structures that are difficult to understand.

Sample Response for Level 2—Weak

[Traditional-character version]

　　如果買東西，送這裏的東西給人，要建議一點兒。嗯，東西很好看，也東西貴一點兒。你想給不給我東西，我不應該要，我是工作人。不管，我都很謝謝你。

[Simplified-character version]

　　如果买东西，送这里的东西给人，要建议一点儿。嗯，东西很好看，也东西贵一点儿。你想给不给我东西，我不应该要，我是工作人。不管，我都很谢谢你。

Sample Response for Level 1—Very Weak

[Traditional-character version]

　　我要有建儀，它是很好的東西。你可以告訴我什麼的建儀，你是很好人。

[Simplified-character version]

　　我要有建仪，它是很好的东西。你可以告诉我什么的建仪，你是很好人。

COMMENTS: The response marginally addresses the question with fragmented sentences. Although the delivery pace is smooth, and the pronunciation is mostly correct, the use of vocabulary and grammatical structures is insufficient.

Sample Response for Level 0—Unacceptable

[Traditional-character version]

　　你能不能再說一次嗎？

[Simplified-character version]

　　你能不能再说一次吗？

COMMENTS: No response.

{Conversation Question 4}

[Traditional-character version]

你認爲做好這份工作要注意什麼？

[Simplified-character version]

你认为做好这份工作要注意什么？

Sample Response for Level 6—Excellent

[Traditional-character version]

一有專業文化知識，就是說，對中國工藝品瞭解，那樣，可以不失時機地給顧客介紹，讓多顧客買我們的東西。二是工作時候很小心。貴重東西，應該輕拿和輕放。要不然，就破壞了。加上，你的服務很重要。服務做好了，顧客會常來買。總之，靠你的知識、熱情和好服務，給我們店裏帶來多的回頭客。

[Simplified-character version]

一有专业文化知识，就是说，对中国工艺品了解，那样，可以不失时机地给顾客介绍，让多顾客买我们的东西。二是工作时候很小心。贵重东西，应该轻拿和轻放。要不然，就破坏了。加上，你的服务很重要。服务做好了，顾客会常来买。总之，靠你的知识、热情和好服务，给我们店里带来多的回头客。

Sample Response for Level 5—Very Good

[Traditional-character version]

最重要的東西是你態度好。你的態度親切，臉上笑，這樣，顧客可以舒服地買東西。你要用一個好心情對待來買東西的人，不管他的文化好不好，也他看起來是不是有錢人。顧客後來沒買東西，你也要對他熱情一些。要是你的附務態度讓他肝動，他會告訴他的朋友來買東西。

[Simplified-character version]

最重要的东西是你态度好。你的态度亲切，脸上笑，这样，顾客可以舒服地买东西。你要用一个好心情对待来买东西的人，不管他的文化好不好，也他看起来是不是有钱人。顾客后来没买东西，你也要对他热情一些。要是你的附务态度让他肝动，他会告诉他的朋友来买东西。

COMMENTS: The response directly addresses the question with a thorough and appropriate answer. The pace is appropriate, with occasional errors in pronunciation, such as "你的附務態度讓他肝動" ("你的附务态度让他肝动").

Sample Response for Level 4—Good

[Traditional-character version]

要知道商店東西房在的地方。骨科買一個東西，他沒看到那個東西，你可以拿快一點兒給他。你對商品的錢應該清楚。骨科想跟你打折，你那個東西可以做主，那個東西應該老闆做主，你要知道。你不能賣錯了東西的錢。不能給老闆賺多錢。

[Simplified-character version]

　　要知道商店东西房在的地方。骨科买一个东西，他没看到那个东西，你可以拿快一点儿给他。你对商品的钱应该清楚。骨科想跟你打折，你那个东西可以做主，那个东西应该老板做主，你要知道。你不能卖错了东西的钱。不能给老板赚多钱。

COMMENTS: The response directly addresses the question with sufficient details. It contains errors that do not interfere with the meaning, such as "骨科" ("骨科") instead of "顧客" ("顾客").

Sample Response for Level 3—Adequate

[Traditional-character version]

　　注意東西很多，很多麻煩事，應該小心一點兒都。工作時候，我來晚，老闆怎麼辦？不能走。別的其他人也不能回家，還是不能去大學上課。那時很麻煩事，真的麻煩。老闆生我氣，也我不能keep一個工作。

[Simplified-character version]

　　注意东西很多，很多麻烦事，应该小心一点儿都。工作时候，我来晚，老板怎么办？不能走。别的其他人也不能回家，还是不能去大学上课。那时很麻烦事，真的麻烦。老板生我气，也我不能keep一个工作。

COMMENTS: The response provides a basic answer. However, limited vocabulary and grammatical structures sometimes get in the way of understanding what is being said.

Sample Response for Level 2—Weak

[Traditional-character version]

　　你問我主義什麼，這是好的事。你商店很多東西，是有一死東西。我喜歡這些個東西，電視看一樣的，中國人喜歡，和美國人喜歡。Like我女朋友。我想買什麼，爲她。

[Simplified-character version]

　　你问我主义什么，这是好的事。你商店很多东西，是有一死东西。我喜欢这些个东西，电视看一样的，中国人喜欢，和美国人喜欢。Like我女朋友。我想买什么，为她。

Sample Response for Level 1—Very Weak

[Traditional-character version]

　　一個工作我想要。你是很好人，也你方裏東西好。我想去中國，上大學晚了，裝錢多以後，去中國玩一下。我practice中文。

[Simplified-character version]

　　一个工作我想要。你是很好人，也你方里东西好。我想去中国，上大学晚了，装钱多以后，去中国玩一下。我practice中文。

COMMENTS: The response minimally addresses the question in very disconnected sentences. The speaker focuses on self-development and one's own goals instead of interaction with the customer or one's job responsibilities. Use of vocabulary and grammatical structures are insufficient. The speaker mistakenly uses "裝錢" ("装钱") instead of "賺錢" ("赚钱").

Sample Response for Level 0—Unacceptable

To my opinion, as waiters, they can't do the bad things to the guest. I think to be a waiter, you should do your best to make your customers happy, and control yourself not to show the angry out when feel upset about things.

COMMENTS: Not in Chinese.

{Conversation Question 5}

[Traditional-character version]
你覺得學生讀書期間打工, 會不會影響學習？

[Simplified-character version]
你觉得学生读书期间打工, 会不会影响学习？

Sample Response for Level 6—Excellent

[Traditional-character version]
關于這個問題，人們看法不同。只要能合理安排好時間，不會影響我學習。我來你這兒工作，除了想賺一些零花錢和減輕父母經濟負擔外，我更想鍛煉自己的能力，可以更好適應社會。我想，打工經歷一定會讓我受益非淺，也對我以後進如社會有幫助。另外，經歷不同事情，我覺得生活很充是。

[Simplified-character version]
关于这个问题，人们看法不同。只要能合理安排好时间，不会影响我学习。我来你这儿工作，除了想赚一些零花钱和减轻父母经济负担外，我更想锻炼自己的能力，可以更好适应社会。我想，打工经历一定会让我受益非浅，也对我以后进如社会有帮助。另外，经历不同事情，我觉得生活很充是。

Sample Response for Level 5—Very Good

[Traditional-character version]
不會啊。要是影響到學習，那我父母一定不同意我。他們..我父母..對我的學習要求很嚴格的 (a long pause) 但是我很聰明，考試考得都很好，每一個考試都得A，他們就讓我隨便怎麼了。..我是很聰明學生，身體也是很胖，不怕累。..你不用擔心，我有辦法做好兩個事。

[Simplified-character version]
不会啊。要是影响到学习，那我父母一定不同意我。他们．．我父母．．对我的学习要求很严格的 (a long pause) 但是我很聪明，考试考得都很好，每一个考试都得A，他们就让我随便怎么了。．．我是很聪明学生，身体也是很胖，不怕累。．．你不用担心，我有办法做好两个事。

COMMENTS: The response addresses the question directly and provides a thorough and appropriate answer in connected sentences. The pace of delivery is generally consistent. Vocabulary is appropriate but with sporadic errors: "一定不同意我" instead of "一定不會同意我繼續工作" ("一定不会同意我继续工作"), "就讓我隨便怎麼了" ("就让我随便怎么了") instead of "就隨便我怎麼安排我的時間了" ("就随便我怎么安排我的时间了")，"身體也是很胖" ("身体也是很胖") instead of "身體也很壯" ("身体也很壮"), and "兩個事" ("两个事") instead of "兩件事". The student uses a variety of grammatical structures and cohesive devices: "要是", "那", "但是".

Sample Response for Level 4—Good

[Traditional-character version]

　　打工對獨立好。我小孩子時候要父母照顧。我長大時候，不能都父母幫忙了。高中快學完，我會去大學。我都是在學校呆，沒看社會的樣子。人可以學書，也應該學社會。打工不是錢，是讓你學到別的社會東西。

[Simplified-character version]

　　打工对独立好。我小孩子时候要父母照顾。我长大时候，不能都父母帮忙了。高中快学完，我会去大学。我都是在学校呆，没看社会的样子。人可以学书，也应该学社会。打工不是钱，是让你学到别的社会东西。

Sample Response for Level 3—Adequate

[Traditional-character version]

　　一便讀書，一便打工，是好辦法。Uh..我學中文，..可以跟一些的人，一些人practice 我的中文.. 學中文。..買東西人是都中國人，是都是中國人，不是 他們說很好中文。..中文difficult，我..不能聽.. 聽懂。.. 你說中文很好，我懂很多。

[Simplified-character version]

　　一便读书，一便打工，是好办法。Uh..我学中文，.. 可以跟一些的人，一些人practice 我的中文.. 学中文。.. 买东西人是都中国人，是都是中国人，不是他们说很好中文。.. 中文difficult，我.. 不能听.. 听懂。.. 你说中文很好，我懂很多。

COMMENTS: The response provides a basic answer with disconnected sentences. Frequent hesitation and repetition interfere and prevent the speaker from completing sentences smoothly. Pronunciation is generally good with the exception of "一便" instead of "一邊" ("一边").Vocabulary and grammatical structures are mostly appropriate but limited and fragmented because of frequent repetition.

Sample Response for Level 2—Weak

[Traditional-character version]

　　你不用擔心啦。打你工不累，沒有印象我。你的店到我家沒有遠，我可以不開車來，那時很好事。我看店的門邊，很麻煩的traffic。要是這裏很潮，顧客不高興。

[Simplified-character version]

　　你不用担心啦。打你工不累，没有印象我。你的店到我家没有远，我可以不开车来，那时很好事。我看店的门边，很麻烦的traffic。要是这里很潮，顾客不高兴。

Sample Response for Level 1—Very Weak

[Traditional-character version]

　　謝謝你。..讀數不難，讀數..時間uh ..不音響。...我uh..不能聽懂..uh謝謝幫忙我。(a long pause) 打工很好。

[Simplified-character version]

谢谢你。. . 读数不难，读数. . 时间uh ..不音响。. . 我uh..不能听懂..uh谢谢帮忙我。(a long pause) 打工很好。

COMMENTS: The response addresses the question only minimally in fragmented sentences. The pace is very labored, with frequent hesitation. It suffers from insufficient vocabulary and very limited control of grammatical structures.

Sample Response for Level 0—Unacceptable

[Traditional-character version]

我不能聽懂你的question. Sorry about that.

[Simplified-character version]

我不能听懂你的question. Sorry about that.

COMMENTS: No response.

{Conversation Question 6}

[Traditional-character version]

爲了安排工作，請問，你一星期中的哪幾天，幾點到幾點可以工作？

[Simplified-character version]

为了安排工作，请问，你一星期中的哪几天，几点到几点可以工作？

Sample Response for Level 6—Excellent

[Traditional-character version]

我最近一點兒都不忙，時間上比較自由。星期一到星期五，我每天的上課的時間是，早上八點到下午兩點半。從學校到這兒，只要十分鐘。老闆，你可以根據這些情況，自由安排我的工作。你完全可以按照對你方便的時間來安排我的工作，不管你安排怎麽，我都言聽計從。

[Simplified-character version]

我最近一点儿都不忙，时间上比较自由。星期一到星期五，我每天的上课的时间是，早上八点到下午两点半。从学校到这儿，只要十分钟。老板，你可以根据这些情况，自由安排我的工作。你完全可以按照对你方便的时间来安排我的工作，不管你安排怎么，我都言听计从。

COMMENTS: The response addresses the question thoroughly and completely. It deserves a high score in spite of an occasional error of "安排怎麽" ("安排怎么") instead of "怎麽安排" ("怎么安排").

Sample Response for Level 5—Very Good

[Traditional-character version]

這個問題有一點難。我每天的課多一點兒，還有，我要考試了，我得復習多。..這是爲什麽我不有自由時間，我想知道，你安排我的工作。可以不可以只在周末？周末工作兩天沒有關係。這樣會對我的學習的印象少。

[Simplified-character version]

　　这个问题有一点难。我每天的课多一点儿，还有，我要考试了，我得复习多。. .这是为什么我不有自由时间，我想知道, 你安排我的工作。可以不可以只在周末？周末工作两天没有关系。这样会对我的学习的印象少。

COMMENTS: The response addresses the question directly. The delivery is generally smooth, and vocabulary is appropriate. It demonstrates good control over grammar, although with sporadic errors that do not interfere with the meaning, such as "我每天的課多一點兒" ("我每天的课多一点儿") instead of "我最近的功課有一點兒多" ("我最近的功课有一点儿多"), "我得復習多" ("我得复习多") instead of "我得多復習" ("我得多复习"), "不有自由時間" ("不有自由时间") instead of "沒有很多空檔" ("没有很多空档"), and "這樣會對我的學習的印象少" ("这样会对我的学习的印象少") instead of "這樣對我的學習來說, 比較沒有影響" ("这样对我的学习来说, 比较没有影响").

Sample Response for Level 4—Good

[Traditional-character version]

　　你看這個情怎麼做，隨便就好了。我都沒有關習，我是隨便，因爲我時間是自由得很。隨便時間，你可以叫我來打工。真沒有那麼多關習，你喜歡決定一個時間，打電話給我吧。謝謝你給我一個工作。我真喜歡做一個工作。

[Simplified-character version]

　　你看这个情怎么做，随便就好了。我都没有关习，我是随便，因为我时间是自由得很。随便时间，你可以叫我来打工。真没有那么多关习，你喜欢决定一个时间，打电话给我吧。谢谢你给我一个工作。我真喜欢做一个工作。

Sample Response for Level 3—Adequate

[Traditional-character version]

　　星期一, 不好..是..星期四..uh..跟星期六，上午還有下午，沒管細..我很free。你是老闆，你隨便。

[Simplified-character version]

　　星期一, 不好．．是．．星期四..uh..跟星期六，上午还有下午..没管细..我很free。你是老板，你随便。

COMMENTS: The response provides a basic answer with disconnected sentences. Frequent hesitation necessitates special listener effort, and pronunciation and grammar errors sometimes obscure the meaning, e.g., "上午還有下午.. 沒管细" ("上午还有下午..没管细") is probably intended to mean "上午或者下午都沒關係" ("上午或者下午都没关系").

Sample Response for Level 2—Weak

[Traditional-character version]

　　我時間不是多，星期..uh....uh..有時間..星期是..是最好。(a long pause) 謝謝你。

[Simplified-character version]
　　我时间不是多，星期..uh...uh..有时间..星期是..是最好。(a long pause) 谢谢你。

COMMENTS: The response directly answers the question, but it is difficult to understand. It is not clear if "星期..uh....uh..有時間" ("星期..uh...uh..有时间") is intended for "星期二有時間" ("星期二有时间"); or whether "星期是..是最好" is intended for "星期四最好".

Sample Response for Level 1—Very Weak

[Traditional-character version]
　　..uh..事件..不難..uh..我有很多事件..uh..很忙..whenever

[Simplified-character version]
　　..uh..事件..不难..uh..我有很多事件..uh..很忙..whenever

COMMENTS: The response seems to start and stop abruptly at a very labored pace. Pronunciation errors and very limited vocabulary make it very difficult to understand, e.g., "事件" seems to mean "時間" ("时间"), but it contradicts "很忙".

Sample Response for Level 0—Unacceptable

[Traditional-character version]
　　我可以買你的東西，是很好。謝謝！

[Simplified-character version]
　　我可以买你的东西，是很好。谢谢！

COMMENTS: The response does not answer the question.

CULTURAL PRESENTATION SAMPLES AND SCORES

Choose ONE famous place in mainland China or Taiwan (for example, The Museum of Terracotta Warriors and Horses, the Great Wall, the Sun Moon Lake, and so on). In your presentation, describe this place and explain its significance.

Similar to the conversation samples described earlier, a presentation that earns the highest mark does not necessarily mean it is perfect or error-free. On the contrary, some samples are deliberately chosen to illustrate that they may still deserve a high mark, as a whole, regardless of some minimal errors, infrequent hesitation, or occasional repetition.

Comments are provided after most samples to further explain how the evaluation is conducted. Some samples may be self-explanatory, and therefore comments are not needed.

Sample Presentation for Level 6—Excellent

[Traditional-character version]

　　大家好！我想借這個機會給大家介紹一下西安的兵馬俑(bìngmǎ　yǒng)博物館。

　　七十年代的時候，在中國西安附近的有個農(nōng)民發現了跟真人、真馬差不多大的陶瓷做的士兵和馬，　原來這就是第一個皇帝秦始皇陪葬的兵馬俑。以後，這兒就成了舉世聞名的秦始皇兵馬俑博物館。這個博物館有三個大小不同的坑，裡面有成千上萬個陪葬的兵馬俑，排得整整齊齊，真的像一個很大的軍隊。據(jǔ)說無論他們身上穿的衣服，還是臉上的表情，都各不相同，千姿百態。兵馬俑博物館除了吸引了無數來自全世界的觀光客，兵馬俑還到世界上二十多個國家和地區展出，聽說也到過美國。遺憾的是，我至今還沒參觀(cánguān)過兵馬俑(bìngmǎ　yǒng)博物館。但我相信，我一定有機會去看看中國的兵馬俑，去感受一下兵馬俑豐富多彩的歷史文化遺產。

[Simplified-character version]

　　大家好！我想借这个机会给大家介绍一下西安的兵马俑(bìngmǎ　yǒng)博物馆。

　　七十年代的时候，在中国西安附近的有个农(nōng)民发现了跟真人、真马差不多大的陶瓷做的士兵和马，原来这就是第一个皇帝秦始皇陪葬的兵马俑。以后，这儿就成了举世闻名的秦始皇兵马俑博物馆。这个博物馆有三个大小不同的坑，里面有成千上万个陪葬的兵马俑，排得整整齐齐，真的像一个很大的军队。据(jǔ)说无论他们身上穿的衣服，还是脸上的表情，都各不相同，千姿百态。兵马俑博物馆除了吸引了无数来自全世界的观光客，兵马俑还到世界上二十多个国家和地区展出，听说也到过美国。遗憾的是，我至今还没参观(cánguān)过兵马俑(bìngmǎ　yǒng)博物馆。但我相信，我一定有机会去看看中国的兵马俑，去感受一下兵马俑丰富多彩的历史文化遗产。

COMMENTS: The response addresses all aspects of the task, describing the place and explaining its significance thoroughly and in great cultural detail. It is organized logically with appropriate conjunctions like "的時候" ("的时候"), "原來" ("原来"), "以後" ("以后"), "無論..都" ("无论..都"), 除了, and 遺憾的是". The delivery is natural and smooth with accurate pronunciation and minimal errors—"參觀" ("参观") is incorrectly pronounced "*cánguān*" instead of "*cānguān*", "兵馬俑" ("兵马俑") "*bìng mā yǒng*" instead of "*bīng mǎ yǒng*", "農民" ("农民") "*nōng mín*" instead of "*nóng mín*", "據說" ("据说") "*jǔ shuō*" instead of "*jù shuō*". The use of vocabulary, idioms, and grammatical structures is rich and appropriate, e.g., "陪葬", "舉世聞名" ("举世闻名"), "成千上萬" ("成千上万"), "豐富多彩" ("丰富多彩"), "文化遺產" ("文化遗产").

It is noteworthy that the speaker makes an excellent effort to present the "兵馬俑博物館" ("兵马俑博物馆"), the *museum*, which is the **place** that the task prompt asks for. Had the speaker chosen to present the "兵馬俑" ("兵马俑") instead, it would have been considered off-topic because "兵馬俑" ("兵马俑") is a *product/artifact*, not a **place**. Any off-topic presentation, regardless how fluent the delivery or perfect the language use, will be awarded a score below 3 for failing to address the prompt directly or completely. Therefore, it is very important to understand what the task prompt is asking for. It may be a place, a product, a practice, or a person. Focus the presentation to address the requirement accordingly.

Sample Presentation for Level 5—Very Good

[Traditional-character version]

今天我想談談中國的長城。長城在中國的北方，uh..長城從東到西，有一萬多里，所以中國人也叫它萬里長城。很久以前，有人要來打中國，秦始皇讓成千上萬的老百姓去蓋長城。你知道蓋長城很難，那時沒有..uh..機器。全部都是靠用手搬。他們好不容易蓋完了長城。這個長城很好用，可以..可以拿來..uh..幫..uh..保護..裡面的人，但是..壞人..很難能打得進來。這就是"一夫當關，萬夫莫開"的故事。中國人還常說..有一句話..常..說：不到長城不是好漢。如果有機會的話，我們一定要去看看中國的萬里長城，做個好漢。

[Simplified-character version]

今天我想谈谈中国的长城。长城在中国的北方，uh..长城从东到西，有一万多里，所以中国人也叫它万里长城。很久以前，有人要来打中国，秦始皇让成千上万的老百姓去盖长城。你知道盖长城很难，那时没有..uh..机器。全部都是靠用手搬。他们好不容易盖完了长城。这个长城很好用，可以..可以拿来..uh..帮..uh..保护..里面的人，但是..坏人..很难能打得进来。这就是"一夫当关，万夫莫开"的故事。中国人还常说..有一句话..常..说：不到长城不是好汉。如果有机会的话，我们一定要去看看中国的万里长城，做个好汉。

COMMENTS: The response addresses all aspects of the task, starting with the objective of the Great Wall, then the significance or value that it represents. Despite some intermittent hesitation, the pace of delivery is generally smooth, and the speaker uses appropriate conjunctions such as "如果", "那時" ("那时"), "這就是" ("这就是"), "很久以前". The presentation includes appropriate vocabulary, idioms—like "一夫當關，萬夫莫開" ("一夫当关，万夫莫开"), "不到長城不是好漢" ("不到长城不是好汉"), "好不容易", "成千上萬" ("成千上万")—and a variety of grammatical structures, with only sporadic errors that do not obscure meaning.

Sample Presentation for Level 4—Good

[Traditional-character version]

我想給你們講講台灣裡有名的風景地方日月潭。日月潭是一個湖，聽說是在台灣最大的湖。日月潭的水很大，也很深，水上非常好看。日月潭中間有一個小島，小島的北半邊看起來像一個太陽，小島的南半邊好像一個月亮，所以大家叫那個湖的名字是日月潭。日月潭的水很藍，人們可以在裡面划船。日月潭四面很漂亮，在那個漂亮的地方，有一個漂亮的傳說：很久以前，有人在山裡看了一隻大鹿，就去追那隻大鹿，鹿很快就跑走了。大家在山裡找了找，找很長時間。他們看見一個湖水，..uh..水裡有小島，把大湖分為兩半，一半像太陽，一半像月亮。這是為什麼它叫"日月潭"。日月潭的一年四季和早晚的景色都不一樣。我最喜歡看雨以後的日月潭。雨以後的日月潭的湖水和四面的山看起來特別乾淨、可愛。怎麼樣，我介紹完了日月潭，你是不是也想去看看了？

[Simplified-character version]

我想给你们讲讲台湾里有名的风景地方日月潭。日月潭是一个湖，听说是在台湾最大的湖。日月潭的水很大，也很深，水上非常好看。日月潭中间有一个小岛，小岛的北半边看起来像一个太阳，小岛的南半边好像一个月亮，所以大家叫那个湖的名字是日月潭。日月潭的水很蓝，人们可以在里面划船。日月潭四面很漂亮，在那个漂亮的地方，有一个漂亮的传说：很久以前，有人在山里看了一只大鹿，就去追那只大鹿，鹿很快就跑走了。大家在山里找了找，找很长时间。他们看见一个湖水，..uh..水里有小岛，把大湖分为两半，一半像太阳，一半像月亮。这是为什么它叫"日月潭"。日月潭的一年四季和早晚的景色都不一样。我最喜欢看雨以后的日月潭。雨以后的日月潭的湖水和四面的山看起来特别干净、可爱。怎么样，我介绍完了日月潭，你是不是也想去看看了？

COMMENTS: The presentation addresses all aspects of the task prompt with some elaboration. It contains some, although inconsistent, transitional elements, and some sentences are loosely connected. The overall structure is tainted by a repeated description of the name origin, suggesting a lack of organization and logic. The quoted legend may be a creative fabrication, or the student may have confused it with some other place. There is no such legend associated with "日月潭". The language use is appropriate and adequate, with errors that do not obscure meaning. For example, in "台灣裡有名的" ("台湾里有名的"), the "裡" ("里") is unnecessary; "大家叫那個湖的名字" ("大家叫那个湖的名字") should be either "大家叫那個湖" ("大家叫那个湖") or "那個湖的名字叫" ("那个湖的名字叫"), "雨以後的" ("雨以后的") should be just "雨後的" ("雨后的").

Sample Presentation for Level 3—Adequate

[Traditional-character version]

少林寺很有名，少林寺在一個陝上，因爲一個中國的皇帝特別有名了。少林武功是中國的一個武術，那個武術，很長歷史了，是中國的傳統武術的一個方面。少林的武術有不同的樣子，有背的少林，和也有nán的少林。中國人們非常..法戰..少林武術，有很多武術學校..歪國人來學習，還到別的歪國表演武功。別的..歪國..別的人..興趣..別的人..對少林的功夫..來說，外國人的別人都感興趣，我也是感興趣。我想學習少林的功夫..有..好處..對身體..有好處，還可以變cŏng明。有一個中國的電影是少林寺，我學少林寺從電影，也是我喜歡少林寺。我想學少林寺功夫，便花一個有名的功夫人。

[Simplified-character version]

少林寺很有名，少林寺在一个陕上，因为一个中国的皇帝特别有名了。少林武功是中国的一个武术，那个武术，很长历史了，是中国的传统武术的一个方面。少林的武术有不同的样子，有背的少林，和也有nàn的少林。中国人们非常...法战..少林武术，有很多武术学校..歪国人来学习，还到别的歪国表演武功。别的..歪国..别的人..兴趣..别的人..对少林的功夫..来说，外国人的别人都感兴趣，我也是感兴趣。我想学习少林的功夫..有..好处..对身体..有好处，还可以变cŏng明。有一个中国的电影是少林寺，我学少林寺从电影，也是我喜欢少林寺。我想学少林寺功夫，便花一个有名的功夫人。

COMMENTS: The presentation addresses the prompt directly, mentioning the long history of "少林寺", and the variety of "少林武術" ("少林武术"). The presentation consists of disconnected sentences that demonstrate the lack of coherence and organization. The delivery pace is inconsistent. It contains frequent pronunciation errors that necessitate listener's efforts. e.g., "陝上" ("陕上") instead of "山上", "背" instead of "北", "nàn的" instead of "南的", "法戰" ("法战") instead of "發展" ("发展"), "歪國" ("歪国") instead of "外國" ("外国"), "*cŏng* 明" instead of "*cōng*明" "聰明" ("聪明"), "便花" instead of "變化" ("变化").

Limited vocabulary, idioms, and simple grammatical structures with frequent errors interrupt the flow and sometimes obscure meaning, such as: "是中國的傳統武術的一個方面" ("是中国的传统武术的一个方面") may be rephrased to "是中國的傳統武術的一種" ("是中国的传统武术的一种"), "有背的少林，和也有nán的少林" may be rephrased to "少林武術分南、北兩派" ("少林武术分南、北两派"), the labored effort about "感興趣" ("感兴趣") may be restructured to "有許多外國人對少林功夫很感興趣，我也是其中一個" ("有许多外国人对少林功夫很感兴趣，我也是其中一个"), "便花一個有名的功夫人" may be rephrased to "成爲一個出色的武術專業人員" ("成为一个出色的武术专业人员").

Sample Presentation for Level 2—Weak

[Traditional-character version]

我要說臺北101。它是一個臺北..高樓，你可以..坐電梯...能在..uh..面，上去快了。英文的名字，很多有意思，也有很好意。(a long pause) 去..101高樓..好了，和那個地方..10分鐘..只走去。101高樓有燈，在晚上，和天天的燈不一樣的（a long pause）像紅的、藍的，和橙的。我看它們，喜歡極了。我完了。

[Simplified-character version]

我要说台北101。它是一个台北..高楼，你可以..坐电梯...能在..uh..面，上去快了。英文的名字，很多有意思，也有很好意。(a long pause) 去..101高楼..好了，和那个地方..10分钟..只走去。101高楼有灯，在晚上，和天天的灯不一样的（a long pause）像红的、蓝的，和橙的。我看它们，喜欢极了。我完了。

COMMENTS: This presentation illustrates a lack of competence in presentational speaking and cultural knowledge. It minimally addresses the prompt with scattered information in fragmented sentences, such as "上去快了", "也有很好意", "和那個地方" ("和那个地方"). The delivery is labored with frequent hesitation, and seems to lose track of the thought. It is hampered by minimal appropriate vocabulary and limited grammatical structures that obscure meaning, e.g., "坐電梯"("坐电梯"), "能在", "和那個地方" ("和那个地方").

Sample Presentation for Level 1—Very Weak

[Traditional-character version]

故宮..在北京。北京..很多老..的有名..okay..在中國。故宮是很高..牆，和很長。(a long pause) 中國人常常去吃，好吃飯，和別的 (inaudible pronunciation)..。(a long pause) 在奧林匹克，很多別的..外國..no..運動人…

[Simplified-character version]

故宫..在北京。北京..很多老..的有名..okay..在中国。故宫是很高..墙，和很长。(a long pause) 中国人常常去吃，好吃饭，和别的 (inaudible pronunciation)..。(a long pause) 在奥林匹克，很多别的..外国..no..运动人…

COMMENTS: This presentation addresses the prompt very minimally with isolated words and disjointed sentences. The delivery is labored, and significantly lacks organization and structure. The language competency is weak, with insufficient vocabulary and grammatical structures that hinder the meaning. It goes from describing the "牆" ("墙") to "好吃飯" ("好吃饭") and "奧林匹克". The last sentence seems to be incomplete.

Sample Presentation for Level 0—Unacceptable

[Traditional-character version]

美國公園很多，黃石國家公園是最大，和最有名。黃石公園在西邊北邊的美國，很漂亮，和很多的動物和旅遊人們。

[Simplified-character version]

美国公园很多，黄石国家公园是最大，和最有名。黄石公园在西边北边的美国，很漂亮，和很多的动物和旅游人们。

COMMENTS: This presentation misses the prompt altogether by describing Yellowstone National Park in the United States instead of a place in China or Taiwan.

SPEAKING TIPS

1. The key to the Speaking test is to address the prompt directly and completely. Therefore it is extremely important to listen to the prompt carefully and understand exactly what the requirements are.

2. To "be fluent" does not mean that students have to speak at a *fast* pace. It means that the pace should be steady and the flow should be smooth. Students should aim to speak at a natural rate of speech. Words, phrases, sentences, and paragraphs should be connected in a logical way. If students can respond appropriately with minimum hesitation, they are likely to receive a high score. If students don't know how to answer a certain question, they should at least address the prompt or topic in a general sense.

3. Students should prepare themselves with as much vocabulary as possible on theme topics. For example, if students are to talk about the Mid-Autumn Festival, it helps to know words like "月餅" ("月饼") and "團圓" ("团圆"). If they are planning an event for a trip, it helps to know words like "景點" ("景点") and "行程." If students don't know enough vocabulary, their speaking responses will likely be compromised. We can't emphasize enough how important it is for students to use appropriate words and phrases to express what they need to say correctly. Incorporating a couple of idioms and/or proverbs enhances the overall impression.

4. Students should pay attention to grammar. The grammar and linguistic structures that students use to communicate should be accurate. If students do not have good syntactic control, it will be very difficult for them to communicate effectively.

5. If students are not native Mandarin Chinese speakers, it is likely that they will have an accent when speaking Mandarin, but their speech should still be understandable. If students have trouble pronouncing certain words in Chinese, they should practice these words often. For example, if they cannot pronounce the third tones, they should find methods to fix their pronunciation.

   The more students listen critically and the more they practice, the better fluency, intonation, and pronunciation they will achieve. For words that students find particularly challenging, even after practicing repeatedly, students may want to avoid using them or find appropriate substitutions for them.

VOCABULARY TIPS

Students can use the following tips to expand their vocabulary:

1. *Reading is the best way to learn vocabulary*. Reading a variety of materials not only helps with learning new words and phrases, but also improves language skills overall.
2. *Make sentences while learning a new word*. Using a new word in sentences will help students memorize the meaning and usage of the word.
3. *Apply new words as much as possible in daily life*.
4. *Study radicals*. Learning just one radical often helps students understand many new words.
5. *Expand vocabulary by learning synonyms and antonyms*. This is very effective for memorizing new words.
6. *Group theme-based words*. Keep practicing and memorizing based on a selected theme or topic.

SPEAKING PREPARATION

Conversation

A conversation differs from simply answering questions. The latter is easy to do as long as one understands the question, but *conversation* consists of more than just a response. It requires students to *elaborate* on a topic to make the conversation interesting. In the Conversation part of the Speaking section, students must keep their responses within 20 seconds. The recording stops after 20 seconds. Anything said after 20 seconds will not be recorded. Students are expected to:

- address the prompt directly, appropriately, and thoroughly;
- keep a natural pace and avoid stumbling;
- demonstrate accurate pronunciation and tones; and
- use a wide range of grammatical structures, vocabulary, and idioms.

Here are some useful hints for participating in conversations. Students should:

1. Understand the prompt without having to translate it in their heads.
2. Include as much information pertaining to the prompt as they can. Avoid any silent moments while responding to the prompt, as silence may indicate that they do not understand the prompt or they lack the words to express themselves.
3. Talk about one word that they do understand if they fail to understand the prompt. Delivering an incomplete answer is much better than saying, "I don't understand," or leaving the recording blank.
4. Keep in mind that their response to the topic should *not* be too brief. Responding to the prompt means providing enough information to show they can carry on a conversation with someone.
5. Forget about being truthful in the response. The purpose of the question is to elicit a speech sample in Chinese. Sometimes, there might not be an absolute correct or incorrect answer. Saying something in Chinese, instead of keeping silent, is highly recommended.

6. Correct any mistake right away if recognized.

7. Practice having spontaneous conversations for added fluency.

Sample Questions

You have a conversation with your friend, Zhang Liping, about learning Chinese.

1. 你學中文學了多長時間？
   你学中文学了多长时间？

2. 你爲什麼學中文？
   你为什么学中文？

3. 你們的中文老師是美國人還是中國人？
   你们的中文老师是美国人还是中国人？

4. 在學習中文過程中，你覺得最有意思的事情是什麼？
   在学习中文过程中，你觉得最有意思的事情是什么？

5. 你在學習中最大的困難是什麼？
   你在学习中最大的困难是什么？

6. 你高中畢業以後還學中文嗎？
   你高中毕业以后还学中文吗？

Suggested Responses

Students should answer the questions directly first and then elaborate on the topic.

1. 你學中文學了多長時間？
   你学中文学了多长时间？

[Traditional-character version]

   First answer directly: 我學中文已經學了兩年了。

   Then elaborate: 我記得兩年前，我們社區開了一所中文學校，我的朋友中很多人都去了，我也去了。上高中以後，我發現學校也有中文課，於是就選了這門課。

[Simplified-character version]

   First answer directly: 我学中文已经学了两年了。

   Then elaborate: 我记得两年前，我们社区开了一所中文学校，我的朋友中很多人都去了，我也去了。上高中以后，我发现学校也有中文课，于是就选了这门课。

2. 你爲什麼學中文？
   你为什么学中文？

[Traditional-character version]

   First answer directly: 剛開始學中文完全是因爲好朋友去了，我也就跟她一起去了。

   Then elaborate: 剛學的時候覺得挺好玩兒，後來越來越喜歡學。我覺得學中文很有挑戰性。

[Simplified-character version]

First answer directly: 刚开始学中文完全是因为好朋友去了，我也就跟她一起去了。

Then elaborate: 刚学的时候觉得挺好玩儿，后来越来越喜欢学。我觉得学中文很有挑战性。

3. 你們的中文老師是美國人還是中國人？
   你们的中文老师是美国人还是中国人？

[Traditional-character version]

First answer directly: 中文學校的老師是在美國長大的中國人，好像是小學四年級的時候從臺灣來的。

Then elaborate: 現在的老師是從大陸來的。她們教得都很好，人也都很友好，特別關心我們的學習。

[Simplified-character version]

First answer directly: 中文学校的老师是在美国长大的中国人，好像是小学四年级的时候从台湾来的。

Then elaborate: 现在的老师是从大陆来的。她们教得都很好，人也都很友好，特别关心我们的学习。

4. 在學習中文過程中，你覺得最有意思的事情是什麼？
   在学习中文过程中，你觉得最有意思的事情是什么？

[Traditional-character version]

First answer directly: 有很多有意思的事情，比如，根據部首猜字義呀，表演成語故事呀什麼的。

Then elaborate: 不過，我覺得最有意思的事情是做遊戲，我在中文學校的那位臺灣老師就特別會帶著學生做遊戲。

[Simplified-character version]

First answer directly: 有很多有意思的事情，比如，根据部首猜字义呀，表演成语故事呀什么的。

Then elaborate: 不过，我觉得最有意思的事情是做游戏，我在中文学校的那位台湾老师就特别会带着学生做游戏。

5. 你在學習中最大的困難是什麼？
   你在学习中最大的困难是什么？

[Traditional-character version]

First answer directly: 對我來說，中文的聽力最難。

Then elaborate: 剛開始的時候，聽力特別糟糕，老師說的話我根本聽不懂。有兩次還因爲沒真聽懂而弄出了笑話。後來，我就多聽錄音，多看中國電影，多跟中國人聊天兒，現在聽力好多了。

[Simplified-character version]

First answer directly: 对我来说，中文的听力最难。

Then elaborate: 刚开始的时候，听力特别糟糕，老师说的话我根本听不懂。有两次还因为没真听懂而弄出了笑话。后来，我就多听录音，多看中国电影，多跟中国人聊天儿，现在听力好多了。

6. 你高中畢業以後還學中文嗎？
   你高中毕业以后还学中文吗？

[Traditional-character version]

    First answer directly: 高中畢業后我肯定會繼續學中文的。

    Then elaborate: 我知道現在美國有很多大學都開設中文課程。我申請大學時也會考慮這一點的。我喜歡學中文，我不會半途而廢的。

[Simplified-character version]

    First answer directly: 高中毕业后我肯定会继续学中文的。

    Then elaborate: 我知道现在美国有很多大学都开设中文课程。我申请大学时也会考虑这一点的。我喜欢学中文，我不会半途而废的。

PRESENTATION

After Conversation, the next task is the Cultural Presentation. The directions will include a topic prompt and a description of the requirements for the presentation. Read the directions carefully. Students should make every effort to address all aspects of the prompt thoroughly and accurately. The presentation should be cohesive and well organized. Any information related to Chinese culture should be accurate and comprehensive.

Generally speaking, a good presentation has the following qualities.

1. ***Captivating.*** To successfully intrigue the audience, students should keep their descriptions and explanations crisp, clear, and adequately detailed. They should be sure to quote relevant facts and examples to support their ideas. The topic prompt typically includes cultural requirements. Students should pay close attention to the requirements and present the related cultural content in a comprehensible manner.

2. ***Purposeful.*** Students should practice stating the purpose, scope, and objectives of the presentation in a clear, concise manner. They should consider how to organize the presentation, including length, key ideas, transitions, and any related stories, including both qualitative and quantitative facts. Students will be given only 2 minutes to record their presentations. Prior to taking the test, they should practice using the time wisely to deliver a well-stated and purposeful presentation.

3. ***Organized.*** Students are encouraged to make their presentations well organized and coherent, develop clear ideas, and use appropriate transitional words and phrases. Both this chapter and the Writing chapter provide lists of frequently used Chinese transition words and phrases. During the presentation, the structure should be apparent to the listener.

4. ***Cultural.*** When addressing the requirements for the Cultural Presentation, students will be able to choose a specific aspect based on a very broad prompt. They should be sure that any cultural information included in their presentations is accurate. It is highly advised that they pick a main focus that they are confident with and know well.

5. *Appropriate.* Students should look for clues in the prompt, especially if the prompt seems to be asking something that they know nothing about. Students should leverage these clues to address the topic and express their own opinions on it. Remember: Don't give up.

6. *Accurate.* During the presentation, students should use language that is accurate, concise but meaningful, diverse, and easy to understand. The last chapter, Cultural Notes, provides cultural information that is specifically designed for written language. When preparing for oral presentations, students need to shift their communication style from written to spoken.

As mentioned above, for the Cultural Presentation, students may pick a specific subject from a broad topic that they are familiar with. Compared with the written parts of the AP Chinese exam, in the Cultural Presentation, students have more freedom to be expressive and creative. For example, as an opening line, they might start with:

- a phrase relevant to the topic—"今天要跟大家談的是.." ("今天要跟大家谈的是..")
- a quote from a famous poem to establish a frame of reference—"每逢佳節倍思親" ("每逢佳节倍思亲"), or
- a simple question—"中秋節是怎麼來的?" ("中秋节是怎么来的?").

A well-organized Cultural Presentation contains an introduction, a main body, and a conclusion.

The **introduction** is the most important part of the presentation; it consists of a greeting and a thesis. Students should include an appropriate greeting and a thesis that captures the audience's attention. A good introduction will notify the audience of the topic right away and stimulate their curiosity about the topic.

The **main body** of the presentation has to be coherent. It should contain sufficient transitions for the audience to distinguish what is primary information and what is secondary.

The **conclusion** should be short. It should restate the main points and also what the student wants the audience to walk away with. A conclusion may include recommendations; for example, if the presentation is about a famous author, recommend one of his/her books.

The presentation must be no more than 2 minutes long. When recording, students should make sure to keep a naturally steady pace. Students should not finish long before the recording time ends, nor should they continue after the recording stops. The latter tends to happen more frequently during classroom practice.

In the classroom, a teacher might give a student more time if his presentation goes beyond 2 minutes. During the actual Speaking test, however, a computer is used for the recording. It will not allow for over-time recording. If the presentation is longer than 2 minutes, the conclusion, which might be the most elaborate and clever part of the presentation, will be cut off. Losing the opportunity to present the conclusion seriously affects the final score.

Here are some common opening remarks and commonly used words in the main body and summary/conclusion, as well as two samples.

Common Opening Remarks

我想談談…	I'm going to talk about…
我想谈谈…	
我演講的題目是…	The title of my presentation is…
我演讲的题目是…	
我談話的主題是…	The topic of my talk is…
我谈话的主题是…	
我想藉這個機會給大家簡單介紹一下…	
我想借这个机会给大家简单介绍一下…	I'd like to take this opportunity to give you an overview of …

Main Body and Summary/Conclusion Words

我演講的內容分爲三個部分	I've divided my talk into (three) parts.
我演讲的内容分为三个部分	
我將從三個方面談談	I'm going to divide my talk into three parts to talk about …
我将从三个方面谈谈	
首先	First
其次	Second
第三	Third
最後 (最后)	Finally
在第一部分	In the first part
在第二部分	Then, in the second part
下面，我談談第一個部分	Let's move to the first part of my talk, which is about …
下面，我谈谈第一个部分	
最後，我再強調一下我的要點	I'd like to end by emphasizing the main points.
最后，我再强调一下我的要点	
我想用…來結束我的演講	I'd like to end with…
我想用…来结束我的演讲	

Cultural Presentation Sample

There are many ancient Chinese stories. Choose one to present. The presentation needs to summarize the story and give your own opinion on the story.

[Traditional-character version]
各位同學：

你們好！我演講的題目是"孟薑女哭長城"。秦朝時候，有一個善良、美麗的女孩子叫孟薑女。孟薑女喜歡一個叫範喜良的小伙子。他們兩人情投意合，不久就結婚了。結婚那天，來了很多客人。到了晚上，喝喜酒的人都走了，新郎、新娘也要入洞房了。突然來了幾個當兵的，把範喜良抓走去修長城。從那以後，孟薑女一個人守在空空的房子裏思念丈夫。後來，孟薑女背上行裝，帶上吃的，找到了長城工地。在工地上，她沒有找到丈夫，卻碰到了一個老鄉。老鄉告訴她，範喜良已經死了，屍體已經埋在了長城的下面。聽到這個消息，孟薑女大哭起來。她哭啊，哭啊，哭得天昏地暗。突然，聽到"嘩啦"一聲，長城倒了，範喜良的屍體露出來。孟薑女終於見到了心愛的丈夫，但丈夫卻永遠也看不到妻子了，因爲他已經被殘暴的秦始皇害死了。這個故事告訴我們，雖然長城是人類最偉大的工程之一，是中華民族的驕傲，但是，長城也凝聚著中國古代勞動人民的血與汗。我的故事講完了，謝謝大家！

[Simplified-character version]

各位同学：

你们好！我演讲的题目是"孟姜女哭长城"。秦朝时候，有一个善良、美丽的女孩子叫孟姜女。孟姜女喜欢一个叫范喜良的小伙子。他们两人情投意合，不久就结婚了。结婚那天，来了很多客人。到了晚上，喝喜酒的人都走了，新郎、新娘也要入洞房了。突然来了几个当兵的，把范喜良抓走去修长城。从那以后，孟姜女一个人守在空空的房子里思念丈夫。后来，孟姜女背上行装，带上吃的，找到了长城工地。在工地上，她没有找到丈夫，却碰到了一个老乡。老乡告诉她，范喜良已经死了，尸体已经埋在了长城的下面。听到这个消息，孟姜女大哭起来。她哭啊，哭啊，哭得天昏地暗。突然，听到"哗啦"一声，长城倒了，范喜良的尸体露出来。孟姜女终于见到了心爱的丈夫，但丈夫却永远也看不到妻子了，因为他已经被残暴的秦始皇害死了。这个故事告诉我们，虽然长城是人类最伟大的工程之一，是中华民族的骄傲，但是，长城也凝聚着中国古代劳动人民的血与汗。我的故事讲完了，谢谢大家！

SPEAKING PRACTICE POINTERS

1. Do jot down idea words and phrases, but do not write out a whole presentation before recording. Students will be given only 4 minutes to determine a topic and to prepare for their presentations. They will not have enough time to write down the full presentation.

2. Do not translate. Some students may be tempted to first compose the presentation in English and then translate it into Chinese. This is not recommended. Not only is it not a productive use of time, but translations do not generally yield the best results. Students should practice thinking and speaking in Chinese to achieve a smooth, natural flow in their speech.

3. Do learn as much vocabulary as possible to cover as many topics as possible.

4. Do use the best vocabulary/idioms as possible. Using a more sophisticated phrase or idiom has a definite advantage over using a single word, or a tediously long and drawn-out description.

5. Do correct a mistake immediately. Self-correction shows that students have mastered the correct grammar.

6. Do practice recording presentations with a variety of topics before taking the exam. This way, students can compare what they think with what they actually speak. Listening to their own voice often helps students become more confident in their abilities. Keep in mind that students will be given 2 minutes to deliver their presentations. They may need to adjust their pace to ensure that they complete their presentations within 2 minutes.

FREE-RESPONSE SECTION: SPEAKING

Type: Free-Response—Speaking
Number of problems: 7
Weight: 25%
Duration: approx. 10 minutes

Directions: You will be asked to present the following two Speaking tasks.
1. **Conversation:** There will be 6 related questions. For each question you hear, you will have 20 seconds to respond.
2. **Cultural Presentation:** You will hear and see the topic for your presentation. You will have 4 minutes to prepare, and 2 minutes to present.

Important Notes:
1. You **cannot** move back and forth between the two tasks.
2. After finishing the last oral question from the first task, you will be moved automatically to the second task.

Knowledge & Skills:
1. Presentation, interpersonal, and interpretive communication.
2. Application of basic cultural knowledge.
3. Speaking.

Strategies:
1. Be focused, and stay on topic.
2. Conversation—be courteous, address your interviewer in the beginning, and thank him/her at the end.
3. Cultural presentation—address the topic, usually a cultural practice, product, place, or person, in detail.
4. Use the displayed clock to gauge the remaining time.
5. Maintain a steady pace and a natural tone.

Fig. 5-1 Speaking Task Breakdown

Speaking Skills Practice

This section contains 20 practice topics. The suggested test prompts are not a definitive list, but they will help students get used to the test format, learn related vocabulary, develop presentation strategies, and build confidence.

The prompts may ask about personal opinions, past experiences, future plans, and so on. Students should keep in mind that these questions will be based on one topic. The topics typically deal with general subjects that high school students are familiar with.

Additional *Useful Words* are provided for each of the selected topics.

The following practice sections are presented in an order similar to the practice sections in the Writing chapter. Students will participate in a simulated conversation and make a cultural presentation.

In the Conversation section, students will be given 20 seconds to record their response for each question. Students should respond as fully and as appropriately as possible. The questions will be centered around one topic.

In the Cultural Presentation section, students will be asked to address a suite of prompts based on a topic in Chinese. Students should imagine the scenario of making an oral presentation in a Chinese class. First, students will read and hear the topic for the presentation. Students will have 4 minutes to prepare for the presentation and another 2 minutes to record the presentation. The presentation should be as complete as possible.

Useful words for each topic are given below and can be used in both conversations and cultural presentations. The question prompts for the Conversation section are scripted, for your reference.

Topic One: School

課程	(课程)	kèchéng	curriculum; course
必修課	(必修课)	bìxiūkè	core course
選修課	(选修课)	xuǎnxiūkè	elective course
基礎課	(基础课)	jīchǔkè	basic course
課外活動	(课外活动)	kèwài huódòng	extracurricular activities
作業	(作业)	zuòyè	assignment
成績	(成绩)	chéngjì	grade; score
學分	(学分)	xuéfēn	credit
寫作	(写作)	xiězuò	writing; composition
體育	(体育)	tǐyù	sport
世界文學	(世界文学)	shìjiè wénxué	world literature
英國文學	(英国文学)	Yīngguó wénxué	English literature
社會學科	(社会学科)	shèhuì xuékē	social studies
歷史	(历史)	lìshǐ	history
世界史		shìjièshǐ	world history
歐洲史	(欧洲史)	Ōuzhōushǐ	European history
美國史	(美国史)	Měiguóshǐ	U.S. history

政府		zhèngfǔ	government
經濟學	(经济学)	jīngjìxué	economics
社會學	(社会学)	shèhuìxué	sociology
心理學	(心理学)	xīnlǐxué	psychology
藝術	(艺术)	yìshù	arts
辯論	(辩论)	biànlùn	debate
樂隊	(乐队)	yuěduì	band
爵士		juéshì	jazz
管弦樂隊	(管弦乐队)	guǎnxián yuèduì	orchestra
戲劇	(戏剧)	xìjù	drama
舞蹈		wǔdǎo	dance
形象藝術	(形象艺术)	xíngxiàng yìshù	graphic arts
年鑒	(年鉴)	niánjiàn	yearbook
數學	(数学)	shùxué	mathematics
代數學	(代数学)	dàishùxué	algebra
幾何學	(几何学)	jǐhéxué	geometry
數學分析	(数学分析)	shùxué fēnxī	math analysis
統計學	(统计学)	tǒngjìxué	statistics
微積分	(微积分)	wēijīfēn	calculus
科學	(科学)	kēxué	science
生物學	(生物学)	shēngwùxué	biology
化學	(化学)	huàxué	chemistry
物理學	(物理学)	wùlǐxué	physics
環境科學	(环境科学)	huánjìng kēxué	environmental science
解剖學	(解剖学)	jiěpōuxué	anatomy
生理學	(生理学)	shēnglǐxué	physiology
體育教育	(体育教育)	tǐyùjiàoyù	physical education
計算機學	(计算机学)	jìsuànjīxué	computer science
電腦	(电脑)	diàn nǎo	computer science
醫學	(医学)	yīxué	medicine

Conversation Prompt

You will have a conversation with a new student about the extracurricular activities offered at your school. She will ask you six questions.

Cultural Presentation Prompt

Track 55

Chinese is a unique language. Choose one characteristic of Chinese characters to present. In your presentation, describe why this aspect of Chinese characters is significant.

Topic Two: Sports

跑步		pǎobù	running
體操	(体操)	tǐcāo	gymnastics
跨欄	(跨栏)	kuàlán	hurdle race
鐵餅	(铁饼)	tiěbǐng	discus
摔跤		shuāijiāo	wrestling
滑冰		huábīng	skating
足球		zúqiú	soccer
壘球	(垒球)	lěiqiú	softball
網球	(网球)	wǎngqiú	tennis
排球		páiqiú	volleyball
棒球		bàngqiú	baseball
旱冰		hànbīng	roller skating
手球		shǒuqiú	handball
鉛球	(铅球)	qiānqiú	shot put
籃球	(篮球)	lánqiú	basketball
橄欖球	(橄榄球)	gǎnlǎnqiú	rugby; football
羽毛球		yǔmáoqiú	badminton
曲棍球		qǔgùnqiú	hockey
乒乓球		pīngpāngqiú	ping-pong
高爾夫球	(高尔夫球)	gāo'ěrfūqiú	golf
比賽	(比赛)	bǐsài	competition
教練	(教练)	jiàoliàn	coach
運動員	(运动员)	yùndòngyuán	athlete
隊	(队)	duì	team
輸	(输)	shū	lose
贏	(赢)	yíng	win

Conversation Prompt

You will have a conversation with Yu Pingping, a reporter from your school newspaper, who is interviewing you about your opinion on sports. She will ask you six questions.

Cultural Presentation Prompt

There are many Chinese martial arts. Choose one art you know (Qigong, Taijiquan, Shaolin Kung Fu, etc.) and describe the particular demographic that is associated with this sport, and any other necessary details, in your presentation.

Topic Three: Lifestyle

生活方式		shēnghuó fāngshì	lifestyle
風格	(风格)	fēnggé	style
財富	(财富)	cáifù	wealth; valuable things
地位		dìwèi	position; status
健康		jiànkāng	health; healthy
文明		wénmíng	civilization; civilized
疾病		jíbìng	disease
心情		xīnqíng	mood
寬容	(宽容)	kuānróng	tolerance; broad-mindedness
氣氛	(气氛)	qìfēn	atmosphere
吸烟		xīyān	smoke
喝酒		hējiǔ	alcoholic drink
毒品		dúpǐn	narcotic drugs; narcotics
吸毒		xīdú	drug-taking
飲食	(饮食)	yǐnshí	food and beverage; diet
衛生	(卫生)	wèishēng	hygiene; health; sanitation
習慣	(习惯)	xíguàn	habit; custom; be used to
習氣	(习气)	xíqì	bad habit; bad practice
睡眠		shuìmián	sleep
充沛		chōngpèi	full of (energy); abundant
充足		chōngzú	abundant; quite sufficient; enough
失眠		shīmián	suffer from insomnia
精力		jīnglì	energy; vigor
精神		jīngshén	spirits
行爲	(行为)	xíngwéi	behavior; conduct; act
危害		wēihài	harm; danger
規律	(规律)	guīlǜ	regular pattern
規則	(规则)	guīzé	rule; regulation
緊張	(紧张)	jǐnzhāng	nervous; tense
效率		xiàolǜ	efficiency
勞累	(劳累)	láolèi	tired; exhausted; fatigued
疲憊	(疲惫)	píbèi	exhausted
疲倦		píjuàn	tired; weary; fatigued
過度	(过度)	guòdù	over; excessive
態度	(态度)	tàidù	attitude; approach
自覺	(自觉)	zìjué	conscious; aware; conscientious
資源	(资源)	zīyuán	natural resources
節約	(节约)	jiéyuē	save; conserve
浪費	(浪费)	làngfèi	waste
負責任	(负责任)	fù zérèn	take responsibility
人生		rénshēng	life
目標	(目标)	mùbiāo	target
遵守		zūnshǒu	observe (rules, regulations, discipline)
公德		gōngdé	social morality
守時	(守时)	shǒushí	be punctual

Conversation Prompt

Track 57

You will have a conversation with your Chinese teacher about students' lifestyles in the United States. She will ask you six questions.

Cultural Presentation Prompt

There are many Chinese idioms and proverbs about health. Choose one to present. Describe the meaning of this expression and explain its relevance in a presentation. Explain how it affects people in everyday life.

Topic Four: Entertainment

節目	(节目)	jiémù	program
新聞	(新闻)	xīnwén	news
商業片	(商业片)	shāngyèpiàn	commercial
藝術片	(艺术片)	yìshùpiàn	art film
紀錄片	(纪录片)	jìlùpiàn	documentary
卡通片		kǎtōngpiàn	cartoon
科幻片		kēhuànpiàn	science fiction film
恐怖片		kǒngbùpiàn	horror movie
悲劇片	(悲剧片)	bēijùpiàn	tragedy film
喜劇片	(喜剧片)	xǐjùpiàn	comedy film
功夫片		gōngfupiàn	kungfu movie
驚險片	(惊险片)	jīngxiǎnpiàn	adventure film
連續劇	(连续剧)	liánxùjù	series drama
肥皂劇	(肥皂剧)	féizàojù	soap opera
脫口秀	(脱口秀)	tuōkǒuxiù	talk show
古典音樂	(古典音乐)	gǔdiǎn yīnyuè	classical music
搖滾樂	(摇滚乐)	yáogǔnyuè	rock
爵士樂	(爵士乐)	juéshìyuè	jazz
電影院	(电影院)	diànyǐngyuàn	movie theatre
禮堂	(礼堂)	lǐtáng	auditorium
導演	(导演)	dǎoyǎn	director
藝人	(艺人)	yìrén	actor; artist
演員	(演员)	yǎnyuán	actor; actress; performer
演技		yǎnjì	acting skill

Conversation Prompt

Track 58

You will have a conversation with Zhang Lin, a school news reporter, about your hobbies and interests. She will ask you six questions.

Cultural Presentation Prompt

There are many Chinese traditional arts. Choose one (such as Peking opera, crosstalk, lion dance, etc.). In your presentation, describe this art and give your own opinion on it.

Topic Five: Jobs

利		lì	advantage; benefit
弊		bì	disadvantage
接觸	(接触)	jiēchù	have contact with
複雜	(复杂)	fùzá	complicated
積累	(积累)	jīlěi	accumulate; build up (knowledge, experience)
經驗	(经验)	jīngyàn	experience
經歷	(经历)	jīnglì	experience; undergo
鍛煉	(锻炼)	duànliàn	temper; toughen; take exercise
實踐	(实践)	shíjiàn	practice
寶貴	(宝贵)	bǎoguì	valuable; precious
分散		fēnsàn	disperse
精力		jīnglì	energy; vigor
賺錢	(赚钱)	zhuànqián	make money
減輕	(减轻)	jiǎnqīng	lighten; ease; reduce
負擔	(负担)	fùdān	burden; load
分憂	(分忧)	fēnyōu	share someone's cares or burdens
學費	(学费)	xuéfèi	tuition fee
生活費	(生活费)	shēnghuófèi	living expenses
零用錢	(零用钱)	língyòngqián	allowance
豐富	(丰富)	fēngfù	rich; enrich
體驗	(体验)	tǐyàn	learn through practice or experience
考驗	(考验)	kǎoyàn	test; testing
觀察	(观察)	guānchá	observe
見識	(见识)	jiànshi	experience; knowledge
基礎	(基础)	jīchǔ	foundation
獨立	(独立)	dúlì	be independent; independent
耽誤	(耽误)	dānwù	delay; hold up; waste
上當受騙	(上当受骗)	shàngdàng shòupiàn	be fooled and tricked
協調	(协调)	xiétiáo	coordinate; concert; bring into line
安排		ānpái	arrange

Conversation Prompt

You will have a conversation with Gu Wei, a reporter from a radio station, who is interviewing people about high school students with part-time jobs. He will ask you six questions.

Cultural Presentation Prompt

There are many social customs. Choose one aspect (being a guest in someone's home, the use of address terms, small talk, etc.). In your presentation, describe this social custom and give your own opinion on it.

Topic Six: Friendship

異性	(异性)	yìxìng	the opposite sex
因素		yīnsù	factor; element
戀愛	(恋爱)	liàn'ài	be in love
幸福		xìngfú	happy; happiness; well-being
彼此		bǐcǐ	each other
瞭解	(了解)	liáojiě	understand; know
信任		xìnrèn	trust; have confidence in
浪漫		làngmàn	romantic
感情		gǎnqíng	feelings; emotions; sentiments
分享		fēnxiǎng	share (joy, rights, etc.)
優秀	(优秀)	yōuxiù	outstanding; excellent
性格		xìnggé	personality
外向		wàixiàng	extroverted
內向		nèixiàng	introverted
脾氣	(脾气)	píqi	temper; temperament
開朗	(开朗)	kāilǎng	outgoing; cheerful
友好		yǒuhǎo	friendly; amicable
急躁		jízào	impetuous; impatient
體貼	(体贴)	tǐtiē	be sensitive to someone's mood or plight; show great care and consideration
溫柔	(温柔)	wēnróu	gentle and soft
溫和	(温和)	wēnhé	gentle
幽默	(幽默)	yōumò	humorous
害羞		hàixiū	shy
勤奮	(勤奋)	qínfèn	diligent; industrious
年齡	(年龄)	niánlíng	age
長相	(长相)	zhǎngxiàng	looks; appearance
身材		shēncái	stature; figure
興趣	(兴趣)	xìngqù	hobbies
習慣	(习惯)	xíguàn	habit
成熟		chéngshú	mature
交往		jiāowǎng	socialize; have dealings with
文化		wénhuà	culture
背景		bèijǐng	background
教育		jiàoyù	education
程度		chéngdù	degree; level (of education, ability)
不同		bùtóng	different; difference
相似		xiāngsì	resemble; be similar; be alike
溝通	(沟通)	gōutōng	communicate
衝突	(冲突)	chōngtū	conflict
爭執	(争执)	zhēngzhí	argue; disagree
吵架		chǎojià	quarrel
分手		fēn shǒu	break up
鬧翻	(闹翻)	nàofān	have a falling out (with somebody)

影響	（影响）	yǐngxiǎng	influence; affect
傳統	（传统）	chuántǒng	tradition; traditional
保守		bǎoshǒu	conservative
責任心	（责任心）	zérènxīn	sense of responsibility (or duty)

Conversation Prompt

Track 60
You will have a conversation with a Chinese teacher, Lu Xiaomin, about friendships and relationships in high school. She will ask you six questions.

Cultural Presentation Prompt

1. There are many Chinese idioms and proverbs about friendship. Choose one to present. In your presentation, describe the meaning of this expression and explain when this idiom or proverb is applicable. Also explain how this expression has helped you with friends.

2. There are many taboo topics in Chinese social rites. Choose one aspect (colors, entertaining guests, private matters, etc.) to present. Describe this taboo and give your own opinion on it.

Topic Seven: Clothing

衣服		yīfu	clothes
襯衫	（衬衫）	chènshān	shirt
褲子	（裤子）	kùzi	pants
牛仔褲	（牛仔裤）	niúzǎikù	jeans; cowboy pants
裙子		qúnzi	skirt
大衣		dàyī	overcoat
夾克	（夹克）	jiákè	jacket
外套		wàitào	coat; jacket
內衣		nèiyī	underwear
西裝	（西装）	xīzhuāng	suit
運動服	（运动服）	yùndòngfú	sportswear; sports clothes
毛衣		máoyī	sweater
T-恤衫		tìxùshān	T-shirt
帽子		màozi	hat
圍巾	（围巾）	wéijīn	scarf
鞋		xié	shoes
襪子	（袜子）	wàzi	socks; stockings
領帶	（领带）	lǐngdài	necktie
件		jiàn	a measure word, typically for garments above the waist, such as shirts, blouses, dresses
條	（条）	tiáo	a measure word, typically for garments below the waist, such as pants, skirts
套		tào	suite; set

雙	(双)	shuāng	a pair
頂	(顶)	dǐng	a measure for hats
大小		dàxiǎo	size
長短	(长短)	chángduǎn	length
厚薄		hòubó	thickness
樣式	(样式)	shìyàng	style
合適	(合适)	héshì	suitable
穿		chuān	to wear (essentials, e.g., shirt, shoes)
戴		dài	to wear (accessories, e.g., hat, jewelry)
顏色	(颜色)	yánsè	color
黃	(黄)	huáng	yellow
綠	(绿)	lǜ	green
紅	(红)	hóng	red
藍	(蓝)	lán	blue
灰		huī	grey
紫		zǐ	purple
黑		hēi	black
白		bái	white
粉紅	(粉红)	fěnhóng	pink
咖啡色		kāfēisè	coffee color
牌子		páizi	brand
名牌		míngpái	name brand
質量	(质量)	zhìliàng	quality
打折		dǎzhé	discount
物美價廉	(物美价廉)	wùměi jiàlián	attractive goods at inexpensive prices

Conversation Prompt

Track 61

You will have a conversation with Wang Yang, a new student at your school, about fashion styles for high school students, and the standard for buying clothes.

Cultural Presentation Prompt

In China, different colors may be associated with different things or events. In your presentation, choose one color (white, red, black, yellow, etc.), describe what the color represents, and introduce related idioms, proverbs, and symbolism.

Topic Eight: Food

中餐		zhōngcān	Chinese food
西餐		xīcān	Western food
素菜		sùcài	vegetarian; vegetable dishes
葷菜	(荤菜)	hūncài	meat or fish dishes
青菜		qīngcài	green leafy vegetable
肉		ròu	meat
雞	(鸡)	jī	chicken
牛肉		niúròu	beef

猪肉		zhūròu	pork
羊肉		yángròu	lamb; mutton
魚		yú	fish
烤鴨	(烤鸭)	kǎoyā	roast duck
家常豆腐		jiācháng dòufu	home-style tofu
糖醋魚		tángcùyú	fish in sweet-and-sour sauce
酸辣湯	(酸辣汤)	suānlàtāng	hot-and-sour soup
米飯	(米饭)	mǐfàn	cooked rice
餃子	(饺子)	jiǎozi	dumplings
麵包	(面包)	miànbāo	bread
麵條	(面条)	miàntiáo	noodles
比薩餅	(比萨饼)	bǐsàbǐng	pizza
空心粉		kōngxīnfěn	spaghetti
漢堡包	(汉堡包)	hànbǎobāo	hamburger
三明治		sānmíngzhì	sandwich
油		yóu	oil; oily
鹽	(盐)	yán	salt
糖		táng	sugar
醋		cù	vinegar
醬油	(酱油)	jiàngyóu	soy sauce
味精		wèijīng	monosodium glutamate (MSG)
味道		wèidào	taste; flavor
酸		suān	sour
甜		tián	sweet
苦		kǔ	bitter
辣		là	spicy
香		xiāng	fragrant; nice-smelling
膩	(腻)	nì	greasy (food)
淡		dàn	bland
鹹	(咸)	xián	salty
清淡		qīngdàn	light in flavor
新鮮	(新鲜)	xīnxiān	fresh
嫩		nèn	tender
老		lǎo	tough
餓	(饿)	è	hungry
渴		kě	thirsty
好吃		hǎochī	delicious
難吃	(难吃)	nánchī	taste bad
牛奶		niúnǎi	milk
酸奶		suānnǎi	yogurt
飲料	(饮料)	yǐnliào	beverage
礦泉水	(矿泉水)	kuàngquánshuǐ	mineral water
汽水		qìshuǐ	soda
純淨水	(纯净水)	chúnjìngshuǐ	spring water
綠茶	(绿茶)	lǜchá	green tea
紅茶	(红茶)	hóngchá	black tea
冰茶		bīngchá	ice tea

檸檬茶	（柠檬茶）	níngméngchá	lemon tea
酒		jiǔ	liquor
白酒		báijiǔ	alcohol
葡萄酒		pútáojiǔ	wine
啤酒		píjiǔ	beer
香檳酒	（香槟酒）	xiāngbīnjiǔ	champagne
果汁		guǒzhī	juice
蘋果汁	（苹果汁）	píngguǒzhī	apple juice
橙汁		chéngzhī	orange juice

Conversation Prompt

Track 62

You will have a conversation with your friend Li Haixia about Chinese food. She will ask you six questions.

Cultural Presentation Prompt

1. Food is an important part of Chinese culture. Choose one well-known dish (Beijing duck, boiled dumplings, sweet-and-sour pork, etc.). In your presentation, describe this dish, including the ingredients, the taste, the history behind it, and any other necessary information. If you have sampled this food before, describe your experience.

2. Chinese food is divided into categories by region and ethnic group. Choose one cuisine (Sichuan cuisine, Shanghai cuisine, Guangdong cuisine, etc.). In your presentation, describe this cuisine, including the ingredients, the tastes, the history behind it, and any other necessary information. If you have sampled this food before, describe your experience.

Topic Nine: Housing

城市		chéngshì	city
鄉村	（乡村）	xiāngcūn	countryside
鎮	（镇）	zhèn	town
安全		ānquán	safe; safety
安靜	（安静）	ānjìng	quiet
乾淨	（干净）	gānjìng	clean
吵		chǎo	noisy
理想		lǐxiǎng	ideal
位置		wèizhi	location
區域	（区域）	qūyù	area; district
住宅區	（住宅区）	zhùzháiqū	residential area
市區	（市区）	shìqū	urban
郊區	（郊区）	jiāoqū	outskirts; suburb
村		cūn	village
公園	（公园）	gōngyuán	park
體育館	（体育馆）	tǐyùguǎn	gymnasium
購物中心	（购物中心）	gòuwù zhōngxīn	shopping center

圖書館	(图书馆)	túshūguǎn	library
醫院	(医院)	yīyuàn	hospital
幼稚園	(幼稚园)	yòuzhìyuán	kindergarten
養老院	(养老院)	yǎnglǎoyuàn	senior citizens' home
學校	(学校)	xuéxiào	school
教堂		jiàotáng	church
馬路	(马路)	mǎlù	road
高速公路		gāosù gōnglù	freeway
交通		jiāotōng	transportation
方便		fāngbiàn	convenient
風景	(风景)	fēngjǐng	scenery
環境	(环境)	huánjìng	environment; surroundings
優美	(优美)	yōuměi	beautiful
設備	(设备)	shèbèi	facilities; equipment
設施	(设施)	shèshī	installations; facilities
公寓		gōngyù	apartment
宿舍		sùshè	dorm
市場	(市场)	shìchǎng	market
劇院	(剧院)	jùyuàn	theatre
博物館	(博物馆)	bówùguǎn	museum
動物園	(动物园)	dòngwùyuán	zoological garden
隔壁		gébì	next door
鄰居	(邻居)	línjū	neighbor
建築	(建筑)	jiànzhù	architecture
樹林	(树林)	shùlín	woods
河		hé	river
湖		hú	lake
海		hǎi	ocean
海濱	(海滨)	hǎibīn	seashore; seaside
山		shān	mountain; hill

Conversation Prompt

You will have a conversation with your friend about your living situation and environment. He will ask you six questions.

Cultural Presentation Prompt

Ancient Chinese architecture established a unique system with highly developed styles. Choose one aspect to present. In your presentation, give a brief history and geography of the architectural work, and describe its characteristics. If you have been to the place, please talk about your own experience.

Topic Ten: Transportation

交通		jiāotōng	transportation
交通管理		jiāotōng guǎnlǐ	traffic control
交通規則	(交通规则)	jiāotōng guīzé	traffic regulation
交通事故		jiāotōng shìgù	accident
公共汽車	(公共汽车)	gōnggòng qìchē	bus
電車	(电车)	diànchē	cable car; trolley bus; tram
出租汽車	(出租汽车)	chūzū qìchē	taxi
計程車	(计程车)	jìchéngchē	taxi
卡車	(卡车)	kǎchē	truck
地鐵	(地铁)	dìtiě	subway
火車	(火车)	huǒchē	train
飛機	(飞机)	fēijī	airplane
船	(船)	chuán	boat; ship
自行車	(自行车)	zìxíngchē	bicycle
摩托車	(摩托车)	mótuōchē	motorcycle
停車場	(停车场)	tíngchēchǎng	parking lot
車站	(车站)	chēzhàn	stop (of bus, train, etc.)
碼頭	(码头)	mǎtóu	wharf; dock
港口		gǎngkǒu	port; harbor
機場	(机场)	jīchǎng	airport
加油站		jiāyóuzhàn	gas station
人行道		rénxíngdào	sidewalk
速度限制		sùdù xiànzhì	speed limit
交通堵塞		jiāotōng dǔsè	traffic jam
暢通無阻	(畅通无阻)	chàngtōng wúzǔ	unobstructed; unimpeded
水泄不通		shuǐxiè bùtōng	overwhelm
高峰時間	(高峰时间)	gāofēng shíjiān	rush hour
街道		jiēdào	street
綫路	(线路)	xiànlù	route
公共		gōnggòng	public
改善		gǎishàn	improve
狀況	(状况)	zhuàngkuàng	state; situation
條件	(条件)	tiáojiàn	condition
道路		dàolù	road
有效		yǒuxiào	efficient
能源		néngyuán	energy
減少		jiǎnshǎo	reduce
污染		wūrǎn	pollution

Conversation Prompt

You will have a conversation with a Chinese friend about the transportation system in your city. She will ask you six questions.

Cultural Presentation Prompt

Bicycles, as well as motorcycles, are very important for many people in their daily lives. Choose one aspect of this topic to present. In your presentation, discuss why these vehicles are important to people, and also the pros and cons of bicycles and motorcycles versus other transportation methods.

Topic Eleven: Family

家庭生活		jiātíng shēnghuó	family life
代		dài	generation
出身		chūshēn	origin
後代	(后代)	hòudài	descendants; later generations
血緣	(血缘)	xuèyuán	consanguinity; blood relationship
成員	(成员)	chéngyuán	member
祖父		zǔfù	father's father
祖母		zǔmǔ	father's mother
外祖父		wàizǔfù	mother's father
外祖母		wàizǔmǔ	mother's mother
父母		fùmǔ	parent
父親	(父亲)	fùqīn	father
母親	(母亲)	mǔqīn	mother
繼父	(继父)	jìfù	stepfather
繼母	(继母)	jìmǔ	stepmother
養父	(养父)	yǎngfù	adopted father
養母	(养母)	yǎngmǔ	adopted mother
哥哥		gēge	elder brother
姐姐		jiějie	elder sister
弟弟		dìdi	younger brother
妹妹		mèimei	younger sister
親屬	(亲属)	qīnshǔ	relations; relatives
親戚	(亲戚)	qīnqi	relatives
姑母		gūmǔ	father's sister
姨媽	(姨妈)	yímā	mother's sister
大伯		dàbó	father's elder brother
叔叔		shūshu	father's younger brother
舅舅		jiùjiu	mother's brother
子女		zǐnǚ	children
尊敬		zūnjìng	respect
長輩	(长辈)	zhǎngbèi	elder member of a family
晚輩	(晚辈)	wǎnbèi	the younger generation
平輩	(平辈)	píngbèi	person of the same generation
平等		píngděng	equality
期望		qīwàng	hope for and expect
單親	(单亲)	dānqīn	single parent
夫婦	(夫妇)	fūfù	husband and wife
婚姻		hūnyīn	marriage

結婚	(结婚)	jiéhūn	get married
離婚	(离婚)	líhūn	divorce
同居		tóngjū	cohabit; live together in common law
關係	(关系)	guānxì	relation; relationship
融洽		róngqià	harmonious; on friendly terms
緊張	(紧张)	jǐnzhāng	strained
嚴格	(严格)	yángé	strict
家教		jiājiào	family upbringing; family instruction
管		guǎn	care about; contral
關愛	(关爱)	guān'ài	care and concern
溺愛	(溺爱)	nì'ài	spoil (a child)
和睦	(和睦)	hémù	harmony
溫暖	(温暖)	wēnnuǎn	warm
快樂	(快乐)	kuàilè	happy; pleased
穩定	(稳定)	wěndìng	stable
操心		cāoxīn	trouble and worry about
分擔	(分担)	fēndān	share (burden)
家務	(家务)	jiāwù	household duties
家庭主婦	(家庭主妇)	jiātíng zhǔfù	housewife
職業婦女	(职业妇女)	zhíyè fùnǚ	career woman

Conversation Prompt

You will have a conversation with your friend about common issues in today's families. She will ask you six questions.

Cultural Presentation Prompt

The average Chinese family has experienced many changes from traditional to modern lifestyles. In your presentation, choose one family issue (family planning, nuclear families, single-parent families, adopted children, etc.), describe this issue and the changes that led to it, and explain how you feel about this topic.

Topic Twelve: Education

普及教育		pǔjí jiàoyù	universal education
義務教育	(义务教育)	yìwù jiàoyù	compulsory education
優點	(优点)	yōudiǎn	strong point; strengths
缺點	(缺点)	quēdiǎn	shortcomings
方式		fāngshì	method
填鴨式	(填鸭式)	tiányāshì	cramming method (in teaching)
啟發式	(启发式)	qǐfāshì	elicitation method (in teaching); heuristic method
主動性	(主动性)	zhǔdòngxìng	initiative

打基礎	(打基础)	dǎ jīchǔ	establish a foundation
上進心	(上进心)	shàngjìnxīn	the desire to be better; aspiration
督促		dūcù	supervise and urge
鼓勵	(鼓励)	gǔlì	encourage
重視	(重视)	zhòngshì	take seriously; view as important
發揮	(发挥)	fāhuī	bring one's (initiative, etc.) into full play
想象力		xiǎngxiànglì	imagination
創造力	(创造力)	chuàngzàolì	creativity
死記硬背	(死记硬背)	sǐjì yìngbèi	mechanical memorizing
讀書	(读书)	dúshū	study; read
本領	(本领)	běnlǐng	skill; capability
競爭	(竞争)	jìngzhēng	compete
態度	(态度)	tàidu	attitude
認真	(认真)	rènzhēn	earnest; serious
自覺	(自觉)	zìjué	self-aware; self-motivated
壓力	(压力)	yālì	pressure
負擔	(负担)	fùdān	burden; load
淘汰		táotài	eliminate through competition
要求		yāoqiú	demand; require
目標	(目标)	mùbiāo	goal; target
補習班	(补习班)	bǔxíbān	"cram" school
輔導	(辅导)	fǔdǎo	tutor
望子成龍	(望子成龙)	wàngzǐ chénglóng	hope for one's child to be very successful
用心良苦		yòngxīn liángkǔ	have really given much thought to the matter; well-meaning

Conversation Prompt

Track 66 You will have a conversation with an exchange student from China about your opinions on the pros and cons of the American education system. He will ask you six questions.

Cultural Presentation Prompt

1. There are many traditional Chinese stories about learning. Choose one to present. In your presentation, explain the meaning of the proverb or idiom and tell an analogous narrative. Then, talk about the effect of this story on yourself.
2. Choose one feature specific to Chinese education to present. Describe the feature in general and explain how it affects students. Give your opinions on this topic.

Topic Thirteen: Festivities

習俗	(习俗)	xísú	custom; convention; habitude
特色		tèsè	special feature
喜慶	(喜庆)	xǐqìng	auspicious occasion
祝願	(祝愿)	zhùyuàn	wish
氣氛	(气氛)	qìfēn	atmosphere
春節	(春节)	Chūnjié	Spring Festival
除夕		chúxī	Chinese New Year's Eve
鞭炮		biānpào	firecracker
拜年		bài nián	pay someone a visit during Chinese New Year
壓歲錢	(压岁钱)	yāsuìqián	money given to children as a gift during Chinese New Year
紅包	(红包)	hóngbāo	a traditional Chinese red packet with money inside
團圓飯	(团圆饭)	tuányuánfàn	family reunion dinner
年糕		niángāo	Chinese New Year cake
元宵節	(元宵节)	Yuánxiāojié	the Lantern Festival
元宵		yuánxiāo	sweet dumplings made of glutinous rice
花燈	(花灯)	huādēng	festive lantern
燈謎	(灯谜)	dēngmí	lantern riddle
端午節	(端午节)	Duānwǔjié	Dragon Boat Festival
粽子		zòngzi	a kind of dumpling wrapped in bamboo leaves eaten during the Dragon Boat Festival
龍舟	(龙舟)	lóngzhōu	dragon boat
中秋節	(中秋节)	Zhōngqiūjié	the Mid-Autumn Festival
月餅	(月饼)	yuèbǐng	moon cake
賞月	(赏月)	shǎng yuè	enjoy looking at the moon
想念		xiǎngniàn	miss
故鄉	(故乡)	gùxiāng	hometown
闔家團圓	(合家团圆)	héjiā tuányuán	family reunion
聯歡	(联欢)	liánhuān	have a get-together; have a party
晚會	(晚会)	wǎnhuì	a party that takes place in the evening
剪紙	(剪纸)	jiǎnzhǐ	paper-cuts
年畫	(年画)	niánhuà	New Year paintings
舞獅	(舞狮)	wǔ shī	lion dance
舞龍	(舞龙)	wǔ lóng	dragon dance
聖誕節	(圣诞节)	Shèngdànjié	Christmas
基督教		Jīdūjiào	Christianity
平安夜		Píng'ānyè	Christmas Eve
禮拜	(礼拜)	lǐbài	religious service
歡樂	(欢乐)	huānlè	happy; joyful

禮物	(礼物)	lǐwù	present
感恩節	(感恩节)	Gǎn'ēnjié	Thanksgiving
古老		gǔlǎo	ancient
豐盛	(丰盛)	fēngshèng	rich; sumptuous
美味佳肴		měiwèi jiāyáo	delicious food
火鷄	(火鸡)	huǒjī	turkey
南瓜餅	(南瓜饼)	nánguābǐng	pumpkin pie
萬聖節	(万圣节)	Wàngshèngjié	Halloween
服飾	(服饰)	fúshì	dress and personal adornment
五顏六色	(五颜六色)	wǔyán liùsè	colorful
千奇百怪		qiānqí bǎiguài	all kinds of strange sights and happenings
面具		miànjù	mask
糖果		tángguǒ	sweets; candies
情人節	(情人节)	Qíngrénjié	Valentine's Day
巧克力		qiǎokèlì	chocolate
鮮花	(鲜花)	xiānhuā	fresh flowers
母親節	(母亲节)	Mǔqīnjié	Mother's Day
父親節	(父亲节)	Fùqīnjié	Father's Day

Conversation Prompt

Track 67

You will have a conversation with an exchange student about holidays in America and China. She will ask you six questions.

Cultural Presentation Prompt

China has many ethnic groups, all of which have different holidays. In your presentation, choose a traditional Chinese holiday (the Spring Festival, the Lantern Festival, the Mid-Autumn Festival, etc.), and describe the history behind this holiday, traditional customs, related cultural myths, and how the Chinese people celebrate it.

Topic Fourteen: Travel

護照	(护照)	hùzhào	passport
簽證	(签证)	qiānzhèng	visa
領事館	(领事馆)	lǐngshìguǎn	consulate
遊客	(游客)	yóukè	tourist
遊覽區	(游览区)	yóulǎnqū	sightseeing district
旅遊景點	(旅游景点)	lǚyóu jǐngdiǎn	tourist attraction
自然景觀	(自然景观)	zìrán jǐngguān	natural splendor
紀念品	(纪念品)	jìniànpǐn	souvenir
國家公園	(国家公园)	guójiā gōngyuán	national park
旅行社		lǚxíngshè	travel agency
導遊	(导游)	dǎoyóu	tour guide

訂	(订)	dìng	reserve
機票	(机票)	jīpiào	plane ticket
國際航班	(国际航班)	guójì hángbān	international flight
國內航班	(国内航班)	guónèi hángbān	domestic flight
航班號	(航班号)	hángbānhào	flight number
行李		xíngli	luggage
往返旅行		wǎngfǎn lǚxíng	round-trip
單程旅行	(单程旅行)	dānchéng lǚxíng	outbound-journey
飛行	(飞行)	fēixíng	flight; flying
起飛	(起飞)	qǐfēi	take off
到達	(到达)	dàodá	arrive
遠足	(远足)	yuǎnzú	excursion; outing
探險	(探险)	tànxiǎn	expedition
旅館	(旅馆)	lǚguǎn	hotel
汽車旅館	(汽车旅馆)	qìchē lǚguǎn	motel
特快車	(特快车)	tèkuàichē	express train
登記	(登记)	dēngjì	check-in
結帳	(结帐)	jiézhàng	check-out
單人房	(单人房)	dānrénfáng	single room
雙人房	(双人房)	shuāngrénfáng	double room
獨具匠心	(独具匠心)	dújù jiàngxīn	exquisite workmanship with an ingenious design
湖光山色		húguāng shānsè	landscape of lakes and hills
依山傍水		yīshān bàngshuǐ	surrounded by hills on one side and water on the other
景色如畫	(景色如画)	jǐngsè rúhuà	picturesque views
山清水秀		shānqīng shuǐxiù	beautiful mountains and clear waters

Conversation Prompt

You will have a conversation with your roommate about travel. He will ask you six questions.

Cultural Presentation Prompt

There are many famous places and landmarks in China that are UNESCO World Heritage sites. Choose one place (Sichuan Giant Panda Sanctuaries, Mount Huangshan, the Landscape of Guilin, etc.). In your presentation, describe the location, the physical characteristics, and the history behind this place. If you have been there before, include your personal experience as well.

Topic Fifteen: Art

藝術	(艺术)	yìshù	art
藝術作品	(艺术作品)	yìshù zuòpǐn	work of art
藝術家	(艺术家)	yìshùjiā	artist

繪畫	(绘画)	huìhuà	painting; drawing
音樂	(音乐)	yīnyuè	music
舞蹈		wǔdǎo	dance
建築	(建筑)	jiànzhù	building
動畫	(动画)	dònghuà	cartoon
漫畫	(漫画)	mànhuà	caricature
攝影	(摄影)	shèyǐng	photography
畫家	(画家)	huàjiā	painter
模特		mótè	model
畫像	(画像)	huàxiàng	portrait
油畫	(油画)	yóuhuà	Chinese painting
風景畫	(风景画)	fēngjǐnghuà	landscape
工藝品	(工艺品)	gōngyìpǐn	craftwork
園林	(园林)	yuánlín	garden
文房四寶	(文房四宝)	wénfáng sìbǎo	the four treasures of the study: writing brush, ink stick, ink slab, paper
琴棋書畫	(琴棋书画)	qín qí shū huà	the four subjects traditionally studied by educated people: a traditional musical instrument, chess, calligraphy, painting
書法	(书法)	shūfǎ	calligraphy
剪紙	(剪纸)	jiǎnzhǐ	paper-cut
風箏	(风筝)	fēngzheng	kites
對聯	(对联)	duìlián	antithetical couplet
刺繡	(刺绣)	cìxiù	embroidery
中國結	(中国结)	Zhōngguójié	Chinese knot
陶器		táoqì	ceramics
瓷器		cíqì	porcelain
武術	(武术)	wǔshù	martial art
京劇	(京剧)	Jīngjù	Beijing opera
豐富多彩	(丰富多彩)	fēngfù duōcǎi	rich and colorful
寶貴	(宝贵)	bǎoguì	valuable
財富	(财富)	cáifù	wealth; fortune
喜愛	(喜爱)	xǐ'ài	like; favor
經典	(经典)	jīngdiǎn	classics
演出		yǎnchū	performance
欣賞	(欣赏)	xīnshǎng	enjoy
博物館	(博物馆)	bówùguǎn	museum
美術館	(美术馆)	měishùguǎn	pinacotheca

Conversation Prompt

Track 69

You will have a conversation with your roommate about different types of art. He will ask you six questions.

Cultural Presentation Prompt

There are many traditional Chinese art forms. In your presentation, choose one specific form of art (kites, Chinese calligraphy, Chinese embroidery, Chinese ceramics, etc.) and describe and explain the basics of this art, its history, and its significance in Chinese culture. If possible, explain your personal experience with this type of art.

Topic Sixteen: Literature & History

文學	(文学)	wénxué	literature
傑作	(杰作)	jiézuò	masterpiece
古典文學	(古典文学)	gǔdiǎn wénxué	classical literature
現代文學	(现代文学)	xiàndài wénxué	contemporary literature
大衆文學	(大众文学)	dàzhòng wénxué	popular literature
民間文學	(民间文学)	mínjiān wénxué	folklore
網絡文學	(网络文学)	wǎngluò wénxué	Internet literature
博客		bókè	blog
小說	(小说)	xiǎoshuō	novel
愛情小說	(爱情小说)	àiqíng xiǎoshuō	love story
偵探小說	(侦探小说)	zhēntàn xiǎoshuō	detective story
幽默小說	(幽默小说)	yōumò xiǎoshuō	humorous story
歷史小說	(历史小说)	lìshǐ xiǎoshuō	historical novel
散文	(散文)	sǎnwén	prose
詩歌	(诗歌)	shīgē	poetry
劇本	(剧本)	jùběn	play; drama; script
隨筆	(随笔)	suíbǐ	essay
遊記	(游记)	yóujì	book of travels
傳記	(传记)	zhuànjì	biography
報告文學	(报告文学)	bàogào wénxué	reportage
寓言	(寓言)	yùyán	fables; allegory
作家		zuòjiā	writer
作者		zuòzhě	author
詩人	(诗人)	shīrén	poet
名人		míngrén	famous people
讀者	(读者)	dúzhě	reader
觀衆	(观众)	guānzhòng	spectator; audience
刻畫	(刻画)	kèhuà	characterize
描述		miáoshù	describe
人物		rénwù	character; literary figure
生動	(生动)	shēngdòng	vividly
反映		fǎnyìng	reflect
現實	(现实)	xiànshí	reality; actuality
史書	(史书)	shǐshū	historical records
暢銷書	(畅销书)	chàngxiāoshū	best seller

Conversation Prompt

You will have a conversation with your friend about your favorite piece of literature and the history behind it. She will ask you six questions.

Cultural Presentation Prompt

1. There are many famous Chinese literary works. In your presentation, choose one work (a novel, poem, screenplay, etc.), introduce the author, give a brief summary, and state your own opinion of this work.
2. There were many famous people in ancient China. In your presentation, choose one person (Confucius, Qin Shi Huang, Qu Yuan, etc.) and give a brief biography, including important things this person accomplished and how they have affected you in your life.

Topic Seventeen: Society

社會	(社会)	shèhuì	society
政府		zhèngfǔ	government
國家	(国家)	guójiā	country
熱門話題	(热门话题)	rèmén huàtí	hot topic
變化	(变化)	biànhuà	change
現象	(现象)	xiànxiàng	phenomenon
機會	(机会)	jīhuì	opportunity
貧富不均	(贫富不均)	pínfù bùjūn	unequal distribution of wealth
種族	(种族)	zǒngzú	race
歧視	(歧视)	qíshì	discriminate against
婦女	(妇女)	fùnǚ	woman; women in general
重男輕女	(重男轻女)	zhòngnán qīngnǚ	regard males as superior to females
同工同酬		tónggōng tóngchóu	equal pay for equal work
失業	(失业)	shīyè	lose one's job
宗教		zōngjiào	religion
平等		píngděng	equal
公平		gōngpíng	fair
槍支	(枪支)	qiāngzhī	firearms
憲法	(宪法)	xiànfǎ	constitution
私人		sīrén	private individual
犯罪		fànzuì	commit a crime
罪犯		zuìfàn	criminal
殺人	(杀人)	shārén	kill someone
死刑		sǐxíng	death penalty
毒品		dúpǐn	narcotic drugs
賭博	(赌博)	dǔbó	gamble
墮胎	(堕胎)	duòtāi	abortion
偷竊	(偷窃)	tōuqiè	steal; pilfer

搶劫	（抢劫）	qiǎngjié	rob; loot
嚴重	（严重）	yánzhòng	serious
危險	（危险）	wēixiǎn	dangerous; danger
解決	（解决）	jiějué	resolve
辦法	（办法）	bànfǎ	method; way (to solve a problem)
提高		tígāo	improve
地位		dìwèi	status
預防	（预防）	yùfáng	prevention
法律		fǎlǜ	the law
保護	（保护）	bǎohù	protect
保障		bǎozhàng	ensure; safeguard
權利	（权利）	quánlì	right
健全		jiànquán	well-developed (of laws, institutions)
理想		lǐxiǎng	ideal

Conversation Prompt

Track 71

You will have a conversation with an exchange student about problems in American society today. He will ask you six questions.

Cultural Presentation Prompt

There are 56 ethnic groups in China, each of which has developed individual customs. Choose one of these groups, and make a presentation about how these people live. If possible, tell a related story.

Topic Eighteen: Geography & Climate

地理		dìlǐ	geography
國家	（国家）	guójiā	country
面積	（面积）	miànjī	area
人口		rénkǒu	population
國旗	（国旗）	guóqí	national flag
州		zhōu	state
省		shěng	province
縣	（县）	xiàn	county
市		shì	city
區	（区）	qū	district
首都		shǒudū	capital
海洋		hǎiyáng	ocean
森林		sēnlín	forest
沙漠		shāmò	desert
山脈		shānmài	mountain
河流		héliú	river
平原		píngyuán	plain; flatlands

高原		gāoyuán	plateau; highland
山谷		shāngǔ	valley
氣候	(气候)	qìhòu	climate
天氣	(天气)	tiānqì	weather
季節	(季节)	jìjié	season
特點	(特点)	tèdiǎn	feature; special characteristic
平均	(平均)	píngjūn	average
溫度	(温度)	wēndù	temperature
乾燥	(干燥)	gānzào	dry
濕潤	(湿润)	shīrùn	wet
風	(风)	fēng	wind
雨		yǔ	rain
雲	(云)	yún	cloud
全球變暖	(全球变暖)	quánqiú biànnuǎn	global warming
溫室效應	(温室效应)	wēnshì xiàoyìng	greenhouse effect
自然災難	(自然灾难)	zìrán zāinàn	natural disaster
洪水		hóngshuǐ	flood
旱災	(旱灾)	hànzāi	drought
火災	(火灾)	huǒzāi	fire (as a disaster)
地震		dìzhèn	earthquake

Conversation Prompt

Track 72

You will have a conversation with your friend about the geography of a country of your choice. He will ask you six questions.

Cultural Presentation Prompt

1. Choose one place (Beijing, Taipei, Xi'an, Hong Kong, Singapore, etc.) to present. In your presentation, give a report on this place. If you have been there, describe your experience there.

2. There are many unique natural landmarks in China. Choose one natural tourist attraction. In your presentation, describe this place. If you have been there, describe your experience there.

Topic Nineteen: Science & Technology

科學	(科学)	kēxué	science
科學家	(科学家)	kēxuéjiā	scientist
電子	(电子)	diànzǐ	electronics
高科技	(高科技)	gāokējì	high technology
機器人	(机器人)	jīqìrén	robot
電腦	(电脑)	diànnǎo	computer
網絡	(网络)	wǎngluò	Internet
電子信	(电子信)	diànzǐxìn	e-mail
手機	(手机)	shǒujī	cell phone
發明	(发明)	fāmíng	invention

克隆		kèlóng	cloning
太陽能	(太阳能)	tàiyángnéng	solar energy
汽車	(汽车)	qìchē	automobile
實現	(实现)	shíxiàn	realize
夢想	(梦想)	mèngxiǎng	dream
改善		gǎishàn	improve
改變	(改变)	gǎibiàn	changed
提高		tígāo	raise; heighten; advance
效率		xiàolǜ	efficiency
積極面	(积极面)	jījímiàn	positive side
消極面	(消极面)	xiāojímiàn	negative side

Conversation Prompt

You will have a conversation with your teacher about how technology affects people's daily lives. He will ask you six questions.

Cultural Presentation Prompt

1. Traditional Chinese medicine is an important part of Chinese culture. Choose one aspect of Chinese medicine and elaborate on this subject.
2. Many inventions of ancient China affect people to this day. Choose one invention (gunpowder, paper, fireworks, compass, etc.), give a brief history of it, and explain its historical significance.

Topic Twenty: Humans & Nature

人類	(人类)	rénlèi	humanity
自然		zìrán	nature
動物	(动物)	dòngwù	animal
生物		shēngwù	biology
植物		zhíwù	plant
環境	(环境)	huánjìng	environment
保護	(保护)	bǎohù	protection
污染		wūrǎn	pollution; pollute
資源	(资源)	zīyuán	resource
能源		néngyuán	energy resources
生態	(生态)	shēngtài	ecology
平衡		pínghéng	balance; balanced
工業	(工业)	gōngyè	industry
化學	(化学)	huàxué	chemistry
廢物	(废物)	fèiwù	wastes
垃圾		lājī	trash; garbage
排放		páifàng	discharge
廢氣	(废气)	fèiqì	waste gas or steam
廢渣	(废渣)	fèizhā	waste residue; solid waste
廢水	(废水)	fèishuǐ	waste water

噪音		zàoyīn	noise
臭氧層	(臭氧层)	chòuyǎngcéng	ozone layer; ozonosphere
酸雨		suānyǔ	acid rain
治理		zhìlǐ	bring under control; manage
回收		huíshōu	recycle
廢物利用	(废物利用)	fèiwù lìyòng	waste use
實驗	(实验)	shíyàn	experiment
解剖	(解剖)	jiěpōu	dissect
人道		réndào	humanitarianism; humane
殘忍	(残忍)	cánrěn	brutal; cruel
忽略		hūlüè	overlook; ignore
意識	(意识)	yìshí	consciousness
薄弱		bóruò	weak; frail
虐待		nüèdài	abuse
野蠻	(野蛮)	yěmán	barbarous; uncivilized
破壞	(破坏)	pòhuài	destroy
熱帶雨林	(热带雨林)	rèdài yǔlín	tropical rain forest
稀有		xīyǒu	rare
珍貴	(珍贵)	zhēnguì	valuable; precious
面臨	(面临)	miànlín	face; be confronted with
瀕臨	(濒临)	bīnlín	be on the verge of
滅絕	(灭绝)	mièjué	exterminate; become extinct
抗議	(抗议)	kàngyì	protest; protection
避免		bìmiǎn	avoid
採取	(采取)	cǎiqǔ	take; adopt (measures, methods, steps)
措施		cuòshī	measure; step
保護區	(保护区)	bǎohùqū	protected area

Conversation Prompt

You will have a conversation with a Chinese student about the environment. She will ask you six questions.

Cultural Presentation Prompt

There are 12 zodiac signs in Chinese, which are used to symbolize the year in which a person is born. In your presentation, talk about your own sign and explain the meaning of your sign in Chinese culture. If possible, tell a related story.

SPEAKING SKILLS

The Conversation scripts are presented in traditional characters first, followed by the simplified version, without labels.

You will participate in several conversations. Each conversation is about a specific topic. After listening to each question, pause your CD player and respond to that question. Allow yourself 20 seconds to respond. Then press the play button to continue on to the next question.

Topic One
You will have a conversation with a new student about the extracurricular activities offered at your school. She will ask you six questions.

1. 你好，我叫孫良。請問你這個學期一共上幾門課？
   你好，我叫孙良。请问你这个学期一共上几门课？

2. 你每天什麼時間上課？
   你每天什么时间上课？

3. 你最喜歡的課是哪一門？最不喜歡的呢？
   你最喜欢的课是哪一门？最不喜欢的呢？

4. 你們學校有哪些課外活動？
   你们学校有哪些课外活动？

5. 你們學校有哪些俱樂部？
   你们学校有哪些俱乐部？

6. 加入俱樂部應該怎麼申請？
   加入俱乐部应该怎么申请？

Topic Two
You will have a conversation with Yu Pingping, a reporter from your school newspaper, who is interviewing you about your opinion on sports. She will ask you six questions.

1. 你好，我是于平平。請問，你們每天都上體育課嗎？
   你好，我是于平平。请问，你们每天都上体育课吗？

2. 你們在體育課上做什麼？
   你们在体育课上做什么？

3. 你最喜歡的體育項目是什麼？
   你最喜欢的体育项目是什么？

4. 你們學校有哪些體育俱樂部？你參加了嗎？
   你们学校有哪些体育俱乐部？你参加了吗？

5. 你能談談最有意思的一次體育課嗎？
   你能谈谈最有意思的一次体育课吗？

6. 學校的哪一場體育比賽給你的印象最深？
   学校的哪一场体育比赛给你的印象最深？

Track 57

Topic Three

You will have a conversation with your Chinese teacher about students' lifestyles in the United States. She will ask you six questions.

1. 你覺得什麼是 "生活方式"？
   你觉得什么是 "生活方式"？

2. 對你來說健康的生活方式是什麼？
   对你来说健康的生活方式是什么？

3. 中學生中有哪些不健康的生活方式？
   中学生中有哪些不健康的生活方式？

4. 你對自己的生活方式滿意嗎？
   你对自己的生活方式满意吗？

5. 你認爲生活方式跟學習有關係嗎？
   你认为生活方式跟学习有关系吗？

6. 關於中學生的生活方式，你有什麼建議？
   关于中学生的生活方式，你有什么建议？

Track 58

Topic Four

You will have a conversation with Zhang Lin, a school news reporter, about your hobbies and interests. She will ask you six questions.

1. 你好，我是張林。請問，你最喜歡看的電視節目是什麼？
   你好，我是张林。请问，你最喜欢看的电视节目是什么？

2. 你最喜歡看哪方面的電影？
   你最喜欢看哪方面的电影？

3. 你經常看電影嗎？經常是跟誰一起看的？
   你经常看电影吗？经常是跟谁一起看的？

4. 給你印象最深的電影是哪一部？
   给你印象最深的电影是哪一部？

5. 你喜歡聽音樂嗎？一般是什麼時候聽？
   你喜欢听音乐吗？一般是什么时候听？

6. 你最喜歡的藝人是誰？爲什麼喜歡他/她？
   你最喜欢的艺人是谁？为什么喜欢他/她？

Topic Five

You will have a conversation with Gu Wei, a reporter from a radio station, who is interviewing people about high school students with part-time jobs. He will ask you six questions.

1. 你好，我叫顧偉。我想問你一個問題，你打過工嗎？
   你好，我叫顾伟。我想问你一个问题，你打过工吗？

2. 同學中打工的多嗎？　中學生通過什麼方式找工作？
   同学中打工的多吗？　中学生通过什么方式找工作？

3. 一般是做些什麼工作？
   一般是做些什么工作？

4. 打工掙的錢怎麼花呢？
   打工挣的钱怎么花呢？

5. 家長同意你們打工嗎？他們怎麼看待這個問題？
   家长同意你们打工吗？他们怎么看待这个问题？

6. 人的精力和時間都是有限的，你怎麼處理工作和學習的關係？
   人的精力和时间都是有限的，你怎么处理工作和学习的关系？

Topic Six

You will have a conversation with a Chinese teacher, Lu Xiaomin, about friendships and relationships in high school. She will ask you six questions.

1. 你好，我是陸小民老師。你最好的朋友是誰呀？你們是怎麼認識的？
   你好，我是陆小民老师。你最好的朋友是谁呀？你们是怎么认识的？

2. 你怎麼跟朋友保持聯繫？
   你怎么跟朋友保持联系？

3. 爲什麼說人應該有朋友？
   为什么说人应该有朋友？

4. 你找朋友的標準是什麼？
   你找朋友的标准是什么？

5. 什麼是真正的朋友？
   什么是真正的朋友？

6. 你是怎麼看待網上交朋友這個問題的？
   你是怎么看待网上交朋友这个问题的？

Topic Seven

You will have a conversation with Wang Yang, a new student at your school, about fashion styles for high school students, and the standard for buying clothes. She will ask you six questions.

1. 你好！我是王陽。我想問你幾個問題，你喜歡買衣服嗎？
   你好！我是王阳。我想问你几个问题，你喜欢买衣服吗？

2. 你一般跟誰一起買衣服？
   你一般跟谁一起买衣服？

3. 你喜歡什麼顏色的衣服？
   你喜欢什么颜色的衣服？

4. 你喜歡什麼樣式的衣服？
   你喜欢什么样式的衣服？

5. 你買衣服的標準是什麼？
   你买衣服的标准是什么？

6. 你買名牌衣服嗎？
   你买名牌衣服吗？

Topic Eight

You will have a conversation with your friend Li Haixia about food. She will ask you six questions.

1. 你最喜歡吃的菜是什麼？
   你最喜欢吃的菜是什么？

2. 你媽媽做什麼菜最拿手？
   你妈妈做什么菜最拿手？

3. 你最喜歡的餐館是哪一家？
   你最喜欢的餐馆是哪一家？

4. 你喜歡吃中國菜嗎？
   你喜欢吃中国菜吗？

5. 有人說中國菜不健康，你怎麼看？
   有人说中国菜不健康，你怎么看？

6. 中國人和美國人飲食習慣有什麼不同？
   中国人和美国人饮食习惯有什么不同？

Topic Nine

You will have a conversation with your friend about your living situation and environment. He will ask you six questions.

1. 你住的地方環境怎麼樣？
   你住的地方环境怎么样？

2. 你住的地方大不大？安不安靜？
   你住的地方大不大？安不安静？

3. 你是一個人住還是跟別人一起住？
   你是一个人住还是跟别人一起住？

4. 你的房間裏有哪些家具？
   你的房间里有哪些家具？

5. 你喜歡什麼樣的房間？
   你喜欢什么样的房间？

6. 上大學以後，你想自己住還是找個同屋一起住？
   上大学以后，你想自己住还是找个同屋一起住？

Topic Ten

You will have a conversation with a Chinese friend about the transportation system in your city. She will ask you six questions.

1. 你每天怎麼去學校？
   你每天怎么去学校？

2. 你們城市的公共交通工具有哪些？
   你们城市的公共交通工具有哪些？

3. 車票貴不貴？
   车票贵不贵？

4. 你們城市的交通狀況怎麼樣？
   你们城市的交通状况怎么样？

5. 交通事故多嗎？
   交通事故多吗？

6. 你對改善交通條件有什麼建議嗎？
   你对改善交通条件有什么建议吗？

Topic Eleven

You will have a conversation with your friend about common issues in today's families. She will ask you six questions.

1. 你家有幾口人？
   你家有几口人？

2. 你的家人有什麼休閒活動？
   你的家人有什么休闲活动？

3. 在家裏，最開心的事是什麼？
   在家里，最开心的事是什么？

4. 對你來說幸福的家庭是什麼？
   对你来说幸福的家庭是什么？

5. 家裏有沒有發生過什麼不愉快的事情？
   家里有没有发生过什么不愉快的事情？

6. 你覺得你的家庭跟別的美國家庭有什麼不一樣嗎？
   你觉得你的家庭跟别的美国家庭有什么不一样吗？

Topic Twelve

Track 66

You will have a conversation with an exchange student from China about your opinions on the pros and cons of the American education system. He will ask you six questions.

1. 你好。我是新來的交換學生。你能給我介紹一下學校老師的情況嗎?
   你好。我是新来的交换学生。你能给我介绍一下学校老师的情况吗?

2. 你最喜歡哪位老師的教學方法?
   你最喜欢哪位老师的教学方法?

3. 哪位老師對你的影響最大?
   哪位老师对你的影响最大?

4. 你準備選哪一所大學?
   你准备选哪一所大学?

5. 你選擇大學的標準是什麼?
   你选择大学的标准是什么?

6. 美國大學招生要考慮哪些因素?
   美国大学招生要考虑哪些因素?

Topic Thirteen

Track 67

You will have a conversation with an exchange student about holidays in America and in China. She will ask you six questions.

1. 你們國家有哪些傳統節日?
   你们国家有哪些传统节日?

2. 你們國家有哪些紀念節日?
   你们国家有哪些纪念节日?

3. 你最喜歡的節日是哪一個?
   你最喜欢的节日是哪一个?

4. 在你們國家,哪些節日是家人團圓的日子?
   在你们国家,哪些节日是家人团圆的日子?

5. 你的家人過節的時候互相送禮物嗎?
   你的家人过节的时候互相送礼物吗?

6. 哪一次節日給你留下的印象最深?
   哪一次节日给你留下的印象最深?

Topic Fourteen

Track 68

You will have a conversation with your roommate about travel. He will ask you six questions.

1. 我看你好像很喜歡旅遊,是不是?
   我看你好像很喜欢旅游,是不是?

2. 你都去過哪些地方旅遊?
   你都去过哪些地方旅游?

3. 哪一次旅遊給你的印象最深？
   哪一次旅游给你的印象最深？

4. 我覺得跟誰一起去旅遊很重要，你最喜歡跟誰去呢？
   我觉得跟谁一起去旅游很重要，你最喜欢跟谁去呢？

5. 有沒有哪次旅遊讓你覺得很沒有意思？
   有没有哪次旅游让你觉得很没有意思？

6. 你們國家的人一般選擇什麼方式旅遊？ 如果出國， 常去哪些國家呢？
   你们国家的人一般选择什么方式旅游？ 如果出国， 常去哪些国家呢？

Topic Fifteen

You will have a conversation with your roommate about different types of art. He will ask you six questions.

1. 學校開設了一些藝術課程，你選了嗎？
   学校开设了一些艺术课程，你选了吗？

2. 你有什麼藝術特長嗎？
   你有什么艺术特长吗？

3. 你最喜歡的藝術家是哪一位？
   你最喜欢的艺术家是哪一位？

4. 哪一部藝術作品給你印象最深刻？
   哪一部艺术作品给你印象最深刻？

5. 人們說，藝術家看起來和普通人不太一樣，是這樣嗎？
   人们说，艺术家看起来和普通人不太一样，是这样吗？

6. 生活離不開藝術，你同意這種說法嗎？
   生活离不开艺术，你同意这种说法吗？

Topic Sixteen

You will have a conversation with your friend about your favorite piece of literature and the history behind it. She will ask you six questions.

1. 你最喜歡的文學作品是什麼？ 誰寫的？
   你最喜欢的文学作品是什么？ 谁写的？

2. 作品主要談論了什麼問題？
   作品主要谈论了什么问题？

3. 書中給你印象最深的是哪一部分？
   书中给你印象最深的是哪一部分？

4. 你想當文學家嗎？
   你想当文学家吗？

5. 哪一位文學家對你的成長最有影響？
   哪一位文学家对你的成长最有影响？

6. 你學了美國歷史，也學了世界歷史，你最喜歡哪位歷史人物？
   你学了美国历史，也学了世界历史，你最喜欢哪位历史人物？

Track
71

Topic Seventeen

You will have a conversation with an exchange student about problems in American society today. He will ask you six questions.

1. 我剛來美國，對美國不太瞭解。我想知道美國當前社會存在哪些問題？
   我刚来美国，对美国不太了解。我想知道美国当前社会存在哪些问题？

2. 我看電視上常常討論槍支問題，還和憲法有關係，是怎麼回事？
   我看电视上常常讨论枪支问题，还和宪法有关系，是怎么回事？

3. 關於死刑問題，你怎麼看？
   关于死刑问题，你怎么看？

4. 在你周圍的中學生中，有人吸毒嗎？
   在你周围的中学生中，有人吸毒吗？

5. 你怎麼看待墮胎問題？
   你怎么看待堕胎问题？

6. 你心目中的理想社會是什麼樣子的？
   你心目中的理想社会是什么样子的？

Track
72

Topic Eighteen

You will have a conversation with your friend about the geography of a country of your choice. He will ask you six questions.

1. 你們國家有多少個州或者省？有哪些大城市？
   你们国家有多少个州或者省？有哪些大城市？

2. 你們的國旗是什麼樣子的？
   你们的国旗是什么样子的？

3. 你住的地方好不好？
   你住的地方好不好？

4. 那裏的氣候有什麼特點？
   那里的气候有什么特点？

5. 談談氣候對你們生活的影響。
   谈谈气候对你们生活的影响。

6. 你覺得你們的國家什麼地方最適合人們居住？
   你觉得你们的国家什么地方最适合人们居住？

Track
73

Topic Nineteen

You will have a conversation with your teacher about how technology affects people's daily lives. He will ask you six questions.

1. 科學課上學的內容，你最喜歡哪部分？
   科学课上学的内容，你最喜欢哪部分？

2. 對你影響最深的科技電影是哪一部？
   对你影响最深的科技电影是哪一部？

3. 歷史上有很多著名的科學家，那麼你最喜愛的科學家是誰？
   历史上有很多著名的科学家，那么你最喜爱的科学家是谁？

4. 你想當科學家嗎？
   你想当科学家吗？

5. 生活中處處是科學，談談你對這個問題的看法。
   生活中处处是科学，谈谈你对这个问题的看法。

6. 有人說科學發展過程中，總會有不好的東西隨著出現，談談你的看法。
   有人说科学发展过程中，总会有不好的东西随着出现，谈谈你的看法。

Topic Twenty

You will have a conversation with a Chinese student about the environment. She will ask you six questions.

1. 目前有哪些比較嚴重的環境污染問題？
   目前有哪些比较严重的环境污染问题？

2. 哪些污染對人體健康造成危害？
   哪些污染对人体健康造成危害？

3. 你對解決環境污染問題有什麼建議？
   你对解决环境污染问题有什么建议？

4. 你自己能爲保護環境做什麼？
   你自己能为保护环境做什么？

5. 人們說動物是人類的朋友，你同意嗎？
   人们说动物是人类的朋友，你同意吗？

6. 你怎麼看待科學家用動物做實驗的問題？
   你怎么看待科学家用动物做实验的问题？

Grammar Review

This chapter reviews a wide range of Chinese grammar, aiming to help students enhance their grammar proficiency in preparation for the AP Chinese exam. The grammar tips in this chapter focus on strengthening students' skills for the Speaking and Writing free-response parts of the AP Chinese test; the chapter also provides 100 examples of common sentence patterns in spoken Chinese. By studying this section, students will not only learn a variety of grammatical structures but also enrich their vocabulary. As we have emphasized throughout this book, the more elaborate students' grammar and vocabulary are, the better prepared they will be for the Listening, Reading, Writing, and Speaking portions of the exam.

All grammar examples presented in this chapter are printed in traditional characters first, followed by simplified characters. The answer explanations will be in traditional characters, followed by simplified characters in parentheses.

COMPLEMENTS

Resultative Complements

In Chinese, a verb can be followed by an adjective or another verb to indicate the result of an action. The adjective or the second verb is called a resultative complement. For example:

> 我吃飽了。
> 我吃饱了。
>
> 不管我的同屋喜不喜歡我，我都不會搬出去。
> 不管我的同屋喜不喜欢我，我都不会搬出去。

Some verbs can only take certain other verbs or adjectives as their resultative complements. Students should remember that each verb and its resultative complements must be viewed as one word: Also note that only verbs and adjectives, because they are able to convey a sense of result, can serve as resultative complements.

Such *verbs* include: "會" ("会"), "完", "見" ("见"), "懂", "開" ("开"), "住", "給" ("给"), "倒", "掉", "死", etc.

Such *adjectives* include: "對" ("对"), "錯" ("错"), "好", "壞" ("坏"), "早", "晚", "清楚", etc.

Again, a resultative complement indicates the result or completion of an action. For example:

> 今天的作業一定要做完。
> 今天的作业一定要做完。

> 我的學生證丟了，我找了半天也沒找到。
> 我的学生证丢了，我找了半天也没找到。

A resultative complement can also clarify an action or a state. For example:

> 你們都聽懂了嗎？
> 你们都听懂了吗？

> 他吃了三個漢堡包還沒吃飽。
> 他吃了三个汉堡包还没吃饱。

Some resultative complements that appear after adjectives or verbs denote psychological state of an extreme degree. For example:

> 她的手提電腦丟了，她快急死了。
> 她的手提电脑丢了，她快急死了。

> 他考上了哈佛，他父母可樂壞了。
> 他考上了哈佛，他父母可乐坏了。

Directional Complements (Indicating Direction)

The simplest directional complements are formed from direction verbs and either "來" ("来") or "去" to indicate motion toward or away from the speaker. There are six basic direction verbs: "上", "下", "進" ("进"), "出", "回", "過" ("过"). When combined with "來"("来") and "去", they yield twelve different complements: "上來" ("上来"), "上去", "下來" ("下来"), "下去", "進來" ("进来"), "進去" ("进去"), "出來 ("出来"), "出去", "回來" ("回来"), "回去", "過來" ("过来"), "過去" ("过去"). These twelve directional complements can serve as compound directional complements when attached to other verbs, such as "走進來" ("走进来"), "站過去" ("站过去"), "坐下來" ("坐下来"), etc. The main verb expresses the action, while the complement describes the direction in which the action is carried out. Any action verb that involves directional movement may become a compound directional complement.

main verb	directional complement
走	進來 (进来)
站	過去 (过去)
坐	下來 (下来)

If the directional complement is followed by an object, the object (noun) can be placed either before or after the main verb, or it can be inserted between the main verb and the direction verb. For example:

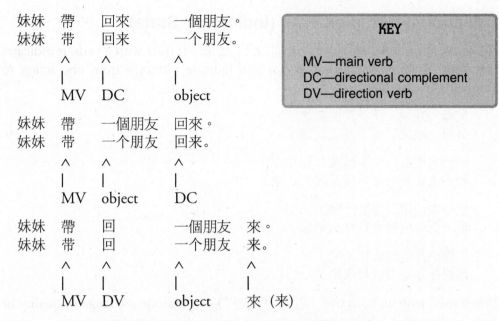

妹妹　帶　回來　　一個朋友。
妹妹　帶　回来　　一个朋友。
　　　∧　∧　　　∧
　　　|　|　　　|
　　　MV　DC　　　object

妹妹　帶　一個朋友　回來。
妹妹　帶　一个朋友　回来。
　　　∧　∧　　　∧
　　　|　|　　　|
　　　MV　object　DC

妹妹　帶　回　一個朋友　來。
妹妹　帶　回　一个朋友　来。
　　　∧　∧　　∧　　∧
　　　|　|　　|　　|
　　　MV　DV　object　來 (来)

KEY

MV—main verb
DC—directional complement
DV—direction verb

If the object signifies a place, it is usually inserted *after* the direction verb, or *between* the main verb and the direction verb. For example:

他明年　回　中國　來。
他明年　回　中国　来。
　　　∧　∧　　∧
　　　|　|　　| |
　　　DV　place　來 (来)

請你們　搬　進　宿舍　去。
请你们　搬　进　宿舍　去。
　　　∧　∧　∧　　∧
　　　|　|　|　　|
　　　MV　DV　object　去

Directional complements can also be used with a 把-sentence. For example:

請你　把　借的書　還　回　圖書館　去。
请你　把　借的书　还　回　图书馆　去。
　　∧　　∧　　∧　∧　　∧　　∧
　　|　　|　　|　|　　|　　|
　　把　　object　MV　DV　object　去

他們　把　椅子　搬　進　客廳裏　來了。
他们　把　椅子　搬　进　客厅里　来了。
　　∧　　∧　　∧　∧　　∧　　∧
　　|　　|　　|　|　　|　　|
　　把　　object　MV　DV　object　來 (来)

Directional Complements (Indicating State)

When the directional complement "起來" ("起来") is used with a verb, it indicates that another action is starting. It can also indicate a change from one action to another. For example:

父母一吵架，孩子就哭起來了。
父母一吵架，孩子就哭起来了。

兩個老朋友一坐下就聊起天兒來。
两个老朋友一坐下就聊起天儿来。

他一看起電視來把什麼都忘了。
他一看起电视来把什么都忘了。

你快把那些書收起來吧。
你快把那些书收起来吧。

When used with an adjective, "起來" ("起來") can indicate a change in quality or state, such as speed, light, temperature, or weight. For example:

水所以深起來是因爲下大雨了。
水所以深起来是因为下大雨了。

美國汽油的價格從上個月高起來了。
美国汽油的价格从上个月高起来了。

這兩年學中文的人一下子多起來了。
这两年学中文的人一下子多起来了。

When the directional complement "下來" ("下来") is used with an adjective, it indicates the decrease of a quality to a lesser state, such as a gradual change from bright to dark, strong to weak, motion to stillness, and so on. For example:

天慢慢地黑下來了。
天慢慢地黑下來了。

只要媽媽生氣，她的聲音就會低下來。
只要妈妈生气，她的声音就会低下来。

燈關了，房間裏黑了下來。
灯关了，房间里黑了下来。

你瘦下來了，我卻胖起來了。
你瘦下来了，我却胖起来了。

When "下來" ("下来") is used with a verb, it indicates that something has become settled or fixed as the result of an action. For example:

父母叫他快點兒把專業定下來。
父母叫他快点儿把专业定下来。

她想在紐約住下來。
她想在纽约住下来。

老師講的語法你都記下來了嗎？
老师讲的语法你都记下来了吗？

The directional complement "下去" indicates the continuation of a state or an action. When "下去" is used with an adjective, it may indicate not just the continuation of a state but its intensification as well. For example:

說下去！
说下去！

這部電影我看不下去了。
这部电影我看不下去了。

看起來天氣會冷下去。
看起来天气会冷下去。

Directional Complements (Indicating Result)

A directional complement used with "V + 出來" ("V + 出来") signifies a change in status. When there is an object, one can often leave out the word "來" ("来").

他	想	出來	一個好辦法。
他	想	出来	一个好办法。
^	^	^	
|	|	|	
MV	DC	object	

This can be rewritten as:

他　想　出　一個好辦法。
他　想　出　一个好办法。

When the directional complement occurs at the end of a sentence, however, one must use the full complement.

她是日本人，	可是以前我一點兒都沒看	出來。
她是日本人，	可是以前我一点儿都没看	出来。
這兩台洗衣機有什麼不同，	我根本看不	出來。
这两台洗衣机有什么不同，	我根本看不	出来。
	^	^
	|	|
	MV	DC

A directional complement with "V + 起來" ("V + 起来") means "seem." For example:

這臺電視機看起來是日本生產的。
这台电视机看起来是日本生产的。

這首歌聽起來不是她唱的。
这首歌听起来不是她唱的。

這個菜吃起來肯定不是你做的，是你媽媽做的吧？
这个菜吃起来肯定不是你做的，是你妈妈做的吧？

Complements of State

A complement of state is usually placed after a verb or an adjective, with the structural particle "得." It expresses a degree, an evaluation, a judgment, or a description related to a verb, an adjective, or a noun preceding "得." For example:

她高興得跳起來。
她高兴得跳起来。

我的功課多得很。
我的功课多得很。

In a negative form, the word "不" or "沒有" ("没有") is placed after a verb or an adjective, preceding the complement. For example:

天氣熱得我吃不下飯。
天气热得我吃不下饭。

To use a complement of state in a sentence with a direct object, the verb is repeated.

我今天考試考得不太理想。
我今天考试考得不太理想。

If the verb is not repeated, the object must be placed before the subject or the verb.

這部電影看得我快睡著了。
这部电影看得我快睡着了。

Potential Complements

Potential complements are formed by inserting "得" or "不" between a verb and a resultative complement. For example:

今天的作業你半個小時做得完嗎？
今天的作业你半个小时做得完吗？

Or, they may appear between a verb and a directional complement to indicate whether a certain result will be realized or not.

開車太難了，我學不下去了。
开车太难了，我学不下去了。

The complements can be constructed as the equivalent of "能" and "不能." Consider an example using #1 from above:

今天的作業你半個小時能做完嗎？
今天的作业你半个小时能做完吗？

Potential complements appear primarily in negative sentences, or in questions. The complements that appear in affirmative sentences become the *resultative* complements discussed earlier. The affirmative form of the resultative complement and the negative form of a potential complement can be put together to form a question. For example:

Q: 那本中文字典你　　買得到　　買不到？
　　那本中文字典你　　买得到　　买不到？

A: 買得到。
　　买得到。

A: 買不到。
　　买不到。

Potential complements have a unique function that cannot be fulfilled by the "不能 + verb + complement" construction. A potential complement cannot be used in a "把"—sentence, either. The following sentences are ***incorrect***.

老師說得太快了，我不能聽清楚。
老师说得太快了，我不能听清楚。

你車太小了，我們五個人不能都坐下。
你车太小了，我们五个人不能都坐下。

我家沒有多少錢，我不能上那麼貴的大學。
我家没有多少钱，我不能上那么贵的大学。

我把今天的功課做不完。
我把今天的功课做不完。

The following sentences are **correct**.

老師說得太快了，我聽不清楚。
老师说得太快了，我听不清楚。

你車太小了，我們五個人坐不下。
你车太小了，我们五个人坐不下。

我家沒有多少錢，我上不了那麼貴的大學。
我家没有多少钱，我上不了那么贵的大学。

我今天的功課做不完。
我今天的功课做不完。

SENTENCES WITH SPECIAL PREDICATES

The "是"—Sentences

Sentences with "是" as the predicate are known as "是"—sentences. The negative form of a "是"—sentence is formed by adding the negative adverb "不" before "是." The subject of the "是"—sentence may be a noun:

華盛頓市是美國的首都。
华盛顿市是美国的首都。

a pronoun:

我是高中二年級的學生。
我是高中二年级的学生。

a verb:

休息也是一種工作。
休息也是一种工作。

an adjective:

熱情是她最大的特點。
热情是她最大的特点。

a numeral–measure word phrase:

二十一點就是晚上九點。
二十一点就是晚上九点。

a verb-object phrase:

學中文是一項艱巨的任務。
学中文是一项艰巨的任务。

a complementary phrase:

努力工作是成功的條件。
努力工作是成功的条件。

or a 的-phrase:

穿黑色衣服的不是我們的歷史老師，穿白衣服的是。
穿黑色衣服的不是我们的历史老师，穿白衣服的是。

The object following the predicate verb "是" may include a noun:

我爸爸是醫生，媽媽是老師。
我爸爸是医生，妈妈是老师。

a pronoun:

把這件事告訴老師的人是她，不是我。
把这件事告诉老师的人是她，不是我。

a verb phrase:

做家庭婦女也是工作。
做家庭妇女也是工作。

an adjective:

那個老師的特點是嚴格。
那个老师的特点是严格。

a numeral-measure word phrase:

今天最高氣溫是98度。
今天最高气温是98度。

a 的-phrase:

那個帥哥是個打籃球的。
那个帅哥是个打篮球的。

a verb-object phrase:

爸爸最不喜歡的事情是逛商店。
爸爸最不喜欢的事情是逛商店。

a complementary phrase

你今天的任務就是休息好。
你今天的任务就是休息好。

a subject-predicate phrase:

這次作業的安排是大家在課堂上一起做。
这次作业的安排是大家在课堂上一起做。

Note that the verb "是" remains unchanged in this form in all situations. It can signify any time, place, person, or thing, and requires no conjugation for tense or gender.

THE PASSIVE VOICE

A sentence whose subject is the receiver of an action is called a passive sentence.

Sentences with the Passive Marker "被"

Pattern: Subject +被+ object + verb + other element
Examples：

我的書被郵局寄丟了。
我的书被邮局寄丢了。

那個小男孩被他爸爸罵了一頓。
那个小男孩被他爸爸骂了一顿。

我家的猫被一隻老鼠咬傷了。
我家的猫被一只老鼠咬伤了。

Note that in a sentence with the passive marker "被," the "doer" may be implicit. For example:

他被叫到老師的辦公室去了。
他被叫到老师的办公室去了。

座位全都被坐了。

那種名牌牛仔褲被買光了。
那种名牌牛仔裤被买光了。

A sentence with the passive marker "被" sometimes refers to unpleasant or undesired situations. For example:

他被女朋友甩了。

我被罰款了。
我被罚款了。

An adverb must be placed before the word "被." For example:

他總是被批評。
他总是被批评。

那個女孩子很乖，常常被大人誇獎。
那个女孩子很乖，常常被大人夸奖。

The passive markers can also be "叫," "讓" ("让"), or "給" ("给"). For example:

洗衣機讓人修好了。
洗衣机让人修好了。

我的車叫誰開走了？
我的车叫谁开走了？

酒都給他喝完了。
酒都给他喝完了。

Unmarked Passive Sentences

Some sentences have no special marker words to indicate the passive voice but nevertheless are notionally passive (passive in meaning). For example:

水果吃完了，應該去買了。
水果吃完了，应该去买了。

房子租好了，明天搬家吧。

護照帶了嗎？
护照带了吗？

這次作業做得不錯。
这次作业做得不错。

THE "把"—SENTENCES

The "把" sentence is used with actions that change the state of a definite object. For example:

老師把我的作業丟了。
老师把我的作业丢了。

請後邊的同學把窗戶關上。
请后边的同学把窗户关上。

There must be another element following the verb, such as:

a complement of result:

她把衣服洗了。

a complement of manner:

她把衣服洗得很乾淨。
她把衣服洗得很干净。

a directional complement:

她把衣服拿回來了。
她把衣服拿回來了。

an aspect particle "了":

她把衣服丟了。

The object in a 把—sentence is usually definite. The speaker is referring to a particular item or items in the real world, which are presumably known to both the speaker and addressee. For example:

你把那扇門打開。
你把那扇门打开。

外面下雨呢，你把我的雨傘帶上吧。
外面下雨呢，你把我的雨伞带上吧。

The main verb in a "把"—sentence must be an action verb, such as "打", "穿", "拉", "準備" ("准备"), "佈置" ("布置"), etc. For example:

今天外面很冷，出門的時候把那件大衣穿上。
今天外面很冷，出门的时候把那件大衣穿上。

太危險了，快把孩子拉回來。
太危险了，快把孩子拉回来。

請大家把筆和紙準備好，我們開始聽寫。
请大家把笔和纸准备好，我们开始听写。

Note that in a "把"—sentence, negative adverbs and modal verbs can be placed before "把." For example:

你不把中文功課做完就不能去看電影。
你不把中文功课做完就不能去看电影。

我想把男朋友送給我的新衣服穿上。
我想把男朋友送给我的新衣服穿上。

Note also, if the object is too long (e.g., contains one or more modifiers), using the "把" pattern may result in a smoother, more natural phrasing than if the long object were to follow the verb. For example:

妹妹把去年我父母從中國給她買的中文書借給同學了。
妹妹把去年我父母从中国给她买的中文书借给同学了。

他把在高中校園裏聽到的那個可怕的消息告訴了我。
他把在高中校园里听到的那个可怕的消息告诉了我。

EXISTENTIAL SENTENCES

Existential sentences indicate the existence of some *thing*(s) at some *location*(s), such as, "There is some *thing* at some *location*," in English. The word order of an existential sentence is rather different from that of other Chinese sentences.

Existential Sentences with "有"

Pattern: Place word + location + 有 + (numerals + measure word) + noun
Examples:

教室的旁邊有一個圖書館。
教室的旁边有一个图书馆。

牆上有一些中文字。
墙上有一些中文字。

Existential Sentences with "是"

Pattern: Place word + location + 是 + (numerals + measure word) + noun
Examples:

床上是一條毯子。
床上是一条毯子。

大學校園的旁邊是一條高速公路。
大学校园的旁边是一条高速公路。

Existential Sentences with "著"("着")

This pattern describes where an object is specifically located. Only verbs that leave an object in an ongoing state can be used in this pattern. For inanimate objects, the verbs that can be used in this pattern include: "放", "掛" ("挂"), "貼" ("贴"), "擺" ("摆"), "停", "寫" ("写"), etc.

Pattern: Place word + verb-"著"("着") + (numerals + measure word) + object
Examples:

桌子上放著一本字典。
桌子上放着一本字典。

衣櫃裏掛著很多衣服。
衣柜里挂着很多衣服。

教室裏坐著很多學生。
教室里坐着很多学生。

Existential Sentences in Describing People

Pattern: Person + place on body + verb-"著"("着")+ (numerals + measure word) + object

Examples:

> 他頭上戴著一頂帽子，身上穿著一件毛衣，腳上穿著一雙皮鞋。
> 他头上戴着一顶帽子，身上穿着一件毛衣，脚上穿着一双皮鞋。

> 姑娘脖子上戴著一條項鏈，手上戴著一塊名牌手錶，肩上卻背著一個非常難看的包。
> 姑娘脖子上戴着一条项链，手上戴着一块名牌手表，肩上却背着一个非常难看的包。

Existential Sentences in Expressing People's Appearance or Disappearance

Pattern: Place word/Time word + verbal phrase + (numerals + measure word) + noun

Examples:

> 昨天我家來了一位客人。
> 昨天我家来了一位客人。

> 那邊跑來一個小男孩。
> 那边跑来一个小男孩。

> 樓上走下來幾個我不認識的人。
> 楼上走下来几个我不认识的人。

SENTENCES WITH VERBAL CONSTRUCTIONS IN A SERIES

This kind of sentence has two or more verbs or verbal structures that are used as the predicate of the same subject.

> 我去圖書館借書。
> 我去图书馆借书。

The negative form is usually made by adding the negative adverb "不" or "沒有" before the first predicate verb.

> 高中學生沒有時間打工。
> 高中学生没有时间打工。

> 他們不來我們學校比賽了。
> 他们不来我们学校比赛了。

If the sentence needs an adverbial adjunct, it is normally placed between the subject and the first predicate verb. For example:

我得去圖書館借幾本書。
我得去图书馆借几本书。

我這學期有時間學中文。
我这学期有时间学中文。

Usually the second verb indicates the purpose of the first verb, or the first verb-object phrase explains the means for achieving the second. For example:

老師要找我談談小考的事情。
老师要找我谈谈小考的事情。

我每天坐校車去學校。
我每天坐校车去学校。

When the second verb indicates the purpose of the first, both verbs typically share a common object; therefore, the second verb usually omits the object. For example:

她用父母給的錢 買 名牌衣服 穿。
她用父母给的钱 买 名牌衣服 穿。

            v1   object   v2

我 借 你的中文字典 用用。
v1 object   v2

PIVOTAL SENTENCES

A pivotal sentence has two predicates. Of the two predicates in the sentence, the object of the first predicate (verb) is at the same time the subject of the second one. This part is called the pivot, and sentences with verb predicates of this sort are identified as pivotal sentences. The basic pattern of pivotal sentences is:

Subject + predicate (verb) + pivot + predicate of the pivot

媽媽說我懶死了。
妈妈说我懒死了。

房東催我交房租。
房东催我交房租。

樓道裏有人大喊大叫。
楼道里有人大喊大叫。

老師要求我們寫一篇關于環境保護的作文。
老师要求我们写一篇关于环境保护的作文。

In the negative form of a pivotal sentence, the adverbs "不" or "沒有" are usually placed between the subject and the first predicate. For example:

父母沒有讓他買那麼貴的車。
父母没有让他买那么贵的车。

In general, verbs indicating a request or a command are used in first predicate; for example: "請" ("请"), "讓" ("让"), "叫," "使," "命令," "禁止," etc. In this case, the pivotal predicate may either be a verbal predicate or an adjectival predicate. For example:

> 我請他在臺灣買本中文字典。
> 我请他在台湾买本中文字典。
>
> 我父母非叫我讀醫科大學不可，他們不讓我學文科。
> 我父母非叫我读医科大学不可，他们不让我学文科。
>
> 朋友離開的事情使我難過了好幾天。
> 朋友离开的事情使我难过了好几天。
>
> 爸爸命令兒子把煙扔了。
> 爸爸命令儿子把烟扔了。
>
> 老師請學生家長們來一趟學校。
> 老师请学生家长们来一趟学校。

Students should note that no other words are allowed to be inserted between the first predicate (verb) and the pivot.

COMPARISON

Expressing Difference

Pattern: A比B + (adverb) + adjective/verb + (numeral + measure word + noun)

Examples:

> 我們學校比你們學校有名。
> 我们学校比你们学校有名。
>
> 我們班比你們班少兩個學生。
> 我们班比你们班少两个学生。
>
> 你比他多學了一年中文。
> 你比他多学了一年中文。
>
> 我比他更喜歡看籃球比賽。
> 我比他更喜欢看篮球比赛。

The negative version of this structure can take one of the following forms:

- adding "不" or "沒有" before "比." For example:

> 我們學校不比你們學校有名。
> 我们学校不比你们学校有名。
>
> 今天沒有比昨天熱。
> 今天沒有比昨天热。

- replacing "比" with "沒有" "不如." For example:

> 他們的高中沒有我們的有名。
> 他们的高中没有我们的有名。

> 紐約的天氣不如加州的好。
> 纽约的天气不如加州的好。

Adverbs such as "很," "非常," "十分" "特別," "真," and "最" cannot be used in this type of sentence. Words such as "一點兒"("一点儿"), "一些," "得多," and "多了" should be used instead. For example:

> 哥哥比弟弟高一點兒。
> 哥哥比弟弟高一点儿。

> 今天比昨天熱多了。
> 今天比昨天热多了。

> 妹妹比姐姐漂亮得多。
> 妹妹比姐姐漂亮得多。

> 我們班的老師比你們的老師年輕一些。
> 我们班的老师比你们的老师年轻一些。

If a verb has an object, the verb should be reduplicated. For example:

> 我開車比她開得好多了。
> 我开车比她开得好多了。

> 你學中文比我學得認真得多。
> 你学中文比我学得认真得多。

Modal verbs like "會" ("会"), and "應該" ("应该") can be placed before the action verb in this type of sentence. For example:

> 弟弟比哥哥會打籃球。
> 弟弟比哥哥会打篮球。

> 老年人比年輕人更應該注意身體。
> 老年人比年轻人更应该注意身体。

The "A比B" structure can be used adverbially. In this case, it can be added between the subject and the adjective or verb. For example:

> 我們這個星期比上個星期忙。
> 我们这个星期比上个星期忙。

> 他在學校比在家裏高興多了。
> 他在学校比在家里高兴多了。

> 孩子一天比一天大了，父母一年比一年老了。

Expressing Similarity

Pattern 1: A跟B + 一樣 (样)

A跟B + 不 + 一樣 (样)

Examples:

我的牛仔褲跟你的牛仔褲一樣。
我的牛仔裤跟你的牛仔裤一样。

東岸跟西岸完全不一樣。
东岸跟西岸完全不一样。

他跟別的中國人有點兒不一樣。
他跟別的中国人有点儿不一样。

Pattern 2: A + 像+ B + (other element)

A + 不像+ B + (other element)

Examples:

他長得很像他爸爸。
他长得很像他爸爸。

英語老師不像四十歲的人，像三十歲的。
英语老师不像四十岁的人，像三十岁的。

今年夏天，紐約像洛杉磯那麼熱。
今年夏天，纽约像洛杉矶那么热。

我不像你那麼喜歡穿名牌的衣服。
我不像你那么喜欢穿名牌的衣服。

Pattern 3: A跟B + 差不多/相似

Examples:

他買的衣服跟你的相似。
他买的衣服跟你的相似。

小張長得跟小王差不多，所以我常看錯人。
小張長得跟小王差不多，所以我常看錯人。

Expressing Similarity with "有"

Pattern: A有B + 那麼/這麼 (那么/这么) + adjective

Examples:

我的房間有你的房間那麼大。
我的房间有你的房间那么大。

他跑得有汽車那麼快。
他跑得有汽车那么快。

EXPRESSING EMPHASIS

Using the "是…的" Construction

To emphasize a past action or a past event, one should use the structure "是…的" to indicate the time, place, manner, or purpose of the occurrence or the agent of the action. "的," which often follows the verb, may be placed either before or after the object.

Patterns: Subject + 是 + time/place + verb + object + 的
　　　　　Subject + 是 + time/place + verb + 的 + object

Examples:

你是幾點吃早飯的？
你是几点吃早饭的？

你是幾點吃的早飯？
你是几点吃的早饭？

你是在什麼地方學的中文？
你是在什么地方学的中文？

你是在什麼地方學中文的？
你是在什么地方学中文的？

Using Rhetorical Questions with "難道" ("难道")

A rhetorical question with "難道" ("难道") is much more emphatic than a non-rhetorical question. For example:

難道可以對自己的行爲不負責任嗎？
难道可以对自己的行为不负责任吗？

難道父母的話都對嗎？
难道父母的话都对吗？

難道你不會寫自己的中文名字嗎？
难道你不会写自己的中文名字吗？

難道今天沒有考試嗎？
难道今天没有考试吗？

Using Double-Negative Sentences

A double-negative is often used in a sentence to indicate affirmation. Common patterns of emphasizing affirmation with double negatives are "不…不…," "沒有…不…," "不…沒有," and "沒有不… ."

Examples:

學生不應該不做功課。
学生不应该不做功课。

我們這次考試沒有人不及格。
我们这次考试没有人不及格。

爸爸不能沒有工作。
爸爸不能没有工作。

哥哥沒有不喜歡的體育運動。
哥哥没有不喜欢的体育运动。

COMPLEX SENTENCES

Complex sentences consist of two or more simple sentences called clauses. Complex sentences are used to express a complete thought and are spoken with a certain intonation. For example:

小王剛走，老張來了。
小王刚走，老张来了。

風停了，雨也不下了。
风停了，雨也不下了。

如果中文太難，我就不學了。
如果中文太难，我就不学了。

她的衣服很漂亮，我的不好看。
她的衣服很漂亮，我的不好看。

Two or more clauses in a complex sentence are separated by a pause when spoken, and indicated by a comma or a semicolon in writing. The sentence is spoken as one entity. If the clauses share a common subject, then the subject does not have to be repeated. For example:

馬克會英文，~~馬克~~會西班牙文，~~馬克~~不會法文。
马克会英文，~~马克~~会西班牙文，~~马克~~不会法文。

我想省钱，~~我~~不想買太貴的電腦。
我想省钱，~~我~~不想买太贵的电脑。

In a complex sentence, clauses have various relationships that are often denoted by conjunctions. For instance:

因爲沒有買到火車票，所以他們得在旅館住一天。
因为没有买到火车票，所以他们得在旅馆住一天。

不但我們喜歡那個歌星，而且我媽媽也很喜歡他。
不但我们喜欢那个歌星，而且我妈妈也很喜欢他。

既然你覺得物理太難了，你今年就別選這門課了。
既然你觉得物理太难了，你今年就别选这门课了。

我是關心她而不是愛她。
我是关心她而不是爱她。

Instead of conjunctions, some adverbs may also connect clauses. Conjunctions or adverbs can be placed either in the first or second clause, depending on the relationship between the clauses. Some conjunction words are used before the subject, and some are used after. For example:

> 我的朋友又學中文，又學日文。
> 我的朋友又学中文，又学日文。

> 要是你們有時間，你們就看這部電影吧。
> 要是你们有时间，你们就看这部电影吧。

> 與其開車這麼麻煩，不如坐公共汽車好。
> 与其开车这么麻烦，不如坐公共汽车好。

> 雖然今天沒有作業，我也要好好復習復習。
> 虽然今天没有作业，我也要好好复习复习。

Clauses in a complex sentence may have various types of predicates. For example:

> 今天星期一，明天星期二。 (*sentence with predicate*)

> 只要有決心，就有學好中文的希望。(*sentence with verbal predicate*)
> 只要有决心，就有学好中文的希望。

> 無論中文多麼難，我都要學好。(*sentence with adjectival predicate*)
> 无论中文多么难，我都要学好。

In a complex sentence, relationships between the clauses can be very complicated. Complex sentences can be roughly divided into two groups: coordinate complex sentences and subordinate complex sentences. These two groups can be further divided into subclasses based on their clauses' relationships.

Coordinate Complex Sentences

Complex sentences indicating coordinate relations are called coordinate sentences. In a coordinate complex sentence, the clauses are equivalent in content and weight. For example:

> 這位是李小姐，那位是張先生。
> 这位是李小姐，那位是张先生。

> 你喜歡吃中國飯還是法國飯？
> 你喜欢吃中国饭还是法国饭？

The relationships between the clauses in a coordinate complex sentence are: *coordinative, successive, progressive,* and *alternative.*

The clauses with the *coordinative* relationship explain or describe several things respectively or explain the different aspects of one thing. For example:

> 他從臺灣來的，我是從新加坡來的。
> 他从台湾来的，我是从新加坡来的。

> 她一邊工作，一邊打工。
> 她一边工作，一边打工。

The clauses with the *successive* relationship are arranged according to the sequence of actions or events. The meanings of the clauses are coherent. For example:

> 他女朋友跟他一分手，他就離開美國了。
> 他女朋友跟他一分手，他就离开美国了。

> 你們應該先做一個演講，再寫一篇讀書報告。
> 你们应该先做一个演讲，再写一篇读书报告。

The clauses with the *progressive* relationship use the second clause to further express the context described in the first one. For example:

> 她不但會說中文，而且還說得很好。
> 她不但会说中文，而且还说得很好。

> 他不但沒在美國的大學學習過，甚至連美國都沒來過。
> 他不但没在美国的大学学习过，甚至连美国都没来过。

The clauses with the *alternative* relationship state alternative options. For example:

> 或者跟媽媽一起生活，或者跟爸爸在一起，對我來說都一樣。
> 或者跟妈妈一起生活，或者跟爸爸在一起，对我来说都一样。

> 我不是上醫學院就是讀法律學院。
> 我不是上医学院就是读法律学院。

Generally speaking, the order of the clauses in the *coordinative* relationship or *alternative* relationship can be changed without affecting the meaning. But the order of the other clauses, *successive* and *progressive*, cannot be reversed at will. For instance:

> 我又喜歡看電視，又喜歡聽音樂。(*coordinative*)
> 我又喜欢看电视，又喜欢听音乐。

> 你們或者吃中餐，或者吃西餐。(*alternative*)
> 你们或者吃中餐，或者吃西餐。

> 我不但會開車，而且會修車。(*progressive*)
> 我不但会开车，而且会修车。

> 我妹妹一高興就唱歌。(*successive*)
> 我妹妹一高兴就唱歌。

Normally, *progressive* and *alternative* clauses should be connected by conjunctions. On the other hand, conjunctions are not always necessary for *coordinative* and *successive* clauses. For example:

> 不但他喜歡游泳，我也喜歡。(*progressive*)
> 不但他喜欢游泳，我也喜欢。

> 這次作文寫400字還是500字？(*alternative*)
> 这次作文写400字还是500字？

他一說完，就走了。(*successive*)
他一说完，就走了。

我說，你們寫。(*successive*)
我说，你们写。

When the subjects of the two clauses are identical, the second occurrence is usually omitted, and the first is positioned at the beginning of the entire sentence. The conjunctions "不但", "還是" ("还是"), and "或者" should be placed after the subjects. When the subjects of the two clauses are different, the conjunctions should be placed before the subject. For example:

小王和小張不但是高中同學，而且是好朋友。
小王和小张不但是高中同学，而且是好朋友。

我們這星期考試，還是下星期考試？
我们这星期考试，还是下星期考试？

不但小王和小張是高中同學，而且小李也跟他們是同學。
不但小王和小张是高中同学，而且小李也跟他们是同学。

你們先休息一下，下午再學。
你们先休息一下，下午再学。

我們一到教室，老師就來了。
我们一到教室，老师就来了。

The conjunctions that are used to identify the *coordinative* and *alternative* relationships, such as "又," "一邊" ("一边"), "一面," "一方面," "不是," "還是" ("还是"), and "或者," can all be used in more than two clauses in a sentence. For example:

她總是一邊吃東西，一邊聽音樂，一邊做功課。
她总是一边吃东西，一边听音乐，一边做功课。

我或者買藍色的，或者買黑色的，或者買黃色，肯定不買紅色的。
我或者买蓝色的，或者买黑色的，或者买黄色，肯定不买红色的。

When the relationships between the clauses are fairly clear, conjunctions are not necessary, and the conjunction "和" should **never** be used between the clauses. For example:

我是從華盛頓來的，他是從芝加哥來的。
我是从华盛顿来的，他是从芝加哥來的。

你們說，我聽。
你们说，我听。

The order of the clauses introduced by "不是...而是..." cannot be switched without altering the meaning. For example:

不是他喜歡那位小姐，而是他哥哥喜歡她。
不是他喜欢那位小姐，而是他哥哥喜欢她。

不是我想學中文，而是我媽讓我學的。
不是我想学中文，而是我妈让我学的。

Listed below are some conjunctions frequently used in coordinate complex sentences. Quiz yourself to see if you can construct a sentence with each of them.

IN A <u>COORDINATIVE</u> RELATIONSHIP

又…, 又…
既…, 又…
既…, 也…
也…, 也…
一會兒…, 一會兒…　　（一会儿…, 一会儿…）
一邊…, 一邊…　　　　（一边…, 一边…）
一面…, 一面…
一方面…, 一方面…
不是…, 而是…
一來…, 二來…　　　　（一来…, 二来…）
有時…, 有時…　　　　（有时…, 有时…）
有的…, 有的…

IN A <u>SUCCESSIVE</u> RELATIONSHIP

…, 就…
一…, 就…
先…, 再…
先…, 又…
…, …然後…　　（…, …然后…）
…, 就…
…, 於是…　　　（…, 于是…）
…, 這才…　　　（…, 这才…）
…, 此後…　　　（…, 此后…）

IN A <u>PROGRESSIVE</u> RELATIONSHIP

…, 還…　　　　（…, 还…）
不但…, 而且…
不僅…, 而且…　　（不仅…, 而且…）
不但…, 反而…
別說…, 就連…　　（别说…, 就连…）
連…都…　　　　　（连…都…）
…, 何況…
…, 甚至…
不僅不…, 還…　　（不仅不…, 还…）

IN AN <u>ALTERNATIVE</u> RELATIONSHIP

是…, 還是…　　（是…, 还是…）
或者…, 或者…
不是…, 就是…
不是…, 而是…
寧願…, 也不…　　（宁愿…, 也不…）
寧可…　　　　　　（宁可…）
…, 要不然…

要麼..., 要麼... （要么..., 要么...）
是..., 不是...

Subordinate Complex Sentences

Complex sentences formed by clauses in a subordinate relationship are called subordinate complex sentences. In a subordinate complex sentence, the clauses are not equally important in terms of their content.

The main clause carries the main idea while the subordinate clause only helps to complete the sentence. For example:

不管你喜歡不喜歡那些課，你都得上。
不管你喜欢不喜欢那些课，你都得上。

因爲我爸爸和媽媽都不能來接我，所以我去了朋友家。
因为我爸爸和妈妈都不能来接我，所以我去了朋友家。

The clauses in a subordinate complex sentence may have different relationships.

Case 1: *Adversative*—The second clause is the main clause, which may oppose or stand in contrast to the first clause (the subordinate clause).

雖然他沒有多少錢，但是他還是把那本很貴的書買回來了。
虽然他没有多少钱，但是他还是把那本很贵的书买回来了。

他考試沒有考好，却上了一個不錯的大學。
他考试没有考好，却上了一个不错的大学。

Case 2: *Causative*—One clause (the subordinate clause) states the reason or premise while the other clause (the main clause) states the result or inference drawn from the premise.

你既然病了，明天就別來上課了。
你既然病了，明天就别来上课了。

由于他們沒有買到飛機票，就在機場旁邊住下來了。
由于他们没有买到飞机票，就在机场旁边住下来了。

Case 3: *Conditional*—One clause (the subordinate clause) may put forward a condition while the other clause (the main clause) states the resulting action.

只要你們努力學習，就能學好中文。
只要你们努力学习，就能学好中文。

不管媽媽同意不同意，我都想去旅遊。
不管妈妈同意不同意，我都想去旅游。

Case 4: *Hypothetical*—One clause (the subordinate clause) puts forward an assumption while the other clause (the main clause) states the result or inference drawn from the assumption.

要是你們學習上有問題，就找我。
要是你们学习上有问题，就找我。

即使他病了，也來上課。
即使他病了，也来上课。

Case 5: *Purposive*—One clause (the subordinate clause) indicates an action for a purpose that is expressed by the other clause (the main clause).

> 我學中文，爲的是以後去中國工作。
> 我学中文，为的是以后去中国工作。

> 爸爸給了我很多錢，以便讓我去臺灣留學。
> 爸爸给了我很多钱，以便让我去台湾留学。

Case 6: *Preferential*—One clause (the subordinate clause) puts forward an extreme course of action while the other clause (the main clause) indicates another course of action that will be adopted after comparison, i.e., to prefer one course to the other.

> 我寧可不睡覺，也要看那場籃球比賽。
> 我宁可不睡觉，也要看那场篮球比赛。

> 妹妹寧願餓死，也不吃爸爸做的飯。
> 妹妹宁愿饿死，也不吃爸爸做的饭。

Subordinate complex sentences are generally made up of two clauses. The order of the clauses normally has the subordinate clause preceding the main clause, but sometimes the main clause comes first, followed by the subordinate clause. In the latter case, it suggests additional explanation. For example:

> 雖然中文很難，但是學的人很多。
> 虽然中文很难，但是学的人很多。

> 因爲那所大學是公立大學，所以不太貴。
> 因为那所大学是公立大学，所以不太贵。

> 我想去東岸讀書，如果父母同意的話。
> 我想去东岸读书，如果父母同意的话。

> 她说芝加哥是一個特別漂亮的城市，雖然她從沒去過。
> 她说芝加哥是一个特别漂亮的城市，虽然她从没去过。

Generally speaking, conjunctions are necessary in a subordinate complex sentence. Listed below are some conjunctions commonly used in subordinate complex sentences.

IN AN <u>ADVERSATIVE</u> RELATIONSHIP

雖然.., 但是...   (虽然.., 但是...)
儘管..., 但是...   (尽管..., 但是...)
..., 其實...   (..., 其实...)
..., 反而...
..., 卻...
是..., 而不是...
不是..., 而是...

IN A <u>CAUSATIVE</u> RELATIONSHIP
由於　　　　　　　（由于）
..., 因此...
..., 於是...　　　　　（..., 于是...）
既然..., 就...
因爲..., 所以...　　　（因为..., 所以...）
所以..., 是因爲　　　（所以..., 是因为）
..., 那麼...　　　　　（..., 那么...）
..., 可見...　　　　　（..., 可见...）
..., 難免...　　　　　（..., 难免...）

IN A <u>CONDITIONAL</u> RELATIONSHIP
只要..., 就...
只有..., 才...
除非..., 才...
一..., 就...
不管..., 都...　　　　（不管..., 都...）
無論..., 也...　　　　（无论..., 也...）
不論..., 也...　　　　（不论..., 也...）

IN A <u>HYPOTHETICAL</u> RELATIONSHIP
要是..., 就...
如果..., 就...
假如..., 就...
假使..., 就...
即使..., 也...

IN A <u>PURPOSIVE</u> RELATIONSHIP
..., 好...
..., 爲的是...　　　　（..., 为的是...）
爲了..., ...　　　　　（为了..., ...）
..., 以便

IN A <u>PREFERENTIAL</u> RELATIONSHIP
寧可..., 也...　　　　（宁可..., 也...）
與其..., 不如...　　　（与其..., 不如...）

When the subjects of the two clauses are identical, conjunctions are often put at the beginning of the sentence. When the subjects of the two clauses are different, conjunctions are normally put before the subject of the first clause.

由于他沒有帶證件，郵局的工作人員不給他包裹。
由于他没有带证件，邮局的工作人员不给他包裹。

假如明天我不來上課，你就跟老師說我病了。
假如明天我不来上课，你就跟老师说我病了。

When the relationship between the clauses is fairly clear, the corrective in the first clause is often omitted. However, the conjunction in the second clause normally cannot be omitted.

（雖然）今天下雪，但是天氣不太冷。
（虽然）今天下雪，但是天气不太冷。

（就是）這個周末沒有時間，我也會參加朋友的生日晚會。
（就是）这个周末没有时间，我也会参加朋友的生日晚会。

Contracted Sentences

A contracted sentence is a special form of complex sentence that has the structure of a simple sentence. The contracted sentence can express what a complex sentence normally states. For example:

你不想吃也得吃。
你不想吃也得吃。

我哥哥非要買那輛難看的汽車不可。
我哥哥非要买那辆难看的汽车不可。

In a contracted sentence, the two predicates share one subject. For example:

外國人學中文非花很多時間不可。
外国人学中文非花很多时间不可。

他们一听说有新电影就很快去了电影院。
他们一听说有新电影就很快去了电影院。

The relationship between the two predicates of the contracted sentence may be *coordinative, alternative, progressive, hypothetical, causative, conditional,* or *successive.* The predicate function in contracted complex sentences are often performed by verbs, V-O phrases, V-C phrases, verbal endocentric phrases, or adjectives. Both the predicate elements in a contracted complex sentence are brief and compact. This kind of structure is often used in speaking without any pause in between clauses. Generally, no comma or semicolon is used. Conjunctions are needed in some of contracted complex sentences, while in others they may not be necessary.

他們越談越高興。
他们越谈越高兴。

明天你們非做完功課不可。
明天你们非做完功课不可。

她昨天病了沒來上課。
她昨天病了没来上课。

The Conjunctive Adverb "越... 越..."

The adverb "越" comes before each predicate (a verb or an adjective) as an adverbial adjunct to show that the degree or the state of the second action changes proportionally to the change in the first. The first predicate is normally a verb and the second an adjective or a gradational verb. For example:

他在家裏越呆越覺得沒有意思。
他在家里越呆越觉得没有意思。

他們都覺得中文越學越容易，可是我怎麼越學越難。
他们都觉得中文越学越容易，可是我怎么越学越难。

你們的中文越學越好，越說越流利。
你们的中文越学越好，越说越流利。

我在高速公路上開車越開越慢。
我在高速公路上开车越开越慢。

The Conjunctive Adverb "一...就 ..."

When the adverbs "一" and "就" are used as adverbial adjuncts before predicates, they may denote the *successive* relationship of actions.

你們一進這個教室就得說中文。
你们一进这个教室就得说中文。

The predicates following "一" and "就" are mainly verbs; however, the predicate after "一" denotes a condition and may be an adjective.

有些中文字一不小心就寫錯。
有些中文字一不小心就写错。

在我們那個城市，天一冷就很難開車。
在我们那个城市，天一冷就很难开车。

The Conjunction "非...不..."

"非...不..." is a double-negative, emphasizing the meaning "如果不...就不行", "一定要..., 才... ." For example:

學好中文非多下功夫不可。
学好中文非多下功夫不可。

你明天非看醫生不可。
你明天非看医生不可。

The predicate following "非" may be a verb, a noun, a pronoun, or a phrase, and the predicate following "不" is often a monosyllabic "可," or "行."

在加州，非有車不可。
在加州，非有车不可。

我媽媽非吃中餐不可。
我妈妈非吃中餐不可。

COMMON SENTENCE PATTERNS IN SPOKEN CHINESE

1. ....才體會到什麼叫... (only then did I realize...)
   ...才体会到什么叫...
   indicates that a certain event caused a realization.

   Example: 到了黃石公園，我才體會到什麼叫自然風景。
   到了黄石公园，我才体会到什么叫自然风景。

2. ...得不得了 (...so much)

is usually placed after an adjective; it used to mean *to a great extent*.

Example: 聽說父母要給他買一輛汽車，他高興得不得了。

聽说父母要给他买一辆汽车，他高兴得不得了。

3. ...的話, 就...(if... then...)

...的话, 就...

is used in a conditional statement.

Example: (要是) 今年暑假我有時間的話，我就去台灣玩玩。

(要是) 今年暑假我有时间的话，我就去台湾玩玩。

4. ...就...點兒吧，... (even if...)

...就...点儿吧，...

is an adjective indicating that even though something has a flaw, there are more pros than cons.

Example: 那件衣服，大就大點兒吧，總比沒有好。

那件衣服，大就大点儿吧，总比没有好。

5. ...來...去 (...here ...there)

...来...去

signifies a repetitive action; it indicates that an action is preformed over and over, without attaining the anticipated result.

Example: 我在網上找來找去，也沒有找到你說的那條新聞。

我在网上找来找去，也没有找到你说的那条新闻。

6. ...了就...了，... (what's done is done)

Example: 錢花了就花了，有什麼可心疼的。

钱花了就花了，有什么可心疼的。

7. ..., 其中... (among them)

is used to refer to a subgroup of a category or of a larger group previously mentioned.

Example: 中國是個能源大國，有煤、石油、天然氣等, 其中煤最便宜。

中国是个能源大国，有煤、石油、天然气等，其中煤最便宜。

8. ...是必不可少的 (... is obliterable)

Example: 要想學好中文，多跟中國人練習是必不可少的。

要想学好中文，多跟中国人练习是必不可少的。

9. ...也得..., 不...也得... (if... or... have to)

indicates in the first clause that whatever one's opinions may be, the situation in the second clause is unavoidable.

Example: 這是必須上的課，你喜歡上也得上，不喜歡上也得上。

这是必须上的课，你喜欢上也得上，不喜欢上也得上。

10. 有什麼好...的, ... (what is there to...)
    有什么好...的, ...
    is a rhetorical expression indicating that there is nothing worthy of a certain action.

    Example: 這兒有什麼好玩的，我們去那邊吃小吃吧。
    这儿有什么好玩的，我们去那边吃小吃吧。

11. ...最好不過了 (cannot be better)
    ...最好不过了
    indicates that something is the best; it is used as a rather advisory expression.

    Example: 要想瞭解中國的古代建築風格，去參觀蘇州園林最好不過了。
    要想了解中国的古代建筑风格，去参观苏州园林最好不过了。

12. A 是 A, B是B (A is A, B is B)
    indicates that two entities should be kept separate.

    Example: 朋友是朋友，工作是工作，不能混爲一談。
    朋友是朋友，工作是工作，不能混为一谈。

13. given A, 不難想像B (... not hard to believe...)
    given A, 不难想象B (... not hard to believe...)
    is used to describe a hypothetical situation.

    Example: 現在經濟那麼不好，不難想像，我畢業時肯定找不到好工作。
    现在经济那么不好，不难想象，我毕业时肯定找不到好工作。

14. given A, 換句話說, B (..., in other words...)
    given A, 换句话说, B

    Example: 生命在於運動，換句話說，多運動對健康有好處。
    生命在于运动，换句话说，多运动对健康有好处。

15. given A, 可見B
    given A, 可见B
    indicates that something can be inferred from the first clause.

    Example: 這麼好的音樂會，他能睡著，可見他對音樂沒有什麼興趣。
    这么好的音乐会，他能睡着，可见他对音乐没有什么兴趣。

16. given A, 況且B
    given A, 况且B
    means that B elaborates a reason that supports the A assessment.

    Example: 我最近很忙，況且芝加哥我早就去過了，所以不想跟你們去那兒旅行了。
    我最近很忙，况且芝加哥我早就去过了，所以不想跟你们去那儿旅行了。

17. given A, 由此體會到了B (by..., realized...)
given A, 由此体会到了B ⋅
indicates realization B by doing A.

Example: 我幫同事照顧了兩天孩子，由此體會到了當媽媽的辛苦。
我帮同事照顾了两天孩子，由此体会到了当妈妈的辛苦。

18. A吧（啊），...
is used to open a conversation; "吧" should be preceded by a subject whereas "啊" may not need one.

Example: 我吧，就不愛逛商店。
我吧，就不爱逛商店。

19. A吧, X; B吧, Y (on one hand..., on the other hand...)
is used to weigh two alternatives when the speaker is indecisive. The two alternatives, A and B, are usually contradictory efforts, and the results of those alternatives, X and Y, are usually both undesirable.

Example: 坐公共汽車吧，太慢；開車吧，停車場很難找。
坐公共汽车吧，太慢；开车吧，停车场很难找。

20. A對B 沒有好處 (A not good for B)
A对B 没有好处

Example: 吸煙對身體沒有好處。
吸烟对身体没有好处。

21. A關係到B (...relating to/affects...)
A关系到B

Example: 這次面試關係到我能不能得到那個工作機會。
这次面试关系到我能不能得到那个工作机会。

22. A和B不無關係 (... and ... are not unrelated)
A和B不无关系
indicates that two things are related using a double-negative.

Example: 一個人的命運和他的性格不無關係，換句話說，性格決定命運。
一个人的命运和他的性格不无关系，换句话说，性格决定命运。

23. A涉及B (A is an element that influences the bigger B)

Example: 物價涉及老百姓的日常生活水平。
物价涉及老百姓的日常生活水平。

24. A也不是, B也不是 (not... not...)
indicates that neither choice is appropriate.

Example: 他送的禮物實在太貴重了，我接受也不是，拒絕也不是。
他送的礼物实在太贵重了，我接受也不是，拒绝也不是。

25. A也不是, 不A也不是 (not... or...)
is used to weigh two undesirable options.

Example: 她送我一件衣服作爲生日禮物，可是我真的不喜歡那種樣式的。穿也不是，不穿也不是，真不知道怎麼辦才好。
她送我一件衣服作为生日礼物，可是我真的不喜欢那种样式的。穿也不是，不穿也不是，真不知道怎么办才好。

26. A也好, B也好 (both...)
is used to weigh two choices that share something in common.

Example: 在美國，東岸也好，西岸也好，房子都貴極了。
在美国，东岸也好，西岸也好，房子都贵极了。

27. A著也是A著, 不如... (should you... might as well)
A着也是A着, 不如...
indicates that there is a better alternative.

Example: 你在家閑著也是閑著，不如找個學校讀讀書。
你在家闲着也是闲着，不如找个学校读读书。

28. 別說...了，就連...都... (can't even..., let alone)
别说...了，就连...都...
is used to belittle one thing in order to emphasize that something else shares a similar consequence.

Example: 別說看電視了，就連吃飯的時間都沒有。
别说看电视了，就连吃饭的时间都没有。

29. 別提...了... (without saying...)
is used in an exclamatory sentence to emphasize an extreme.

Example: 中國西安的兵馬俑別提多壯觀了。
中国西安的兵马俑别提多壮观了。

30. 並不... or 並沒... (absolutely not, certainly not, indeed not)
并不... or 并没...
appears before negative verbs to assert something contrary to expectation or assumption.

Example: 大家都說星巴克咖啡味道好，我並不覺得好喝。
大家都说星巴克咖啡味道好，我并不觉得好喝。

31. 不大...可是 (not very...but)
is an adverb used to express the idea that the outcome does not necessarily reflect the situation.

Example: 他不大喜歡學工科，可是他父母希望他學。
他不大喜欢学工科，可是他父母希望他学。

32. 不過話又說回來, ... (Having said that, ...)
不过话又说回来, ...

Example: 你說得對。不過話又說回來，他說的也不是一點兒道理都沒
有。
你说得对。不过话又说回来，他说的也不是一点儿道理都没
有。

33. 不見得 (not necessarily)
不见得

is often preceded in colloquial speech by "都" or "也," especially when
contradicting someone else's statement or assumption.

Example: 中國人也不見得都會說中文。
中国人也不见得都会说中文。

34. 不就是...嗎？ (Isn't it just...?)
不就是...吗？ (Isn't it just...?)

is a rhetorical pattern used to express surprise that something is not in accord
with the speaker's assumptions.

Example: 不就是一個小考嗎？你爲什麼這麼緊張？
不就是一个小考吗？你为什么这么紧张？

35. 不是A就是 B (if not A then B; it's either A or B)

Example: 我這學期選的課都不好。不是太難，就是作業太多。
我这学期选的课都不好。不是太难，就是作业太多。

36. ... 不算，還... (...not only, but also...)
....不算，还...

Example: 我丢了錢不算，還把車鑰匙丢了。
我丢了钱不算，还把车钥匙丢了。

37. 不只..., 還... (not only... but also)
不只..., 还...

Example: 能不能上好大學，不只看SAT成績，還要看社區工作方面做得怎
麼樣。
能不能上好大学，不只看SAT成绩，还要看社区工作方面做得怎
么样。

38. 除非 (unless)

indicates that only when a condition is met does the 才- clause occur.

Example: 除非我父母同意，我才參加那個體育俱樂部，要不然我就什麼
都不參加。
除非我父母同意，我才参加那个体育俱乐部，要不然我就什么
都不参加。

39. 除了A以外, 都... (except for)

Example: 我的同學除了小王以外，都去過中國。
我的同学除了小王以外，都去过中国。

40. 除了A以外, 還B (in addition to; also; either)
除了A以外, 还B

Example: 我除了有個弟弟以外，還有兩個妹妹。
我除了有个弟弟以外，还有两个妹妹。

41. 從...方面來看，還是...好 (looking at this from... it is... better)
从...方面来看，还是...好
indicates that something may be better when viewed from a different perspective.

Example: 從保護環境方面來看，還是少開車好。
从保护环境方面来看，还是少开车好。

42. 從A的角度來看,... (looking from ...'s point of view)
从A的角度来看,...
indicates an opinion from someone else other than the speaker.

Example: 這件事，從男人的角度來看，是小事一件。從女人的角度來看，卻是天大的事。
这件事，从男人的角度来看，是小事一件。从女人的角度来看，却是天大的事。

43. 從整體上來說,... (overall...)
从整体上来说,...

Example: 從整體上來說,中國這幾年發展得很快。
从整体上来说,中国这几年发展得很快。

44. 到...爲止...(until; up to)
到...为止...
is used to indicate the duration of an action or event.

Example: 到昨天爲止，我一直在忙那件事。
到昨天为止，我一直在忙那件事。

45. 動不動就... (easily; at every turn)
动不动就...
is used to describe how often something unfavorable happens.

Example: 他在學習上不怎麼努力，動不動就不來上課了。
他在学习上不怎么努力，动不动就不来上课了。

46. 對...的印象 (impression of...)

对...的印象

is used to indicate one's impression about someone or some event.

Example: 我對他的印象很不好。

我对他的印象很不好。

47. 對...來說 (to...)

对...来说

indicates an opinion that is directed toward a certain person or thing.

Example: 對我來說，上一個有名的大學是最重要的。

对我来说，上一个有名的大学是最重要的。

48. 放著...不... (prefer the latter)

放着...不...

is used in the first clause of a sentence with two or more clauses; expresses that one chooses a less desirable option over a more superior one.

Example: 放著家裏的大房子不住，他偏要住到學生宿舍裏去。

放着家里的大房子不住，他偏要住到学生宿舍里去。

49. 非...不可 (have to, must)

is used to indicate an action that one must take.

Example: 我爸爸病了，我非回家不可。

50. 給...印象 (give...impression)

给...印象

is used to indicate an impression that is left with someone.

Examples: 他給我了一個很不好的印象。

他给我了一个很不好的印象。

51. 管...叫... (called)

indicates the name of something.

Example: 在中國，有些地方管女子結婚叫 "出門子"。

在中国，有些地方管女子结婚叫 "出门子"。

52. 害得... (causing such harm that...)

is used to indicate an event that contributes directly to a harmful result.

Example: 弟弟把我的車開走了，害得我走路去上學。

弟弟把我的车开走了，害得我走路去上学。

53. 好 (不) 容易... (with great difficulty)

indicates that something was difficult to accomplish; "好不容易" and "好容易" both mean the same thing.

Example: 那本書很難買，我跑了很多書店，好不容易才買到。

那本书很难买，我跑了很多书店，好不容易才买到。

54. 還A呢, ... (It is also..., and even...)
还A呢, ...
uses a rhetorical predicate to express something which is not satisfactory.

Example: 還美國人呢，連紐約在哪兒都不知道！
还美国人呢，连纽约在哪儿都不知道！

55. 還是...吧 (It's better if...)
还是...吧
suggests the best of several alternative actions; it is gentler and more polite than "最好."

Example: 學文科找不到好工作，你還是學電腦或者醫學吧。
学文科找不到好工作，你还是学电脑或者医学吧。

56. 還是...的, 就是...(it may be..., it's just...)
还是...的, 就是...
concedes that the subject has a positive quality, but there is also something negative.

Example: 洛杉磯這個城市還是不錯的，就是那兒的空氣污染太嚴重了。
洛杉矶这个城市还是不错的，就是那儿的空气污染太严重了。

57. 就拿...來說 (take... for example)
就拿...来说
is used to illustrate a general statement with a specific example.

Example: 在美國，男女同工不同酬的現象哪兒都有。就拿我姐姐和她男朋友來說，他們做相同的工作，姐姐的薪水卻少得多。
在美国，男女同工不同酬的现象哪儿都有。就拿我姐姐和她男朋友来说，他们做相同的工作，姐姐的薪水却少得多。

58. 就 (算) 是...,也...(even if..., still...)
expresses supposition; it usually comes at the beginning of a sentence, but will sometimes come directly before the verb; the clause that follows "就 (算)是" may be either a sentence or a noun phrase.

Example: 我今天特別累，不想去看電影。就(算)是電影票不要錢，我也不去。
我今天特别累，不想去看电影。就(算)是电影票不要钱，我也不去。

59. 看把...的 (see how...)
describes to a greater extent.

Example: 兒子比賽得了冠軍，看把爸爸媽媽高興的。
儿子比赛得了冠军，看把爸爸妈妈高兴的。

60. 可...了／可...呢 (very...)

is an adverb that describes to a greater extent.

Examples: 我們學校的女子籃球隊可有名了。

我们学校的女子篮球队可有名了。

你看，小寶寶睡得可香呢。

你看，小宝宝睡得可香呢。

61. 可以說... (one may say...)

可以说...

is used to summarize the thought leading to a conclusion.

Example: 中國古代的科學技術可以說在當時是數一數二的。

中国古代的科学技术可以说在当时是数一数二的。

62. 連...也／都... (even)

连...也／都...

is used to indicate that something surprising or unexpected is about to happen.

Example: 那場比賽真是太精彩了，連奶奶都跟著我們一起大喊大叫。

那场比赛真是太精彩了，连奶奶都跟着我们一起大喊大叫。

63. 每當...的時候 (whenever...)

每当...的时候

is used to indicate that something always happens during a certain event or time.

Examples: 每當中秋節的時候，家裏的人都盡可能地回家團圓。

每当中秋节的时候，家里的人都尽可能地回家团圆。

64. 你...你的吧 (you do what you're doing)

Example: 你吃你的吧，我坐坐就走。

65. 你說什麼也得... (whatever you say, you have to...)

你说什么也得...

indicates one's obligations.

Example: 你就是不在我這兒吃飯，你說什麼也得喝了水再走。

你就是不在我这儿吃饭，你说什么也得喝了水再走。

66. 稍微有一點兒... (a bit too...)

稍微有一点儿...

is a euphemism used to point out a flaw or problem.

Example: 住在學生宿舍很方便，就是稍微有點兒不自由。

住在学生宿舍很方便，就是稍微有点儿不自由。

67. 實話跟你說吧,... / 老實告訴你吧 (to tell you the truth...)
實话跟你说吧,... / 老实告诉你吧

Example: 實話跟你說吧,你這樣下去很麻煩。
實话跟你说吧,你这样下去很麻烦。

68. 說 ...就 ... (whenever)
说 ...就 ...
indicates that a certain action or event happens unexpectedly.

Example: 媽媽脾氣很不好,說發火就發火。
妈妈脾气很不好,说发火就发火。

69. 說不上... (...cannot really count for)
说不上...
indicates that something is not up to a certain standard.

Example: 我只是偶爾聽聽音樂,說不上多喜歡。
我只是偶尔听听音乐,说不上多喜欢。

70. 所以...是因爲... (the reason that... is because ...)
所以...是因为...
is used to give the reason for a situation that is already known to the speaker and listener.

Example: 我所以經常去中國城,是因爲我想跟那兒的中國人練習中文。
我所以经常去中国城,是因为我想跟那儿的中国人练习中文。

71. 特別是... (especially)
when followed by a noun phrase, extends the meaning of the preceding sentence.

Example: 我的同屋不喜歡起床,特別是天冷的時候。
我的同屋不喜欢起床,特别是天冷的时候。

72. 我說你... (I'll say...you...)
我说你...
indicates that someone is able to point out some flaws about the other person.

Example: 我說你怎麼老看電視呀。
我说你怎么老看电视呀。

73. 無所謂A不A (doesn't matter if...)
无所谓A不A

Example: 我餓極了,有吃的就行,無所謂好吃不好吃。
我饿极了,有吃的就行,无所谓好吃不好吃。

74. 反之... (conversely...)

is used to indicate an assessment from two sides.

Example: 你願意幫助別人，別人也會幫助你。反之，你不跟人家來往，
人家也離你遠遠的。
你愿意帮助别人，别人也会帮助你。反之，你不跟人家来往，
人家也离你远远的。

75. 想像不出...到什麼程度 (couldn't imagine how (+ adjective)....)
想象不出...到什么程度

expresses that a situation is at an unbelievable degree.

Example: 你想像不出中國的人多到什麼程度。
你想象不出中国的人多到什么程度。

76. 要A沒A, 要B沒B (there isn't... nor...)
要A没A, 要B没B

indicates that neither A nor B is available to someone or something.

Example: 你看我這個人，要房沒房，要車沒車，誰會喜歡我呀。
你看我这个人，要房没房，要车没车，谁会喜欢我呀。

77. 要A有A, 要B有B (there is... and...)

indicates that both A and B are available to someone or something.

Example: 那個男孩子，要個子有個子，要學問有學問。
那个男孩子，要个子有个子，要学问有学问。

78. 要不是...就...(if not for..., ...probably...)

is used to express a hypothetical situation; it is a conditional statement.

Example: 要不是為了照顧我們這個家，媽媽早就出去工作了。
要不是为了照顾我们这个家，妈妈早就出去工作了。

79. 要麼...要麼... (either... or...)
要么...要么...

is a *selective* conjunction, used before two predicates or clauses to indicate a
choice between two or more possibilities.

Example: 今天下午，我要麼去看電影，要麼去朋友家玩。
今天下午，我要么去看电影，要么去朋友家玩。

80. 要是..., 看你...? (if... let's see ...)

indicates a possible unsatisfactory outcome.

Example: 你要是考不上大學，看你以後怎麼辦？
你要是考不上大学，看你以后怎么办？

81. 一 ... 就... (as soon as)
indicates a quick succession of related actions

Example: 昨天我一出門，女朋友就給我打電話了。
昨天我一出门，女朋友就给我打电话了。

82. 一來...二來...(first of all... second of all)
is used to list causes, reasons, goals, etc.

Example: 姐姐沒有買那件衣服，一來顏色不太好，二來太貴了。
姐姐没有买那件衣服，一来颜色不太好，二来太贵了。

83. 以...的方式 (來)... (via...)
以...的方式 (来)...
indicates how or by what means something is done.

Example: 他跟朋友們常以上網聊天的方式進行交流。
他跟朋友们常以上网聊天的方式进行交流。

84. 應該說明的是, ... (it should be made clear that...)
应该说明的是, ...
is used to clarify a point.

Example: 應該說明的是，中國在環境方面還存在很多問題。
应该说明的是，中国在环境方面还存在很多问题。

85. 有的...有的... (some... some...)
links two or more clauses to indicate differences.

Example: 有的人喜歡熱鬧，有的人喜歡安靜。
有的人喜欢热闹，有的人喜欢安静。

86. 又 A又 B (not only... but also...)
can be used to indicate two concurrent situations or actions; A and B can be
verbs or adjectives.

Example: 這個週末我忙死了，又得準備下周的考試，又得打工。
这个周末我忙死了，又得准备下周的考试，又得打工。

87. 在...有這樣一種說法：... (in... there is a saying...)
在...有这样一种说法：...
is used to open a conversation.

Example: 在中國有這樣一種說法：入鄉隨俗。到了這兒就要習慣這裏的
生活方式。
在中国有这样一种说法：入乡随俗。到了这儿就要习惯这里的
生活方式。

88. 在...的同時，也/還... (at the same time... there is still...)
在...的同时，也/还...
indicates that there are two actions happening at the same time.

Example: 我在上電腦課的同時，還上一門藝術課。
我在上电脑课的同时，还上一门艺术课。

89. 在...上 (in terms of...)
can be used after abstract nouns; it is commonly used with "性格," "興趣"
("兴趣,") "工作"、"學習" ("学习,") "經濟" ("经济").

Example: 在選擇專業上，我和父母的看法完全不一樣。
在选择专业上，我和父母的看法完全不一样。

90. 早也不...，晚也不...，偏偏...(not then... or now...)
indicates that something will not happen.

Example: 你早也不來晚也不來，偏偏在我最忙的時候來了。
你早也不来晚也不来，偏偏在我最忙的时候来了。

91. 這就要看... (it depends on)
这就要看...
is always followed by a question, which may be a "verb-not-verb" or
"adjective-not-adjective" structure or a question word, but never a "嗎-
question."

Example: Q: 你打算不打算去中國旅行？
你打算不打算去中国旅行？
A: 這就要看我父母給不給我錢了。
这就要看我父母给不给我钱了。

92. 這也不...那也不... (neither... nor...)
这也不...那也不...

Example: 到了商店，這也不讓買，那也不讓買，那你把我帶到商店來做
什麼?
到了商店，这也不让买，那也不让买，那你把我带到商店来做
什么?

93. 正如...所說, ... (just as he/she said ...)
正如...所说, ...
is used to quote someone to make a conclusion.

Example: 正如我們老師所說，高中的課程沒有容易上的，我這學期選的
課，門門課都學得不怎麼樣。
正如我们老师所说，高中的课程没有容易上的，我这学期选的
课，门门课都学得不怎么样。

94. 只靠...不行 (just... is not enough)

Example: 要想減肥，只靠走走路不行，你還得跑跑步，游游泳什麼的。
要想减肥，只靠走走路不行，你还得跑跑步，游游泳什么的。

95. 只是... (it's just that...)

is a conjunctive used to connect two clauses, similar to "but"; it appears in the second clause, and is used to introduce a qualification, problem, or exception to the preceding statement.

Example: 我確實想買那件毛衣，只是我剛剛買了條牛仔褲，不能再花錢了。

我确实想买那件毛衣，只是我刚刚买了条牛仔裤，不能再花钱了。

96. 衆所周知, ... (as we all know...)
众所周知, ...

is used to start conversations.

Example: 衆所周知，美國的汽油價格漲得很厲害。
众所周知，美国的汽油价格涨得很厉害。

97. 自從...以來 (ever since...)
自从...以来

indicates the duration of time since an event or action occurred; it always refers to the past.

Example: 自從上高中以來, 我一直都在選修中文課。
自从上高中以来, 我一直都在选修中文课。

98. ...., 自然就... (naturally, over the course of time)

is used to indicate that an outcome comes about naturally after a period of time; the first clause describes an action or process, which is the condition for the second clause.

Example: 只要你多聽、多說、多寫，自然就能學好中文。
只要你多听、多说、多写，自然就能学好中文。

99. 綜上所述, ... (to sum it up)
综上所述, ...

is used to indicate that the following will be a summary.

Example: 綜上所述，我認爲選專業還是應該多聽聽父母的建議比較好。
综上所述，我认为选专业还是应该多听听父母的建议比较好。

100. 作爲..., ... (being...)
作为..., ...

indicates that a certain status results in a certain action or opinion.

Example: 作爲中國人，我爲2008年奧運會在北京召開感到驕傲。
作为中国人，我为2008年奥运会在北京召开感到骄傲。

Cultural Notes

Chinese culture makes up a large part of the AP Chinese Language and Culture exam. The materials in this chapter have been selected to help you review the Chinese culture, including social practices and products.

This chapter also covers some topics that may be relevant to the Writing and Speaking sections of the AP Chinese exam. For example, both Writing and Speaking sections evaluate the student's mastery of Chinese idioms. The last section of this chapter provides 50 idioms and 25 proverbs that are commonly used in a typical AP Chinese course. Students who practice these idioms will be more confident applying them on the AP Chinese exam.

Whenever Chinese characters are used in this chapter, the traditional version is presented first, followed by the simplified within parentheses. If there are no parentheses, the characters in both versions are identical. Other texts in Chinese are clearly labeled as "Traditional," "Simplified," and "Pinyin."

PHYSICAL GEOGRAPHY OF CHINA

[Traditional-character version]

地理

　　中國，全稱中華人民共和國，位於亞洲東部、太平洋西岸。中國陸地的總面積爲960萬平方公里，是亞洲國家中面積最大的，居世界第三位。

　　中國地勢的特點是西高東低、山脈衆多。著名的山脈有喜瑪拉雅山、昆侖山、天山、太行山、秦嶺、大興安嶺等，其中喜馬拉雅山脈的主峰珠穆朗瑪峰的海拔高達8848米，有"世界屋脊"的稱號。

　　中國是世界上河流最多的國家之一，許多大江大河源遠流長。中國的第一大河是長江，全長6300公里，流域面積180.9萬平方公里。長江中下游地區，氣候溫暖濕潤，雨量充足，土地肥沃，是中國重要的農業區之一，在水上交通方面也發揮了重要作用。中國第二大河爲黃河，全長5464公里，流域面積75.2萬平方公里。位於長江和黃河之間還有一條大河叫淮河，是中國的第三大河流。淮河還是中國南北方自然氣候的分界線。以淮河幹流爲界，淮河北部是暖溫、半濕潤地帶，南部則是亞熱帶濕潤地區。中國也是一個湖泊衆多的國家，其中太湖、鄱陽湖、洞庭湖和洪澤湖被稱爲中國的四大湖泊。

[Simplified-character version]

地理

　　中国，全称中华人民共和国，位于亚洲东部、太平洋西岸。中国陆地的总面积为960万平方公里，是亚洲国家中面积最大的，居世界第三位。

　　中国地势的特点是西高东低、山脉众多。著名的山脉有喜玛拉雅山、昆仑山、天山、太行山、秦岭、大兴安岭等，其中喜马拉雅山脉的主峰珠穆朗玛峰的海拔高达8848米，有"世界屋脊"的称号。

　　中国是世界上河流最多的国家之一，许多大江大河源远流长。中国的第一大河是长江，全长6300公里，流域面积180.9万平方公里。长江中下游地区，气候温暖湿润，雨量充足，土地肥沃，是中国重要的农业区之一，在水上交通方面也发挥了重要作用。中国第二大河为黄河，全长5464公里，流域面积75.2万平方公里。位于长江和黄河之间还有一条大河叫淮河，是中国的第三大河流。淮河还是中国南北方自然气候的分界线。以淮河干流为界，淮河北部是暖温、半湿润地带，南部则是亚热带湿润地区。中国也是一个湖泊众多的国家，其中太湖、鄱阳湖、洞庭湖和洪泽湖被称为中国的四大湖泊。

[Pinyin version]

Dìlǐ

Zhōngguó, quánchēng Zhōnghuá Rénmín Gònghéguó, wèiyú Yàzhōu dōngbù, Tàipíngyáng xī'àn. Zhōngguó lùdì de zǒng miànjī wéi jiǔbǎi liùshí wàn píngfāng gōnglǐ, shì Yàzhōu guójiā zhōng miànjī zuìdà de, jū shìjiè dì sān wèi.

　　Zhōngguó dìshì de tèdiǎn shì xī gāo dōng dī, shānmài zhòngduō. Zhùmíng de shānmài yǒu Xǐmǎlāyǎshān, Kūnlúnshān, Tiānshān, Tàixíngshān, Qínlǐng, Dàxīng'ānlǐng děng, qízhōng Xǐmǎlāyǎ shānmài de zhǔfēng Zhūmùlǎngmǎ fēng de hǎibá gāodá bābǎi sìshíbā mǐ, yǒu "shìjiè wūjí" de chēnghào.

　　Zhōngguó shì shìjièshang héliú zuì duō de guójiā zhīyī, xǔduō dàjiāng dàhé yuányuǎn liúcháng. Zhōngguó de dì yī dàhé shì Chángjiāng, quáncháng liùqiān sānbǎi gōnglǐ, liúyù miànjī yìbǎi bāshídiǎnjiǔ wàn píngfāng gōnglǐ. Chángjiāng zhòngxià yóu dìqū, qìhòu wēnnuǎn shīrùn, yǔliàng chōngzú, tǔdì féiwò, shì Zhōngguó zhòngyào de nóngyèqū zhīyī, zài shuǐshàng jiāotōng fāngmiàn yě fāhuīle zhòngyào zuòyòng. Zhōngguó dì èr dàhé wéi Huánghé, quáncháng wǔqiān sìbǎi liùshísì gōnglǐ, liúyù miànjī qīshíwǔ diǎn èr wàn píngfāng gōnglǐ. Wèiyú Chángjiāng hé Huánghé zhījiān hái yǒu yì tiáo dàhé jiào Huáihé, shì Zhōngguó de dì sān dà héliú. Huáihé háishì Zhōngguó nánběifāng zìrán qìhòu de fēnjièxiàn. Yǐ Huáihé gànliú wèijiè, Huáihé běibù shì nuǎnwēn, bàn shīrùn dìdài, nánbù zé shì yàrèdài shīrùn dìqū. Zhōngguó yěshì yígè húbó zhòngduō de guójiā, qízhōng Tàihú, Póyánghú, Dòngtínghú hé Hóngzéhú bèi chēngwéi Zhōngguó de sì dà húbó.

[Traditional-character version]

氣候

　　中國屬於大陸季風性氣候，大部分地區四季分明，南北溫差較大。夏季炎熱多雨，冬季寒冷乾燥。一月份平均氣溫相差近50˚C，七月份平均氣溫相差在20˚C以上。受到地勢的影響，各地降雨情況不完全一樣，東南沿海地區的年降水量多在1600毫米以上，而西北地區的年降水量卻不到50毫米。

[Simplified-character version]

气候

中国属于大陆季风性气候，大部分地区四季分明，南北温差较大。夏季炎热多雨，冬季寒冷干燥。一月份平均气温相差近50°C，七月份平均气温相差在20°C以上。受到地势的影响，各地降雨情况不完全一样，东南沿海地区的年降水量多在1600毫米以上，而西北地区的年降水量却不到50毫米。

[Pinyin vesion]

Qìhòu

Zhōngguó shǔyú dàlù jìfēng xìng qìhòu, dà bùfèn dìqū sìjì fēnmíng, nánběi wēnchā jiào dà. Xiàjì yánrè duōyǔ, dōngjì hánlěng gānzào. Yī yuèfèn píngjūn qìwēn xiāngchà jìn wǔshí shèshìdù, qī yuèfèn píngjūn qìwēn xiāngchà zài èrshí shèshìdù yǐshàng. Shòudào dìshì de yǐngxiǎng, gèdì jiàngyǔ qíngkuàng bù wánquán yíyàng, dōngnán yánhǎi dìqū de nián jiàngshuǐ liàng duō zài yìqiān liùbǎi háomǐ yǐshàng, ér xīběi dìqū de nián jiàngshuǐ liàng què bú dào wǔshí háomǐ.

[Traditional-character version]

自然資源

中國的自然資源總量豐富，但是由於人口衆多，人均資源的佔有量不足。中國的礦產資源豐富，種類齊全。中國的石油資源和石油產量不斷增長。中國的煤炭資源也很豐富，中國是世界上煤炭產量最高的國家，煤炭的儲存量占世界第一位。但是煤炭在開發和利用的過程中造成的環境污染是中國急需解決的問題。水資源是人類生產、生活的最基本的資源。雖然中國水資源總量占世界第四位，但人均佔有量僅爲世界平均水平的四分之一，使中國成爲全球嚴重缺水的國家之一。此外，中國還存在水污染嚴重、水土流失等問題。日趨嚴重的水污染不僅降低了水體的使用功能，也加劇了水資源短缺的矛盾。

[Simplified-character version]

自然资源

中国的自然资源总量丰富，但是由于人口众多，人均资源的占有量不足。中国的矿产资源丰富，种类齐全。中国的石油资源和石油产量不断增长。中国的煤炭资源也很丰富，中国是世界上煤炭产量最高的国家，煤炭的储存量占世界第一位。但是煤炭在开发和利用的过程中造成的环境污染是中国急需解决的问题。水资源是人类生产、生活的最基本的资源。虽然中国水资源总量占世界第四位，但人均占有量仅为世界平均水平的四分之一，使中国成为全球严重缺水的国家之一。此外，中国还存在水污染严重、水土流失等问题。日趋严重的水污染不仅降低了水体的使用功能，也加剧了水资源短缺的矛盾。

[Pinyin version]

Zìrán Zīyuán

Zhōngguó de zìrán zīyuán zǒngliàng fēngfù, dànshì yóuyú rénkǒu zhòngduō, rénjūn zīyuán de zhànyǒuliàng bùzú. Zhōngguó de kuàngchǎn zīyuán fēngfù, zhǒnglèi qíquán. Zhōngguó de shíyóu zīyuán hé shíyóu chǎnliàng búduàn zēngzhǎng. Zhōngguó de méitàn zīyuán yě hěn fēngfù, Zhōngguó shì shìjièshang méitàn chǎnliàng zuìgāo de guójiā, méitàn de chǔcún liàng zhàn shìjiè dìyī wèi. Dànshì méitàn zài kāifā hé lìyòng de guòchéng zhōng zàochéng de huánjìng wūrǎn shì Zhōngguó jíxū jiějué de wèntí. Shuǐ zīyuán shì rénlèi shēngchǎn, shēnghuó de zuì jīběn de zīyuán. Suīrán Zhōngguó shuǐ zīyuán zǒngliàng zhàn shìjiè dìsì wèi, dàn rénjūn zhànyǒu liàng jǐn wéi shìjiè píngjūn shuǐpíng de sìfēn zhīyī, shǐ Zhōngguó chéngwéi quánqiú yánzhòng quēshuǐ de guójiā zhīyī. Cǐwài, Zhōngguó hái cúnzài shuǐ wūrǎn yánzhòng, shuǐtǔ liúshī děng wèntí. Rìqū yánzhòng de shuǐ wūrǎn bùjǐn jiàngdīle shuǐtǐ de shǐyòng gōngnéng, yě jiājùle shuǐ zīyuán duǎnquē de máodùn.

[Traditional-character version]

野生動物和植物

中國面積遼闊，地形複雜，河流衆多，氣候多樣，這些天然條件爲各種野生動物、植物提供了優越的生存環境。生活在中國境內的脊椎動物約占世界總數的10%，還有大熊貓、金絲猴、華南虎等幾百種動物爲中國所特有。中國木本植物居世界第三，其中喬木多達2000種以上，而水杉、銀杉、銀杏樹等也是中國所特有的植物。

爲保護自然資源與自然環境，中國政府對具有代表性的自然環境地帶和稀有動物的自然棲息地劃出界限，如四川的臥龍，福建的武夷山、吉林的長白山以及湖北神農架等地都已成爲國家自然保護區。

[Simplified-character version]

野生动物和植物

中国面积辽阔，地形复杂，河流众多，气候多样，这些天然条件为各种野生动物、植物提供了优越的生存环境。生活在中国境内的脊椎动物约占世界总数的10%，还有大熊猫、金丝猴、华南虎等几百种动物为中国所特有。中国木本植物居世界第三，其中乔木多达2000种以上，而水杉、银杉、银杏树等也是中国所特有的植物。

为保护自然资源与自然环境，中国政府对具有代表性的自然环境地带和稀有动物的自然栖息地划出界限，如四川的卧龙，福建的武夷山、吉林的长白山以及湖北神农架等地都已成为国家自然保护区。

[Pinyin version]

Yěshēng Dòngwù hé Zhíwù

Zhōngguó miànjī liáokuò, dìxíng fùzá, héliú zhòngduō, qìhòu duōyàng, zhèxiē tiānrán tiáojiàn wèi gèzhǒng yěshēng dòngwù, zhíwù tígōngle yōuyuè de shēngcún huánjìng. Shēnghuó zài Zhōngguó jìngnèi de jǐzhuī dòngwù yuē zhàn shìjiè zǒngshǔ de bǎi fēn zhī shí, háiyǒu dàxióngmāo, jīnsīhóu, huánánhǔ děng jǐbǎi zhǒng dòngwù wéi Zhōngguó suǒ tèyǒu. Zhōngguó mùběn zhíwù jū shìjiè dì sān, qízhōng qiáomù duōdá liǎngqiān zhǒng yǐshàng, ér shuǐshān, yínshān, yínxìngshù děng yěshì Zhōngguó suǒ tèyǒu de zhíwù.

Wèi bǎohù zìrán zīyuán yǔ zìrán huánjìng, Zhōngguó zhèngfǔ duì jùyǒu dàibiǎoxìng de zìrán huánjìng dìdài hé xīyǒu dòngwù de zìrán qīxīdì huàchū jièxiàn, rú Sìchuān de Wòlóng, Fújiàn de Wǔyíshān, Jílín de Chángbáishān yǐjí Húběi Shénnóngjià děngdì dōu yǐ chéngwéi guójiā zìrán bǎohùqū.

[Traditional-character version]

大熊貓

　　大熊貓，也叫貓熊，顧名思義，像貓一樣的熊。大熊貓長得頭圓尾短、身體肥胖，頭部和身體的毛色黑白相間，憨態可掬，很是惹人喜愛。

　　大熊貓是中國特有的物種，被譽爲中國的國寶。大熊貓的棲息地曾經分佈廣泛，覆蓋中國東部和南部的大部分地區，而如今，它們的分佈範圍變得十分狹窄，主要生活在四川等地的一些山區。大熊貓的食譜非常特殊，主要吃各種竹子。除了睡眠或短距離活動外，大熊貓每天取食時間長達十幾小時。大熊貓的食量十分驚人，一隻大熊貓每天進食最多可達三十公斤。

　　由於對生活環境的要求極高，大熊貓的生育率較低，再加上人類的濫捕、濫殺，大熊貓的數量急劇減少。據統計，目前世界上的野生大貓熊不到2000只，大熊貓也因此被列爲瀕臨滅絕的動物。

[Simplified-character version]

大熊猫

　　大熊猫，也叫猫熊，顾名思义，像猫一样的熊。大熊猫长得头圆尾短、身体肥胖，头部和身体的毛色黑白相间，憨态可掬，很是惹人喜爱。

　　大熊猫是中国特有的物种，被誉为中国的国宝。大熊猫的栖息地曾经分布广泛，覆盖中国东部和南部的大部分地区，而如今，它们的分布范围变得十分狭窄，主要生活在四川等地的一些山区。大熊猫的食谱非常特殊，主要吃各种竹子。除了睡眠或短距离活动外，大熊猫每天取食时间长达十几小时。大熊猫的食量十分惊人，一只大熊猫每天进食最多可达三十公斤。

　　由于对生活环境的要求极高，大熊猫的生育率较低，再加上人类的滥捕、滥杀，大熊猫的数量急剧减少。据统计，目前世界上的野生大猫熊不到2000只，大熊猫也因此被列为濒临灭绝的动物。

[Pinyin version]

Dàxióngmāo

Dàxióngmāo, yě jiào māoxióng, gùmíng sīyì, xiàng māo yíyàng de xióng. Dàxióngmāo zhǎngde tóuyuán wěiduǎn, shēntǐ féipàng, tóubù hé shēntǐ de máosè hēibái xiàngjiān, hāntài kějū, hěn shì rěrén xǐ'ài.

　　Dàxióngmāo shì Zhōngguó tèyǒu de wùzhǒng, bèi yùwéi Zhōngguó de guóbǎo. Dàxióngmāo de qīxidì céngjīng fēnbù guǎngfàn, fùgài Zhōngguó dōngbù hé nánbù de dà bùfèn dìqū, ér rújīn, tāmen de fēnbù fànwéi biànde shífēn xiázhǎi, zhǔyào shēnghuó zài Sìchuān děng dì de yīxiē shānqū. Dàxióngmāo de shípǔ fēicháng tèshū, zhǔyào chī gèzhǒng zhúzi. Chúle shuìmián huò duǎn jùlí huódòng wài, dàxióngmāo měitiān qǔshí shíjiān chángdá shíjǐ xiǎoshí. Dàxióngmāo de shíliàng shífēn jīngrén, yī zhǐ dàxióngmāo měitiān jìnshí zuìduō kě dá sānshí gōngjīn.

　　Yóuyú duì shēnghuó huánjìng de yāoqiú jígāo, dàxióngmāo de shēngyùlǜ jiàodī, zài jiāshang rénlèi de lànbǔ, lànshā, dàxióngmāo de shùliàng jíjù jiǎnshǎo. Jù tǒngjì, mùqián shìjièshang de yěshēng dàmāoxióng bú dào liǎngqiān zhǐ, dàxióngmāo yě yīncǐ bèi lièwéi bīnlín mièjué de dòngwù.

[Traditional-character version]

行政區域劃分

中國行政區域的劃分從古到今多次變更。爲了便於行政管理，中國的行政區域以省、市、縣等單位分級劃分。目前，中國有二十多個省，五個民族自治區。除此之外，中國還有北京、上海、天津和重慶四個直轄市以及香港、澳門兩個特別行政區。

中國的首都是北京，北京是著名的歷史文化古城，金、元、明、清等幾個朝代都建都於北京。北京也是世界上擁有文化遺產專案數量最多的城市之一。今日的北京，還是全國的政治、經濟、文化、教育的中心。目前，北京的常住人口已達2000萬。不斷增長的人口給北京人的住房、交通、資源等方面帶來巨大的壓力，也使北京的人口調控成爲急需解決的問題。

[Simplified-character version]

行政区域划分

中国行政区域的划分从古到今多次变更。为了便于行政管理，中国的行政区域以省、市、县等单位分级划分。目前，中国有二十多个省，五个民族自治区。除此之外，中国还有北京、上海、天津和重庆四个直辖市以及香港、澳门两个特别行政区。

中国的首都是北京，北京是著名的历史文化古城，金、元、明、清等几个朝代都建都于北京。北京也是世界上拥有文化遗产项目数量最多的城市之一。今日的北京，还是全国的政治、经济、文化、教育的中心。目前，北京的常住人口已达2000万。不断增长的人口给北京人的住房、交通、资源等方面带来巨大的压力，也使北京的人口调控成为急需解决的问题。

[Pinyin version]

Xíngzhèng Qūyù Huàfēn

Zhōngguó xíngzhèng qūyù de huàfēn cónggǔ dàojīn duōcì biàngēng. Wèile biànyú xíngzhèng guǎnlǐ, Zhōngguó de xíngzhèng qūyù yǐ shěng, shì, xiàn děng dānwèi fēnjí huàfēn. Mùqián, Zhōngguó yǒu èrshí duō gè shěng, wǔ gè mínzú zìzhìqū. Chúcǐ zhīwài, Zhōngguó háiyǒu Běijīng, Shànghǎi, Tiānjīn hé Chóngqìng sì gè zhíxiáshì yǐjí Xiānggǎng, Ào'mén liǎng gè tèbié xíngzhèngqū.

Zhōngguó de shǒudū shì Běijīng, Běijīng shì zhùmíng de lìshǐ wénhuà gǔchéng, Jīn, Yuán, Míng, Qīng děng jǐ gè cháodài dōu jiàn dū yú Běijīng. Běijīng yěshì shìjièshang yōngyǒu wénhuà yíchǎn xiàngmù shùliàng zuìduō de chéngshì zhīyī. Jīnrì de Běijīng, háishì quánguó de zhèngzhì, jīngjì, wénhuà, jiàoyù de zhōngxīn. Mùqián, Běijīng de chángzhù rénkǒu yǐ dá liǎngqiān wàn. Búduàn zēngzhǎng de rénkǒu gěi Běijīngrén de zhùfáng, jiāotōng, zīyuán děng fāngmiàn dài lái jùdà de yālì, yě shǐ Běijīng de rénkǒu tiáokòng chéngwéi jíxū jiějué de wèntí.

[Traditional-character version]

人口

根據2010年第六次全國人口普查結果，中國人口總數爲13.7億。同2000年的第五次人口普查相比，增長了5.84%。目前，中國仍是世界上人口最多的國家，約占世界總人口的20%。中國人口分佈不均衡，東部沿海地區人口密集，西部高原地區人口稀少。在性別比例上，男性人口占總人口的51.27%，女性人口占48.73%。居住在城鎮的人口占總人口的49%，跟2000年相比，上升了

13.5%。從2000年到2010年，是中國人口從農村向城市轉移速度最快的10年。目前，城鄉人口比例基本持平。在人口年齡段的劃分上，60歲以上的人口占人口總數的11.3%，標誌著中國已經成爲世界上老年人最多的國家。

[Simplified-character version]

人口

根据2010年第六次全国人口普查结果，中国人口总数为13.7亿。同2000年的第五次人口普查相比，增长了5.84%。目前，中国仍是世界上人口最多的国家，约占世界总人口的20%。中国人口分布不均衡，东部沿海地区人口密集，西部高原地区人口稀少。在性别比例上，男性人口占总人口的51.27%，女性人口占48.73%。居住在城镇的人口占总人口的49%，跟2000年相比，上升了13.5%。从2000年到2010年，是中国人口从农村向城市转移速度最快的10年。目前，城乡人口比例基本持平。在人口年龄段的划分上，60岁以上的人口占人口总数的11.3%，标志着中国已经成为世界上老年人最多的国家。

[Pinyin version]

Rénkǒu

Gēnjù èr líng yī lín nián dì-liù cì quánguó rénkǒu pǔchá jiéguǒ, Zhōngguó rénkǒu zǒngshù wéi shí sān diǎn qī yì. Tóng liǎng qiān nián de dì wǔ cì rénkǒu pǔchá xiāngbǐ, zēngzhǎngle bǎifēnzhī wǔ diǎn bā sì. Mùqián, Zhōngguó réng shì shìjièshang rénkǒu zuìduō de guójiā, yuē zhàn shìjiè zǒng rénkǒu de bǎifēnzhī érshí. Zhōngguó rénkǒu fēnbù bù jūnhéng, dōngbù yánhǎi dìqū rénkǒu mìjí, xībù gāoyuán dìqū rénkǒu xīshǎo. Zài xìngbié bǐlì shang, nánxìng rénkǒu zhàn zǒng rénkǒu de bǎifēnzhī wǔshíyī diǎn è qī, nǚxìng rénkǒu zhàn bǎifēnzhī sìshíbā diǎn qīsān. Jūzhù zài chéngzhèn de rénkǒu zhàn zǒng rénkǒu de bǎifēnzhī sìshíjiǔ, gēn liǎngqiān nián xiāngbǐ, shàngshēngle shísān diǎn wu. Cóng liǎng qiān nián dào èr líng yī líng nián, shì zhōngguó rénkǒu cóng nóngcūn xiàng chéngshì zhuǎnyí sùdù zuìkuài de shí nián. Mùqián, chéngxiāng rénkǒu bǐlì jīběn chípíng. Zài rénkǒu niánlíngduàn de huàfēn shang, liùshí suì yǐshàng de rénkǒu zhàn rénkǒu zǒng shǔ de shíyī diǎn sān, biāozhìzhe Zhōngguó yǐjīng chéngwéi shìjièshang lǎoniánrén zuìduō de guójiā.

[Traditional-character version]

民族

中國是一個統一的多民族國家，由56個民族組成。漢族人口最多，其他55個民族人口較少，所以人口較少的民族被稱爲少數民族。中國民族的分佈是"大雜居，小聚居"，這一分佈特點有利於各民族之間的相互交往和團結合作。

中國根據歷史發展、文化特點、民族關係和民族分佈等具體情況以及各民族人民的共同利益和發展要求採用民族區域自治的政治制度。

[Simplified-character version]

民族

中国是一个统一的多民族国家，由56个民族组成。汉族人口最多，其他55个民族人口较少，所以人口较少的民族被称为少数民族。中国民族的分布是"大杂居，小聚居"，这一分布特点有利于各民族之间的相互交往和团结合作。

中国根据历史发展、文化特点、民族关系和民族分布等具体情况以及各民族人民的共同利益和发展要求采用民族区域自治的政治制度。

[Pinyin version]

Mínzú

Zhōngguó shì yí gè tǒngyī de duō mínzú guójiā, yóu wǔshíliù gè mínzú zǔchéng. Hànzú rénkǒu zuìduō, qítā wǔshíwǔ gè mínzú rénkǒu jiàoshǎo, suǒyǐ rénkǒu jiào shǎo de mínzú bèi chēngwéi shǎoshù mínzú. Zhōngguó mínzú de fēnbù shì "dà zájū, xiǎo jùjū", zhè yī fēnbù tèdiǎn yǒulìyú gè mínzú zhījiān de xiānghù jiāowǎng hé tuánjié hézuò.

Zhōngguó gēnjù lìshǐ fāzhǎn, wénhuà tèdiǎn, mínzú guānxì hé mínzú fēnbù děng jùtǐ qíngkuàng yǐjí gè mínzú rénmín de gòngtóng lìyì hé fāzhǎn yāoqiú cǎiyòng mínzú qūyù zìzhì de zhèngzhì zhìdù.

SURVEY OF MODERN HISTORY

[Traditional-character version]

孫中山

孫中山，本名孫文，號逸仙，1866年出生於中國的廣東省，1925年3月12日在北京逝世，葬于南京紫金山的中山陵。孫中山逝世後，被世人尊稱爲"中華民國國父"。

孫中山早期接受中國傳統教育，後來到西方教會學校讀書，對東西方世界都有深刻的認識。早在青年時代，孫中山就提出改革時政，但他的思想不被當時的滿清政府所接受。後來，他赴檀香山學習，在華僑中宣傳革命，並建立革命組織。孫中山是中國最早提出用革命形式推翻滿清統治、建立中華民國的發起者和領導者，提出"民族、民權、民生"的"三民主義"等政治綱領，在中國社會產生了深遠影響，推動了整個社會的發展。

[Simplified-character version]

孙中山

孙中山，本名孙文，号逸仙，1866年出生于中国的广东省，1925年3月12日在北京逝世，葬于南京紫金山的中山陵。孙中山逝世后，被世人尊称为"中华民国国父"。

孙中山早期接受中国传统教育，后来到西方教会学校读书，对东西方世界都有深刻的认识。早在青年时代，孙中山就提出改革时政，但他的思想不被当时的满清政府所接受。后来，他赴檀香山学习，在华侨中宣传革命，并建立革命组织。孙中山是中国最早提出用革命形式推翻满清统治、建立中华民国的发起者和领导者，提出"民族、民权、民生"的"三民主义"等政治纲领，在中国社会产生了深远影响，推动了整个社会的发展。

[Pinyin version]

Sūn Zhōngshān

Sūn Zhōngshān, běnmíng Sūn Wén, hào Yìxiān, yī bā liù liù nián chūshēng yú Zhōngguó de Guǎngdōng shěng, yī jiǔ èr wǔ nián sān yuè shí èr rì zài Běijīng shìshì, zàngyú Nánjīng Zǐjīnshān de Zhōngshānlíng. Sūnzhōngshān shìshì hòu, bèi shìrén zūnchēng wéi "Zhōnghuá Mínguó Guófù".

Sūn Zhōngshān zǎoqī jiēshòu Zhōngguó chuántǒng jiàoyù, hòulái dào xīfāng jiàohuì xuéxiào dúshū, duì dōngxīfāng shìjiè dōu yǒu shēnkè de rènshi. Zǎozài qīngnián shídài, Sūn Zhōngshān jiù tíchū gǎigé shízhèng, dàn tā de sīxiǎng bú bèi dāngshí de mǎnqīng zhèngfǔ suǒ jiēshòu. Hòulái, tā fù Tánxiāngshān xuéxí, zài huáqiáo zhōng xuānchuán gémìng, bìng jiànlì gémìng zǔzhī. Sūn Zhōngshān shì Zhōngguó zuìzǎo tíchū yòng gémìng xíngshì tuīfān mǎnqīng tǒngzhì, jiànlì Zhōnghuá Mínguó de fāqǐzhě hé lǐngdǎozhě, tíchū "Mínzú, mínquán, mínshēng" de "Sānmín Zhǔyì" děng zhèngzhì gānglǐng, zài Zhōngguó shèhuì chǎnshēngle shēnyuǎn yǐngxiǎng, tuīdòngle zhěnggè shèhuì de fāzhǎn.

[Traditional-character version]

辛亥革命

辛亥革命是指發生在1911年至1912年間的一場以推翻清朝專制統治、建立共和政體的全國性的革命。由於1911年是中國農曆的辛亥年,所以這場革命被稱爲辛亥革命。

中國歷史上的辛亥革命分狹義的和廣義的。狹義的辛亥革命是指自1911年10月爆發的武昌起義到孫中山擔任中華民國臨時大總統前後時間裏發生的革命事件,而廣義的辛亥革命指以推翻滿清統治爲目標的一系列革命運動。1911年由孫中山發起的辛亥革命成功地推翻了清朝的統治,結束了中國的帝制,開啓了民主共和的新紀元,推動了中國的憲政與法治的發展,在建立國內各民族間的良好關係上起到關鍵作用。

[Simplified-character version]

辛亥革命

辛亥革命是指发生在1911年至1912年间的一场以推翻清朝专制统治、建立共和政体的全国性的革命。由于1911年是中国农历的辛亥年,所以这场革命被称为辛亥革命。

中国历史上的辛亥革命分狭义的和广义的。狭义的辛亥革命是指自1911年10月爆发的武昌起义到孙中山担任中华民国临时大总统前后时间里发生的革命事件,而广义的辛亥革命指以推翻满清统治为目标的一系列革命运动。1911年由孙中山发起的辛亥革命成功地推翻了清朝的统治,结束了中国的帝制,开启了民主共和的新纪元,推动了中国的宪政与法治的发展,在建立国内各民族间的良好关系上起到关键作用。

[Pinyin version]

Xīnhài Gémìng

Xīnhài gémìng shì zhǐ fāshēng zài yī jiǔ yī yī nián zhì yī jiǔ yī èr nián jiān de yì chǎng yǐ tuīfān Qīngcháo zhuānzhì tǒngzhì, jiànlì gònghé zhèngtǐ de quánguóxìng de gémìng. Yóuyú yī jiǔ yī yī nián shì Zhōngguó nónglì de xīnhài nián, suǒyǐ zhè chǎng gémìng bèi chēngwéi Xīnhài gémìng. Zhōngguó lìshǐshang de Xīnhài gémìng fēn xiáyì de hé guǎngyì de. Xiáyì de Xīnhài gémìng shì zhǐ zì yī jiǔ yī yī nián shí yuè bàofā de Wǔchāng qǐyì dào Sūn Zhōngshān dānrèn Zhōnghuá Mínguó línshí dà zǒngtǒng qiánhòu shíjiānli fāshēng de gémìng shìjiàn, ér guǎngyì de Xīnhài gémìng zhǐ yǐ tuīfān mǎnqīng tǒngzhì wéi mùbiāo de yíxìliè gémìng yùndòng. Yī jiǔ yī yī nián yóu Sūn Zhōngshān fāqǐ de Xīnhài gémìng chénggōng de tuīfānle

Qīngcháo de tǒngzhì, jiéshùle Zhōngguó de dìzhì, kāiqǐle mínzhǔ gònghé de xīnjìyuán, tuīdòngle Zhōngguó de xiànzhèng yǔ fǎzhì de fāzhǎn, zài jiànlì guónèi gè mínzú jiān de liánghǎo guānxìshang qǐdào guānjiàn zuòyòng.

FESTIVALS AND CUSTOMS

[Traditional-character version]

春節

　　春節是中國最重要的傳統節日。春節也叫新年、大年，口語中也說過年。古代的時候，中國人使用農曆，春節曾經是指節氣中的立春，農曆的新年叫"元旦"，就是一年中的第一天的意思。"辛亥革命"以後，中國採用了公曆。爲了區別農曆和公曆的新年，人們把農曆的新年叫"春節"，而把公曆的新年叫"元旦"。據說，中國人過春節已有四千多年的歷史。由于中國是多民族的國家，各民族過新年的形式各有不同。漢族、滿族等過春節的風俗習慣比較相似。過春節的時候，全家團圓。人們吃年糕、餃子以及各種豐盛的飯菜。春節期間的慶祝活動很豐富，放鞭炮、舞獅子、貼春聯、挂年畫、耍龍燈、拜年賀喜等習俗至今流行。

[Simplified-character version]

春节

　　春节是中国最重要的传统节日。春节也叫新年、大年，口语中也说过年。古代的时候，中国人使用农历，春节曾经是指节气中的立春，农历的新年叫"元旦"，就是一年中的第一天的意思。"辛亥革命"以后，中国采用了公历。为了区别农历和公历的新年，人们把农历的新年叫"春节"，而把公历的新年叫"元旦"。据说，中国人过春节已有四千多年的历史。由于中国是多民族的国家，各民族过新年的形式各有不同。汉族、满族等过春节的风俗习惯比较相似。过春节的时候，全家团圆。人们吃年糕、饺子以及各种丰盛的饭菜。春节期间的庆祝活动很丰富，放鞭炮、舞狮子、贴春联、挂年画、耍龙灯、拜年贺喜等习俗至今流行。

[Pinyin version]

Chūnjié

Chūnjié shì Zhōngguó zuì zhòngyào de chuántǒng jiérì. Chūnjié yě jiào xīnnián, dànián, kǒuyǔ zhōng yě shuō guònián. Gǔdài de shíhou, Zhōngguórén shǐyòng nónglì, chūnjié céngjīng shì zhǐ jiéqì zhōng de lìchūn, nónglì de xīnnián jiào "Yuándàn", jiùshì yì nián zhōng de dì yī tiān de yìsi. "Xīnhài gémìng" yǐhòu, Zhōngguó cǎiyòngle gōnglì. Wèile qūbié nónglì hé gōnglì de xīnnián, rénmen bǎ nónglì de xīnnián jiào "chūnjié", ér bǎ gōnglì de xīnnián jiào "yuándàn". Jùshuō, Zhōngguórén guò chūnjié yǐ yǒu sìqiān duō nián de lìshǐ. Yóuyú Zhōngguó shì duō mínzú de guójiā, gè mínzúguò xīnnián de xíngshì gè yǒu bùtóng. Hànzú, Mǎnzú děng guò chūnjié de fēngsú xíguàn bǐjiào xiāngsì. Guò chūnjié de shíhou, quánjiā tuányuán. Rénmen chī niángāo, jiǎozǐ yǐjí gèzhǒng fēngshèng de fàncài. Chūnjié qījiān de qìngzhù huódòng hěn fēngfù, fàng biānpào, wǔ shīzi, tiē chūnlián, guà niánhuà, shuǎ lóngdēng, bàinián hèxǐ děng xísú zhìjīn liúxíng.

[Traditional-character version]

元宵節

　　元宵節在農曆的正月十五日。正月是農曆的元月，古人把它叫做"宵"。正月十五日是一年中的第一個月圓之夜，所以人們稱它爲"元宵節"。元宵節也叫燈節、上元節，它是春節之後的第一個重要節日，也標誌著春節活動的結束。元宵節已經有兩千多年的歷史了。元宵節的重要習俗是吃元宵。元宵是一種用糯米粉做成的圓圓的食品，象徵著"團圓"。除了吃元宵以外，中國人還有賞花燈、猜燈謎、舞龍、舞獅等節日習俗。

[Simplified-character version]

元宵节

　　元宵节在农历的正月十五日。正月是农历的元月，古人把它叫做"宵"。正月十五日是一年中的第一个月圆之夜，所以人们称它为"元宵节"。元宵节也叫灯节、上元节，它是春节之后的第一个重要节日，也标志着春节活动的结束。元宵节已经有两千多年的历史了。元宵节的重要习俗是吃元宵。元宵是一种用糯米粉做成的圆圆的食品，象征着"团圆"。除了吃元宵以外，中国人还有赏花灯、猜灯谜、舞龙、舞狮等节日习俗。

[Pinyin version]

Yuánxiāo Jié

Yuánxiāo Jié zài nónglì de zhēngyuè shíwǔ rì. Zhēngyuè shì nónglì de yuányuè, gǔrén bǎ tā jiàozuò "xiāo". Zhēngyuè shíwǔ rì shì yì nián zhōng de dì yī gè yuèyuán zhīyè, suǒyǐ rénmen chēng tā wéi "Yuánxiāo Jié". Yuánxiāo Jié yě jiào Dēng Jié, Shàngyuán Jié, tā shì chūnjié zhīhòu de dì yī gè zhòngyào jiérì, yě biāozhìzhe chūnjié huódòng de jiéshù. Yuánxiāo Jié yǐjīng yǒu liǎngqiān duō nián de lìshǐle. Yuánxiāo Jié de zhòngyào xísú shì chī yuánxiāo. Yuánxiāo shì yì zhǒng yòng nuòmǐfěn zuòchéngde yuányuán de shípǐn, xiàngzhēngzhe "tuányuán". Chúle chī yuánxiāo yǐwài, Zhōngguórén háiyǒu shǎng huādēng, cāi dēngmí, wǔlóng, wǔshī děng jiérì xísú.

[Traditional-character version]

清明節

　　清明節在陽歷每年的4月5日前後，是祭祀祖先和掃墓的日子。漢族和一些少數民族大多都有清明節掃墓的習俗。按照舊的習俗，掃墓時，人們要帶酒和食品以及紙錢等物品到墓地，把食物放在死去的親人墓前，再把紙錢燒掉，爲墳墓培上新土，插幾枝新樹枝在墳上，然後叩頭、祭拜。除了祭祀家人以外，現在人們也在清明節悼念烈士。清明節已經有二千多年的歷史了。清明時節正是春耕、春種的大好時節，所以中國有"清明前後，種瓜種豆"的俗語。清明節的時候，天氣開始變暖，人們開始踏青、蕩秋千、放風箏等，所以清明節也叫"踏青節"。

[Simplified-character version]

清明节

　　清明节在阳历每年的4月5日前后，是祭祀祖先和扫墓的日子。汉族和一些少数民族大多都有清明节扫墓的习俗。按照旧的习俗，扫墓时，人们要带酒和食品以及纸钱等物品到墓地，把食物放在死去的亲人墓前，再把纸钱烧掉，为坟墓培上新土，插几枝新树枝在坟上，然后叩头、祭拜。除了祭祀家人以外，现在人们也在清明节悼念烈士。清明节已经有二千多年的历史了。清明时节正是春耕、春种的大好时节，所以中国有"清明前后，种瓜种豆"的俗语。清明节的时候，天气开始变暖，人们开始踏青、荡秋千、放风筝等，所以清明节也叫"踏青节"。

[Pinyin version]

Qīngmíng Jié

Qīngmíng Jié zài yánglì měi nián de sì yuè wǔ rì qiánhòu, shì jìsì zǔxiān hé sǎomù de rìzi. Hànzú hé yìxiē shǎoshù mínzú dàduō dōu yǒu Qīngmíng Jié sǎomù de xísú. Ànzhào jiù de xísú, sǎomù shí, rénmen yào dài jiǔ hé shípǐn yǐjí zhǐqián děng wùpǐn dào mùdì, bǎ shíwù fàng zài sǐqù de qīnrén mùqián, zài bǎ zhǐqián shāodiào, wèi fénmù péishang xīn tǔ, chā jǐ zhī xīn shùzhī zài fénshang, ránhòu kòutóu, jìbài. Chúle jìsì jiārén yǐwài, xiànzài rénmen yě zài Qīngmíng Jié dàoniàn lièshì. Qīngmíng Jié yǐjīng yǒu èrqiān duō nián de lìshǐ le. Qīngmíng shíjié zhèng shì chūngēng, chūnzhǒng de dàhǎo shíjié, suǒyǐ Zhōngguó yǒu "Qīngmíng qiánhòu, zhǒngguā zhǒngdòu" de súyǔ. Qīngmíng Jié de shíhou, tiānqì kāishǐ biàn nuǎn, rénmen kāishǐ tàqīng, dàng qiūqiān, fàng fēngzheng děng, suǒyǐ Qīngmíng Jié yě jiào "Tàqīng Jié".

[Traditional-character version]

端午節

端午節是中國傳統節日，在農曆五月初五，所以叫"端午節"。關于端午節的由來有很多傳說，其中比較流行的說法是端午節是紀念屈原的節日。

屈原是戰國時期楚國的大臣。屈原憂國憂民，希望國家富強，希望人才得到重用。屈原給楚王提出了很多合理的建議，卻遭到一些貴族的反對，因此被趕出都城，流放到別處。屈原在流放中寫下了著名的愛國詩歌《離騷》、《九歌》等。後來，秦國打敗了楚國。屈原眼看著自己的祖國被侵略，心如刀割，在五月五日那一天投江自殺，用生命表達自己的愛國熱情。傳說，屈原死後，楚國的老百姓非常難過，大家紛紛劃著龍舟來到江邊，尋找屈原的屍體。有一位漁夫拿出爲屈原準備的飯團、鶏蛋等食品，把它們丟進江裏，給水中的魚蝦吃，以使它們不再去咬屈原的身體。後來，飯團變成了今天的棕子，于是就有了端午節賽龍舟、吃粽子的民間風俗。由於地域廣大，民族衆多，中國人過端午節的習俗不完全一樣。而且，有些活動的意義已經發生變化，如賽龍舟這一習俗，已經有了新的發展，它突破了時間、地域的界綫，成爲國際性的體育賽事了。

[Simplified-character version]

端午节

端午节是中国传统节日，在农历五月初五，所以叫"端午节"。关于端午节的由来有很多传说，其中比较流行的说法是端午节是纪念屈原的节日。

屈原是战国时期楚国的大臣。屈原忧国忧民，希望国家富强，希望人才得到重用。屈原给楚王提出了很多合理的建议，却遭到一些贵族的反对，因此被赶出都城，流放到别处。屈原在流放中写下了著名的爱国诗歌《离骚》、《九歌》等。后来，秦国打败了楚国。屈原眼看着自己的祖国被侵略，心如刀割，在五月五日那一天投江自杀，用生命表达自己的爱国热情。　传说，屈原死后，楚国的老百姓非常难过，大家纷纷划着龙舟来到江边，寻找屈原的尸体。有一位渔夫拿出为屈原准备的饭团、鸡蛋等食品，把它们丢进江里，给水中的鱼虾吃，以使它们不再去咬屈原的身体。后来，饭团变成了今天的棕子，于是就有了端午节赛龙舟、吃棕子的民间风俗。由于地域广大，民族众多，中国人过端午节的习俗不完全一样。而且，有些活动的意义已经发生变化，如赛龙舟这一习俗，已经有了新的发展，它突破了时间、地域的界线，成为国际性的体育赛事了。

[Pinyin version]

Duānwǔ jié

Duānwǔ jié shì Zhōngguó de chuántǒng jiérì, zài nónglì wǔyuè chū wǔ, suǒyǐ jiào "Duānwǔ Jié". Guānyú Duānwǔ Jié de yóulái, yǒu hěnduō chuánshuō, qízhōng bǐjiào liúxíng de shuōfǎ shì Duānwǔ Jié shì jìniàn Qū Yuán de jiérì.

Qū Yuán shì Zhànguó shíqī Chǔguó de dàchén. Qū Yuán yōuguó yōumín, xīwàng guójiā fùqiáng, xīwàng réncái dédào zhòngyòng. Qū Yuán gěi Chǔwáng tíchūle hěnduō hélǐ de jiànyì, què zāodào yīxiē guìzú de fǎnduì, yīncǐ bèi gǎnchū dūchéng, liúfàng dào biéchù. Qū Yuán zài liúfàng zhōng xiěxiàle zhùmíng de àiguó shīgē "Lísāo", "Jiǔgē" děng. Hòulái, Qínguó dǎbàile Chǔguó. Qū Yuán yǎnkànzhe zìjǐ de zǔguó bèi qīnlüè, xīnrú dāogē, zài wǔyuè wǔrì nà yī tiān tóujiāng zìshā, yòng shēngmìng biǎodá zìjǐ de àiguó rèqíng. Chuánshuō, Qū Yuán sǐhòu, Chǔguó de lǎobǎixìng fēicháng nánguò, dàjiā fēnfēn huázhe lóngzhōu láidào jiāngbiān, xúnzhǎo Qū Yuán de shītǐ. Yǒu yí wèi yúfū náchū wèi Qū Yuán zhǔnbèi de fàntuán, jīdàn děng shípǐn, bǎ tāmen diūjìn jiānglǐ, gěi shuǐzhōng de yúxiā chī, yǐ shǐ tāmen bù zài qù yǎo Qū Yuán de shēntǐ. Hòulái, fàntuán biànchéngle jīntiān de zōngzi, yúshì jiù yǒule Duānwǔ Jié sài lóngzhōu, chī zòngzi de mínjiān fēngsú. Yóuyú dìyù guǎngdà, mínzú zhòngduō, Zhōngguórén guò Duānwǔ Jié de xísú bù wánquán yíyàng. Érqiě, yǒuxiē huódòng de yìyì yǐjīng fāshēng biànhuà, rú sài lóngzhōu zhè yī xísú, yǐjīng yǒule xīnde fāzhǎn, tā tūpòle shíjiān, dìyù de jièxiàn, chéngwéi guójìxìng de tǐyù sàishì le.

[Traditional-character version]

中秋節

每年的農曆八月十五日是中國傳統的中秋節。在中國的農曆裏，一年分爲四季，每季又分爲孟、仲、季三個階段，因而中秋也叫仲秋。八月十五這一天的月亮最圓、最亮，在這天晚上，一家人圍坐在院子裏，一邊吃著香甜的月餅，一邊欣賞圓圓的月亮。因爲月餅是圓的，月亮也是圓的，象徵著一家人的團圓，所以中國人也把這一天叫作"團圓節"。每當中秋節到來的時候，在外面工作、學習的人都會儘量趕回家，與家人團圓。

中秋節的習俗很多，慶祝中秋節的形式各不相同，但都寄托著人們對美好生活的無限熱愛和向往。

[Simplified-character version]

中秋节

每年的农历八月十五日是中国传统的中秋节。在中国的农历里，一年分为四季，每季又分为孟、仲、季三个阶段，因而中秋也叫仲秋。八月十五这一天的月亮最圆、最亮，在这天晚上，一家人围坐在院子里，一边吃着香甜的月饼，一边欣赏圆圆的月亮。因为月饼是圆的，月亮也是圆的，象征着一家人的团圆，所以中国人也把这一天叫作"团圆节"。每当中秋节到来的时候，在外面工作、学习的人都会尽量赶回家，与家人团圆。

中秋节的习俗很多，庆祝中秋节的形式各不相同，但都寄托着人们对美好生活的无限热爱和向往。

[Pinyin version]

Zhōngqiū Jié

Měinián de nónglì bāyuè shíwǔ rì shì Zhōngguó chuántǒng de Zhōngqiū Jié. Zài Zhōngguó de nónglì lǐ, yì nián fēnwéi sìjì, měi jì yòu fēnwéi mèng, zhòng, jì sān ge jiēduàn, yīn'ér zhōngqiū yě jiào zhòngqiū. Bāyuè shíwǔ zhè yītiān de yuèliàng zuìyuán, zuìliàng, zài zhè tiān wǎnshang, yìjiā rén wéizuò zài yuànzi lǐ, yìbiān chīzhe xiāngtián de yuèbǐng, yìbiān xīnshǎng yuányuán de yuèliàng. Yīnwèi yuèbǐng shì yuánde, yuèliàng yěshì yuánde, xiàngzhēngzhe yìjiārén de tuányuán, suǒyǐ Zhōngguórén yě bǎ zhè yìtiān jiàozuò "Tuányuán Jié". Měidāng Zhōngqiū Jié dàolái de shíhou, zài wàimiàn gōngzuò, xuéxí de rén dū huì jǐnliàng gǎn huíjiā, yǔ jiārén tuányuán.

Zhōngqiū Jié de xísú hěnduō, qìngzhù Zhōngqiū Jié de xíngshì gèbù xiāngtóng, dàn dōu jìtuōzhe rénmen duì měihǎo shēnghuó de wúxiàn rè'ài hé xiàngwǎng.

[Traditional-character version]

重陽節

農曆九月九日是中國傳統的重陽節。按照中國的古老傳說，九是陽數，九月九日，兩個九相重，所以叫重陽，也叫重九。

中國古人認爲，重陽是個吉祥的日子，所以中國人很早就開始過重陽節了。慶祝重陽節的活動豐富多彩，一般包括出遊賞景、登高遠眺、觀賞菊花、吃重陽糕、飲酒等活動。因爲"九九"跟"久久"同音，九在數位中又是最大的數，所以重陽還有"長久，"、"長壽"的意思。1989年，中國把每年的九月九日定爲"老人節"，把傳統與現代結合起來，成爲尊老、愛老、助老的老年人節日。

[Simplified-character version]

重阳节

农历九月九日是中国传统的重阳节。按照中国的古老传说，九是阳数，九月九日，两个九相重，所以叫重阳，也叫重九。

中国古人认为，重阳是个吉祥的日子，所以中国人很早就开始过重阳节了。庆祝重阳节的活动丰富多彩，一般包括出游赏景、登高远眺、观赏菊花、吃重阳糕、饮酒等活动。因为"九九"跟"久久"同音，九在数位中又是最大的数，所以重阳还有"长久，"、"长寿"的意思。1989年，中国把每年的九月九日定为"老人节"，把传统与现代结合起来，成为尊老、爱老、助老的老年人节日。

[Pinyin version]

Chóngyáng Jié

Nónglì jiǔyuè jiǔrì shì Zhōngguó chuántǒng de Chóngyáng Jié. Ànzhào Zhōngguó de gǔlǎo chuánshuō, jiǔ shì yángshù, jiǔyuè jiǔrì, liǎng gè jiǔ xiāngchóng, suǒyǐ jiào Chóngyáng, yě jiào Chóngjiǔ.

Zhōngguó gǔrén rènwéi, Chóngyáng shì gè jíxiáng de rìzi, suǒyǐ Zhōngguórén hěnzǎo jiù kāishǐ guò Chóngyáng Jié le. Qìngzhù Chóngyáng Jié de huódòng fēngfù duōcǎi, yìbān bāokuò chūyóu shǎngjǐng, dēnggāo yuǎntiào, guānshǎng júhuā, chī chóngyánggāo, yǐnjiǔ děng huódòng. Yīnwèi "jiǔjiǔ" gēn "jiǔjiǔ" tóngyīn, jiǔ zài shùwèi zhōng yòu shì zuìdà de shù, suǒyǐ Chóngyáng háiyǒu "chángjiǔ", "chángshòu" de yìsi. yī jiǔ bā jiǔ nián, Zhōngguó bǎ měinián de jiǔyuè jiǔrì dìngwéi "Lǎorén Jié", bǎ chuántǒng yǔ xiàndài jiéhé qǐlai, chéngwéi zūnlǎo, àilǎo, zhùlǎo de lǎoniánrén jiérì.

CHINESE FAMILY VIRTUES

[Traditional-character version]

包公棄官

中國古人說：百善孝爲先，意思是說孝敬父母是至關重要的品德。父母爲養育子女付出所有心血，作爲兒女，就要報答父母養育之恩。歷史上因孝順揚名天下、留名史冊的人不計其數，包公爲父母棄官的故事流傳至今。

包公是中國古代一個有名的清官，也是民間最能代表公平和正義的化身，而他孝敬父母的故事也爲人稱道。包公從小就顯出才氣，年僅28歲就考中進士，並在遠離家鄉的地方得到一份官職。但是當年老的父母不願跟他離開家鄉時，包公毫不猶豫地辭去官職，留在家裏照顧父母。包公的孝心受到了官員們的一致好評。

[Simplified-character version]

包公弃官

中国古人说：百善孝为先，意思是说孝敬父母是至关重要的品德。父母为养育子女付出所有心血，作为儿女，就要报答父母养育之恩。历史上因孝顺扬名天下、留名史册的人不计其数，包公为父母弃官的故事流传至今。

包公是中国古代一个有名的清官，也是民间最能代表公平和正义的化身，而他孝敬父母的故事也为人称道。包公从小就显出才气，年仅28岁就考中进士，并在远离家乡的地方得到一份官职。但是当年老的父母不愿跟他离开家乡时，包公毫不犹豫地辞去官职，留在家里照顾父母。包公的孝心受到了官员们的一致好评。

[Pinyin version]

Bāogōng Qìguān

Zhōngguó gǔrén shuō: Bǎi shàn xiào wèi xiān, yìsi shì shuō xiàojìng fùmǔ shì zhìguān zhòngyào de pǐndé. Fùmǔ wèi yǎngyù zǐnǚ fùchū suǒyǒu xīnxuè, zuòwéi érnǚ, jiùyào bàodá fùmǔ yǎngyù zhī'ēn. Lìshǐ shang yīn xiàoshùn yángmíng tiānxià, liúmíng shǐcè de rén bùjì qíshù, Bāogōng wèi fùmǔ qìguān de gùshì liúchuán zhìjīn.

Bāogōng shì Zhōngguó gǔdài yígè yǒumíng de qīngguān, yěshì mínjiān zuì néng dàibiǎo gōngpíng hé zhèngyì de huàshēn, ér tā xiàojìng fùmǔ de gùshì yě wéirén chēngdào. Bāogōng cóngxiǎo jiù xiǎnchū cáiqì, nián jǐn èrshíbā suì jiù kǎozhōng jìnshì, bìng zài yuǎnlí jiāxiāng de dìfāng dédào yí fèn guānzhí. Dànshì dāng niánlǎo de fùmǔ búyuàn gēn tā líkāi jiāxiāng shí, Bāogōng háobù yóuyù de cíqù guānzhí, liúzài jiālǐ zhàogù fùmǔ. Bāogōng de xiàoxīn shòudàole guānyuánmen de yízhì hǎopíng.

[Traditional-character version]

親嘗湯藥

中國古代的漢文帝劉恒是一個有名的大孝子。劉恒非常孝順母親，不管自己多忙，也都把母親的事情放在首位。有一次，母親得了大病，而且一病就是三年。在這三年中，劉恒在處理好國家大事後，常常守護在母親床前照顧。每次宮女們把爲母親熬的湯藥端來以後，劉恒都要親自嘗一嘗，看看湯藥苦不苦、燙不燙，然後一勺一勺地喂給母親喝。三年後，母親的病終於好了，他自己卻因爲操勞過度累倒了。

皇帝親嘗湯藥的故事在當時婦孺皆知，皇帝的孝順感動了全國。受到他的影響，整個漢朝的孝子層出不窮。

[Simplified-character version]

亲尝汤药

中国古代的汉文帝刘恒是一个有名的大孝子。刘恒非常孝顺母亲，不管自己多忙，也都把母亲的事情放在首位。有一次，母亲得了大病，而且一病就是三年。在这三年中，刘恒在处理好国家大事后，常常守护在母亲床前照顾。每次宫女们把为母亲熬的汤药端来以后，刘恒都要亲自尝一尝，看看汤药苦不苦、烫不烫，然后一勺一勺地喂给母亲喝。三年后，母亲的病终于好了，他自己却因为操劳过度累倒了。

皇帝亲尝汤药的故事在当时妇孺皆知，皇帝的孝顺感动了全国。受到他的影响，整个汉朝的孝子层出不穷。

[Pinyin version]

Qīncháng Tāngyào

Zhōngguó gǔdài de Hàn Wéndì Liú Héng shì yí gè yǒumíng de dà xiàozǐ. Liú Héng fēicháng xiàoshùn mǔqīn, bùguǎn zìjǐ duōmáng, yě dū bǎ mǔqīn de shìqing fàngzài shǒuwèi. Yǒu yí cì, mǔqīn déle dàbìng, érqiě yí bìng jiùshì sānnián. Zài zhè sānnián zhōng, Liú Héng zài chǔlǐhǎo guójiā dàshì hòu, chángcháng shǒuhù zài mǔqīn chuángqián zhàogù. Měi cì gōngnǚmen bǎ wèi mǔqīn áode tāngyào duānlai yǐhòu, Liú Héng dōu yào qīnzì chángyicháng, kànkan tāngyào kǔbukǔ, tàngbutàng, ránhòu yìsháo yìsháo de wèigěi mǔqīn hē. Sānnián hòu, mǔqīn de bìng zhōngyú hǎole, tā zìjǐ què yīnwèi cāoláo guòdù lèidǎole. Huángdì qīncháng tāngyào de gùshì zài dāngshí fùrú jiēzhī, huángdì de xiàoshùn gǎndòngle quánguó. Shòudào tā de yǐngxiǎng, zhěnggè Hàncháo de xiàozǐ céngchū bùqióng.

[Traditional-character version]

子路負米

　　孔子的學生子路非常孝敬父母。因爲是在貧窮的家庭中長大的，子路在生活上非常節儉，經常靠吃野菜度日，但是他擔心父母常吃野菜影響身體健康，想買些米給父母吃，補充營養。爲了讓父母吃到米，子路不辭辛勞地跑到百里之外買米，然後背回家做成飯給父母吃。無論酷暑寒冬，都沒能阻止他爲父母去背米。後來，子路的父母相繼過世了，他才到了楚國做官。

　　在楚國做官的日子裏，子路的生活條件很好。一日三餐山珍海味，出門百輛馬車跟隨。子路不但沒有爲富足的生活感到高興，反而經常感歎父母過世太早，否則，就可以跟他過上好日子了。

[Simplified-character version]

子路负米

　　孔子的学生子路非常孝敬父母。因为是在贫穷的家庭中长大的，子路在生活上非常节俭，经常靠吃野菜度日，但是他担心父母常吃野菜影响身体健康，想买些米给父母吃，补充营养。为了让父母吃到米，子路不辞辛劳地跑到百里之外买米，然后背回家做成饭给父母吃。无论酷暑寒冬，都没能阻止他为父母去背米。后来，子路的父母相继过世了，他才到了楚国做官。

　　在楚国做官的日子里，子路的生活条件很好。一日三餐山珍海味，出门百辆马车跟随。子路不但没有为富足的生活感到高兴，反而经常感叹父母过世太早，否则，就可以跟他过上好日子了。

[Pinyin version]

Zǐlù Fùmǐ

Kǒngzǐ de xuéshēng Zǐ Lù fēicháng xiàojìng fùmǔ. Yīnwéi shì zài pínqióng de jiātíng zhōng zhǎngdà de, Zǐ Lù zài shēnghuó shang fēicháng jiéjiǎn, jīngcháng kào chī yěcài dùrì, dànshì tā dānxīn fùmǔ cháng chī yěcài, yǐngxiǎng shēntǐ jiànkāng, xiǎng mǎi xiē mǐ gěi fùmǔ chī, bǔchōng yíngyǎng. Wèile ràng fùmǔ chīdào mǐ, Zǐ Lù bùcí xīnláo de pǎodào bǎilǐ zhīwài mǎimǐ, ránhòu bēihuí jiā zuòchéng fàn gěi fùmǔ chī. Wúlùn kùshǔ hándōng, dōu méi néng zǔzhǐ tā wèi fùmǔ qù bèimǐ. Hòulái, Zǐ Lù de fùmǔ xiāngjì guòshìle, tā cái dàole Chǔguó zuòguān.

　　Zài Chǔguó zuòguān de rìzi lǐ, Zǐ Lù de shēnghuó tiáojiàn hěn hǎo. Yírì sāncān shānzhēn hǎiwèi, chūmén bǎiliàng mǎchē gēnsuí. Zǐ Lù búdàn méiyǒu wèi fùzú de shēnghuó gǎndào gāoxìng, fǎn'ér jīngcháng gǎntàn fùmǔ guòshì tài zǎo, fǒuzé, jiù kěyǐ gēn tā guòshang hǎo rìzi le.

[Traditional-character version]

孔融讓梨

　　漢朝時有一個孩子叫孔融，孔融從小聰明伶俐、勤奮好學。有一天，父親的一個朋友到家裏做客，並帶來一些梨子給孔家的孩子們。父親把孔融叫過來，讓他把梨子分給兄弟們吃。孔融首先挑了一個最小的梨子留給自己，然後把其餘的梨子按照年齡順序分給哥哥和弟弟們。父親問孔融爲什麼這樣分梨，孔融說：「哥哥們的年紀比我大，應該把大梨分給他們。」父親好奇地問：「可是弟弟們都比你小呀，爲什麼他們的梨子也比你的大呢？」孔融說：“正是因爲弟弟們比我小，所以我應該讓著他們，把大的分給他們。”父親聽後，滿意地點了點頭。

孔融讓梨的故事在當時家喻戶曉，孔融謙讓的精神流傳至今。

[Simplified-character version]

孔融让梨

汉朝时有一个孩子叫孔融，孔融从小聪明伶俐、勤奋好学。有一天，父亲的一个朋友到家里做客，并带来一些梨子给孔家的孩子们。父亲把孔融叫过来，让他把梨子分给兄弟们吃。孔融首先挑了一个最小的梨子留给自己，然后把其余的梨子按照年龄顺序分给哥哥和弟弟们。父亲问孔融为什么这样分梨，孔融说：“哥哥们的年纪比我大，应该把大梨分给他们。”父亲好奇地问：“可是弟弟们都比你小呀，为什么他们的梨子也比你的大呢？”孔融说：“正是因为弟弟们比我小，所以我应该让着他们，把大的分给他们。”父亲听后，满意地点了点头。

孔融让梨的故事在当时家喻户晓，孔融谦让的精神流传至今。

[Pinyin version]

Kǒng Róng Rànglí

Hàncháo shí yǒu yí gè háizi jiào Kǒng Róng, Kǒng Róng cóngxiǎo cōngmíng línglì, qínfèn hàoxué. Yǒu yí tiān, fùqīn de yí gè péngyǒu dào jiālǐ zuòkè, bìng dàilai yí xiē lízi gěi Kǒngjiā de háizimen. Fùqīn bǎ Kǒng Róng jiào guòlai, ràng tā bǎ lízi fēngěi xiōngdìmen chī. Kǒng Róng shǒuxiān tiāole yí gè zuì xiǎo de lízi liúgěi zìjǐ, ránhòu bǎ qíyú de lízi ànzhào niánlíng shùnxù fēngěi gēgē hé dìdìmen. Fùqīn wèn Kǒng Róng wèi shénme zhèyàng fēnlí, Kǒng Róng shuō: "Gēgēmen de niánjì bǐ wǒ dà, yīnggāi bǎ dàlí fēngěi tāmen." Fùqīn hàoqí de wèn:"Kěshì dìdìmen dōu bǐ nǐ xiǎo ya, wèi shénme tāmen de lízi yě bǐ nǐ de dà ne?" Kǒng Róng shuō:"Zhèngshì yīnwèi dìdìmen bǐ wǒ xiǎo, suǒyǐ wǒ yīnggāi ràngzhe tāmen, bǎ dàde fēngěi tāmen." Fùqīn tīnghòu, mǎnyì de diǎnlediǎn tóu.

Kǒng Róng rànglí de gùshì zài dāngshí jiāyù hùxiǎo, Kǒng Róng qiānràng de jīngshén liúchuán zhìjīn.

CHINESE MYTHOLOGY

[Traditional-character version]

女媧補天

女媧是中國古代化育萬物、造福人類的女神。傳說有了天地以後，大地上只有山川湖泊、花草鳥獸，而沒有人類。爲了造人，女媧抓起黃土，仿照自己映在水中的樣子，捏成小人的形狀。這個泥人一放到地面上，就有了生命。于是女媧就繼續捏了男男女女的人。由於用手捏得太慢，女媧就拿起一根草繩，攪拌黃泥，拋了出去，結果泥點到的地方，都變成了一個個活生生的人。以後，女媧讓那些男女生育後代，延伸下去。後來，宇宙發生了大變動，半邊天塌了下來，出現一個個可怕的黑洞。地上也出現了一道道大裂口。山林著起大火，地面流出很多水。野獸們也都出來危害人類。女媧看到人類受這樣的災禍，就全力補修天地。她先用五彩石把天上的大洞補好，又殺了一隻大龜，把龜的四隻腳放在大地的四個角上，把天空支了起來。後來，她還殺了黑龍，趕走了野獸，堵住了洪水。從此，災難被平息了，人類得到了拯救，人世間又有了欣欣向榮的景象。

女媧補天的神話反映了中國古代勞動人民對人類起源和自然現象的最初認識。

[Simplified-character version]

女娲补天

女娲是中国古代化育万物、造福人类的女神。传说有了天地以后，大地上只有山川湖泊、花草鸟兽，而没有人类。为了造人，女娲抓起黄土，仿照自己映在水中的样子，捏成小人的形状。这个泥人一放到地面上，就有了生命。于是女娲就继续捏了男男女女的人。由于用手捏得太慢，女娲就拿起一根草绳，搅拌黄泥，抛了出去，结果泥点到的地方，都变成了一个个活生生的人。以后，女娲让那些男女生育后代，延伸下去。后来，宇宙发生了大变动，半边天塌了下来，出现一个个可怕的黑洞。地上也出现了一道道大裂口。山林着起大火，地面流出很多水。野兽们也都出来危害人类。女娲看到人类受这样的灾祸，就全力补修天地。她先用五彩石把天上的大洞补好，又杀了一只大龟，把龟的四只脚放在大地的四个角上，把天空支了起来。后来，她还杀了黑龙，赶走了野兽，堵住了洪水。从此，灾难被平息了，人类得到了拯救，人世间又有了欣欣向荣的景象。

女娲补天的神话反映了中国古代劳动人民对人类起源和自然现象的最初认识。

[Pinyin version]

Nǚwā Bǔtiān

Nǚwā shì Zhōngguó gǔdài huàyù wànwù, zàofú rénlèi de nǚshén. Chuānshuō, yǒule tiāndì yǐhòu, dàdìshang zhǐyǒu shānchuān húbó, huācǎo niǎoshòu, ér méiyǒu rénlèi. Wèile zàorén, Nǚwā zhuāqǐ huángtǔ, fǎngzhào zìjǐ yìngzài shuǐzhōng de yàngzi, niēchéng xiǎorén de xíngzhuàng. Zhège nírén yī fàngdào dìmiànshang, jiù yǒule shēngmìng. Yúshì Nǚwā jiù jìxù niēle nánnán nǚnǚ de rén. Yóuyú yòngshǒu niē de tài màn, Nǚwā jiù náqǐ yì gēn cǎoshéng, jiǎobàn huángní, pāole chūqu, jiéguǒ ní diǎndào de dìfāng, dōu biànchéngle yí gège huóshēngshēng de rén. Yǐhòu, Nǚwā ràng nàxiē nánnǚ shēngyù hòudài, yánshēn xiàqu. Hòulái, yǔzhòu fāshēngle dà biàndòng, bàn biān tiān tāle xiàlai, chūxiàn yí gège kěpà de hēidòng. Dìshang yě chūxiànle yídàodao dà lièkǒu. Shānlín zháoqi dàhuǒ, dìmiàn liúchū hěnduō shuǐ. Yěshòumen yě dōu chūlai wēihài rénlèi. Nǚwā kàndào rénlèi shòu zhèyàng de zāihuò, jiù quánlì bǔxiū tiāndì. Tā xiān yòng wǔcǎishí bǎ tiānshang de dàdòng bǔhǎo, yòu shāle yì zhī dàguī, bǎ guī de sì zhǐ jiǎo fàng zài dàdì de sì gè jiǎoshang, bǎ tiānkōng zhīle qǐlai. Hòulái, tā hái shāle hēilóng, gǎnzǒule yěshòu, dǔzhùle hóngshuǐ. Cóngcǐ, zāinàn bèi píngxīle, rénlèi dédàole zhěngjiù, rénshìjiān yòu yǒule xīnxīn xiàngróng de jǐngxiàng.

Nǚwā bǔtiān de shénhuà fǎnyìngle Zhōngguó gǔdài láodòng rénmín duì rénlèi qǐyuán hé zìrán xiànxiàng de zuìchū rènshi.

[Traditional-character version]

精衛填海

太陽神炎帝的女兒去東海邊玩，不小心掉到大海裏淹死了。她死了以後變成一隻小鳥，叫做精衛。精衛鳥不僅長得活潑、可愛，心地還很善良。爲了不讓別人也掉到大海裏，精衛鳥不斷地從西山叼來一根根的樹枝、一顆顆的石頭，丟進海裏，想要把大海填平。她一刻不停地在西山和東海之間飛來飛去。

精衛善良的願望和宏偉的志向受到人們的尊敬。中國歷代文學作品中都有詩文贊揚精衛敢於向大海抗爭的精神。

[Simplified-character version]

精卫填海

太阳神炎帝的女儿去东海边玩，不小心掉到大海里淹死了。她死了以后变成一只小鸟，叫做精卫。精卫鸟不仅长得活泼、可爱，心地还很善良。为了不让别人也掉到大海里，精卫鸟不断地从西山叼来一根根的树枝、一颗颗的石头，丢进海里，想要把大海填平。她一刻不停地在西山和东海之间飞来飞去。

精卫善良的愿望和宏伟的志向受到人们的尊敬。中国历代文学作品中都有诗文赞扬精卫敢于向大海抗争的精神。

[Pinyin version]

Jīngwèi Tiánhǎi

Tàiyángshén Yándì de nǚ'ér qù dōnghǎibiān wán, bùxiǎoxīn diàodao dàhǎili yānsǐle. Tā sǐle yǐhòu biànchéng yì zhǐ xiǎoniǎo, jiàozuò Jīngwèi. Jīngwèiniǎo bùjǐn zhǎngde huópō, kě'ài, xīndì hái hěn shànliáng. Wèile bú ràng biérén yě diàodao dàhǎili, Jīngwèiniǎo búduàn de cóng xīshān diāolai yì gēngēn de shùzhī, yì kēkē de shítou, diūjìn hǎili, xiǎng yào bǎ dàhǎi tiánpíng. Tā yíkè bùtíng de zài xīshān hé dōnghǎi zhījiān fēilai fēiqu.

Jīngwèi shànliáng de yuànwàng hé hóngwěi de zhìxiàng shòudào rénmen de zūnjìng. Zhōngguó lìdài wénxué zuòpǐn zhōng dōu yǒu shīwén zànyáng Jīngwèi gǎnyú xiàng dàhǎi kàngzhēng de jīngshén.

[Traditional-character version]

后羿射日

后羿是傳說中擅長射箭的天神。堯當皇帝的時候，天上有十個太陽。太陽把禾苗都曬死了，野獸也跑出來傷害人類，給人類帶來了嚴重的災難。於是，皇帝叫后羿到人間去解救人民。后羿到了人間，受到人民的歡迎。他拿起弓箭，對準天上的火球射去，過了一會，火球爆炸，一團東西落在地面上。人們跑去觀看，原來是太陽精魂。天上的太陽少了一個，空氣也涼爽了，人們齊聲歡呼。后羿受到鼓舞後又開始射日，天空中火球一個個破裂了，滿天是火。堯想到人們不能沒有太陽，就命令后羿留下一個太陽，爲人類造福。

[Simplified-character version]

后羿射日

后羿是传说中擅长射箭的天神。尧当皇帝的时候，天上有十个太阳。太阳把禾苗都晒死了，野兽也跑出来伤害人类，给人类带来了严重的灾难。于是，皇帝叫后羿到人间去解救人民。后羿到了人间，受到人民的欢迎。他拿起弓箭，对准天上的火球射去，过了一会，火球爆炸，一团东西落在地面上。人们跑去观看，原来是太阳精魂。天上的太阳少了一个，空气也凉爽了，人们齐声欢呼。后羿受到鼓舞后又开始射日，天空中火球一个个破裂了，满天是火。尧想到人们不能没有太阳，就命令后羿留下一个太阳，为人类造福。

[Pinyin version]

Hòuyì Shèrì

Hòuyì shì chuánshuō zhōng shàncháng shèjiàn de tiānshén. Yáo dāng Huángdì de shíhou, tiānshang yǒu shí gè tàiyáng. Tàiyáng bǎ hémiáo dōu shàisǐle, yěshòu yě pǎochūlai shānghài rénlèi, gěi rénlèi dàiláile yánzhòng de zāinàn. Yúshì, Huángdì jiào Hòuyì dào rénjiān qù jiějiù rénmín. Hòuyì dàole rénjiān, shòudào rénmín de huānyíng. Tā náqi gōngjiàn, duìzhǔn tiānshang de huǒqiú shèqu, guòle yíhuǐ, huǒqiú bàozhà, yì tuán dōngxi luòzài dìmiànshang. Rénmen pǎoqu guānkàn, yuánlái shì tàiyáng jīnghún. Tiānshang de tàiyáng shǎole yí gè, kōngqì yě liángshuǎng le, rénmen qíshēng huānhū. Hòuyì shòudào gǔwǔ hòu yòu kāishǐ shèrì, tiānkōng zhōng huǒqiú yígège pòlièle, mǎntiān shì huǒ. Yáo xiǎngdào rénmen bùnéng méiyǒu tàiyáng, jiù mìnglìng Hòuyì liúxia yí ge tàiyáng, wèi rénlèi zàofú.

[Traditional-character version]

嫦娥奔月

傳說嫦娥是天上的女神，是后羿的妻子。有一天，后羿帶回家一種長生不死的靈藥。后羿把藥交給嫦娥，並告訴她，這種藥如果兩人一起吃，就可以長生不死。如果一人獨吃，就能變成神。后羿告訴妻子說，等到一個吉祥的日子他們兩個人一起吃。可是在一個晚上，嫦娥趁后羿不在家，獨自把靈藥吃了。藥一吃下去，嫦娥的身體就不由自主地飄出窗戶，飛向天空，飛到月宮裏了。在月宮裏，嫦娥很寂寞，只有一隻白兔陪伴著她。嫦娥非常思念自己的丈夫后羿。後來，天帝封后羿爲天將，在中秋節的時候讓他們兩個人重逢、團圓。從此，嫦娥和后羿在天上過起了幸福、美滿的生活。天帝還規定，月亮每月十五日圓一次，用來祝願花好月圓夜，天下有情人成眷屬。

[Simplified-character version]

嫦娥奔月

传说嫦娥是天上的女神，是后羿的妻子。有一天，后羿带回家一种长生不死的灵药。后羿把药交给嫦娥，并告诉她，这种药如果两人一起吃，就可以长生不死。如果一人独吃，就能变成神。后羿告诉妻子说，等到一个吉祥的日子他们两个人一起吃。可是在一个晚上，嫦娥趁后羿不在家，独自把灵药吃了。药一吃下去，嫦娥的身体就不由自主地飘出窗户，飞向天空，飞到月宫里了。在月宫里，嫦娥很寂寞，只有一只白兔陪伴着她。嫦娥非常思念自己的丈夫后羿。后来，天帝封后羿为天将，在中秋节的时候让他们两个人重逢、团圆。从此，嫦娥和后羿在天上过起了幸福、美满的生活。天帝还规定，月亮每月十五日圆一次，用来祝愿花好月圆夜，天下有情人成眷属。

[Pinyin version]

Cháng'é Bēnyuè

Chuánshuō Cháng'é shì tiānshang de nǔshén, shì Hòuyì de qīzi. Yǒu yì tiān, Hòuyì dàihuí jiā yì zhǒng chángshēng bùsǐ de língyào. Hòuyì bǎ yào jiāogěi Cháng'é, bìng gàosu tā, zhè zhǒng yào rúguǒ liǎng rén yìqǐ chī, jiù kěyǐ chángshēng bùsǐ. Rúguǒ yìrén dú chī, jiù néng biànchéng shén. Hòuyì gàosu qīzi shuō, děngdào yí gè jíxiáng de rìzi tāmen liǎnggerén yìqǐ chī. Kěshì zài yí gè wǎnshang, Cháng'é chèn Hòuyì bú zàijiā, dúzì bǎ língyào chīle. Yào yì chīxiàqu, Cháng'é de shēntǐ jiù bùyóu zìzhǔ de piāochu chuānghu, fēixiàng tiānkōng, fēi dào yuègōngli le. Zài yuègōng li, Cháng'é hěn jìmò, zhǐyǒu yì zhī báitù péibànzhe tā. Cháng'é fēicháng sīniàn zìjǐ de zhāngfu Hòuyì. Hòulái, tiāndì fēng Hòuyì wéi tiānjiàng, zài Zhōngqiū Jié de shíhou ràng tāmen liǎng gèrén chóngféng, tuányuán. Cóngcǐ, Cháng'é hé Hòuyì zài tiānshang guòqǐle xìngfú měimǎn de shēnghuó. Tiāndì hái guīdìng, yuèliàng měiyuè shíwǔ rì yuán yí cì, yònglái zhùyuàn huāhǎo yuèyuán yè, tiānxià yǒuqíngrén chéng juànshǔ.

[Traditional-character version]

大禹治水

　　古代的時候，大地上一片汪洋，人類沒有居住的地方。有的人到山上尋找洞穴居住，有的人在樹上用鳥窩來藏身。後來，天帝命令大禹去治理洪水、挽救人類。大禹先動員衆神把水神趕走，又帶領他們堆出一座座山，挖出一條條河道，把洪水引到江海裏去。因爲治水繁忙，大禹三次路過家門口都沒有進去。經過艱苦的勞動，大禹終于治好了洪水。從此，天下太平了，人民安居樂業了，大禹也因此做了天子，用自己的一生爲人類謀求安寧和幸福，受到人們的愛戴。

[Simplified-character version]

大禹治水

　　古代的时候，大地上一片汪洋，人类没有居住的地方。有的人到山上寻找洞穴居住，有的人在树上用鸟窝来藏身。后来，天帝命令大禹去治理洪水、挽救人类。大禹先动员众神把水神赶走，又带领他们堆出一座座山，挖出一条条河道，把洪水引到江海里去。因为治水繁忙，大禹三次路过家门口都没有进去。经过艰苦的劳动，大禹终于治好了洪水。从此，天下太平了，人民安居乐业了，大禹也因此做了天子，用自己的一生为人类谋求安宁和幸福，受到人们的爱戴。

[Pinyin version]

Dàyǔ Zhìshuǐ

Gǔdài de shíhou, dàdìshang yí piàn wāngyáng, rénlèi méiyǒu jūzhù de dìfāng. Yǒuderén dào shānshang xúnzhǎo dòngxué jūzhù, yǒuderén zài shùshang yòng niǎowō lái cángshēn. Hòulái, Tiāndì mìnglìng Dàyǔ qù zhìlǐ hóngshuǐ, wǎnjiù rénlèi. Dàyǔ xiān dòngyuán zhòngshén bǎ shuǐshén gǎnzǒu, yòu dàilǐng tāmen duīchū yí zuòzuò shān, wāchū yì tiáotiáo hédào, bǎ hóngshuǐ yǐndào jiānghǎi li qù. Yīnwèi zhìshuǐ fánmáng, Dàyǔ sān cì lùguò jiāménkǒu dōu méiyǒu jìnqu. Jīngguò jiānkǔ de láodòng, Dàyǔ zhōngyú zhìhǎole hóngshuǐ. Cóngcǐ, tiānxià tàipíng le, rénmín ānjū lèyè le, Dàyǔ yě yīncǐ zuòle Tiānzǐ, yòng zìjǐ de yìshēng wèi rénlèi móuqiú ānníng hé xìngfú, shòudào rénmen de àidài.

IDIOM STORY

[Traditional-character version]

鐵杵磨針

　　李白小時不喜歡讀書，常常逃學。有一天，李白又沒有去上課，而是獨自一人跑到街上玩耍。在街上，他東瞧瞧、西看看，不知不覺地來到了一個破草屋前。李白看見一個白髮蒼蒼的老奶奶坐在屋前，手裏拿著一根粗粗的鐵棍子在磨。李白很好奇，就走過去問到：“老奶奶，你在做什麼？”老奶奶擡起頭說：“我要把這根鐵棍子磨成一根繡花針。”說完，老奶奶又低下頭，繼續磨著她的針。

"繡花針？鐵棍子這麼粗，你什麼時候才能磨成繡花針呢？"

老奶奶說："滴水可以穿透石頭，愚公可以移走大山，我爲什麼不能把鐵棍子磨成針呢？只要下的功夫深，就沒有做不到的事情。"

聽完老奶奶的話，李白感到很慚愧，默默地離開草屋，回去上課。從此以後，李白再也沒有逃過學。每天刻苦讀書，終於成爲歷史上著名的詩仙。

鐵杵磨針這個故事告訴我們：無論做什麼事情，只要堅持到底,就一定能夠成功。

[Simplified-character version]

铁杵磨针

李白小时不喜欢读书，常常逃学。有一天，李白又没有去上课，而是独自一人跑到街上玩耍。在街上，他东瞧瞧、西看看，不知不觉地来到了一个破草屋前。李白看见一个白发苍苍的老奶奶坐在屋前，手里拿着一根粗粗的铁棍子在磨。李白很好奇，就走过去问到："老奶奶，你在做什么？"老奶奶抬起头说："我要把这根铁棍子磨成一根绣花针。"说完，老奶奶又低下头，继续磨着她的针。

"绣花针？铁棍子这么粗，你什么时候才能磨成绣花针呢？"

老奶奶说："滴水可以穿透石头，愚公可以移走大山，我为什么不能把铁棍子磨成针呢？只要下的功夫深，就没有做不到的事情。"

听完老奶奶的话，李白感到很惭愧，默默地离开草屋，回去上课。从此以后，李白再也没有逃过学。每天刻苦读书，终于成为历史上著名的诗仙。

铁杵磨针这个故事告诉我们：无论做什么事情，只要坚持到底,就一定能够成功。

[Pinyin version]

Tiěchǔ Mózhēn

Lǐ Bái xiǎoshí bù xǐhuan dúshū, chángcháng táoxué. Yǒu yītiān, Lǐ Bái yòu méiyǒu qù shàngkè, érshì dúzì yì rén pǎodào jiēshang wánshuǎ. Zài jiēshang, tā dōng qiáoqiáo, xī kànkàn, bùzhī bùjué de lái daole yí gè pò cǎowū qián. Lǐ Bái kànjiàn yí gè báifà cāngcāng de lǎonǎinai zuòzài wū qián, shǒuli názhe yì gēn cūcū de tiě gùnzi zài mó. Lǐ Bái hěn hàoqí, jiù zǒu guòqù wèndao:"Lǎonǎinai, nǐ zài zuò shénme?"Lǎonǎinai tái qǐtóu shuō:"Wǒ yào bǎ zhè gēn tiě gùnzi móchéng yì gēn xiùhuāzhēn." Shuōwán, lǎonǎinai yòu dīxiatou, jìxù mózhe tāde zhēn.

"Xiùhuāzhēn? Tiě gùnzi zhème cū, nǐ shénme shíhou cáinéng móchéng xiùhuā zhēn ne?"

Lǎonǎinai shuō:"Dīshuǐ kěyǐ chuāntòu shítou, yúgōng kěyǐ yízǒu dàshān, wǒ wèishénme bùnéng bǎ tiě gùnzi móchéng zhēn ne? Zhǐyào xiàde gōngfu shēn, jiù méiyǒu zuòbudào de shìqíng."

Tīngwán lǎonǎinai de huà, Lǐ Bái gǎndào hěn cánkuì, mòmòde líkāi cǎowū, huíqù shàngkè. Cóngcǐ yǐhòu, Lǐ Bái zàiyě méiyǒu táoguoxué. Měitiān kèkǔ dúshū, zhōngyú chéngwéi lìshǐ shang zhùmíng de Shīxiān.

Tiěchǔ mózhēn zhège gùshì gàosu wǒmen: Wúlùn zuò shénme shìqíng, zhǐyào jiānchí dàodǐ, jiù yídìng nénggòu chénggōng.

[Traditional-character version]

掩耳盜鈴

　　古時候，有一個小偷跑到一個有錢人家裏偷東西。一進院門，這個小偷就看見這戶人家的院子裏挂著一口精致的大鍾。小偷高興極了，心想一定要把這口大鍾背回家去。可是那口鍾又大又重，他一個人怎麽背也背不動。忽然，他想出一個好辦法來：把鍾砸碎了，然後分幾次背回家不就行了嗎？於是，小偷跑回家找來一把大錘子，使出全身力氣朝大鍾砸去，只聽到"咣當"一聲，把他自己也嚇了一大跳。小偷心想：這下子可糟了，這不等於告訴大家我正在這裏偷鍾嗎？不行，我得想個辦法讓鐘聲停止。他想呀想，不由自主地用雙手捂住耳朵，"太好了，聲音變小了，聽不見了！"小偷又高興起來了，又跑回家，找了一些布把自己的耳朵堵起來，又回到那戶人家，放心地砸起鍾來。鐘聲傳到了很遠的地方，人們一聽到鐘聲就都跑過來，把這個小偷抓了起來。

　　掩耳盜鈴這個故事告訴我們：客觀存在的東西是不會以人的主觀意志而改變的。如果一定那麽做，就是自欺欺人。

[Simplified-character version]

掩耳盗铃

　　古时候，有一个小偷跑到一个有钱人家里偷东西。一进院门，这个小偷就看见这户人家的院子里挂着一口精致的大钟。小偷高兴极了，心想一定要把这口大钟背回家去。可是那口钟又大又重，他一个人怎么背也背不动。忽然，他想出一个好办法来：把钟砸碎了，然后分几次背回家不就行了吗？于是，小偷跑回家找来一把大锤子，使出全身力气朝大钟砸去，只听到"咣当"一声，把他自己也吓了一大跳。小偷心想：这下子可糟了，这不等于告诉大家我正在这里偷钟吗？不行，我得想个办法让钟声停止。他想呀想，不由自主地用双手捂住耳朵，"太好了，声音变小了，听不见了！"小偷又高兴起来了，又跑回家，找了一些布把自己的耳朵堵起来，又回到那户人家，放心地砸起钟来。钟声传到了很远的地方，人们一听到钟声就都跑过来，把这个小偷抓了起来。

　　掩耳盗铃这个故事告诉我们：客观存在的东西是不会以人的主观意志而改变的。如果一定那么做，就是自欺欺人。

[Pinyin version]

Yǎn'ěr Dàolíng

Gǔ shíhou, yǒu yí gè xiǎotōu pǎodào yígè yǒuqiánrén jiāli tōu dōngxi. Yī jìn yuànmén, zhège xiǎotōu jiù kànjiàn zhè hù rénjiā de yuànzi li guàzhe yì kǒu jīngzhì de dàzhōng. Xiǎotōu gāoxìng jíle, xīn xiǎng yídìng yào bǎ zhè kǒu dàzhōng bēi huíjiā qu. Kěshì nà kǒu zhōng yòudà yòuzhòng, tā yí gè rén zěnme bēi yě bēibudòng. Hūrán, tā xiǎngchu yí gè hǎo bànfǎ lái: Bǎ zhōng zásuìle, ránhòu fēn jǐ cì biē huíjiā, bú jiùxíng le ma? Yúshì, xiǎotōu pǎo huíjiā zhǎolai yì bǎ dà chuízi, shǐchū quánshēn lìqì cháo dàzhōng záqu, zhǐ tīngdao "guāngdāng" yì shēng, bǎ tā zìjǐ yě xiàle yí dà tiào. Xiǎotōu xīn xiǎng: Zhè xià zi kě zāole, zhè bù děngyú gàosu dàjiā wǒ zhèngzài zhèli tōu zhōng ma? Bùxíng, wǒ děi xiǎngge bànfǎ ràng zhōngshēng tíngzhǐ. Tā xiǎng ya xiǎng, bùyóu zìzhǔ de yòng shuāngshǒu wǔzhù ěrduo,"tài hǎole, shēngyīn biàn xiǎole, tīngbujiàn le!"Xiǎotōu yòu gāoxīng qǐlaile, yòu pǎo huíjiā, zhǎole yìxiē bù bǎ zìjǐ de ěrduo dǔ qǐlai, yòu huídào nà hù rénjiā, fàngxīn de záqi zhōng lai. Zhōngshēng chuán dàole hěnyuǎn de dìfāng, rénmen yì tīngdao zhōngshēng jiù dōu pǎoguòlai, bǎ zhège xiǎotōu zhuāle qǐlai.

Yǎn'ěr dàolíng zhège gùshì gàosu wǒmen: Kèguān cúnzài de dōngxi shì bù huì yǐ rénde zhǔguān yìzhì ér gǎibiàn de. Rúguǒ yídìng nàme zuò, jiùshì zìqī qīrén.

[Traditional-character version]

拔苗助長

　　古時候，有一個農夫總是擔心自己田裏的苗子長得比別人的慢。有一天清晨，他扛著鋤頭來到田裏，看到田地裏稻苗好像一點也沒有長高，心裏很著急。怎樣才能讓苗子長得快一點呢？他想啊想，終於想出了一個好主意。他走到稻苗前，用手把稻苗一棵棵地向上拔高。就這樣，忙了一整天，到了傍晚的時候，農夫終於把所有的稻苗都拔高了。雖然身上很累，但是看到田裏的稻苗都長高了不少，農夫的心裏甜滋滋的。那天晚上，農夫激動得一夜都沒有睡著覺。第二天，農夫又早早地來到田裏，滿懷希望地察看稻苗生長的情況。讓他沒有想到的是，田地裏的稻苗都死了。

　　拔苗助長的故事告訴我們：做事情不能急於求成，更不能違反事物發展的客觀規律。

[Simplified-character version]

拔苗助长

　　古时候，有一个农夫总是担心自己田里的苗子长得比别人的慢。有一天清晨，他扛着锄头来到田里，看到田地里稻苗好像一点也没有长高，心里很着急。怎样才能让苗子长得快一点呢？他想啊想，终于想出了一个好主意。他走到稻苗前，用手把稻苗一棵棵地向上拔高。就这样，忙了一整天，到了傍晚的时候，农夫终于把所有的稻苗都拔高了。虽然身上很累，但是看到田里的稻苗都长高了不少，农夫的心里甜滋滋的。那天晚上，农夫激动得一夜都没有睡着觉。第二天，农夫又早早地来到田里，满怀希望地察看稻苗生长的情况。让他没有想到的是，田地里的稻苗都死了。

　　拔苗助长的故事告诉我们：做事情不能急于求成，更不能违反事物发展的客观规律。

[Pinyin version]

Bámiáo Zhùzhǎng

Gǔ shíhou, yǒu yí gè nóngfū zǒngshì dānxīn zìjǐ tiánli de miáozi zhǎngde bǐ biérén de màn. Yǒu yí tiān qīngchén, tā kángzhe chútóu láidao tiánli, kàndao tiándì li dàomiáo hǎoxiàng yìdiǎn yě méiyǒu zhǎnggāo, xīnli hěn zhāojí. Zěnyàng cáinéng ràng miáozi zhǎngde kuài yìdiǎn ne? Tā xiǎng a xiǎng, zhōngyú xiǎngchūle yí gè hǎo zhǔyì. Tā zǒudao dàomiáo qián, yòng shǒu bǎ dàomiáo yì kēkēde xiàngshàng bágāo. Jiù zhèyàng, mángle yìzhěngtiān, dàole bàngwǎn de shíhou, nóngfū zhōngyú bǎ suǒyǒu de dàomiáo dōu bágāole. Suīrán shēnshang hěnlèi, dànshì kàndào tiánli de dàomiáo dōu zhǎnggāo le bùshǎo, nóngfū de xīnlǐ tiánzīzī de. Nà tiān wǎnshang, nóngfū jīdòng de yí yè dōu méiyǒu shuìzháo jiào. Dì èr tiān, nóngfū yòu zǎozǎode láidao tiánli, mǎnhuái xīwàng de chákàn dàomiáo shēngzhǎng de qíngkuàng. Ràng tā méiyǒu xiǎngdào de shì, tiándìl de dàomiáo dōu sǐle.

Bámiáo Zhùzhǎng de gùshì gàosu wǒmen: Zuò shìqíng bùnéng jíyú qiúchéng, gèng bùnéng wéifǎn shìwù fāzhǎn de kèguān guīlǜ.

[Traditional-character version]

對牛彈琴

古代的時候，有一個人叫公明儀。公明儀是一位有名的音樂家，可以演奏各種各樣的樂器，尤其是彈琴彈得好。有一天，公明儀帶著琴在田野中散步，忽然發現遠處有一頭牛正在吃草。公明儀突然想爲那頭牛彈一首曲子，於是，他快步走到牛的身邊，拿出琴，對著那頭正在吃草的牛興致勃勃地彈了起來。雖然公明儀彈奏的曲子無比優美，但是那頭牛始終無動於衷，一點也沒被那悅耳動聽的曲子所打動，一直專心致志地吃著它的草。

對牛彈琴這個故事告訴我們：不要對愚蠢的人講深刻的道理，也不要對外行的人說內行話。否則，就會白白地浪費時間。這個故事也諷刺了那些說話不看物件的人。

[Simplified-character version]

对牛弹琴

古代的时候，有一个人叫公明仪。公明仪是一位有名的音乐家，可以演奏各种各样的乐器，尤其是弹琴弹得好。有一天，公明仪带着琴在田野中散步，忽然发现远处有一头牛正在吃草。公明仪突然想为那头牛弹一首曲子，于是，他快步走到牛的身边，拿出琴，对着那头正在吃草的牛兴致勃勃地弹了起来。虽然公明仪弹奏的曲子无比优美，但是那头牛始终无动于衷，一点也没被那悦耳动听的曲子所打动，一直专心致志地吃着它的草。

对牛弹琴这个故事告诉我们：不要对愚蠢的人讲深刻的道理，也不要对外行的人说内行话。否则，就会白白地浪费时间。这个故事也讽刺了那些说话不看对象的人。

[Pinyin version]

Duìniú Tánqín

Gǔdài de shíhou, yǒu yí gè rén jiào Gōngmíng Yí. Gōngmíng Yí shì yí wèi yǒumíng de yīnyuèjiā, kěyǐ yǎnzòu gèzhǒng gèyàng de yuèqì, yóuqí shì tánqín tánde hǎo. Yǒu yì tiān, Gōngmíng Yì dàizhe qín zài tiányězhōng sànbù, hūrán fāxiàn yuǎnchù yǒu yí tóu niú zhèngzài chīcǎo. Gōngmíng Yì tūrán xiǎng wèi nà tóu niú tán yì shǒu qǔzi, yúshì, tā kuàibù zǒudào niúde shēnbiān, náchū qín, duìzhe nà tóu zhèngzài chīcǎo de niú xìngzhì bóbó de tánle qǐlai. Suīrán Gōngmíng Yí tánzòu de qǔzǐ wúbǐ yōuměi, dànshì nà tóu niú shǐzhōng wúdòng yúzhōng, yìdiǎn yě méi bèi nà yuè'ěr dòngtīng de qǔzi suǒ dǎdòng, yìzhí zhuānxīn zhìzhì de chīzhe tāde cǎo.

Duìniú Tánqín zhège gùshì gàosu wǒmen: Búyào duì yúchǔn de rén jiǎng shēnkè de dàolǐ, yě búyào duì wàiháng de rén shuō nèi hánghuà. Fǒuzé, jiù huì báibái de làngfèi shíjiān. Zhège gùshì yě fěngcìle nàxiē shuōhuà bú kàn duìxiàng de rén.

[Traditional-character version]

畫蛇添足

　　古代的時候，一家有錢人在祭祀完祖宗後準備把剩下的一壺酒作爲獎品賞給手下的人喝。可是手下的人太多，而酒又太少，怎麼辦呢？這時候，有個人提出一個建議：每個人都在地上畫一條蛇，那麼誰畫得最快、最好，這壺酒就賞給誰。於是，大家都蹲在地上，拿起筆畫起蛇來。沒過多久，就有一個人畫完了。這個人走過去，端起酒壺，正要喝的時候，才發現其他人都沒有畫完呢。他想："沒想到他們畫得那麼慢。那好吧，我就再多展示一些我的本領吧。"於是，他放下酒壺，拿起畫筆，在自己已經畫完的蛇的身上畫起腳來。正在他認真地給蛇畫上一隻只腳的時候，另外一個人把他的畫畫完了。那個人馬上走到酒壺前，端起酒壺，一口氣把那壺酒喝完了。

　　畫蛇添足這個故事告訴我們：不要做多餘的事情。否則，不但不能把事情做好，反而會把事情做壞了。

[Simplified-character version]

画蛇添足

　　古代的时候，一家有钱人在祭祀完祖宗后准备把剩下的一壶酒作为奖品赏给手下的人喝。可是手下的人太多，而酒又太少，怎么办呢？这时候，有个人提出一个建议：每个人都在地上画一条蛇，那么谁画得最快、最好，这壶酒就赏给谁。于是，大家都蹲在地上，拿起笔画起蛇来。没过多久，就有一个人画完了。这个人走过去，端起酒壶，正要喝的时候，才发现其他人都没有画完呢。他想："没想到他们画得那么慢。那好吧，我就再多展示一些我的本领吧。"于是，他放下酒壶，拿起画笔，在自己已经画完的蛇的身上画起脚来。正在他认真地给蛇画上一只只脚的时候，另外一个人把他的画画完了。那个人马上走到酒壶前，端起酒壶，一口气把那壶酒喝完了。

　　画蛇添足这个故事告诉我们：不要做多余的事情。否则，不但不能把事情做好，反而会把事情做坏了。

[Pinyin version]

Huàshé Tiānzú

Gǔdài de shíhou, yì jiā yǒuqiánrén zài jìsìwán zǔzōng hòu zhǔnbèi bǎ shèngxia de yì hú jiǔ zuòwéi jiǎngpǐn shǎnggěi shǒuxià de rén hē. Kěshì shǒuxià de rén tài duō, ér jiǔ yòu tài shǎo, zěnme bàn ne? Zhè shíhou, yǒugerén tíchū yí gè jiànyì: Měigèrén dōu zài dìshang huà yì tiáo shé, nàme shuí huàde zuìkuài, zuìhǎo, zhè hú jiǔ jiù shǎnggěi shuí. Yúshì, dàjiā dōu dūnzài dìshang, náqi bǐ huàqi shé lai. Méiguò duōjiǔ, jiù yǒu yí gè rén huàwánle. Zhège rén zǒu guòqu, duānqi jiǔhú, zhèngyào hē de shíhou, cái fāxiàn qítārén dōu méiyǒu huàwán ne. Tā xiǎng:"Méi xiǎngdào tāmen huàde nàme màn. Nà hǎo ba, wǒ jiù zài duō zhǎnshì yíxiē wǒ de běnlǐng ba."Yúshì, tā fàngxia jiǔhú, náqi huàbǐ, zài zìjǐ yǐjīng huàwán de shéde shēnshang huà qǐ jiǎo lai. Zhèngzài tā rènzhēn de gěi shé huàshang yì zhǐzhǐ jiǎo de shíhou, lìngwài yí gè rén bǎ tāde huà huàwánle. Nàgè rén mǎshàng zǒudào jiǔhú qián, duānqi jiǔhú, yìkǒuqì bǎ nà hú jiǔ hēwánle.

Huàshé Tiānzú zhège gùshì gàosu wǒmen: Búyào zuò duōyú de shìqíng. Fǒuzé, búdàn bùnéng bǎ shìqíng zuòhǎo, fǎn'ér huì bǎ shìqíng zuòhuài le.

[Traditional-character version]

東施效顰

　　春秋時代，有一個女子叫西施，長得非常漂亮，因此，一舉一動都特別吸引別人。遺憾的是，西施的身體很不好，經常生病。有一天，西施走在回家的路上，胸口又疼了起來，她趕緊用手捂住自己的胸口，不由自主地皺起了眉頭。雖然西施的身體很難受，但她手捂胸口、眉頭皺起的樣子在旁邊的人看來非常美麗，讓人愛憐不已。人群中有一個姑娘叫東施，長得很難看。東施看到大家誇讚西施手捂胸口的樣子好看，就學著西施的樣子，也用手捂住胸口、皺起眉頭，在人們面前慢慢地走來走去，希望也得到大家的誇讚。可是，因爲東施本來就長得很醜，加上刻意地學著西施的動作，令人更加地不喜歡她了。

　　東施效顰的故事告訴我們：如果刻意地去模仿別人，只會給別人留下壞影響，甚至成爲大家的笑料。

[Simplified-character version]

东施效颦

　　春秋时代，有一个女子叫西施，长得非常漂亮，因此，一举一动都特别吸引别人。遗憾的是，西施的身体很不好，经常生病。有一天，西施走在回家的路上，胸口又疼了起来，她赶紧用手捂住自己的胸口，不由自主地皱起了眉头。虽然西施的身体很难受，但她手捂胸口、眉头皱起的样子在旁边的人看来非常美丽，让人爱怜不已。人群中有一个姑娘叫东施，长得很难看。东施看到大家夸赞西施手捂胸口的样子好看，就学着西施的样子，也用手捂住胸口、皱起眉头，在人们面前慢慢地走来走去，希望也得到大家的夸赞。可是，因为东施本来就长得很丑，加上刻意地学着西施的动作，令人更加地不喜欢她了。

　　东施效颦的故事告诉我们：如果刻意地去模仿别人，只会给别人留下坏影响，甚至成为大家的笑料。

[Pinyin version]

Dōngshī Xiàopín

Chūnqiū shídài, yǒu yí gè nǚzǐ jiào Xīshī, zhǎngde fēicháng piàoliang, yīncǐ, yìjǔ yídòng dōu tèbié xīyǐn biérén. Yíhàn de shì, Xīshī de shēntǐ hěnbuhǎo, jīngcháng shēngbìng. Yǒu yì tiān, Xīshī zǒuzài huíjiā de lùshang, xiōngkǒu yòu téngle qǐlai, tā gǎnjǐn yòng shǒu wǔzhù zìjǐ de xiōngkǒu, bùyóu zìzhǔ de zhòuqǐle méitóu. Suīrán Xīshī de shēntǐ hěn nánshòu, dàn tā shǒuwǔ xiōngkǒu, méitóu zhòuqǐ de yàngzi zài pángbiānde rén kànlai fēicháng měilì, ràngrén àilián bùyǐ. Rénqún zhōng yǒu yí gè gūniang jiào Dōngshī, zhǎngde hěn nánkàn. Dōngshī kàndao dàjiā kuāzàn Xīshī shǒuwǔ xiōngkǒu de yàngzi hǎokàn, jiù xuézhe Xīshī de yàngzi, yě yòngshǒu wǔzhù xiōngkǒu, zhòuqǐ méitóu, zài rénmen miànqián mànman de zǒulái zǒuqù, xīwàng yě dédào dàjiā de kuāzàn. Kěshì, yīnwèi Dōngshī běnlái jiù zhǎngde hěn chǒu, jiāshàng kèyì de xuézhe Xīshī de dòngzuò, lìngrén gèngjiā de bù xǐhuan tā le.

Dōngshī Xiàopín de gùshì gàosu wǒmen: Rúguǒ kèyì de qù mófǎng biérén, zhǐ huì gěi biérén liúxià huài yǐngxiǎng, shènzhì chéngwéi dàjiā de xiàoliào.

[Traditional-character version]

懸梁刺股

　　孫敬是中國東漢時期著名的政治家。孫敬年輕時勤奮好學，讀起書來廢寢忘食。由於讀書時間長，又捨不得休息，有時他就累得打瞌睡。總打瞌睡不但浪費了時間，也影響讀書的效果，孫敬爲此很著急。後來，他終於想出了一個好辦法。中國古代的時候，男子跟女人一樣留著長髮，孫敬找來一根繩子，把繩子的一頭牢牢地綁在房梁上，另一頭綁在自己的頭髮上。他打一下瞌睡，就低一次頭，繩子就拉一下頭髮，這樣頭皮就被繩子拉疼了，於是他就清醒了。孫敬就是用這個辦法讀書的。

　　中國戰國時期有一位著名的政治家，叫蘇秦。蘇秦年輕的時候沒有什麼學問，做什麼都不被重視，家人也看不起他。於是，蘇秦決心刻苦讀書，以後幹一番大事業。每當蘇秦讀書讀到深夜的時候，他總是困得打盹。後來，他就在自己打盹的時候，用錐子往大腿上刺一下，讓自己清醒。

　　孫敬和蘇秦的"懸梁刺股"的故事讓後人很感動，他們刻苦讀書的精神在民間流傳下來。

[Simplified-character version]

悬梁刺股

　　孙敬是中国东汉时期著名的政治家。孙敬年轻时勤奋好学，读起书来废寝忘食。由于读书时间长，又舍不得休息，有时他就累得打瞌睡。总打瞌睡不但浪费了时间，也影响读书的效果，孙敬为此很着急。后来，他终于想出了一个好办法。中国古代的时候，男子跟女人一样留着长发，孙敬找来一根绳子，把绳子的一头牢牢地绑在房梁上，另一头绑在自己的头发上。他打一下瞌睡，就低一次头，绳子就拉一下头发，这样头皮就被绳子拉疼了，于是他就清醒了。孙敬就是用这个办法读书的。

　　中国战国时期有一位著名的政治家，叫苏秦。苏秦年轻的时候没有什么学问，做什么都不被重视，家人也看不起他。于是，苏秦决心刻苦读书，以后干一番大事业。每当苏秦读书读到深夜的时候，他总是困得打盹。后来，他就在自己打盹的时候，用锥子往大腿上刺一下，让自己清醒。

　　孙敬和苏秦的"悬梁刺股"的故事让后人很感动，他们刻苦读书的精神在民间流传下来。

[Pinyin version]

Xuánliáng Cìgǔ

Sūn Jìng shì Zhōngguó Dōnghàn shíqī zhùmíng de zhèngzhìjiā. Sūn jìng niánqīng shí qínfèn hàoxué, dúqi shū lai fèiqǐn wàngshí. Yóuyú dúshū shíjiān cháng, yòu shěbude xiūxi, yǒushí tā jiù lèide dǎ kēshuì. Zǒng dǎ kēshuì bùdàn làngfèi le shíjiān, yě yǐngxiǎng dúshū de xiàoguǒ, Sūn Jìng wèicǐ hěn zhāojí. Hòulái, tā zhōngyú xiǎng chūle yí gè hǎo bànfǎ. Zhōngguó gǔdài de shíhou, nánzǐ gēn nǚrén yíyàng liúzhe chángfā, Sūn Jìng zhǎolai yì gēn shéngzi, bǎ shéngzi de yì tóu láoláode bǎngzài fángliángshang, lìng yì tóu bǎngzài zìjǐ de tóufa shang. Tā dǎ yí xià kēshuì, jiù dī yí cì tóu, shéngzi jiù lā yí xià tóufa, zhèyàng tóupí jiù bèi shéngzi lāténgle, yúshì tā jiù qīngxǐngle. Sūn Jìng jiùshì yòng zhège bànfǎ dúshū de.

Zhōngguó Zhànguó shíqī yǒu yí wèi zhùmíng de zhèngzhìjiā, jiào Sū Qín. Sū Qín niánqīng de shíhou méiyǒu shénme xuéwèn, zuò shénme dōu bù bèi zhòngshì, jiārén yě kànbuqǐ tā. Yúshì, Sū Qín juéxīn kèkǔ dúshū, yǐhòu gàn yì fān dà shìyè. Měidāng Sū Qín dúshū dúdào shēnyè de shíhou, tā zǒngshì kùnde dǎdǔn. Hòulái, tā jiù zài zìjǐ dǎdǔn de shíhou, yòng zhuīzi wǎng dàtuǐshang cì yí xià, ràng zìjǐ qīngxǐng.

Sūn Jìng hé Sū Qín de "Xuánliáng cìgǔ"de gùshì ràng hòurén hěn gǎndòng, tāmen kèkǔ dúshū de jīngshén zài mínjiān liúchuán xiàlai.

[Traditional-character version]

鑿壁偷光

西漢有個叫匡衡的人特別喜歡讀書，但是他的家裏非常窮，根本買不起蠟燭。晚上屋裏太黑，匡衡沒有辦法讀書。匡衡的鄰居家，日子過得不錯，點著蠟燭的屋子總是亮堂堂的。匡衡很想到鄰居家去讀書，可是怕人家不同意。後來，他想出一個好主意，他在牆上鑿了一個小洞，這樣，鄰居家的光就過來了，匡衡把書對著光讀起書來。匡衡讀的書越來越多，可是因爲沒有錢，不能買書，怎麼辦呢？他想起有個有錢人家，家裏的書很多，於是，他就去幫那家人幹活，但是不要錢。人家很奇怪，就問他爲什麼。匡衡說："我幫你幹活，其實是想借你家的書看看，不知你答應不答應？"人家非常高興，就把書借給他看。後來，匡衡成了一個有學問的人。"鑿壁偷光"這個成語也因此而流傳下來。

[Simplified-character version]

凿壁偷光

西汉有个叫匡衡的人特别喜欢读书，但是他的家里非常穷，根本买不起蜡烛。晚上屋里太黑，匡衡没有办法读书。匡衡的邻居家，日子过得不错，点着蜡烛的屋子总是亮堂堂的。匡衡很想到邻居家去读书，可是怕人家不同意。后来，他想出一个好主意，他在墙上凿了一个小洞，这样，邻居家的光就过来了，匡衡把书对着光读起书来。匡衡读的书越来越多，可是因为没有钱，不能买书，怎么办呢？他想起有个有钱人家，家里的书很多，于是，他就去帮那家人干活，但是不要钱。人家很奇怪，就问他为什么。匡衡说："我帮你干活，其实是想借你家的书看看，不知你答应不答应？"人家非常高兴，就把书借给他看。后来，匡衡成了一个有学问的人。"凿壁偷光"这个成语也因此而流传下来。

[Pinyin version]

Záobì Tōuguāng

Xīhàn yǒu gè jiào Kuāng Héng de rén tèbié xǐhuan dúshū, dànshì tā de jiāli fēicháng qióng, gēnběn mǎibuqǐ làzhú. Wǎnshang wūli tài hēi, Kuāng Héng méiyǒu bànfǎ dúshū. Kuāng Héng de línjū jiā, rìzi guòde búcuò, diǎnzhe làzhú de wūzi zǒngshì liàng tángtáng de. Kuāng Héng hěn xiǎng dào línjūjiā qù dúshū, kěshì pà rénjiā bù tóngyì. Hòulái, tā xiǎngchu yí gè hǎo zhǔyì, tā zài qiángshang záole yí gè xiǎodòng, zhèyàng, línjū jiā de guāng jiù guòlaile, Kuāng Héng bǎ shū duìzhe guāng dúqi shūlai. Kuāng Héng dúde shū yùelái yùeduō, kěshì yīnwèi méiyǒu qián, bùnéng mǎishū, zěnme bàn ne? Tā xiǎngqǐ yǒu gè yǒuqián rénjiā, jiāli de shū hěnduō, yúshì, tā jiù qù bāng nà jiā rén gànhuó, dànshì bú yào qián. Rénjiā hěn qíguài, jiù wèn tā wèishénme. Kuāng Héng shuō:"Wǒ bāng nǐ gànhuó, qíshí shì xiǎng jiè nǐ jiā de shū kànkàn, bùzhī nǐ dāyìng bu dāyìng?"Rénjiā fēicháng gāoxìng, jiù bǎ shū jiègěi tā kàn. Hòulái, Kuāng Héng chéngle yí gè yǒu xuéwèn de rén. "Záobì tōuguāng"zhège chéngyǔ yě yīncǐ ér liúchuán xiàlái.

FOUR GRAND WORKS IN CHINESE LITERATURE

[Traditional-character version]

《紅樓夢》

《紅樓夢》的作者是清朝偉大的文學家曹雪芹。《紅樓夢》通過對一個封建貴族大家庭的變化的描寫，揭露了中國封建社會末期的黑暗及矛盾，從而展示出封建社會必然走向滅亡的歷史命運。作品結構規模宏大、內容豐富，代表了中國古典小說藝術的最高成就。《紅樓夢》對後世的影響深遠。

《紅樓夢》中主要人物是賈寶玉。賈寶玉是賈家的嫡派子孫，也是這個大家庭寄予希望的繼承人。雖然寶玉生活在封建的大家庭中，但是他看不起功名利祿，不願意走"學而優則仕"的道路。他輕視世俗的男性，尊重社會下層的女性。他背離封建家庭給他安排的人生道路，要求婚姻自主。雖然與林黛玉的愛情最終以悲劇收場，但是體現了賈寶玉的叛逆性格。小說的另一主要人物是林黛玉。林黛玉聰明美麗、天真率直、才華橫溢。她從小失去父母，寄居於賈家。雖然賈母對她非常疼愛，但清高、自尊的性格使她變得多愁善感。她與寶玉有共同的理想和志趣。她深愛寶玉，但受到封建禮教的約束，不能表白，在寶玉結婚之日鬱鬱而死。《紅樓夢》的男女主人公受時代的局限，沒有找到現實生活的出路。他們要擺脫封建社會的建制，但又不得不依靠貴族階級生活，這使他們的思想性格具有悲劇性的矛盾。

[Simplified-character version]

《红楼梦》

《红楼梦》的作者是清朝伟大的文学家曹雪芹。《红楼梦》通过对一个封建贵族大家庭的变化的描写，揭露了中国封建社会末期的黑暗及矛盾，从而展示出封建社会必然走向灭亡的历史命运。作品结构规模宏大、内容丰富，代表了中国古典小说艺术的最高成就。《红楼梦》对后世的影响深远。

《红楼梦》中主要人物是贾宝玉。贾宝玉是贾家的嫡派子孙，也是这个大家庭寄予希望的继承人。虽然宝玉生活在封建的大家庭中，但是他看不起功名利禄，不愿意走"学而优则仕"的道路。他轻视世俗的男性，尊重社会下层的女性。他背离封建家庭给他安排的人生道路，要求婚姻自主。虽然与林黛玉的爱情最终以悲剧收场，但是体现了贾宝玉的叛逆性格。小说的另一主要人物是林黛玉。林黛玉聪明美丽、天真率直、才华横溢。她从小失去父母，寄居于贾家。虽然贾母对她非常疼爱，但清高、自尊的性格使她变得多愁善感。她与宝玉有共同的理想和志趣。她深爱宝玉，但受到封建礼教的约束，不能表白，在宝玉结婚之日郁郁而死。《红楼梦》的男女主人公受时代的局限，没有找到现实生活的出路。他们要摆脱封建社会的建制，但又不得不依靠贵族阶级生活，这使他们的思想性格具有悲剧性的矛盾。

[Pinyin version]

Hónglóumèng

"Hónglóumèng" de zuòzhě shì Qīngcháo wěidà de wénxuéjiā Cáo Xuěqín. "Hónglóumèng" tōngguò duì yí gè fēngjiàn guìzú dà jiātíng de biànhuà de miáoxiě, jiēlùle Zhōngguó fēngjiàn shèhuì mòqī de hēi'àn jí máodùn, cóng'ér zhǎnshì chū fēngjiàn shèhuì bìrán zǒuxiàng mièwáng de lìshǐ mìngyùn. Zuòpǐn jiégòu guīmó hóngdà, nèiróng fēngfù, dàibiǎole Zhōngguó gǔdiǎn xiǎoshuō yìshù de zuìgāo chéngjiù. "Hónglóumèng" duì hòushì de yǐngxiǎng shēnyuǎn.

"Hónglóumèng" zhōng zhǔyào rénwù shì Jiǎ Bǎoyù. Jiǎ Bǎoyù shì Jiǎjiā de dípài zǐsūn, yěshì zhège dà jiātíng jìyǔ xīwàng de jìchéngrén. Suīrán Bǎoyù shēnghuó zài fēngjiàn de dà jiātíng zhōng, dànshì tā kànbuqǐ gōngmíng lìlù, bú yuànyì zǒu "Xué ér yōu zé shì" de dàolù. Tā qīngshì shìsú de nánxìng, zūnzhòng shèhuì xiàcéng de nǚxìng. Tā bèilí fēngjiàn jiātíng gěi tā ānpái de rénshēng dàolù, yāoqiú hūnyīn zìzhǔ. Suīrán yǔ Lín Dàiyù de àiqíng zuìzhōng yǐ bēijù shōuchǎng, dànshì tǐxiànle Jiǎ Bǎoyù de pànnì xìnggé. Xiǎoshuō de lìng yí zhǔyào rénwù shì Lín Dàiyù. Lín Dàiyù cōngmíng měilì, tiānzhēn shuàizhí, cáihuá héngyì. Tā cóngxiǎo shīqù fùmǔ, jìjū yú Jiǎ jiā. Suīrán Jiǎ mǔ duì tā fēicháng téng'ài, dàn qīnggāo, zìzūn de xìnggé shǐ tā biànde duōchóu shàngǎn. Tā yǔ Bǎoyù yǒu gòngtóng de lǐxiǎng hé zhìqù. Tā shēn ài Bǎoyù, dàn shòudào fēngjiàn lǐjiào de yuēshù, bùnéng biǎobái, zài Bǎoyù jiéhūn zhīrì yùyù ér sǐ. "Hónglóumèng" de nánnǚ zhǔréngōng shòu shídài de júxiàn, méiyǒu zhǎodào xiànshí shēnghuó de chūlù. Tāmen yào bǎituō fēngjiàn shèhuì de jiànzhì, dàn yòu bùdébù yīkào guìzú jiējí shēnghuó, zhè shǐ tāmen de sīxiǎng xìnggé jùyǒu bēijùxìng de máodùn.

[Traditional-character version]

《三國演義》

　　明代通俗小說家羅貫中的《三國演義》描寫了從東漢到西晉的歷史故事，尤其集中描寫了魏、蜀、吳三國的鬥爭，爲人們提供了一幅豐富多彩的歷史人物的形象圖。

　　小說中諸葛亮的形象最爲突出，在讀者心中留下了深刻印象，成爲家喻戶曉、婦孺皆知的人物，受到世人的喜愛和推崇。由諸葛亮產生的成語、俗語數不勝數。如當人們誇獎別人聰明時，往往稱其爲"賽諸葛"、"小諸葛"或者說"三個臭皮匠，合成一個諸葛亮"。人們把諸葛亮看成了智慧的化身。

　　據小說描述，蜀漢開國皇帝劉備聽說諸葛亮很有才識，就帶著禮物去他家請他出山。那一天正好諸葛亮不在家，只能失望而歸。不久，劉備又和關羽、張飛冒著大風雪第二次去請，沒想到諸葛亮還不在家。又過了一段時間，劉備吃了三天素，第三次探訪諸葛亮。到他家時，諸葛亮正在睡覺。劉備沒有驚動他，直到他醒來才坐下跟他談話。諸葛亮見劉備態度誠懇，就與他分析天下形勢。聽完諸葛亮的分析，劉備非常敬佩，懇請諸葛亮出山，幫助他完成大業。諸葛亮見劉備心胸開闊，禮賢下士，抱負遠大，于是答應了劉備的請求。《三顧茅廬》的典故就是由此而來的。

[Simplified-character version]

《三国演义》

　　明代通俗小说家罗贯中的《三国演义》描写了从东汉到西晋的历史故事，尤其集中描写了魏、蜀、吴三国的斗争，为人们提供了一幅丰富多彩的历史人物的形象图。

　　小说中诸葛亮的形象最为突出，在读者心中留下了深刻印象，成为家喻户晓、妇孺皆知的人物，受到世人的喜爱和推崇。由诸葛亮产生的成语、俗语数不胜数。如当人们夸奖别人聪明时，往往称其为"赛诸葛"、"小诸葛"或者说"三个臭皮匠，合成一个诸葛亮"。人们把诸葛亮看成了智慧的化身。

　　据小说描述，蜀汉开国皇帝刘备听说诸葛亮很有才识，就带着礼物去他家请他出山。那一天正好诸葛亮不在家，只能失望而归。不久，刘备又和关羽、张飞冒着大风雪第二次去请，没想到诸葛亮还不在家。又过了一段时间，刘备吃了三天素，第三次探访诸葛亮。到他家时，诸葛亮正在睡觉。刘备没有惊动他，直到他醒来才坐下跟他谈话。诸葛亮见刘备态度诚恳，就与他分析天下形势。听完诸葛亮的分析，刘备非常敬佩，恳请诸葛亮出山，帮助他完成大业。诸葛亮见刘备心胸开阔，礼贤下士，抱负远大，于是答应了刘备的请求。《三顾茅庐》的典故就是由此而来的。

[Pinyin version]

Sānguó Yǎnyì

Míngdài tōngsú xiǎoshuōjiā Luō Guànzhōng de "Sānguó Yǎnyì" miáoxiěle cóng Dōnghàn dào Xījìn de lìshǐ gùshì, yóuqí jízhōng miáoxiěle Wèi, Shǔ, Wú sānguó de dòuzhēng, wèi rénmen tígōngle yì fú fēngfù duōcǎi de lìshǐ rénwù de xíngxiàngtú.

　　Xiǎoshuō zhōng Zhūgé Liàng de xíngxiàng zuìwéi tūchū, zài dúzhě xīnzhōng liúxiàle shēnkè yìnxiàng, chéngwéi jiāyù hùxiǎo, fùrú jiēzhī de rénwù, shòudào shìrén de xǐ'ài hé tuīchóng. Yóu Zhūgé Liàng chǎnshēng de chéngyǔ, súyǔ shǔbù shēngshǔ. Rú dāng rénmen kuājiǎng biérén cōngmíng shí, wǎngwǎng chēng qí wéi "sài Zhūgé", "xiǎo Zhūgé", huòzhě shuō "Sān gè chòu píjiang, héchéng yí gè Zhūgé Liàng". Rénmen bǎ Zhūgé Liàng kànchéng le zhìhuì de huàshēn.

　　Jù xiǎoshuō miáoshù, Shǔ Hàn kāiguó huángdì Liú Bèi tīngshuō Zhūgé Liàng hěn yǒu cáishì, jiù dàizhe lǐwù qù tā jiā qǐng tā chūshān. Nà yí tiān zhènghǎo Zhūgé Liàng bú zàijiā, zhǐ néng shīwàng ér guī. Bùjiǔ, Liú Bèi yòu hé Guān Yǔ, Zhāng Fēi màozhe dàfēngxuě dì èr cì qù qǐng, méi xiǎngdào Zhūgé Liàng hái bú zàijiā. Yòu guòle yí duàn shíjiān, Liú Bèi chīle sān tiān sù, dì sān cì tànfǎng Zhūgé Liàng. Dào tā jiā shí, Zhūgé Liàng zhèngzài shuìjiào. Liú Bèi méiyǒu jīngdòng tā, zhídào tā xǐnglai cái zuòxià gēn tā tánhuà. Zhūgé Liàng jiàn Liú Bèi tàidù chéngkěn, jiù yǔ tā fēnxī tiānxià xíngshì. Tīngwán Zhūgé Liàng de fēnxī, Liú Bèi fēicháng jìngpèi, kěnqǐng Zhūgé Liàng chūshān, bāngzhù tā wánchéng dàyè. Zhūgé Liàng jiàn Liú Bèi xīnxiōng kāikuò, lǐxián xiàshì, bàofù yuǎndà, yúshì dāyìngle Liú Bèi de qǐngqiú. "Sāngù Máolú" de diǎngù jiùshì yóucǐ érlái de.

[Traditional-character version]

《水滸傳》

　　生活在元末明初的文學家施耐庵寫的《水滸傳》被認爲是中國英雄傳奇作品中的典範，也是中國第一部反映民衆反抗鬥爭的長篇小說。《水滸傳》以其獨有的藝術的形式真實地反映了封建社會的黑暗，揭示了官逼民反的社會現實。小說以口語爲基礎語言，顯示了濃厚的生活氣息。

　　武松是《水滸傳》中的重要人物之一。他從小就練習武功，技藝高強。有一次，武松在回家探望哥哥的途中，在一個酒店喝了很多酒後，在路旁的一塊大石頭上躺下，剛要睡著的時候，忽然聽到一陣狂風呼嘯，與此同時，一隻猛虎朝他凶猛地撲了過來。武松急忙閃開，躲到了老虎的背後。老虎縱身一跳，武松又躲開了。老虎氣急敗壞地大吼一聲，用它的尾巴向武松抽來，武松又一次地躲開了，幷趁老虎轉身的時候舉起棍棒，用足力氣朝老虎的頭部打去。當老虎又一次地朝武松撲來時，武松機警地扔掉棍棒，靈敏地騎到虎背上，抓住老虎的頭猛烈打擊，直到把它打死爲止。武松打虎的故事流傳至今，武松也從此威名大震。

[Simplified-character version]

《水浒传》

　　生活在元末明初的文学家施耐庵写的《水浒传》被认为是中国英雄传奇作品中的典范，也是中国第一部反映民众反抗斗争的长篇小说。《水浒传》以其独有的艺术的形式真实地反映了封建社会的黑暗，揭示了官逼民反的社会现实。小说以口语为基础语言，显示了浓厚的生活气息。

　　武松是《水浒传》中的重要人物之一。他从小就练习武功，技艺高强。有一次，武松在回家探望哥哥的途中，在一个酒店喝了很多酒后，在路旁的一块大石头上躺下，刚要睡着的时候，忽然听到一阵狂风呼啸，与此同时，一只猛虎朝他凶猛地扑了过来。武松急忙闪开，躲到了老虎的背后。老虎纵身一跳，武松又躲开了。老虎气急败坏地大吼一声，用它的尾巴向武松抽来，武松又一次地躲开了，并趁老虎转身的时候举起棍棒，用足力气朝老虎的头部打去。当老虎又一次地朝武松扑来时，武松机警地扔掉棍棒，灵敏地骑到虎背上，抓住老虎的头猛烈打击，直到把它打死为止。武松打虎的故事流传至今，武松也从此威名大震。

[Pinyin version]

Shuǐhǔzhuàn

Shēnghuó zài Yuánmò Míngchū de wénxuéjiā Shī Nài'ān xiě de "Shuǐhǔzhuàn" bèi rènwéi shì Zhōngguó yīngxióng chuánqí zuòpǐn zhōng de diǎnfàn, yěshì Zhōngguó dì yī bù fǎnyìng mínzhòng fǎnkàng dòuzhēng de chángpiān xiǎoshuō. "Shuǐhǔzhuàn" yǐ qí dúyǒu de yìshù de xíngshì zhēnshí de fǎnyìngle fēngjiàn shèhuì de hēi'àn, jiēshìle guānbī mínfǎn de shèhuì xiànshí. Xiǎoshuō yǐ kǒuyǔ wéi jīchǔ yǔyán, xiǎnshìle nónghòu de shēnghuó qìxí.

　　Wǔ Sōng shì "Shuǐhǔzhuàn" zhōng de zhòngyào rénwù zhīyī. Tā cóngxiǎo jiù liànxí wǔgōng, jìyì gāoqiáng. Yǒu yí cì, Wǔ Sōng zài huíjiā tànwàng gēge de túzhōng, zài yí gè jiǔdiàn hēle hěnduō jiǔ hòu, zài lùpáng de yí kuài dà shítou shang tǎngxia, gāngyào shuìzháo de shíhou, hūrán tīngdào yí zhèn kuángfēng hūxiào, yǔcǐ tóngshí, yì zhī měnghǔ cháo tā xiōngměng de pūle guòlai. Wǔ Sōng jímáng shǎnkāi, duǒdào le lǎohǔ de bèihòu. Lǎohǔ zòngshēn yí tiào, Wǔ Sōng yòu duǒkāi le. Lǎohǔ qìjí bàihuài de dàhǒu yì shēng, yòng tā de wěiba xiàng Wǔ Sōng chōulai, Wǔ Sōng yòu yí cì de duǒkāi le, bìng chèn lǎohǔ zhuǎnshēn de shíhou juǒqi gùnbàng, yòngzú lìqì cháo lǎohǔ de tóubù dǎqu. Dāng lǎohǔ yòu yí cì de cháo Wǔ Sōng pūlai shí, Wǔ Sōng jījǐng de rēngdiào gùnbàng, língmǐn de qídào hǔbèi shang, zhuāzhù lǎohǔ de tóu měngliè dǎjī, zhídào bǎ tā dǎsǐ wéizhǐ. Wǔ Sōng dǎhǔ de gùshì liúchuán zhìjīn, Wǔ Sōng yě cóngcǐ wēimíng dàzhèn.

[Traditional-character version]

《西遊記》

　　《西遊記》的作者是明代的吳承恩。小說根據唐代玄奘和尚取經的故事，用神性、人性和物性三者合一的方式講述故事，塑造形象。小說通過豐富的藝術想象，塑造了一個神話世界和一個個栩栩如生的文學形象。小說的語言是在口語的基礎上加工而成的，富于表現力。

　　《西遊記》的主要人物孫悟空給人們留下深刻的印象。孫悟空善良、活潑、頑皮、樂觀，非常注重名譽。他第一次打出天門就是因爲被封的官銜太小，讓他臉上無光。第二次大鬧天宮也是因爲齊天大聖的官職有名無實，讓他氣惱。在跟隨唐僧取經的途中，他常因顧全名譽而與他人決鬥。除了好名以外，孫悟空還勇敢機智、爭强好鬥。他的敢爭、敢拼、敢鬥的反抗性格在大鬧天宮、三打白骨精、大鬧黑風山等故事情節中被形象地描述出來。孫悟空有勇、有謀，在取經途中鏟除妖魔鬼怪，救助貧民百姓，克服種種困難，終于完成任務。《西遊記》的故事告訴我們：在漫漫的人生道路上，不可能是一帆風順的。要像孫悟空一樣，爲追求自己的理想而努力奮鬥。

[Simplified-character version]

《西游记》

　　《西游记》的作者是明代的吴承恩。小说根据唐代玄奘和尚取经的故事，用神性、人性和物性三者合一的方式讲述故事，塑造形象。小说通过丰富的艺术想象，塑造了一个神话世界和一个个栩栩如生的文学形象。小说的语言是在口语的基础上加工而成的，富于表现力。

　　《西游记》的主要人物孙悟空给人们留下深刻的印象。孙悟空善良、活泼、顽皮、乐观，非常注重名誉。他第一次打出天门就是因为被封的官衔太小，让他脸上无光。第二次大闹天宫也是因为齐天大圣的官职有名无实，让他气恼。在跟随唐僧取经的途中，他常因顾全名誉而与他人决斗。除了好名以外，孙悟空还勇敢机智、争强好斗。他的敢争、敢拼、敢斗的反抗性格在大闹天宫、三打白骨精、大闹黑风山等故事情节中被形象地描述出来。孙悟空有勇、有谋，在取经途中铲除妖魔鬼怪，救助贫民百姓，克服种种困难，终于完成任务。《西游记》的故事告诉我们：在漫漫的人生道路上，不可能是一帆风顺的。要像孙悟空一样，为追求自己的理想而努力奋斗。

[Pinyin version]

Xīyóujì

"Xīyóujì" de zuòzhě shì Míngdài de Wú Chéng'ēn. Xiǎoshuō gēnjù Tángdài Xuánzàng héshàng qǔjīng de gùshì, yòng shénxìng, rénxìng hé wùxìng sānzhě héyī de fāngshì jiǎngshù gùshì, sùzào xíngxiàng. Xiǎoshuō tōngguò fēngfù de yìshù xiǎngxiàng, sùzàole yí gè shénhuà shìjiè hé yí gègè xǔxǔ rúshēng de wénxué xíngxiàng. Xiǎoshuō de yǔyán shì zài kǒuyǔ de jīchǔ shang jiāgōng érchéng de, fùyú biǎoxiàn lì.

"Xīyóujì" de zhǔyào rénwù Sūn Wùkōng gěi rénmen liúxia shēnkè de yìnxiàng. Sūn Wùkōng shànliáng, huópō, wánpí, lèguān, fēicháng zhùzhòng míngyù. Tā dì yí cì dǎchū tiānmén jiùshì yīnwèi bèifēng de guānxián tàixiǎo, ràng tā liǎnshang wúguāng. Dì èr cì dànào tiāngōng yěshì yīnwèi qítiān dàshèng de guānzhí yǒumíng wúshí, ràng tā qìnǎo. Zài gēnsuí Tángsēng qǔjīng de túzhōng, tā cháng yīn gùquán míngyù ér yǔ tārén juédòu. Chúle hǎomíng yǐwài, Sūn Wùkōng hái yǒnggǎn jīzhì, zhēngqiáng hàodòu. Tā de gǎnzhēng, gǎnpīn, gǎndòu de fǎnkàng xìnggé zài Dànào tiāngōng, Sāndǎ báigǔjīng, Dànào hēifēngshān děng gùshì qíngjié zhōng bèi xíngxiàng de miáoshù chūlai. Sūn Wùkōng yǒuyǒng, yǒumóu, zài qǔjīng túzhōng chǎnchú yāomó guǐguài, jiùzhù pínmín bǎixìng, kèfú zhǒngzhǒng kùnnán, zhōngyú wánchéng rènwù. "Xīyóujì" de gùshì gàosu wǒmen: Zài mànmàn de rénshēng dàolù shang, bù kěnéng shì yīfān fēngshùn de. Yào xiàng Sūn Wùkōng yíyàng, wèi zhuīqiú zìjǐ de lǐxiǎng ér nǔlì fèndòu.

CHINESE CHARACTER

[Traditional-character version]

漢字

　　漢字是記錄漢語的文字，也是世界上最古老的文字之一。漢字以象形字爲基礎，形、音、義結合於一體，成爲一種獨特的方塊形的表意體系文字。現在發現的最早、最成熟的漢字是中國商代的甲骨文。從甲骨文發展到今天使用的漢字，又經歷了大篆、小篆、隸書、楷書、草書、行書等演變過程。在形體上，漢字逐漸由圖畫變爲筆畫，由象形變爲象徵，由複雜變得簡單。

　　漢字的造字方法有"象形"、"指事"、"會意"、"形聲"。根據中國古代"六書"的說法，造字法還包括"轉注"和"假借"。"象形法"是指用文字的綫條或筆畫，把要表達物體的外形特徵畫出來。例如"月"像一個明月的形狀。"指事字"是把含有抽象中的東西劃出來，如"刃"字是在"刀"上加上一點。"形聲字"由形旁和聲旁兩部份組成。形旁是字的意思，聲旁表示字的發音。例如"楊"字，形旁是"木"，表示它是一種樹木，聲旁是"易"，表示它的發音與"易"字一樣。"會意字"是由兩個或多個獨體字組成的，合並起來表達字的意思。例如"休"字，由"人"和"木"合起來，表示人靠在樹上休息。轉注和假借實際上都是用字的方法。

　　漢字的最小構成單位是筆畫。寫漢字時要按照先後次序寫，即筆順。筆順的基本規則是先橫後豎，先撇後捺，從上到下，從左到右，先外後內，再封口，先中間後兩邊。

　　由於一個漢字一般具有多種含義，也有很強的組詞能力，這使得漢字有極高的使用效率。2000左右的常用字就可覆蓋98%以上的書面表達方式。

　　語言是文化的載體，漢字在歷史上對中國文化的傳播起到了重要作用。在漢字發展過程中，留下了大量的文學、文化作品，並形成了獨特的漢字書法藝術。

[Simplified-character version]

汉字

　　汉字是记录汉语的文字，也是世界上最古老的文字之一。汉字以象形字为基础，形、音、意结合于一体，成为一种独特的方块形的表意体系文字。现在发现的最早、最成熟的汉字是中国商代的甲骨文。从甲骨文发展到今天使用的汉字，又经历了大篆、小篆、隶书、楷书、草书、行书等演变过程。在形体上，汉字逐渐由图画变为笔画，由象形变为象征，由复杂变得简单。

　　汉字的造字方法有"象形"、"指事"、"会意"、"形声"。根据中国古代"六书"的说法，造字法还包括"转注"和"假借"。"象形法"是指用文字的线条或笔画，把要表达物体的外形特征画出来。例如"月"像一个明月的形状。"指事字"是把含有抽象中的东西划出来，如"刃"字是在"刀"上加上一点。"形声字"由形旁和声旁两部份组成。形旁是字的意思，声旁表示字的发音。例如"杨"字，形旁是"木"，表示它是一种树木，声旁是"易"，表示它的发音与"易"字一样。"会意字"是由两个或多个独体字组成的，合并起来表达字的意思。例如"休"字，由"人"和"木"合起来，表示人靠在树上休息。转注和假借实际上都是用字的方法。

　　汉字的最小构成单位是笔画。写汉字时要按照先后次序写，即笔顺。笔顺的基本规则是先横后竖，先撇后捺，从上到下，从左到右，先外后内，再封口，先中间后两边。

　　由于一个汉字一般具有多种含义，也有很强的组词能力，这使得汉字有极高的使用效率。2000左右的常用字就可覆盖98%以上的书面表达方式。

　　语言是文化的载体，汉字在历史上对中国文化的传播起到了重要作用。在汉字发展过程中，留下了大量的文学、文化作品，并形成了独特的汉字书法艺术。

[Pinyin version]

Hànzì

Hànzì shì jìlù Hànyǔ de wénzì, yěshì shìjiè shang zuì gǔlǎo de wénzì zhīyī. Hànzì yǐ xiàngxíngzì wéi jīchǔ, xíng, yīn, yì jiéhé yú yītǐ, chéngwéi yì zhǒng dútè de fāngkuàixíng de biǎoyì tǐxì wénzì. Xiànzài fāxiàn de zuìzǎo, zuì chéngshú de hànzì shì Zhōngguó Shāngdài de Jiǎgǔwén. Cóng Jiǎgǔwén fāzhǎn dào jīntiān shǐyòng de hànzì, yòu jīnglìle dàzhuàn, xiǎozhuàn, lìshū, kǎishū, cǎoshū, hángshū děng yǎnbiàn guòchéng. Zài xíngtǐ shang, hànzì zhújiàn yóu túhuà biànwéi bǐhuà, yóu xiàngxíng biànwéi xiàngzhēng, yóu fùzá biànde jiǎndān.

Hànzì de zàozì fāngfǎ yǒu "xiàngxíng", "zhǐshì", "huìyì", "xíngshēng". Gēnjù Zhōngguó gǔdài "Liùshū" de shuōfǎ, zàozìfǎ hái bāokuò "zhuǎnzhù" hé "jiǎjiè". "xiàngxíngfǎ" shì zhǐ yòng wénzì de xiàntiáo huò bǐhuà, bǎ yào biǎodá wùtǐ de wàixíng tèzhēng huàchūlai. Lìrú "yuè" xiàng yí gè míngyuè de xíngzhuàng. "Zhǐshìzì" shì bǎ hányǒu chōuxiàng zhōng de dōngxi huàchūlai, rú "rèn" zì shì zài "dāo" shang jiāshang yí diǎn. "Xíngshēngzì" yóu xíngpáng hé shēngpáng liǎng bùfèn zǔchéng. Xíngpáng shì zì de yìsi, shēngpáng biǎoshì zì de fāyīn. Lìrú "yáng" zì, xíngpáng shì "mù", biǎoshì tā shì yí zhǒng shùmù, shēngpáng shì "yáng", biǎoshì tā de fāyīn yǔ "yáng" zì yí yàng. "Huìyìzì" shì yóu liǎng gè huò duō gè dútǐzì zǔchéng de, hébìng qǐlai biǎodá zì de yìsi. Lìrú "xiū" zì, yóu "rén" hé "mù" hé qǐlai, biǎoshì rén kàozài shùshang xiūxi. Zhuǎnzhù hé jiǎjiè shíjì shang dōu shì yòng zì de fāngfǎ.

Hànzì de zuìxiǎo gòuchéng dānwèi shì bǐhuà. Xiě hànzì shí yào ànzhào xiānhòu cìxù xiě, jí bǐshùn. Bǐshùn de jīběn guīzé shì xiānhéng hòushù, xiānpiē hòunà, cóngshàng dàoxià, cóngzuǒ dàoyòu, xiānwài hòunèi, zài fēngkǒu, xiān zhōngjiān hòu liǎngbiān.

Yóuyú yí gè hànzì jùyǒu duōzhǒng hányì, yěyǒu hěn qiáng de zǔcí nénglì, zhè shǐde hànzì yǒu jígāo de shǐyòng xiàolǜ. liǎngqiān zuǒyòu de chángyòngzì jiù kě fùgài bǎifēnzhī jiǔshíbā yǐshàng de shūmiàn biǎodá fāngshì.

Yǔyán shì wénhuà de zàitǐ, hànzì zài lìshǐ shang duì Zhōngguó wénhuà de chuánbò qǐdàole zhòngyào zuòyòng. Zài hànzì fāzhǎn guòchéng zhōng, liúxiàle dàliàng de wénxué, wénhuà zuòpǐn, bìng xíngchéngle dútè de hànzì shūfǎ yìshù.

CALLIGRAPHY

[Traditional-character version]

書法

　　書法是漢字的書寫藝術，是漢字在漫長的演變發展過程中形成的獨特的造型藝術。中國的書法藝術歷史悠久，源遠流長，影響深遠。中國書法是一門古老的藝術，從甲骨文、金文演變而爲大篆、小篆、隸書，到定型于東漢、魏、晉的草書、楷書、行書各種書寫體，書法一直散發著藝術的魅力。

　　中國書法的工具和材料基本上是由筆、墨、紙、硯構成的，人們稱之爲“文房四寶”。筆，就是毛筆，是中國特有的書寫用具。目前，最好的毛筆是湖筆，產於浙江湖州。墨是書寫、繪畫所用的黑色顏料，產於安徽徽州的徽墨最有名。唐朝初年，安徽宣州生產出一種高級書畫用紙，就是有名的宣紙。這種紙，白而柔軟，經久不變。硯是用來研磨的工具，在中國有5000年的歷史，其中端硯是中國最有名的硯。

　　書法藝術的審美要素大體由以下幾個方面構成：

　　一是字的結構。各種書體、流派都有自己獨特的結構。書法像建造房屋一樣，結體講究空間美。

　　二是書法作品的整體布局，這是書法家追求的最高境界。

　　三是行筆的方式、方法。一般來說有方筆、圓筆、尖筆等。行筆要求有力度和質感，富於曲綫美和形象美。

　　四是墨的著色程度。

　　五是韻律，也就是筆畫、線條的動靜、起伏等變化有節奏。

　　六是風格。這是由結體、章法、用筆、用墨、韵律等共同組成的總的藝術效果。

　　書法藝術的審美特徵大體上有下面幾個方面：

　　一是造型性。書法藝術是通過點綫組合來進行美的造型的藝術。

　　二是抽象性。書法藝術對現實美的反映，是靠點線和字形結構來完成的。它不像繪畫那樣具體地去描繪某一種事物。

　　三是表情性。書法藝術浸透著書法家的思想感情，反映作者的品格情趣，是一種表情的藝術。

[Simplified-character version]

书法

　　书法是汉字的书写艺术，是汉字在漫长的演变发展过程中形成的独特的造型艺术。中国的书法艺术历史悠久，源远流长，影响深远。中国书法是一门古老的艺术，从甲骨文、金文演变而为大篆、小篆、隶书，到定型于东汉、魏、晋的草书、楷书、行书各种书写体，书法一直散发着艺术的魅力。

中国书法的工具和材料基本上是由笔、墨、纸、砚构成的，人们称之为"文房四宝"。笔，就是毛笔，是中国特有的书写用具。目前，最好的毛笔是湖笔，产于浙江湖州。墨是书写、绘画所用的黑色颜料，产于安徽徽州的徽墨最有名。唐朝初年，安徽宣州生产出一种高级书画用纸，就是有名的宣纸。这种纸，白而柔软，经久不变。砚是用来研磨的工具，在中国有5000年的历史，其中端砚是中国最有名的砚。

书法艺术的审美要素大体由以下几个方面构成：

一是字的结构。各种书体、流派都有自己独特的结构。书法像建造房屋一样，结体讲究空间美。

二是书法作品的整体布局，这是书法家追求的最高境界。

三是行笔的方式方法。一般来说有方笔、圆笔、尖笔等。行笔要求有力度和质感，富于曲线美和形象美。

四是墨的着色程度。

五是韵律，也就是笔画、线条的动静、起伏等变化有节奏。

六是风格。这是由结体、章法、用笔、用墨、韵律等共同组成的总的艺术效果。

书法艺术的审美特征大体上有下面几个方面：

一是造型性。书法艺术是通过点线组合来进行美的造型的艺术。

二是抽象性。书法艺术对现实美的反映，是靠点线和字形结构来完成的。它不像绘画那样具体地去描绘某一种事物。

三是表情性。书法艺术浸透着书法家的思想感情，反映作者的品格情趣，是一种表情的艺术。

[Pinyin version]

Shūfǎ

Shūfǎ shì hànzì de shūxiě yìshù, shì hànzì zài màncháng de yǎnbiàn fāzhǎn guòchéng zhōng xíngchéng de dútè de zàoxíng yìshù. Zhōngguó de shūfǎ yìshù lìshǐ yōujiǔ, yuányuǎn liúcháng, yǐngxiǎng shēnyuǎn. Zhōngguó shūfǎ shì yì mén gǔlǎo de yìshù, cóng Jiǎgǔwén, Jīnwén yǎnbiàn érwéi dàzhuàn, xiǎozhuàn, lìshū, dào dìngxíng yú Dōnghàn, Wèi, Jìn de cǎoshū, kǎishū, hánshū gèzhǒng shūxiětǐ, shūfǎ yìzhí sànfàzhe yìshù de mèilì.

Zhōngguó shūfǎ de gōngjù hé cáiliào jīběnshang shì yóu bǐ, mò, zhǐ, yàn gòuchéng de, rénmen chēngzhī wéi "wénfáng sìbǎo". Bǐ, jiùshì máobǐ, shì Zhōngguó tèyǒu de shūxiě yòngjù. Mùqián, zuìhǎo de máobǐ shì húbǐ, chǎnyú Zhèjiāng Húzhōu. Mò shì shūxiě, huìhuà suǒyòng de hēisè yánliào, chǎnyú Āhuī Huīzhōu de huīmò zuì yǒumíng. Tángcháo chūnián, Ānhuī Xuānzhōu shēngchǎn chū yí zhǒng gāojí shūhuà yòngzhǐ, jiùshì yǒumíng de xuānzhǐ. Zhè zhǒng zhǐ, bái ér róuruǎn, jīngjiǔ bú biàn. Yàn shì yònglái yánmó de gōngjù, zài Zhōngguó yǒu 5000 nián de lìshǐ, qízhōng duānyàn shì Zhōngguó zuì yǒumíng de yàn.

Shūfǎ yìshù de shěnměi yàosù dàtǐ yóu yǐxià jǐ gè fāngmiàn gòuchéng:

Yī shì zì de jiégòu. Gè zhǒng shūtǐ, liúpài dōu yǒu zìjǐ dútè de jiégòu. Shūfǎ xiàng jiànzào fángwū yí yàng, jiétǐ jiǎngjiù kōngjiānměi.

Èr shì shūfǎ zuòpǐn de zhěngtǐ bùjú, zhè shì shūfǎjiā zhuīqiú de zuìgāo jìngjiè.

Sān shì xíngbǐ de fāngshì fāngfǎ. Yìbān láishuō yǒu fāngbǐ, yuánbǐ, jiānbǐ děng. Xíngbǐ yāoqiú yǒu lìdù hé zhìgǎn, fùyú qūxiànměi hé xíngxiàngměi.

Sì shì mò de zhuósè chéngdù.

Wǔ shì yùnlǜ, yě jiùshì bǐhuà, xiàntiáo de dòngjìng, qǐfú děng biànhuà yǒu jiézòu.

Liù shì fēnggé. Zhè shì yóu jiétǐ, zhāngfǎ, yòngbǐ, yòngmò, yùnlǜ děng gòngtóng zǔchéng de zǒng de yìshù xiàoguǒ.

Shūfǎ yìshù de shěnměi tèzhēng dàtǐshang yǒu xiàmiàn jǐ gè fāngmiàn:

Yī shì zàoxíngxìng. Shūfǎ yìshù shì tōngguò diǎnxiàn zǔhé lái jìnxíng měide zàoxíng de yìshù.

Èr shì chōuxiàngxìng. Shūfǎ yìshù duì xiànshí měide fǎnyìng, shì kào diǎnxiàn hé zìxíng jiégòu lái wánchéng de. Tā bú xiàng huìhuà nàyàng jùtǐ de qù miáohuì mǒu yí zhǒng shìwù.

Sān shì biǎoqíngxìng. Shūfǎ yìshù jìntòuzhe shūfǎjiā de sīxiǎng gǎnqíng, fǎnyìng zuòzhě de pǐngé qíngqù, shì yí zhǒng biǎoqíng de yìshù.

CHINESE ARTS AND CRAFTS

[Traditional-character version]

景泰藍

　　景泰藍是中國著名的傳統手工藝品，已有600多年的歷史。景泰藍是由金銀銅等貴重金屬通過燒焊、燒藍、磨光、鍍金等多種工藝精製而成的，同時又引進了傳統繪畫和雕刻技藝，可是說結合了中國的歷史、文化、藝術等傳統的精華。景泰藍工藝品，古樸典雅，精美華貴。現存最早的景泰藍是元代的產品。北京是景泰藍技術的發源地，北京人喜歡用景泰藍工藝品裝飾居室。景泰藍產品既有欣賞價值，同時還可作爲日常生活用品來使用。

[Simplified-character version]

景泰蓝

　　景泰蓝是中国著名的传统手工艺品，已有600多年的历史。景泰蓝是由金银铜等贵重金属通过烧焊、烧蓝、磨光、镀金等多种工艺精制而成的，同时又引进了传统绘画和雕刻技艺，可是说结合了中国的历史、文化、艺术等传统的精华。景泰蓝工艺品，古朴典雅，精美华贵。现存最早的景泰蓝是元代的产品。北京是景泰蓝技术的发源地，北京人喜欢用景泰蓝工艺品装饰居室。景泰蓝产品既有欣赏价值，同时还可作为日常生活用品来使用。

[Pinyin version]

Jǐngtàilán

Jǐngtàilán shì Zhōngguó zhùmíng de chuántǒng shǒu gōngyìpǐn, yǐ yǒu liùbǎi duō nián de lìshǐ. Jǐngtàilán shì yóu jīn yín tóng děng guìzhòng jīnshǔ tōngguò shāohàn, shāolán, móguāng, dùjīn děng duō zhǒng gōngyì jīngzhì érchéng de, tóngshí yòu yǐnjìnle chuántǒng huìhuà hé diāokè jìyì, kěshì shuō jiéhéle Zhōngguó de lìshǐ, wénhuà, yìshù děng chuántǒng de jīnghuá. Jǐngtàilán gōngyìpǐn, gǔpú diǎnyǎ, jīngměi huáguì. Xiàncún zuìzǎo de jǐngtàilán shì Yuándài de chǎnpǐn. Běijīng shì jǐngtàilán jìshù de fāyuándì, Běijīngrén xǐhuan yòng jǐngtàilán gōngyìpǐn zhuāngshì jūshì. Jǐngtàilán chǎnpǐn jì yǒu xīnshǎng jiàzhí, tóngshí hái kě zuòwéi rìcháng shēnghuó yòngpǐn lái shǐyòng.

[Traditional-character version]

剪紙

剪紙是中國流行的民間藝術。剪紙常用的方法有剪刀剪和刀剪。前者借助於剪刀，剪完後把幾張剪紙貼起來，再用剪刀對圖案進行加工；後者是先把紙張折成幾疊，放在鬆軟的東西上，用小刀慢慢刻。在中國農村，剪紙曾是每個女孩必須掌握的手工藝術，但是職業的剪紙藝人常常是男人。剪紙常用於宗教儀式、裝飾和造型藝術等方面。過去，人們經常用紙做成不同形態的人和物，與死者一起下葬或在葬禮上燃燒，可見，剪紙藝術是有象徵意義的。今天，剪紙更多地是用於裝飾牆壁、門窗、鏡子等，也可作爲禮品送給他人。

[Simplified-character version]

剪纸

剪纸是中国流行的民间艺术。剪纸常用的方法有剪刀剪和刀剪。前者借助于剪刀，剪完后把几张剪纸贴起来，再用剪刀对图案进行加工；后者是先把纸张折成几叠，放在松软的东西上，用小刀慢慢刻。在中国农村，剪纸曾是每个女孩必须掌握的手工艺术，但是职业的剪纸艺人常常是男人。剪纸常用于宗教仪式、装饰和造型艺术等方面。过去，人们经常用纸做成不同形态的人和物，与死者一起下葬或在葬礼上燃烧，可见，剪纸艺术是有象征意义的。今天，剪纸更多地是用于装饰墙壁、门窗、镜子等，也可作为礼品送给他人。

[Pinyin version]

Jiǎnzhǐ

Jiǎnzhǐ shì Zhōngguó liúxíng de mínjiān yìshù. Jiǎnzhǐ chángyòng de fāngfǎ yǒu jiǎndāojiǎn hé dāojiǎn. Qiánzhě jièzhùyú jiǎndāo, jiǎnwán hòu bǎ jǐ zhāng jiǎnzhǐ tiē qǐlai, zài yòng jiǎndāo duì tú'àn jìnxíng jiāgōng; hòuzhě shì xiān bǎ zhǐzhāng zhéchéng jǐ dié, fàngzài sōngruǎn de dōngxi shang, yòng xiǎodāo mànman kè. Zài Zhōngguó nóngcūn, jiǎnzhǐ céngshì měi gè nǚhái bìxū zhǎngwò de shǒugōng yìshù, dànshì zhíyè de jiǎnzhǐ yìrén chángcháng shì nánrén. Jiǎnzhǐ chángyòngyú zōngjiào yíshì, zhuāngshì hé zàoxíng yìshù děng fāngmiàn. Guòqù, rénmen jīngcháng yòng zhǐ zuòchéng bùtóng xíngtài de rén hé wù, yǔ sǐzhě yì qǐ xiàzàng huò zài zànglǐ shang ránshāo, kějiàn, jiǎnzhǐ yìshù shì yǒu xiàngzhēng yìyì de. Jīntiān, jiǎnzhǐ gèngduō de shì yòngyú zhuāngshì qiángbì, ménchuāng, jìngzi děng, yě kě zuòwéi lǐpǐn sòng gěi tārén.

[Traditional-character version]

風箏

風箏是中國古老的一種民間藝術，放風箏是中國傳統的一種休閒活動。相傳，在春秋戰國時期，墨子就用木板製成風箏。東漢蔡倫發明造紙術後，民間才開始用紙做風箏。

據說，中國人放風箏最早是爲了圖吉利。人們把風箏放得高高的，等它快要鑽進雲裏的時候，就把風箏綫剪斷，風箏就飛走了，表示把不好的事情也帶走了。據記載，北京人放風箏已有很長時間的歷史了。明清時北京人的風箏製作技術已經相當成熟，還形成了不同的風箏流派。今天，放風箏已經成爲一項休閒活動。放風箏的好處在於既能在近處觀賞，又能在遠處賞玩，而且全身運動，利於養性強身。

[Simplified-character version]

风筝

　　风筝是中国古老的一种民间艺术，放风筝是中国传统的一种休闲活动。相传，在春秋战国时期，墨子就用木板制成风筝。东汉蔡伦发明造纸术后，民间才开始用纸做风筝。

　　据说，中国人放风筝最早是为了图吉利。人们把风筝放得高高的，等它快要钻进云里的时候，就把风筝线剪断，风筝就飞走了，表示把不好的事情也带走了。据记载，北京人放风筝已有很长时间的历史了。明清时北京人的风筝制作技术已经相当成熟，还形成了不同的风筝流派。今天，放风筝已经成为一项休闲活动。放风筝的好处在于既能在近处观赏，又能在远处赏玩，而且全身运动，利于养性强身。

[Pinyin version]

Fēngzheng

Fēngzheng shì Zhōngguó gǔlǎo de yì zhǒng mínjiān yìshù, fàng fēngzhēng shì Zhōngguó chuántǒng de yì zhǒng xiūxián huódòng. Xiāngchuán, zài Chūnqiū Zhànguó shíqī, Mòzi jiù yòng mùbǎn zhìchéng fēngzheng. Dōnghàn Cài Lún fāmíng zàozhǐshù hòu, mínjiān cái kāishǐ yòng zhǐ zuò fēngzheng.

Jùshuō, Zhōngguórén fàng fēngzheng zuìzǎo shì wèile tú jílì. Rénmen bǎ fēngzheng fàngde gāogāo de, děng tā kuàiyào zuānjìn yúnli de shíhou, jiù bǎ fēngzhengxiàn jiǎnduàn, fēngzheng jiù fēizǒule, biǎoshì bǎ bùhǎo de shìqíng yě dàizǒule. Jù jìzǎi, Běijīngrén fàng fēngzheng yǐ yǒu hěncháng shíjiān de lìshǐ le. Míng Qīng shí Běijīngrén de fēngzheng zhìzuò jìshù yǐjīng xiāngdàng chéngshú, hái xíngchéng le bùtóng de fēngzheng liúpài. Jīntiān, fàng fēngzheng yǐjīng chéngwéi yí xiàng xiūxián huódòng. Fàng fēngzheng de hǎochù zàiyú jì néng zài jìnchù guānshǎng, yòu néng zài yuǎnchù shǎngwán, érqiě quánshēn yùndòng, lìyú yǎngxìng qiángshēn.

FOUR GREAT INVENTIONS OF ANCIENT CHINA

[Traditional-character version]

指南針

　　戰國時期，中國古人利用天然磁鐵和齒輪製造了能指示方向的指南車。宋朝時代，中國人發明了人工磁鐵，製造出磁針，也製作了指南針。後來，又把磁針和方位盤結合起來，製造出了羅盤針。指南針的發明與運用對發展航海事業和經濟文化的交流起了推動作用。

[Simplified-character version]

指南针

　　战国时期，中国古人利用天然磁铁和齿轮制造了能指示方向的指南车。宋朝时代，中国人发明了人工磁铁，制造出磁针，也制作了指南针。后来，又把磁针和方位盘结合起来，制造出了罗盘针。指南针的发明与运用对发展航海事业和经济文化的交流起了推动作用。

[Pinyin version]

Zhǐnánzhēn

Zhànguó shíqī, Zhōngguó gǔrén lìyòng tiānrán cítiě hé chǐlún zhìzàole néng zhǐshì fāngxiàng de zhǐnánchē. Sòngcháo shídài, Zhōngguórén fāmíngle réngōng cítiě, zhìzào chu cízhēn, yě zhìzuòle zhǐnánzhēn. Hòulái, yòu bǎ cízhēn hé fāngwèipán jiéhé qǐlai, zhìzào chūle luópánzhēn. Zhǐnánzhēn de fāmíng yǔ yùnyòng duì fāzhǎn hánghǎi shìyè hé jīngjì wénhuà de jiāoliú qǐle tuīdòng zuòyòng.

[Traditional-character version]

造紙術

　　在紙沒有發明以前，世界各地使用不同的方式記事，如古印度人用樹葉，古巴比倫人用泥磚，古羅馬人用蠟板等。中國商朝把文字刻在甲骨和青銅器上。到了東漢時期，蔡倫在總結前人經驗的基礎上發明了造紙術。他用樹皮、麻頭、破布、舊魚網等原料製成了纖維紙。蔡倫發明的紙，原材料多，成本低，質量高，深受歡迎。紙的發明和應用，在社會歷史的記錄與保存、文化思想的交流與傳播方面都發揮了重要作用，對人類文明做出了巨大的貢獻。

[Simplified-character version]

造纸术

　　在纸没有发明以前，世界各地使用不同的方式记事，如古印度人用树叶，古巴比伦人用泥砖，古罗马人用蜡板等。中国商朝把文字刻在甲骨和青铜器上。到了东汉时期，蔡伦在总结前人经验的基础上发明了造纸术。他用树皮、麻头、破布、旧鱼网等原料制成了纤维纸。蔡伦发明的纸，原材料多，成本低，质量高，深受欢迎。纸的发明和应用，在社会历史的记录与保存、文化思想的交流与传播方面都发挥了重要作用，对人类文明做出了巨大的贡献。

[Pinyin version]

Zàozhǐshù

Zài zhǐ méiyǒu fāmíng yǐqián, shìjiè gèdì shǐyòng bùtóng de fāngshì jìshì, rú gǔ Yìndù rén yòng shùyè, gǔ Bābǐlún rén yòng nízhuān, gǔ Luómǎ rén yòng làbǎn děng. Zhōngguó Shāngcháo bǎ wénzì kèzài jiǎgǔ hé qīngtóngqì shang. Dàole Dōnghàn shíqī, Cài Lún zài zǒngjié qiánrén jīngyàn de jīchǔshang fāmíngle zàozhǐshù. Tā yòng shùpí, mátóu, pòbù, jiù yúwǎng děng yuánliào zhìchéngle xiānwéizhǐ. Cài Lún fāmíng de zhǐ, yuáncáiliào duō, chéngběn dī, zhìliàng gāo, shēnshòu huānyíng. Zhǐ de fāmíng hé yìngyòng, zài shèhuì lìshǐ de jìlù yǔ bǎocún, wénhuà sīxiǎng de jiāoliú yǔ chuánbō fāngmiàn dōu fāhuīle zhòngyào zuòyòng, duì rénlèi wénmíng zuòchūle jùdà de gòngxiàn.

[Traditional-character version]

火藥

　　火藥是由中國古人發明的。中國古代的帝王貴族都希望自己長生不老，於是讓一些道士煉仙丹，煉製仙丹的過程中產生了火藥的配方。古代煉丹家們利用早在漢代就已掌握的硝石和硫磺，經過長期的煉丹實踐，在唐朝時便發明了火藥。到了唐朝末年，火藥已經在軍事上使用。後來，火藥和火藥武器傳到阿拉伯國家，然後又傳到歐洲的一些國家。火藥的發明對中國與世界科技的發展起了重要作用。

[Simplified-character version]

火药

　　火药是由中国古人发明的。中国古代的帝王贵族都希望自己长生不老，于是让一些道士炼仙丹，炼制仙丹的过程中产生了火药的配方。古代炼丹家们利用早在汉代就已掌握的硝石和硫磺，经过长期的炼丹实践，在唐朝时便发明了火药。到了唐朝末年，火药已经在军事上使用。后来，火药和火药武器传到阿拉伯国家，然后又传到欧洲的一些国家。火药的发明对中国与世界科技的发展起了重要作用。

[Pinyin version]

Huǒyào

Huǒyào shì yóu Zhōngguó gǔrén fāmíng de. Zhōngguó gǔdài de dìwáng guìzú dōu xīwàng zìjǐ chángshēng bùlǎo, yúshì ràng yìxiē dàoshì liàn xiāndān, liànzhì xiāndān de guòchéng zhōng chǎnshēngle huǒyào de pèifāng. Gǔdài liàndānjiāmen lìyòng zǎo zài Hàndài jiù yǐ zhǎngwò de xiāoshí hé liúhuáng, jīngguò chángqī de liàndān shíjiàn, zài Tángcháo shí biàn fāmíngle huǒyào. Dàole Tángcháo mònián, huǒyào yǐjīng zài jūnshì shang shǐyòng. Hòulái, huǒyào hé huǒyào wǔqì chuán dào Ālābó guójiā, ránhòu yòu chuándào Ōuzhōu de yìxiē guójiā. Huǒyào de fāmíng duì Zhōngguó yǔ shìjiè kējì de fāzhǎn qǐle zhòngyào zuòyòng.

[Traditional-character version]

印刷術

　　中國在唐朝初年就已出現採用雕版印刷術印製的書，《金剛經》是世界上現存最早的、有刻印時間的印刷品。宋朝人畢升在雕版印刷的基礎上發明了活字印刷術。它是用膠泥刻字，每字一個印，燒好後製成字印。把一個個字印排列在鐵板之上，經過燒烤、壓平等工藝製成印版，用來印刷。活字印版的字印可以反復使用的特點已經具備了現代印刷的基本過程。印刷術的發明，促進了人類文明的發展和傳播。

[Simplified-character version]

印刷术

　　中国在唐朝初年就已出现采用雕版印刷术印制的书，《金刚经》是世界上现存最早的、有刻印时间的印刷品。宋朝人毕升在雕版印刷的基础上发明了活字印刷术。它是用胶泥刻字，每字一个印，烧好后制成字印。把一个个字印排列在铁板之上，经过烧烤、压平等工艺制成印版，用来印刷。活字印版的字印可以反复使用的特点已经具备了现代印刷的基本过程。印刷术的发明，促进了人类文明的发展和传播。

[Pinyin version]

Yìnshuā shù

Zhōngguó zài Tángcháo chūnián jiù yǐ chūxiàn cǎiyòng diāobǎn yìnshuāshù yìnzhì de shū, "Jīngāngjīng" shì shìjiè shang xiàncún zuìzǎo de, yǒu kèyìn shíjiān de yìnshuāpǐn. Sòngcháorén Bì Shēng zài diāobǎn yìnshuā de jīchǔ shang fāmíngle huózì yìnshuāshù. Tā shì yòng jiāoní kèzì, měi zì yí gè yìn, shāohǎo hòu zhìchéng zìyìn. Bǎ yí gège zìyìn páiliè zài tiěbǎn zhīshàng, jīngguò shāokǎo, yāpíng děng gōngyì zhìchéng yìnbǎn, yònglái yìnshuā. Huózì yìnbǎn de zìyìn kěyǐ fǎnfù shǐyòng de tèdiǎn yǐjīng jùbèile xiàndài yìnshuā de jīběn guòchéng. Yìnshuāshù de fǎmíng, cùjìnle rénlèi wénmíng de fǎzhǎn hé chuánbò.

TRADITIONAL CHINESE MEDICINE

[Traditional-character version]

傳統醫學

　　中國傳統醫學的歷史已有幾千年。中國的傳統醫學由中醫學、民族醫學和中藥學三部分組成，其中，中醫學是中國傳統醫學的代表。中國傳統醫學把陰陽五行學說作爲理論的基礎，通過"望"、"聞"、"問"、"切"四種診察方法分析和判斷人體的生理狀況及病理變化，對疾病做出診斷，並採取相應的治療措施，使人體得到康復。"望"是對病人的神、色、形、態等幾個方面進行有目的的觀察，來判斷內臟的病變。"聞"就是聽患者語言氣息的高低、強弱、緩急等變化來分辨病情。"問"是通過詢問患者，瞭解病情。"切"是醫生運用指端的觸覺，在病人的一定部位進行觸、摸、按、壓，瞭解病情的方法。

[Simplified-character version]

传统医学

　　中国传统医学的历史已有几千年。中国的传统医学由中医学、民族医学和中药学三部分组成，其中，中医学是中国传统医学的代表。中国传统医学把阴阳五行学说作为理论的基础，通过"望"、"闻"、"问"、"切"四种诊察方法分析和判断人体的生理状况及病理变化，对疾病做出诊断，并采取相应的治疗措施，使人体得到康复。"望"是对病人的神、色、形、态等几个方面进行有目的的观察，来判断内脏的病变。"闻"就是听患者语言气息的高低、强弱、缓急等变化来分辨病情。"问"是通过询问患者，了解病情。"切"是医生运用指端的触觉，在病人的一定部位进行触、摸、按、压，了解病情的方法。

[Pinyin version]

Chuántǒng yīxué

Zhōngguó chuántǒng yīxué de lìshǐ yǐyǒu jǐqiān nián. Zhōngguó de chuántǒng yīxué yóu zhōngyīxué, mínzú yīxué hé zhōngyàoxué sān bùfèn zǔchéng, qízhōng, zhōngyīxué shì Zhōngguó chuántǒng yīxué de dàibiǎo. Zhōngguó chuántǒng yīxué bǎ yīnyáng wǔháng xuéshuō zuòwéi lǐlùn de jīchǔ, tōngguò "wàng", "wén", "wèn", "qiè" sì zhǒng zhěnchá fāngfǎ fēnxī hé pànduàn réntǐ de shēnglǐ zhuàngkuàng jí bìnglǐ biànhuà, duì jíbìng zuòchū zhěnduàn, bìng cǎiqǔ xiāngyìng de zhìliáo cuòshī, shǐ réntǐ dédào kāngfù. "Wàng" shì duì bìngrén de shén, sè, xíng, tài děng jǐ gè fāngmiàn jìnxíng yǒu mùdì de guānchá, lái pànduàn nèizàng de bìngbiàn. "Wén" jiùshì tīng huànzhě yǔyán qìxí de gāodī, qiángruò, huǎnjí děng biànhuà lái fēnbiàn bìngqíng. "Wèn" shì tōngguò xúnwèn huànzhě, liǎojiě bìngqíng. "Qiè" shì yīshēng yùnyòng zhǐ duānde chùjué, zài bìngrén de yīdìng bùwèi jìnxíng chù, mō, àn, yā, liǎojiě bìngqíng de fāngfǎ.

[Traditional-character version]

古代名醫

傳說扁鵲是黃帝時代的名醫，是中國傳統醫學的祖先。扁鵲年輕時虛心好學，刻苦鑽研醫術。在總結前人醫療經驗的基礎上，他創立了"望"、"聞"、"問"、"切"診斷疾病的方法。扁鵲遍遊各地行醫，擅長各科，醫術高超，名揚天下。

華佗是漢朝的醫學家。華佗生活的時代，軍閥混亂，水旱成災，疫病流行，人民處於水深火熱之中。華佗非常同情受壓迫、受剝削的勞動人民，熱心爲人民解脫疾苦。華佗在接受古代的醫療經驗外，還很好地應用了民間的醫療經驗。他一生遊歷了不少地方，到處採集草藥，學習醫藥知識。在總結前人經驗的基礎上，華佗發明了麻醉術，提高了外科手術的技術和療效，擴大了手術治療的範圍。華佗還創立了一套使全身肌肉和關節都能得到舒展的醫療體操"五禽之戲"。

在中國古代豐富的醫藥學遺產中，有許多著名的科學著作，其中《本草綱目》就是一部聞名世界的藥物學巨著。《本草綱目》的作者是明代醫藥學家李時珍。李時珍出生在一個世代行醫的家庭，祖父、父親都是當地名醫。李時珍從小跟隨父親到病人家看病，上山採集草藥，對醫學產生了濃厚的興趣。在長期的醫療實踐中，李時珍治好了不少疑難病，累積了豐富的醫藥知識。在行醫過程中，李時珍讀了許多醫藥著作，感到歷代的藥物學著作存有不少缺點，他決心編著一部藥物學著作。爲了編書，他走訪了很多地方，虛心向他人請教，採集藥物標本，收集民間驗方。他花了二十七年工夫，參考了八百多種書籍，終於寫成了一部新的藥物學巨著《本草綱目》。《本草綱目》記載了近兩千種藥物，每一種藥物都對它的產地、形狀、顏色、功用加以說明。書裏還附了一千多幅藥物圖，記載了一萬多個醫方。這部書對藥物學的發展起了很大的作用。

[Simplified-character version]

古代名医

传说扁鹊是黄帝时代的名医，是中国传统医学的祖先。扁鹊年轻时虚心好学，刻苦钻研医术。在总结前人医疗经验的基础上，他创立了"望"、"闻""、"问"、"切"诊断疾病的方法。扁鹊遍游各地行医，擅长各科，医术高超，名扬天下。

华佗是汉朝的医学家。华佗生活的时代，军阀混乱，水旱成灾，疫病流行，人民处于水深火热之中。华佗非常同情受压迫、受剥削的劳动人民，热心为人民解脱疾苦。华佗在接受古代的医疗经验外，还很好地应用了民间的医疗经验。他一生游历了不少地方，到处采集草药，学习医药知识。在总结前人经验的基础上，华佗发明了麻醉术，提高了外科手术的技术和疗效，扩大了手术治疗的范围。华佗还创立了一套使全身肌肉和关节都能得到舒展的医疗体操"五禽之戏"。

在中国古代丰富的医药学遗产中，有许多著名的科学著作，其中《本草纲目》就是一部闻名世界的药物学巨著。《本草纲目》的作者是明代医药学家李时珍。李时珍出生在一个世代行医的家庭，祖父、父亲都是当地名医。李时珍从小跟随父亲到病人家看病，上山采集草药，对医学产生了浓厚的兴趣。在长期的医疗实践中，李时珍治好了不少疑难病，积累了丰富的医药知识。在行医过程中，李时珍读了许多医药著作，感到历代的药物学著作存有不少缺点，他决心编著一部药物学著作。为了编书，他走访了很多地方，虚心向他人请教，采集药物标本，收集民间验方。他花了二十七年工夫，参考了八百多种书籍，终于写成了一部新的药物学巨著《本草纲目》。《本草纲目》记载了近两千种药物，每一种药物都对它的产地、形状、颜 色、功用加以说明。书里还附了一千多幅药物图，记载了一万多个医方。这部书对药物学的发展起了很大的作用。

[Pinyin version]

Gǔdài Míngyī

Chuánshuō Biǎn Què shì huángdì shídài de míngyī, shì Zhōngguó chuántǒng yīxué de zǔxiān. Biǎn Què niánqīng shí xūxīn hàoxué, kèkǔ zuānyán yīshù. Zài zǒngjié qiánrén yīliáo jīngyàn de jīchǔ shang, tā chuànglìle "wàng", "wén", "wèn", "qiè" zhěnduàn jíbìng de fāngfǎ. Biǎn Què biànyóu gèdì xíngyī, shàncháng gèkē, yīshù gāochāo, míngyáng tiānxià.

Huà Tuó shì Hàncháo de yīxuéjiā. Huá Tuó shēnghuó de shídài, jūnfá hǔnluàn, shuǐhàn chéngzāi, yìbìng liúxíng, rénmín chǔyú shuǐshēn huǒrè zhīzhōng. Huà Tuó fēicháng tóngqíng shòu yāpò, shòu bōxuē de láodòng rénmín, rèxīn wèi rénmín jiětuō jíkǔ. Huà Tuó zài jiēshòu gǔdài de yīliáo jīngyàn wài, hái hěnhǎo de yìngyòngle mínjiān de yīliáo jīngyàn. Tā yìshēng yóulì le bùshǎo dìfang, dàochù cǎijí cǎoyào, xuéxí yīyào zhīshì. Zài zǒngjié qiánrén jīngyàn de jīchǔ shang, Huà Tuó fāmíngle mázuìshù, tígāole wàikē shǒushù de jìshù hé liáoxiào, kuòdàle shǒushù zhìliáo de fànwéi. Huà Tuó hái chuànglìle yí tào shǐ quánshēn jīròu hé guānjié dōu néng dédào shūzhǎn de yīliáo tǐcāo "Wǔqín zhīxì".

Zài Zhōngguó gǔdài fēngfù de yīyàoxué yíchǎn zhōng, yǒu xǔduō zhùmíng de kēxué zhùzuò, qízhōng "Běncǎo Gāngmù" jiùshì yí bù wénmíng shìjiè de yàowùxué jùzhù. "Běncǎo Gāngmù" de zuòzhě shì Míngdài yīyào xuéjiā Lǐ Shízhēn. Lǐ Shízhēn chūshēng zài yí gè shìdài xíngyī de jiātíng, zǔfù, fuqīn dōu shì dāngdì míngyī. Lǐ Shízhēn cóngxiǎo gēnsuí fuqīn dào bìngrén jiā kànbìng, shàngshān cǎijí cǎoyào, duì yīxué chǎnshēngle nónghòu de xìngqù. Zài chángqī de yīliáo shíjiàn zhōng, Lǐ Shízhēn zhìhǎo le bùshǎo yínánbìng, jīlěile fēngfù de yīyào zhīshì. Zài xíngyī guòchéng zhōng, Lǐ Shízhēn dúle xǔduō yīyào zhùzuò, gǎndào lìdài de yàowùxué zhùzuò cúnyǒu bùshǎo quēdiǎn, tā juéxīn biānzhù yí bù yàowùxué zhùzuò. Wèile biānshū, tā zǒufǎngle hěnduō dìfang, xūxīn xiàng tārén qǐngjiào, cǎijí yàowù biāoběn, shōují mínjiān yànfāng. Tā huāle èrshíqī nián gōngfū, cānkǎole bābǎi duō zhǒng shūjí, zhōngyú xiěchéngle yí bù xīnde yàowùxué jùzhù "Běncǎo Gāngmù". "Běncǎo Gāngmù" jìzǎile jìn liǎngqiān zhǒng yàowù, měi yì zhǒng yàowù dōu duì tā de chǎndì, xíngzhuàng, yánsè, gōngyòng jiāyǐ shuōmíng. Shūli hái fùle yìqiān duō fú yàowùtú, jìzǎile yíwàn duō gè yīfāng. Zhè bù shū duì yàowùxué de fāzhǎn qǐle hěndà de zuòyòng.

TRADITIONAL CHINESE ARCHITECTURE

[Traditional-character version]

傳統建築風格

中國建築已有六、七千年的歷史。中國建築的藝術特點是多方面的。首先，中國建築使用木柱、木梁構成房屋的框架，屋頂與房檐的重量通過梁架傳遞到立柱上，墙壁承受不了房屋的重量。其次，中國建築具有庭院式的組群佈局。中國傳統的住宅、宮殿、官衙、寺廟等都是由若干單座建築和一些圍廊、圍牆之類環繞成一個個庭院而組成的。庭院式的組群與結構使用均衡對稱的方式進行設計，如北京故宮和北方的四合院。這種結構和中國封建社會的宗法和禮教制度有密切關係。中國傳統建築不僅重視建築技術科學，同時也顯示了建築者的藝術水準。中國古代建築吸收了中國繪畫、雕刻、工藝美術等藝術特點，創造了豐富多彩的藝術形象，並形成自己的特點，如富有裝飾性的屋頂，襯托性建築的應用（宮殿正門前的華表、石獅）和色彩的運用。

[Simplified-character version]

传统建筑风格

中国建筑已有六、七千年的历史。中国建筑的艺术特点是多方面的。首先，中国建筑使用木柱、木梁构成房屋的框架，屋顶与房檐的重量通过梁架传递到立柱上，墙壁承受不了房屋的重量。其次，中国建筑具有庭院式的组群布局。中国传统的住宅、宫殿、官衙、寺庙等都是由若干单座建筑和一些围廊、围墙之类环绕成一个个庭院而组成的。庭院式的组群与结构使用均衡对称的方式进行设计，如北京故宫和北方的四合院。这种结构和中国封建社会的宗法和礼教制度有密切关系。中国传统建筑不仅重视建筑技术科学，同时也显示了建筑者的艺术水平。中国古代建筑吸收了中国绘画、雕刻、工艺美术等艺术特点，创造了丰富多彩的艺术形象，并形成自己的特点，如富有装饰性的屋顶，衬托性建筑的应用（宫殿正门前的华表、石狮）和色彩的运用。

[Pinyin version]

Chuántǒng Jiànzhú Fēnggé

Zhōngguó jiànzhú yǐyǒu liùqīqiān nián de lìshǐ. Zhōngguó jiànzhù de yìshù tèdiǎn shì duō fāngmiàn de. Shǒuxiān, Zhōngguó jiànzhù shǐyòng mùzhù, mùliáng gòuchéng fángwū de kuàngjià, wūdǐng yǔ fángyán de zhòngliàng tōngguò liángjià chuándì dào lìzhù shang, qiángbì chéngshòu bùliǎo fángwū de zhòngliàng. Qícì, Zhōngguó jiànzhú jùyǒu tíngyuànshì de zǔqún bùjú. Zhōngguó chuántǒng de zhùzhái, gōngdiàn, guānyá, sìmiào děng dōushì yóu ruògān dānzuò jiànzhú hé yìxiē wéiláng, wéiqiáng zhīlèi huánràochéng yí gège tíngyuàn ér zǔchéng de. Tíngyuànshì de zǔqún yǔ jiégòu shǐyòng jūnhéng duìchèn de fāngshì jìnxíng shèjì, rú Běijīng Gùgōng hé běifāng de sìhéyuàn. Zhè zhǒng jiégòu hé Zhōngguó fēngjiàn shèhuì de zōngfǎ hé lǐjiào zhìdù yǒu mìqiè guānxì. Zhōngguó chuántǒng jiànzhú bùjǐn zhòngshì jiànzhú jìshù kēxué, tóngshí yě xiǎnshìle jiànzhúzhě de yìshù shuǐpíng. Zhōngguó gǔdài jiànzhù xīshōule Zhōngguó huìhuà, diāokè, gōngyì měishù děng yìshù tèdiǎn, chuàngzàole fēngfù duōcǎi de yìshù xíngxiàng, bìng xíngchéng zìjǐ de tèdiǎn, rú fùyǒu zhuāngshìxìng de wūdǐng, chèntuōxìng jiànzhù de yìngyòng (gōngdiàn zhèngménqián de huábiǎo, shíshī) hé sècǎi de yùnyòng.

[Traditional-character version]

故宮

故宮又叫紫禁城，是中國明、清兩代的皇宮，也是中國現存最大、最完整的古建築群。

故宮占地72萬多平方米，共有宮殿9000多間，都是木結構、黃琉璃瓦頂、青白石底座，並用彩畫加以裝飾。故宮的四面是城牆，四角各有一個角樓，城牆外面由寬52米的護城河環繞。故宮宮殿的建築分外朝和內廷，它們的建築氣氛也完全不同。外朝是封建皇帝行使權力、舉行盛典的地方。內廷是帝王與家人居住的地方。故宮建築氣勢雄偉、豪華壯麗，是中國古代建築藝術的精華。

[Simplified-character version]

故宫

故宫又叫紫禁城，是中国明、清两代的皇宫，也是中国现存最大、最完整的古建筑群。

故宫占地72万多平方米，共有宫殿9000多间，都是木结构、黄琉璃瓦顶、青白石底座，并用彩画加以装饰。故宫的四面是城墙，四角各有一个角楼，城墙外面由宽52米的护城河环绕。故宫宫殿的建筑分外朝和内廷，它们的建筑气氛也完全不同。外朝是封建皇帝行使权力、举行盛典的地方。内廷是帝王与家人居住的地方。故宫建筑气势雄伟、豪华壮丽，是中国古代建筑艺术的精华。

[Pinyin version]

Gùgōng

Gùgōng yòu jiào Zǐjìnchéng, shì Zhōngguó Míng, Qīng liǎng dài de huánggōng, yěshì Zhōngguó xiàncún zuìdà, zuìwánzhěng de gǔ jiànzhúqún.

Gùgōng zhàndì liùbǎi wànduō píngfāng mǐ, gòngyǒu gōngdiàn jiǔqiān duō jiān, dōu shì mùjiégòu, huáng liúlíwǎ dǐng, qīngbáishí dǐzuò, bìng yòng cǎihuà jiāyǐ zhuāngshì. Gùgōng de sìmiàn shì chéngqiáng, sìjiǎo gèyǒu yí gè jiǎolóu, chéngqiáng wàimiàn yóu kuān wǔshíèr mǐ de hùchénghé huánrào. Gùgōng gōngdiàn de jiànzhú fēn wàicháo hé nèitíng, tāmen de jiànzhù qìfēn yě wánquán bùtóng. Wàicháo shì fēngjiàn huángdì xíngshǐ quánlì, jǔxíng shèngdiǎn de dìfāng. Nèitíng shì dìwáng yǔ jiārén jūzhù de dìfāng. Gùgōng jiànzhù qìshì xióngwěi, háohuá zhuànglì, shì Zhōngguó gǔdài jiànzhù yìshù de jīnghuá.

[Traditional-character version]

四合院

四合院是中國的一種傳統民居建築形式。它的院子的四面都建有房屋，從四面把庭院圍在中間，因此被稱爲"四合院"。四合院歷史悠久，建造廣泛。最早的四合院出現在3000多年前的西周。華北和西北地區建造的四合院比較多。四合院的特徵是外觀規矩，中綫對稱。大的四合院可以建成皇宮、王府，小的四合院就是老百姓的普通住宅，以北京的四合院爲代表。

四合院所以有名，首先是因爲它歷史悠久，其次在於它的構成有獨特之處。四合院蘊含著深刻的文化內涵，在人們心中留下了深刻的印象。但是，由於傳統的四合院沒有基本的衛生設施，更沒有空調、車庫等現代化的設備，很難滿足現代生活的需要。另外，傳統的幾代同堂的大家庭越來越少，現代的年輕人希望生活在自己獨立的生活空間，寧可到郊區購買交通方便的別墅，也不願意繼續生活在擁擠的市內。因此，作爲老百姓普通宅居的四合院是否還有存在價值，是一個爭論的問題。

[Simplified-character version]

四合院

四合院是中国的一种传统民居建筑形式。它的院子的四面都建有房屋，从四面把庭院围在中间，因此被称为"四合院"。四合院历史悠久，建造广泛。最早的四合院出现在3000多年前的西周。华北和西北地区建造的四合院比较多。四合院的特征是外观规矩，中线对称。大的四合院可以建成皇宫、王府，小的四合院就是老百姓的普通住宅，以北京的四合院为代表。

四合院所以有名，首先是因为它历史悠久，其次在于它的构成有独特之处。四合院蕴含着深刻的文化内涵，在人们心中留下了深刻的印象。但是，由于传统的四合院没有基本的卫生设施，更没有空调、车库等现代化的设备，很难满足现代生活的需要。另外，传统的几代同堂的大家庭越来越少，现代的年轻人希望生活在自己独立的生活空间。宁可到郊区购买交通方便的别墅，也不愿意继续生活在拥挤的市内。因此，作为老百姓普通宅居的四合院是否还有存在价值，是一个争论的问题。

[Pinyin version]

Sìhéyuàn

Sìhéyuàn shì Zhōngguó de yì zhǒng chuántǒng mínjū jiànzhù xíngshì. Tāde yuànzi de sìmiàn dōu jiànyǒu fángwū, cóng sìmiàn bǎ tíngyuàn wéizài zhōngjiān, yīncǐ bèi chēngwéi "Sìhéyuàn". Sìhéyuàn lìshǐ yōujiǔ, jiànzào guǎngfàn. Zuìzǎo de sìhéyuàn chūxiàn zài sānqiān duōnián qián de Xīzhōu. Huáběi hé xīběi dìqū jiànzào de sìhéyuàn bǐjiào duō. Sìhéyuàn de tèzhēng shì wàiguān guīju, zhōngxiàn duìchèn. Dàde sìhéyuàn kěyǐ jiànchéng huánggōng, wángfǔ, xiǎode sìhéyuàn jiùshì lǎobǎixìng de pǔtōng zhùzhái, yǐ Běijīng de sìhéyuàn wéi dàibiǎo.

Sìhéyuàn suǒyǐ yǒumíng, shǒuxiān shì yīnwèi tā lìshǐ yōujiǔ, qícì zàiyú tāde gòuchéng yǒu dútè zhīchù. Sìhéyuàn yùnhánzhe shēnkè de wénhuà nèihán, zài rénmen xīnzhōng liúxiale shēnkè de yìnxiàng. Dànshì, yóuyú chuántǒng de sìhéyuàn méiyǒu jīběn de wèishēng shèshī, gèng méiyǒu kòngtiáo, chēkù děng xiàndàihuà de shèbèi, hěnnán mǎnzú xiàndài shēnghuó de xūyào. Lìngwài, chuántǒng de jǐdài tóngtáng de dà jiātíng yuèlái yuèshǎo, xiàndài de niánqīngrén xīwàng shēnghuó zài zìjǐ dúlì de shēnghuó kōngjiān. Nìngkě dào jiāoqū gòumǎi jiāotōng fāngbiàn de biéshù, yě bú yuànyì jìxù shēnghuó zài yōngjǐ de shìnèi. Yīncǐ, zuòwéi lǎobǎixìng pǔtōng zháijū de sìhéyuàn shìfǒu háiyǒu cúnzài jiàzhí, shì yí gè zhēnglùn de wèntí.

CLASSICAL GARDENS

[Traditional-character version]

古典園林風格

中國古典園林可以分爲皇家園林和私家園林。皇家園林主要是供帝王休息享樂的園林，其特點是規模宏大，真山、真水較多，園中建築色彩富麗堂皇，建築體型高大。著名的皇家園林有北京的頤和園和河北承德的避暑山莊。私家園林是供豪門世家休閑的園林，其特點是規模較小，常用假山、假水，建築小巧玲瓏，色彩淡雅。現存的私家園林如北京的恭王府、蘇州的拙政園、上海的豫園等。園林所處地理位置不同，建築風格也不一樣。北方園林建築富麗堂皇，但不夠秀美。北方園林的代表大多集中在北京、西安、洛陽、開封等地，

其中以北京爲首。南方人口較密集，所以園林地域範圍小。又因爲河湖、常綠
樹較多，所以園林精緻、細膩。南方園林的代表大多集中在南京、上海、蘇
州、揚州等地，特別是蘇州園林舉世聞名，最具特色。

[Simplified-character version]

古典园林风格

中国古典园林可以分为皇家园林和私家园林。皇家园林主要是供帝王休息
享乐的园林，其特点是规模宏大，真山、真水较多，园中建筑色彩富丽堂皇，
建筑体型高大。著名的皇家园林有北京的颐和园和河北承德的避暑山庄。私家
园林是供豪门世家休闲的园林，其特点是规模较小，常用假山、假水，建筑小
巧玲珑，色彩淡雅。现存的私家园林如北京的恭王府、苏州的拙政园、上海的
豫园等。园林所处地理位置不同，建筑风格也不一样。北方园林建筑富丽堂
皇，但不够秀美。北方园林的代表大多集中在北京、西安、洛阳、开封等地，
其中以北京为首。南方人口较密集，所以园林地域范围小。又因为河湖、常绿
树较多，所以园林精致、细腻。南方园林的代表大多集中在南京、上海、苏
州、扬州等地，特别是苏州园林举世闻名，最具特色。

[Pinyin version]

Gǔdiǎn Yuánlín Fēnggé

Zhōngguó gǔdiǎn yuánlín kěyǐ fēnwéi huángjiā yuánlín hé sījiā yuánlín. Huángjiā
yuánlín zhǔyào shì gōng dìwáng xiūxí xiǎnglè de yuánlín, qí tèdiǎn shì guīmó
hóngdà, zhēnshān, zhēnshuǐ jiàoduō, yuánzhōng jiànzhù sècǎi fùlì tánghuáng,
jiànzhù tǐxíng gāodà. Zhùmíng de huángjiā yuánlín yǒu Běijīng de Yíhéyuán hé
Héběi Chéngdé de Bìshǔ Shānzhuāng. Sījiā yuánlín shì gōng háomén shìjiā xiūxián
de yuánlín, qí tèdiǎn shì guīmó jiàoxiǎo, chángyòng jiǎshān, jiǎshuǐ, jiànzhù
xiǎoqiǎo línglóng, sècǎi dànyǎ. Xiàncún de sījiā yuánlín rú Běijīng de Gōngwángfǔ,
Sūzhōu de Zhuōzhèngyuán, Shànghǎi de Yùyuán děng. Yuánlín suǒchǔ dìlǐ wèizhì
bùtóng, jiànzhù fēnggé yě bù yí yàng. Běifāng yuánlín jiànzhù fùlì tánghuáng, dàn
búgòu xiùměi. Běifāng yuánlín de dàibiǎo dàduō jízhōng zài Běijīng, Xī'ān,
Luòyáng, Kāifēng děng dì, qízhōng yǐ Běijīng wéishǒu. Nánfāng rénkǒu jiào mìjí,
suǒyǐ yuánlín dìyù fànwéi xiǎo. Yòu yīnwèi héhú, chánglùshù jiàoduō, suǒyǐ
yuánlín jīngzhì, xìnì. Nánfāng yuánlín de dàibiǎo dàduō jízhōng zài Nánjīng,
Shànghǎi, Sūzhōu, Yángzhōu děng dì, tèbié shì Sūzhōu yuánlín jǔshì wénmíng,
zuìjù tèsè.

[Traditional-character version]

頤和園

頤和園位於北京西郊，是世界著名園林之一。頤和園是由清朝慈禧太后挪
用海軍經費建造的皇家園林。頤和園由萬壽山、昆明湖和環繞在山湖之間的一
組精美的建築物群組成，其中包括政治活動區、主體生活區和萬壽山、昆明湖
組成的風景遊覽區。頤和園全園的背景是西山群峰，建築群與園內山湖融爲一
體，使景色富於變化。萬壽山的佛香閣是頤和園的象徵。以排雲殿爲中心的宮
殿式建築群是當年慈禧太后過生日的地方。萬壽山下是昆明湖，昆明湖畔有273
間房子，還有全長728米的長廊，把政治活動區、生活區和遊覽區結合在一起。

長廊繪畫精美無比，以"世界上最長的長廊"列入吉尼斯世界之最。頤和園既集中了中國古典建築的精華，又容納了不同地區的園林風格，被稱爲"園林建築博物館"。

[Simplified-character version]

颐和园

　　颐和园位于北京西郊，是世界著名园林之一。颐和园是由清朝慈禧太后挪用海军经费建造的皇家园林。颐和园由万寿山、昆明湖和环绕在山湖之间的一组精美的建筑物群组成，其中包括政治活动区、主体生活区和万寿山、昆明湖组成的风景游览区。颐和园全园的背景是西山群峰，建筑群与园内山湖融为一体，使景色富于变化。万寿山的佛香阁是颐和园的象征。以排云殿为中心的宫殿式建筑群是当年慈禧太后过生日的地方。万寿山下是昆明湖，昆明湖畔有273间房子，还有全长728米的长廊，把政治活动区、生活区和游览区结合在一起。长廊绘画精美无比，以"世界上最长的长廊"列入吉尼斯世界之最。颐和园既集中了中国古典建筑的精华，又容纳了不同地区的园林风格，被称为"园林建筑博物馆"。

[Pinyin version]

Yíhéyuán

Yíhéyuán wèiyú Běijīng xījiāo, shì shìjiè zhùmíng yuánlín zhīyī. Yíhéyuán shì yóu Qīngcháo Cíxǐ tàihòu nuóyòng hǎijūn jīngfèi jiànzào de huángjiā yuánlín. Yíhéyuán yóu Wànshòushān, Kūnmínghú hé huánrào zài shānhú zhījiān de yì zǔ jīngměi de jiànzhùwù qún zǔchéng, qízhōng bāokuò zhèngzhì huódòngqū, zhǔtǐ shēnghuóqū hé Wànshòushān, Kūnmínghú zǔchéng de fēngjǐng yóulǎnqū. Yíhéyuán quányuán de bèijǐng shì Xīshān qúnfēng, jiànzhùqún yǔ yuánnèi shānhú róngwéi yìtǐ, shǐ jǐngsè fùyú biànhuà. Wànshòushān de Fóxiānggé shì Yíhéyuán de xiàngzhēng. Yǐ Páiyúndiàn wéi zhōngxīn de gōngdiànshì jiànzhùqún shì dāngnián Cíxǐ tàihòu guò shēngrì de dìfāng. Wànshòushānxià shì Kūnmínghú, kūnmínghúpàn yǒu èrbǎi qīshísān jiān fángzi, háiyǒu quáncháng qībǎi èrshíbāmǐ de chángláng, bǎ zhèngzhì huódòngqū, shēnghuóqū hé yóulǎnqū jiéhé zài yìqǐ. Chángláng huìhuà jīngměi wúbǐ, yǐ "Shìjiè shang zuì cháng de chángláng" lièrù Jínísī Shìjiè Zhīzuì. Yíhéyuán jì jízhōngle Zhōngguó gǔdiǎn jiànzhù de jīnghuá, yòu róngnàle bùtóng dìqū de yuánlín fēnggé, bèi chēngwéi "Yuánlín jiànzhù bówùguǎn".

TRADITIONAL PERFORMING ARTS

[Traditional-character version]

京劇

　　中國京劇已有200年的歷史。清朝的時候，安徽四大著名的戲班子來到北京，他們的曲藝與北京的昆曲、漢劇等劇種經過了幾十年的融合，逐漸演變成爲中國最大的戲曲劇種——京劇。

　　京劇是一種綜合性的表演藝術。京劇把唱、念、做、打、舞結合在一體，通過程式化的表演手段叙演故事，刻畫人物，表達思想。京劇的角色可分爲"生"（男人）、"旦"（女人）、"淨"（男人）、"醜"（男、女人都有）。京劇中的人物有美、醜、善、惡之分。

中國京劇的臉譜是一門傳統藝術，是演員面部化妝的一種程式。京劇中的各種人物都有特定的樣式和色彩，突出不同的人物性格。臉譜的演變和發展是藝術家們在長期藝術實踐中，對生活現象的觀察、體驗、綜合以及對劇中角色的不斷分析、判斷，逐步形成的完整的藝術手法。

中國京劇有四大名旦的說法。1927年，北京的一份報紙舉辦評選"首屆京劇旦角最佳演員"活動，梅蘭芳、程硯秋、尚小雲、荀慧生被選爲京劇"四大名旦"。梅蘭芳（1894—1961），江蘇人，出生於京劇世家。代表作有《霸王別姬》、《貴妃醉酒》等。他曾率京劇團多次赴日、美等國演出，是享有國際聲譽的戲曲表演藝術家。程硯秋（1904—1958），北京人，從小就跟隨梅蘭芳學習京劇。他的代表作品有《英台抗婚》、《寶娥冤》等戲，劇情大多表現封建社會婦女的悲慘命運。尚小雲（1900—1976），河北人，14歲就被稱爲"第一童伶"。他的代表作品有《二進宮》、《昭君出塞》等，在劇中，他塑造了一批女英雄形象。荀慧生（1900—1968），河北人，擅長扮演天真、活潑、溫柔的婦女角色，以演《紅娘》、《紅樓二尤》等劇著名。

[Simplified-character version]

京剧

中国京剧已有200年的历史。清朝的时候，安徽四大著名的戏班子来到北京，他们的曲艺与北京的昆曲、汉剧等剧种经过了几十年的融合，逐渐演变成为中国最大的戏曲剧种——京剧。

京剧是一种综合性的表演艺术。京剧把唱、念、做、打、舞结合在一体，通过程式化的表演手段叙演故事，刻画人物，表达思想。京剧的角色可分为"生"（男人）、"旦"（女人）、"净"（男人）、"丑"（男、女人都有）。京剧中的人物有美、丑、善、恶之分。

中国京剧的脸谱是一门传统艺术，是演员面部化妆的一种程式。京剧中的各种人物都有特定的样式和色彩，突出不同的人物性格。脸谱的演变和发展是艺术家们在长期艺术实践中，对生活现象的观察、体验、综合以及对剧中角色的不断分析、判断，逐步形成的完整的艺术手法。

中国京剧有四大名旦的说法。1927年，北京的一份报纸举办评选"首届京剧旦角最佳演员"活动，梅兰芳、程砚秋、尚小云、荀慧生被选为京剧"四大名旦"。梅兰芳（1894—1961），江苏人，出生于京剧世家。代表作有《霸王别姬》、《贵妃醉酒》等。他曾率京剧团多次赴日、美等国演出，是享有国际声誉的戏曲表演艺术家。程砚秋（1904—1958），北京人，从小就跟随梅兰芳学习京剧。他的代表作品有《英台抗婚》、《窦娥冤》等戏，剧情大多表现封建社会妇女的悲惨命运。尚小云（1900—1976），河北人，14岁就被称为"第一童伶"。他的代表作品有《二进宫》、《昭君出塞》等，在剧中，他塑造了一批女英雄形象。荀慧生（1900—1968），河北人，擅长扮演天真、活泼、温柔的妇女角色，以演《红娘》、《红楼二尤》等剧著名。

[Pinyin version]

Jīngjù

Zhōngguó jīngjù yǐyǒu èrbǎi nián de lìshǐ. Qīngcháo de shíhou, Ānhuī sìdà zhùmíng de xìbānzi láidào Běijīng, tāmen de qǔyì yǔ Běijīng de kūnqǔ, hànjù děng jùzhǒng jīngguòle jǐshí nián de rónghé, zhújiàn yǎnbiàn chéngwéi Zhōngguó zuìdà de xìqǔ jùzhǒng—Jīngjù.

Jīngjù shì yí zhǒng zònghéxìng de biǎoyǎn yìshù. Jīngjù bǎ chàng, niàn, zuò, dǎ, wǔ jiéhé zài yìtǐ, tōngguò chéngshìhuà de biǎoyǎn shǒuduàn xùyǎn gùshì, kèhuà rénwù, biǎodá sīxiǎng. Jīngjù de juésè kě fēnwéi "shēng" (nánrén), "dàn" (nǚrén), "jìng" (nánrén), "chǒu" (nán, nǚrén dōuyǒu). Jīngjù zhōng de rénwù yǒu měi, chǒu, shàn, è zhīfēn.

Zhōngguó jīngjù de liǎnpǔ shì yì mén chuántǒng yìshù, shì yǎnyuán miànbù huàzhuāng de yì zhǒng chéngshì. Jīngjù zhōng de gè zhǒng rénwù dōuyǒu tèdìng de yàngshì hé sècǎi, tūchū bùtóng de rénwù xìnggé. Liǎnpǔ de yǎnbiàn hé fāzhǎn shì yìshùjiāmen zài chángqī yìshù shíjiàn zhōng, duì shēnghuó xiànxiàng de guānchá, tǐyàn, zònghé yǐjí duì jùzhōng juésè de búduàn fēnxī, pànduàn, zhúbù xíngchéng de wánzhěng de yìshù shǒufǎ.

Zhōngguó jīngjù yǒu sìdà míngdàn de shuōfǎ. Yī jiǔ èr qī nián, Běijīng de yí fèn bàozhǐ jǔbàn píngxuǎn "Shǒujiè jīngjù dànjué zuìjiā yǎnyuán" huódòng, Méi Lánfāng, Chéng Yànqiū, Shàng Xiǎoyún, Xún Huìshēng bèi xuǎnwéi jīngjù "Sìdà míngdàn". Méi Lánfāng (1894—1961), Jiāngsūrén, chūshēng yú jīngjù shìjiā. Dàibiǎozuò yǒu "Bàwáng biéjī", "Guìfēi zuìjiǔ" děng. Tā céng shuài jīngjùtuán duō cì fù Rì, Měi děngguó yǎnchū, shì xiǎngyǒu guójì shēngyù de xìqǔ biǎoyǎn yìshùjiā. Chéng Yànqiū (1904—1958), Běijīngrén, cóngxiǎo jiù gēnsuí Méi Lánfāng xuéxí jīngjù. Tā de dàibiǎo zuòpǐn yǒu "Yīng tái kànghūn", "Dòu'é yuān" děng xì, jùqíng dàduō biǎoxiàn fēngjiàn shèhuì fùnǚ de bēicǎn mìngyùn. Shàng Xiǎoyún (1900—1976), Héběirén, 14 suì jiù bèi chēngwéi "Dìyī tónglíng". Tā de dàibiǎo zuòpǐn yǒu "Èrjìngōng", "Zhāojūn chūsāi" děng, zài jùzhōng, tā sùzàole yí pī nǚyīngxióng xíngxiàng. Xún Huìshēng (1900—1968), Héběirén, shàncháng bànyǎn tiānzhēn, huópō, wēnróu de fùnǚ juésè, yǐ yǎn "Hóngniáng", "Hónglóu èr yóu" děng jù zhùmíng.

[Traditional-character version]

相聲

相聲是中國傳統的曲藝表演藝術，起源於華北地區的民間說唱曲藝，在明朝時已經盛行。相聲按內容分類，可分爲諷刺型、歌頌型和娛樂型等。按表演形式分，相聲有單口相聲、對口相聲和群口相聲，其中，對口相聲是最受觀眾喜愛的形式。"說"、"學"、"逗"、"唱"是相聲演員的四個基本功。"說"，就是講故事。"學"，就是模仿生活中的各種人物、方言和自然界中的各種聲音。"逗"，就是製造笑料，引人發笑。"唱"，常被認爲是唱戲和唱歌，實際上是北京的一種民間小曲。

[Simplified-character version]

相声

相声是中国传统的曲艺表演艺术，起源于华北地区的民间说唱曲艺，在明朝时已经盛行。相声按内容分类，可分为讽刺型、歌颂型和娱乐型等。按表演形式分，相声有单口相声、对口相声和群口相声，其中，对口相声是最受观众喜爱的形式。"说"、"学"、"逗"、"唱"是相声演员的四个基本功。"说"，就是讲故事。"学"，就是模仿生活中的各种人物、方言和自然界中的各种声音。"逗"，就是制造笑料，引人发笑。"唱"，常被认为是唱戏和唱歌，实际上是北京的一种民间小曲。

[Pinyin version]

Xiàngsheng

Xiàngsheng shì Zhōngguó chuántǒng de qǔyì biǎoyǎn yìshù, qǐyuán yú huáběi dìqū de mínjiān shuōchàng qǔyì, zài Míngcháo shí yǐjīng shèngxíng. Xiàngsheng àn nèiróng fēnlèi, kě fēnwéi fèngcìxíng, gēsòngxíng hé yúlèxíng děng. Àn biǎoyǎn xíngshì fēn, xiàngsheng yǒu dānkǒu xiàngshēng, duìkǒu xiàngshēng hé qúnkǒu xiàngshēng, qízhōng, duìkǒu xiàngshēng shì zuì shòu guānzhòng xǐ'ài de xíngshì. "Shuō", "xué", "dòu", "chàng" shì xiàngsheng yǎnyuán de sì gè jīběngōng. "Shuō", jiùshì jiǎng gùshì. "Xué", jiùshì mófǎng shēnghuó zhōng de gèzhǒng rénwù, fāngyán hé zìránjiè zhōng de gèzhǒng shēngyīn. "Dòu", jiùshì zhìzào xiàoliào, yǐnrén fāxiào. "Chàng", cháng bèi rènwéi shì chàngxì hé chànggē, shíjìshang shì Běijīng de yì zhǒng mínjiān xiǎoqǔ.

EDUCATION

[Traditional-character version]

私塾

中國古代的"私塾"教育是中國封建社會的主要教育體系。從漢朝開始，中國有了培養選拔官吏的"官學"，宋代以後著名文人辦"書院"開始增多。清朝末年，中國開始出現了現代教育方式的學校。現代教育體系在20世紀不斷完善。進入90年代，中國的教育體系又有了很大的變化，私人辦學現象重新開始出現。

[Simplified-character version]

私塾

中国古代的"私塾"教育是中国封建社会的主要教育体系。从汉朝开始，中国有了培养选拔官吏的"官学"，宋代以后著名文人办"书院"开始增多。清朝末年，中国开始出现了现代教育方式的学校。现代教育体系在20世纪不断完善。进入90年代，中国的教育体系又有了很大的变化，私人办学现象重新开始出现。

[Pinyin version]

Sīshú

Zhōngguó gǔdài de "sīshú" jiàoyù shì Zhōngguó fēngjiàn shèhuì de zhǔyào jiàoyù tǐxì. Cóng Hàncháo kāishǐ, Zhōngguó yǒule péiyǎng xuǎnbá guānlì de "guānxué", Sòngdài yǐhòu zhùmíng wénrén bàn "shūyuàn" kāishǐ zēngduō. Qīngcháo mònián, Zhōngguó kāishǐ chūxiànle xiàndài jiàoyù fāngshì de xuéxiào. Xiàndài jiàoyù tǐxì zài èrshí shìjì búduàn wánshàn. Jìnrù jiǔshí niándài, Zhōngguó de jiàoyù tǐxì yòu yǒule hěndà de biànhuà, sīrén bànxué xiànxiàng chóngxīn kāishǐ chūxiàn.

[Traditional-character version]

科舉制度

科舉是中國古代封建社會在讀書人中選拔官吏的一種考試制度。因爲採用分科取士的辦法，所以叫做科舉。中國科舉制度最早起源於隋朝，在唐朝進一步完善，宋朝時進行了改革，明朝是科舉制度的鼎盛時期，到了清朝，這一古代科舉制度走向滅亡，歷經一千三百多年。

明清兩代的科舉考試分爲鄉試、會試、殿試三級。鄉試是地方考試，會試是全國考試。這兩種考試主要考八股文和詩等。殿試在會試後當年舉行,由皇帝主考。科舉考試的主要內容是八股文，也就是從《詩》、《書》、《禮》、《易》、《春秋》裏選擇題目進行寫作。題目和寫作方式都有一定格式。會試的地方是貢院。各地舉人來此應試，如同向皇帝貢獻名產，所以叫貢院。

科舉制度對中國以及東亞、世界都產生了積極的影響。科舉原來的目的是從民間爲政府提拔人材，相對來說是一種公平、公開及公正的方法。最初日本、韓國、越南等國也都模仿中國的科舉考試。傳教士還把中國科舉制度，通過他們的遊記介紹到歐洲國家。科舉制度的消極影響主要在它的考試內容和形式上。考試內容僵化，限制了考生的創造能力和獨立思考能力。雖然科舉制度已被廢除，但它仍然在中國社會中留下不少痕迹。今天的考試制度在一定程度上仍是科舉制度的延續。

[Simplified-character version]

科举制度

科举是中国古代封建社会在读书人中选拔官吏的一种考试制度。因为采用分科取士的办法，所以叫做科举。中国科举制度最早起源于隋朝，在唐朝进一步完善，宋朝时进行了改革，明朝是科举制度的鼎盛时期，到了清朝，这一古代科举制度走向灭亡，历经一千三百多年。

明清两代的科举考试分为乡试、会试、殿试三级。乡试是地方考试，会试是全国考试。这两种考试主要考八股文和诗等。殿试在会试后当年举行,由皇帝主考。科举考试的主要内容是八股文，也就是从《诗》、《书》、《礼》、《易》、《春秋》里选择题目进行写作。题目和写作方式都有一定格式。会试的地方是贡院。各地举人来此应试，如同向皇帝贡献名产，所以叫贡院。

科举制度对中国以及东亚、世界都产生了积极的影响。科举原来的目的是从民间为政府提拔人材，相对来说是一种公平、公开及公正的方法。最初日本、韩国、越南等国也都模仿中国的科举考试。传教士还把中国科举制度，通过他们的游记介绍到欧洲国家。科举制度的消极影响主要在它的考试内容和形式上。考试内容僵化，限制了考生的创造能力和独立思考能力。虽然科举制度已被废除，但它仍然在中国社会中留下不少痕迹。今天的考试制度在一定程度上仍是科举制度的延续。

[Pinyin version]

Kējǔ zhìdù

Kējǔ shì Zhōngguó gǔdài fēngjiàn shèhuì zài dúshūrén zhōng xuǎnbá guānlì de yì zhǒng kǎoshì zhìdù. Yīnwèi cǎiyòng fēnkē qǔshì de bànfǎ, suǒyǐ jiàozuò kējǔ. Zhōngguó kējǔ zhìdù zuìzǎo qǐyuányú Suícháo, zài Tángcháo jìnyíbù wánshàn, Sòngcháo shí jìnxíngle gǎigé, Míngcháo shì kējǔ zhìdù de dǐngshèng shíqí, dàole Qīngcháo, zhè yī gǔdài kējǔ zhìdù zǒuxiàng mièwáng, lìjīng yìqiān sānbǎi duō nián.

Míng Qīng liǎngdài de kējǔ kǎoshì fēnwéi xiāngshì, huìshì, diànshì sānjí. Xiāngshì shì dìfāng kǎoshì, huìshì shì quánguó kǎoshì. Zhè liǎng zhǒng kǎoshì zhǔyào kǎo bāgǔwén hè shī děng. Diànshì zài huìshì hòu dāngnián jǔxíng, yóu huángdì zhǔkǎo. Kējǔ kǎoshì de zhǔyào nèiróng shì bāgǔwén, yě jiùshì cóng "Shī", "Shū", "Lǐ", "Yì", "Chūnqiū" lǐ xuǎnzé tímù jìnxíng xiězuò. Tímù hé xiězuò fāngshì dōu yǒu yídìng géshì. Huìshì de dìfāng shì gòngyuàn. Gèdì jǔrén láicǐ yìngshì, rútóng xiàng huángdì gòngxiàn míngchǎn, suǒyǐ jiào gòngyuàn.

Kējǔ zhìdù duì Zhōngguó yǐjí dōngyà, shìjiè dōu chǎnshēngle jījí de yǐngxiǎng. Kējǔ yuánlái de mùdì shì cóng mínjiān wèi zhèngfǔ tíbá réncái, xiāngduì láishuō shì yì zhǒng gōngpíng, gōngkāi jí gōngzhèng de fāngfǎ. Zuìchū Rìběn, Hánguó, Yuènán děng guó yě dū mófǎng Zhōngguó de kējǔ kǎoshì. Chuánjiàoshì hái bǎ Zhōngguó kējǔ zhìdù, tōngguò tāmen de yóujì jièshào dào Ōuzhōu guójiā. Kējǔ zhìdù de xiāojí yǐngxiǎng zhǔyào zài tā de kǎoshì nèiróng hé xíngshì shang. Kǎoshì nèiróng jiānghuà, xiànzhìle kǎoshēng de chuàngzào nénglì hé dúlì sīkǎo nénglì. Suīrán kējǔ zhìdù yǐ bèi fèichú, dàn tā réngrán zài Zhōngguó shèhuì zhōng liúxia bùshǎo hénjī. Jīntiān de kǎoshì zhìdù zài yídìng chéngdù shang réngshì kējǔ zhìdù de yánxù.

[Traditional-character version]

貢院

　　貢院是中國古代國家舉行科舉考試的地方。爲什麼叫"貢院"呢？原來要把通過這個考試選拔出來的人才貢獻給皇帝或國家。北京的順天貢院和南京的江南貢院是當時規模最大的考場。按照明清時的科舉制度，考試分三級，也就是鄉試、會試和殿試。鄉試每三年考一次，每次考試連續考三場，每場三天。鄉試在農曆八月舉行。通過鄉試的人叫舉人，舉人可以在第二年三月參加京城的會試和殿試。會試在貢院舉行，也是連考三場，每場三天。通過會試的人叫貢士。得到貢士資格的人可以參加同年四月的殿試。貢院考試很嚴格。考生進入考場後，要把門鎖上。三天考期結束前考生不許離開考場，吃、喝、睡都得在裏面。

[Simplified-character version]

贡院

　　贡院是中国古代国家举行科举考试的地方。为什么叫"贡院"呢？原来要把通过这个考试选拔出来的人才贡献给皇帝或国家。北京的顺天贡院和南京的江南贡院是当时规模最大的考场。按照明清时的科举制度，考试分三级，也就是乡试、会试和殿试。乡试每三年考一次，每次考试连续考三场，每场三天。乡试在农历八月举行。通过乡试的人叫举人，举人可以在第二年三月参加京城的会试和殿试。会试在贡院举行，也是连考三场，每场三天。通过会试的人叫贡士。得到贡士资格的人可以参加同年四月的殿试。贡院考试很严格。考生进入考场后，要把门锁上。三天考期结束前考生不许离开考场，吃、喝、睡都得在里面。

[Pinyin version]

Gòngyuàn

Gòngyuàn shì Zhōngguó gǔdài guójiā jǔxíng kējǔ kǎoshì de dìfāng. Wèishénme jiào "Gòngyuàn" ne? Yuánlái yào bǎ tōngguò zhège kǎoshì xuǎnbá chūlái de réncái gòngxiàn gěi huángdì huò guójiā. Běijīng de Shùntiān gòngyuàn hé Nánjīng de Jiāngnán gòngyuàn shì dāngshí guīmó zuìdà de kǎochǎng. Ànzhào Míng Qīng shí de kējǔ zhìdù, kǎoshì fēn sānjí, yě jiùshì xiāngshì, huìshì hé diànshì. Xiāngshì měi sānnián kǎo yí cì, měicì kǎoshì liánxù kǎo sānchǎng, měichǎng sān tiān. Xiāngshì zài nónglì bāyuè jǔxíng. Tōngguò xiāngshì de rén jiào jǔrén, jǔrén kěyǐ zài dìernián sānyuè cānjiā jīngchéng de huìshì hé diànshì. Huìshì zài gòngyuàn jǔxíng, yěshì lián kǎo sānchǎng, měichǎng sān tiān. Tōngguò huìshì de rén jiào gòngshì. Dédào gòngshì zīgé de rén kěyǐ cānjiā tóngnián sìyuè de diànshì. Gòngyuàn kǎoshì hěn yángé. Kǎoshēng jìnrù kǎochǎng hòu, yào bǎ mén suǒshang. Sāntiān kǎoqī jiéshù qián kǎoshēng bùxǔ líkāi kǎochǎng, chī, hē, shuì dōuděi zài lǐmian.

[Traditional-character version]

九年義務教育

　　中國實行從小學到初中的九年義務教育，從法律上保護學生接受義務教育的權利。中國的小學分爲六年。小學開設的課程爲語文（中文）、數學、英語、體育、社會（含地理、歷史和政治常識）、自然（含物理、化學和生物常識）、音樂、美術和電腦。中學分爲初中和高中兩個階段。初中階段需要學習的課程有語文、數學、英語、體育、物理、化學、生物、地理、歷史、思想政治，條件好的學校還開設電腦課程。在初三年級結束時，學生有一個升學考試，即中考。中考的科目爲語文、數學、英語、物理、化學和體育。學生初中畢業後可以升入高中繼續學習，爲上大學做準備，也可以上中等專業學校和職業中學。在高中，學生需要學習語文、數學、英語、物理、化學、生物、地理、歷史、政治、體育和電腦。一般情況下，在高一學習結束後，學生就要確立今後的學習方向是理科還是文科。到了高二，如果選擇理科，將學習語文、數學、英語、物理、化學、生物、政治和體育。如果選擇文科，就要學習語文、英語、歷史等科目。高二需要通過一定科目的畢業考試，高三之後學生將爲大學考試做準備。

[Simplified-character version]

九年义务教育

　　中国实行从小学到初中的九年义务教育，从法律上保护学生接受义务教育的权利。中国的小学分为六年。小学开设的课程为语文（中文）、数学、英语、体育、社会（含地理、历史和政治常识）、自然（含物理、化学和生物常识）、音乐、美术和电脑。中学分为初中和高中两个阶段。初中阶段需要学习的课程有语文、数学、英语、体育、物理、化学、生物、地理、历史、思想政治，条件好的学校还开设电脑课程。在初三年级结束时，学生有一个升学考试，即中考。中考的科目为语文、数学、英语、物理、化学和体育。学生初中毕业后可以升入高中继续学习，为上大学做准备，也可以上中等专业学校和职业中学。在高中，学生需要学习语文、数学、英语、物理、化学、生物、地理、历史、政治、体育和电脑。一般情况下，在高一学习结束后，学生就要确立今后的学习方向是理科还是文科。到了高二，如果选择理科，将学习语文、数学、英语、物理、化学、生物、政治和体育。如果选择文科，就要学习语文、英语、历史等科目。高二需要通过一定科目的毕业考试，高三之后学生将为大学考试做准备。

[Pinyin version]

Jiǔnián Yìwù Jiàoyù

Zhōngguó shíxíng cóng xiǎoxué dào chūzhōng de jiǔnián yìwù jiàoyù, cóng fǎlǜshang bǎohù xuéshēng jiēshòu yìwù jiàoyù de quánlì. Zhōngguó de xiǎoxué fēnwéi liùnián. Xiǎoxué kāishè de kèchéng wéi yǔwén (zhōngwén), shùxué, yīngyǔ, tǐyù, shèhuì (hán dìlǐ, lìshǐ hé zhèngzhì chángshì), zìrán (hán wùlǐ, huàxué hé shēngwù chángshì), yīnyuè, měishù hé diànnǎo. Zhōngxué fēnwéi chūzhōng hé gāozhōng liǎnggè jiēduàn. Chūzhōng jiēduàn xūyào xuéxí de kèchéng yǒu yǔwén, shùxué, yīngyǔ, tǐyù, wùlǐ, huàxué, shēngwù, dìlǐ, lìshǐ, sīxiǎng zhèngzhì, tiáojiàn hǎode xuéxiào hái kāishè diànnǎo kèchéng. Zài chūsān niánjí jiéshù shí, xuéshēng yǒu yí gè shēngxué kǎoshì, jí zhōngkǎo. Zhōngkǎo de kēmù wéi yǔwén, shùxué, yīngyǔ, wùlǐ, huàxué hé tǐyù. Xuéshēng chūzhōng bìyè hòu kěyǐ shēngrù gāozhōng jìxù xuéxí, wèi shàng dàxué zuò zhǔnbèi, yě kěyǐ shàng zhōngděng zhuānyè xuéxiào hé zhíyè zhōngxué. Zài gāozhōng, xuéshēng xūyào xuéxí yǔwén, shùxué, yīngyǔ, wùlǐ, huàxué, shēngwù, dìlǐ, lìshǐ, zhèngzhì, tǐyù hé diànnǎo. Yìbān qíngkuàng xia, zài gāoyī xuéxí jiéshù hòu, xuéshēng jiù yào quèlì jīnhòu de xuéxí fāngxiàng shì lǐkē háishì wénkē. Dàole gāo'èr, rúguǒ xuǎnzé lǐkē, jiāng xuéxí yǔwén, shùxué, yīngyǔ, wùlǐ, huàxué, shēngwù, zhèngzhì hé tǐyù. Rúguǒ xuǎnzé wénkē, jiùyào xuéxí yǔwén, yīngyǔ, lìshǐ děng kēmù. Gāo'èr xūyào tōngguò yídìng kēmù de bìyè kǎoshì, gāosān zhīhòu xuéshēng jiāng wèi dàxué kǎoshì zuò zhǔnbèi.

[Traditional-character version]

高考

　　高考，就是中國的高等學校入學考試，是考生選擇大學和進入大學資格的平臺之一。從1952年開始，中國在普通高校實行全國統一招生考試。然而，從1966年到1976年的文化大革命期間，高等學校停止統一招生，直到文革結束後的1977年，高考才得以恢復。目前，中國的大學入學考試採用教育部統一命題和各地自由命題的方式。無論選擇哪種方式，基本上是每年僅舉行一次考試。高考的科目包括語文、數學、外語三門主科和一門綜合考試。綜合考試部分主要指考生根據自己的意願從文科中的政治、歷史、地理或理科中的物理、化學、生物等學科中選擇一個考試科目。這一考試方案是目前中國應用最廣泛、最成熟的，也是最大程度被考生接受的。

　　高考最大限度地實現了選拔人才的公平性、合理性，爲普通百姓的孩子，特別是農村學子改變命運，提高自身經濟地位提供了條件。然而，僅憑一次考試就決定一個人的終生，是不利於個人發展的。因此，中國現行的高考制度還需要不斷完善。

[Simplified-character version]

高考

　　高考，就是中国的高等学校入学考试，是考生选择大学和进入大学资格的平台之一。从1952年开始，中国在普通高校实行全国统一招生考试。然而，从1966年到1976年的文化大革命期间，高等学校停止统一招生，直到文革结束后的1977年，高考才得以恢复。目前，中国的大学入学考试采用教育部统一命题和各地自由命题的方式。无论选择哪种方式，基本上是每年仅举行一次考试。高考的科目包括语文、数学、外语三门主科和一门综合考试。综合考试部分主要指考生根据自己的意愿从文科中的政治、历史、地理或理科中的物理、化学、生物等学科中选择一个考试科目。这一考试方案是目前中国应用最广泛、最成熟的，也是最大程度被考生接受的。

高考最大限度地实现了选拔人才的公平性、合理性，为普通百姓的孩子，特别是农村学子改变命运，提高自身经济地位提供了条件。然而，仅凭一次考试就决定一个人的终生，是不利于个人发展的。因此，中国现行的高考制度还需要不断完善。

[Pinyin version]

Gāokǎo

Gāokǎo, jiùshì Zhōngguó de gāoděng xuéxiào rùxué kǎoshì, shì kǎoshēng xuǎnzé dàxué hé jìnrù dàxué zīgé de píngtái zhīyī. Cóng yī jiǔ wǔ èr nián kāishǐ, Zhōngguó zài pǔtōng gāoxiào shíxíng quánguó tǒngyī zhāoshēng kǎoshì. Rán'ér, cóng yī jiǔ liù liù nián dào yī jiǔ qī liù nián de wénhuà dàgémìng qījiān, gāoděng xuéxiào tíngzhǐ tǒngyī zhāoshēng, zhídào wéngé jiéshù hòu de yī jiǔ qīqī nián, gāokǎo cái déyǐ huīfù. Mùqián, Zhōngguó de dàxué rùxué kǎoshì cǎiyòng Jiàoyùbù tǒngyī mìngtí hé gèdì zìyóu mìngtí de fāngshì. Wúlùn xuǎnzé nǎ zhǒng fāngshì, jīběn shang shì měinián jǐn jǔxíng yí cì kǎoshì. Gāokǎo de kēmù bāokuò yǔwén, shùxué, wàiyǔ sānmén zhǔkē hé yì mén zònghé kǎoshì. Zònghé kǎoshì bùfèn zhǔyào zhǐ kǎoshēng gēnjù zìjǐ de yìyuàn cóng wénkē zhōng de zhèngzhì, lìshǐ, dìlǐ huò lǐkē zhōng de wùlǐ, huàxué, shēngwù děng xuékē zhōng xuǎnzé yí gè kǎoshì kēmù. Zhè yī kǎoshì fāng'àn shì mùqián Zhōngguó yìngyòng zuì guǎngfàn, zuì chéngshú de, yěshì zuìdà chéngdù bèi kǎoshēng jiēshòu de. Gāokǎo zuìdà xiàndù de shíxiànle xuǎnbá réncái de gōngpíngxìng, hélǐxìng, wèi pǔtōng bǎixìng de háizi, tèbié shì nóngcūn xuézǐ gǎibiàn mìngyùn, tígāo zìshēn jīngjì dìwèi tígōngle tiáojiàn. Rán'é, jǐn píng yí cì kǎoshì jiù juédìng yí gè rén de zhōngshēng, shì búlìyú gèrén fāzhǎn de. Yīncǐ, Zhōngguó xiànxíng de gāokǎo zhìdù hái xūyào búduàn wánshàn.

[Traditional-character version]

高等教育

中國高等教育包括高等職業學校，大學專科和大學本科。職高和大專畢業沒有學位，本科畢業可以獲得學士學位。本科畢業可以考研究所。一般來說，研究生3年畢業獲得碩士學位，以後是博士學位。

中國的教育系列也包括成人教育。中國成人教育是對已經有工作的人員和待業人員進行文化知識、專業技能的教育和培訓，爲專業技術人員和管理人員提供繼續教育的機會。成人教育的辦學形式是多種多樣的，成人教育的學校已成爲目前中國的重要教育資源之一。

[Simplified-character version]

高等教育

中国高等教育包括高等职业学校，大学专科和大学本科。职高和大专毕业没有学位，本科毕业可以获得学士学位。本科毕业可以考研究所。一般来说，研究生3年毕业获得硕士学位，以后是博士学位。

中国的教育系列也包括成人教育。中国成人教育是对已经有工作的人员和待业人员进行文化知识、专业技能的教育和培训，为专业技术人员和管理人员提供继续教育的机会。成人教育的办学形式是多种多样的，成人教育的学校已成为目前中国的重要教育资源之一。

[Pinyin version]

Gāoděng jiàoyù

Zhōngguó gāoděng jiàoyù bāokuò gāoděng zhíyè xuéxiào, dàxué zhuānkē hé dàxué běnkē. Zhígāo hé dàzhuān bìyè méiyǒu xuéwèi, běnkē bìyè kěyǐ huòdé xuéshì xuéwèi. Běnkē bìyè kěyǐ kǎo yánjiūsuǒ. Yìbān láishuō, yánjiūshēng sān nián bìyè huòdé shuòshì xuéwèi, yǐhòu shì bóshì xuéwèi.

Zhōngguó de jiàoyù xìliè yě bāokuò chéngrén jiàoyù. Zhōngguó chéngrén jiàoyù shì duì yǐjīng yǒu gōngzuò de rényuán hé dàiyè rényuán jìnxíng wénhuà zhīshì, zhuānyè jìnéng de jiàoyù hé péixùn, wèi zhuānyè jìshù rényuán hé guǎnlǐ rényuán tígōng jìxù jiàoyù de jīhuì. Chéngrén jiàoyù de bànxué xíngshì shì duōzhǒng duōyàng de, chéngrén jiàoyù de xuéxiào yǐ chéngwéi mùqián Zhōngguó de zhòngyào jiàoyù zīyuán zhīyī.

CHINESE MARTIAL ARTS

[Traditional-character version]

武術

武術，也叫功夫，是中華民族在長期歷史變革中形成的一個運動項目。中國武術起源於原始社會。那時，人類用棍棒等工具與野獸搏鬥，逐漸積累了一些攻防的經驗。中國南北地理氣候和人體形態的不同而形成了中國不同的武術流派。北方人身材高大，北方天氣寒冷，所以北方武術有氣勢雄勁的特點。南方多水，南方人身材矮小，形成南方武術細膩的風格。

中國武術的流派沒有統一的命名方法。有的按山脈命名，如武當派。有的按宗師姓氏命名，如楊氏太極拳。中國武術門派修煉方法不同，但大體上都包括基本功、套路和內外功的修煉。練內功對身體器官及調整身體部分有好處。中國老百姓已經把練氣功作爲強身健體的一種方法。武術套路運動和搏鬥運動，以技擊爲中心內容，起到了增強體質的作用，也能提高人們防身自衛的能力。長期練習基本功，對培養人們勤奮、刻苦、頑强、勇于進取的意志品德有幫助。

今天，武術成爲傳播中國文化的橋梁，各國武術愛好者通過練武也瞭解了中國文化。武術通過體育競技、文化交流等途徑，在與世界各國人民友好交往中發揮著越來越大的作用。

[Simplified-character version]

武术

武术，也叫功夫，是中华民族在长期历史变革中形成的一个运动项目。中国武术起源于原始社会。那时，人类用棍棒等工具与野兽搏斗，逐渐积累了一些攻防的经验。中国南北地理气候和人体形态的不同而形成了中国不同的武术流派。北方人身材高大，北方天气寒冷，所以北方武术有气势雄劲的特点。南方多水，南方人身材矮小，形成南方武术细腻的风格。

中国武术的流派没有统一的命名方法。有的按山脉命名，如武当派。有的按宗师姓氏命名，如杨氏太极拳。中国武术门派修炼方法不同，但大体上都包括基本功、套路和内外功的修炼。练内功对身体器官及调整身体部分有好处。中国老百姓已经把练气功作为强身健体的一种方法。武术套路运动和搏斗运动，以技击为中心内容，起到了增强体质的作用，也能提高人们防身自卫的能力。长期练习基本功，对培养人们勤奋、刻苦、顽强、勇于进取的意志品德有帮助。

今天，武术成为传播中国文化的桥梁，各国武术爱好者通过练武也了解了中国文化。武术通过体育竞技、文化交流等途径，在与世界各国人民友好交往中发挥着越来越大的作用。

[Pinyin version]

Wǔshù

Wǔshù, yě jiào gōngfu, shì Zhōnghuá mínzú zài chángqī lìshǐ biàngé zhōng xíngchéng de yí gè yùndòng xiàngmù. Zhōngguó wǔshù qǐyuán yú yuánshǐ shèhuì. Nàshí, rénlèi yòng gùnbàng děng gōngjù yǔ yěshòu bódòu, zhújiàn jīlěile yìxiē gōngfáng de jīngyàn. Zhōngguó nánběi dìlǐ qìhòu hé réntǐ xíngtài de bùtóng ér xíngchéngle Zhōngguó bùtóng de wǔshù liúpài. Běifāngrén shēncái gāodà, běifāng tiānqì hánlěng, suǒyǐ běifāng wǔshù yǒu qìshì xióngjìng de tèdiǎn. Nánfāng duōshuǐ, nánfāngrén shēncái ǎixiǎo, xíngchéng nánfāng wǔshù xìnì de fēnggé.

Zhōngguó wǔshù de liúpài méiyǒu tǒngyī de mìngmíng fāngfǎ. Yǒude àn shānmài mìngmíng, rú wǔdāngpài. Yǒude àn zōngshī xìngshì mìngmíng, rú yángshì tàijíquán. Zhōngguó wǔshù ménpài xiūliàn fāngfǎ bùtóng, dàn dàtǐ shang dōu bāokuò jīběngōng, tàolù hé nèiwàigōng de xiūliàn. Liàn nèigōng duì shēntǐ qìguān jí tiáozhěng shēntǐ bùfèn yǒu hǎochù. Zhōngguó lǎobǎixìng yǐjīng bǎ liàn qìgōng zuòwéi qiángshēn jiàntǐ de yí zhǒng fāngfǎ. Wǔshù tàolù yùndòng hé bódòu yùndòng, yǐ jìjī wéi zhōngxīn nèiróng, qǐdàole zēngqiáng tǐzhì de zuòyòng, yě néng tígāo rénmen fángshēn zìwèi de nénglì. Chángqī liànxí jīběngōng, duì péiyǎng rénmen qínfèn, kèkǔ, wánqiáng, yǒngyú jìnqǔ de yìzhì pǐndé yǒu bāngzhù.

Jīntiān, wǔshù chéngwéi chuánbò Zhōngguó wénhuà de qiáoliáng, gèguó wǔshù àihàozhě tōngguò liànwǔ yě liáojiěle Zhōngguó wénhuà. Wǔshù tōngguò tǐyù jìngjì, wénhuà jiāoliú děng tújìng, zài yǔ shìjiè gèguó rénmín yǒuhǎo jiāowǎng zhōng fāhuīzhe yuèlái yuèdà de zuòyòng.

[Traditional-character version]

少林寺

少林寺是中國有名的佛教寺院。北魏皇帝爲了安排印度僧人傳播佛教而建造了這座寺廟。因爲這座寺廟坐落在河南省少室山的密林叢中，所以人們把它稱爲"少林寺"。後來，另一位印度高僧也到了少林寺。這位高僧主張普渡眾生，於是他在少林寺收了很多信徒，傳播禪宗。不久禪宗在中國普及，少林寺也被稱爲禪宗的祖庭。隋末唐初，少林寺因十三僧人救了唐王李世民，立下大功，因而受到朝廷的推崇，少林武術也從此聞名天下，寺院也因此得到很快的發展，號稱"天下第一名剎"。俗話說，中國功夫冠天下，天下武功出少林。可見，少林武術是舉世公認的中國武術的正宗流派。

少林寺的常住院是少林寺的核心，總面積三萬多平方米。大雄寶殿是全寺的中心建築，是僧人進行佛事活動的場所。少林寺西面有中國現存的最大的塔林，是歷代少林寺和尚的墓塔。這些墓塔因它們建築年代的不同而各具風格。少林寺塔林對研究古代中外文化交流和少林武功有極大的參考價值。

[Simplified-character version]

少林寺

少林寺是中国有名的佛教寺院。北魏皇帝为了安排印度僧人传播佛教而建造了这座寺庙。因为这座寺庙坐落在河南省少室山的密林丛中，所以人们把它称为"少林寺"。后来，另一位印度高僧也到了少林寺。这位高僧主张普渡众生，于是他在少林寺收了很多信徒，传播禅宗。不久禅宗在中国普及，少林寺也被称为禅宗的祖庭。隋末唐初，少林寺因十三僧人救了唐王李世民，立下大功，因而受到朝廷的推崇，少林武术也从此闻名天下，寺院也因此得到很快的发展，号称"天下第一名刹"。俗话说，中国功夫冠天下，天下武功出少林。可见，少林武术是举世公认的中国武术的正宗流派。

少林寺的常住院是少林寺的核心，总面积三万多平方米。大雄宝殿是全寺的中心建筑，是僧人进行佛事活动的场所。少林寺西面有中国现存的最大的塔林，是历代少林寺和尚的墓塔。这些墓塔因它们建筑年代的不同而各具风格。少林寺塔林对研究古代中外文化交流和少林武功有极大的参考价值。

[Pinyin version]

Shàolínsì

Shàolínsì shì Zhōngguó yǒumíng de fójiào sìyuàn. Běiwèi huángdì wèile ānpái Yìndù sēngrén chuánbō fójiào ér jiànzàole zhè zuò sìmiào. Yīnwèi zhè zuò sìmiào zuòluò zài Hénán shěng Shǎoshìshān de mìlín cóng zhōng, suǒyǐ rénmen bǎ tā chēngwéi "Shàolínsì". Hòulái, lìng yí wèi Yìndù gāosēng yě dàole Shàolínsì. Zhè wèi gāosēng zhǔzhāng pǔdù zhòngshēng, yúshì tā zài Shàolínsì shōule hěnduō xìntú, chuánbō chánzōng. Bùjiǔ chánzōng zài Zhōngguó pǔjí, Shàolínsì yě bèi chēngwéi chánzōng de zǔtíng. Suímò Tángchū , Shàolínsì yīn shísān sēngrén jiùle Tángwáng Li Shìmín, lìxià dàgōng, yīn'ér shòudào cháotíng de tuīchóng, Shàolín wǔshù yě cóngcǐ wénmíng tiānxià, sìyuàn yě yīncǐ dédào hěnkuài de fāzhǎn, hàochēng "Tiānxià dì yī míngchà". Súhuà shuō, Zhōngguó gōngfu guān tiānxià, tiānxià wǔgōng chū Shàolín. Kějiàn, Shàolín wǔshù shì jǔshì gōngrèn de Zhōngguó wǔshù de zhèngzōng liúpài.

Shàolínsì de Chángzhùyuàn shì Shàolínsì de héxīn, zǒng miànjī sānwàn duō píngfāngmǐ. Dàxióng bǎodiàn shì quánsì de zhōngxīn jiànzhú, shì sēngrén jìnxíng fóshì huódòng de chǎngsuǒ. Shàolínsì xīmiàn yǒu Zhòngguó xiàncún de zuìdà de tǎlín, shì lìdài Shàolínsì héshang de mùtǎ. Zhèxiē mùtǎ yīn tāmen jiànzhú niándài de bùtóng ér gèjù fēnggé. Shàolínsì tǎlín duì yánjiū gǔdài zhōngwài wénhuà jiāoliú hé shàolín wǔgōng yǒu jídà de cānkǎo jiàzhí.

TRADITIONAL ENTERTAINMENT

[Traditional-character version]

麻將

玩麻將是中國傳統的文娛活動。關於麻將的由來，眾說紛紜。有人認爲麻將是春秋戰國時出現的，也有人覺得麻將產生于明朝，但是麻將是中國的國粹這一點不容置疑。

麻將原叫"麻雀"，是由四個人一起玩的一種遊戲。玩麻將有很多規則，但由於各地的風俗與文化的不同，麻將的規則也不統一，玩法各不一樣。中國的麻將運動有著豐富的文化內涵。它不僅是一種獨特的、趣味性很強的遊戲，也對開發人的智力有好處。玩麻將在中國十分普及，流行範圍涉及到社會各個階層、各個領域，已經進入到千家萬戶，成爲中國最有影響力的智力活動。目前世界上很多地區都有玩麻將的風俗。

[Simplified-character version]

麻将

　　玩麻将是中国传统的文娱活动。关于麻将的由来，众说纷纭。有人认为麻将是春秋战国时出现的，也有人觉得麻将产生于明朝，但是麻将是中国的国粹这一点不容置疑。

　　麻将原叫"麻雀"，是由四个人一起玩的一种游戏。玩麻将有很多规则，但由于各地的风俗与文化的不同，麻将的规则也不统一，玩法各不一样。中国的麻将运动有着丰富的文化内涵。它不仅是一种独特的、趣味性很强的游戏，也对开发人的智力有好处。玩麻将在中国十分普及，流行范围涉及到社会各个阶层、各个领域，已经进入到千家万户，成为中国最有影响力的智力活动。目前世界上很多地区都有玩麻将的风俗。

[Pinyin version]

Májiàng

Wán májiàng shì Zhōngguó chuántǒng de wényú huódòng. Guānyú májiàng de yóulái, zhòngshuō fēnyún. Yǒurén rènwéi májiàng shì Chūnqiū Zhànguó shí chūxiàn de, yě yǒurén juéde májiàng chǎnshēng yú Míngcháo, dànshì májiàng shì Zhōngguó de guócuì zhè yí diǎn bùróng zhìyí.

　　Májiàng yuán jiào "máquè", shì yóu sì ge rén yìqǐ wánde yì zhǒng yóuxì. Wán májiàng yǒu hěnduō guīzé, dàn yóuyú gèdì de fēngsú yǔ wénhuà de bùtóng, májiàng de guīzé yě bù tǒngyī, wánfǎ gèbù yíyàng. Zhōngguó de májiàng yùndòng yǒuzhe fēngfù de wénhuà nèihán. Tā bùjǐn shì yì zhǒng dútè de, qùwèixìng hěnqiáng de yóuxì, yě duì kāifā rénde zhìlì yǒu hǎochù. Wán májiàng zài Zhōngguó shífēn pǔjí, liúxíng fànwéi shèjí dào shèhuì gège jiēcéng, gège lǐngyù, yǐjīng jìnrù dào qiānjiā wànhù, chéngwéi Zhōngguó zuì yǒu yǐngxiǎnglì de zhìlì huódòng. Mùqián shìjièshang hěnduō dìqū dōu yǒu wán májiàng de fēngsú.

[Traditional-character version]

舞龍

　　傳說浙江有一座山，山下有一條大河。那裏的老百姓每天都用河裏的水澆田、煮飯。有一天，當地的一位縣官來到鄉間，半路上看見幾個大漢擡著一個大籠子，籠子裏有一條流著眼淚的大蛇。縣官看了以後很難過，就對幾個大漢說："你們能不能把這條大蛇賣給我？"幾位大漢見縣官要買蛇，連忙答應了。縣官把大蛇帶回家裏養了起來。開始的時候，縣官讓人給大蛇肉吃，可是大蛇不吃，後來才知道，原來大蛇和人類一樣，只吃糧食。

　　有一年的夏天，天一直很熱，很少下雨。河裏的水都乾了，地裏的莊稼也都曬死了，老百姓的生活因此受到嚴重影響。一天晚上，縣官做了一個夢，夢中有人告訴他，如果把那條大蛇放到河裏，天自然就會下雨了。縣官醒了以後，馬上讓人把大蛇放到河裏去。果然過了沒幾天，天就下起雨來了。人們爲了感謝大蛇，就燒香祭拜它，還把糧食丟到河裏，希望第二年有個大豐收。可是人們並不知道，這樣做是犯了天上的規矩。原來那條大蛇是山上的巨龍，是主要負責糧食問題的天神。因爲老百姓把糧食丟到河中用於祭拜，糟蹋了糧食，被玉帝知道了，玉帝憤怒極了，於是就把巨龍殺了。巨龍被殺了後，那個地方天天下雨，雨水簡直和血一樣。後來，人們知道了巨龍被殺的原因，十分後悔，就在正月十五那一天舞龍，希望能把巨龍的身體接合起來。舞龍這個習俗從此而流傳下來。

[Simplified-character version]

舞龙

传说浙江有一座山，山下有一条大河。那里的老百姓每天都用河里的水浇田、煮饭。有一天，当地的一位县官来到乡间，半路上看见几个大汉抬着一个大笼子，笼子里有一条流着眼泪的大蛇。县官看了以后很难过，就对几个大汉说："你们能不能把这条大蛇卖给我？"几位大汉见县官要买蛇，连忙答应了。县官把大蛇带回家里养了起来。开始的时候，县官让人给大蛇肉吃，可是大蛇不吃，后来才知道，原来大蛇和人类一样，只吃粮食。

有一年的夏天，天一直很热，很少下雨。河里的水都干了，地里的庄稼也都晒死了，老百姓的生活因此受到严重影响。一天晚上，县官做了一个梦，梦中有人告诉他，如果把那条大蛇放到河里，天自然就会下雨了。县官醒了以后，马上让人把大蛇放到河里去。果然过了没几天，天就下起雨来了。人们为了感谢大蛇，就烧香祭拜它，还把粮食丢到河里，希望第二年有个大丰收。可是人们并不知道，这样做是犯了天上的规矩。原来那条大蛇是山上的巨龙，是主要负责粮食问题的天神。因为老百姓把粮食丢到河中用于祭拜，糟蹋了粮食，被玉帝知道了，玉帝愤怒极了，于是就把巨龙杀了。巨龙被杀了后，那个地方天天下雨，雨水简直和血一样。后来，人们知道了巨龙被杀的原因，十分后悔，就在正月十五那一天舞龙，希望能把巨龙的身体接合起来。舞龙这个习俗从此而流传下来。

[Pinyin version]

Wǔ lóng

Chuánshuō Zhèjiāng yǒu yí zuò shān, shānxia yǒu yí tiáo dàhé. Nàli de lǎobǎixìng měitiān dū yòng héli de shuǐ jiāotián, zhǔfàn. Yǒu yí tiān, dāngdì de yí wèi xiànguān láidao xiāngjiān, bànlùshang kànjiàn jǐ gè dàhàn táizhe yí gè dà lóngzi, lóngzi li yǒu yí tiáo liúzhe yǎnlèi de dàshé. Xiànguān kànle yǐhòu hěn nánguò, jiù duì jǐ gè dàhàn shuō: "Nǐmen néngbunéng bǎ zhè tiáo dàshé màigěi wǒ?" Jǐ wèi dàhàn jiàn xiànguān yào mǎishé, liánmáng dāyingle. Xiànguān bǎ dàshé dàihuí jiāli yǎngle qǐlai. Kāishǐ de shíhou, xiànguān ràng rén gěi dàshé ròu chī, kěshì dàshé bùchī, hòulai cái zhīdào, yuánlái dàshé hé rénlèi yíyàng, zhǐ chī liángshi.

Yǒu yí nián de xiàtiān, tiān yìzhí hěnrè, hěnshǎo xiàyǔ. Héli de shuǐ dōu gānle, dìli de zhuāngjia yě dōu shàisǐle, lǎobǎixìng de shēnghuó yīncǐ shòudào yánzhòng yǐngxiǎng. Yìtiān wǎnshang, xiànguān zuòle yí gè mèng, mèngzhōng yǒurén gàosu tā, rúguǒ bǎ nà tiáo dàshé fàngdao héli, tiān zìrán jiù huì xiàyǔ le. Xiànguān xǐngle yǐhòu, mǎshàng ràng rén bǎ dàshé fàngdao héli qu. Guǒrán guòle méi jǐ tiān, tiān jiù xiàqi yǔ laile. Rénmen wèile gǎnxiè dàshé, jiù shāoxiāng jìbài tā, hái bǎ liángshí diūdao héli, xīwàng dì èr nián yǒu gè dà fēngshōu. Kěshì rénmen bìng bù zhīdào, zhèyàng zuò shì fànle tiānshang de guījǔ. Yuánlái nà tiáo dàshé shì shānshang de jùlóng, shì zhǔyào fùzé liángshí wèntí de tiānshén. Yīnwèi lǎobǎixìng bǎ liángshí diūdao hézhōng yòngyú jìbài, zāotale liángshí, bèi Yùdì zhīdàole, Yùdì fènnù jíle, yúshì jiù bǎ jùlóng shāle. Jùlóng bèi shāle hòu, nàgè dìfāng tiāntiān xiàyǔ, yǔshuǐ jiǎnzhí hé xuè yíyàng. Hòulái, rénmen zhīdàole jùlóng bèi shā de yuányīn, shífēn hòuhuǐ, jiù zài zhēngyuè shíwǔ nà yì tiān wǔlóng, xīwàng néng bǎ jùlóng de shēntǐ jiēhé qǐlai. Wǔlóng zhège xísú cóngcǐ ér liúchuán xiàlai.

[Traditional-character version]

舞獅

　　舞獅是中國優秀的民間藝術。每到元宵節或者集會慶典的時候，民間都有舞獅助興的習俗。這一習俗流傳至今，已有一千多年的歷史。

　　舞獅在發展過程中形成了南獅與北獅兩種不同的表演風格。北獅以安徽、河北爲代表。北獅舞以表演"武獅"爲主，小獅子由一個人舞，大獅子由雙人舞，一個人站立舞獅頭，一人彎腰舞獅身和獅子尾巴。另外，還有一個人扮成武士，在獅子面前引導它表演各種技巧。南方舞獅表演時講究表情及各種逗人喜愛的動作。南獅以廣東爲中心，並流行於香港、澳門及東南亞地區。獅子形象雄偉，中國古人把它當作勇敢和力量的象徵，認爲它能保佑人類平安。中國人在元宵節及其它重大活動裏用舞獅子的方式期盼生活吉祥如意、事事平安。

[Simplified-character version]

舞狮

　　舞狮是中国优秀的民间艺术。每到元宵节或者集会庆典的时候，民间都有舞狮助兴的习俗。这一习俗流传至今，已有一千多年的历史。

　　舞狮在发展过程中形成了南狮与北狮两种不同的表演风格。北狮以安徽、河北为代表。北狮舞以表演"武狮"为主，小狮子由一个人舞，大狮子由双人舞，一个人站立舞狮头，一人弯腰舞狮身和狮子尾巴。另外，还有一个人扮成武士，在狮子面前引导它表演各种技巧。南方舞狮表演时讲究表情及各种逗人喜爱的动作。南狮以广东为中心，并流行于香港、澳门及东南亚地区。狮子形象雄伟，中国古人把它当作勇敢和力量的象征，认为它能保佑人类平安。中国人在元宵节及其它重大活动里用舞狮子的方式期盼生活吉祥如意、事事平安。

[Pinyin version]

Wǔshī

Wǔshī shì Zhōngguó yōuxiù de mínjiān yìshù. Měidao Yuánxiāojié huòzhě jíhuì qìngdiǎn de shíhou, mínjiān dōu yǒu wǔshī zhùxìng de xísú. Zhè yí xísú liúchuán zhìjīn, yǐ yǒu yìqiān duō nián de lìshǐ.

Wǔshī zài fāzhǎn guòchéng zhōng xíngchéngle nánshī yǔ běi shī liǎng zhǒng bùtóng de biǎoyǎn fēnggé. Běishī yǐ Ānhuī, Héběi wéi dàibiǎo. Běishīwǔ yǐ biǎoyǎn "wǔshī" wéizhǔ, xiǎo shīzi yóu yí gè rén wǔ, dà shīzi yóu shuāngrén wǔ, yí gè rén zhànlì wǔ shītóu, yì rén wānyāo wǔ shīshēn hé shīzǐ wěiba. Lìngwài, háiyǒu yí gè rén bànchéng wǔshì, zài shīzi miànqián yǐndǎo tā biǎoyǎn gèzhǒng jìqiǎo. Nánfāng wǔshī biǎoyǎn shí jiǎngjiu biǎoqíng jí gèzhǒng dòurén xǐ'ài de dòngzuò. Nánshī yǐ Guǎngdōng wéi zhōngxīn, bìng liúxíng yú Xiānggǎng, Àomén jí dōngnányà dìqū. Shīzǐ xíngxiàng xióngwěi, Zhōngguó gǔrén bǎ tā dàngzuò yǒnggǎn hé lìliàng de xiàngzhēng, rènwéi tā néng bǎoyòu rénlèi píng'ān. Zhōngguórén zài Yuánxiāojié jí qítā zhòngdà huódòng li yòng wǔ shīzi de fāngshì qīpàn shēnghuó jíxiáng rúyì, shìshì píng'ān.

CULTURAL HERITAGE

[Traditional-character version]

周口店北京人遺址

　　周口店北京人遺址位於北京南部的房山區周口店。上世紀20年代，人們在周口店發現了第一塊北京人頭蓋骨，爲研究古人類提供了堅實的基礎。

　　研究結果顯示，北京人生活在距今70萬年至20萬年之間。據推算，北京人身高爲男156釐米，女150釐米。北京人的壽命較短，大部分人死於14歲以前，超過50歲的人微乎其微。北京人屬石器時代，是最早使用火的古人類，並能捕獵動物。

[Simplified-character version]

周口店北京人遗址

　　周口店北京人遗址位于北京南部的房山区周口店。上世纪20年代，人们在周口店发现了第一块北京人头盖骨，为研究古人类提供了坚实的基础。

　　研究结果显示，北京人生活在距今70万年至20万年之间。据推算，北京人身高为男156厘米，女150厘米。北京人的寿命较短，大部分人死于14岁以前，超过50岁的人微乎其微。北京人属石器时代，是最早使用火的古人类，并能捕猎动物。

[Pinyin version]

Zhōukǒudiàn Běijīngrén Yízhǐ

Zhōukǒudiàn Běijīngrén Yízhǐ wèiyú Běijīng nánbù de Fángshān qū Zhōukǒudiàn. Shàng shìjì èrshí niándài, rénmen zài Zhōukǒudiàn fāxiànle dì yī kuài Běijīngrén tóugàigǔ, wèi yánjiū gǔrénlèi tígōngle jiānshí de jīchǔ.

　Yánjiū jiéguǒ xiǎnshì, Běijīngrén shēnghuó zài jùjīn qīshí wàn nián zhì èrshí wàn nián zhījiān. Jù tuīsuàn, Běijīngrén shēngāo wéi nán yìbǎi wǔshíliù límǐ, nǚ yìbǎi wǔshí límǐ. Běijīngrén de shòumìng jiàoduǎn, dàbùfèn rén sǐyú shísì suì yǐqián, chāoguò wǔshí suì de rén wéihū qíwēi. Běijīngrén shǔ shíqì shídài, shì zuìzǎo shǐyòng huǒ de gǔrénlèi, bìng néng bǔliè dòngwù.

[Traditional-character version]

黃山

　　黃山位於中國安徽省的南部，南北約40公里，東西約30公里，面積約1200平方公里。黃山的主峰蓮花峰，海拔1864米。黃山景區分溫泉、雲谷、松谷、北海、玉屏和鈎橋六個部分。黃山的奇松、怪石、雲海和溫泉被稱爲“四絕”。黃山集中了中國各大名山的美景，所以，中國古代著名的旅行家徐霞客說：“五岳歸來不看山，黃山歸來不看岳”，可見，黃山的景色是多麼的美麗。除了自然景觀，黃山在人文景觀方面也佔有重要地位。黃山是個資源豐富、生態完整、有重要科學和生態環境價值的國家級風景名勝區和避暑勝地。

[Simplified-character version]

黄山

　　黄山位于中国安徽省的南部，南北约40公里，东西约30公里，面积约1200平方公里。黄山的主峰莲花峰，海拔1864米。黄山景区分温泉、云谷、松谷、北海、玉屏和钓桥 六个部分。黄山的奇松、怪石、云海和温泉被称为"四绝"。黄山集中了中国各大名山的美景，所以，中国古代著名的旅行家徐霞客说："五岳归来不看山，黄山归来不看岳"，可见，黄山的景色是多么的美丽。除了自然景观，黄山在人文景观方面也占有重要地位。黄山是个资源丰富、生态完整、有重要科学和生态环境价值的国家级风景名胜区和避暑胜地。

[Pinyin version]

Huángshān

Huángshān wèiyú Zhōngguó Āhuī shěng de nánbù, nánběi yuē sìshí gōnglǐ, dōngxi yuē sānshí gōnglǐ, miànjī yuē yìqiān èrbǎi píngfāng gōnglǐ. Huángshān de zhǔfēng Liánhuāfēng, hǎibá yìqiān bābǎi liùshísìmǐ. Huángshān jǐngqū fēn Wēnquán, Yúngǔ, Sōnggǔ, Běihǎi, Yùpíng hé Diàoqiáo liù gè bùfen. Huángshān de qísōng, guàishí, yúnhuǎ hé wēnquán bèi chēngwéi "Sì jué". Huángshān jízhōngle Zhōngguó gèdà míngshān de měijǐng, suǒyǐ, Zhōngguó gǔdài zhùmíng de lǚxíngjiā Xú Xiákè shuō: "Wǔyuè guīlai bú kànshān, Huángshān guīlai bú kànyuè", kějiàn, Huángshān de jǐngsè shì duōme de měilì. Chúle zìrán jǐngguān, Huángshān zài rénwén jǐngguān fāngmiàn yě zhànyǒu zhòngyào dìwèi. Huángshān shì gè zīyuán fēngfù, shēngtài wánzhěng, yǒu zhòngyào kēxué hé shēngtài huánjìng jiàzhí de guójiājí fēngjǐng míngshèng qū hé bìshǔ shèngdì.

[Traditional-character version]

四川大熊貓棲息地

中國四川省內的大熊貓棲息地，面積9245平方公里，地跨省內幾個市、自治州和縣。大熊貓棲息地擁有豐富的植物種類，居住著全世界30%以上的野生大熊貓，是世界上最大、最完整的大熊貓棲息地。另外，那裏也是小熊貓、雪豹等瀕危物種棲息的地方。在幾個自然保護區中，臥龍自然保護區主要保護大熊貓及森林生態系統。四姑娘山自然保護區主要保護野生動物及高山生態系統。金山脈自然保護區主要保護珍稀動物及生態環境。

[Simplified-character version]

四川大熊猫栖息地

中国四川省内的大熊猫栖息地，面积9245平方公里，地跨省内几个市、自治州和县。大熊猫栖息地拥有丰富的植物种类，居住着全世界30%以上的野生大熊猫，是世界上最大、最完整的大熊猫栖息地。另外，那里也是小熊猫、雪豹等濒危物种栖息的地方。在几个自然保护区中，卧龙自然保护区主要保护大熊猫及森林生态系统。四姑娘山自然保护区主要保护野生动物及高山生态系统。金山脉自然保护区主要保护珍稀动物及生态环境。

[Pinyin version]

Sìchuān Dàxióngmāo Qīxīdì

Zhōngguó Sìchuānshěng nèide dàxióngmāo qīxīdì, miànjī jiǔqiān èrbǎi sìshíwǔ píngfāng gōnglǐ, dìkuà shěngnèi jǐ gè shì, zìzhìzhōu hé xiàn. Dàxióngmāo qīxīdì yōngyǒu fēngfù de zhíwù zhǒnglèi, jūzhùzhe quán shìjiè bǎifēnzhī sānshí yǐshàng de yěshēng dàxióngmāo, shì shìjiè shang zuìdà, zuì wánzhěng de dàxióngmāo qīxīdì. Lìngwài, nàlǐ yěshì xiǎoxióngmāo, xuěbào děng bīnwēi wùzhǒng qīxī de dìfāng. Zài jǐ gè zìrán bǎohùqū zhōng, Wòlóng zìrán bǎohù qū zhǔyào bǎohù dàxióngmāo jí sēnlín shēngtài xìtǒng. Sìgūniángshān zìrán bǎohùqū zhǔyào bǎohù yěshēng dòngwù jí gāoshān shēngtài xìtǒng. Jīnshānmài zìrán bǎohùqū zhǔyào bǎohù zhēnxī dòngwù jí shēngtài huánjìng.

TRADITIONAL CLOTHING

[Traditional-character version]

漢服

漢服，也叫漢裝，是漢族的傳統民族服裝。漢民族服飾傳統延續了幾千年，並隨著時代的變遷和民族的交融而發展出了豐富多彩的樣式，但是漢服的"交領右衽，上衣下裳"這一最主要特徵一直保留下來。漢服代表了中國古老民族的華麗、優雅和博大的氣質。漢服的基本形式爲東方世界提供了標準，韓國的傳統服裝與日本的和服都是在漢服的基礎上發展而來的。

[Simplified-character version]

汉服

汉服，也叫汉装，是汉族的传统民族服装。汉民族服饰传统延续了几千年，并随着时代的变迁和民族的交融而发展出了丰富多彩的样式，但是汉服的"交领右衽，上衣下裳"这一最主要特征一直保留下来。汉服代表了中国古老民族的华丽、优雅和博大的气质。汉服的基本形式为东方世界提供了标准，韩国的传统服装与日本的和服都是在汉服的基础上发展而来的。

[Pinyin version]

Hànfú

Hànfú, yě jiào hànzhuāng, shì hànzú de chuántǒng mínzú fúzhuāng. Hànmínzú fúshì chuántǒng yánxùle jǐqiān nián, bìng suízhe shídài de biànqiān hé mínzú de jiāoróng ér fāzhǎnchūle fēngfù duōcǎi de yàngshì, dànshì hànfú de "jiāolǐng yòurèn, shàngyī xiàshāng" zhè yí zuì zhǔyào tèzhēng yìzhí bǎoliú xiàlai. Hànfú dàibiǎole Zhōngguó gǔlǎo mínzú de huálì, yōuyǎ hé bódà de qìzhi. Hànfú de jīběn xíngshì wéi dōngfāng shìjiè tígōngle biāozhǔn, Hánguó de chuántǒng fúzhuāng yǔ Rìběn de héfú dōushì zài hànfú de jīchǔ shang fāzhǎn ér lái de.

[Traditional-character version]

中山裝

中山裝在國際上被稱爲中國男式禮服的代表性服裝。孫中山先生居住日本期間，看到日本學生所穿的服裝簡單樸素、方便、大方，就請服裝師將它加以改造，創造了中山裝。中山裝的標志是，它的上衣，左右上下各有一個帶蓋子和扣子的口袋。中山裝做工講究，造型對稱，外形美觀、大方，穿著高雅、穩重，活動方便，起了保暖護身的作用。中山裝的色彩很豐富，除常見的藍色、灰色外，還有黑色、白色、米色等。一般來說，南方人偏愛淺色，北方人偏愛深色。中山裝既可作禮服，又可作便裝。作禮服用的中山裝色彩要莊重、沉著，而作便服用時色彩可以鮮明活潑些。

1949年10月1日，毛澤東主席穿著中山裝，站在天安門城樓向世界莊嚴宣布中華人民共和國成立了。從此，中山裝進入老百姓的家裏，成了那個時代的"國服"。因毛主席一直堅持穿中山裝，所以外國人又稱中山裝爲"毛服"或"毛裝"。

[Simplified-character version]

中山装

中山装在国际上被称为中国男式礼服的代表性服装。孙中山先生居住日本期间，看到日本学生所穿的服装简单朴素、方便、大方，就请服装师将它加以改造，创造了中山装。中山装的标志是，它的上衣，左右上下各有一个带盖子和扣子的口袋。中山装做工讲究，造型对称，外形美观、大方，穿着高雅、稳重，活动方便，起了保暖护身的作用。中山装的色彩很丰富，除常见的蓝色、灰色外，还有黑色、白色、米色等。一般来说，南方人偏爱浅色，北方人偏爱深色。中山装既可作礼服，又可作便装。作礼服用的中山装色彩要庄重、沉着，而作便服用时色彩可以鲜明活泼些。

1949年10月1日，毛泽东主席穿着中山装，站在天安门城楼向世界庄严宣布中华人民共和国成立了。从此，中山装进入老百姓的家里，成了那个时代的"国服"。因毛主席一直坚持穿中山装，所以外国人又称中山装为"毛服"或"毛装"。

[Pinyin version]

Zhōngshānzhuāng

Zhōngshānzhuāng zài guójì shang bèi chēngwéi Zhōngguó nánshì lǐfú de dàibiǎoxìng fúzhuāng. Sūn Zhōngshān xiānshēng jūzhù Rìběn qījiān, kàndào Rìběn xuéshēng suǒ chuānde fúzhuāng jiǎndān pǔsù, fāngbiàn, dàfāng, jiù qǐng fúzhuāngshī jiāng tā jiāyǐ gǎizào, chuàngzàole zhōngshānzhuāng. Zhōngshānzhuāng de biāozhì shì, tāde shàngyī, zuǒyòu shàngxià gèyǒu yí gè dài gàizi hé kòuzi de kǒudài. Zhōngshānzhuāng zuògōng jiǎngjiu, zàoxíng duìchèn, wàixíng měiguān, dàfāng, chuānzhuó gāoyǎ, wěnzhòng, huódòng fāngbiàn, qǐle bǎonuǎn hùshēn de zuòyòng. Zhōngshānzhuāng de sècǎi hěn fēngfù, chú chángjiàn de lánsè, huīsè wài, háiyǒu hēisè, báisè, mǐsè děng. Yībān láishuō, nánfāngrén piān'ài qiǎnsè, běifāngrén piān'ài shēnsè. Zhōngshānzhuāng jì kě zuò lǐfú, yòu kě zuò biànzhuāng. Zuò lǐfú yòngde zhōngshānzhuāng sècǎi yào zhuāngzhòng, chénzhuó, ér zuò biànfú yòng shí sècǎi kěyǐ xiānmíng huópō xiē.

Yī jiǔ sì jiǔ nián shí yuè yī rì, Máo Zédōng zhǔxí chuānzhe zhōngshānzhuāng, zhànzai Tiān'ānmén chénglóu xiàng shìjiè zhuāngyán xuānbù Zhōnghuá Rénmín Gònghéguó chénglìle. Cóngcǐ, zhōngshānzhuāng jìnrù lǎobǎixìng de jiāli, chéngle nàge shídài de "guófú". Yīn Máo zhǔxí yìzhí jiānchí chuān zhōngshānzhuāng, suǒyǐ wàiguórén yòu chēng zhōngshānzhuāng wéi "máofú" huò "máozhuāng".

[Traditional-character version]

旗袍

旗袍是中國女性的傳統服裝，源於清朝旗人的著裝。今天的旗袍大多是經過改良而來的。改良後的旗袍種類繁多，但主要結構特徵是立領、右大襟、緊腰身等。

在中國，選購旗袍有一定的講究，要根據需要來決定穿什麼樣的旗袍。如結婚旗袍，不僅面料質地要好，色彩也要鮮艷。迎賓、赴宴的旗袍，外觀要穩重而高雅；便服旗袍可以隨心所欲，只要能突出個性、展現體型美、穿著舒適大方就行了。由於市場上賣的旗袍大都是按照大眾化的身材和體型製作的，所以買到合適的旗袍不是一件容易的事。由於每個人的身材都不一樣，購買旗袍前必須準確地量出自己的胸圍、腰圍和臀圍。另外，還要看領子、衣身、袖子的長短與肥瘦是否合適。

因爲旗袍可以充分展示女性身體特徵，所以，從上一世紀20年代到今天，旗袍一直深受廣大女性朋友的青睞。

[Simplified-character version]

旗袍

旗袍是中国女性的传统服装，来源于清朝旗人的着装。今天的旗袍大多是经过改良而来的。改良后的旗袍种类繁多，但主要结构特征是立领、右大襟、紧腰身等。

在中国，选购旗袍有一定的讲究，要根据需要来决定穿什么样的旗袍。如结婚旗袍，不仅面料质地要好，色彩也要鲜艳。迎宾、赴宴的旗袍，外观要稳重而高雅；便服旗袍可以随心所欲，只要能突出个性、展现体型美、穿着舒适大方就行了。由于市场上卖的旗袍大都是按照大众化的身材和体型制作的，所以买到合适的旗袍不是一件容易的事。由于每个人的身材都不一样，购买旗袍前必须准确地量出自己的胸围、腰围和臀围。另外，还要看领子、衣身、袖子的长短与肥瘦是否合适。

因为旗袍可以充分展示女性身体特征，所以，从上一世纪20年代到今天，旗袍一直深受广大女性朋友的青睐。

[Pinyin version]

Qípáo

Qípáo shì Zhōngguó nǚxìng de chuántǒng fúzhuāng, láiyuán yú Qīngcháo qírén de zhuózhuāng. Jīntiān de qípáo dàduō shì jīngguò gǎiliáng érlái de. Gǎiliáng hòu de qípáo zhǒnglèi fánduō, dàn zhǔyào jiégòu tèzhēng shì lìlǐng, yòudàjīn, jǐnyāoshēn děng.

Zài Zhōngguó, xuǎngòu qípáo yǒu yídìng de jiǎngjiu, yào gēnjù xūyào lái juédìng chuān shénmeyàng de qípáo. Rú jiéhūn qípáo, bùjǐn miànliào zhídì yào hǎo, sècǎi yě yào xiānyàn. Yíngbīn, fùyàn de qípáo, wàiguān yào wěnzhòng ér gāoyǎ; biànfú qípáo kěyǐ suíxīn suǒyù, zhǐyào néng tūchū gèxìng, zhǎnxiàn tǐxíngměi, chuānzhuó shūshì dàfāng jiù xíng le. Yóuyú shìchǎng shang màide qípáo dà dōu shì ànzhào dàzhònghuà de shēncái hé tǐxíng zhìzuò de, suǒyǐ mǎidao héshì de qípáo búshì yí jiàn róngyì de shì. Yóuyú měi gè rén de shēncái dōu bù yíyàng, gòumǎi qípáo qián bìxū zhǔnquè de liàngchū zìjǐ de xiōngwéi, yāowéi hé túnwéi. Lìngwài, hái yào kàn lǐngzi, yī shēn, xiùzi de chángduǎn yǔ féishòu shìfǒu héshì.

Yīnwèi qípáo kěyǐ chōngfèn zhǎnshì nǚxìng shēntǐ tèzhēng, suǒyǐ, cóng shàng yī shìjì èrshí niándài dào jīntiān, qípáo yìzhí shēnshòu guǎngdà nǚxìng péngyǒu de qīnglài.

TRADITIONAL FOOD

[Traditional-character version]

四大菜系

由於地理環境、氣候物產、文化傳統以及民族習俗等因素的不同，中國地方風味也各具特色，形成了不同的菜系。魯菜、川菜、蘇菜和粵菜被稱爲中國著名的"四大菜系"。

魯菜也叫山東菜。山東省依山傍海，物產豐富，爲飲食文化發展提供了良好條件。魯菜用料廣泛，選料講究，刀工精細，烹飪技藝全面。魯菜風味，鹹鮮適口，清香脆嫩。魯菜注重用湯，"清湯全家福"就是一道有名的魯菜。魯菜在烹製海鮮方面有獨到之處，"蟹黃魚翅"、"雞蓉魚骨"等都是獨具特點的海味食品。

粵菜也叫廣東菜，據說起源於西漢時期。粵菜用料較廣、花色繁多、善於變化，講究鮮嫩。粵菜的材料多達幾千種。家裏養的禽畜、水裏的魚蝦都是粵菜的烹調材料，甚至別的菜系從來不用的蛇、鼠、貓等，粵菜都能把它們做成美味佳肴。著名的粵菜有"蛇油牛肉"、"烤乳豬"和"冬瓜盅"等。隨著中外文化的交流，粵菜走向世界，據說僅美國紐約就有幾千家粵菜館。

川菜出現於秦漢時期，唐宋時發展迅速，到了明清，川菜已很有名氣了。川菜在味道方面獨具特色，特別是在辣味的運用上講求多樣，調味靈活多變。在用料上，辣椒是川菜最普遍的調味品。川菜在烹調方法上，講究刀工和火候。"水煮牛肉"、"麻婆豆腐"等都是有名的川菜。正宗的川菜以四川成都、重慶兩地的菜肴爲代表。現今，不僅川菜流傳全國，川菜館也遍佈世界各地。

蘇菜又叫淮揚菜。淮揚菜的特點是講究火工，味道醇厚，保持原汁原味，並以烹製山野海味而聞名於世。在選料方面，淮揚菜注重選料的廣泛性及科學地調配營養。在工藝方面，淮陽菜注重烹飪火工。在造型方面，注重色彩器皿的結合，展現出精美的藝術性。著名的菜肴品種有"天下第一球"、"葫蘆八寶"、"一蝦兩味"等。

[Simplified-character version]

四大菜系

由于地理环境、气候物产、文化传统以及民族习俗等因素的不同，中国地方风味也各具特色，形成了不同的菜系。鲁菜、川菜、苏菜和粤菜被称为中国著名的"四大菜系"。

鲁菜也叫山东菜。山东省依山傍海，物产丰富，为饮食文化发展提供了良好条件。鲁菜用料广泛，选料讲究，刀工精细，烹饪技艺全面。鲁菜风味，咸鲜适口，清香脆嫩。鲁菜注重用汤，"清汤全家福"就是一道有名的鲁菜。鲁菜在烹制海鲜方面有独到之处，"蟹黄鱼翅"、"鸡蓉鱼骨"等都是独具特点的海味食品。

粤菜也叫广东菜，据说起源于西汉时期。粤菜用料较广、花色繁多、善于变化，讲究鲜嫩。粤菜的材料多达几千种。家里养的禽畜、水里的鱼虾都是粤菜的烹调材料，甚至别的菜系从来不用的蛇、鼠、猫等，粤菜都能把它们做成美味佳肴。著名的粤菜有"蛇油牛肉"、"烤乳猪"和"冬瓜盅"等。随着中外文化的交流，粤菜走向世界，据说仅美国纽约就有几千家粤菜馆。

川菜出现于秦汉时期，唐宋时发展迅速，到了明清，川菜已很有名气了。川菜在味道方面独具特色，特别是在辣味的运用上讲求多样，调味灵活多变。

在用料上，辣椒是川菜最普遍的调味品。川菜在烹调方法上，讲究刀工和火候。"水煮牛肉"、"麻婆豆腐"等都是有名的川菜。正宗的川菜以四川成都、重庆两地的菜肴为代表。现今，不仅川菜流传全国，川菜馆也遍布世界各地。

苏菜又叫淮扬菜。淮扬菜的特点是讲究火工，味道醇厚，保持原汁原味，并以烹制山野海味而闻名于世。在选料方面，淮扬菜注重选料的广泛性及科学地调配营养。在工艺方面，淮阳菜注重烹饪火工。在造型方面，注重色彩器皿的结合，展现出精美的艺术性。著名的菜肴品种有"天下第一球"、"葫芦八宝"、"一虾两味"等。

[Pinyin version]

Sìdà Càixì

Yóuyú dìlǐ huánjìng, qìhòu wùchǎn, wénhuà chuántǒng yǐjí mínzú xísú děng yīnsù de bùtóng, Zhōngguó dìfāng fēngwèi yě gèjù tèsè, xíngchéngle bùtóng de càixì. Lǔcài, chuāncài, sūcài hé yuècài bèi chēngwéi Zhōngguó zhùmíng de "Sìdà Càixì".

Lǔcài yě jiào shāndōngcài. Shāndōng shěng yīshān bànghǎi, wùchǎn fēngfù, wèi yǐnshí wénhuà fāzhǎn tígòngle liánghǎo tiáojiàn. Lǔcài yòngliào guǎngfàn, xuǎnliào jiǎngjiu, dāogōng jīngxì, pēngrèn jìyì quánmiàn. Lǔcài fēngwèi, xiánxiān shìkǒu, qīngxiāng cuìnèn. Lǔcài zhùzhòng yòngtāng,"Qīngtāng quánjiāfú" jiùshì yí dào yǒumíng de lǔcài. Lǔcài zài pēngzhì hǎixiān fāngmiàn yǒu dúdào zhīchù,"Xièhuáng yúchì", "jīróng yúgǔ" děng dōushì dújù tèdiǎn de hǎiwèi shípǐn.

Yuècài yě jiào guǎngdōngcài, jùshuō qǐyuán yú Xīhàn shíqī. Yuècài yòngliào jiǎoguǎng, huāsè fánduō, shànyú biànhuà, jiǎngjiu xiānnèn. Yuècài de cáiliào duōdá jǐqiān zhǒng. Jiāli yǎngde qínchù, shuǐli de yúxiā dōu shì yuècài de pēngtiáo cáiliào, shènzhì biéde càixì cónglái búyòng de shé, shǔ, māo děng, yuècài dōu néng bǎ tāmen zuòchéng měiwèi jiāyáo. Zhùmíng de yuècài yǒu "Shéyóu niúròu", "Kǎo rǔzhū" hé "Dōngguāzhōng" děng. Suízhe zhōngwài wénhuà de jiāoliú, yuècài zǒuxiàng shìjiè, jùshuō jǐn Měiguó Niǔyuē jiù yǒu jǐqiān jiā yuècàiguǎn.

Chuāncài chūxiàn yú Qín Hàn shíqī, Táng Sòng shí fāzhǎn xùnsù, dàole Míng Qīng, chuāncài yǐ hěn yǒu míngqìle. Chuāncài zài wèidào fāngmiàn dújù tèsè, tèbié shì zài làwèi de yùnyòng shang jiǎngqiú duōyàng, tiáowèi línghuó duōbiàn. Zài yòngliào shang, làjiāo shì chuāncài zuì pǔbiàn de tiáowèipǐn. Chuāncài zài pēngtiáo fāngfǎ shang, jiǎngjiu dāogōng hé huǒhou. "Shuǐzhǔ niúròu", "Mápó dòufu"děng dōushì yǒumíng de chuāncài. Zhèngzōng de chuāncài yǐ Sìchuān Chéngdū, Chóngqìng liǎng dì de càiyáo wéi dàibiǎo. Xiànjīn, bùjǐn chuāncài liúchuán quánguó, chuāncàiguǎn yě biànbù shìjiè gèdì.

Sūcài yòu jiào huáiyángcài. Huáiyángcài de tèdiǎn shì jiǎngjiu huǒgōng, wèidào chúnhòu, bǎochí yuánzhī yuánwèi, bìng yǐ pēngzhì shānyě hǎiwèi ér wénmíng yú shì. Zài xuǎnliào fāngmiàn, huáiyángcài zhùzhòng xuǎnliào de guǎngfànxìng jí kēxué de tiáopèi yíngyǎng. Zài gōngyì fāngmiàn, huáiyángcài zhùzhòng pēngrèn huǒgōng. Zài zàoxíng fāngmiàn, zhùzhòng sècǎi qìmǐn de jiéhé, zhǎnxiànchu jīngměi de yìshùxìng. Zhùmíng de càiyáo pǐnzhǒng yǒu "Tiānxià dìyī qiú", "Húlu bābǎo", "Yīxiā liǎngwèi" děng.

[Traditional-character version]

八大菜系

中國菜肴由於受到各地不同氣候、物産及飲食風俗的影響，在選料、切配及烹飪技藝上有不同特點，形成不同流派。魯菜、川菜、蘇菜和粵菜等四大菜系形成歷史較早，隨後又產生浙菜、湘菜、徽菜、閩菜等八大菜系。

浙菜，也叫浙江菜，是在杭州、寧波、溫州等地方菜肴的基礎上形成的。由於浙江臨海，盛産魚蝦，所以浙菜具有清、香、嫩、鮮等特點。著名的浙菜有"西湖醋魚"、"叫化童雞"、"爆墨魚卷"等。

湘菜，又叫湖南菜，是歷史悠久的一個地方風味菜。早在漢朝時代，湘菜的烹調技藝就已有相當高的水平。湘菜的特點是，品味上講究香鮮、酸辣，視覺上注重外形美觀。湘菜風味多達1000餘種，其中有代表性的菜肴有古老肉、蓮子鍋、香酥雞等。

徽菜，又叫徽州菜，主要是在皖南、沿江、沿淮三個地方風味上形成的。受徽州古樸典雅的地方風格影響，徽菜善於烹製山野海味，注重保持原汁原味。"清燉馬蹄"、"雪冬燒山雞"、"奶汁肥王魚"等徽菜風味久負盛名。

閩菜在福州菜的基礎上融合了福建其他地方菜肴的特點。閩菜具有色調美觀、滋味清鮮等風味特點。由於福建地處東南沿海，盛産多種海鮮，因此，閩菜多是以海鮮爲原材料烹製出來的。著名閩菜有"佛跳牆"、"酸辣爛魷魚"、"太極明蝦"等。

[Simplified-character version]

八大菜系

中国菜肴由于受到各地不同气候、物产及饮食风俗的影响，在选料、切配及烹饪技艺上有不同特点，形成不同流派。鲁菜、川菜、苏菜和粤菜等四大菜系形成的历史较早，随后又产生浙菜、湘菜、徽菜、闽菜等八大菜系。

浙菜，也叫浙江菜，是在杭州、宁波、温州等地方菜肴的基础上形成的。由于浙江临海，盛产鱼虾，所以浙菜具有清、香、嫩、鲜等特点。著名的浙菜有"西湖醋鱼"、"叫化童鸡"、"爆墨鱼卷"等。

湘菜，又叫湖南菜，是历史悠久的一个地方风味菜。早在汉朝时代，湘菜的烹调技艺就已有相当高的水平。湘菜的特点是，品味上讲究香鲜、酸辣，视觉上注重外形美观。湘菜风味多达1000余种，其中有代表性的菜肴有古老肉、莲子锅、香酥鸡等。

徽菜，又叫徽州菜，主要是在皖南、沿江、沿淮三个地方风味上形成的。受徽州古朴典雅的地方风格影响，徽菜善于烹制山野海味，注重保持原汁原味。"清炖马蹄"、"雪冬烧山鸡"、"奶汁肥王鱼"等徽菜风味久负盛名。

闽菜在福州菜的基础上融合了福建其他地方菜肴的特点。闽菜具有色调美观、滋味清鲜等风味特点。由于福建地处东南沿海，盛产多种海鲜，因此，闽菜多是以海鲜为原材料烹制出来的。著名闽菜有"佛跳墙"、"酸辣烂鱿鱼"、"太极明虾"等。

[Pinyin version]

Bādà Càixì

Zhōngguó càiyáo yóuyú shòudào gèdì bùtóng qìhòu, wùchǎn jí yǐnshí fēngsú de yǐngxiǎng, zài xuǎnliào, qièpèi jí pēngrèn jìyì shang yǒu bùtóng tèdiǎn, xíngchéng bùtóng liúpài. Lǔcài, chuāncài, sūcài hé yuècài děng sìdà càixì xíngchéng de lìshǐ jiàozǎo, suíhòu yòu chǎnshēng zhècài, xiāngcài, huīcài, mǐncài děng bādà càixì.

Zhècài, yě jiào zhèjiāngcài, shì zài Hángzhōu, Níngbō, Wēnzhōu děng dìfāng càiyáo de jīchǔshang xíngchéng de. Yóuyú Zhèjiāng línhǎi, shèngchǎn yúxiā, suǒyǐ zhècài jùyǒu qīng, xiāng, nèn, xiān děng tèdiǎn. Zhùmíng de zhècài yǒu "Xīhú cùyú", "Jiàohuā tóngjī", "Bào mòyújuǎn" děng.

Xiāngcài, yòu jiào húnáncài, shì lìshǐ yōujiǔ de yí gè dìfāng fēngwèicài. Zǎozài Hàncháo shídài, xiāngcài de pēngtiáo jìyì jiù yǐ yǒu xiāngdānggāo de shuǐpíng. Xiāngcài de tèdiǎn shì, pǐnwèi shang jiǎngjiu xiāngxiān, suānlà, shìjué shang zhùzhòng wàixíng měiguān. Xiāngcài fēngwèi duōdá yìqiān yú zhǒng, qízhōng yǒu dàibiǎoxìng de càiyáo yǒu Gǔlǎoròu, Liánzǐguō, Xiāngsūjī děng.

Huīcài, yòu jiào huīzhōucài, zhǔyào shì zài Wǎnnán, Yánjiāng, Yánhuái sān gè dìfāng fēngwèi shang xíngchéng de. Shòudào Huīzhōu gǔpú diǎnyǎ de dìfāng fēnggé yǐngxiǎng, huīcài shànyú pēngzhì shānyě hǎiwèi, zhùzhòng bǎochí yuánzhī yuánwèi. "Qīngdùn mǎtí", "Xuědōng shāo shānjī", "Nǎizhī féiwángyú" děng huīcài fēngwèi jiǔfù shèngmíng.

Mǐncài zài fúzhōucài de jīchǔ shang rónghéle Fújiàn qítā dìfāng càiyáo de tèdiǎn. Mǐncài jùyǒu sèdiào měiguān, zīwèi qīngxiān děng fēngwèi tèdiǎn. Yóuyú Fújiàn dìchù dōngnán yánhǎi, shèngchǎn duōzhǒng hǎixiān, yīncǐ, mǐncài duō shì yǐ hǎixiǎn wéi yuáncáiliào pēngzhì chūlai de. Zhùmíng mǐncài yǒu "Fótiàoqiáng", "Suānlà lànyóuyú", "Tàijí míngxiā" děng.

[Traditional-character version]

麻婆豆腐

麻婆豆腐是中國傳統風味之一，至今已有一百多年的歷史。據說，麻婆豆腐是在清朝時期由四川成都的一個小飯店創制的。飯店主人陳老闆的妻子臉上長了很多麻點，大家都叫她陳麻婆。陳麻婆發明的燒豆腐，被稱爲"陳麻婆豆腐"。後來，他們把小飯店的名字就改爲"陳麻婆豆腐店"。

麻婆豆腐的主要原料有豆腐、青蒜苗、牛肉，還有油、鹽、醬油、料酒、葱、薑、蒜、鷄精等。麻婆豆腐的燒法很有特色。在雪白細嫩的豆腐上，加上棕紅色的牛肉末和油綠的青蒜苗，再加一些亮晶晶的紅油。人們用"麻、辣、燙、鮮、嫩、香、酥"七個字形象地概括了麻婆豆腐的特點。

很多書籍也都記述了陳麻婆發明麻婆豆腐的歷史。上世紀初，"陳麻婆豆腐店"被列入"成都著名食品店"，麻婆豆腐由此很快在全國流傳，後來又傳到日本、新加坡等地。如今，麻婆豆腐已經是世界聞名的美味佳肴。

[Simplified-character version]

麻婆豆腐

麻婆豆腐是中国传统风味之一，至今已有一百多年的历史。据说，麻婆豆腐是在清朝时期由四川成都的一个小饭店创制的。饭店主人陈老板的妻子脸上长了很多麻点，大家都叫她陈麻婆。陈麻婆发明的烧豆腐，被称为"陈麻婆豆腐"。后来，他们把小饭店的名字就改为"陈麻婆豆腐店"。

麻婆豆腐的主要原料有豆腐、青蒜苗、牛肉，还有油、盐、酱油、料酒、葱、姜、蒜、鸡精等。麻婆豆腐的烧法很有特色。在雪白细嫩的豆腐上，加上棕红色的牛肉末和油绿的青蒜苗，再加一些亮晶晶的红油。人们用"麻、辣、烫、鲜、嫩、香、酥"七个字形象地概括了麻婆豆腐的特点。

很多书籍也都记述了陈麻婆发明麻婆豆腐的历史。上世纪初，"陈麻婆豆腐店"被列入"成都著名食品店"，麻婆豆腐由此很快在全国流传，后来又传到日本、新加坡等地。如今，麻婆豆腐已经是世界闻名的美味佳肴。

[Pinyin version]

Mápó dòufu

Mápó dòufu shì Zhōngguó chuántǒng fēngwèi zhīyī, zhìjīn yǐ yǒu yìbǎi duōnián de lìshǐ. Jùshuō, mápó dòufu shì zài Qīngcháo shíqī yóu Sìchuān Chéngdū de yí gè xiǎo fàndiàn chuàngzhì de. Fàndiàn zhǔrén Chén lǎobǎn de qīzǐ liǎnshang zhǎngle hěnduō mádiǎn, dàjiā dōu jiào tā Chén Mápó. Chén Mápó fāmíng de shāodòufu, bèi chēngwéi "Chén mápó dòufu". Hòulái, tāmen bǎ xiǎofàndiàn de míngzì jiù gǎiwéi "Chén mápó dòufudiàn".

Mápó dòufu de zhǔyào yuánliào yǒu dòufu, qīngsuànmiáo, niúròu, háiyǒu yóu, yán, jiàngyóu, liàojiǔ, cōng, jiāng, suàn, jījīng děng. Mápó dòufu de shāofǎ hěn yǒu tèsè. Zài xuěbái xìnèn de dòufu shang, jiāshang zōnghóngsè de niúròumò hé yóulǜ de qīng suànmiáo, zài jiā yì xiē liàngjīngjīng de hóngyóu. Rénmen yòng "má, là, tàng, xiān, nèn, xiāng, sū" qī gè zì xíngxiàng de gàikuòle mápó dòufu de tèdiǎn.

Hěnduō shūjí yě dōu jìshùle Chén mápó fāmíng mápó dòufu de lìshǐ. Shàng shìjì chū,"Chén mápó dòufudiàn" bèi lièrù "Chéngdū zhùmíng shípǐndiàn", mápó dòufu yóucǐ hěnkuài zài quánguó liúchuán, hòulái yòu chuándao Rìběn, Xīnjiāpō děng dì. Rújīn, mápó dòufu yǐjīng shì shìjiè wénmíng de měiwèi jiāyáo.

CHINESE ASTROLOGY

[Traditional-character version]

十二生肖

十二生肖來源於原始時代人們對動物的崇拜，也與十二地支有著密切的關係。在中國的傳統觀念中，如果牛、羊、馬、豬、狗、鷄等六種家畜興旺，就代表了家族人丁的興旺，家庭的吉祥美好。虎、兔、猴、鼠、蛇等野生動物也與人們的生活密切相關。虎、蛇是人們所害怕的，鼠是人們所厭惡和忌諱的，兔和猴子是人們所喜愛的。龍是中國傳統文化中的吉祥物，它的身上集中了許多動物的特性，代表了富貴和吉祥。由此可見，中國人選擇十二生肖的動物是從不同角度選擇的，並帶有一定的意義。

關於生肖動物的排列，民間說法不太一樣。據說，當年黃帝要選十二個動物做衛士，猫讓老鼠幫它報名，老鼠卻給忘了，結果猫沒有被選上，從此以後，猫把老鼠看成了敵人。大象也來參加比賽了，却被老鼠鑽進鼻子趕跑了。開始的時候，大家推選牛做第一個，老鼠却跳到牛背上，豬也跟著去了，於是老鼠排第一，豬排最後。虎和龍分別是山裏的大王和海中之王，對排在老鼠和牛的後面怎麼能服氣呢？兔子也不服氣，就和龍賽跑，結果排在了龍的前面。狗一氣之下咬了兔子，結果受到懲罰，被安排在倒數第二的位置上。蛇、馬、羊、猴、鷄也都經過一番較量，一一排定了位置，最後形成了鼠、牛、虎、兔、龍、蛇、馬、羊、猴、鷄、狗、豬的順序。

文化背景不同，人們對動物詞語的文化內涵的理解及用法也不完全一樣。中國人用十二生肖動物來比喻人，如用"老黃牛"、"膽小如鼠"等來比喻肯幹的人和膽小怯懦的人。英語中同樣可用十二生肖動物作比喻，但所表達的意思不完全一樣。

[Simplified-character version]

十二生肖

十二生肖来源于原始时代人们对动物的崇拜，也与十二地支有着密切的关系。在中国的传统观念中，如果牛、羊、马、猪、狗、鸡等六种家畜兴旺，就代表了家族人丁的兴旺，家庭的吉祥美好。虎、兔、猴、鼠、蛇等野生动物也与人们的生活密切相关。虎、蛇是人们所害怕的，鼠是人们所厌恶和忌讳的，兔和猴子是人们所喜爱的。龙是中国传统文化中的吉祥物，它的身上集中了许多动物的特性，代表了富贵和吉祥。由此可见，中国人选择十二生肖的动物是从不同角度选择的，并带有一定的意义。

关于生肖动物的排列，民间说法不太一样。据说，当年黄帝要选十二个动物做卫士，猫让老鼠帮它报名，老鼠却给忘了，结果猫没有被选上，从此以后，猫把老鼠看成了敌人。大象也来参加比赛了，却被老鼠钻进鼻子赶跑了。开始的时候，大家推选牛做第一个，老鼠却跳到牛背上，猪也跟着去了，于是老鼠排第一，猪排最后。虎和龙分别是山里的大王和海中之王，对排在老鼠和牛的后面怎么能服气呢？兔子也不服气，就和龙赛跑，结果排在了龙的前面。狗一气之下咬了兔子，结果受到惩罚，被安排在倒数第二的位置上。蛇、马、羊、猴、鸡也都经过一番较量，一一排定了位置，最后形成了鼠、牛、虎、兔、龙、蛇、马、羊、猴、鸡、狗、猪的顺序。

文化背景不同，人们对动物词语的文化内涵的理解及用法也不完全一样。中国人用十二生肖动物来比喻人，如用"老黄牛"、"胆小如鼠"等来比喻肯干的人和胆小怯懦的人。英语中同样可用十二生肖动物作比喻，但所表达的意思不完全一样。

[Pinyin version]

Shí'èr Shēngxiào

Shí'èr shēngxiào láiyuán yú yuánshǐ shídài rénmen duì dòngwù de chóngbài, yě yǔ shí'èr dìzhī yǒuzhe mìqiè de guānxì. Zài Zhōngguó de chuántǒng guānniàn zhōng, rúguǒ niú, yáng, mǎ, zhū, gǒu, jī děng liù zhǒng jiāchù xīngwàng, jiù dàibiǎole jiāzú réndīng de xīngwàng, jiātíng de jíxiáng měihǎo. Hǔ, tù, hóu, shǔ, shé děng yěshēng dòngwù yě yǔ rénmen de shēnghuó mìqiè xiāngguān. Hǔ, shé shì rénmen suǒ hàipà de, shǔ shì rénmen suǒ yànwù hé jìhuì de, tù hé hóuzi shì rénmen suǒ xǐ'ài de. Lóng shì Zhōngguó chuántǒng wénhuà zhōng de jíxiángwù, tā de shēnshang jízhōngle xǔduō dòngwù de tèxìng, dàibiǎole fùguì hé jíxiáng. Yóucǐ kějiàn, Zhōngguórén xuǎnzé shí'èr shēngxiào de dòngwù shì cóng bùtóng jiǎodù xuǎnzé de, bìng dài yǒu yídìng de yìyì.

Guānyú shēngxiào dòngwù de páiliè, mínjiān shuōfǎ bù tài yíyàng. Jùshuō, dāngnián huángdì yào xuǎn shí'èr gè dòngwù zuò wèishì, māo ràng lǎoshǔ bāng tā bàomíng, lǎoshǔ quègěi wàngle, jiéguǒ māo méiyǒu bèi xuǎnshang, cóngcǐ yǐhòu, māo bǎ lǎoshǔ kànchéngle dírén. Dàxiàng yě lái cānjiā bǐsàile, què bèi lǎoshǔ zuānjìn bízi gǎnpǎole. Kāishǐ de shíhou, dàjiā tuīxuǎn niú zuò dì yī gè, lǎoshǔ què tiàodao niúbèi shang, zhū yě gēnzhe qùle, yúshì lǎoshǔ pái dì yī, zhū pái zuìhòu. Hǔ hé lóng fēnbié shì shānli de dàwáng hé hǎizhōng zhīwáng, duì páizài lǎoshǔ hé niú de hòumiàn zěnme néng fúqì ne? Tùzi yě bù fúqì, jiù hé lóng sàipǎo, jiéguǒ pái zàile lóng de qiánmiàn. Gǒu yíqì zhīxià yǎole tùzi, jiéguǒ shòudào chéngfá, bèi ānpái zài dàoshǔ dì èr de wèizhi shang. Shé, mǎ, yáng, hóu, jī yě dōu jīngguò yì fān jiàoliàng, yīyī páidìngle wèizhi, zuìhòu xíngchéngle shǔ, niú, hǔ, tù, lóng, shé, mǎ, yáng, hóu, jī, gǒu, zhū de shùnxù.

Wénhuà bèijǐng bùtóng, rénmen duì dòngwù cíyǔ de wénhuà nèihán de lǐjiě jí yòngfǎ yě bù wánquán yíyàng. Zhōngguórén yòng shí'èr shēngxiào dòngwù lái bǐyù rén, rú yòng "lǎohuángniú", "dǎn xiǎo rúshǔ" děng lái bǐyù kěngàn de rén hé dǎnxiǎo qiènuò de rén. Yīngyǔ zhōng tóngyàng kěyòng shí'èr shēngxiào dòngwù zuò bǐyù, dàn suǒ biǎodá de yìsi bù wánquán yíyàng.

CHINESE TABOOS

[Traditional-character version]

顏色禁忌

　　顏色在中國文化中有明確的象徵意義。黃色、紫色都是貴族色，曾經是皇室貴族的專用顏色，老百姓是不能把那些顏色用在服裝上的。中國歷代皇帝大都喜歡黃色，所以登基做皇帝被叫做"黃袍加身"。中國人把白色和黑色看成是不吉利的顏色，是與死人、陰間的鬼魂有關係的顏色。以前中國人辦喪事，就要穿白色的孝服，今天也還有帶黑紗、戴白花的習俗。中國傳統中，人們在婚嫁、生育、過年等喜慶日子裏忌諱穿純白、純黑色的衣裳，害怕不吉利。紅色是吉利的顏色，中國人喜歡在喜慶的日子裏穿紅色的服裝。由於紅色與血的顏色一樣，容易引起傷害、流血的恐怖感，所以，在中國傳統中，喪葬期間人們不能穿紅衣服，害怕沖犯了神靈。

[Simplified-character version]

颜色禁忌

　　颜色在中国文化中有明确的象征意义。黄色、紫色都是贵族色，曾经是皇室贵族的专用颜色，老百姓是不能把那些颜色用在服装上的。中国历代皇帝大都喜欢黄色，所以登基做皇帝被叫做"黄袍加身"。中国人把白色和黑色看成是不吉利的颜色，是与死人、阴间的鬼魂有关系的颜色。以前中国人办丧事，就要穿白色的孝服，今天也还有带黑纱、戴白花的习俗。中国传统中，人们在婚嫁、生育、过年等喜庆日子里忌讳穿纯白、纯黑色的衣裳，害怕不吉利。红色是吉利的颜色，中国人喜欢在喜庆的日子里穿红色的服装。由于红色与血的颜色一样，容易引起伤害、流血的恐怖感，所以，在中国传统中，丧葬期间人们不能穿红衣服，害怕冲犯了神灵。

[Pinyin version]

Yánsè Jìnjì

Yánsè zài Zhōngguó wénhuà zhōng yǒu míngquè de xiàngzhēng yìyì. Huángsè, zǐsè dōu shì guìzúsè, céngjīng shì huángshì guìzú de zhuānyòng yánsè, lǎobǎixìng shì bùnéng bǎ nàxiē yánsè yòngzài fúzhuāng shang de. Zhōngguó lìdài huángdì dàdōu xǐhuan huángsè, suǒyǐ dēngjī zuò huángdì bèi jiàozuò "huángpáo jiāshēn". Zhōngguórén bǎ báisè hé hēisè kànchéng shì bù jílì de yánsè, shì yǔ sǐrén, yīnjiān de guǐhún yǒu guānxì de yánsè. Yǐqián Zhōngguórén bàn sāngshì, jiù yào chuān báisè de xiàofú, jīntiān yě háiyǒu dài hēi shā, dài báihuā de xísú. Zhōngguó chuántǒng zhōng, rénmen zài hūnjià, shēngyù, guònián děng xǐqìng rìzi li jìhuì chuān chúnbái, chúnhēisè de yīshang, hàipà bù jílì. Hóngsè shì jílì de yánsè, Zhōngguórén xǐhuan zài xǐqìng de rìzi li chuān hóngsè de fúzhuāng. Yóuyú hóngsè yǔ xuè de yánsè yíyàng, róngyì yǐnqǐ shānghài, liúxuè de kǒngbùgǎn, suǒyǐ, zài

Zhōngguó chuántǒng zhōng, sāngzàng qījiān rénmen bùnéng chuān hóng yīfu, hàipà chōngfànle shénlíng.

[Traditional-character version]

數字禁忌

中國的數字文化源遠流長、博大精深，中國人對數字的使用非常小心。

"一"是一個單數，如果給結婚、過生日的人送禮，應該儘量避免送單數，因爲中國人的禮物中寄托著"好事成雙"的美好願望。跟文字的諧音一樣，中國的數字諧音也是一門藝術，它從傳統文化一直影響到現代的生活。"九"的諧音是"久"，九是中國古代帝王崇拜的數字，因此，皇宮的台階有九級，朝廷的官員有九品。在中國的一些地方，"八"是一個吉利的數字。據說"八"文化來自於廣東話，因爲它與"發"同音，對於做生意的人來說，就意味著以後會發財。"三"的諧音是"散"，很多人過生日或者結婚的時候會回避和這個數字有關係的日子。祝壽、賀喜送禮的時候也會有意回避這個數字。"四"的諧音是"死"，於是有些中國人不願意在門牌號、汽車牌號上使用這個數字，以免遭遇不順利的事情。

[Simplified-character version]

数字禁忌

中国的数字文化源远流长、博大精深，中国人对数字的使用非常小心。

"一"是一个单数，如果给结婚、过生日的人送礼，应该尽量避免送单数，因为中国人的礼物中寄托着"好事成双"的美好愿望。跟文字的谐音一样，中国的数字谐音也是一门艺术，它从传统文化一直影响到现代的生活。"九"的谐音是"久"，九是中国古代帝王崇拜的数字，因此，皇宫的台阶有九级，朝廷的官员有九品。在中国的一些地方，"八"是一个吉利的数字。据说"八"文化来自于广东话，因为它与"发"同音，对于做生意的人来说，就意味着以后会发财。"三"的谐音是"散"，很多人过生日或者结婚的时候会回避和这个数字有关系的日子。祝寿、贺喜送礼的时候也会有意回避这个数字。"四"的谐音是"死"，于是有些中国人不愿意在门牌号、汽车牌号上使用这个数字，以免遭遇不顺利的事情。

[Pinyin version]

Shùzì Jìnjì

Zhōngguó de shùzì wénhuà yuányuǎn liúcháng, bódà jīngshēn, Zhōngguórén duì shùzì de shǐyòng fēicháng xiǎoxīn.

"Yī" shì yí gè dānshù, rúguǒ gěi jiéhūn, guò shēngrì de rén sònglǐ, yīnggāi jǐnliàng bìmiǎn sòng dānshù, yīnwéi Zhōngguórén de lǐwù zhōng jìtuōzhe "hǎoshì chéngshuāng" de měihǎo yuànwàng. Gēn wénzì de xiéyīn yíyàng, Zhōngguó de shùzì xiéyīn yěshì yí mén yìshù, tā cóng chuántǒng wénhuà yìzhí yǐngxiǎng dao xiàndài de shēnghuó. "Jiǔ" de xiéyīn shì "jiǔ", jiǔ shì Zhōngguó gǔdài dìwáng chóngbài de shùzì, yīncǐ, huánggōng de táijiē yǒu jiǔjí, cháotíng de guānyuán yǒu jiǔpǐn. Zài Zhōngguó de yìxiē dìfāng, "bā" shì yí gè jílì de shùzì. Jùshuō "bā" wénhuà láizì yú Guǎngdōnghuà, yīnwèi tā yǔ "fā" tóngyīn, duìyú zuò shēngyì de rén láishuō, jiù yìwèizhe yǐhòu huì fācái. "Sān" de xiéyīn shì "sàn", hěnduō rén guò shēngrì huòzhě jiéhūn de shíhou huì huíbì hé zhège shùzì yǒu guānxì de rìzi.

Zhùshòu, hèxǐ sònglǐ de shíhou yě huì yǒuyì huíbì zhège shùzì. "Sì" de xiéyīn shì "sǐ", yúshì yǒuxiē Zhōngguórén bú yuànyì zài ménpáihào, qìchē páihào shang shǐyòng zhège shùzì, yǐmiǎn zāoyù bú shùnlì de shìqíng.

[Traditional-character version]

飲食禁忌

中國人講究"入鄉隨俗",所以到中國人家裏做客,一定要清楚當地的飲食習俗。不然的話,就會鬧出笑話,甚至發生誤會。

中國是個多民族的國家,不同民族有不同飲食文化的習慣與風俗。到回族人家做客,吃飯的時候千萬不能提到豬肉。在維吾爾族人家中做客,吃飯時,不能隨便地撥盤子裏的食物。吃抓飯前要先洗手,通常要洗三下,然後用手帕擦乾,千萬不能爲了省事,亂甩手上的水,這是對主人的不尊敬。哈薩克族人不能用手背摸食物,也不能坐在裝有食物的東西上。另外,哈薩克的青年人當著老人的面喝酒被看作是一種不禮貌的行爲。在漢族人家吃飯有"客不翻魚"的說法,人們覺得吃魚時把魚翻過來是一件不吉利的事情。

中國漢族人請客吃飯,在飯前要給客人遞上熱毛巾,請客人洗臉、擦手。主人要把客人安排到首席的座位上。吃飯時,主人要親自給客人夾菜、敬酒。盛飯時,勺子不能往外翻,爲的是家裏的財不流到外邊去。在招待客人的時候,主人應該始終陪坐,不要提前離開飯桌。吃飯的時候,也不能把空碗、空盤子提前收走,容易產生"趕客"的誤解。過去,雞蛋是招待客人的貴重食品。家裏來了客人,不能做兩個雞蛋,因爲"二蛋"是"傻瓜"的意思。招待客人吃水果時,不能兩人分吃一個梨,因爲會有"分離"的意思。

[Simplified-character version]

饮食禁忌

中国人讲究"入乡随俗",所以到中国人家里做客,一定要清楚当地的饮食习俗。不然的话,就会闹出笑话,甚至发生误会。

中国是个多民族的国家,不同民族有不同饮食文化的习惯与风俗。到回族人家做客,吃饭的时候千万不能提猪肉。在维吾尔族人家中做客,吃饭时,不能随便地拨盘子里的食物。吃抓饭前要先洗手,通常要洗三下,然后用手帕擦干,千万不能为了省事,乱甩手上的水,这是对主人的不尊敬。哈萨克族人不能用手背去摸食物,也不能坐在装有食物的东西上。另外,哈萨克的青年人当着老人的面喝酒被看作是一种不礼貌的行为。在汉族人家吃饭有"客不翻鱼"的说法,人们觉得吃鱼时把鱼翻过来是一件不吉利的事情。

中国汉族人请客吃饭,在饭前要给客人递上热毛巾,请客人洗脸、擦手。主人要把客人安排到首席的座位上。吃饭时,主人要亲自给客人夹菜、敬酒。盛饭时,勺子不能往外翻,为的是家里的财不流到外边去。在招待客人的时候,主人应该始终陪坐,不要提前离开饭桌。吃饭的时候,也不能把空碗、空盘子提前收走,容易产生"赶客"的误解。过去,鸡蛋是招待客人的贵重食品。家里来了客人,不能做两个鸡蛋,因为"二蛋"是"傻瓜"的意思。招待客人吃水果时,不能两人分吃一个梨,因为会有"分离"的意思。

[Pinyin version]

Yǐnshí Jìnjì

Zhōngguórén jiǎngjiu "rùxiān gsuísú", suǒyǐ dào Zhōngguórén jiāli zuòkè, yídìng yào qīngchu dāngdì de yǐnshí xísú. Bùrán de huà, jiù huì nàochu xiàohuà, shènzhì fāshēng wùhuì.

Zhōngguó shì gè duō mínzú de guójiā, bùtóng mínzú yǒu bùtóng yǐnshí wénhuà de xíguàn yǔ fēngsú. Dào Huízú rénjiā zuòkè, chīfàn de shíhou qiānwàn bùnéng tídao zhūròu. Zài Wéiwú'ěrzúrén jiāzhōng zuòkè, chīfàn shí, bùnéng suíbiàn de bō pánzi lǐ de shíwù. Chī zhuāfàn qián yào xiān xǐshǒu, tōngcháng yào xǐ sān xià, ránhòu yòng shǒupà cāgān, qiānwàn bùnéng wèile shěngshì, luàn shuǎi shǒushang de shuǐ, zhè shì duì zhǔrén de bù zūnjìng. Hāsàkèzúrén bùnéng yòng shǒubèi qù mō shíwù, yě bùnéng zuò zài zhuāngyǒu shíwù de dōngxi shang. Lìngwài, Hāsàkè de qīngniánrén dāngzhe lǎorén de miàn hējiǔ bèi kànzuò shì yìzhǒng bù lǐmào de xíngwéi. Zài Hànzú rénjiā chīfàn yǒu "Kè bù fānyú" de shuōfǎ, rénmen juéde chīyú shí bǎ yú fānguolai shì yí jiàn bù jílì de shìqíng.

Zhōngguó hànzúrén qǐngkè chīfàn, zài fànqián yào gěi kèrén dìshang rè máojīn, qǐng kèrén xǐliǎn, cāshǒu. Zhǔrén yào bǎ kèrén ānpái dao shǒuxí de zuòwèi shang. Chīfàn shí, zhǔrén yào qīnzì gěi kèrén jiācài, jìngjiǔ. Chéng fànshí, sháozi bùnéng wǎngwài fān, wèi de shì jiāli de cái bù liúdao wàibian qù. Zài zhāodài kèrén de shíhou, zhǔrén yīnggāi shǐzhōng péizuò, búyào tíqián líkāi fànzhuō. Chīfàn de shíhou, yě bùnéng bǎ kōngwǎn, kōngpánzi tíqián shōuzǒu, róngyì chǎnshēng "gǎnkè" de wùjiě. Guòqù, jīdàn shì zhāodài kèrén de guìzhòng shípǐn. Jiālǐ láile kèrén, bùnéng zuò liǎng gè jīdàn, yīnwèi "èrdàn" shì "shǎguā" de yìsi. Zhāodài kèrén chī shuǐguǒ shí, bùnéng liǎngrén fēnchī yí gè lí, yīnwèi huì yǒu "fēnlí" de yìsi.

[Traditional-character version]

吃魚不"翻魚"

在中國沿海地區,有很多以漁業為生的漁民,他們最擔心的事情是出海打魚時遇到風浪翻船,而"翻魚"會讓人聯想到"翻船",那是不吉利的事情。所以,在那些地區就有了吃魚忌翻的餐飲習俗。有的地方不僅忌諱"翻魚"的動作,甚至忌諱說出"翻"字,當需要把魚翻過來時,他們就說"順魚"。當把魚上面的一面吃完後,用筷子把魚骨和魚刺挑開,再吃下麵一面的魚肉。這樣,既避免了"翻魚",也避免了浪費。

[Simplified-character version]

吃鱼不"翻鱼"

在中国沿海地区,有很多以渔业为生的渔民,他们最担心的事情是出海打鱼时遇到风浪翻船,而"翻鱼"会让人联想到"翻船",那是不吉利的事情。所以,在那些地区就有了吃鱼忌翻的餐饮习俗。有的地方不仅忌讳"翻鱼"的动作,甚至忌讳说出"翻"字,当需要把鱼翻过来时,他们就说"顺鱼"。当把鱼上面的一面吃完后,用筷子把鱼骨和鱼刺挑开,再吃下面一面的鱼肉。这样,既避免了"翻鱼",也避免了浪费。

[Pinyin version]

Chīyú bù Fānyú

Zài Zhōngguó yánhǎi dìqū, yǒu hěnduō yǐ yúyè wéishēng de yúmín, tāmen zuì dānxīn de shìqing shì chūhǎi dǎyú shí yùdao fēnglàng fānchuán, ér "fānyú" huì ràng rén liánxiǎng dao "fānchuán", nà shì bù jílì de shìqing. Suǒyǐ, zài nàxiē dìqū jiù yǒu le chīyú jìfān de cānyǐn xísú. Yǒude dìfāng bùjǐn jìhuì "fānyú" de dòngzuò, shènzhì jìhuì shuōchu "fān" zì, dāng xūyào bǎ yú fānguolai shí, tāmen jiù shuō "shùnyú". Dāng bǎ yú shàngmian de yīmiàn chīwán hòu, yòng kuàizi bǎ yúgǔ hé yúcì tiāokāi, zài chī xiàmiàn yímiàn de yúròu. Zhèyàng, jì bìmiǎn le "fānyú", yě bìmiǎn le làngfèi.

[Traditional-character version]

稱謂禁忌

　　在中國，自古以來都有直接稱呼祖先和長輩的名字的忌諱。一些民族認爲，直呼祖先的名字是對祖先的不尊敬，會給子孫帶來災難。對於長輩，也不能直接叫名字，甚至不能把長輩的名字告訴別人。否則，家中就會生下不健康的孩子。如果晚輩中有人與長輩的名字相同，就要把晚輩的名字改了，否則會影響壽命。晚輩稱呼長輩，一般的做法是用輩份稱謂代替名字，例如叫爺爺、奶奶、姥爺、姥姥、爸爸、媽媽等等。這樣既可以明確輩份之間的關係，也有尊敬的意思。即使是同輩人之間，有時也有稱謂上的禁忌。

　　在人際交往中，中國人出於對對方的尊敬，往往不直接叫名字，而是以兄、弟、姐、妹、先生、女士、師傅等相稱。在有些民族中，連夫妻間都不能互相叫名字。還有的民族，一旦結了婚生了孩子，別人就不能再叫名字了，而是稱爲"某某他爸"、"某某他媽"什麼的。漢族也有類似的習俗，甚至一結婚就改了稱呼。比如妻子叫丈夫"當家的"，丈夫把妻子叫做"屋裏的"。要不然就什麼都不叫，而互相用"哎"、"嗯"打招呼。外人稱呼他們，也是用"某某他老公"、"某某的老婆"來稱呼。

[Simplified-character version]

称谓禁忌

　　在中国，自古以来都有直接称呼祖先和长辈的名字的忌讳。一些民族认为，直呼祖先的名字是对祖先的不尊敬，会给子孙带来灾难。对于长辈，也不能直接叫名字，甚至不能把长辈的名字告诉别人。否则，家中就会生下不健康的孩子。如果晚辈中有人与长辈的名字相同，就要把晚辈的名字改了，否则会影响寿命。晚辈称呼长辈，一般的做法是用辈份称谓代替名字，例如叫爷爷、奶奶、姥爷、姥姥、爸爸、妈妈等等。这样既可以明确辈份之间的关系，也有尊敬的意思。即使是同辈人之间，有时也有称谓上的禁忌。

　　在人际交往中，中国人出于对对方的尊敬，往往不直接叫名字，而是以兄、弟、姐、妹、先生、女士、师傅等相称。在有些民族中，连夫妻间都不能互相叫名字。还有的民族，一旦结了婚生了孩子，别人就不能再叫名字了，而是称为"某某他爸"、"某某他妈"什么的。汉族也有类似的习俗，甚至一结婚就改了称呼。比如妻子叫丈夫"当家的"，丈夫把妻子叫做"屋里的"。要不然就什么都不叫，而互相用"哎"、"嗯"打招呼。外人称呼他们，也是用"某某他老公"、"某某的老婆"来称呼。

[Pinyin version]

Chēngwèi Jìnjì

Zài Zhōngguó, zìgǔ yǐlái dōuyǒu zhíjiē chēnghu zǔxiān hé zhǎngbèi de míngzì de jìhuì. Yìxiē mínzú rènwéi, zhíhū zǔxiān de míngzì shì duì zǔxiān de bù zūnjìng, huì gěi zǐsūn dàilai zāinàn. Duìyú zhǎngbèi, yě bùnéng zhíjiē jiào míngzì, shènzhì bùnéng bǎ zhǎngbèi de míngzì gàosu biérén. Fǒuzé, jiāzhōng jiù huì shēngxia bú jiànkāng de háizi. Rúguǒ wǎnbèi zhōng yǒurén yǔ zhǎngbèi de míngzì xiāngtóng, jiù yào bǎ wǎnbèi de míngzì gǎile, fǒuzé huì yǐngxiǎng shòumìng. Wǎnbèi chēnghu zhǎngbèi, yìbān de zuòfǎ shì yòng bèifèn chēngwèi dàitì míngzì, lìrú jiào yéye, nǎinai, lǎoye, lǎolao, bàba, māmā děngděng. Zhèyàng jì kěyǐ míngquè bèifèn zhījiān de guānxì, yěyǒu zūnjìng de yìsi. Jíshǐ shì tóngbèirén zhījiān, yǒushí yěyǒu chēngwèi shàng de jìnjì.

Zài rénjì jiāowǎng zhōng, Zhōngguórén chūyú duì duìfāng de zūnjìng, wǎngwǎng bù zhíjiē jiào míngzì, érshì yǐ xiōng, dì, jie, mèi, xiānsheng, nǔshì, shīfu děng xiāngchēng. Zài yǒuxiē mínzú zhōng, lián fūqī jiān dōu bù néng hùxiāng jiào míngzì. Hái yǒude mínzú, yídàn jiélehūn shēngle háizi, biérén jiù bùnéng zài jiào míngzìle, érshì chēng wéi "mǒumǒu tābà", "mǒumǒu tāmā" shénme de. Hànzú yěyǒu lèisì de xísú, shènzhì yì jiéhūn jiù gǎile chēnghu. Bǐrú qīzi jiào zhàngfu "dāngjiāde", zhàngfu bǎ qīzi jiàozuò "wūlide". Yàoburán jiù shénme dōu bú jiào, ér hùxiāng yòng "āi", "en" dǎ zhāohū. Wàirén chēnghu tāmen, yěshì yòng "mǒumǒu tā lǎogōng", "mǒumǒu de lǎopo"lái chēnghu.

[Traditional-character version]

語言禁忌

在中國文化中，人們在涉及某種事物時需要回避，當不方便用語言表達的時候，可能會通過身體語言來表達。如果這樣還是不能準確地表達意思的時候，人們就會用某種變通的說法來暗示自己需要表達的意思，這就是語言禁忌。例如死亡，這是人們普遍恐懼、忌諱的一件事情，所以，在一般情況下，人們是不願意提到"死"的，於是就把"死"稱爲"疾終"、"謝世"、"走了"什麼的。在戰場上爲國家和民族而死的人，被大家稱作是"殉國"、"犧牲"或者"光榮了"。人們用這些含有褒義的詞語代替"死"字。在日常生活中，爲了避免"死"字，有的地區把"氣死我"說成"激生我"，把"笑死我"說成"笑生我"。有的地區的人連跟"死"字同音的一些字也都要避開。例如，有的地區的人把姓"史"的男士叫"吏先生"，把姓"施"的女士稱爲"盛太太"。

[Simplified-character version]

语言禁忌

在中国文化中，人们在涉及某种事物时需要回避，当不方便用语言表达的时候，可能会通过身体语言来表达。如果这样还是不能准确地表达意思的时候，人们就会用某种变通的说法来暗示自己需要表达的意思，这就是语言禁忌。例如死亡，这是人们普遍恐惧、忌讳的一件事情，所以，在一般情况下，人们是不愿意提到"死"的，于是就把"死"称为"疾终"、"谢世"、"走了"什么的。在战场上为国家和民族而死的人，被大家称作是"殉国"、"牺牲"或者"光荣了"。人们用这些含有褒义的词语代替"死"字。在日常生活中，为了避免"死"字，有的地区把"气死我"说成"激生我"，把"笑死我"说成"笑生我"。有的地区的人连跟"死"字同音的一些字也都要避开。例如，有的地区的人把姓"史"的男士叫"吏先生"，把姓"施"的女士称为"盛太太"。

[Pinyin version]

Yǔyán Jìnjì

Zài Zhōngguó wénhuà zhōng, rénmen zài shèjí mǒuzhǒng shìwù shí xūyào húibì, dāng bù fāngbiàn yòng yǔyán biǎodá de shíhou, kěnéng huì tōngguò shēntǐ yǔyán lái biǎodá. Rúguǒ zhèyàng háishì bùnéng zhǔnquè de biǎodá yìsi de shíhou, rénmen jiù huì yòng mǒuzhǒng biàntōng de shuōfǎ lái ànshì zìjǐ xūyào biǎodá de yìsi, zhè jiùshi yǔyán jìnjì. Lìrú sǐwáng, zhè shì rénmen pǔbiàn kǒngjù, jìhuì de yíjiàn shìqing, suǒyǐ, zài yìbān qíngkuàng xia, rénmen shì bú yuànyì tídao "sǐ" de, yúshì jiù bǎ "sǐ" chēngwéi "jízhōng", "xièshì", "zǒule" shénme de. Zài zhànchǎng shang wèi guójiā hé mínzú ér sǐde rén, bèi dàjiā chēngzuò shì "xùnguó", "xīshēng" huòzhě "guāngróng le". Rénmen yòng zhèxiē hányǒu bāoyì de cíyǔ dàitì "sǐ" zì. Zài rìcháng shēnghuó zhōng, wèile bìmiǎn "sǐ" zì, yǒude dìqū bǎ "qìsǐwǒ" shuōchéng "jīshēngwǒ", bǎ "xiàosǐwǒ" shuōchéng "xiàoshēngwǒ". Yǒude dìqū de rén lián gēn "sǐ" zì tóngyīn de yìxiē zì yě dōu yào bìkāi. Lìrú, yǒude dìqū de rén bǎ xìng "Shǐ" de nánshì jiào "Lì Xiānshēng", bǎ xìng "Shī" de nǚshì chēngwéi "Shèng Tàitài".

[Traditional-character version]

做客禁忌

　　中國人熱情好客。家裏來了客人，一定要禮貌待客，否則會被人嘲笑。客人進門時，主人要主動上前打招呼，並請客人坐。對客人不言不語，或者只站著說話而不請客人坐，都是不禮貌的行爲。客人坐下以後，主人不能光說請客人喝茶却不沏茶，或說了半天話以後，才想起來沏茶讓客。這些都是對客人不歡迎、不尊敬的表現。請客人吃飯，講究"淺茶、滿酒、整盒煙"，也就是說，茶水要沏得淺一點，酒要倒滿杯子，煙要給整盒烟。遞煙、酒、茶，都要用雙手，不能單手遞。招待客人的菜也要雙數，是"好事成雙"的意思。

　　在座位安排上，也是很有講究的。首先，席位的方向要擺正，首席座位總是面向屋門口的方向。主要賓客要面朝南，坐在首席上。其他的座位也得按照一定順序排列。在宴席上，客人要尊敬主人，一定讓主人先開始吃，就是俗話所說的"主不動，客不吃"、"主不吃，客不飲"。

[Simplified-character version]

做客禁忌

　　中国人热情好客。家里来了客人，一定要礼貌待客，否则会被人嘲笑。客人进门时，主人要主动上前打招呼，并请客人坐。对客人不言不语，或者只站着说话而不请客人坐，都是不礼貌的行为。客人坐下以后，主人不能光说请客人喝茶却不沏茶，或说了半天话以后，才想起来沏茶让客。这些都是对客人不欢迎、不尊敬的表现。请客人吃饭，讲究"浅茶、满酒、整盒烟"，也就是说，茶水要沏得浅一点，酒要倒满杯子，烟要给整盒烟。递烟、酒、茶，都要用双手，不能单手递。招待客人的菜也要双数，是"好事成双"的意思。

在座位安排上，也是很有讲究的。首先，席位的方向要摆正，首席座位总是面向屋门口的方向。主要宾客要面朝南，坐在首席上。其他的座位也得按照一定顺序排列。在宴席上，客人要尊敬主人，一定让主人先开始吃，就是俗话所说的"主不动，客不吃"、"主不吃，客不饮"。

[Pinyin version]

Zuòkè Jìnjì

Zhōngguórén rèqíng hàokè. Jiāli láile kèrén, yídìng yào lǐmào dài kè, fǒuzé huì bèirén cháoxiao. Kèrén jìnmén shí, zhǔrén yào zhǔdòng shàngqián dǎ zhāohū, bìng qǐng kèrén zuò. Duì kèrén bùyán bùyǔ, huòzhě zhǐ zhànzhe shuōhuà ér bù qǐng kèrén zuò, dōu shì bù lǐmào de xíngwéi. Kèrén zuòxia yǐhòu, zhǔrén bùnéng guāng shuō qǐng kèrén hēchá què bù qīchá, huò shuōle bàntiān huà yǐhòu, cái xiǎngqilai qīchá ràngkè. Zhèxiē dōu shì duì kèrén bù huānyíng, bù zūnjìng de biǎoxiàn. Qǐng kèrén chīfàn, jiǎngjiu "qiǎnchá, mǎnjiǔ, zhěnghéyān", yě jiùshì shuō, cháshuǐ yào qīde qiǎnyidiǎn, jiǔ yào dàomǎn bēizi, yān yào gěi zhěnghé. Dì yān, jiǔ, chá, dōu yào yòng shuāngshǒu, bùnéng dānshǒu dì. Zhāodài kèrén de cài yě yào shuāngshù, shì "hǎoshì chéngshuāng" de yìsi.

Zài zuòwèi ānpái shang, yěshì hěn yǒu jiǎngjiu de. Shǒuxiān, xíwèi de fāngxiàng yào bǎizhèng, shǒuxí zuòwèi zǒngshì miànxiàng wūménkǒu de fāngxiàng. Zhǔyào bīnkè yào miàn cháonán, zuòzài shǒuxí shang. Qítā de zuòwèi yě děi ànzhào yídìng shùnxù páiliè. Zài yànxí shang, kèrén yào zūnjìng zhǔrén, yídìng ràng zhǔrén xiān kāishǐ chī, jiùshì súhuà suǒshuōde "Zhǔ búdòng, kè bù chī", "Zhǔ bù chī, kè bù yǐn".

IMPORTANT IDIOMS

Chinese idioms are closely linked to Chinese culture. Idioms express a speaker's feelings with very few words. They enrich the Chinese language and offer a glimpse into people's thoughts.

A list of idioms, including their pronunciation and examples of their usage, is provided below. Students should practice using these idioms in their writing and speaking.

1. 愛不釋手　(爱不释手) àibù-shìshǒu
   to be too fond of something to part with it; mainly used to describe things

   Example: 她對姑媽送的生日禮物愛不釋手。
   　　　　 她对姑妈送的生日礼物爱不释手。

2. 愛憎分明　(爱憎分明) àizēng-fēnmíng
   to be clear about whom or what to love or hate

   Example: 我爸爸是個愛憎分明、敢愛敢恨的人。
   　　　　 我爸爸是个爱憎分明、敢爱敢恨的人。

3. 安然無恙 （安然无恙）ānrán-wúyàng
to be in a good situation without any problems, usually pertaining to health; refers to a person who has gone through an unforeseen event unscathed

Example: 經歷了一場那麼大的車禍，他却安然無恙，真是一個奇蹟。
經历了一场那么大的车祸，他却安然无恙，真是一个奇迹。

4. 按部就班 ànbù-jiùbān
in accordance with the prescribed order; the act of following a schedule

Example: 雖然父親去世了，但家裏的一切事情還在按部就班地進行著。
虽然父亲去世了，但家里的一切事情还在按部就班地进行着。

5. 半途而廢 （半途而废）bàntú-érfèi
to give up halfway; to leave something unfinished

Example: 要想做好一件事情，就要不斷努力，而不能半途而廢。
要想做好一件事情，就要不断努力，而不能半途而废。

6. 本末倒置 （本末倒置）běnmò-dàozhì
to reverse the primary and secondary tasks

Example: 你們不先解決環境問題，却把時間、金錢都花費在這些小事情上，簡直是本末倒置。
你们不先解决环境问题，却把时间、金钱都花费在这些小事情上，简直是本末倒置。

7. 必不可少 bìbù-kěshǎo
absolutely necessary

Example: 如今，個人電腦已經成爲學生必不可少的學習工具了。
如今，个人电脑已经成为学生必不可少的学习工具了。

8. 變化無常 （变化无常）biànhuà-wúcháng
irregular; capricious

Example: 這兒的天氣變化無常，剛才還是晴空萬里，現在却已經烏雲密布了。
这儿的天气变化无常，刚才还是晴空万里，现在却已经乌云密布了。

9. 別具一格 （别具一格）biéjù-yìgé
to have a unique style; describes literature, art, and architecture

Example: 那家博物館的設計別具一格。
那家博物馆的设计别具一格。

10. 不言而喻 bùyán-éryù
obvious

Example: 保護環境是每個公民的義務，這是不言而喻的。
保护环境是每个公民的义务，这是不言而喻的。

11. 不約而同　（不约而同）bùyuē-értóng

to do something synchronized without previous arrangement; a coincidence

Example: 老師一走進教室，同學們就不約而同地安靜下來。
　　　　老师一走进教室，同学们就不约而同地安静下来。

12. 不知所措　bùzhī-suǒcuò

to not know what to do; refers to an awkward or confusing situation

Example: 每當碰到麻煩的事情，我就會不知所措。
　　　　每当碰到麻烦的事情，我就会不知所措。

13. 參差不齊　（参差不齐) cēncī-bùqí

Non-uniformity; non-standard

Example: 大家的英文水平差不多，但是中文水平參差不齊。
　　　　大家的英文水平差不多，但是中文水平参差不齐。

14. 成千上萬　（成千上万) chéngqiān-shàngwàn

a massive amount

Example: 每天都有成千上萬的人參觀故宮博物院。
　　　　每天都有成千上万的人参观故宫博物院。

15. 寸步不離　（寸步不离) cùnbù-bùlí

very close; inseparable, usually refers to two or more people

Example: 他們是一對寸步不離的好朋友。
　　　　他们是一对寸步不离的好朋友。

16. 大吃一驚　（大吃一惊) dàchī-yìjīng

to be surprised

Example: 聽說她要結婚了，我大吃一驚。
　　　　听说她要结婚了，我大吃一惊。

17. 大海撈針　（大海捞针) dàhǎi-lāozhēn

hard to find; like finding a needle in a haystack

Example: 現在要想找到一個理想的工作，簡直是大海撈針。
　　　　现在要想找到一个理想的工作，简直是大海捞针。

18. 大失所望　dàshī-suǒwàng

extremely disappointing

Example: 他們輸了那場比賽，讓我大失所望。
　　　　他们输了那场比赛，让我大失所望。

19. 大同小異　（大同小异) dàtóng-xiǎoyì

similar in essential aspects, different in minor details

Example: 我的看法跟他的看法大同小異，沒有什麼根本的區別。
　　　　我的看法跟他的看法大同小异，没有什么根本的区别。

20. 丟三落四 diūsān-làsì

to be forgetful

Example: 姐姐最近總是丟三落四的，好像有什麼心事。
姐姐最近总是丢三落四的，好像有什么心事。

21. 獨一無二 (独一无二) dúyī-wú'èr

unlike any other; to be unique; one of a kind

Example: 中國的長城在世界建築史上是獨一無二的。
中国的长城在世界建筑史上是独一无二的。

22. 豐富多彩 (丰富多彩) fēngfù-duōcǎi

diverse

Example: 中學生的生活應該是豐富多彩的。
中学生的生活应该是丰富多彩的。

23. 風和日麗 (风和日丽) fēnghé-rìlì

gentle breeze and beautiful sun; describes the weather

Example: 在一個風和日麗的星期六，我們見面了。
在一个风和日丽的星期六，我们见面了。

24. 各抒己見 (各抒己见) gèshū-jǐjiàn

a discussion where everyone has equal say

Example: 課堂討論的時候，同學們各抒己見，提出了不少建議。
课堂讨论的时候，同学们各抒己见，提出了不少建议。

25. 和藹可親 (和蔼可亲) hé'ǎi-kěqīn

friendly and amicable; usually refers to an elderly person

Example: 他雖然是個有名的人，但是對人和藹可親，特別是對孩子們。
他虽然是个有名的人，但是对人和蔼可亲，特别是对孩子们。

26. 記憶猶新 (记忆犹新) jìyì-yóuxīn

to remain fresh in one's memory; remember vividly

Example: 雖然幾年過去了，但是我對那天發生的事記憶猶新。
虽然几年过去了，但是我对那天发生的事记忆犹新。

27. 今非昔比 jīnfēi-xībǐ

to see improvement in the present compared to the past; can be a fact or an opinion

Example: 這次到中國一看，真是今非昔比。特別是上海，完全不是我記憶中的樣子了。
这次到中国一看，真是今非昔比。特别是上海，完全不是我记忆中的样子了。

28. 口是心非 kǒushì-xīnfēi

saying something that one does not mean

Example: 我怎麼會跟這種口是心非的人做朋友呢。
我怎么会跟这种口是心非的人做朋友呢。

29. 力不從心 (力不从心) lìbù-cóngxīn

describes one whose abilities or skills are not adequate to fulfill one's desires

Example: 我很想幫他，可是實在是力不從心。
我很想帮他，可是实在是力不从心。

30. 兩全其美 (两全其美) liǎngquán-qíměi

to the satisfaction of both parties

Example: 我們想不出一個兩全其美的辦法。
我们想不出一个两全其美的办法。

31. 亂七八糟 (乱七八糟) luànqī -bāzāo

messy; describes both concrete and abstract things

Example: 他的同屋總是把房間弄得亂七八糟的。
他的同屋总是把房间弄得乱七八糟的。

32. 馬到成功 (马到成功) mǎdào-chénggōng

to wish someone good luck

Example: 我祝你們馬到成功！
我祝你们马到成功！

33. 沒精打采 méijīng-dǎcǎi

to be listless or apathetic

Example: 她一整天都沒精打采的，原來是考試沒考好。
她一整天都没精打采的，原来是考试没考好。

34. 美中不足 měizhōng-bùzú

having only one small flaw

Example: 加州是個很適合居住的地方，美中不足的是房子太貴了。
加州是个很适合居住的地方，美中不足的是房子太贵了。

35. 面目一新 miànmù-yìxīn

to change for the better

Example: 經過大家的共同努力，我們的宿舍樓面目一新。
经过大家的共同努力，我们的宿舍楼面目一新。

36. 千差萬別 (千差万别) qiānchā -wànbié

unlike any other; different

Example: 這兩件事表面上看起來千差萬別，卻有著內在的聯繫。
这两件事表面上看起来千差万别，却有着内在的联系。

37. 千言萬語　(千言万语) qiānyán-wànyǔ
having much to say

Example: 就是用千言萬語也表達不了我對你的感激之情。
就是用千言万语也表达不了我对你的感激之情。

38. 人山人海　rénshān-rénhǎi
large crowds of people

Example: 每到周末，迪斯尼樂園裏人山人海。
每到周末，迪斯尼乐园里人山人海。

39. 日新月異　(日新月异) rìxīn-yuèyì
to change very quickly

Example: 這幾年，我們家鄉的建設日新月異。
这几年，我们家乡的建设日新月异。

40. 十拿九穩　(十拿九稳) shíná-jiǔwěn
very likely to happen; success within reach

Example: 他學習那麼好，考上哈佛大學是十拿九穩的事。
他学习那么好，考上哈佛大学是十拿九稳的事。

41. 十全十美　shíquán-shíměi
perfect; flawless

Example: 世界上很難找到十全十美的人。
世界上很难找到十全十美的人。

42. 事半功倍　shìbàn-gōngbèi
to achieve success with little effort

Example: 找到科學的學習方法，可以達到事半功倍的效果。
找到科学的学习方法，可以达到事半功倍的效果。

43. 數一數二　(数一数二) shǔyī-shǔ'èr
one of the best; outstanding

Example: 李白是中國文學史上數一數二的詩人。
李白是中国文学史上数一数二的诗人。

44. 討價還價　(讨价还价) tǎojià-huánjià
to haggle over a price

Example: 經過一番討價還價，他只用10 塊錢就把那幅名畫買回來了。
经过一番讨价还价，他只用10 块钱就把那幅名画买回来了。

45. 同舟共濟　(同舟共济) tóngzhōu-gòngjì
to get through a time of difficulty by settling one's differences and working together

Example: 真正的朋友應該同舟共濟。
真正的朋友应该同舟共济。

46. 無價之寶　(无价之宝) wújià-zhībǎo
an object that is priceless or an asset; can also refer to abstract things

Example: 健康是無價之寶，可是遺憾的是，人們在年輕的時候往往不懂得
這個道理。
健康是无价之宝，可是遗憾的是，人们在年轻的时候往往不懂得
这个道理。

47. 心直口快　(心直口快) xīnzhí-kǒukuài
outspoken

Example: 她是個心直口快的人，有什麼說什麼。
她是个心直口快的人，有什么说什么。

48. 一見鍾情　(一见钟情) yíjiàn-zhōngqíng
to fall in love at first sight

Example: 聽說她跟她男朋友是一見鍾情。
听说她跟她男朋友是一见钟情。

49. 自食其果　zìshí-qíguǒ
to reap what one sows; karma

Example: 人們爲了發展經濟而把環境都破壞了，總有一天，我們人類會自
食其果的。
人们为了发展经济而把环境都破坏了，总有一天，我们人类会自
食其果的。

50. 走馬觀花　(走马观花) zǒumǎ-guānhuā
to give a quick glance

Example: 我這次來美國時間不長，只是走馬觀花地看了看。
我这次来美国时间不长，只是走马观花地看了看。

USEFUL PROVERBS

Proverbs are an integral part of the folklore of a country. As with idioms, proverbs give students a glimpse into Chinese culture. Students should try to understand them, memorize the ones they like, and practice using them in both writing and speaking activities.

1. 百聞不如一見
百闻不如一见
bǎi wén bù rú yí jiàn
(To see once is better than to hear a hundred times.)
expresses that one should see something for himself

Example: 雖然都知道大峽谷很壯觀，但是百聞不如一見，有機會你還是應
該親自去看看。
虽然都知道大峡谷很壮观，但是百闻不如一见，有机会你还是应
该亲自去看看。

2. 冰凍三尺，非一日之寒
冰冻三尺，非一日之寒
bīng dòng sān chǐ fēi yí rì zhī hán
(Ice is not formed by one day's cold.)
equivalent of "Rome was not built in a day"

Example: 俗話說，冰凍三尺，非一日之寒。　他身上的這些壞習慣，肯定不是一天兩天養成的。
俗话说，冰冻三尺，非一日之寒。　他身上的这些坏习惯，肯定不是一天两天养成的。

3. 好書如摯友
好书如挚友
hǎo shū rú zhì yǒu
(A good book is the best of friends, the same today and forever.)
indicates the importance of reading good books

Example: 書可以指導人們工作、學習和生活，因爲好書如摯友。
书可以指导人们工作、学习和生活，因为好书如挚友。

4. 恨鐵不成鋼
恨铁不成钢
hèn tiě bù chéng gāng
(Pitying iron will not change it into steel.)
to set high goals for someone to help him achieve success after a setback; usually describes the actions of the guardian of a child

Example: 不是父母不愛你，而是他們恨鐵不成鋼啊。
不是父母不爱你，而是他们恨铁不成钢啊。

5. 病從口入
病从口入
bìng cóng kǒu rù
(Sickness comes from the mouth.)
used to explain the causes and effects of health-related problems

Example: 難道你不懂病從口入的道理嗎？你總是這麼不講衛生，早晚得生病。
难道你不懂病从口入的道理吗？你总是这么不讲卫生，早晚得生病。

6. 患難見真情
患难见真情
huàn nàn jiàn zhēn qíng
(A friend in need is a friend indeed.)
used to describe the relationship between people

Example: 俗話說，患難見真情。困境中認識的朋友才是真正的朋友。
俗话说，患难见真情。困境中认识的朋友才是真正的朋友。

7. 禍從口出，言多必失
禍从口出，言多必失
huò cóng kǒu chū, yán duō bì shī
(Careless talk leads to trouble. The more one talks, the more is lost.)
indicates that gossip causes misfortune

Example: 他這個人，做人太謹慎。他相信禍從口出，言多必失的道理，所
以，平時他盡量少說話，多做事。
他这个人，做人太谨慎。他相信祸从口出，言多必失的道理，所
以，平时他尽量少说话，多做事。

8. 家家有本難念的經
家家有本难念的经
jiā jiā yǒu běn nán niàn de jīng
(Every family has a scripture that is hard to recite.)
indicates that every family has its own problems

Example: 我一直以爲只有美國才存在著那麽多的家庭問題，到了中國一
看，家庭問題也不少，比如離婚呀，兒女出走呀什麽的。真是家
家有本難念的經。
我一直以为只有美国才存在着那么多的家庭问题，到了中国一
看，家庭问题也不少，比如离婚呀，儿女出走呀什么的。真是 家
家有本难念的经。

9. 撿了芝麻丢了西瓜
捡了芝麻丢了西瓜
Jiǎn le zhī ma diū le xī guā
(To lose a watermelon trying to pick up a sesame seed.)
describes losing something significant while obtaining something trivial

Example: 你爲了掙幾個小錢把學習耽誤了，這不是撿了芝麻丢了西瓜嘛。
你为了挣几个小钱把学习耽误了，这不是捡了芝麻丢了西瓜嘛。

10. 健康是最大的財富
健康是最大的财富
jiàn kāng shì zuì dà de cái fù
(Good health is the greatest treasure.)
indicates that good health is more valuable than anything else

Example: 身體是生存的本錢，健康是最大的財富，所以，我們一定要注意
身體健康。
身体是生存的本钱，健康是最大的财富，所以，我们一定要注意
身体健康。

11. 金無足赤，人無完人
    金无足赤，人无完人
    jīn wú zú chì, rén wú wán rén
    (There is no pure gold. Every man has his flaws.)
    used to indicate that no one is perfect

    Example: 金無足赤，人無完人。生活中怎麼可能找到一個完全沒有缺點的
    人呢？
    金无足赤，人无完人。生活中怎么可能找到一个完全没有缺点的
    人呢？

12. 禮輕情意重
    礼轻情意重
    lǐ qīng qíng yì zhòng
    (A small gift can show good intentions.)
    indicates that it's the thought that counts

    Example: 教師節那天，小明把親手做的一朵小花給老師戴在胸前。　禮輕情
    意重，老師非常感動。
    教师节那天，小明把亲手做的一朵小花给老师戴在胸前。　礼轻情
    意重，老师非常感动。

13. 男兒有淚不輕彈
    男儿有泪不轻弹
    nánr yǒu lèi bù qīng tán
    (Men don't easily cry.)

    Example: 俗話說，男兒有淚不輕彈。你一個大小伙子，怎麼說哭就哭？
    俗话说，男儿有泪不轻弹。你一个大小伙子，怎么说哭就哭？

14. 千里之行，始於足下
    千里之行，始于足下
    qiān lǐ zhī xíng,　shǐ yú zú xià
    (A journey of a thousand miles begins with one step.)

    Example: 千里之行，始於足下。只有把小事做好了，才可能成就大事業。
    千里之行，始于足下。只有把小事做好了，才可能成就大事业。

15. 前人栽樹，後人乘涼
    前人栽树，后人乘凉
    qián rén zāi shù, hòu rén chéng liáng
    (The previous generation plants the trees so the later generation will benefit
    from the shade.)
    describes doing something for someone else later on

    Example: 前人栽樹，　後人乘涼。我們應該節約能源，保護環境，爲我們的
    子孫後代留下一個生存空間。
    前人栽树，后人乘凉。我们应该节约能源，保护环境，为我们的子
    孙后代留下一个生存空间。

16. 少小不努力，老大徒傷悲
少小不努力，老大徒伤悲
shào xiǎo bù nǔ lì, lǎo dà tú shāng bēi
(A young idler will become an old beggar.)
used to indicate that one should work hard to have a good life in the future

Example: 古人說：少小不努力，老大徒傷悲。你現在不好好學習，將來一
事無成。到那時，你後悔都來不及了。
古人说：少小不努力，老大徒伤悲。你现在不好好学习，将来一
事无成。到那时，你后悔都来不及了。

17. 失敗是成功之母
失败是成功之母
shī bài shì chéng gōng zhī mǔ
(Failure is the mother of success.)
expresses that failures prepare you for success

Example: 我覺得失敗並不是可怕的事情，只要你能不斷地從失敗中吸取經
驗教訓，總有一天你會成功的，因爲失敗是成功之母。
我觉得失败并不是可怕的事情，只要你能不断地从失败中吸取经
验教训，总有一天你会成功的，因为失败是成功之母。

18. 事實勝於雄辯
事实胜于雄辩
shì shí shèng yú xióng biàn
(Facts speak louder than words.)
indicates that facts matter more than opinions

Example: 他們犯下的罪行是事實，他們再怎麼否定那段歷史也是沒有用的，
因爲人們堅信"事實勝於雄辯"這個道理。
他们犯下的罪行是事实，他们再怎么否定那段历史也是没有用的，
因为人们坚信"事实胜于雄辩"这个道理。

19. 書山有路勤爲徑
书山有路勤为径
shū shān yǒu lù qín wéi jìng
(One must work hard to climb a mountain.)
indicates that to achieve success, one must work hard

Example: 書山有路勤爲徑。一個人不管他多聰明，如果不努力，也很難成
就一番事業。只有勤奮好學，才能把成功變成現實。
书山有路勤为径。一个人不管他多聪明，如果不努力，也很难成
就一番事业。只有勤奋好学，才能把成功变成现实。

20. 天下沒有不散的宴席
天下没有不散的宴席
tiān xià méi yǒu bú sàn de yàn xí
(All good things come to an end.)
equivalent to good things don't last forever

Example: 雖然我懂得“天下沒有不散的宴席”這個道理，但是跟最好的朋友分別，對我來說，還是一件很難接受的事情。
虽然我懂得“天下没有不散的宴席”这个道理，但是跟最好的朋友分别，对我来说，还是一件很难接受的事情。

21. 天下興亡，匹夫有責
天下兴亡，匹夫有责
tiān xià xīng wáng, pǐ fū yǒu zé
(A country's condition is the result of both the noble and the peasant's actions.)
indicates that everybody is responsible for the fate of his country

Example: 天下興亡，匹夫有責。作爲一個中國人，我們都應該爲國家的強盛做出自己的貢獻。
天下兴亡，匹夫有责。作为一个中国人，我们都应该为国家的强盛做出自己的贡献。

22. 天有不測風雲
天有不測风云
tiān yǒu bú cè fēng yún
(The sky may not be consistent.)
equivalent to expect the unexpected

Example: 本來小王有個幸福的家庭：妻子漂亮，女兒聰明，一家人生活得快快樂樂的。誰知天有不測風雲，一場車禍把一切都毀了。
本来小王有个幸福的家庭：妻子漂亮，女儿聪明，一家人生活得快快乐乐的。谁知天有不测风云，一场车祸把一切都毁了。

23. 笑一笑，十年少；愁一愁，白了頭
笑一笑，十年少；愁一愁，白了头
xiào yi xiào, shí nián shào; chóu yi chóu, bái le tóu
(A smile can make you ten years younger, but worry turns your hair gray.)
expresses that one's lifestyle affects his health

Example: 人的情緒直接影響健康。俗話說得好，笑一笑，十年少；愁一愁，白了頭。我們應該從中獲得啓發，尋找積極的人生態度，讓自己的身心更健康。
人的情绪直接影响健康。俗话说得好，笑一笑，十年少；愁一愁，白了头。我们应该从中获得启发，寻找积极的人生态度，让自己的身心更健康。

24. 行動勝於空談

行动胜于空谈

xíng dòng shèng yú kōng tán

(Actions speak louder than words.)

indicates that action is much more important than just talking

Example: 人在一生中，總會有各種理想、願望和計劃。如果人們能在抓住
它們的時候馬上拿出行動來，那一定會取得很多成就。可惜的
是，人們的許多計劃都停留在空談上。我想告訴年輕朋友，人生
目標不要立得太多，重要的是有了目標馬上就去做，畢竟行動勝
於空談。

人在一生中，总会有各种理想、愿望和计划。如果人们能在抓住
它们的时候马上拿出行动来，那一定会取得很多成就。可惜的
是，人们的许多计划都停留在空谈上。我想告诉年轻朋友，人生
目标不要立得太多，重要的是有了目标马上就去做，毕竟行动胜于
空谈。

25. 這山望到那山高

这山望到那山高

zhè shān wàng dào nà shān gāo

(The other mountain always looks taller than the one you're standing on.)

the equivalent of "the grass always looks greener on the other side"

Example: 你既然從事這個行業，就應該好好學習，好好工作，可不能這山
望到那山高 啊！

你既然从事这个行业，就应该好好学习，好好工作，可不能这山
望到那山高 啊！

Model Exam 1
ANSWER SHEET

Section I–Part A: Multiple Choice (Listening)

1 Ⓐ Ⓑ Ⓒ Ⓓ   9 Ⓐ Ⓑ Ⓒ Ⓓ   17 Ⓐ Ⓑ Ⓒ Ⓓ   25 Ⓐ Ⓑ Ⓒ Ⓓ
2 Ⓐ Ⓑ Ⓒ Ⓓ   10 Ⓐ Ⓑ Ⓒ Ⓓ   18 Ⓐ Ⓑ Ⓒ Ⓓ   26 Ⓐ Ⓑ Ⓒ Ⓓ
3 Ⓐ Ⓑ Ⓒ Ⓓ   11 Ⓐ Ⓑ Ⓒ Ⓓ   19 Ⓐ Ⓑ Ⓒ Ⓓ   27 Ⓐ Ⓑ Ⓒ Ⓓ
4 Ⓐ Ⓑ Ⓒ Ⓓ   12 Ⓐ Ⓑ Ⓒ Ⓓ   20 Ⓐ Ⓑ Ⓒ Ⓓ   28 Ⓐ Ⓑ Ⓒ Ⓓ
5 Ⓐ Ⓑ Ⓒ Ⓓ   13 Ⓐ Ⓑ Ⓒ Ⓓ   21 Ⓐ Ⓑ Ⓒ Ⓓ   29 Ⓐ Ⓑ Ⓒ Ⓓ
6 Ⓐ Ⓑ Ⓒ Ⓓ   14 Ⓐ Ⓑ Ⓒ Ⓓ   22 Ⓐ Ⓑ Ⓒ Ⓓ   30 Ⓐ Ⓑ Ⓒ Ⓓ
7 Ⓐ Ⓑ Ⓒ Ⓓ   15 Ⓐ Ⓑ Ⓒ Ⓓ   23 Ⓐ Ⓑ Ⓒ Ⓓ
8 Ⓐ Ⓑ Ⓒ Ⓓ   16 Ⓐ Ⓑ Ⓒ Ⓓ   24 Ⓐ Ⓑ Ⓒ Ⓓ

Section I–Part B: Multiple Choice (Reading)

31 Ⓐ Ⓑ Ⓒ Ⓓ   40 Ⓐ Ⓑ Ⓒ Ⓓ   49 Ⓐ Ⓑ Ⓒ Ⓓ   58 Ⓐ Ⓑ Ⓒ Ⓓ
32 Ⓐ Ⓑ Ⓒ Ⓓ   41 Ⓐ Ⓑ Ⓒ Ⓓ   50 Ⓐ Ⓑ Ⓒ Ⓓ   59 Ⓐ Ⓑ Ⓒ Ⓓ
33 Ⓐ Ⓑ Ⓒ Ⓓ   42 Ⓐ Ⓑ Ⓒ Ⓓ   51 Ⓐ Ⓑ Ⓒ Ⓓ   60 Ⓐ Ⓑ Ⓒ Ⓓ
34 Ⓐ Ⓑ Ⓒ Ⓓ   43 Ⓐ Ⓑ Ⓒ Ⓓ   52 Ⓐ Ⓑ Ⓒ Ⓓ   61 Ⓐ Ⓑ Ⓒ Ⓓ
35 Ⓐ Ⓑ Ⓒ Ⓓ   44 Ⓐ Ⓑ Ⓒ Ⓓ   53 Ⓐ Ⓑ Ⓒ Ⓓ   62 Ⓐ Ⓑ Ⓒ Ⓓ
36 Ⓐ Ⓑ Ⓒ Ⓓ   45 Ⓐ Ⓑ Ⓒ Ⓓ   54 Ⓐ Ⓑ Ⓒ Ⓓ   63 Ⓐ Ⓑ Ⓒ Ⓓ
37 Ⓐ Ⓑ Ⓒ Ⓓ   46 Ⓐ Ⓑ Ⓒ Ⓓ   55 Ⓐ Ⓑ Ⓒ Ⓓ   64 Ⓐ Ⓑ Ⓒ Ⓓ
38 Ⓐ Ⓑ Ⓒ Ⓓ   47 Ⓐ Ⓑ Ⓒ Ⓓ   56 Ⓐ Ⓑ Ⓒ Ⓓ   65 Ⓐ Ⓑ Ⓒ Ⓓ
39 Ⓐ Ⓑ Ⓒ Ⓓ   48 Ⓐ Ⓑ Ⓒ Ⓓ   57 Ⓐ Ⓑ Ⓒ Ⓓ   66 Ⓐ Ⓑ Ⓒ Ⓓ

Model Exam 1

SECTION I—PART A: LISTENING COMPREHENSION

Conversations 1 through 15.
Time–Approximately 20 minutes

> **Directions:** You will hear several short conversations. Each conversation will be played once along with four choices of response (A), (B), (C), and (D). You will have 5 seconds to choose a response that completes the conversation in a logical and culturally appropriate way.

MODEL EXAM I
SECTION I—PART A: LISTENING COMPREHENSION

Selections for questions 16 through 30.

> You will listen to several listening selections. Each selection will be played either once or twice. You may take notes. After each selection, you will have twelve seconds to read the question and choose the most appropriate response (A), (B), (C), or (D) in English from the answer sheet.

16. What is the purpose of the message?

 (A) To explain the reason for the flight delay
 (B) To book a plane ticket
 (C) To ask for a pick-up
 (D) To describe the traffic

17. What was the speaker's original flight plan?

 (A) New York—San Francisco
 (B) San Francisco—Los Angeles
 (C) New York—Los Angeles
 (D) Los Angeles—San Francisco

18. Where is the speaker calling from?

 (A) New York
 (B) San Francisco
 (C) Los Angeles
 (D) Home

19. What time did the speaker make the phone call?

 (A) 1:20 AM
 (B) 8:10 PM
 (C) 10:10 PM
 (D) 11:30 PM

20. What is the topic of the conversation?

 (A) Parents
 (B) Choosing a major
 (C) Looking for a job
 (D) Differences between literature and science

21. What do the woman's parents consider when choosing a major?

    (A) Interest
    (B) Stress
    (C) Money
    (D) Enjoyment

22. What does the woman want to study?

    (A) Literature
    (B) History
    (C) Medicine
    (D) Computer science

23. What do the man's parents want him to choose as a major ?

    (A) Literature
    (B) Medicine
    (C) Computer science
    (D) History

 Track 78

24. What is the passage mainly about?

    (A) Testing times
    (B) Testing sites
    (C) Registration information
    (D) Registration sites and times

25. When is the test?

    (A) February 19
    (B) March 2
    (C) April 3
    (D) May 20

26. Which is not required for registration?

    (A) Student ID
    (B) Photo
    (C) Transcript
    (D) Registration form

27. Which statement is false?

    (A) Students must come during the registration time.
    (B) Students from other schools cannot register.
    (C) Any photo is acceptable.
    (D) Students must pay the registration fee.

28. What were the results that the sociologist came up with?

   (A) The cost of raising a child from birth to adulthood in Shanghai
   (B) The cost of raising a child from birth to death in Shanghai
   (C) The cost of raising a child from birth to adulthood in China
   (D) The cost of raising a child from birth to death in China

29. In China, what is the second-highest expense?

   (A) Housing
   (B) Medical care
   (C) Education
   (D) Retirement fund

30. What did the bank's results show?

   (A) Citizens need to save money for retirement.
   (B) Saving money is a very quick process.
   (C) In China, most citizens save money mainly for their kids.
   (D) In China, most people enjoy saving money.

END OF PART A

SECTION I—PART B: READING COMPREHENSION

Time–Approximately 60 minutes

> **Directions:** For each reading selection, answer the accompanying questions by choosing the best response.

Sign for questions 31 and 32.

[Traditional-character version]

室內禁止大聲喧嘩。

[Simplified-character version]

室内禁止大声喧哗。

31. Where would the sign most likely appear?

 (A) In a department store
 (B) On a train
 (C) In a library
 (D) In a park

32. What is the purpose of the sign?

 (A) To inform people of a regulation
 (B) To advertise a new product
 (C) To introduce people to new music
 (D) To give directions

Story for questions 33 through 37.

[Traditional-character version]

　　中國唐代的文學家韓愈很小的時候父母就死了，他是跟著哥哥和嫂子長大的。哥哥和嫂子對他很好，像自己的兒子一樣。韓愈的哥哥有一個兒子，因爲是大家庭中的第十二個男孩子，所以大家叫他十二郎。十二郎跟韓愈在一起玩得很好。韓愈的哥哥在四十二歲的時候得了一場大病，不久就死了。當時，韓愈只有十一歲，十二郎就更小了。從那以後，韓愈和十二郎相依爲命。韓愈十九歲的時候離開了家鄉，在以後的十年中，韓愈跟十二郎只見過三次面。正當韓愈打算回到家鄉，跟十二郎永遠生活在一起的時候，卻聽到了十二郎死去的消息。韓愈非常難過，於是寫了一篇懷念十二郎的文章。

[Simplified-character version]

　　中国唐代的文学家韩愈很小的时候父母就死了，他是跟着哥哥和嫂子长大的。哥哥和嫂子对他很好，像自己的儿子一样。韩愈的哥哥有一个儿子，因为是大家庭中的第十二个男孩子，所以大家叫他十二郎。十二郎跟韩愈在一起玩得很好。韩愈的哥哥在四十二岁的时候得了一场大病，不久就死了。当时，韩愈只有十一岁，十二郎就更小了。从那以后，韩愈和十二郎相依为命。韩愈十九岁的时候离开了家乡，在以后的十年中，韩愈跟十二郎只见过三次面。正当韩愈打算回到家乡，跟十二郎永远生活在一起的时候，却听到了十二郎死去的消息。韩愈非常难过，于是写了一篇怀念十二郎的文章。

33. What is this story about?

   (A) Han Yu and his older brother
   (B) Han Yu and his sister-in-law
   (C) Han Yu and his nephew
   (D) Han Yu's brother's family

34. Why did Han Yu live with his brother?

   (A) His sister-in-law thought he was their son.
   (B) His parents died.
   (C) He wanted to play with Shi'er Lang.
   (D) He had to look after Shi'er Lang.

35. How old was Han Yu when his brother died?

   (A) 11
   (B) 12
   (C) 19
   (D) 42

36. Which statement is true?

   (A) Han Yu's brother has 12 kids.
   (B) Han Yu's brother died from an illness.
   (C) Han Yu was not close to his nephew.
   (D) Han Yu left his hometown when he was nine.

37. Why did Han Yu write the article?

   (A) To talk about his own experiences
   (B) To tell his brother's story
   (C) To coin a new proverb
   (D) To mourn his nephew

Advertisement for questions 38 through 42.

[Traditional-character version]

　　有公寓房一套，位於市中心。交通方便，安全、安靜。兩室一廳，兩個浴室。不帶家具，有地毯、洗衣機、烘乾機及高速網綫。月租$1500，不包水電，交一個月押金。　房客不可吸烟及養寵物，夫妻帶一到兩個孩子的家庭及女學生優先考慮。有意者請於早7點以後晚10點以前打電話: 555-555-5555。

[Simplified-character version]

　　有公寓房一套，位于市中心。交通方便，安全、安静。两室一厅，两个浴室。不带家具，有地毯、洗衣机、烘干机及高速网线。月租$1500，不包水电，交一个月押金。房客不可吸烟及养宠物，夫妻带一到两个孩子的家庭及女学生优先考虑。有意者请于早7点以后晚10点以前打电话：555-555-5555。

38. What kind of people cannot rent the apartment?

   (A) Couples with kids
   (B) Smokers
   (C) Couples without kids
   (D) Male students

39. What statement about the ad is true?

   (A) Comes with furniture
   (B) Safe, but transportation is inconvenient
   (C) Comes with high-speed Internet
   (D) Comes with a washing machine, but no dryer

40. Which aspect of the apartment is not mentioned?

   (A) Location
   (B) Parking
   (C) Deposit
   (D) Rent

41. Who has priority for renting the apartment?

   (A) Nonsmokers
   (B) People without pets
   (C) Male students
   (D) Female students

42. What time should one call?

   (A) 7:00 AM or 10:00 PM
   (B) between 10:00 AM and 7:00 PM
   (C) between 7:00 AM and 10:00 PM
   (D) between 7:00 AM and 10:00 AM

Policies for questions 43 through 47.

[Traditional-character version]

　　一、本館爲全校會議、體育教學、比賽活動場地。
　　二、進入本館要穿運動服裝、運動鞋。
　　三、禁止在館內喧嘩、吸烟或亂丟果皮、紙屑、口香糖等物。
　　四、愛護館內器材，如有損壞，照價賠償。
　　五、器材使用後放回原處。

[Simplified-character version]

一、本馆为全校会议、体育教学、比赛活动场地。

二、进入本馆要穿运动服装、运动鞋。

三、禁止在馆内喧哗、吸烟或乱丢果皮、纸屑、口香糖等物。

四、爱护馆内器材，如有损坏，照价赔偿。

五、器材使用后放回原处。

43. Where would these policies appear?

(A) Cafeteria
(B) Conference hall
(C) Gym
(D) Restaurant

44. What is not allowed in this building?

(A) Gym class
(B) Science labs
(C) Competitions
(D) Meetings

45. Which policy is not mentioned?

(A) Students cannot litter in the gym.
(B) Students cannot leave paper lying on the floor.
(C) Students cannot throw fruit peels on the floor.
(D) Students have to throw away all empty bottles.

46. Which statement is true?

(A) Food is allowed in the building.
(B) Smoking is not allowed.
(C) A fine will be imposed if any property is damaged.
(D) People cannot move the equipment around.

47. What is not mentioned in the policy?

(A) The purpose of the building
(B) Business hours
(C) Equipment
(D) Attire

Article for questions 48 though 53.

[Traditional-character version]

中國的老年婦女問題是人們討論的重要話題。目前在中國，60歲以上的老年人口將近1.5億，占總人數的10%。在今後的20到30年之間，中國老年婦女將會占女性人口的25%。也就是說，每四個女性中就會有一位是老年人。女性老人存在的最大問題是貧困問題。有27%的老年婦女每月的生活費不到100元。女性老人存在的第二個問題是退休金問題。城市老年婦女只有55%的人有退休金，而農村婦女都沒有退休金。精神孤獨也是女性老年人普遍存在的問題。60歲以上的老年婦女中，42%的老人的丈夫死亡。女性老人的家務繁重，更是一個需要全社會都來關心的問題。

[Simplified-character version]

中国的老年妇女问题是人们讨论的重要话题。目前在中国，60岁以上的老年人口将近1.5亿，占总人数的10%。在今后的20到30年之间，中国老年妇女将会占女性人口的25%。也就是说，每四个女性中就会有一位是老年人。女性老人存在的最大问题是贫困问题。有27%的老年妇女每月的生活费不到100元。女性老人存在的第二个问题是退休金问题。城市老年妇女只有55%的人有退休金，而农村妇女都没有退休金。精神孤独也是女性老年人普遍存在的问题。60岁以上的老年妇女中，42%的老人的丈夫死亡。女性老人的家务繁重，更是一个需要全社会都来关心的问题。

48. What does the passage mainly talk about?

    (A) Elderly people
    (B) Women
    (C) Elderly women
    (D) Ratios between men and women

49. What is the population of people over 60 in China?

    (A) More than fifteen hundred million
    (B) Close to fifteen hundred million
    (C) Close to fifteen hundred
    (D) Exactly fifteen hundred

50. Currently, elderly people make up what percent of the total population?

    (A) 10%
    (B) 20%
    (C) 25%
    (D) 30%

51. What is a major issue regarding elderly women?

    (A) Marriage
    (B) Poverty
    (C) Retirement funds
    (D) Loneliness

52. What is not mentioned in the passage?

    (A) Widows
    (B) Retirement funds
    (C) Social interaction
    (D) Chores

53. Which statement is correct?

(A) 10% of the total population is elderly women.
(B) There will eventually be fewer elderly women.
(C) 27% of elderly people receive a salary of 100 yuan or less.
(D) Many elderly women are lonely.

Passage for questions 54 through 59.

[Traditional-character version]

　　體育除了可以鍛煉身體以外，還能培養人的自信心，鼓勵人們迎接挑戰。在美國的大學裏，學習好、品德好、體育成績好的學生很多。在同學中，有一項出色的體育技能是很讓人羨慕的。美國的很多家長鼓勵自己的孩子從小參加學校和社區的足球隊、排球隊和籃球隊什麼的，爲的是培養孩子的自信心。孩子們的家庭體育教練也常常是由家長當的。相比之下，從中國大陸或台灣來的很多學生，雖然學習名列前茅，但是他們在體育、創造性、社交等方面往往感到信心不夠。這並不奇怪，因爲中國來的很多學生是在父母長期地保護中生活的，是在對體育普遍不重視的環境中長大的。這些中國家庭的學生，想克服身體的不適應和心理上的信心不足，還需要時間。

[Simplified-character version]

　　体育除了可以锻炼身体以外，还能培养人的自信心，鼓励人们迎接挑战。在美国的大学里，学习好、品德好、体育成绩好的学生很多。在同学中，有一项出色的体育技能是很让人羡慕的。美国的很多家长鼓励自己的孩子从小参加学校和社区的足球队、排球队和篮球队什么的，为的是培养孩子的自信心。孩子们的家庭体育教练也常常是由家长当的。相比之下，从中国大陆或台湾来的很多学生，虽然学习名列前茅，但是他们在体育、创造性、社交等方面往往感到信心不够。这并不奇怪，因为中国来的很多学生是在父母长期地保护中生活的，是在对体育普遍不重视的环境中长大的。这些中国家庭的学生，想克服身体的不适应和心理上的信心不足，还需要时间。

54. Which of the following titles fits the passage best?

(A) "Sports and Family"
(B) "Sports and Confidence"
(C) "Exercise and Challenges"
(D) "Good Students"

55. Which is the main idea of this passage?

(A) Sports improve students' physical and mental states.
(B) Sports challenge people.
(C) Chinese and American families have different views on sports.
(D) Chinese and American children receive different grades in gym class.

56. Which statement is correct?

(A) In the United States, few students receive good grades.
(B) In schools, excelling in sports is admirable.
(C) American families hire sports professionals to coach their kids.
(D) Parents with sports-related occupations require their kids to participate in sports at a young age.

57. In which area does the article say Chinese students usually excel?

(A) Sports
(B) Creativity
(C) Social activities
(D) Studying

58. What is the author's attitude about the difference between Chinese and American students?

(A) Disappointed
(B) Worried
(C) Not surprised
(D) Confident

59. What does the author imply in the last sentence of the passage?

(A) Chinese parents want their children to be independent.
(B) This problem can be solved easily.
(C) This problem cannot be solved in a short amount of time.
(D) Chinese families should spoil their kids.

E-mail for questions 60 through 66.

[Traditional-character version]

發件人：王月
收件人：彼得
主題：漢語橋獎學金
發送日期: 2013年3月18日

彼得同學：

　　你好！你來信說想申請"漢語橋獎學金"的事情。我給你介紹一下有關申請資格、申請辦法和需要準備的材料等方面的情況。

　　"漢語橋獎學金"的申請人應該是在"漢語橋世界大學生中文比賽"中取得好成績的學生。主要有下面四種情況：1) "漢語橋世界大學生中文比賽"決賽的3個一等獎的學生可以申請"漢語橋學位獎學金"；2) 決賽中的5個二等獎的學生可以申請"漢語橋暑期學習獎學金"；3) 決賽中的 7個三等獎的學生可以申請"漢語橋中華文化旅行獎學金"；4) 在"漢語橋世界大學生中文比賽" 海外預賽中表現好，但沒有得到決賽資格的學生可以申請"漢語橋預賽優秀選手獎學金"。海外預賽在每年3月到5月舉行，決賽時間在7月。有資格申請的學生一定在12月31日以前提出申請。申請人要按要求填寫申請表，並交成績單和推薦信的複印件。申請材料一定要在規定的時間內寄到。特別注意的是，申請人所交的材料都不退還。以上信息希望對你有幫助。

祝你成功！
王月

[Simplified-character version]

发件人：王月
收件人：彼得
主题：汉语桥奖学金
发送日期：2013年3月18日

彼得同学：

　　你好！你来信说想申请"汉语桥奖学金"的事情。我给你介绍一下有关申请资格、申请办法和需要准备的材料等方面的情况。

　　"汉语桥奖学金"的申请人应该是在"汉语桥世界大学生中文比赛"中取得好成绩的学生。主要有下面四种情况：1）"汉语桥世界大学生中文比赛"决赛的3个一等奖的学生可以申请"汉语桥学位奖学金"；2）决赛中的5个二等奖的学生可以申请"汉语桥暑期学习奖学金"；3）决赛中的 7个三等奖的学生可以申请"汉语桥中华文化旅行奖学金"；4）在"汉语桥世界大学生中文比赛"海外预赛中表现好，但没有得到决赛资格的学生可以申请"汉语桥预赛优秀选手奖学金"。海外预赛在每年3月到5月举行，决赛时间在7月。有资格申请的学生一定在12月31日以前提出申请。申请人要按要求填写申请表，并交成绩单和推荐信的复印件。申请材料一定要在规定的时间内寄到。特别注意的是，申请人所交的材料都不退还。以上信息希望对你有帮助。

祝你成功！
王月

60. Why did Wang Yue write this letter?

(A) Wang Yue wants to apply for a scholarship.
(B) Wang Yue wants to help Peter apply for a scholarship.
(C) Wang Yue wants to advertise the scholarship.
(D) Wang Yue is introducing this scholarship.

61. Which area is not discussed in the e-mail?

(A) Mailing address
(B) Types of scholarships
(C) Documents for applying
(D) Registration process

62. Who are candidates for this scholarship?

(A) International students who study Chinese
(B) International Chinese competition winners
(C) Chinese students in America
(D) International students

63. How many people can receive scholarships to China to get a degree?

    (A) 3
    (B) 5
    (C) 7
    (D) Not mentioned

64. When is the final competition?

    (A) March
    (B) May
    (C) July
    (D) December

65. What is not required in the application?

    (A) Transcript
    (B) Application form
    (C) Recommendation letter
    (D) Degree certificate

66. What is particularly noted in the e-mail?

    (A) Students can apply online.
    (B) Original forms are preferred, but copies are okay.
    (C) Applications can be sent at any time.
    (D) Documents will not be returned.

END OF SECTION I

SECTION II—PART A: WRITING

Time–Approximately 30 minutes.

Directions: You will produce several written works in Chinese in different formats. You will write specifically for a certain purpose and to a certain person. Your work should be as complete and culturally appropriate as possible.

Story Narration

These pictures present a sequence of events. Write a complete story based on these pictures from beginning to end.

1.

2.

3.

4.

E-Mail Response
Read this e-mail from a friend and then type a response.

[Traditional-character version]
發件人：孫小民
郵件主題：什麼時候考SAT？

　　我父母計劃送我到美國讀書。我想等到了美國以後再參加SAT考試，然後申請大學，可是我父母說應該先在中國把SAT考了。我想聽聽你的看法。另外，請你幫我想幾個理由來說服我父母，希望能很快收到你的來信。

[Simplified-character version]
发件人：孙小民
邮件主题：什么时候考SAT？

　　我父母计划送我到美国读书。我想等到了美国以后再参加SAT考试，然后申请大学，可是我父母说应该先在中国把SAT考了。我想听听你的看法。另外，请你帮我想几个理由来说服我父母，希望能很快收到你的来信。

END OF PART A

SECTION II—PART B: SPEAKING, CONVERSATION

Time-Approximately 11 minutes

> You will have a conversation with Li Ping, an interviewer, about your application for a High School Study Abroad Program in China. She will ask you six questions. After eacher question, you will have 20 seconds to respond. Respond as fully and as appropriately as possible.

> **Directions:** You will make a presentation in Chinese on a given topic. You will be given 4 minutes to plan your presentation and 2 minutes to record your presentation. Your presentation should be as complete as possible.

Cultural Presentation
Choose ONE Chinese folk custom that is associated with a particular holiday (firecrackers, dragon boat racing, etc.). In your presentation, describe this custom and explain its significance.

End of Section II

Model Exam 1
ANSWER KEY

Section I–Part A: Multiple Choice (Listening)

1	D	9	B	17	C	25	D
2	C	10	C	18	B	26	C
3	B	11	B	19	B	27	C
4	C	12	B	20	B	28	A
5	B	13	D	21	C	29	D
6	C	14	B	22	A	30	C
7	B	15	D	23	C		
8	C	16	C	24	C		

Section I–Part B: Multiple Choice (Reading)

31	C	40	B	49	B	58	C
32	A	41	D	50	A	59	C
33	C	42	C	51	B	60	B
34	B	43	C	52	C	61	A
35	A	44	B	53	D	62	B
36	B	45	D	54	B	63	A
37	D	46	B	55	A	64	C
38	B	47	B	56	B	65	D
39	C	48	C	57	D	66	D

ANSWERS AND ANSWER EXPLANATIONS

Section I—Part A: Listening

1. **(D)** This is the only response that answers the question, "I'm from New York. How about you?" which essentially is the same as the question, "Where are you from?" (A) is wrong because the man just said he is from New York. (B) and (C) indicate where the woman does want to go, and where she is from.

2. **(C)** This is the only appropriate response to the woman's suggestion. (A) and (D) are wrong because they have nothing to do with the actual present. (B) is wrong because the woman never said that computers were expensive.

3. **(B)** The woman suggests that she and the man go see a movie. The man's response is a rhetorical question, which means "there aren't any good movies out." The woman then says, "Lately there's been lots of good movies." (A) and (C) are wrong because they both take the man's question literally. (D) is wrong because the man already implied that he does not want to see a movie.

4. **(C)** The man says that he tends to get lost in a book. The woman should respond with "That means you get too into the book." (A) and (B) are wrong because they both take the man literally. (D) is wrong because it is both irrelevant and rude.

5. **(B)** The woman says, "Sorry, I'm late because we had a family problem." (B) is correct because the man says, "It's okay, I've only been here for a little while, too," which is the most reasonable and polite answer. (A) is therefore not appropriate. (C) is wrong because the man should not apologize for no reason. (D) is wrong because the woman already explained why she was late.

6. **(C)** The man answers why he is alone: His brother is playing soccer with a friend. (A) is wrong because the man tells the woman what he and his brother did but never answers her question. (B) is wrong because he still does not answer the question. (D) is wrong because the man talks about his brother's behavior, but again, does not answer the question.

7. **(B)** This response answers the question, "What do you think of that professor?" (A), (C), and (D) are wrong because they are all facts about the professor, not opinions.

8. **(C)** This answers that the professor teaches Chinese. (A), (B), and (D) don't answer the question.

9. **(B)** The man retorts, "I think the traffic is bad all the time," to the woman's statement, "It depends on during what hours you're on the highway." (A), (C), and (D) are not completely relevant to the conversation.

10. **(C)** Choices (A), (B), and (D) have already all been answered by the woman in her first statement.

11. **(B)** This is the only answer that tells the man where the movie theatre is located. (A) and (C) do not answer the question, and (D) is just repeating the man's question.

12. **(B)** This answers how many classes the woman is taking. (A), (C), and (D) don't answer the question.

13. **(D)** The man is telling the woman where the Chinese restaurant is located. (A) is wrong because it does not appropriately respond to the woman's statement. (B) and (C) have already been answered by the woman.

14. **(B)** The man asks the woman what kind of movies she likes to watch. (A) and (C) are related to music, but the woman did not say anything about music. (D) is wrong, because the woman just said that she has not watched any movies recently.

15. **(D)** The woman commented that the man does not look well. The man admits in (D) that he did not do well on his test. (A), (B), and (C) take the woman's statement "臉色這麼難看" ("脸色这么难看") too literally.

16. **(C)** "我想麻煩你到機場接我一趟" ("我想麻烦你到机场接我一趟") means that the woman needs to be picked up from the airport.

17. **(C)** "我本來應該中午從紐約直飛洛杉磯" ("我本来应该中午从纽约直飞洛杉矶") means that the woman was originally going to fly from New York to Los Angeles.

18. **(B)** "我現在在舊金山機場等著坐飛機回洛杉磯" ("我现在在旧金山机场等着坐飞机回洛杉矶") means that the woman is currently in San Francisco.

19. **(B)** "飛機兩個小時以後，也就是10:10起飛" ("飞机两个小时以后，也就是10:10起飞") means that the flight will leave in two hours, at 10:10, which indicates that it is currently 8:10 PM.

20. **(B)** The opening sentence, "大學的專業你選好了嗎" ("大学的专业你选好了吗"), is about choosing a major.

21. **(C)** "可是我父母說，選專業不能只靠興趣，而應該看將來好不好找工作，能不能賺錢" ("可是我父母说，选专业不能只靠兴趣，而应该看将来好不好找工作，能不能赚钱") shows that the salary is important.

22. **(A)** "我特別喜歡文學" ("我特别喜欢文学") means that the woman enjoys literature.

23. **(C)** "可我父母非讓我學工程技術或電腦不可" ("可我父母非让我学工程技术或电脑不可") means that, although the man wants to study history, his parents want him to major in either computer science or engineering.

24. **(C)** Choices (A), (B), and (D) are specific items included in (C).

25. **(D)** The correct answer is directly stated in the announcement.

26. **(C)** Nowhere in the announcement does it say anything about a transcript.

27. **(C)** The announcement states "交近期照片," which means only recent photos are acceptable. All of the other answers are confirmed directly.

28. **(A)** The correct answer is directly stated in the passage. (B) is not logical because one usually does not raise a child from birth all the way until death, only to adulthood. (C) and (D) are wrong, because the statistics only apply to Shanghai, not the entire country of China.

29. **(D)** The correct answer is directly stated in the passage: "超過了養老和住房" ("超过了养老和住房"). "養老" ("养老") is, therefore, considered second, and "住房" is considered third.

30. **(C)** "中國銀行的調查結果也告訴我們，中國人存錢主要是爲了子女學習" ("中国银行的调查结果也告诉我们，中国人存钱主要是为了子女学习") means that most people save all their money for their children.

Section I—Part B: Reading

31. **(C)** The sign says, "Do not talk loudly indoors," which eliminates (B) and (D). It is not likely that such a sign would appear in (A), a department store, so (C) is the most logical answer.

Model Exam 1

32. **(A)** Choices (B) and (D) have no relevance to the sign. (C) is wrong because the sign has to do with noise but not with music in particular.

33. **(C)** The story talks about Han Yu and his brother's son (his nephew). (A) is wrong because his older brother died at the age of 42, and after that, his sister-in-law (B) and brother's family (D) are never mentioned again.

34. **(B)** The correct answer is directly stated in the story.

35. **(A)** The correct answer is directly stated in the story.

36. **(B)** The sentence "韓愈的哥哥在四十二歲的時候得了一場大病，不久就死了" ("韩愈的哥哥在四十二岁的时候得了一场大病，不久就死了") indicates that his brother died from an illness, which is (B). There were 12 children in his extended family, but not all of those were necessarily his own, so (A) is wrong. The story says, "韓愈和十二郎相依爲命" ("韩愈和十二郎相依为命"), which means that Han Yu had a very close relationship with his nephew, which makes (C) wrong. Han Yu left his hometown when he was nineteen, so (D) is also wrong.

37. **(D)** The correct answer is directly stated in the story.

38. **(B)** The advertisement directly states, "Smokers are not allowed." The article states that females are preferred, but that doesn't necessarily mean that men are not allowed. Therefore, (D) is not the answer.

39. **(C)** The correct answer is directly stated in the advertisement. (A) is not true. (B) is false because transportation is convenient. (D) is wrong because the apartment has both a dryer and a washer.

40. **(B)** No information about parking is given.

41. **(D)** The correct answer is directly stated in the advertisement.

42. **(C)** "有意者請於早7點以後晚10點以前打電話" ("有意者请于早7点以后晚10点以前打电话") means that (C) is correct.

43. **(C)** The first rule says, "穿運動服裝、運動鞋" ("穿运动服装、运动鞋"), which would only appear in a gym. Logically speaking, such a rule would not apply at a cafeteria, a conference hall, or a restaurant.

44. **(B)** The first line states, "本館爲全校會議、體育教學、比賽活動場地" ("本馆为全校会议、体育教学、比赛活动场地,") which means that (A), (C), and (D) are allowed.

45. **(D)** The third policy, "禁止在館內喧嘩、吸烟或亂丟果皮、紙屑、口香糖等物" ("禁止在馆内喧哗、吸烟或乱丢果皮、纸屑、口香糖等物"), does not mention anything about empty bottles.

46. **(B)** The regulations state, "禁止在館內喧嘩、吸烟或亂丟果皮、紙屑、口香糖等物" ("禁止在馆内喧哗、吸烟或乱丢果皮、纸屑、口香糖等物"). (A) is not mentioned, so it is not true. (C) is wrong because "如有損壞，照價賠償" ("如有损坏，照价赔偿") means that the person will have to pay for the damage, not a fine. (D) is incorrect because "器材使用後放回原處" ("器材使用后放回原处") means that people are free to move the equipment around, but they should put it back in its original spot when they are done.

47. **(B)** The first line states, "本館爲全校會議、體育教學、比賽活動場地" ("本馆为全校会议、体育教学、比赛活动场地"), which is (A). (C) is mentioned in the sentence "器材使用後放回原處" ("器材使用后放回原处"). (D) appears in "進入本館要穿運動服裝、運動鞋" ("进入本馆要穿运动服装、运动鞋").

48. **(C)** The first sentence states, "中國的老年婦女問題是人們討論的重要話題" ("中国的老年妇女问题是人们讨论的重要话题").

49. **(B)** The correct answer is stated in the sentence "60歲以上的老年人口將近1.5億" ("60岁以上的老年人口将近1.5亿"). The adverb "將近" ("将近) means "close."

50. **(A)** The correct answer is directly stated in the sentence "目前在中國，60歲以上的老年人口將近1.5億，占總人數的10%" ("目前在中国，60岁以上的老年人口将近1.5亿，占总人数的10%"). 25% (C) is the estimated percentage of the total population of elderly people in the next 20 to 30 years. (B) and (D) are irrelevant.

51. **(B)** The correct answer is stated in the first sentence of the second paragraph, "女性老人存在的最大問題是貧困問題" ("女性老人存在的最大问题是贫困问题").

52. **(C)** The text states the problems, "退休金問題" ("退休金问题"), "42%的老人的丈夫死亡," and "女性老人的家務繁重" ("女性老人的家务繁重")，which are (A), (B), and (D).

53. **(D)** The correct answer is directly stated in the passage. (A) is wrong because "60歲以上的老年人口將近1.5億，占總人數的10%" ("60岁以上的老年人口將近1.5亿，占总人数的10%") includes both women and men, not just women. (B) is not true. (C) only applies to elderly women, not everyone.

54. **(B)** These sentences indicate that the passage is about sports and confidence: "體育除了可以鍛煉身體以外，還能培養人的自信心，鼓勵人們迎接挑戰" ("体育除了可以锻炼身体以外，还能培养人的自信心，鼓励人们迎接挑战") and "爲的是培養孩子的自信心" ("为的是培养孩子的自信心").

55. **(A)** The phrases "在美國的大學裏" ("在美国的大学里"), "在同學中" ("在同學中"), "從中國大陸或臺灣來的很多學生" ("从中国大陆或台湾来的很多学生"), and "中國家庭的學生" ("中国家庭的学生") show that the passage is all about students. (B) is too general, and (C) and (D) are only examples, not the main idea.

56. **(B)** The passage states, "在同學中，有一項出色的體育技能是很讓人羨慕的" ("在同学中，有一项出色的体育技能是很让人羡慕的"). (A) is not true. The passage states that "在美國的大學裏，學習好、品德好、體育成績好的學生很多" ("在美国的大学里，学习好、品德好、体育成绩好的学生很多"). (C) is incorrect because "孩子們的家庭體育教練也常常是由家長當的" ("孩子们的家庭体育教练也常常是由家长当的") means that parents often coach their kids themselves, not that they hire coaches. (D) is wrong because "美國的很多家長鼓勵自己的孩子從小參加學校和社區的足球隊、排球隊和籃球隊等什麼的" ("美国的很多家长鼓励自己的孩子从小参加学校和社区的足球队、排球队和篮球队等什么的") means that parents in general often want their kids to participate in sports, not parents with sports-related occupations specifically.

57. **(D)** The passage states that "從中國大陸或台灣來的很多學生，雖然學習名列前茅，但是他們在體育、創造性、社交等方面往往感到信心不够" ("从中国大陆或台湾来的很多学生，虽然学习名列前茅，但是他们在体育、创造性、社交等方面往往感到信心不够"), which means that, while Chinese students are good at studying, they do not excel at other subjects.

58. **(C)** "這並不奇怪" ("这并不奇怪") means "not surprising."

59. **(C)** The phrase "還需要時間" ("还需要时间") means that this problem cannot be solved in a short amount of time. (A) and (B) are the opposite of what the author is trying to say. (D) has nothing to do with time.

60. **(B)** The correct answer can be found in these two sentences: "你來信說想申請'漢語橋獎學金'的事情" ("你来信说想申请'汉语桥奖学金'的事情") and "以上信息希望對你有幫助" ("以上信息希望对你有帮助").

61. **(A)** The e-mail never mentions where one should mail his or her application.

62. **(B)** One can only apply for this scholarship if he or she has already won a competition: "'漢語橋獎學金'的申請人應該是在'漢語橋世界大學生中文比賽'中取得好成績的學生" ("'汉语桥奖学金'的申请人应该是在'汉语桥世界大学生中文比赛'中取得好成绩的学生").

63. **(A)** As directly stated in the e-mail, "漢語橋世界大學生中文比賽決賽的3個一等獎的學生可以申請'漢語橋學位獎學金'" ("汉语桥世界大学生中文比赛决赛的3个一等奖的学生可以申请'汉语桥学位奖学金'").

64. **(C)** The correct answer is directly stated in the e-mail.

65. **(D)** Nowhere in the e-mail is anything about a degree certificate mentioned. (A), (B), and (C) are all mentioned.

66. **(D)** The e-mail states: "申請人所交的材料都不退還" ("申请人所交的材料都不退还"), which means that the documents will not be returned. (A) is wrong because the e-mail doesn't mention anything about online applications. (B) is wrong because the writer of the e-mail asked for copies, not originals. (C) is wrong because applications can only be sent during registration times.

SCRIPTS

(Narrator) Model Exam 1. Section I–Part A: Listening Comprehension. Conversations 1 through 15.

You will hear several short conversations. Each conversation will be played once along with four choices of response (A), (B), (C), and (D). You will have 5 seconds to choose a response that completes the conversation in a logical and culturally appropriate way.

Conversation 1

[Traditional-character version]

(Woman)	你是從哪個城市來的？
(Man)	我是從紐約來的。你呢？
(Woman)	(A) 什麼？你沒去過紐約？
	(B) 我哪兒都想去。
	(C) 我可不想去那兒。
	(D) 我也是從那兒來的。

[Simplified-character version]

(Woman)	你是从哪个城市来的？
(Man)	我是从纽约来的。你呢？
(Woman)	(A) 什么？你没去过纽约？
	(B) 我哪儿都想去。
	(C) 我可不想去那儿。
	(D) 我也是从那儿来的。

Conversation 2

[Traditional-character version]

(Man)	我妹妹要過生日了，你說我送她什麼禮物？
(Woman)	她正在上大學，是吧？送她電腦比較有用。
(Man)	(A) 好，我就送她上大學。
	(B) 你說得對，電腦都很貴。
	(C) 電腦太貴了，我沒有那麼多錢。
	(D) 我妹妹是在上大學。

[Simplified-character version]

(Man)	我妹妹要过生日了，你说我送她什么礼物？
(Woman)	她正在上大学，是吧？ 送她电脑比较有用。
(Man)	(A) 好，我就送她上大学。
	(B) 你说得对，电脑都很贵。
	(C) 电脑太贵了，我没有那么多钱。
	(D) 我妹妹是在上大学。

Conversation 3

[Traditional-character version]

(Woman)	咱們去看場電影吧。
(Man)	有什麼好看的。
(Woman)	(A) 你覺得哪部電影好看？
	(B) 最近上演了不少好電影呀。
	(C) 我也不知道哪部電影好看。
	(D) 你也喜歡看電影嗎？

[Simplified-character version]

(Woman)	咱们去看场电影吧。
(Man)	有什么好看的。
(Woman)	(A) 你觉得哪部电影好看？
	(B) 最近上演了不少好电影呀。
	(C) 我也不知道哪部电影好看。
	(D) 你也喜欢看电影吗？

Conversation 4

[Traditional-character version]

(Man)	我這個人一看起書來就什麼都忘了。
(Woman)	(A) 你忘了看什麼？
	(B) 你爲什麼忘了看書？
	(C) 你看書看得太專心了。
	(D) 你能記住什麼？

[Simplified-character version]

(Man)	我这个人一看起书来就什么都忘了。
(Woman)	(A) 你忘了看什么？
	(B) 你为什么忘了看书？
	(C) 你看书看得太专心了。
	(D) 你能记住什么？

Conversation 5

[Traditional-character version]

(Woman)	對不起，家裏有點兒事，來晚了。
(Man)	(A) 我到了很長時間了。
	(B) 沒關係，我也剛到一會兒。
	(C) 不好意思，打擾你了。
	(D) 你怎麼來晚了。

[Simplified-character version]

(Woman)　　对不起，家里有点儿事，来晚了。
(Man)　　　(A) 我到了很长时间了。
　　　　　　(B) 没关系，我也刚到一会儿。
　　　　　　(C) 不好意思，打扰你了。
　　　　　　(D) 你怎么来晚了。

Conversation 6

[Traditional-character version]

(Woman)　　你怎麼一個人回來了？你弟弟呢？
(Man)　　　(A) 我跟我弟弟去看了一場球賽。
　　　　　　(B) 我回來了，他沒回來。
　　　　　　(C) 我弟弟找朋友踢球去了。
　　　　　　(D) 我弟弟看球賽的時候大喊大叫。

[Simplified-character version]

(Woman)　　你怎么一个人回来了？ 你弟弟呢？
(Man)　　　(A) 我跟我弟弟去看了一场球赛。
　　　　　　(B) 我回来了，他没回来。
　　　　　　(C) 我弟弟找朋友踢球去了。
　　　　　　(D) 我弟弟看球赛的时候大喊大叫。

Conversation 7

[Traditional-character version]

(Woman)　　你覺得那位教授怎麼樣？
(Man)　　　(A) 他在這所大學工作快二十年了。
　　　　　　(B) 他對學生非常負責。
　　　　　　(C) 我去年秋季學期選了他的課。
　　　　　　(D) 他每天都有課。

[Simplified-character version]

(Woman)　　你觉得那位教授怎麼样？
(Man)　　　(A) 他在这所大学工作快二十年了。
　　　　　　(B) 他对学生非常负责。
　　　　　　(C) 我去年秋季学期选了他的课。
　　　　　　(D) 他每天都有课。

Conversation 8

[Traditional-character version]

(Woman)	那位穿裙子的老師教你們什麼？
(Man)	(A) 她叫張小雲。
	(B) 她教二年級。
	(C) 她教中文。
	(D) 我們都叫她"張老師"。

[Simplified-character version]

(Woman)	那位穿裙子的老师教你们什么？
(Man)	(A) 她叫张小云。
	(B) 她教二年级。
	(C) 她教中文。
	(D) 我们都叫她"张老师"。

Conversation 9

[Traditional-character version]

(Man)	現在走哪條高速公路都堵車。
(Woman)	那就要看你什麼時候走高速公路了。
(Man)	(A) 在高速公路上可以開快車。
	(B) 我覺得什麼時候都堵車。
	(C) 我經常在高速公路上開車。
	(D) 我不喜歡開車。

[Simplified-character version]

(Man)	现在走哪条高速公路都堵车。
(Woman)	那就要看你什么时候走高速公路了。
(Man)	(A) 在高速公路上可以开快车。
	(B) 我觉得什么时候都堵车。
	(C) 我经常在高速公路上开车。
	(D) 我不喜欢开车。

Conversation 10

[Traditional-character version]

(Woman)	我下星期要去紐約。一是爲了出差，二是可以順便看看我住在紐約的姑媽。
(Man)	(A) 你去紐約做什麼？
	(B) 你去哪兒出差？
	(C) 你姑媽做什麼工作？
	(D) 你姑媽住在哪兒？

[Simplified-character version]

(Woman)　　我下星期要去纽约。一是为了出差，二是可以顺便看看我住在纽
　　　　　　约的姑妈。

(Man)　　　(A) 你去纽约做什么？
　　　　　　(B) 你去哪儿出差？
　　　　　　(C) 你姑妈做什么工作？
　　　　　　(D) 你姑妈住在哪儿？

Conversation 11

[Traditional-character version]

(Man)　　　你能告訴我電影院怎麼走嗎？
(Woman)　　(A) 那個電影院大不大？
　　　　　　(B) 從這兒一直走，到了第一個路口向左拐就到了。
　　　　　　(C) 你去電影院做什麼？
　　　　　　(D) 對不起，怎麼去電影院？

[Simplified-character version]

(Man)　　　你能告诉我电影院怎么走吗？
(Woman)　　(A) 那个电影院大不大？
　　　　　　(B) 从这儿一直走，到了第一个路口向左拐就到了。
　　　　　　(C) 你去电影院做什么？
　　　　　　(D) 对不起，怎么去电影院？

Conversation 12

[Traditional-character version]

(Woman)　　你這學期選了幾門課？
(Man)　　　我選了三門，其中一門是物理。你呢？
(Woman)　　(A) 我也沒選中文課。
　　　　　　(B) 我比你多選了一門。
　　　　　　(C) 什麼時候選課？
　　　　　　(D) 聽說物理課很難得A。

[Simplified-character version]

(Woman)　　你这学期选了几门课？
(Man)　　　我选了三门，其中一门是物理。你呢？
(Woman)　　(A) 我也没选中文课。
　　　　　　(B) 我比你多选了一门。
　　　　　　(C) 什么时候选课？
　　　　　　(D) 听说物理课很难得A。

Conversation 13

[Traditional-character version]

(Woman)　我找了好半天，也不知道你說的中國餐館到底在哪兒。
(Man)　(A) 那家中國餐館的飯好吃嗎？
　　　　(B) 那家餐館好找嗎？
　　　　(C) 你找到那家餐館了嗎？
　　　　(D) 那家餐館就在電影院旁邊呀。

[Simplified-character version]

(Woman)　我找了好半天，也不知道你说的中国餐馆到底在哪儿。
(Man)　(A) 那家中国餐馆的饭好吃吗？
　　　　(B) 那家餐馆好找吗？
　　　　(C) 你找到那家餐馆了吗？
　　　　(D) 那家餐馆就在电影院旁边呀。

Conversation 14

[Traditional-character version]

(Man)　　我周末的時候上上網，跟朋友看看電影或者聽聽音樂什麼的。
(Woman)　我也喜歡看電影，不過最近兩個星期太忙，一部電影也沒看。
(Man)　(A) 你喜歡聽什麼音樂？
　　　　(B) 你喜歡看什麼電影？
　　　　(C) 你喜歡聽中國音樂還是美國音樂？
　　　　(D) 你這兩天看了什麼電影？

[Simplified-character version]

(Man)　　我周末的时候上上网，跟朋友看看电影或者听听音乐什么的。
(Woman)　我也喜欢看电影，不过最近两个星期太忙，一部电影也没看。
(Man)　(A) 你喜欢听什么音乐？
　　　　(B) 你喜欢看什么电影？
　　　　(C) 你喜欢听中国音乐还是美国音乐？
　　　　(D) 你这两天看了什么电影？

Conversation 15

[Traditional-character version]

(Woman)　你怎麼了？臉色這麼難看。
(Man)　(A) 我的臉本來就不好看。
　　　　(B) 我的臉本來就是這種顏色。
　　　　(C) 我在太陽下呆的時間太長了。
　　　　(D) 嗯, 考試沒考好。

[Simplified-character version]

(Woman)　你怎么了？脸色这么难看。
(Man)　　(A) 我的脸本来就不好看。
　　　　 (B) 我的脸本来就是这种颜色。
　　　　 (C) 我在太阳下呆的时间太长了。
　　　　 (D) 嗯，考试没考好。

(Narrator) *Model Exam 1*—Section I—Part A: Listening Comprehension-Selections for questions 16 through 30. You will listen to several listening selections. Each selection will be played either once or twice. You may take notes. After each selection, you will have twelve seconds to read the question and choose the most appropriate response (A), (B), (C), or (D) in English from the answer sheet.

Track 76

Listening selection 1. Now you will listen to a voice message twice. First time.

[Traditional-character version]

(Woman)　喂，王力，我是張華。我本來應該中午從紐約直飛洛杉磯,可是在去機場的高速公路上堵車堵了很長時間, 沒趕上飛機, 只好改坐紐約飛往舊金山的航班。我現在在舊金山機場等著坐飛機回洛杉磯。飛機兩個小時以後, 也就是10:10起飛, 飛1小時20分鐘, 到洛杉磯大約是晚上11:30。我想麻煩你到機場接我一趟。你回家聽到留言後請馬上給我打個電話。我的手機號是: 555-555-555。謝謝！

[Simplified-character version]

(Woman)　喂，王力，我是张华。我本来应该中午从纽约直飞洛杉矶,可是在去机场的高速公路上堵车堵了很长时间, 没赶上飞机, 只好改坐纽约飞往旧金山的航班。我现在在旧金山机场等着坐飞机回洛杉矶。飞机两个小时以后, 也就是10:10起飞, 飞1小时20分钟, 到洛杉矶大约是晚上11:30。我想麻烦你到机场接我一趟。你回家听到留言后请马上给我打个电话。我的手机号是: 555-555-555。谢谢！

(Narrator)　Now the second time.
　　　　　 Now answer question 16.
　　　　　 Now answer question 17.
　　　　　 Now answer question 18.
　　　　　 Now answer question 19.

Track 77

(Narrator) Listening Selection 2. Now you will listen to a conversation between two students. Once only.

[Traditional-character version]

(Woman)	怎麼樣，大學的專業你選好了嗎？
(Man)	還沒有。你呢？
(Woman)	不是學醫學就是學文學吧，還沒最後決定。
(Man)	為什麼？
(Woman)	我特別喜歡文學，希望將來當個作家什麼的，可是我父母說，選專業不能只靠興趣，而應該看將來好不好找工作，能不能賺錢。他們希望我念醫學院。我最不喜歡當醫生了，整天跟病人打交道，多沒意思呀！再說，當醫生也太累了。
(Man)	我父母跟你父母的想法差不多，他們也反對我學文科。他們說什麼學文科以後找不著好工作。我喜歡歷史，以後當個歷史老師，可我父母非讓我學工程技術或電腦不可。

[Simplified-character version]

(Woman)	怎么样，大学的专业你选好了吗？
(Man)	还没有。你呢？
(Woman)	不是学医学就是学文学吧，还没最后决定。
(Man)	为什么？
(Woman)	我特别喜欢文学，希望将来当个作家什么的，可是我父母说，选专业不能只靠兴趣，而应该看将来好不好找工作，能不能赚钱。他们希望我念医学院。我最不喜欢当医生了，整天跟病人打交道，多没意思呀！再说，当医生也太累了。
(Man)	我父母跟你父母的想法差不多，他们也反对我学文科。他们说什么学文科以后找不着好工作。我喜欢历史，以后当个历史老师，可我父母非让我学工程技术或电脑不可。

(Narrator)	Now answer question 20.
	Now answer question 21.
	Now answer question 22.
	Now answer question 23.

Track 78

(Narrator) Listening Selection 3. Now you will listen to an announcement twice. First time.

[Traditional-character version]

(Woman)	各位考生: 漢語水平考試 (HSK) 將在2007年5月20日舉行，請同學們在規定的時間內報名。 1. 報名時間：2月19日至3月2日 2. 報名地點：教學樓403室 3. 報名要求：1) 到教學辦公室領取報名表格; 2) 報名時請帶本人學生證、身份證; 3) 每位考生報名時需交近期照片一張; 4) 每位考生需交報名費40元; 5) 不接受外校考生報名。

[Simplified-character version]

(Woman)　　　各位考生：汉语水平考试 (HSK) 将在2007年5月20日举行，请同
　　　　　　　学们在规定的时间内报名。
　　　　　　　1. 报名时间：2月19日至3月2日
　　　　　　　2. 报名地点：教学楼403室
　　　　　　　3. 报名要求：1) 到教学办公室领取报名表格; 2) 报名时请带本人
　　　　　　　学生证、身份证; 3) 每位考生报名时需交近期照片一张; 4) 每
　　　　　　　位考生需交报名费40元; 5) 不接受外校考生报名。

(Narrator)　　　Now the second time.
　　　　　　　Now answer question 24.
　　　　　　　Now answer question 25.
　　　　　　　Now answer question 26.
　　　　　　　Now answer question 27.

(Narrator) Listening Selection 4. Now you will listen to a report twice. First
time.

Track 79

[Traditional-character version]

(Woman)　　　上海的一位社會學家統計：在上海，培養一個孩子從出生到成年
　　　　　　　一共要49萬元。最近的另一份報告也說明，中國家庭用在子女教
　　　　　　　育方面的錢最多，超過了養老和住房。中國銀行的調查結果也告
　　　　　　　訴我們，中國人存錢主要是爲了子女學習。

[Simplified-character version]

(Woman)　　　上海的一位社会学家统计：在上海，培养一个孩子从出生到成年
　　　　　　　一共要49万元。最近的另一份报告也说明，中国家庭用在子女教
　　　　　　　育方面的钱最多，超过了养老和住房。中国银行的调查结果也告
　　　　　　　诉我们，中国人存钱主要是为了子女学习。

(Narrator)　　　Now the second time.
　　　　　　　Now answer question 28.
　　　　　　　Now answer question 29.
　　　　　　　Now answer question 30.

(Narrator) Model Exam 1 Section II–Part B: Speaking, *Conversation*

You will have a conversation with Li Ping, an interviewer, about your application for a High School Study Abroad Program in China. She will ask you six questions. After each question, you will have 20 seconds to respond. Respond as fully and as appropriately as possible.

1. 你好，我是李平。你是怎麼知道這個項目的？
   你好，我是李平。你是怎么知道这个项目的？

2. 如果申請到了，你打算去哪個城市？哪一所中學？
   如果申请到了，你打算去哪个城市？哪一所中学？

3. 你準備在中國的學校選什麼課程？
   你准备在中国的学校选什么课程？

4. 你今後會不會申請中國的大學？
   你今后会不会申请中国的大学？

5. 這個項目要求在中國留學期間要當志願者，對此你有什麼打算？
   这个项目要求在中国留学期间要当志愿者，对此你有什么打算？

6. 關於這個項目，你還有什麼問題嗎？
   关于这个项目，你还有什么问题吗？

Model Exam 2
ANSWER SHEET

Section I–Part A: Multiple Choice (Listening)

1 Ⓐ Ⓑ Ⓒ Ⓓ	9 Ⓐ Ⓑ Ⓒ Ⓓ	17 Ⓐ Ⓑ Ⓒ Ⓓ	25 Ⓐ Ⓑ Ⓒ Ⓓ
2 Ⓐ Ⓑ Ⓒ Ⓓ	10 Ⓐ Ⓑ Ⓒ Ⓓ	18 Ⓐ Ⓑ Ⓒ Ⓓ	26 Ⓐ Ⓑ Ⓒ Ⓓ
3 Ⓐ Ⓑ Ⓒ Ⓓ	11 Ⓐ Ⓑ Ⓒ Ⓓ	19 Ⓐ Ⓑ Ⓒ Ⓓ	27 Ⓐ Ⓑ Ⓒ Ⓓ
4 Ⓐ Ⓑ Ⓒ Ⓓ	12 Ⓐ Ⓑ Ⓒ Ⓓ	20 Ⓐ Ⓑ Ⓒ Ⓓ	28 Ⓐ Ⓑ Ⓒ Ⓓ
5 Ⓐ Ⓑ Ⓒ Ⓓ	13 Ⓐ Ⓑ Ⓒ Ⓓ	21 Ⓐ Ⓑ Ⓒ Ⓓ	29 Ⓐ Ⓑ Ⓒ Ⓓ
6 Ⓐ Ⓑ Ⓒ Ⓓ	14 Ⓐ Ⓑ Ⓒ Ⓓ	22 Ⓐ Ⓑ Ⓒ Ⓓ	30 Ⓐ Ⓑ Ⓒ Ⓓ
7 Ⓐ Ⓑ Ⓒ Ⓓ	15 Ⓐ Ⓑ Ⓒ Ⓓ	23 Ⓐ Ⓑ Ⓒ Ⓓ	
8 Ⓐ Ⓑ Ⓒ Ⓓ	16 Ⓐ Ⓑ Ⓒ Ⓓ	24 Ⓐ Ⓑ Ⓒ Ⓓ	

Section I–Part B: Multiple Choice (Reading)

31 Ⓐ Ⓑ Ⓒ Ⓓ	40 Ⓐ Ⓑ Ⓒ Ⓓ	49 Ⓐ Ⓑ Ⓒ Ⓓ	58 Ⓐ Ⓑ Ⓒ Ⓓ
32 Ⓐ Ⓑ Ⓒ Ⓓ	41 Ⓐ Ⓑ Ⓒ Ⓓ	50 Ⓐ Ⓑ Ⓒ Ⓓ	59 Ⓐ Ⓑ Ⓒ Ⓓ
33 Ⓐ Ⓑ Ⓒ Ⓓ	42 Ⓐ Ⓑ Ⓒ Ⓓ	51 Ⓐ Ⓑ Ⓒ Ⓓ	60 Ⓐ Ⓑ Ⓒ Ⓓ
34 Ⓐ Ⓑ Ⓒ Ⓓ	43 Ⓐ Ⓑ Ⓒ Ⓓ	52 Ⓐ Ⓑ Ⓒ Ⓓ	61 Ⓐ Ⓑ Ⓒ Ⓓ
35 Ⓐ Ⓑ Ⓒ Ⓓ	44 Ⓐ Ⓑ Ⓒ Ⓓ	53 Ⓐ Ⓑ Ⓒ Ⓓ	62 Ⓐ Ⓑ Ⓒ Ⓓ
36 Ⓐ Ⓑ Ⓒ Ⓓ	45 Ⓐ Ⓑ Ⓒ Ⓓ	54 Ⓐ Ⓑ Ⓒ Ⓓ	63 Ⓐ Ⓑ Ⓒ Ⓓ
37 Ⓐ Ⓑ Ⓒ Ⓓ	46 Ⓐ Ⓑ Ⓒ Ⓓ	55 Ⓐ Ⓑ Ⓒ Ⓓ	64 Ⓐ Ⓑ Ⓒ Ⓓ
38 Ⓐ Ⓑ Ⓒ Ⓓ	47 Ⓐ Ⓑ Ⓒ Ⓓ	56 Ⓐ Ⓑ Ⓒ Ⓓ	65 Ⓐ Ⓑ Ⓒ Ⓓ
39 Ⓐ Ⓑ Ⓒ Ⓓ	48 Ⓐ Ⓑ Ⓒ Ⓓ	57 Ⓐ Ⓑ Ⓒ Ⓓ	66 Ⓐ Ⓑ Ⓒ Ⓓ

Model Exam 2

Model Exam 2

CHAPTER 9

SECTION I—PART A: LISTENING COMPREHENSION

Conversations 1 through 15.
Time–Approximately 20 minutes

Track
81

You will hear several short conversations. Each conversation will be played once along with four choices of response (A), (B), (C), and (D). You will have 5 seconds to choose a response that completes the conversation in a logical and culturally appropriate way.

Model Exam II
SECTION I—PART A: LISTENING COMPREHENSION

Selections for questions 16–30.

> You will listen to several listening selections. Each selection will be played either once or twice. You may take notes. After each selection, you will have twelve seconds to read the question and choose the most appropriate response (A), (B), (C), or (D) in English from the answer sheet.

16. What is the purpose of the message?

    (A) To notify the receiver that there will be a presentation
    (B) To discuss issues in society with the receiver
    (C) To plan to go to class together
    (D) To introduce a famous professor

17. What is the topic of the presentation?

    (A) Development of society
    (B) Family education
    (C) Discipline
    (D) Scientific development

18. When will the presentation begin?

    (A) 3:30
    (B) 2:10
    (C) 3:10
    (D) 4:00

19. What is the relationship between the man and the woman?

    (A) Friends
    (B) Classmates
    (C) Roommates
    (D) No relation

20. Where might Wang Qiang be right now?

    (A) In a library
    (B) In class
    (C) At his dorm
    (D) At home

Model Exam 2

21. What does the woman plan on doing?

    (A) Going home
    (B) Going to the library to look for Wang Qiang
    (C) Waiting for him at his dorm
    (D) Calling Wang Qiang

22. What is the purpose of the announcement?

    (A) To announce the flight times
    (B) To announce a delayed flight
    (C) To announce a canceled flight
    (D) To inform people of the weather

23. Where is it snowing?

    (A) Nowhere
    (B) Beijing
    (C) Xinjiang
    (D) Lanzhou

24. What time should the plane take off according to the schedule change?

    (A) 15:50
    (B) 17:50
    (C) 18:00
    (D) 20:00

25. What is the flight number?

    (A) 2371
    (B) 1732
    (C) 2337
    (D) 7123

26. Where might this report most likely appear?

    (A) On the radio
    (B) On TV
    (C) In a newspaper
    (D) In a magazine

27. Which of the following is not mentioned in the report?

    (A) People love Taijiquan.
    (B) There are many Taijiquan schools.
    (C) Taijiquan has a long history.
    (D) There is Taijiquan all over the world.

28. What kind of a person is Mr. Chen?

    (A) Someone who loves Taijiquan
    (B) A professional Taijiquan coach
    (C) Someone who enjoys watching Taijiquan
    (D) A person who is about to retire

29. When does he go to the park?

    (A) Every day
    (B) Three mornings a week
    (C) Every Thursday and Tuesday
    (D) Every Saturday

30. Which statement is false?

    (A) There is no way to calculate how many people do Taijiquan.
    (B) Mr. Chen has been doing Taijiquan for 20 years.
    (C) Taijiquan is very important to Mr. Chen.
    (D) Mr. Chen is happy to watch people do Taijiquan.

END OF PART A

SECTION I—PART B: READING COMPREHENSION

Time–Approximately 60 minutes

> **Directions:** For each reading selection, answer the accompanying questions by choosing the best response.

Sign for questions 31 and 32.

[Traditional-character version]

車輛啓動，請勿與司機交談。

[Simplified-character version]

车辆启动，请勿与司机交谈。

31. Where would the sign most likely appear?

   (A) In a car
   (B) On a bus
   (C) On a train
   (D) On an airplane

32. What is the purpose of the sign?

   (A) To prohibit people from driving cars
   (B) To prohibit people from using cell phones
   (C) To inform people about public transportation
   (D) To prevent people from disrupting the driver

Note for questions 33 through 37.

[Traditional-character version]

老王：

　　我剛接到張麗的電話，說她感覺很不好，得去看醫生，可是她丈夫出差不在家，我得送她去醫院，她還讓我幫她去幼稚園接兒子。我得趕快去醫院了。你下班回來後把晚飯做了，吃完飯，別讓女兒看電視，叫她趕快寫作業。我什麼時候回來還不知道，到時候再給你打電話。要是她的病很嚴重，我今晚就住在她家照顧她。

[Simplified-character version]

老王：

　　我刚接到张丽的电话，说她感觉很不好，得去看医生，可是她丈夫出差不在家，我得送她去医院，她还让我帮她去幼稚园接儿子。我得赶快去医院了。你下班回来后把晚饭做了，吃完饭，别让女儿看电视，叫她赶快写作业。我什么时候回来还不知道，到时候再给你打电话。要是她的病很严重，我今晚就住在她家照顾她。

33. What is the main purpose of this note?

    (A) To tell someone the reason for not being at home
    (B) To tell someone that there is a sick person
    (C) To tell someone that their child watches too much television
    (D) To discuss what should be eaten for dinner

34. What is the relationship between the writer of the note and the receiver?

    (A) The writer of the note is a father and the receiver is a daughter.
    (B) The writer of the note is a father and the receiver is a son.
    (C) The writer of the note and the receiver of the note are good friends.
    (D) The writer of the note is a wife and the receiver is her husband.

35. Who is sick?

    (A) Zhang Li
    (B) Zhang Li's husband
    (C) The son
    (D) The daughter

36. What might the writer be doing right now?

    (A) The writer is on a business trip.
    (B) The writer is watching television.
    (C) The writer is at the hospital.
    (D) The writer is at his or her workplace.

37. What should the receiver do?

    (A) The receiver should cook dinner for the family.
    (B) The receiver should go to the hospital.
    (C) The receiver should go to the kindergarten.
    (D) The receiver should do homework.

Story for questions 38 through 43.

[Traditional-character version]

　　蘇東坡是中國古代著名的詩人、散文家和書法家，還是一位受老百姓歡迎的政治家。

　　蘇東坡在杭州做官的時候，帶領民工治理了西湖，爲老百姓做了一件好事。爲了感謝蘇東坡，到過年的時候，老百姓帶著豬肉和酒來給他拜年。蘇東坡叫人把肉切成方塊，燒得紅紅的，然後給那些民工家送去。大家很高興，就把他送來的豬肉叫"東坡肉"。杭州有一家飯館，老闆是一個非常聰明的人。他看人們都說蘇東坡好，就讓廚師把豬肉也切成方塊，做成紅燒肉，也叫"東坡肉"。從此以後，那家飯館的生意特別好。別的飯館的老闆也看到這是一道可以賺錢的菜，於是，都學著做起來。從此，杭州的飯館，家家都賣"東坡肉"。

Model Exam 2

[Simplified-character version]

　　苏东坡是中国古代著名的诗人、散文家和书法家，还是一位受老百姓欢迎的政治家。

　　苏东坡在杭州做官的时候，带领民工治理了西湖，为老百姓做了一件好事。为了感谢苏东坡，到过年的时候，老百姓带着猪肉和酒来给他拜年。苏东坡叫人把肉切成方块，烧得红红的，然后给那些民工家送去。大家很高兴，就把他送来的猪肉叫 "东坡肉"。杭州有一家饭馆，老板是一个非常聪明的人。他看人们都说苏东坡好，就让厨师把猪肉也切成方块，做成红烧肉，也叫"东坡肉"。从此以后，那家饭馆的生意特别好。别的饭馆的老板也看到这是一道可以赚钱的菜，于是，都学着做起来。从此，杭州的饭馆，家家都卖 "东坡肉"。

38. What is the story mainly about?

    (A) A recipe for a certain dish
    (B) The place where this dish is sold
    (C) The related person of a dish
    (D) The history of the dish

39. Which was not one of Su Dongpo's occupations?

    (A) Politician
    (B) Prose writer
    (C) Chef
    (D) Calligrapher

40. Why did people give Su Dongpo so much pork?

    (A) He is a politician that the common people liked.
    (B) Everybody knew that he enjoyed pork.
    (C) Delivering someone pork is a traditional Chinese New Year custom.
    (D) He needed pork.

41. Who named this dish?

    (A) Su Dongpo named the dish himself.
    (B) The owner of the restaurant named the dish.
    (C) The chef of the restaurant named the dish.
    (D) The public named the dish.

42. Why did the owner of the restaurant decide to include this dish as part of his menu?

    (A) Because he thought Su Dongpo was a good politician, too
    (B) Because this dish was very popular
    (C) Because this dish could earn the restaurant a lot of money
    (D) Because this dish was easy to make

Model Exam 2

43. Which statement is true?

    (A) The workers gave Su Dongpo this dish as a treat.
    (B) The owner gave Su Dongpo this dish as a gift.
    (C) The owner of the restaurant is very smart.
    (D) Many restaurants in China sell this dish.

Article for questions 44 through 49.

[Traditional-character version]

　　冰心，1900年出生在福建，是中國有名的小說家、散文家和詩人。冰心出生7個月以後，全家搬到上海。1905年，又搬到山東。從那以後，他們生活在大海旁邊很長時間。冰心的父親還辦過一所海軍學校。1923年，冰心到美國留學。在美國，她的代表作散文集《寄小讀者》出版了。

　　冰心只是她的筆名，真正的名字是謝婉瑩。1919年，她發表第一篇小說時用了"冰心"這個筆名。她說，當時她不想讓同學們知道文章是她寫的，所以用了筆名。爲什麽叫"冰心"呢？因爲這兩個字筆劃少，容易寫，又跟她的名字中"瑩"的意思相同，所以取了"冰心"這個筆名。

[Simplified-character version]

　　冰心，1900年出生在福建，是中国有名的小说家、散文家和诗人。冰心出生7个月以后，全家搬到上海。1905年，又搬到山东。从那以后，他们生活在大海旁边很长时间。冰心的父亲还办过一所海军学校。1923年，冰心到美国留学。在美国，她的代表作散文集《寄小读者》出版了。

　　冰心只是她的笔名，真正的名字是谢婉莹。1919年，她发表第一篇小说时用了"冰心"这个笔名。她说，当时她不想让同学们知道文章是她写的，所以用了笔名。为什么叫"冰心"呢？因为这两个字笔划少，容易写，又跟她的名字中"莹"的意思相同，所以取了"冰心"这个笔名。

44. Which identity is not related to Bing Xin?

    (A) Novelist
    (B) Screenwriter
    (C) Prose writer
    (D) Poet

45. Where was Bing Xin at the age of three?

    (A) Bin Xin was in Fujian when she was three years old.
    (B) Bin Xin was in Shanghai with her family at the age of three.
    (C) Bin Xin lived in Shandong when she was three years old.
    (D) Bin Xin came to America with her father at the age of three.

46. When did she publish her first work?

    (A) She published her first work in 1900.
    (B) She published her first work in 1904, when she lived in Shanghai.
    (C) She published her first work under a pen name in 1919.
    (D) She published her first work in 1923, while she was in America.

47. Why does Bing Xin use a pen name?

    (A) She wants to become a famous writer.
    (B) She doesn't want her classmates to know that she wrote the article.
    (C) She doesn't like her real name.
    (D) Her father wanted her to use a pen name.

48. Why did she choose Bing Xin as her pen name?

    (A) It has many strokes.
    (B) It sounds nice.
    (C) It has a better meaning than her real name.
    (D) It is easy to write.

49. Which statement is correct?

    (A) Her most famous work is a novel.
    (B) She started a school.
    (C) When she was seven months old, her family moved to Shandong.
    (D) She lived next to the ocean for a very long time.

Advertisement for questions 50 through 55.

[Traditional-character version]

　　暑期即將來臨，我成才學校補習班開始招生。補習班現開設小學部、初中部和高中部課程，分別招生80人班、100人班和120人班。

開設課程：小學部開設的課程爲語文、數學和英語課程。初中部開設數學、化學、英語和地理課程。高中部除初中部開設的課程外，還增開生物課。

上課日期：7月5日－8月25日

上課時間：小學部，周二、周四，上午8:30-12:30

　　　　　初中部，每周一、三、四，上午8:30-12:30

　　　　　高中部，每周二、三、五，上午8:30-12:30

報名及上課地點：本市第六中學

報名時間：6月25日至6月30日

[Simplified-character version]

　　暑期即将来临，我成才学校补习班开始招生。补习班现开设小学部、初中部和高中部课程，分别招生80人班、100人班和120人班。

开设课程：小学部开设的课程为语文、数学和英语课程。初中部开设数学、化学、英语和地理课程。高中部除初中部开设的课程外，还增开生物课。

上课日期：7月5日- 8月25日

上课时间：小学部，周二、周四，上午8:30 –12:30

　　　　　初中部，每周一、三、四，上午8:30 –12:30

　　　　　高中部，每周二、三、五，上午8:30-12:30

报名及上课地点：本市第六中学

报名时间：6月25日至6月30日

50. What is this advertisement promoting?

(A) College preparation classes
(B) Adult school
(C) After-school programs
(D) Summer school

51. How many high school students will this program accept?

(A) 80
(B) 100
(C) 120
(D)180

52. Which program offers a Chinese class?

(A) Middle school
(B) Elementary school
(C) High school
(D) None

53. What is the deadline for registration?

(A) June 25
(B) June 30
(C) July 5
(D) August 25

54. Which program offers a biology class?

(A) High school
(B) Middle school
(C) Elementary school
(D) None

Model Exam 2

55. What other information should the advertisement provide?

    (A) The advertisement should inform students of the location.
    (B) The advertisement should tell people the registration fees.
    (C) The time of registration should be provided in the advertisement.
    (D) A class list should be given in the advertisement.

Policies for questions 56 through 60.

[Traditional-character version]

　　一、開放時間 8:30–18:00，周末、節假日不休息。
　　二、票價：每張100元。學生及60歲以上(含60歲)可用學生證或者身份證購買半價票。跟父母一起來的1米以下的兒童、殘疾人、軍人以及記者可免費參觀。
　　三、如下雨、下雪，爲保護文物，本舘不開放。
　　四、請把包、照相機、攝相機等存在寄存處，不得帶入舘內。
　　五、愛護文物，請不要觸摸舘內物品。

[Simplified-character version]

　　一、开放时间 8:30–18:00，周末、节假日不休息。
　　二、票价：每张100元。学生及60岁以上 (含60岁)可用学生证或者身份证购买半价票。跟父母一起来的1米以下的儿童、残疾人、军人以及记者可免费参观。
　　三、如下雨、下雪，为保护文物，本馆不开放。
　　四、请把包、照相机、摄相机等存在寄存处，不得带入馆内。
　　五、爱护文物，请不要触摸馆内物品。

56. What kind of a document might this be?

    (A) A brief history of a museum
    (B) Information about the admission fees
    (C) Information regarding the gift shop at a museum
    (D) Museum policy

57. Who is eligible for a discounted ticket?

    (A) Babies
    (B) Disabled people
    (C) Journalists
    (D) People over 60

58. What do we not know from the document?

    (A) People can't bring their bags into the museum.
    (B) People can't use cell phones in the museum.
    (C) Cameras can't be brought into the museum.
    (D) Video cameras can't be used in the museum.

59. Which statement is correct?

   (A) All tickets cost ¥100.
   (B) The museum is never closed.
   (C) Lockers will be provided for storing personal items.
   (D) The museum is closed during holidays.

60. Which issue is not mentioned?

   (A) Business hours
   (B) Tickets
   (C) Attire
   (D) Prohibited items

Letter for questions 61 through 66.

[Traditional-character version]

斯蒂夫：

　　你好！你信中提到中學生打工問題，關於這個問題，目前中國社會存有兩種完全不同的看法。支持打工的人認爲，中學生打工可以增長知識、培養獨立性、瞭解社會，還能掙一些錢。學習很重要，但是打工積累的經驗更重要。反對中學生打工的人覺得，學生打工一定會影響學習，而且，並不是所有的工作對中學生都有好處。我認爲後一種看法不是沒有道理的。學生的主要任務還是學習。當然，學生也可以參加學校組織的一些志願者活動，像撿垃圾、種樹、幫助殘疾兒童學習等等，這些活動十分安全，在時間安排上也比較合理。斯蒂夫，你同意我的看法嗎？

　　　　　　　　　　　　　　　　　　　　　　　　　　黃　岩
　　　　　　　　　　　　　　　　　　　　　　　　　2013年5月9日

[Simplified-character version]

斯蒂夫：

　　你好！你信中提到中学生打工问题，关于这个问题，目前中国社会存有两种完全不同的看法。支持打工的人认为，中学生打工可以增长知识、培养独立性、了解社会，还能挣一些钱。学习很重要，但是打工积累的经验更重要。反对中学生打工的人觉得，学生打工一定会影响学习，而且，并不是所有的工作对中学生都有好处。我认为后一种看法不是没有道理的。学生的主要任务还是学习。当然，学生也可以参加学校组织的一些志愿者活动，像捡垃圾、种树、帮助残疾儿童学习等等，这些活动十分安全，在时间安排上也比较合理。斯蒂夫，你同意我的看法吗？

　　　　　　　　　　　　　　　　　　　　　　　　　　黃　岩
　　　　　　　　　　　　　　　　　　　　　　　　　2013年5月9日

61. How does the general public feel about high school students with part-time jobs?

    (A) Everyone has the same opinion.
    (B) Everyone's opinions vary.
    (C) There are generally two different opinions.
    (D) No one has the same opinion.

62. What do people who support high school workers think is the most important?

    (A) Education
    (B) Work experience
    (C) Understanding society
    (D) Helping with family

63. Which statement is true?

    (A) Having a part-time job might affect a student's health.
    (B) Students are required to do volunteer work.
    (C) Not all jobs are beneficial for students.
    (D) Schools don't plan events very well.

64. Which is the least likely reason that students take jobs?

    (A) To gain knowledge
    (B) To gain independence
    (C) To meet new people
    (D) To earn money

65. Which volunteer project is not mentioned?

    (A) Planting trees
    (B) Babysitting
    (C) Picking up trash
    (D) Tutoring disabled kids

66. How would you describe the author's attitude toward working students?

    (A) Supportive
    (B) Against
    (C) Unbiased
    (D) Indifferent

END OF SECTION I

SECTION II—PART A: WRITING

Time-Approximately 30 minutes.

> **Directions:** You will produce several written works in Chinese in different formats. You will write specifically for a certain purpose and to a certain person. Your work should be as complete and culturally appropriate as possible.

Story Narration

These pictures present a sequence of events. Write a complete story based on these pictures from beginning to end.

1.

2.

3.

4.

Model Exam 2

E-Mail Response
Read this e-mail from a friend and then type a response.

[Traditional-character version]
發件人：趙大偉
郵件主題：應該住在哪里？

　　我將作爲交換學生到你們學校學習一年。在這一年中，我可以住在學校安排的美國人家裏，也可以跟其他國際學生一起住在學生宿舍裏。你覺得我選哪一個比較好？爲什麼？另外，請你告訴我，住在美國人家裏要注意哪些事情。謝謝你！

[Simplified-character version]
发件人：赵大伟
邮件主题：应该住在哪里？

　　我将作为交换学生到你们学校学习一年。在这一年中，我可以住在学校安排的美国人家里，也可以跟其他国际学生一起住在学生宿舍里。你觉得我选哪一个比较好？为什么？另外，请你告诉我，住在美国人家里要注意哪些事情。谢谢你！

END OF PART A

Track
86

SECTION II—PART B: SPEAKING, CONVERSATION

Time–Approximately 11 minutes

> You will have a conversation with Lin Yue, an interviewer, about traveling in China. She will ask you six questions. After each question, you will have 20 seconds to respond. Respond as fully and as appropriately as possible.

> **Directions:** You will make a presentation in Chinese on a given topic. You will be given 4 minutes to plan your presentation and 2 minutes to record your presentation. Your presentation should be as complete as possible.

Cultural Presentation
There are many famous landmarks in mainland China and in Taiwan. Choose one (The Great Wall, Emperor Qin Shihuang's Tomb, Sun Moon Lake, etc.) to present. In your presentation, describe this landmark and explain its significance.

End of Section II

Model Exam 2
ANSWER KEY

SECTION I—Part A: Multiple Choice (Listening)

1 C	9 D	17 B	25 D
2 D	10 D	18 A	26 A
3 B	11 C	19 D	27 B
4 D	12 A	20 B	28 A
5 C	13 B	21 A	29 B
6 C	14 C	22 B	30 B
7 D	15 D	23 D	
8 B	16 A	24 C	

Section I—Part B: Multiple Choice (Reading)

31 B	40 A	49 D	58 B
32 D	41 D	50 D	59 C
33 A	42 C	51 C	60 C
34 D	43 C	52 B	61 C
35 A	44 B	53 B	62 B
36 C	45 B	54 A	63 C
37 A	46 C	55 B	64 C
38 D	47 B	56 D	65 B
39 C	48 D	57 D	66 B

ANSWERS AND ANSWER EXPLANATIONS

Section I—Part A: Listening

1. **(C)** This response answers the man's question. (A) and (B) do not answer the question, and (D) implies that the man is not a sophomore, when he is.

2. **(D)** The man tells the woman where his father is and also answers her question at the same time. (A) and (C) are irrelevant to the conversation. (B) was already stated by the woman.

3. **(B)** This is the correct answer because it answers the woman's question. (A), (C), and (D) are not relevant.

4. **(D)** The man says, "No, my mom was mad, so I couldn't go," which answers the woman's question. (A) and (C) are irrelevant. (B) doesn't answer the question.

5. **(C)** This is the correct answer because it answers what the professor teaches. (A), (B), and (D) are irrelevant to what he teaches.

6. **(C)** This is the correct answer because it answers where the bicycle is from. (A), (B), and (D) do not answer the question.

7. **(D)** This is the correct answer because it responds to the woman's question. (A), (B), and (C) are information about the friend; however, they don't answer the question.

8. **(B)** The correct answer explains why they like to watch these movies. The phrase "有什麼好的" ("有什么好的") means that the woman does not like kung fu movies. Therefore, (A) is wrong because it implies that the woman likes them. (C) and (D) are irrelevant.

9. **(D)** The woman says, "I looked for a long time, but I still couldn't find that restaurant you were talking about." In (D), the man says, "It's not that hard to find. It's right next to the movie theater," which is an appropriate response to the woman's statement. (B) and (C) have already been answered by the woman. (A) is wrong because the woman already clearly knows about the restaurant.

10. **(D)** Only (D) is relevant to the woman's trip to China. (A), (B), and (C) have already been answered by the woman's first statement.

Model Exam 2

11. **(C)** This is the appropriate response because the man has not said anything about a bathroom yet, and all the others have already been answered.

12. **(A)** The woman asks the man if he is going to the movies or not, and the man says, "I want to, but I can't, because I haven't finished my homework." (B) doesn't answer the question. (C) and (D) are irrelevant.

13. **(B)** Only (B) answers the man's question. (A) and (C) don't answer the question, and (D) is wrong because it implies that the man did not pick this class, which is not true.

14. **(C)** This answers why the woman's roommate is not here. (A), (B), and (D) do not answer the man's question.

15. **(D)** The man answers that he likes to watch the same sports that she mentioned. (A) and (C) are wrong because the woman's favorite sports are different. (B) is wrong because the man implied that the woman doesn't like volleyball, even though she does.

16. **(A)** "明天下午3:30，學校有一個講座" ("明天下午3:30, 学校有一个讲座") shows that there will be a presentation tomorrow.

17. **(B)** "中國社會家庭中的子女教育" ("中国社会家庭中的子女教育") shows that the main topic of the presentation is family education.

18. **(A)** The phone message directly states that it will begin tomorrow at 3:30.

19. **(D)** The conversation shows that the man did not previously know the woman.

20. **(B)** The man says, "今天星期三，他有課。現在他應該在上課" ("今天星期三，他有课。现在他应该在上课"), which means that Wang Qiang is most likely in class.

21. **(A)** The woman says, "我得回家了，" which shows that she is going to go home. "王强回來以後，請你告訴他給我打個電話" ("王强回来以后，请你告诉他给我打个电话") means that Wang Qiang will call the woman, so (D) is incorrect.

22. **(B)** "由北京飛往蘭州的中國東方航空公司MU7123航班因此推遲起飛時間" ("由北京飞往兰州的中国东方航空公司MU7123航班因此推迟起飞时间") is meant to announce a delayed flight.

23. **(D)** "蘭州地區今日有大雪" ("兰州地区今日有大雪") shows that it is snowing in Lanzhou.

24. **(C)** "現根據蘭州地區的天氣情況，將航班起飛時間改爲18：00，預計到達蘭州的時間爲20：00"("现根据兰州地区的天气情况，将航班起飞时间改为18：00，预计到达兰州的时间为20：00") shows the original times and then states the new takeoff time, which is 18:00.

25. **(D)** The correct answer is directly stated in the announcement.

26. **(A)** "各位聽衆" ("各位听众") shows that there is an audience, so this report is most likely from the radio.

27. **(B)** Nowhere in the report is anything about Taijiquan schools mentioned. (A) is stated in the sentence "太極拳是一種深受中國老百姓和海外朋友普遍歡迎的體育運動" ("太极拳是一种深受中国老百姓和海外朋友普遍欢迎的体育运动"). "太極拳歷史悠久,流傳世界" ("太极拳历史悠久,流传世界") confirms (C) and (D).

28. **(A)** "陳老先生就是這衆多的愛好者中的一位" ("陈老先生就是这众多的爱好者中的一位") shows that Mr. Chen enjoys Taijiquan. (B) is wrong because Mr. Chen is just a "業餘教練" ("业余教练"), not a professional coach. (C) is incorrect because "陳老先生從二十幾歲開始打太極拳，四十多年來，從來沒有停止過" ("陈老先生从二十几岁开始打太极拳，四十多年来，从来没有停止过") shows that Mr. Chen likes to do Taijiquan, not just watch it. (D) is wrong because he has already retired.

29. **(B)** The correct answer is stated in the sentence "每個星期的二、四、六早晨，他都會到中國城附近的公園裏教人們打太極拳" ("每个星期的二、四、六早晨，他都会到中国城附近的公园里教人们打太极拳"), which shows that he goes to the park three times a week in the mornings.

30. **(B)** "從二十幾歲開始打太極拳，四十多年來，從來沒有停止過" ("从二十几岁开始打太极拳，四十多年来，从来没有停止过") means that Mr. Chen started at the age of 20, more than 40 years ago. (A) "不計其數" ("不计其数") means that it is impossible to calculate. (C) is correct because it is stated that "太極拳已經成爲陳老先生生活中不可缺少的一部分"("太极拳已经成为陈老先生生活中不可缺少的一部分"). (D) is true because it is stated that "看到那麼多的人學中國的太極拳，就是再累他也高興" ("看到那么多的人学中国的太极拳，就是再累他也高兴").

Section I—Part B: Reading

31. **(B)** The sign says, "Once the vehicle has started moving, please do not talk to the driver." (C) and (D) are wrong because passengers cannot talk to the conductor or pilot on a train or an airplane. This sign is not appropriate for a car, (A).

32. **(D)** The sign reminds people not to disrupt the driver. (A) is not logical because it has nothing to do with public transportation. (B) is irrelevant. (C) is wrong because the sign does not inform anyone of anything.

33. **(A)** The context implies that a wife is leaving her husband a note, to tell him why she is not home. (B) is the reason why she is not home. "別讓女兒看電視" ("别让女儿看电视") means that their child should not watch television, not that she watches too much, (C). (D) is wrong because the woman never says what he should make for dinner.

34. **(D)** The correct answer is implied by clues like "別讓女兒看電視," ("别让女儿看电视") and "我今晚就住在她家照顧她"("我今晚就住在她家照顾她").

35. **(A)** The correct answer is directly stated in the note.

36. **(C)** "我得送她去醫院" ("我得送她去医院") means "I have to go to the hospital," so the writer is most likely at the hospital.

37. **(A)** The correct answer is stated in "你下班回來後把晚飯做了" ("你下班回来后把晚饭做了."

38. **(D)** is the correct answer. (A), (C), and (B) are all included in (D).

39. **(C)** "蘇東坡叫人把肉切成方塊，燒得紅紅的，然後給那些民工家送去" ("苏东坡叫人把肉切成方块，烧得红红的，然后给那些民工家送去") shows that Su Dongpo asked other people to cook the pork, not that he did it himself. All the other occupations are mentioned directly.

40. **(A)** "爲了感謝蘇東坡" ("为了感谢苏东坡") means that people gave him pork to thank him.

41. **(D)** The correct answer is directly stated in the passage: "大家很高興，就把他送來的豬肉叫'東坡肉'" ("大家很高兴，就把他送来的猪肉叫'东坡肉'").

42. **(C)** "他看人們都說蘇東坡好，就讓廚師把豬肉也切成方塊，做成紅燒肉，也叫'東坡肉'。從此以後，那家飯館的生意特別好" ("他看人们都说苏东坡好，就让厨师把猪肉也切成方块，做成红烧肉，也叫'东坡肉'。从此以后，那家饭馆的生意特别好" means that the dish was very profitable.

43. **(C)** The correct answer is directly stated in the passage. (A) and (B) are wrong because Su Dongpo gave this dish to his workers as a treat. Many restaurants in Hanzhou sell this dish, but it's not sold throughout China, so (D) is not correct.

44. **(B)** The passage never mentions anything about a screenwriter.

45. **(B)** The correct answer is stated in "冰心出生7個月以後，全家搬到上海。1905年，又搬到山東" ("冰心出生7个月以后，全家搬到上海。1905年，又搬到山东").

46. **(C)** The correct answer is directly stated in the passage.

47. **(B)** The correct answer is directly stated in the passage.

48. **(D)** The correct answer is directly stated in the passage.

49. **(D)** The correct answer is directly stated in the passage. (A) is wrong because her most famous work is in prose. (B) is wrong because her father was the one who started a school. (C) is wrong because when she was seven months old she moved to Shanghai, not Shandong.

50. **(D)** "暑期即將來臨" ("暑期即将来临") means that the class will take place in the summer.

51. **(C)** The correct answer is directly stated in the advertisement.

52. **(B)** This is the correct answer, as the advertisement lists a Chinese class.

53. **(B)** The correct answer is directly stated in the advertisement.

54. **(A)** This is the correct answer, as the advertisement states, "還增開生物課" ("还增开生物课").

55. **(B)** The advertisement does not mention anything about fees.

56. **(D)** "開放時間" ("开放时间"), "票價" ("票价"), "本舘不開放" ("本馆不开放"), and "請不要觸摸舘內物品" ("请不要触摸馆内物品") show that this is a museum policy.

57. **(D)** It says in the passage that people over 60 are eligible for a discounted ticket. (A), (B), and (C) are eligible for a free ticket.

58. **(B)** All the other answers are mentioned in item 4.

59. **(C)** "請把包、照相機、攝相機等存在寄存處" ("请把包、照相机、摄相机等存在寄存处") means that lockers will be provided for bags, cameras, and video cameras. (A) is wrong because there are discounted tickets and free tickets for certain people. (B) is wrong because the museum is closed on days with bad weather. (D) is wrong because the museum "周末、節假日不休息" ("周末、节假日不休息").

60. **(C)** All the other issues are mentioned.

61. **(C)** The correct answer is directly stated: "目前中國社會存有兩種完全不同的看法" ("目前中国社会存有两种完全不同的看法").

62. **(B)** "但是打工積累的經驗更重要" ("但是打工积累的经验更重要") shows that work experience is important.

63. **(C)** Not all jobs are beneficial, as stated by "並不是所有的工作對中學生都有好處" ("并不是所有的工作对中学生都有好处"). (A) is wrong because the passage says that a student's schoolwork will be affected, but it says nothing about health. (B) is wrong because students can do volunteer work but are not required to do it. (D) is wrong because it is irrelevant.

64. **(C)** All the other answers are mentioned.

65. **(B)** The passage mentions nothing about babysitting.

66. **(B)** "反對中學生打工的人覺得， … 我認爲後一種看法不是沒有道理的" ("反对中学生打工的人觉得， … 我认为后一种看法不是没有道理的") means that the author agrees with the second opinion, that jobs are not beneficial for students.

SCRIPTS

(Narrator) Model Exam 2. Section I—Part A: Listening Comprehension. Conversations 1 through 15.

You will hear several short conversations. Each conversation will be played once along with four choices of response (A), (B), (C), and (D). You will have 5 seconds to choose a response that completes the conversation in a logical and culturally appropriate way.

Conversation 1

[Traditional-character version]

(Woman)	你是幾年級的學生？
(Man)	我是二年級的學生。你呢？
(Woman)	(A) 我今天的功課不太多。
	(B) 我聽說二年級的課不太難。
	(C) 我也是二年級的學生。
	(D) 我也不是二年級的。

[Simplified-character version]

(Woman)	你是几年级的学生？
(Man)	我是二年级的学生。你呢？
(Woman)	(A) 我今天的功课不太多。
	(B) 我听说二年级的课不太难。
	(C) 我也是二年级的学生。
	(D) 我也不是二年级的。

Conversation 2

[Traditional-character version]

(Woman)	你怎麼一個人回來了？你爸沒去接你嗎？
(Man)	(A) 我爸早晨送我的時候遲到了。
	(B) 我自己回來的。
	(C) 我今天的作業多極了。
	(D) 接了，他把我放下又去買東西了。

[Simplified-character version]

(Woman)	你怎么一个人回来了？你爸没去接你吗？
(Man)	(A) 我爸早晨送我的时候迟到了。
	(B) 我自己回来的。
	(C) 我今天的作业多极了。
	(D) 接了，他把我放下又去买东西了。

Conversation 3

[Traditional-character version]

(Woman) 你媽媽會說中文嗎？

(Man) (A) 我喜歡學中文。

(B) 她會說，可是沒有爸爸說得好。

(C) 中文沒有法文難。

(D) 我們全家人都會說法文。

[Simplified-character version]

(Woman) 你妈妈会说中文吗？

(Man) (A) 我喜欢学中文。

(B) 她会说，可是没有爸爸说得好。

(C) 中文没有法文难。

(D) 我们全家人都会说法文。

Conversation 4

[Traditional-character version]

(Woman) 昨天你看那場電影了嗎？

(Man) (A) 我有一個朋友特別想當電影演員。

(B) 我特別喜歡看電影。

(C) 有些演員演得真的不怎麼樣。

(D) 沒有，因為媽媽生氣了，不讓我去。

[Simplified-character version]

(Woman) 昨天你看那场电影了吗？

(Man) (A) 我有一个朋友特别想当电影演员。

(B) 我特别喜欢看电影。

(C) 有些演员演得真的不怎么样。

(D) 没有，因为妈妈生气了，不让我去。

Conversation 5

[Traditional-character version]

(Woman) 那位個子高高的老師教什麼？

(Man) (A) 那位老師叫趙方。

(B) 那位老師教四年級。

(C) 那位老師教生物。

(D) 我們給他起了個外號，叫"大個子老師"。

[Simplified-character version]

(Woman) 那位个子高高的老师教什么？

(Man) (A) 那位老师叫赵方。

(B) 那位老师教四年级。

(C) 那位老师教生物。

(D) 我们给他起了个外号，叫"大个子老师"。

Conversation 6

[Traditional-character version]

(Man)	這輛自行車是誰給你買的？
(Woman)	(A) 我確實需要一輛自行車。
	(B) 騎自行車可以鍛煉身體。
	(C) 是我男朋友送的生日禮物。
	(D) 我也覺得這輛自行車很漂亮。

[Simplified-character version]

(Man)	这辆自行车是谁给你买的？
(Woman)	(A) 我确实需要一辆自行车。
	(B) 骑自行车可以锻炼身体。
	(C) 是我男朋友送的生日礼物。
	(D) 我也觉得这辆自行车很漂亮。

Conversation 7

[Traditional-character version]

(Woman)	你高中畢業典禮的時候，你朋友會來嗎？
(Man)	(A) 我們是在學校認識的。
	(B) 她想和我讀同一所大學。
	(C) 我們倆同歲。
	(D) 她來不了。

[Simplified-character version]

(Woman)	你高中毕业典礼的时候，你朋友会来吗？
(Man)	(A) 我们是在学校认识的。
	(B) 她想和我读同一所大学。
	(C) 我们俩同岁。
	(D) 她来不了。

Conversation 8

[Traditional-character version]

(Woman)	你們都喜歡看功夫片，打打鬧鬧的，有什麼好的。
(Man)	(A) 我也覺得功夫片挺好的。
	(B) 看這類電影可以放鬆。
	(C) 你說的那個演員我知道，他叫成龍。
	(D) 哪兒演功夫片？

[Simplified-character version]

(Woman)	你们都喜欢看功夫片，打打闹闹的，有什么好的。
(Man)	(A) 我也觉得功夫片挺好的。
	(B) 看这类电影可以放松。
	(C) 你说的那个演员我知道，他叫成龙。
	(D) 哪儿演功夫片？

Conversation 9

[Traditional-character version]

(Woman)　　我找了好半天，也不知道你說的那家飯館在哪兒。
(Man)　　　(A) 你不知道那家飯館嗎？
　　　　　　(B) 那家飯館好找嗎？
　　　　　　(C) 你找到那家飯館了嗎？
　　　　　　(D) 就在電影院的旁邊。

[Simplified-character version]

(Woman)　　我找了好半天，也不知道你说的那家饭馆在哪儿。
(Man)　　　(A) 你不知道那家饭馆吗？
　　　　　　(B) 那家饭馆好找吗？
　　　　　　(C) 你找到那家饭馆了吗？
　　　　　　(D) 就在电影院的旁边。

Conversation 10

[Traditional-character version]

(Woman)　　我這次去中國主要是出差，順便旅遊。
(Man)　　　(A) 你去中國做什麼？
　　　　　　(B) 你去中國旅遊嗎？
　　　　　　(C) 你不想利用出差的機會旅遊嗎？
　　　　　　(D) 你打算什麼時候去？

[Simplified-character version]

(Woman)　　我这次去中国主要是出差，顺便旅游。
(Man)　　　(A) 你去中国做什么？
　　　　　　(B) 你去中国旅游吗？
　　　　　　(C) 你不想利用出差的机会旅游吗？
　　　　　　(D) 你打算什么时候去？

Conversation 11

[Traditional-character version]

(Man)　　　我幫你找的那套公寓，客廳挺大，臥室也不小，環境很安靜，但是不帶家具。
(Woman)　　(A) 臥室大不大？
　　　　　　(B) 有客廳嗎？
　　　　　　(C) 沒有浴室嗎？
　　　　　　(D) 環境怎麼樣？

[Simplified-character version]

(Man)	我帮你找的那套公寓，客厅挺大，卧室也不小，环境很安静，但是不带家具。
(Woman)	(A) 卧室大不大？
	(B) 有客厅吗？
	(C) 没有浴室吗？
	(D) 环境怎么样？

Conversation 12

[Traditional-character version]

(Woman)	你到底去不去看電影了？
(Man)	(A) 想去，可是功課沒做完，去不了。
	(B) 安娜也去呀？
	(C) 你最近怎麼樣？忙不忙？
	(D) 演電影的人都有錢。

[Simplified-character version]

(Woman)	你到底去不去看电影了？
(Man)	(A) 想去，可是功课没做完，去不了。
	(B) 安娜也去呀？
	(C) 你最近怎么样？忙不忙？
	(D) 演电影的人都有钱。

Conversation 13

[Traditional-character version]

(Woman)	你這學期選電腦課了？
(Man)	我選了，還選了生物課。你呢？
(Woman)	(A) 你選了那麼多課。
	(B) 選生物了，電腦課太難，沒選。
	(C) 電腦課難不難？
	(D) 我也沒選生物課。

[Simplified-character version]

(Woman)	你这学期选电脑课了？
(Man)	我选了，还选了生物课。你呢？
(Woman)	(A) 你选了那么多课。
	(B) 选生物了，电脑课太难，没选。
	(C) 电脑课难不难？
	(D) 我也没选生物课。

Conversation 14

[Traditional-character version]

(Woman)   對不起，來晚了。路上車太多了。
(Man)   沒關係，我也剛到一會兒。你同屋沒來嗎？
(Woman)   (A) 我同屋開車比我好。
        (B) 這個地方的交通不太好。
        (C) 我同屋有課，不能來。
        (D) 你來的路上車多不多？

[Simplified-character version]

(Woman)   对不起，来晚了。路上车太多了。
(Man)   没关系，我也刚到一会儿。你同屋没来吗？
(Woman)   (A) 我同屋开车比我好。
        (B) 这个地方的交通不太好。
        (C) 我同屋有课，不能来。
        (D) 你来的路上车多不多?

Conversation 15

[Traditional-character version]

(Man)   你最喜歡看什麼體育比賽？
(Woman)   網球、足球、排球什麼的，我都愛看，不過最喜歡的還是NBA籃球。你呢？
(Man)   (A) 我最喜歡看的也是網球。
        (B) 我也不喜歡看排球比賽。
        (C) 跟你一樣，我也最愛看足球。
        (D) 跟你一樣。

[Simplified-character version]

(Man)   你最喜欢看什么体育比赛？
(Woman)   网球、足球、排球什么的，我都爱看，不过最喜欢的还是NBA篮球。你呢？
(Man)   (A) 我最喜欢看的也是网球。
        (B) 我也不喜欢看排球比赛。
        (C) 跟你一样，我也最爱看足球。
        (D) 跟你一样。

(Narrator) *Model Exam 2*—Section I–PART A Listening Comprehension-Selections for questions 16 through 30. You will listen to several listening selections. Each selection will be played either once or twice. You may take notes. After each selection, you will have twelve seconds to read the question and choose the most appropriate response (A), (B), (C), or (D) in English from the answer sheet.

Listening selection 1. Now you will listen to a telephone message twice. First time.

[Traditional-character version]

(Woman)　　顧全，你好！我是胡平。明天下午3:30，學校有一個講座，題目是 "中國社會家庭中的子女教育"。演講的人是北方大學人類學系一個著名教授，地點在學校主樓三層4101教室。我知道你正在寫這方面的論文，你一定會感興趣的，我也會去聽聽。3:10的時候，我們在主樓門前見面，好嗎？請給我回個電話。

[Simplified-character version]

(Woman)　　顾全，你好！我是胡平。明天下午3:30, 学校有一个讲座，题目是 "中国社会家庭中的子女教育"。演讲的人是北方大学人类学系一个著名教授，地点在学校主楼三层4101教室。我知道你正在写这方面的论文，你一定会感兴趣的,我也会去听听。3:10的时候，我们在主楼门前见面，好吗？请给我回个电话。

(Narrator)　　Now the second time.
　　　　　　　Now answer question 16.
　　　　　　　Now answer question 17.
　　　　　　　Now answer question 18.

(Narrator) Listening Selection 2. Now you will listen to a conversation between a man and a woman once only.

[Traditional-character version]

(Woman)　　請問，王強住在這兒嗎？
(Man)　　　對，他就住在這兒，可是他不在。我是他的同屋，叫建國。
(Woman)　　我是王強的同學，叫李平。王強去哪兒了？
(Man)　　　可能去圖書館了。啊，不對，今天星期三，他有課。現在他應該在上課。
(Woman)　　他幾點回來？
(Man)　　　大概兩個小時以後。你進來等吧。
(Woman)　　我得回家了。王強回來以後，請你告訴他給我打個電話。

[Simplified-character version]

(Woman)	请问，王强住在这儿吗？
(Man)	对，他就住在这儿，可是他不在。我是他的同屋，叫建国。
(Woman)	我是王强的同学，叫李平。王强去哪儿了？
(Man)	可能去图书馆了。啊，不对，今天星期三，他有课。现在他应该在上课。
(Woman)	他几点回来？
(Man)	大概两个小时以后。你进来等吧。
(Woman)	我得回家了。王强回来以后，请你告诉他给我打个电话。

(Narrator)   Now answer question 19.
Now answer question 20.
Now answer question 21.

Track 84

(Narrator) Listening Selection 3. Now you will listen to an announcement twice. First time

[Traditional-character version]

(Woman)   各位旅客請注意，因爲受到新疆冷空氣的影響，蘭州地區今日有大雪。由北京飛往蘭州的中國東方航空公司MU7123航班因此推遲起飛時間。此航班原定15:50從北京起飛，17:50到達蘭州機場，現根據蘭州地區的天氣情況，將航班起飛時間改爲18:00，預計到達蘭州的時間爲20:00。

[Simplified-character version]

(Woman)   各位旅客请注意，因为受到新疆冷空气的影响，兰州地区今日有大雪。由北京飞往兰州的中国东方航空公司MU7123航班因此推迟起飞时间。此航班原定15:50从北京起飞，17:50到达兰州机场，现根据兰州地区的天气情况，将航班起飞时间改为18:00，预计到达兰州的时间为20:00。

(Narrator)   Now the second time.
Now answer question 22.
Now answer question 23.
Now answer question 24.
Now answer question 25.

Report (Questions 26–30)

(Narrator) Listening Selection 4. Now you will listen to a report twice. First time

[Traditional-character version]

(Woman)　各位聽眾，你們好。大家都知道，太極拳是一種深受中國老百姓和海外朋友普遍歡迎的體育運動。太極拳歷史悠久，流傳世界。練習太極拳的人更是不計其數。今天我們要給大家介紹的陳老先生就是這眾多的愛好者中的一位。陳老先生從二十幾歲開始打太極拳，四十多年來，從來沒有停止過，太極拳已經成爲陳老先生生活中不可缺少的一部分。陳老先生不但是太極拳的愛好者，還是一位熱心的業餘教練。退休以後，陳老先生熱心教太極拳。每個星期的二、四、六早晨，他都會到中國城附近的公園裏教人們打太極拳。他說，看到那麼多的人學中國的太極拳，就是再累他也高興。

[Simplified-character version]

(Woman)　各位听众，你们好。大家都知道，太极拳是一种深受中国老百姓和海外朋友普遍欢迎的体育运动。太极拳历史悠久，流传世界。练习太极拳的人更是不计其数。今天我们要给大家介绍的陈老先生就是这众多的爱好者中的一位。陈老先生从二十几岁开始打太极拳，四十多年来，从来没有停止过，太极拳已经成为陈老先生生活中不可缺少的一部分。陈老先生不但是太极拳的爱好者，还是一位热心的业余教练。退休以后，陈老先生热心教太极拳。每个星期的二、四、六早晨，他都会到中国城附近的公园里教人们打太极拳。他说，看到那么多的人学中国的太极拳，就是再累他也高兴。

(Narrator)　Now the second time.
　　　　　　Now answer question 26.
　　　　　　Now answer question 27.
　　　　　　Now answer question 28.
　　　　　　Now answer question 29.
　　　　　　Now answer question 30.

(Narrator) Model Exam 2. Section II—Part B: Speaking, *Conversation*

You will have a conversation with Lin Yue, an interviewer, about traveling in China. She will ask you six questions. After each question, you will have 20 seconds to respond. Respond as fully and as appropriately as possible.

1. 你好，我叫林越。你喜歡旅遊嗎？
   你好，我叫林越。你喜欢旅游吗？

2. 談談你去中國旅遊的計劃。
   谈谈你去中国旅游的计划。

3. 你這次主要去中國的哪些地方旅遊？
   你这次主要去中国的哪些地方旅游？

4. 你爲去中國旅遊安排一個什麼樣的行程？
   你为去中国旅游安排一个什么样的行程？

5. 你打算一個人去還是跟別人一起去？
   你打算一个人去还是跟别人一起去？

6. 去中國旅遊以前，你還需要做哪些準備？
   去中国旅游以前，你还需要做哪些准备？

Success on Advanced Placement Tests Starts with Help from BARRON'S

Each May, thousands of college-bound students take one or more Advanced Placement Exams to earn college credits—and for many years, they've looked to Barron's, the leader in Advanced Placement test preparation. You can get Barron's user-friendly manuals for 23 different AP subjects, most with optional CD-ROMs.

*BONUS ONLINE PRACTICE TEST: Free access to one additional full-length online test with purchase.

AP: Art History, 2nd Ed., w/optional CD-ROM
Book: ISBN 978-0-7641-4691-6, $18.99, Can$21.99
Book w/CD-ROM: ISBN 978-1-4380-7125-1, $29.99, Can$34.50

AP: Biology, 5th Ed., w/optional CD-ROM*
Book: ISBN 978-1-4380-0500-3, $18.99, Can$21.99
Book w/CD-ROM: ISBN 978-1-4380-7518-1, $29.99, Can$34.50

AP: Calculus, 13th Ed., w/optional CD-ROM*
Book: ISBN 978-1-4380-0497-6, $18.99, Can$21.99
Book w/CD-ROM: ISBN 978-1-4380-7516-7, $29.99, Can$34.50

AP: Chemistry, 7th Ed., w/optional CD-ROM
Book: ISBN 978-1-4380-0271-2, $18.99, Can$21.99
Book w/CD-ROM: ISBN 978-1-4380-7382-8, $29.99, Can$34.50

AP: Chinese Language and Culture, w/3 Audio CDs, 2nd Ed.
ISBN 978-1-4380-7388-0, $29.99, Can$34.50

AP: Computer Science, 7th Ed., w/optional CD-ROM*
Book: ISBN 978-1-4380-0594-2, $18.99, Can$21.99
Book w/CD-ROM: ISBN 978-1-4380-7553-2, $29.99, Can$34.50

AP: English Language and Composition, 6th Ed., w/optional CD-ROM*
Book: ISBN 978-1-4380-0496-9, $16.99, Can$19.50
Book w/CD-ROM: ISBN 978-1-4380-7515-0, $29.99, Can$34.50

AP: English Literature and Composition, 5th Ed., w/optional CD-ROM
Book: ISBN 978-1-4380-0278-1, $16.99, Can$19.50
Book w/CD-ROM: ISBN 978-1-4380-7386-6, $29.99, Can$34.50

AP: Environmental Science, 6th Ed., w/optional CD-ROM*
Book: ISBN 978-1-4380-0552-2, $18.99, Can$21.99
Book w/CD-ROM: ISBN 978-1-4380-7534-1, $29.99, Can$34.50

AP: European History, 7th Ed., w/optional CD-ROM
Book: ISBN 978-1-4380-0277-4, $18.99, Can$21.99
Book w/CD-ROM: ISBN 978-1-4380-7385-9, $29.99, Can$34.50

AP: French Language and Culture, w/3 Audio CDs
ISBN 978-1-4380-7259-3, $26.99, Can$31.00

AP: Human Geography, 5th Ed., w/optional CD-ROM
Book: ISBN 978-1-4380-0282-8, $16.99, Can$19.50
Book w/CD-ROM: ISBN 978-1-4380-7390-3, $29.99, Can$34.50

AP: Italian Language and Culture, w/3 Audio CDs
ISBN 978-0-7641-9368-2, $26.99, Can$32.50

AP: Microeconomics/Macroeconomics, 5th Ed.
ISBN 978-1-4380-0495-2, $16.99, Can$19.50

AP: Music Theory, w/4 Audio CDs, 2nd Ed.
ISBN 978-1-4380-7389-7, $34.99, Can$39.99

AP: Physics 1 and 2, w/optional CD-ROM
Book: ISBN 978-1-4380-0268-2, $18.99, Can$21.99
Book w/CD-ROM: ISBN 978-1-4380-7379-8, $29.99, Can$34.50

AP: Physics C, 3rd Ed.
ISBN 978-0-7641-4707-4, $18.99, Can$21.99

AP: Psychology, 6th Ed., w/optional CD-ROM
Book: ISBN 978-1-4380-0270-5, $16.99, Can$19.50
Book w/CD-ROM: ISBN 978-1-4380-7381-1, $29.99, Can$34.50

AP: Spanish Language and Culture w/4 Audio CDs, 8th Ed., and w/optional CD-ROM
Book w/4 audio CDs: ISBN 978-1-4380-7391-0, $26.99, Can$31.00
Book w/4 audio CDs and CD-ROM: ISBN 978-1-4380-7392-7, $34.99, Can$39.99

AP: Statistics, 8th Ed., w/optional CD-ROM*
Book: ISBN 978-1-4380-0498-3, $18.99, Can$21.00
Book w/CD-ROM: ISBN 978-1-4380-7517-4, $29.99, Can$34.50

AP: U.S. Government and Politics, 8th Ed., w/optional CD-ROM
Book: ISBN 978-1-4380-0279-8, $16.99, Can$19.50
Book w/CD-ROM: ISBN 978-1-4380-7387-3, $29.99, Can$34.50

AP: U.S. History, 2nd Ed., w/optional CD-ROM
Book: ISBN 978-1-4380-0269-9, $18.99, Can$21.99
Book w/CD-ROM: ISBN 978-1-4380-7380-4, $29.99, Can$34.50

AP: World History, 6th Ed., w/optional CD-ROM
Book: ISBN 978-1-4380-0272-9, $18.99, Can$21.99
Book w/CD-ROM: ISBN 978-1-4380-7383-5, $29.99, Can$34.50

Barron's Educational Series, Inc.
250 Wireless Blvd.
Hauppauge, NY 11788
Order toll-free: 1-800-645-3476

Prices subject to change without notice.

In Canada:
Georgetown Book Warehouse
34 Armstrong Ave.
Georgetown, Ontario L7G 4R9
Canadian orders: 1-800-247-7160

Available at your local book store or visit **www.barronseduc.com**

(#93 R10/14)

BARRON'S—the first place to look for instruction in Mandarin Chinese

Modern Mandarin Chinese for Beginners with 2 Audio CDs

This program introduces students and travelers to Mandarin Chinese by presenting a virtual "guided tour" of China's different regions. Enclosed audio CDs present the text's dialogues and teach correct Mandarin pronunciation and listening comprehension.

ISBN 978-0-7641-9456-6, $24.99, Can$29.99

Barron's Children's English-Chinese/Chinese-English Dictionary

Written for English-speaking elementary-school-level boys and girls, this book is divided into three sections: an English to Chinese dictionary; a Chinese to English dictionary; and a section giving bilingual entries for telling time, days of the week, months, names of continents and oceans, numbers, and other useful designations.

ISBN 978-0-7641-4106-5, $14.99, Can$17.99

Mandarin Chinese at a Glance, 3rd Ed.

This illustrated phrasebook for travelers is perfect as a take-along guide for visitors to the Far East. It features city maps, information on public transportation systems, general information for visitors to China, and bilingual lists of more than 1,500 most-often-used words and expressions for travelers, in the form of phonetic spellings of Mandarin words with their English translations.

ISBN 978-0-7641-3556-9, $8.99, Can$10.99

Mandarin Chinese the Easy Way, 2nd Ed. Book with Audio CD

This book-and-CD combination introduces basic sentence patterns and practical vocabulary for students of Mandarin Chinese. Includes humorous and dramatic spoken dialogues to aid listening comprehension. An introduction to Chinese written characters is also presented.

ISBN 978-0-7641-9369-9, 23.99, Can$27.50

Now You're Talking! Mandarin Chinese in No Time, 3rd Ed. Book with Audio CD

This traveler's aid consists of a Mandarin Chinese language phrasebook, *Mandarin Chinese At a Glance*, described above, with one accompanying audio compact disc. The CD gives travelers approximately 70 minutes of bilingual dialogue that dramatizes situations and conversations at airports, hotels, stores, taxicabs, and more.

ISBN 978-0-7641-7954-9, $18.99, Can$22.99

Available at your
local book store or visit
www.barronseduc.com

Barron's Educational Series, Inc.
250 Wireless Blvd.
Hauppauge, N.Y. 11788
Call toll-free: 1-800-645-3476

In Canada:
Georgetown Book Warehouse
34 Armstrong Ave.
Georgetown, Ontario L7G 4R9
Call toll-free: 1-800-247-7160

Prices subject to change without notice.

(#187) R 9/14

MOVE TO THE HEAD OF YOUR CLASS
THE EASY WAY!

Barron's presents **THE E-Z SERIES** (formerly THE EASY WAY SERIES)—specially prepared by top educators, it maximizes effective learning while minimizing the time and effort it takes to raise your grades, brush up on the basics, and build your confidence. Comprehensive and full of clear review examples, **THE E-Z SERIES** is your best bet for better grades, quickly!

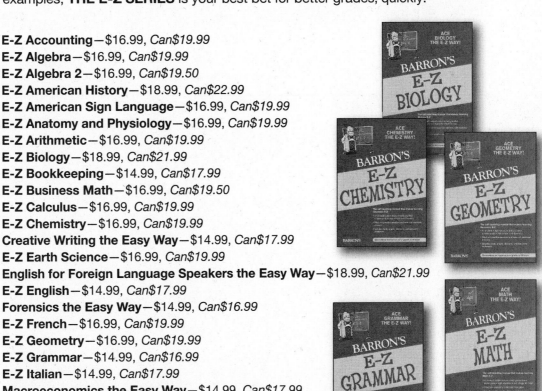

SBN 978-0-7641-4256-7	**E-Z Accounting**—$16.99, *Can$19.99*		
SBN 978-0-7641-4257-4	**E-Z Algebra**—$16.99, *Can$19.99*		
SBN 978-1-4380-0039-8	**E-Z Algebra 2**—$16.99, *Can$19.50*		
SBN 978-0-7641-4258-1	**E-Z American History**—$18.99, *Can$22.99*		
SBN 978-0-7641-4458-5	**E-Z American Sign Language**—$16.99, *Can$19.99*		
SBN 978-0-7641-4468-4	**E-Z Anatomy and Physiology**—$16.99, *Can$19.99*		
SBN 978-0-7641-4466-0	**E-Z Arithmetic**—$16.99, *Can$19.99*		
SBN 978-0-7641-4134-8	**E-Z Biology**—$18.99, *Can$21.99*		
SBN 978-0-7641-4133-1	**E-Z Bookkeeping**—$14.99, *Can$17.99*		
SBN 978-0-7641-4259-8	**E-Z Business Math**—$16.99, *Can$19.50*		
SBN 978-0-7641-4461-5	**E-Z Calculus**—$16.99, *Can$19.99*		
SBN 978-0-7641-4128-7	**E-Z Chemistry**—$16.99, *Can$19.99*		
SBN 978-0-7641-2579-9	**Creative Writing the Easy Way**—$14.99, *Can$17.99*		
SBN 978-0-7641-4464-6	**E-Z Earth Science**—$16.99, *Can$19.99*		
SBN 978-0-7641-3736-5	**English for Foreign Language Speakers the Easy Way**—$18.99, *Can$21.99*		
SBN 978-0-7641-4260-4	**E-Z English**—$14.99, *Can$17.99*		
SBN 978-0-7641-3050-2	**Forensics the Easy Way**—$14.99, *Can$16.99*		
SBN 978-0-7641-4455-4	**E-Z French**—$16.99, *Can$19.99*		
SBN 978-0-7641-3918-5	**E-Z Geometry**—$16.99, *Can$19.99*		
SBN 978-0-7641-4261-1	**E-Z Grammar**—$14.99, *Can$16.99*		
SBN 978-0-7641-4454-7	**E-Z Italian**—$14.99, *Can$17.99*		
SBN 978-0-7641-3237-7	**Macroeconomics the Easy Way**—$14.99, *Can$17.99*		
SBN 978-0-7641-9369-9	**Mandarin Chinese the Easy Way**—$23.99, *Can$27.50*		
SBN 978-0-7641-4132-4	**E-Z Math**—$14.99, *Can$17.99*		
SBN 978-0-7641-4456-1	**E-Z Microbiology**—$18.99, *Can$22.99*		
SBN 978-0-7641-4467-7	**E-Z Organic Chemistry**—$18.99, *Can$21.99*		
SBN 978-0-7641-4126-3	**E-Z Physics**—$16.99, *Can$19.99*		
SBN 978-1-4380-0011-4	**E-Z Pre-Algebra**—$14.99, *Can$16.99*		
SBN 978-0-7641-4465-3	**E-Z Precalculus**—$16.99, *Can$19.99*		
SBN 978-0-7641-4462-2	**E-Z Psychology**—$16.99, *Can$19.99*		
SBN 978-0-7641-4129-4	**E-Z Spanish**—$16.99, *Can$19.99*		
SBN 978-0-7641-4249-9	**E-Z Spanish Grammar**—$16.99, *Can$19.99*		
SBN 978-0-7641-4459-2	**E-Z Spelling**—$14.99, *Can$17.99*		
SBN 978-0-7641-3978-9	**E-Z Statistics**—$16.99, *Can$19.99*		
SBN 978-0-7641-4251-2	**E-Z Trigonometry**—$16.99, *Can$19.99*		
SBN 978-0-8120-9765-8	**World History the Easy Way, Vol. One**—$18.99, *Can$22.99*		
SBN 978-0-8120-9766-5	**World History the Easy Way, Vol. Two**—$21.99, *Can$26.50*		

Available at your local book store or visit **www.barronseduc.com**

Barron's Educational Series, Inc.
250 Wireless Blvd.
Hauppauge, NY 11788
Order toll-free: 1-800-645-3476
Order by fax: 1-631-434-3217

Prices subject to change without notice.

In Canada:
Georgetown Book Warehouse
34 Armstrong Ave.
Georgetown, Ontario L7G 4R9
Canadian orders: 1-800-247-7160
Order by fax: 1-800-887-1594

(#45) R10/14